THE
REAL
ALE
P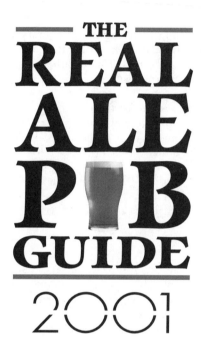B
GUIDE

2001

GRAHAM TITCOMBE
& NICOLAS ANDREWS

foulsham
LONDON • NEW YORK • TORONTO • SYDNEY

foulsham

The Publishing House, Bennetts Close,
Cippenham, Berkshire, SL1 5AP, England.

Printed in Great Britain by St. Edmundsbury Press, Bury St. Edmunds, Suffolk.

CONTENTS

CONTENTS

Cans, kegs and widgets, sparklers, gases – even a slice of lime. The multi-national conglomerates that still dictate much of the British beer-drinking market will stop at nothing in their determined drive to make their latest product appear new, exciting and the ultimate accessory for the sophisticated drinker. Presentation and image are all: huge sums are spent on advertising and packaging; film stars and stand-up comedians are employed to try and make you, the consumer, believe that whatever they finally force down your neck really is the last word in state-of-the-art British brewing. It ain't what you drink, it's who sees you drinking it.

As the trends move relentlessly on, from Third-World imports to ice beers to can-conditioned creamy confections that in one case, apparently, doubles up as moisturiser, the shallowness of all this image control becomes increasingly clear. Alcoholic lemonade is all very well, but will they be encouraging you to drink it in 12 months time? And if not, why not?

Fortunately, at the same time, there is an ever-increasing band of independent micro-brewers and discerning drinkers who have discovered that the best way to move forward is in fact to take a step back. Modern methods and the latest in brewing expertise can be successfully allied to a product that has served us well for centuries. The problems associated with producing *real* real ale, which the big drinks companies were so keen to exaggerate 30 years ago, can be and have been overcome. The best beers in Britain are now brewed, transported and then served to perfection. They need no advance advertising or heavy promotion for these are products that speak for themselves.

The exclusive world of truly traditional brewing is closer to that of the makers of fine wines than of fine television commercials. Once tasted, these beers will hook you forever and draw you in. All other ales will be exposed as the pale and unsophisticated imitations that they really are.

The Real Ale Pub Guide is a celebration of these brews and of the brewers for whom quality, not quantity, is all that matters. Other guides do an admirable job in listing those pubs with handpumps or by telling you about the impressive architecture, decor and food to be found at inns around the country. In this book, it is quite simply the beer that counts – and not just any old beer at that. Use this guide and lose yourself in an exhilarating world of exceptional craftsmen and exquisite tastes. Timeless techniques and sufficient attention to detail ensure that never again need you be disappointed by the product in your glass.

We tell you where to go to find beers of the finest character and complexity, served by enthusiasts who really care about what you are drinking. We explain why the way it is stored and served is as important as the contents of the barrel itself. And we invite you to help us to put the very best beers in Britain, and the brewers and barmen responsible for them, on the map so that, having travelled to the pubs we list, hopefully, that first sip from the first pint will tell you that you have truly arrived.

THE HISTORY OF BEER

Possibly discovered as a result of airborne wild yeast infecting open food, the art of brewing originated in Mesopotamia, between 8000 and 6000 BC. Slowly, the secret spread to Greece, Egypt and eventually to Rome. It was Caesar's invading army that brought beer to Britain in 55 AD.

Roman aristocracy still preferred to drink wine but, over the centuries, beer became an important source of nutrition for the native Britons and was often safer to drink than water. Beer continued to thrive long after the Romans had gone, and more than 40 breweries were listed in the Domesday Book of 1086.

Hops, which impart flavour and aroma, and act as a preservative, were initially introduced from Scandinavia in the middle of the tenth century, but they were not widely used until the fifteenth century, when growing became widespread in Kent.

Brewing took place in monasteries and the monks improved brewing techniques and introduced better varieties of barley. But, during Henry VIII's break with Rome in the 1530s, the monasteries were abolished and their land and assets seized by the Crown. The noble art passed into the hands of farmers and owners of landed estates, who installed private brewhouses which provided beer for farm workers and staff. These were the forerunners of the breweries we have today.

Commercial breweries began to set up in business during the latter part of the sixteenth century, growing steadily in number until around 30,000 breweries were registered in Great Britain in the 1870s, when beer drinking per head of the population was at its peak. Breweries were then found serving local communities throughout the British Isles. Even small towns could support such establishments. The Beer Act of 1830 permitted any householder to obtain a licence from the excise authorities allowing them to brew and sell beer on the premises. But, gradually, home-brewing went into decline. New taxes were levied on malt and hops which accelerated this demise until, by the end of the nineteenth century, the market was dominated by commercial brewers.

Many of these, too, have now gone, either bought up and closed down by large national breweries or, unable to survive in an increasingly competitive market, have simply faded away. A considerable number of excellent breweries have been lost with them and only 55 of the independent breweries that were in operation at the turn of the century still brew today.

Of these, Shepherd Neame Ltd at Faversham in Kent is believed to be the oldest. Beer has been produced on the same site without interruption since the brewery's official foundation in 1698. Britain's oldest surviving brewpub is believed to be the Blue Anchor at Helston in Cornwall. It first became a pub around the middle of the sixteenth century, although it seems certain that monks were already brewing beer on the premises long before then.

The title of the oldest pub in Britain probably belongs to the Trip to Jerusalem in Nottingham, part of which is cut into the rock of the castle and dates from 1189. This was once the malthouse for the castle brewery.

Although brewing technology may have progressed over the centuries, the process and basic ingredients have changed very little. Today, real ales still arrive at the pub with live yeast and fermentable sugars present in the brew, allowing the final stages of fermentation to take place in the cellar. This produces a fresh, pert, rounded flavour and natural effervescence. This is beer at its very best, and part of the proud tradition which spans the centuries.

Happily, new breweries are again setting up across the land and total around 400, a considerable improvement on the situation of just 20 years ago. The real ale cause is a rare triumph for quality and tradition in an age of all-consuming commercialism.

WHAT WENT WRONG?

Many pubs originally brewed their own beer in an outbuilding or similar adjacent place, often drawing water from a spring or well beneath. Frequently it was the lady of the house who did the brewing while her husband worked elsewhere.

But cask-conditioned beers tended to be unreliable and were too often not properly looked after in the cellar. To overcome this problem, the larger brewers turned to bottles and keg beers which, though bland and characterless by comparison, were consistent and had a much longer shelf life. They were easy to transport and easy to look after. Huge investments were made in kegs, equipment and advertising and, by the middle of the 1960s, real ale had all but disappeared from the British pub. Watneys Red Barrel, Worthington E and Double Diamond became the order of the day.

Just four of the once ubiquitous brewpubs remained and, as recently as 1985, there were fewer than 150 independent breweries in operation. Lager, too, although a poor imitation of some of the excellent continental brews, became increasingly successful in Britain, due largely to massive advertising campaigns which targeted the trend-conscious younger drinker. The national breweries had imposed their corporate will to increase profits at the expense of quality. Real ale sales continued to decline to the verge of extinction.

Though consistent, keg beer is a disappointing substitute for the natural product. It starts life as real ale but, prior to filling into containers, the beer is filtered, pasteurised and chilled. This process destroys and removes the yeast, preventing any further fermentation, and ensures that the beer is clear and bright in the keg.

But the beer is now dead. It produces no natural carbon dioxide and lacks the depth of character that cask-conditioned beers offer. In an effort to overcome this problem, it is now frequently served using a mixture of nitrogen and carbon dioxide, which gives the beer a tighter, creamy head in the glass while reducing the overall fizziness associated with carbon dioxide. The result can be compared with drinking cappuccino, which often uses the cheapest coffee beans available but becomes acceptable when frothed.

Additionally, no work is required in the pub cellar to bring keg beer into condition. It can be dispensed upon receipt and will remain servable, under the layer of gas used to dispense it, for many weeks. Consequently, no skill is required of the cellarman and very few keg beers are unfit to be served, necessitating their return to the brewery.

Little wonder that the national brewers, and some publicans too, would prefer it if cask-conditioned beers quietly faded away.

THE REAL ALE REVIVAL

Over the past 20 years, due to the dedication of a number of small brewery owners and the campaigning efforts of CAMRA (Campaign for Real Ale), the country's excellent real ales have gradually been rediscovered and Britain's great heritage of independent breweries is now thriving once more.

A change in the law known as The Beer Orders has helped, too, permitting pubs previously tied to one brewery for all beer supplies to take one guest beer from elsewhere. This has increased considerably the potential market for the smaller independent suppliers.

While some would argue that the tied pub system works against the smaller breweries which are unable to supply beer at sufficiently competitive prices, if at all, there is a strongly held view among larger independents and regional brewers that complete abolition of the system could result in the closure of some breweries which would no longer be able to rely on the necessary guaranteed outlets for their brews.

Meanwhile, new micro-breweries are springing up all over the country. These operate on a much smaller scale, so costs and overheads are much smaller. The micro-brewers concentrate, at least initially, on supplying a limited range of pubs. Some brewpubs produce beer on the premises that is not available anywhere else.

Not to be outdone, most existing brewers are adding new beers to their portfolios too. Today, there are approximately 400 independent breweries in Britain providing well over 1000 beers of widely varying styles and character, plus a plethora of one-off special or occasional brews. Wheat, tandoori, garlic, vanilla, melon, coriander, lemon, orange, strawberry and liquorice are just a few of the flavours on offer, in addition to the whole raft of more traditional beers.

Fortunately, more and more enterprising publicans are now offering these delightful brews and the revived interest in cask-conditioned beers has produced a new breed of drinker, the 'Scooper' or 'Ticker', who will often travel many miles just to find a new beer.

The market should easily be able to support the current crop of independents, and those that produce good brews of consistent quality and possess sufficient marketing and distribution skills should continue to thrive. But the national brewers have not gone to sleep. Keg beer, dispensed using mixed gases in an effort to mimic the character of real ale, is gaining ground on the back of multi-million pound marketing campaigns. But why drink a substitute when the real thing is available from the independent breweries in so many pubs throughout Britain?

If you take the trouble to search those pubs out, you will undoubtedly enjoy the best beer that Britain has to offer and help to prevent a return to the dark days of the 1960s and 70s.

THE BREWING PROCESS

The brewing process is a delicate one and most brewers inevitably experience occasional problems. The very nature of ale makes it impossible to produce a consistently uniform product, barrel after barrel, month after month. Also, brewers will be constantly striving to improve and refine the quality of the beer they produce.

Of course, this is part of the attraction for the real ale drinker. There is nothing like the experience of discovering new tastes and drinking sensations, and it places a premium on the skills and experience of both the brewer and the publican. But this inconsistency is something that the makers of bland, uniform keg beers are also keen to emphasise.

The slightest variation in established practice or, more commonly, yeast infections, equipment failures, changes in water or ingredient sources can upset the brewing process and affect the resulting beer. Often, a combination of these elements causes problems. No matter how much care is taken, it is simply not feasible to expect every new brew to taste and behave just the same as it did the last time. But each one must be of a similar high standard and as consistent as possible.

Even renowned, award-winning beers are sometimes unacceptably inconsistent in quality and flavour. Increased demand during the summer months can lead to beer being sent out 'green' or too soon. Some may even be contract-brewed and lose subtle, but important, characteristics.

Barley, which the Mesopotamians were lucky enough to have growing wild, is still an important ingredient for beer making today. It is soaked in water, then spread over the floor of the malthouse and gently heated to promote germination. This releases sugars, which are vital for fermentation. The barley is constantly raked to ensure even germination throughout. Once the grains start to produce rootlets, they are roasted to prevent further germination. The higher the temperature, the darker the malt will be, and the beer produced from it will be darker, with a more roasted flavour. Pale malt will impart a sweeter, more delicate flavour to the brew.

MALT MILL
At the brewery, the malt is passed through rollers in the malt mill, which crushes the grains releasing the soluble starch.

MASH TUN
The malt is passed from the malt mill into the mash tun where it is mixed with hot water or 'liquor'. This is known as 'mashing' and converts the soluble starches into fermentable and non-fermentable sugars. Depending on the type of beer required a mix of malts may be used.

Water used in the brewing process is usually treated in order to remove any unwanted characteristics, and to emulate water found in other areas, which is considered most suitable to the style of beer required.

The 'mash' is thoroughly stirred, then allowed to stand until it becomes clear, when it is known as 'wort'.

THE COPPER
The wort is then run into the copper, where it is boiled and hops are added. At this stage, various 'adjuncts' may be added to the wort, such as invert sugar, to increase fermentability, but any additive is considered by many to be an insult to the brewer's art.

Depending on the variety used, hops impart bitterness of flavour or aroma and help to prevent infection in the wort. A mixture of hops may be used.

But they were not always popular with everyone. Henry VIII objected to this foreign habit of putting hops into beer and suggested that it should be outlawed. Fortunately, the noble hop survived.

Of the many varieties available, those most commonly used in Britain are still the

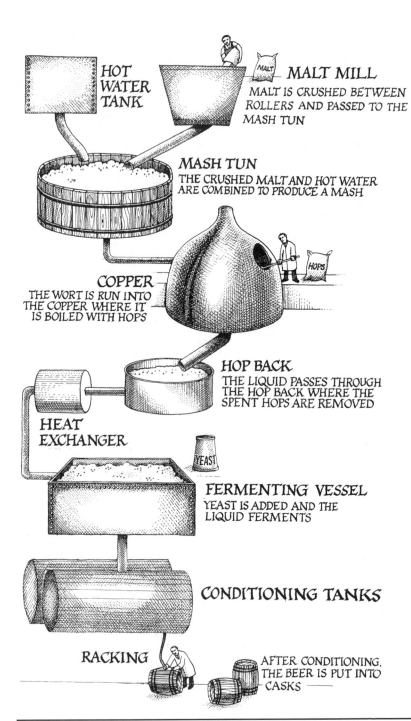

HOT WATER TANK

MALT MILL
MALT IS CRUSHED BETWEEN ROLLERS AND PASSED TO THE MASH TUN

MASH TUN
THE CRUSHED MALT AND HOT WATER ARE COMBINED TO PRODUCE A MASH

COPPER
THE WORT IS RUN INTO THE COPPER WHERE IT IS BOILED WITH HOPS

HOP BACK
THE LIQUID PASSES THROUGH THE HOP BACK WHERE THE SPENT HOPS ARE REMOVED

HEAT EXCHANGER

FERMENTING VESSEL
YEAST IS ADDED AND THE LIQUID FERMENTS

CONDITIONING TANKS

RACKING
AFTER CONDITIONING, THE BEER IS PUT INTO CASKS

Golding and the Fuggle, although other types are rapidly finding favour.

Unfortunately, some brewers substitute hop oils but it is widely felt that this has a detrimental effect on the flavour of the finished brew. Perhaps we should learn from some of our continental friends where this practice would contravene purity laws.

The wort will remain in the copper for one to two hours.

HOP BACK

From the copper the wort is then passed through the hop back where the spent hops are removed.

HEAT EXCHANGER

On its way to the fermenting vessel, the wort is passed through a heat exchanger, where its temperature is reduced to 20°C. This is important for producing ideal conditions for the yeast. Extremes of temperature will either kill the yeast or result in a sluggish fermentation.

FERMENTING VESSEL

The wort is now 'pitched' or has yeast added. It will remain here for around five days, the yeast feeding on the fermentable sugars, while excreting alcohol and producing carbon dioxide.

A thick creamy head of yeast builds up in the fermentation vessel, and this is skimmed and retained for further use. But, as the yeast in the brew becomes tired and much of the sugar has been converted to alcohol, the process slows down. The primary fermentation is now over, and it is at this point that beer produced for the keg will go its separate way.

CONDITIONING TANKS

At this stage, beer is said to be 'green' and the flavour is harsh. It is passed into conditioning tanks, where it will remain for several days, and much of the remaining sugar will ferment out to produce a more rounded flavour.

RACKING

At last, the beer is ready to be put into the cask, or 'racked'. By now, any harsh or undesirable flavours will have disappeared, but the brew will be crisp and fresh.

Finings, which draw the dying yeast cells to the bottom of the cask, are added allowing the beer to 'drop bright' or clear down.

Some fermentable sugars and living yeast cells remain, so the beer continues to ferment in the cask. Sometimes, priming sugar will be added to assist this secondary fermentation. Hops may also be added to impart a hoppy aroma to the brew.

Once in the pub cellar, the beer will continue to ferment, producing carbon dioxide, which gives real ale its natural vitality.

The finings will clear the beer down until it is bright, and the cask will then be tapped, in preparation for use. This final stage, which is known as cask-conditioning, typically takes two or three days and brings the beer naturally to perfection. It should now be served as soon as possible.

TRAVELLING BEER

Assuming that a beer is in the proper condition when it leaves the brewery, plenty of damage can still be done during distribution. Most beers will 'travel' providing that they are properly handled.

The brew within the cask is a living product that must be treated with respect if it is ultimately to be served at its best. Every time a cask is rolled, the finings, which draw all the solid matter to the bottom of the cask, are activated and these will work effectively for approximately five cask rollings.

Better quality finings are available which will allow far more cask rollings, but they are significantly more expensive and many, shortsighted, brewers still fail to understand the full implications of their cost cutting.

Therefore, a cask from a brewer in Scotland arriving at a pub in Cornwall may well have been moved between wholesalers and rolled a number of times. It may also have been in transit too long, having been left in various stores en route, and so be nearing the end of its life even before it arrives. The result will almost certainly be a lifeless, dull brew lacking in any subtlety of flavour.

Extremes of temperature can also prevent a brew from getting into condition properly and dropping clear and bright. Casks may be left in very hot or cold conditions, in warehouses, garages or on the back of vehicles where there is no temperature control equipment. This, too, may result in a brew being damaged before it arrives at the pub and, unfortunately, the publican will not know about this until it is too late.

Co-operation is the answer. Regional and larger independent brewers have, for some time, also offered beers from other breweries and an increasing number of the smaller independents are now offering their product wholesale in an effort to improve turnover and distribution. Delivering beers to a brewery in another part of the country, while collecting that brewery's beer for sale with one's own, is obviously of great benefit to both parties. These beers are likely to be subjected to a minimum amount of movement and a shorter transit time, resulting in beer reaching the pub in a much better condition than if it had been shipped from wholesaler to wholesaler.

So, it is very much in a publican's interest to deal directly with the breweries wherever possible and to avoid brews from wholesalers which may arrive via a devious route. It is important, too, to boycott any source of supply if it proves necessary to return more than the occasional cask. Having said that, there are some excellent real ale wholesalers operating in Britain. The key is to find them and then deal with them only, even if this ultimately limits the range of beers on offer.

IN THE CELLAR

During the hot summer of 1995, pubs were on the receiving end of an unusually high proportion of brews that were sour or, more usually, that would not 'drop bright'. With limited cellar capacity, this can cause problems. Many publicans pursuing a more adventurous guest beer policy found it necessary to restrict the range of beers on offer in order to maintain quality and availability at the bar.

Unlike keg beer, cask-conditioned brews are alive and have not finished fermenting when they are delivered to the pub. The final stages of the conditioning process take place in the cellar before the beer is served. Temperature control and cleanliness are therefore vital if the beer is to drop clear and bright and without infection. Additionally, good stock control and rapid turnover combined with regular beer line cleaning are essential if each pint is to be served in peak condition.

A small amount of beer is inevitably lost when spilling and tapping each cask and, no matter how carefully it may be stooped, some beer will always be unservable. For this reason, many licensees prefer to buy larger casks in order to minimise wastage, but this often results in casks remaining on-line in the cellar for too long. Once a beer has worked into condition, it will remain at its best for a relatively short period of time. Every pint pulled draws more air into the cask, increasing the rate of oxidisation. If a beer remains on-line for four or five days, not unusual in some pubs, although still drinkable, it will be well past its best.

Controversially, in order to prevent air being taken into the cask, some cellarmen use a cask breather system, which maintains a blanket of carbon dioxide on top of the beer. The gas is at a much lower pressure than that used for the dispensing of keg beer, so there is relatively little absorbence, although it is often detectable as a pint is served.

Some drinkers also believe that the flavour of the beer is impaired by this, although blind tasting tests have not proved that this is so. While it is certainly better than serving a beer that is out of condition, this process inevitably offends the purist and so it is surely preferable to use smaller containers that allow the beer to be served naturally and at its best.

The method of dispensing beer has also become a very contentious issue and there are few hard and fast rules. Many people object to long 'swan necks' or multi-holed sparklers on the end of a handpump, although some beers are brewed specifically to be served in this way. Some beer is at its best served through the conventional slit-type sparkler and short neck, although some brews lose much of their condition and hoppiness if served through any form of sparkler at all. In such cases, the beer should be served straight from the barrel if all its subtleties of flavour are to be enjoyed to the full.

Different beers are at their best served in different ways. To insist that all sparklers are an abomination, or that all beer is at its best straight from the wood, is to misunderstand the nature of cask-conditioned beers.

SMALL IS BEAUTIFUL

So many things can go wrong between the start of the brewing process and the presentation of the pint at the bar, and inconsistency, for whatever reason, inevitably plays right into the hands of the big, national brewers. They have the ability to undercut smaller breweries on price and to capitalise on first-class marketing and distribution expertise.

The introduction of nitro-keg products to the market has proved a great success. Keg beer is served using a mixture of carbon dioxide and nitrogen to give it a tighter, creamier head. The beer itself may be bland, but such products are very popular. With all the investment tied up in kegs and plant, national and larger independent brewers will understandably continue to look for new ways to utilise existing equipment.

Most so-called freehouses still retain some type of trading agreement with a particular brewery and many emerging brewers have difficulty finding regular outlets for their beers. Frequently unable to raise money to buy a pub, a publican will borrow additional funds from a national brewer. Conditions will obviously be attached to such loans, usually in the form of stipulated barrelage figures. A pub will be required to serve a certain amount of a particular well-known beer.

Such a policy leaves the publican with little room for manoeuvre. A guest beer may prove more popular than the permanent offering and it will then be difficult to honour the commitment to the national brewer, resulting in stiff financial penalties. National brewers have also been know to offer financial inducements to a publican to drop a guest beer not supplied by them if it becomes too popular. Additionally, most trading agreements provide discounts, which may be substantial in certain cases.

A publican operating a true freehouse, free of all ties and agreements, and providing a constantly changing range of unusual guest beers, will probably not deal with any one source in sufficient volume to receive much, if any, discount. Even by reducing profit margins to significantly below the accepted norm, the publican may struggle to sell beers at a competitive rate. Only by then increasing the volume of beer sold can they hope to survive.

Little wonder then that most publicans are not prepared to take such risks and so stick to a regular range of guest beers upon which good discounts are available. In areas where beer is traditionally cheaper, or where there are high levels of unemployment, these discounts can be critical to a pub's survival and so few publicans are likely to risk their livelihood by pursuing an adventurous guest beer policy.

THE NEXT 1000 YEARS

One priceless commodity that the small, independent brewer can use in their favour is the British drinking public's insatiable curiosity. The pub remains an integral part of our way of life, just as it has done for several hundred years, and the national brewers know only too well that there will always be a market for something new and exciting.

So, the brewer who puts the quality of the product first will always find a market of potential pub-goers eager to try something different and something which represents good value for money. Seasonal ales and celebration brews are an excellent way to revive flagging interest.

Even for those drinkers who believe they already know what they like, a degree of variety remains the key. And once the pub-goer knows that a particular publican can be trusted, whether they know the beer in question or not, a bond is established that can be nurtured and strengthened.

When it comes to real ale, you cannot have too much of a good thing, so

independent pub chains that can afford to are rapidly adding new sites to their estates. Many large towns and cities now boast a number of group-owned pubs offering a good range of brews from the independent breweries. Their purchasing power allows them to be very competitive, although they are usually still subject to some trading agreements which can limit the range of beers available.

One day, perhaps, everyone will get the message, but it can still prove frustratingly difficult to find good-quality beers from the smaller and new independent breweries even when visiting the area in which they are produced. Independent brewers today still supply less than 15 per cent of the beer found in Britain's pubs and clubs.

Fortunately, there are true freehouses, some with an interesting range of tried and tested beers and others serving a constantly changing range of guest beers from across the British Isles, including those from the smallest and newest breweries.

The pubs that you will find in the pages that follow vary in character from the basic back-street boozer to the idyllic country inn, but all offer beer well worth searching out. So, while we enjoy British beer at its best, let us spare a thought for brews unlucky enough to be sent to the keg. Cold, devoid of character and flavour and dependent on a gas cylinder for life ... a sad existence indeed.

Even today's commercial giants have been unable to substitute their lifeless, pale imitations for the real thing. Instinctively, one recognises the genuine article, regardless of hype and advertising. Britain's independent brewers have been producing traditional ales for 1000 years. They have withstood the test of time, even through adversity, with banners held high. Let us drink to them, and the next 1000 years.

Most regular drinkers still appreciate a first-class pint that they may have tried before more than an indifferent brew, no matter how new or exotic. But fortunately, there are pubs where both of these needs can be satisfied. For an increasing number of publicans serving beer in peak condition, an interesting guest beer policy remains paramount, and so it is possible to find beers from Orkney in Cornwall, and brews from Jersey in Cumbria.

We all have our favourite real ales but, given the amazing variety of characters and flavours that are produced from such a limited number of ingredients, these obviously vary from individual to individual.

Lighter, paler brews are generally more popular during the summer months, while porters come into their own when the weather is colder. There are, however, certain brews that, regardless of style and time of year, prove to be most popular.

Graham Titcombe, who until recently owned the Bell Inn at Pensax, Worcestershire, served a constantly changing range of brews from the independent breweries. From records kept of almost 3000 different beers served there and at his previous pub, over a seven-year period, it has been possible to compile a list of drinkers' favourite 100 brews.

The picture is constantly changing, with many new beers and breweries appearing, so although many of the beers displayed here are familiar favourites, there are a number of welcome newcomers.

1 ARCHERS: GOLDEN BITTER
WILTSHIRE

2 WOODFORDE'S: WHERRY
NORFOLK

3 HARVIESTOUN:
SCHIEHALLION
SCOTLAND

4 CALEDONIAN: R & D
DEUCHARS IPA
SCOTLAND

5 HOP BACK:
SUMMER LIGHTNING
WILTSHIRE

6 OTTER: BRIGHT
DEVON

7 RCH: PITCHFORK
SOMERSET

8 BATHAMS:
BEST BITTER
WEST MIDLANDS

9 TIMOTHY TAYLOR:
LANDLORD
YORKSHIRE

10 EXMOOR: GOLD
SOMERSET

11 FULLER'S:
LONDON PRIDE
LONDON

12 ENVILLE: WHITE
WEST MIDLANDS

13 BLACK SHEEP:
SPECIAL BITTER
YORKSHIRE

14 BURNTISLAND:
DOCKYARD RIVETS
SCOTLAND

15 HOBSONS: TOWN CRIER
HEREFORD & WORCESTER

16 HOOK NORTON:
OLD HOOKY
OXFORDSHIRE

17 ENVILLE:
CZECHMATE SAAZ
WEST MIDLANDS

18 WADWORTH: 6X
WILTSHIRE

19 ADNAMS: BITTER
SUFFOLK

 MOORHOUSE'S: PENDLE
WITCHES BREW
LANCASHIRE

21 SKINNER'S:
CORNISH KNOCKER
CORNWALL

22 ENVILLE: PHOENIX
WEST MIDLANDS

 BULLMASTIFF:
SON OF A BITCH
WALES

 ENVILLE: ALE
WEST MIDLANDS

 WOOD'S:
SHROPSHIRE LAD
SHROPSHIRE

 RINGWOOD:
FORTYNINER
HAMPSHIRE

27 CHERITON:
POTS ALE
HAMPSHIRE

 HOLDEN'S:
SPECIAL BITTER
WEST MIDLANDS

 COTLEIGH:
HARRIER
SOMERSET

30 ADNAMS:
EXTRA
SUFFOLK

31 EXMOOR: ALE
SOMERSET

 CHERITON:
DIGGERS GOLD
HAMPSHIRE

 HOP BACK:
GFB
WILTSHIRE

 KELHAM ISLAND:
PALE RIDER
YORKSHIRE

 BRAKSPEAR:
SPECIAL
OXFORDSHIRE

SARAH HUGHES:
DARK RUBY MILD
WEST MIDLANDS

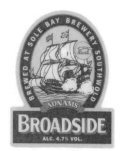

 ADNAMS:
BROADSIDE
SUFFOLK

 TITANIC:
WHITE STAR
STAFFORDSHIRE

MAULDONS:
WHITE ADDER
SUFFOLK

 BATEMAN'S:
VICTORY ALE
LINCOLNSHIRE

WOODBURY:
WHITE GROUSE
HEREFORD & WORCESTER

ECCLESHALL:
SLATERS SUPREME
STAFFORDSHIRE

GOFF'S:
JOUSTER
GLOUCESTERSHIRE

 WADWORTH:
FARMERS GLORY
WILTSHIRE

45 BARNSLEY:
BITTER
YORKSHIRE

46 MORDUE:
WORKIE TICKET
TYNE & WEAR

 WYRE PIDDLE:
PIDDLE IN THE WIND
HEREFORD & WORCESER

48 WYE VALLEY:
HPA
HEREFORD & WORCESTER

49 HARDY & HANSONS:
KIMBERLEY CLASSIC
NOTTINGHAMSHIRE

 OTTER: BITTER
DEVON

51 GODDARDS:
FUGGLE DEE DUM
ISLE OF WIGHT

52 RINGWOOD:
XXXX PORTER
HAMPSHIRE

 BUNCES:
DANISH DYNAMITE
WILTSHIRE

54 CROUCH VALE:
MILLENNIUM GOLD
ESSEX

55 DARK HORSE:
FALLEN ANGEL
HERTFORDSHIRE

56 RIDLEYS:
RUMPUS
ESSEX

57 BERROW:
TOPSY TURVY
SOMERSET

58 JOLLYBOAT:
PLUNDER
DEVON

59 CONCERTINA:
BENGAL TIGER
YORKSHIRE

60 EVERARDS:
TIGER
LEICESTERSHIRE

61 SARAH HUGHES:
SEDGLEY SURPRISE
WEST MIDLANDS

62 CHARLES WELLS:
BOMBARDIER
BEDFORDSHIRE

63 BRAINS:
SA
WALES

64 STONEHENGE:
OLD SMOKEY
WILTSHIRE

65 JENNINGS:
COCKER HOOP
CUMBRIA

66 ARKELL'S:
KINGSDOWN
WILTSHIRE

67 ORKNEY:
DARK ISLAND
SCOTLAND

68   ROBINSON'S:
OLD TOM
CHESHIRE

69   LEES:
MOONRAKER
MANCHESTER

70   INVERALMOND:
OSSIAN'S ALE
SCOTLAND

71   BORDER:
FARNE ISLAND
NORTHUMBERLAND

72   REBELLION:
MUTINY
BUCKINGHAMSHIRE

73   KING & BARNES:
FESTIVE ALE
SUSSEX

74   CANNON ROYALL:
BUCKSHOT
HEREFORD & WORCESTER

75   HESKET NEWMARKET:
DORIS'S 90TH BIRTHDAY
CUMBRIA

76   RINGWOOD:
OLD THUMPER
HAMPSHIRE

77   ABBEY:
BELLRINGER
SOMERSET

78   HOGS BACK:
HOP GARDEN GOLD
SURREY

79   FERNANDES:
WAKEFIELD PRIDE
YORKSHIRE

80 BALLARD'S:
TROTTON
HAMPSHIRE

81 BIGFOOT:
GAINSBOROUGH GOLD
LINCOLNSHIRE

82 CHURCH END:
WHAT THE FOX'S HAT
WARWICKSHIRE

83 BALLARD'S:
WASSAIL
HAMPSHIRE

84 VALE:
EDGAR'S GOLDEN ALE
BUCKINGHAMSHIRE

85 WOLF:
GRANNY WOULDN'T LIKE IT
NORFOLK

86 ECCLESHALL:
TOP TOTTY
STAFFORDSHIRE

87 BATH:
BARNSTORMER
SOMERSET

88 GREENE KING:
ABBOT ALE
SUFFOLK

89 FROG ISLAND:
BEST BITTER
NORTHAMPTONSHIRE

90 OAKHAM:
JHB
LEICESTERSHIRE

91 TEME VALLEY:
T'OTHER
HEREFORD & WORCESTER

 LEATHERBRITCHES:
ASHBOURNE ALE
DERBYSHIRE

 TRAQUAIR:
BEAR ALE
SCOTLAND

 MORLAND:
OLD SPECKLED HEN
OXFORDSHIRE

 BURTONWOOD:
JAMES FORSHAW'S BITTER
CHESHIRE

 DENT:
T'OWD TUP
CUMBRIA

 ICENI:
GOLD
NORFOLK

HOP BACK:
THUNDERSTORM
WILTSHIRE

TITANIC:
PREMIUM
STAFFORDSHIRE

ROBINSON'S:
FREDERICS
CHESHIRE

Once, pub shelves heaved under the weight of bottles of light and brown ales, stouts and IPAs. Now, these have largely disappeared, relegated to the corner of the cold cabinet, the bottling lines closed down and dispatched to brewing history. Like keg beer, they were dead, pasteurised and filtered, bland and tasteless.

But in recent years a renaissance has taken place, largely led by the independent breweries, many of whom are now very successfully bottling real ale. Shelves are full again and although there are some pubs and brewery shops offering a good selection of these beers, you are more likely to find them in the supermarket.

Real ale in a bottle or bottle-conditioned beer, like cask ale, contains live yeast and fermentable sugars. A secondary fermentation takes place in the bottle which develops the beer naturally and maintains its condition. Despite the almost hysterical passion for sell-by dates nowadays, these beers actually mature in the bottle and are likely to be in prime condition for some time. Beers like Fuller's Vintage Ale, produced in 1997 with a sell-by date of the end of 2000, is drinking beautifully now and probably will do so for a long while yet. Obviously, though, you should make your own decision as to whether your particular bottle *is* drinkable and will not cause you any upset.

Like cask beer, to allow enjoyment of the full complexity of flavour they should be between 55–59 degrees when consumed. The bottle should be allowed to stand for a sufficient period to allow the sediment to drop to the bottom, then poured carefully, to prevent the sediment rising and clouding the beer. They should never be drunk straight from the bottle. Some, less hoppy, continental beers, can be drunk cloudy, but British bottle-conditioned beers generally should not.

The Hogs Back Brewery at Tongham has an excellent selection of bottle-conditioned beers and the following list represents their top fifty best-sellers. Tasting notes were produced with the kind assistance of David Underwood, Pete Arguile, Mo Rolfe, Keith Brothwell and Alison Titcombe.

ALES OF KENT STILTMAN 4.3% ABV
Pale ruby colour, light body with sweet malt and chocolate notes in the aroma. Malt flavour gives way to hoppiness in the finish.

ALES OF KENT SMUGGLERS GLORY 4.8% ABV
Golden orange colour and light-bodied, with pears and hop aroma. Powerful, bitter apples flavour.

ASH VINE SWEET FA 4.0% ABV
Bronze colour and good body, with delicate hoppy aroma. Smooth with good hoppy bitterness throughout which gives way to a clean, slightly dry finish.

ASH VINE TOUCHDOWN 4.0% ABV
Light brown and medium-bodied with slight fruit aroma. Fruity flavour with a little bitterness.

ASH VINE HOP & GLORY 5.0% ABV
Very pale gold colour and light-bodied, with hoppy herby aroma and hoppy, dry bitter flavour.

BALLARD'S NYEWOOD GOLD 5.0% ABV
Pale gold colour and light-bodied with hoppy aroma. Hops come through in the flavour, leaving a dryish finish.

BALLARD'S PLEASURE DOME 10.0% ABV
Red/brown colour and full-bodied with caramel and chocolate aroma. Sweet and smooth, well-rounded caramel and chocolate flavour.

BARNGATES TAG LAG 4.4% ABV
Yellow/golden and light-bodied, with faint hop aroma. Hops developing with malt on the back palate and well-hopped aftertaste.

BRAKSPEAR VINTAGE HENLEY 5.5% ABV
Mid-brown colour and medium-bodied with delicate aroma and rounded malt flavour.

BURTON BRIDGE EMPIRE PALE ALE 7.5% ABV
Pale and light-bodied with fresh aroma. Dry with complex herby flavours.

BURTON BRIDGE TICKLE BRAIN ALE 8.0% ABV
Amber-coloured and relatively light-bodied, with fruity aroma and cidery, Belgian-style flavour.

BUTTS BLACKGUARD PORTER 4.5% ABV
Ruby red colour and light body with smoky aroma. Bitter chocolate and fruit flavour with dry aftertaste.

BUTTS BARBUS BARBUS 4.6% ABV
Golden colour and light body with delicate, fruity hop aroma. Initial sweetness quickly gives way to hoppy citrus fruit flavour. Smooth and mellow.

CONISTON BLUE BIRD 4.2% ABV
Pale amber colour and light-bodied with cherryade aroma. Initial light flavour has good hop/malt balance and hoppy, fading finish.

CROPTON KING BILLY BITTER 3.6% ABV
Honeyed gold colour and full-bodied for gravity with malt and honey aroma. The initial rounded maltiness gives way to intense, lingering bitter aftertaste.

CROPTON HONEY FARM BITTER 4.2% ABV
Golden and light-bodied with honeyed aroma. Delicate hoppiness, little sweetness and dry, bitter finish.

CROPTON SCORESBY STOUT 4.2% ABV
Dark ruby colour and full-bodied for gravity with chocolate malt and molasses aroma. Chocolate flavour with hops following through in the aftertaste. Drying on the palate with malt sweetness.

CROPTON BACKWOODS BITTER 5.1% ABV
Cola/darkish brown colour and full-bodied, with raisin, roast and malt aroma. Balanced and rounded roast malt flavour and good bitterness.

FREEMINER SPECULATION 4.8% ABV
Dark brown colour and full-bodied, sweetish, malt flavour. Balancing hoppiness gives way to dry finish.

FREEMINER SHAKEMANTLE 5.0% ABV
Pale colour and cloudy with light body. Ginger flavour throughout with hoppy hints.

FREEMINER DEEP SHAFT STOUT 6.2% ABV
Very dark and relatively light-bodied, with smoked wood aroma and smoked apple barrel flavour.

GALES HSB 4.8% ABV
Amber-coloured and light-bodied with a slight
Cheddary aroma. Initial nutty, malt and hop
flavour is followed by creamy hop finish in the
aftertaste.

GALES PRIZE OLD ALE 9.0% ABV
Mahogany-coloured and medium-bodied with
fresh, fruity, vanilla and caramel aroma.
Balanced sherry-like flavour.

HAMPSHIRE KING ALFRED'S ALE 3.8% ABV
Golden and light-bodied with a fresh hop
aroma. Astringent, dry, fruity flavour.

HAMPSHIRE 1066 6.0% ABV
Mid-gold colour and full-bodied with slight
butterscotch aroma. Soft, light bitterness,
smooth and succulent.

HOGS BACK TEA 4.2% ABV
Pale bronze colour and rounded good body with
delicate, hoppy aroma. Smooth and beautifully
balanced with refreshing, clean hoppy finish.

HOGS BACK BSA 4.5% ABV
Copper-coloured and medium-bodied with hop
and fruit aroma. Initial hoppy bitterness gives
way to smooth malt with a hint of fruit,
followed by lingering, dry hoppy aftertaste.

HOGS BACK BREWSTERS BUNDLE 7.4% ABV
Medium-bodied with delicate malt and hop
aroma, honeyed malt flavour and orange pith
notes.

HOGS BACK WOBBLE IN A BOTTLE 7.5% ABV
Amber-coloured and inviting, malt and hop
aroma. Balanced and smooth with an explosion
of hoppiness, giving way to some sweetness in
the finish.

HOGS BACK A OVER T 9.0% ABV
Amber-coloured and full-bodied with light malty
aroma. Tasty, honeyed sweetness and malt
flavour.

HOP BACK TAIPHOON 4.2% ABV
Pale straw-coloured and light-bodied with
intriguing lemongrass aroma. Dry, subtle, clean
spicy flavour

HOP BACK SUMMER LIGHTNING 5.0% ABV
Very pale/straw-coloured and medium-bodied. A
fresh, citrus, herbal aroma with well-balanced,
crisp clean hoppy flavour and finish.

HOP BACK THUNDERSTORM 5.0% ABV
Straw-coloured and light-bodied with distinctive
aroma. Slight hoppy flavour develops with malt
in the aftertaste, fading quickly.

KING & BARNES HARVEST 4.7% ABV
Golden colour and light-bodied with little
aroma. Refreshing and balanced.

KING & BARNES IPA 5.0% ABV
Pale amber colour and light-bodied. Bitter but
balanced hoppiness, followed by hoppy, gently
dry palate.

KING & BARNES FESTIVE 5.3% ABV
Dark chestnut/red colour with medium body.
Malt and slight fruit aroma, and rounded, well-
balanced flavour.

KING & BARNES OLD PORTER 5.5% ABV
Mahogany colour and full-bodied with milky,
malt aroma. Chocolate malt flavour, like liquid
Milky Way!

PITFIELD EAST KENT GOLDINGS 4.2% ABV
Golden/amber colour and light-bodied with
honey and orange aroma. The flavour is light,
fresh and tasty.

PITFIELD BLACK EAGLE 5.0% ABV
Dark chestnut colour, light to medium body and
malty aroma with some hoppiness. Malty flavour
with slight vanilla notes and rounded, smooth
finish.

RINGWOOD FORTYNINER 4.9% ABV
Mid-gold colour and medium body with
honeyed nose, some fruity bitterness and slight
honeyed flavour.

**SULWATH KNOCKENDOCH GALLOWAY ALE
5.0% ABV**
Chestnut colour and good body, with malt and
fig aroma. Sweet and very malty flavour.

SWALE WHITSTABLE OYSTER STOUT 4.5% ABV
Very dark brown colour and medium body.
Pleasant coffee/roast aroma and smooth and
balanced roast malt flavour with long finish.

SWALE KENTISH GOLD 5.0% ABV
Yellow-coloured and light-bodied with sweet,
fresh, slightly perfumed aroma. Slight hoppy
taste, with hops in the aftertaste developing into
dryness.

TISBURY STONEHENGE 4.2% ABV
Ginger colour and light-bodied with apple and
honey aroma. Hoppy flavour with pert
bitterness.

TISBURY ALE FRESCO 4.5% ABV
Golden/yellow colour, light body with
honeydew and slight hop aroma. Honey and
faint hop flavour, drying on the palate with
tangy aftertaste.

TISBURY REAL NUT ALE 4.5% ABV
Chestnut colour and good body, with hoppy
aroma. Smooth, malty flavour and dry hoppy
aftertaste.

WICKWAR DOGS HAIR 4.0% ABV
Pale colour and light-bodied with hoppy aroma.
Hops predominate throughout, leaving drier
finish.

WICKWAR STATION PORTER 6.1% ABV
Ruby red colour and medium-bodied with
smooth hoppy aroma. Initially mouth-filling yet
delicately sweet malty flavour and fruity hints.
Surprisingly easy to drink for gravity.

**WYE VALLEY DOROTHY GOODBODY'S GOLDEN
SUMMERTIME ALE 4.2% ABV**
Straw-coloured and light-bodied with fresh,
slightly honeyed aroma. Hoppy citrus fruit
flavour and long finish.

**WYE VALLEY DOROTHY GOODBODY'S
WHOLESOME STOUT 4.6% ABV**
Ruby red and light-bodied with hoppy aroma.
Slight chocolate malt flavour with distinctive,
hoppy dry finish.

YOUNG'S SPECIAL LONDON ALE 6.4% ABV
Brass-coloured and medium-bodied with herby
aroma. Complex, hoppy flavour with initial
sweetness. Hops come through leaving a
bittersweet aftertaste.

The Real Ale Pub Guide is a celebration of the rejuvenated art of brewing in Great Britain. Our concern, deliberately, is not with the often bland and certainly mass-produced market leaders, but simply with the smaller, independent makers of what we consider to be the *real* real ales. For this reason, we do not tell you about the big, multi-national brewers and their products, good or bad. Nor do we tell you about the pubs whose reputation owes more to their impressive location, their excellent cooking or their extensive range of malt whiskies, although we may mention their claim in passing. This is a book about beer and is aimed squarely at those who love drinking it, who want to know more about it and who want to know where to find it at its best. The entries within England are arranged alphabetically by county, taking into account the boundary changes that came into force in 1996. Since plenty of people never got used to the last round of boundary changes this will envitably cause some confusion.

For example, Avon, Cleveland and Humberside now no longer exist. Parts of these counties have been swallowed up by their recent neighbours and towns have returned to what many have always considered to be their spiritual homes. Elsewhere a large number of new unitary authorities have been established. Bristol, for example, is no longer at the heart of Avon, but nor has it returned to its Gloucestershire roots. Leicester has an authority of its own, despite being located in the middle of the county of Leicestershire.

We have attempted to adopt a logical approach (incorporating Bristol within Gloucestershire and Leicester within Leicestershire, etc.) to minimise this confusion. Some border towns and villages may still surprise you, however. The postal address may be in one county whereas the actual place is over the boundary. We have tried to place all entries in the counties to which they actully belong (and not where the post office may indicate that they should be), so be prepared for a bit of county-hopping along the borders.

The brewery entries come first, at the beginning of the county, followed by the pubs and brewpubs, organised alphabetically by town or village. We have attempted to give as full an address as possible and a telephone number in most cases. Brief directions may also be found within the entry itself but, if you do get lost and there is no one available to ask, a call ahead should keep the inconvenience to a minimum.

Our primary aim is to make this guide as useful to people looking for a place to drink real ale as possible. The criteria, therefore, is that a selection of real ales in proportion to the number of beers sold in total is always available. Tied houses, even those tied to national breweries, are included if they meet this criteria. However, because cask ales are the focus of our project we have usually excluded details of the keg beers available.

Where possible, we have sought to include the licensee's name for we believe that the character and quality of a pub owes much to the person who runs it. Inevitably, these people move on and many enjoy the challenge of taking on a new pub and establishing its place on the map. While every acknowledgement should be made of the nation's finest innkeepers, this is more than just a chance for publicans to see their names in print. We hope that readers will recognise the people who run particularly successful pubs and, as they move, need no other recommendations to visit than that person's name.

Because we believe the beers are the most important thing to be found in a pub, we have sought to give an indication of the names and numbers of ales that you are likely to find when you walk through the door. Of course, there are few hard and fast rules. Availability varies and, on some days, the choice will probably be wider than on others. Nevertheless, a pub that says it has 12 beers on tap should come reasonably close to doing just that. If you discover this is not the case, then we want to know.

There is a short description of the type of pub to be found with each entry, intended to give you an idea of what to expect. If they have told us they specialise in a certain type of food, or have accommodation or other features then we have sought to pass that on. However, as this is not the purpose of our guide we have kept the details to a minimum.

Opening hours are another feature that will inevitably vary, particularly as the Government relaxes the licensing laws. An increasing number of pubs are opening for longer and later than was the case just a few years ago. However, we suggest that, if you are proposing to visit in the middle of the afternoon, a telephone call ahead will ensure that you are not disappointed.

Unfortunately, for a number of reasons it has not been possible to include an entry for every real ale pub in the country. Similarly, there are many pubs about which we have heard favourable reports but which we have been unable to verify first hand. A selection of those pubs appears at the end of each county under the heading 'You Tell Us'. Perhaps if you visit them you can let us know your findings by returning one of the questionnaires at the back of the book. Similarly, If you find a pub does not live up to your expectations or you know of a good pub which is not included, we'd love to hear from you. The pubs already recommended by readers are highlighted with a little 'Reader's Report' logo. Send us your completed questionnaire, or visit our web site at www.foulsham.com and leave us your comments.

Graham Titcombe and Nicolas Andrews

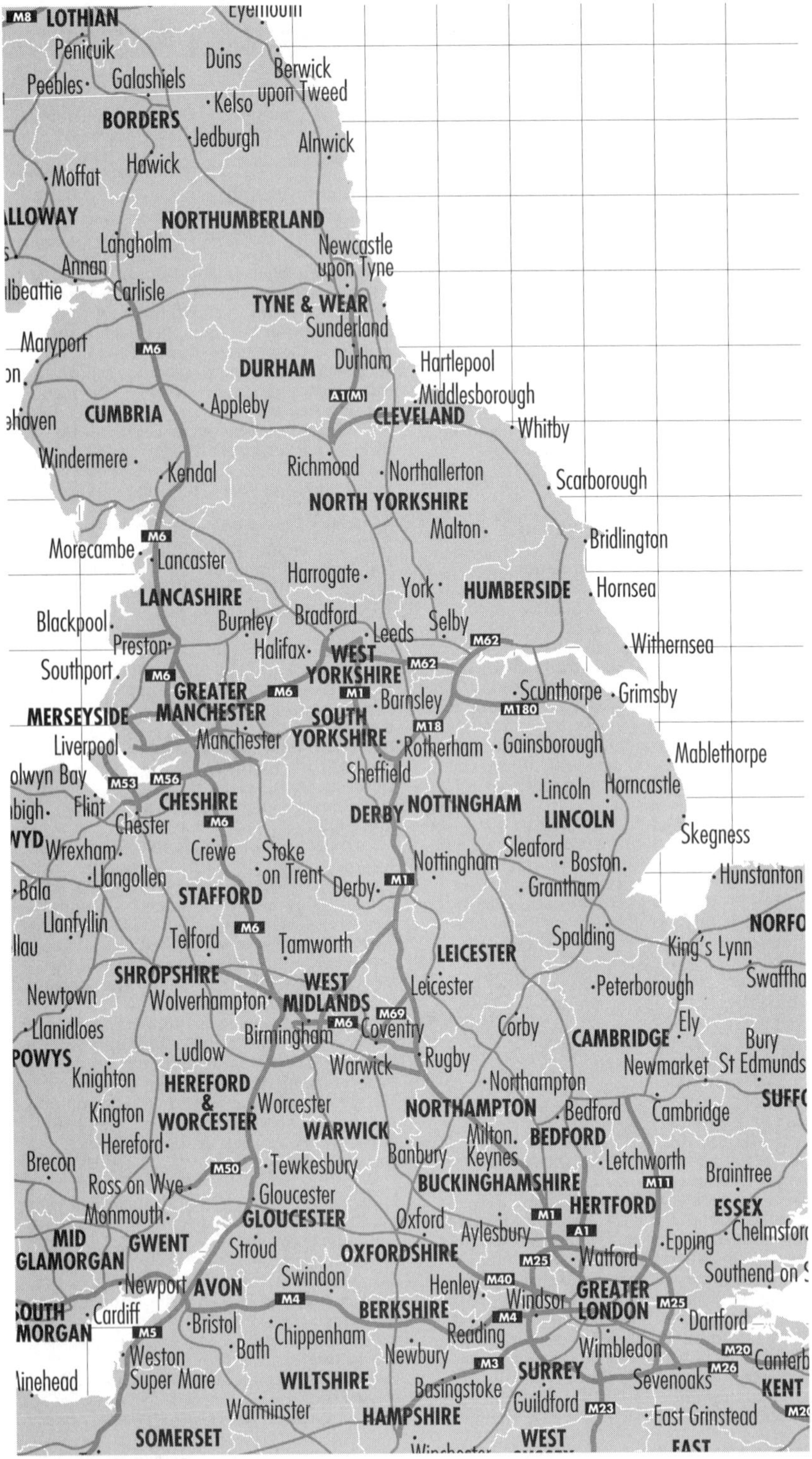
LOTHIAN
Penicuik
Peebles
Galashiels
Duns
Berwick upon Tweed
Kelso
BORDERS
Jedburgh
Alnwick
Moffat
Hawick
NORTHUMBERLAND
Langholm
Newcastle upon Tyne
Annan
Carlisle
TYNE & WEAR
Sunderland
Maryport
M6
DURHAM
Durham
Hartlepool
A1(M)
Middlesborough
Appleby
CUMBRIA
CLEVELAND
Whitby
Windermere
Kendal
Richmond
Northallerton
Scarborough
NORTH YORKSHIRE
Malton
Bridlington
Morecambe
Lancaster
Harrogate
York
HUMBERSIDE
Hornsea
LANCASHIRE
Blackpool
Burnley
Bradford
Leeds
Selby
M62
Preston
Halifax
WEST YORKSHIRE
Withernsea
Southport
GREATER MANCHESTER
M1
Barnsley
Scunthorpe
Grimsby
MERSEYSIDE
SOUTH YORKSHIRE
M18
M180
Liverpool
Manchester
Rotherham
Gainsborough
Mablethorpe
Sheffield
M53
M56
Lincoln
Horncastle
Flint
CHESHIRE
DERBY
NOTTINGHAM
LINCOLN
Chester
Skegness
Wrexham
Crewe
Stoke on Trent
Nottingham
Sleaford
Boston
Llangollen
Derby
Grantham
Hunstanton
Bala
STAFFORD
Llanfyllin
Telford
Tamworth
LEICESTER
Spalding
King's Lynn
SHROPSHIRE
WEST MIDLANDS
Leicester
Peterborough
Newtown
Wolverhampton
M69
Llanidloes
Birmingham
Coventry
Corby
CAMBRIDGE
Ely
POWYS
Ludlow
Warwick
Rugby
Newmarket
Bury St Edmunds
Knighton
HEREFORD & WORCESTER
Northampton
Kington
Worcester
NORTHAMPTON
Bedford
Cambridge
Hereford
WARWICK
Milton Keynes
BEDFORD
Brecon
M50
Tewkesbury
Banbury
Letchworth
Braintree
Ross on Wye
Gloucester
BUCKINGHAMSHIRE
M11
Monmouth
GLOUCESTER
Oxford
HERTFORD
ESSEX
MID GLAMORGAN
GWENT
Stroud
Aylesbury
A1
Epping
OXFORDSHIRE
M25
Watford
Newport
AVON
Swindon
Henley
M40
Windsor
GREATER LONDON
M4
Cardiff
Bristol
BERKSHIRE
Reading
Dartford
M5
Bath
Chippenham
Newbury
Wimbledon
M20
Weston Super Mare
WILTSHIRE
M3
SURREY
Sevenoaks
M26
KENT
Basingstoke
Guildford
M23
East Grinstead
Warminster
HAMPSHIRE
SOMERSET
WEST

Lowestoft
Norwich
Swaffham
King's Lynn
Spalding
Eye
Ipswich · Felixstowe
SUFFOLK
Bury St Edmunds
Newmarket
Peterborough
CAMBRIDGE
Ely
Cambridge
Braintree
Chelmsford
ESSEX
Southend on Sea
Bedford
Letchworth
HERTFORD
Epping
Watford
GREATER LONDON
Dartford
Canterbury
Dover
KENT
M26
Sevenoaks
East Grinstead
Hastings
Eastbourne
EAST SUSSEX
Brighton
Bognor Regis
WEST SUSSEX
Guildford
SURREY
Wimbledon
Windsor
M25
M23
M11
A1
M1
M40
M4
M3
Northampton
NORTHAMPTON
Milton Keynes
BUCKINGHAMSHIRE
Aylesbury
Banbury
Oxford
Henley
OXFORDSHIRE
Reading
Newbury
BERKSHIRE
Basingstoke
Winchester
HAMPSHIRE
Portsmouth
Sandown
Southampton
Bournemouth
Poole
M27
Corby
Rugby
LEICESTER
Leicester
WARWICK
Warwick
Coventry
M69
WEST MIDLANDS
Birmingham
Wolverhampton
M6
Tamworth
Telford
SHROPSHIRE
Ludlow
Knighton
HEREFORD & WORCESTER
Worcester
Tewkesbury
Gloucester
GLOUCESTER
Stroud
M50
Kington
Hereford
Ross on Wye
Monmouth
GWENT
Newport
AVON
Bristol
Bath
Chippenham
Swindon
M4
WILTSHIRE
Warminster
Weston Super Mare
SOMERSET
Taunton
Yeovil
DORSET
Weymouth
Lyme Regis
Honiton
Exmouth
Exeter
M5
DEVON
Torquay
Dartmouth
Barnstaple
Bideford
Bude
Okehampton
Tavistock
Plymouth
Liskeard
CORNWALL
Bodmin
Launceston
Padstow
Newquay
St Ives
Penzance
Helston
Falmouth
Truro
Barmouth
Dolgellau
Towyn
Aberystwyth
Aberayron
Lampeter
Llandovery
POWYS
Newtown
Llanidloes
Brecon
DYFED
New Quay
Cardigan
Fishguard
Haverfordwest
Pembroke
WEST GLAMORGAN
Swansea
Porthcawl
MID GLAMORGAN
SOUTH GLAMORGAN
Cardiff
Minehead
Ilfracombe
Ilminster
Bognor
M5

MAP OF ENGLAND   25

Places Featured:

Bedford
Biggleswade
Dunstable
Great Barford
Henlow
Leighton Buzzard
Luton

Millbrook Village
Ridgmont
Shefford
Stotfold
Studham
Wingfield

THE BREWERIES

B & T BREWERY LTD

The Brewery, Shefford SG17 5DZ
☎ *01462 815080*

MIDSUMMER ALE 3.5% ABV
Seasonal, easy-drinking brew.
SHEFFORD BITTER 3.8% ABV
Golden and hoppy with dry hop finish.
SHEFFORD DARK MILD 3.8% ABV
Rich, mellow, dry and hoppy dark mild.
BARLEY MOW 3.8% ABV
Seasonal, quenching hoppy brew.
BEDFORDSHIRE CLANGER 3.8% ABV
Seasonal, crisp and well-hopped.
SANTA'S SLAYER 4.0% ABV
Seasonal, with sweeter fruit and malt flavour.
TURKEY'S TRAUMA 4.0% ABV
Seasonal, well-balanced beer.
BODYSNATCHER 4.5% ABV
Seasonal, sweetness with balancing hops.
EASTER EGGSTRA 4.5% ABV
Seasonal, with malt throughout.
GUY FAWKES 4.5% ABV
Seasonal, amber malty beer with good
hoppiness.
ROMEO'S RUIN 4.5% ABV
Seasonal, hoppy and bitter.
DRAGONSLAYER 4.5% ABV
Sharp, light and golden with good body.
SHEFFORD PALE ALE 4.5% ABV
Hoppy with balancing malt and dry finish.
EDWIN TAYLOR'S EXTRA STOUT 4.5% ABV
Creamy and full-bodied.
EMERALD ALE 5.0% ABV
Seasonal, green-coloured and rounded.
JULIET'S REVENGE 5.0% ABV
Seasonal, smooth and rounded.
SHEFFORD OLD DARK 5.0% ABV
Deep red, sweet caramel and malt flavour.
SHEFFORD OLD STRONG 5.0% ABV
Hoppy with bitter malty flavour.
BLACK BAT 6.0% ABV
Ruby black, malt and fruit flavour.
2XS 6.0% ABV
Golden, rich aroma and fruit undertones.
SHEFFORD 2000 6.5% ABV
Powerful barley wine.
Plus regular commemorative and celebratory brews.

CHARLES WELLS LTD

*The Eagle Brewery, Havelock Street, Bedford
MK40 4LU*
☎ *01234 272766*

EAGLE 3.6% ABV
Balanced, dry, full-flavoured IPA.
BOMBARDIER 4.3% ABV
Hoppy, well-balanced with dry finish.
FARGO 5.0% ABV
Bittersweet, fruity flavour with dryness in
the finish.

POTTON BREWING CO.

*10 Shannon Place, Potton, Sandy
SG19 2PZ*
☎ *01767 261042*

SHANNON IPA 3.6% ABV
Traditional, hoppy IPA.
PHOENIX 3.8% ABV
Soft, smooth and hoppy.
SHAMBLES 4.3% ABV
Hoppy bitterness with balancing sweetness.
VILLAGE BIKE 4.3% ABV
Hoppy brew.
PRIDE OF POTTON 6.0% ABV
Warming and dry-hopped.

BEDFORD

The Castle

17 Newnham Street, Bedford MK40 3JR
☎ *(01234) 353295* Michael Holmes

A Charles Wells tenancy. Four guest beers available from a range of 12 per year including Morland Old Speckled Hen, Marston's Pedigree, Young's Special, Brains Bitter and Badger Tanglefoot.

A two-bar public house with country pub atmosphere. Bar food available at lunchtime and evenings. Car park, accommodation. Well-behaved children allowed.

12–3pm and 5.30–11pm Mon–Thurs and Sun; all day Fri–Sat.

De Parys Hotel

45 De Parys Avenue, Bedford MK40 2UA
☎ *(01234) 352121* Joanna Worthy

A freehouse with Castle Eden, Potton Brewery and Fenland Brewery ales regularly available plus Fuller's London Pride. Beers changed weekly with emphasis on smaller breweries.

Hotel with bar, garden, 100-seater restaurant and 20 rooms. Situated near the park. Food available at lunchtimes and evenings Mon–Sat, and all day Sun. Children allowed.

All day, every day.

The Wellington Arms

Wellington Street, Bedford MK40 2JA
☎ *(01234) 308033* Eric Mills (Manager)

A B&T tied house, with Shefford Bitter, Dragonslayer, Shefford Dark Mild, Shefford Old Strong and Adnams Bitter always available, plus three guests from microbreweries such as Rebellion, Border, North Yorkshire and Mighty Oak. Hoegarden and real cider also served.

This Mecca for real ale drinkers is a traditional local with wooden floors. Large collection of real ale memorabilia, including bottles and pump clips. Patio and small car park. Darts and dominoes. Bar snacks available all day. Children allowed outside only. Situated near the prison.

12pm–11pm (10.30pm Sun).

BIGGLESWADE

The Brown Bear

29 Hitchin Street, Biggleswade SG18 8BE
☎ *(01767) 316161*
Mary and Alan Hamilton

Eight hand pumps serving a constantly changing range of real ales (1,200 in two years) from micro and other small breweries. Recent examples include beers from Maypole, Cottage, Bank Top, Salopian, Teignworthy and Eccleshall.

A two-bar, open-plan pub with a large non-smoking eating area. Two annual beer festivals and a mini festival on the second weekend of every month. Homemade food available all day. Located on the main street, off the market square.

12–3pm and 5–11pm Mon–Thurs; 11am–11pm Fri–Sat; 12–3pm and 7–10.30pm Sun.

The Wheatsheaf

5 Lawrence Road, Biggleswade SG18 0LS
☎ *(01767) 222220* Mr R E Stimson

Greene King IPA and XX Mild regularly available.

Simple, unspoilt, small and friendly pub known for its well-kept beer. No food. Beer garden and children's play area.

11am–4pm and 7–11pm Mon–Fri; 11am–11pm Sat; 12–10.30pm Sun.

DUNSTABLE

The Victoria

69 West Street, Dunstable LU6 1ST
☎ *(01582) 662682* Ian Mackay

Five hand pumps regularly serving a house beer (Victoria Ale) from the Tring Brewery, plus a range of guest beers (approx. 200 per year) from independent breweries such as Fuller's, Vale, Mauldons, Cottage, Wye Valley, York and Fernandes.

A traditional pub just outside the town centre. Bar food is served at lunchtimes only (12–2.30pm), with roasts on Sundays. Well-behaved children allowed. The landlord's policy is to have a session, a premium and a mind-blowing beer always on sale! Regular beer festivals are held in the barn at the rear of the pub. Small patio-style garden where regular barbecues are held in summer.

All day, every day.

GREAT BARFORD

The Golden Cross

2–4 Bedford Road, Great Barford MK44 3JD
☎ *(01234) 870439* Mr Older

Greene King IPA permanently available, plus four guest beers changed weekly including Hop Back Summer Lightning and brews from Charles Wells, Bateman, Shepherd Neame, Morland and Wadworth, among others.

A traditional pub on the main road with an unconventional twist as the rear houses a Chinese restaurant. There is only Chinese food available. Children allowed in restaurant.

OPEN *12.30–2.30pm and 5–11pm Mon–Fri; 11am–11pm Sat; 12–10.30pm Sun.*

HENLOW

The Engineers Arms

68 High Street, Henlow SG16 6AA
☎ *(01462) 812284* Kevin Macuin

Everards Tiger, Timothy Taylor Landlord and Fuller's London Pride usually available. Six guest beers are usually served, changing twice weekly, and may include Hop Back Summer Lightning and beers from Cottage, Wolf, Kitchen and many micro-breweries from around the country.

P opular village local with pleasant beer terrace. Sky TV in separate room. Rolls, sandwiches and traditional hot pies available. Children welcome in separate room and garden. Pub in Henlow village, not Henlow Camp.

OPEN *12–11pm (12–10.30pm Sun).*

LEIGHTON BUZZARD

The Stag

1 Heath Road, Leighton Buzzard LU7 8AB
☎ *(01525) 372710* Bob Patrick

Serves the full range of Fuller's beers, including seasonal specials such as Honey Dew, Summer Ale, Red Fox and Old Winter Ale.

A traditional town pub with food served Mon–Sat lunchtimes (12–2pm) and evenings (6–9.30pm). Children not allowed.

OPEN *12–2.30pm and 6–11pm.*

LUTON

The Bricklayers Arms

High Town Road, Luton LU2 0DD
☎ *(01582) 611017* Alison Taylor

Everards Beacon and Tiger, and Bateman Mild usually available with two weekly changing guest beers, perhaps from B&T, Nethergate, Dent, Crouch Vale, Rebellion, Burton Bridge and many others.

B are boards and barrels set the tone for this traditional pub, first known to be trading in 1834. Lunchtime bar snacks. Car park. No children.

OPEN *12–2.30pm and 5–11pm Mon–Thurs; 12–11pm Fri–Sat; 12–10.30pm Sun.*

The Globe

26 Union Street, Luton LU1 3AN
☎ *(01582) 728681*

Greene King IPA always available, plus one guest from an ever-changing range.

F riendly one-bar pub, situated just outside town centre. Strong local support, with bar games and teams a regular feature. All major sporting events shown. Beer festivals held. Car park. Food served 12–3pm and 5–8pm Mon–Sat, plus breakfast 8am–12 and Sunday lunches 12–4pm. No children.

OPEN *All day, every day.*

The Two Brewers

43 Dumfries Street, Luton LU1 5AY
☎ *(01582) 616008* Andy Gill

Four B&T brews always available (Shefford Bitter, Dragonslayer, Edwin Taylor's Extra Stout and Shefford Old Strong), plus three changing guest ales perhaps including Timothy Taylor Landlord or brews from Adnams, Titanic, Tisbury, Wye Valley, Woods, Hoskins, Nethergate, Mansfield or Everards.

A welcoming, old-style, back-street pub just two minutes from the town centre. No food. Children allowed.

OPEN *12–11pm (10.30pm Sun).*

MILLBROOK VILLAGE

The Chequers

Millbrook Village MK45 2JB
☎ *(01525) 403835* Mr G Polti

Fuller's London Pride and Hook Norton Old Hooky are regulars, others appear occasionally.

A n Italian family-run pub specialising in pasta and chargrilled food, which is available every day (12–3pm and 6.30–11pm) except Sunday. Children allowed in the restaurant. Located off A507 from Ridgmont, opposite the Vauxhall proving ground.

OPEN *11.30am–3pm and 6.30–11pm Mon–Sat (10.30pm Sun).*

RIDGMONT

The Rose & Crown

89 High Street, Ridgmont MK43 0TY
☎ *(01525) 280245* Neil McGregor

Adnams Broadside and Mansfield Riding Bitter are regularly available, while other guests may include Morland's Old Speckled Hen or a Young's brew.

A traditional, rural pub with food available (12–2pm and 7–9pm). Children allowed.

10.30am–2.30pm and 6–11pm Mon–Sat (10.30pm Sun).

SHEFFORD

Brewery Tap

14 North Bridge Street, Shefford SG17 5DH
☎ *(01462) 628448* David Mortimer

B&T's Shefford Bitter, Dragonslayer and Dark Mild are always available plus two guests, which change every week, but might include brews from Dent, Crouch Vale, Leatherbritches, Yorkshire or Burton Bridge.

A traditional alehouse and, as the name suggests, the B&T brewery tap. Snacks available, but no bar food. Small children's room and garden.

11am–11pm Mon–Sat; 12–10.30pm Sun.

STOTFOLD

The Stag Inn

Brook Street, Stotfold SG5 4LA
☎ *(01462) 730261* Ray Rudzki

Home of Abel Brown's Brewery, which was launched in 1995 and is named after the first publican of The Stag. Full range of home beers brewed and sold on the premises plus various guests, three or four served at any one time (250 per year), to include ales from Titanic and Hop Back.

B uilt in 1920, the pub is set in a rural location. Thai and Indian food is available in evenings. Accommodation. Children allowed. One mile from A1 junction 10.

JACK OF HEARTS 4.0%
A premium bitter with dry finish.
LITTLE BILLY 4.0%
A light, pale ale.
POCOLOCO 5.0%
PLOUGHMAN'S PICKLE 5.0%
A strong, brown ale

12–2.30pm and 5–11pm Mon–Thurs; all day Fri–Sat; 12–10.30pm Sun.

STUDHAM

The Red Lion at Studham

Church Road, Studham LU6 2QA
☎ *(01582) 872530* Philip Potts

Five real ales available, perhaps including Timothy Taylor Landlord, Greene King Abbot Ale, Fuller's London Pride, Wadworth 6X and Farmers Glory, plus Black Sheep Bitter and Thwaites or Marston brews. The selection changes on a weekly basis.

T raditional country pub with food at lunchtimes and evenings (12–2.30pm and 7–9.30pm). Children allowed at lunchtimes only.

11.30am–3pm and 5.30–11pm Mon–Fri; 11am–11pm Sat; 12–10.30pm Sun.

WINGFIELD

The Plough Inn

Tebworth Road, Wingfield, Leighton Buzzard LU7 9QH
☎ *(01525) 873077* Mr and Mrs Worsley

Six beers permanently available including B&T Shefford Bitter, Fuller's London Pride, Brakspear Special and a Hook Norton brew. Also a large number of guests per year including B&T Black Bat, Vale Notley Bitter and many more.

A thatched olde-English pub. CAMRA South Bedfordshire Pub of the Year 1993 and 1994. Bar and restaurant food available at lunchtimes and evenings. Garden with children's play area. From M1 junction 12, follow the A5120 through Toddington to Houghton Regis. Turn off to Wingfield.

11am–3pm and 5.30–11pm Mon–Fri; 11am–11pm Sat; 12–10.30pm Sun.

YOU TELL US

★ *The Cock*, 23 High Street, Broom
★ *The Countryman*, Shefford
★ *The Old Bell*, Church Road, Totternhoe
★ *The Queen's Head*, The Lane, Tebworth
★ *The Swan with Two Necks*, High Street, Sharnbrook
★ *The White Hart*, Mill Lane, Campton

Places Featured:

Aldworth
Brimpton
Broad Laying
Caversham
Chieveley
Cookham
Eton
Frilsham
Hurley
Littlewick Green
Lower Inkpen
Maidenhead

Newbury
Reading
Shinfield
Slough
Sonning
Stanford Dingley
Sunningdale
Sunninghill
Tidmarsh
Twyford
White Waltham
Winterbourne

THE BREWERIES

BUTTS BREWERY LTD

*Unit 6a, Northfield Farm, Wantage Road,
Great Shefford, Hungerford RG17 7BY*
☎ *01488 648133*

 JESTER 3.5% ABV
Light, easy-drinking.
BITTER 4.0% ABV
Golden and fruity.
BLACKGUARD 4.5% ABV
Smooth chocolate malt flavour.
BARBUS BARBUS 4.6% ABV
Hoppy throughout.
GOLDEN BROWN 5.0% ABV
Hoppy spice flavour.
Plus occasional brews.

THE WEST BERKSHIRE BREWERY CO.

*Pot Kiln Lane, Frilsham, Yattendon, Newbury
RG18 0XX*
☎ *01635 202638*

 SKIFF 3.6% ABV
Refreshing session beer.
GOOD OLD BOY 4.0% ABV
Hop flavours throughout.
BRICK KILN BITTER 4.0% ABV
Fruity. Only brewed for the Pot Kiln.
OLD TYLER 4.0% ABV
Brewed for The Bell at Aldworth.
DR HEXTER'S WEDDING 4.1% ABV
Golden and refreshing.
GRAFT BITTER 4.3% ABV
Hoppy, with bitterness in the finish.
GOLDSTAR 5.0% ABV
Brewed with honey.
DR HEXTER'S HEALER 5.0% ABV
Pale and fruity.
Plus occasional brews.

THE PUBS

ALDWORTH

The Bell
Aldworth, Nr Reading RG8 9SE
☎ *(01635) 578272* Mr and Mrs IJ Macaulay

Arkell's 3B and Kingsdown Ale, West Berkshire's Old Tyler and Magnificent Mild plus Crouch Vale Best always available.

A small, unaltered inn dating from 1340 in good walking country. Bar food available at lunchtimes and evenings. Well-behaved children allowed in the tap room. Country garden with adjacent cricket ground. Two miles from Streatley on B4009 to Newbury.

Closed all day Mon (except bank holidays). 11am–3pm and 6–11pm Tue–Sat; 12–3pm and 7–10.30pm Sun.

BRIMPTON

The Three Horseshoes
Brimpton Lane, Brimpton
☎ *(0118) 971 2183* Mr J O'Keeffe

Fuller's London Pride and a guest beer regularly available, perhaps from Adnams, Wadworth or a seasonal Fuller's beer.

Small, country pub with public and lounge bar, situated off the A4 between Thatcham and Midgham. Food served 12–2pm Mon–Sat. Beer garden. Car park. Well-behaved children welcome, but no special facilities.

11am–3pm and 6–11pm Mon–Sat; 12–3pm and 7–10.30pm Sun.

The Rampant Cat

Broad Laying, Wootton Hill, Nr Newbury RG20 9TP
☎ *(01635) 253474*
Mr JP and Mrs NJ Molyneux

Greene King Abbot Ale and IPA and Fuller's London Pride regularly available, plus a guest beer changed every eight weeks, such as Charles Wells Bombardier.

A well-presented pub with good atmosphere and magnificent gardens, set in the beautiful Berkshire countryside. Food served lunchtimes and evenings Tues–Sat, evenings only Mon and lunchtimes only Sun. Car park. Children welcome if eating.

OPEN *12–3pm and 6–11pm Mon–Sat; 12–3pm and 7–10.30pm Sun.*

Baron Cadogan

22–4 Prospect Street, Caversham, Reading RG4 8JG
☎ *(0118) 947 0626* Philip Ashby

Three hand pumps serving a constantly changing range of guests, with four or five different beers each week. Regulars include Fuller's London Pride, Greene King Abbot, Shepherd Neame Spitfire, Archers Golden, Hogs Back TEA and Morland Old Speckled Hen.

A modern town freehouse with food available all day. No children.

OPEN *All day, every day.*

Olde Red Lion

Green Lane, Chieveley RG20 8XB
☎ *(01635) 248379* Lance and Jackie Headley

Arkell's 3B and Kingsdown Ale always available plus other, seasonal Arkell's brews.

A traditional pub with bar food available (12–2.30pm and 6.30–10pm). Children welcome. Located north off M4 J13, near the services. Coach parties welcome.

OPEN *11am–3pm and 6–11pm (10.30pm Sun).*

Cookham Tavern

Lower Road, Cookham SL6 9HJ
☎ *(01628) 529519* Marilyn Rothwell

A Whitbread tied house. Up to six cask ales including Brakspear's Bitter, Greene King Abbot Ale, Marston's Pedigree and Young's ales. Changed monthly.

A traditional, community local with food available (12–2.30pm and 6–9.30pm). Children allowed. Near Cookham station.

OPEN *11.30am–2.30pm and 5.30–11pm Mon–Thur; 11.30am–11pm Fri–Sat; 12–10.30pm Sun.*

Waterman's Arms

Brocas Street, Eton SL4 6BW
☎ *(01753) 861001* Mr Collibee

Greene King IPA, Wadworth 6X, Charles Wells Bombardier and a Brakspear brew always available, plus guests from Bateman, Gales and Felinfoel.

An old English-style pub with food served in a separate restaurant at lunchtimes and evenings. Children allowed.

OPEN *11am–2.30pm and 6–11pm Mon–Fri; all day Sat–Sun.*

Pot Kiln

Yattendon, Frilsham RG18 0XX
☎ *(01635) 201366* Philip Gent

West Berkshire Brick Kiln Bitter only available here, plus Morland Original, Arkell's 3B and others. Seasonal brews and specials, usually from West Berkshire brewery.

A traditional pub with the West Berkshire micro-brewery in an out-building at the back. Food available (12–1.45pm and 7–9.30pm). Children allowed. From Newbury take B4009 into Hermitage. Turn right at The Fox, follow Yattendon sign. Take second turning on right and continue for a mile. Pub is on the right.

OPEN *12–2.30pm (except Tues) and 6.30–11pm Mon–Sat; 12–3pm and 7–10.30pm Sun.*

HURLEY

The Dew Drop Inn

Batts Green, Honey Lane, Hurley SL6 6RB
☎ *(01628) 824327* CH and BD Morley

Brakspear Mild, Bitter, Special and the seasonal ale regularly available.

Recently refurbished and sensitively extended, cottage-style country pub in an idyllic woodland setting. Fresh, home-cooked food served every lunchtime and evening. Large car park and garden. Well-behaved children welcome. To find the pub, look for a sharp turning halfway along Honey Lane with a smaller lane leading off. Follow this for 300 yards. Pub will be found on the right-hand side.

OPEN *12–3pm and 6–11pm Mon–Sat; 12–3pm and 7–10.30pm Sun.*

LITTLEWICK GREEN

The Cricketers

Coronation Road, Littlewick Green SL6 3RA
☎ *(01628) 822888* Mr Carter

Timothy Taylor Landlord, Fuller's London Pride and Brakspear Pale Ale always available. Other brews rotating regularly may include Shepherd Neame Spitfire, Wadworth 6X, Morland Old Speckled Hen or something from Timothy Taylor..

A traditional village pub situated on the village green close to the old Bath Road (A4). Food available (12–2pm and 7–9pm). Cricket regularly played at weekends. Children allowed.

OPEN *11am–11pm Mon–Sat; 12–10.30pm Sun.*

LOWER INKPEN

Swan Inn

Lower Inkpen, Hungerford RG17 9DX
☎ *(01488) 668326* Mr Harris

Hook Norton Bitter and Mild and Butts Brewery's Traditional and Blackguard regularly available, plus a range of guest beers.

A traditional village hotel with 'free house' bar. Ten bedrooms and a restaurant. Bar food also available with organic food a speciality. Organic farm shop and butchery on the premises. Children allowed.

OPEN *All day, every day.*

MAIDENHEAD

The Hobgoblin

High Street, Maidenhead SL6 1QE
☎*(01628) 636510* D Dean (Manager)

A Wychwood tied house with at least two seasonal Wychwood ales always available, plus three guests changing weekly, such as Fuller's London Pride, Rebellion ales, Hooray Henley, or Ow'sthat (a cricket celebration ale).

A lively town pub with a young clientele, particularly at weekends. One bar, beer garden. Food available 12–2pm. Children allowed in the garden only.

OPEN *12–11pm Mon–Sat; 3–10.30pm Sun.*

NEWBURY

The Hobgoblin

Bartholomew Street, Newbury RG14 5HB
☎ *(01635) 47336* Gay Diss

A Wychwood special always available, plus up to five guest ales such as Wadworth 6X, Brakspear Special or other Wychwood brew. Beers changed every fortnight.

A traditional town pub with one bar, beams and wooden floors. Food available at lunchtime only. Children allowed.

OPEN *12–11pm (10.30pm Sun).*

The Monument

57 Northbrook Street, Newbury RG14 1AN
☎ *(01635) 41964* Simon Owens

Tap & Spile Premium, Gales HSB, Butts Traditional and Butts Barbus Barbus permanently available.

This 350-year-old pub is the oldest in Newbury. Until recently, it was owned by the Tap & Spile chain and has only just changed back to its original name. Good food available all day, including Sunday roasts. Children and dogs very welcome.

OPEN *11am–11pm Mon–Sat; 12–10.30pm Sun.*

READING

3B's Bar

Old Town Hall, Blagrave Street, Reading RG1 1QH
☎ *(0118) 939 9803* Stefano Buratta

Four real ales at any one time often including Bunces Old Smokey and Pigswill, and Timothy Taylor Landlord. Guests changed weekly from breweries such as Ash Vine, Ushers, Greene King and others.

A friendly café bar right next to the station. Families welcome. Food available all day.

OPEN *11am–11pm Mon–Sat; 12–10.30pm Sun.*

Back of Beyond

104–8 Kings Road, Reading RG4 8DT
☎ *(0118) 959 5906* Sean Pickering

Fuller's London Pride is among the beers always available. Regular guests include Archers Golden and Hogs Back Traditional English Ale plus others from independent breweries such as Cains, Caledonian, Cotleigh, Exmoor, Hardys & Hansons, Smiles, Wychwood and Timothy Taylor.

A traditional JD Wetherspoon's pub with garden, located five minutes from the railway station. Food available all day. No children.

[OPEN] *10am–11pm Mon–Sat; 12–10.30pm Sun.*

The Brewery Tap

27 Castle Street, Reading RG1 7SB
☎ *(0118) 957 6280*
Mike Moore (brewer and landlord)

Shepherd Neame Masterbrew and Spitfire, plus Marston's Pedigree usually available.

Traditional-style city-centre pub, home to the Tudor Brewing Co. Presently not brewing, although brewery tours are still available. Food served 12–3pm Mon–Fri. No children.

[OPEN] *11am–11pm Mon–Sat; 12–10.30pm Sun.*

The Hobgoblin

2 Broad Street, Reading RG1 2BH
☎ *(01734) 508119* Duncan Ward

Wychwood beers always available plus up to 700 guests per year exclusively from small independent brewers. No national products are stocked. Also real cider, perry and genuine German lager.

Small, friendly town-centre pub. No jukebox, but background R&B etc. Occasional live music, traditional pub games. Bar food at lunchtimes. Supervised children allowed up to 7pm.

[OPEN] *All permitted hours.*

The Hop Leaf

163–5 Southampton Street, Reading RG1 2QZ
☎ *(0118) 931 4700*

The full range of Hop Back ales brewed and served on the premises.

This formerly derelict pub on the edge of the town centre was taken over and revitalised as a brewpub by the Hop Back Brewery. A late Victorian building, recently refurbished. Parking can be difficult.

MILD	3.0% ABV
GFB	3.5% ABV
HOP LEAF	4.0% ABV
EXTRA STOUT	4.0% ABV
SUMMER LIGHTNING	5.0% ABV
RYE BEER	5.0% ABV
WHEAT BEER	5.0% ABV

[OPEN] *All permitted hours.*

Sweeney & Todd

10 Castle Street, Reading RG1 7RD
☎ *(0118) 958 6466* Catherine J Hayward

Wadworth 6X usually available, plus one guest such as Eldridge Pope Royal Oak, Adnams Best and brews from Butts, Itchen Valley, Brakspear, Gales, Greene King and Young's.

A traditional 'pie and pint' pub. A huge range of pies is served all day in the dedicated restaurant. Children allowed in the restaurant.

[OPEN] *11am–11pm Mon–Sat; 12–10.30pm Sun.*

Wheelwright's Arms

Davis Way, St Nicholas Hurst, Reading RG10 0TR
☎ *(0118) 934 4100* Kevin Morley

Four Wadworth brews always available, plus four guests perhaps including Adnams Extra, Badger Tanglefoot and others. Guests are changed monthly.

A traditional pub on the Twyford Road with low beams and a real fire. Food available 12–2pm and 6.30–9pm. Children allowed in restaurant only.

[OPEN] *11.30am–2.30pm and 5.30–11pm Mon–Fri; 11am–11pm Sat; 12–10.30pm Sun.*

Bell & Bottle

School Green, Shinfield, Reading RG2 9EE
☎ *(0118) 988 3563* Fran Jane

Nine cask ales available, regularly featuring beers from Beckett's, Cottage, Wychwood, Butts, Smiles, plus Marston's Pedigree, Archers Village and Golden, Rebellion Mild and Wadworth 6X from time to time. Beers rotated weekly.

A traditional pub with food available. Children and dogs welcome.

[OPEN] *11.30am–11.30pm Mon–Sat; 12–10.30pm Sun.*

Moon & Spoon

86–8 High Street, Slough SL1 1EL
☎ *(01753) 531650*
Alan and Nyki Martin

Shepherd Neame Spitfire always available, plus two guest beers, changed when the barrel runs out!

A themed JD Wetherspoon's pub with a lively clientele. Food served all day, every day. Children not allowed. At the end of the High Street, opposite the library.

[OPEN] *10.30am–11pm Mon–Sat; 12–10.30pm Sun.*

SONNING

The Bull

High Street, Sonning, Reading RG4 6UP
☎ *(0118) 969 3901*
Christine and Dennis Mason

A George Gale tied house, permanently serving Gales HSB, Best and Butser, plus Gales seasonal specials. Marston's Pedigree often available as a guest.

An old country pub with log fires. Food available lunchtimes and evenings. Children allowed.

OPEN *11am–3pm and 5.30–11pm Mon–Fri; all day Sat–Sun.*

STANFORD DINGLEY

The Boot

Stanford Dingley, Reading RG7 6LT
☎ *(0118) 974 4292* John Haley

Real ales rotated fortnightly usually from Smiles, Archers or West Berkshire breweries.

A traditional, olde-worlde freehouse. Bar food available (12–2.15pm and 7–9.15pm). Children welcome.

OPEN *11am–3pm and 6–11pm Mon–Sat (7–10pm Sun).*

The Bull

Stanford Dingley, Reading RG7 6LS
☎ *(0118) 974 4409* Pat Langdon

West Berkshire's Good Old Boy, Skiff and Gold Star plus Brakspear Bitter regularly available. Also West Berkshire specials as and when available.

A traditional freehouse with food available (12–2.30pm and 7.30–10pm). Well-behaved children allowed in the saloon bar at lunchtimes and early evenings. Six miles from J12 of M4.

OPEN *12–3pm and 7–11pm (10.30pm Sun); closed Mon lunchtime except bank holidays.*

SUNNINGDALE

The Nags Head

28 High Street, Sunningdale SL5 0NG
☎ *(01344) 622725* Dave and Denise West

Harveys Sussex Mild, Pale Ale and Best Bitter usually available plus a Harveys seasonal brew.

Traditional village pub and the only Harveys pub in Berkshire. Games-orientated public bar and spacious lounge bar. Cask Marque award. 'Pub grub' with daily special served 12–2pm Mon–Sat. Car park. Well-behaved children welcome in lounge bar. Play equipment in large garden. Between A30/A329 in Sunningdale village, nearly opposite the church.

OPEN *11.30am–11pm Mon–Sat; 12–10.30pm Sun.*

SUNNINGHILL

The Dukes Head

Upper Village Road, Sunninghill SL5 7AG
☎ *(01344) 626949* Philip Durrant

Marston's Pedigree and Greene King Abbot permanently available, plus Greene King seasonal ales as and when available.

A traditional village pub specialising in Thai food (12–2pm and 7–10pm). Owned by Greene King. Well-behaved children allowed. Upper Village Road runs parallel to the High Street. A beer festival is held once a year.

OPEN *11am–11pm Mon–Sat; 12–10.30pm Sun.*

TIDMARSH

Greyhound

The Street, Tidmarsh RG8 8ER
☎ *(0118) 984 3557* Martin Ford

Five real ales including Fuller's London Pride and others rotated monthly from Shepherd Neame, Rebellion, West Berkshire, Morland, Coniston, Wadworth and other breweries.

A traditional, twelfth-century village pub serving food at lunchtimes. Children allowed. On the main A340.

OPEN *11am–3pm and 5.30–11pm Mon–Fri; 11am–11pm Sat; 12–10.30pm Sun.*

TWYFORD

The Golden Cross

38 Waltham Road, Twyford, Reading RG10 9EG
☎ *(0118) 934 0180* Duncan Campbell

Brakspear brews and Fuller's London Pride permanently available, plus guests regularly including Greene King IPA, Marston's Pedigree, and Wadworth 6X.

A locals' pub with restaurant area and beer garden. Food served every lunchtime and Tues–Sat evenings. Children allowed in the garden and restaurant only.

OPEN *All day, every day.*

WHITE WALTHAM

The Beehive

Waltham Road, White Waltham SL6 3SH
☎ *(01628) 822877* Guy Martin

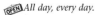 A Whitbread tied house with four cask ales always available, including Fuller's London Pride, a Brakspear brew, plus twice-weekly changing guests perhaps from the Cottage Brewery, Hampshire Brewery and Rebellion.

A rural pub under new management. Two large gardens, one south-facing overlooking cricket pitch, separate restaurant. Food available all day at weekends, lunchtimes and evenings on weekdays. Children welcome.

OPEN *All day, every day.*

WINTERBOURNE

The Winterbourne Arms

Winterbourne, Newbury RG20 8BB
☎ *(01635) 248200* Alan Hodge

Three hand pumps serving a constantly changing range of real ales such as West Berkshire Brewery's Good Old Boy and Morrells Oxford. All independent breweries considered.

A one-bar freehouse with restaurant and attractive garden. Food available every lunchtime and Tues–Sat evenings. Children allowed in the restaurant area. Located off the B4494.

OPEN *11am–3pm and 6–11pm Tues–Sat; 12–3pm Sun. Closed Sun evening and all day Mon.*

YOU TELL US

★ *The Belgian Arms*, Holyport Street, Holyport, Nr Maidenhead
★ *The Cooper's Arms*, 39 Bartholomew Street, Newbury
★ *The Cricketers*, Cricketer's Lane, Warfield
★ *The Crooked Billet*, Honey Hill, Wokingham
★ *The Flower Pot Hotel*, Ferry Lane, Aston
★ *The Horse & Jockey*, 120 Castle Street, Reading
★ *The Vansittart Arms*, 105 Vansittart Road, Windsor

Places Featured:

Ashenden
Asheridge
Beaconsfield
Bradwell Common
Chesham
Cublington
Haddenham
Hedgerley
Ibstone
Little Marlow
Little Missenden
Littleworth Common
Loudwater

Marlow
New Bradwell
Newport Pagnell
North Crawley
Prestwood
Stoke Poges
Stony Stratford
Tatling End
The Lee
Thornborough
Wendover
Wheeler End
Wing

THE BREWERIES

THE CHILTERN BREWERY

Nash Lee Road, Terrick, Aylesbury HP17 0TQ
☎ *(01296) 613647*

CHILTERN ALE 3.7% ABV
Pale, smooth and refreshing clean finish.
BEECHWOOD BITTER 4.3% ABV
Well-rounded, with nut flavours and a long finish.
THREE HUNDREDS OLD ALE 5.0% ABV
Dark, good body and long finish.

REBELLION BEER CO.

Bencombe Farm, Marlow Bottom Road,
Marlow SL7 3LT
☎ *(01628) 476594*

IPA 3.7% ABV
Balanced easy quaffer.
SMUGGLER 4.1% ABV
Well-rounded and full-flavoured.
BLONDE BOMBSHELL 4.3% ABV
Summer brew.
OVERDRAFT ALE 4.3% ABV
Available Jan–Mar.
MUTINY 4.5% ABV
Smooth and hoppy.
RED OKTOBER 4.7% ABV
Autumn ale.
ZEBEDEE 4.7% ABV
Spring ale.
OLD CODGER 5.0% ABV
Winter ale.
Plus seasonal and monthly brews.

SAM TRUEMAN'S BREWERY

The Little Brewery, Henley House, School Lane,
Medmenham SL7 2HJ
☎ *(01491) 576100*

BEST 3.5% ABV
BEE'S KNEES 4.2% ABV
TIPPLE 4.2% ABV
GOLD 5.0% ABV

VALE BREWERY CO. LTD

Thame Road, Haddenham HP17 8BY
☎ *(01844) 290008*

BLACK SWAN 3.3% ABV
Dark mild with lots of roast flavour.
NOTLEY ALE 3.3% ABV
Bitter and refreshing.
WYCHERT ALE 3.9% ABV
Smooth and mellow flavours.
HADDA'S SUMMER GLORY 4.0% ABV
HADDA'S WINTER SOLSTICE 4.1% ABV
Soft, malty flavour. Dec–Feb.
BLACK BEAUTY 4.3% ABV
Malty, full-bodied porter.
EDGAR'S GOLDEN ALE 4.3% ABV
Pale and hoppy.
HADDA'S AUTUMN ALE 4.5% ABV
HADDA'S SPRING GOLD 5.0% ABV
GOOD KING SENSELESS 5.2% ABV

ASHENDEN

Gatehangers

Lower End, Ashenden HP18 0HE
☎ *(01296) 651296*

Wadworth IPA and 6X, Adnams Best and a Badger brew always available plus a guest beer (up to 30 per year) from breweries such as Mole's, Elgood's, Hook Norton, Felinfoel, Everard's, Bateman's, Smiles, or Marston's.

A 300-year-old country pub with traditional atmosphere. Beamed in part with open fires and large L-shaped bar. Bar food at lunchtime and evenings. Car park and garden. Children allowed. Twenty minutes to Oxford. Between the A41 and A418 west of Aylesbury, near the church.

OPEN *12–2.30pm and 7–11pm.*

ASHERIDGE

The Blue Ball

Asheridge, Chesham HP5 2UX
☎ *(01494) 758263* Peter George

A freehouse, whose June beer festival offers at least 32 real ales. Greene King IPA and Fuller's London Pride are always available plus two guest beers, changed weekly, which may come from Adnams, Brakspear, Cottage, Orkney, Rebellion or Arundel breweries.

A traditional pub built in 1851, two miles north of Chesham, with a mixed clientele. Non-smoking function room, big garden. Food served at lunchtime and evenings. Children allowed in dining area.

OPEN *12–2.30pm and 5.30–11pm Mon–Thur; 11am–11pm Fri–Sat; 12–10.30pm Sun.*

BEACONSFIELD

The Greyhound

33 Windsor End, Beaconsfield HP9 2JN
☎ *(01494) 673823* Jamie Godrich

A freehouse, with Fuller's London Pride and Wadworth 6X always on sale. Two guest beers are also available, one changed weekly, one monthly, which may include Brakspear Special, Timothy Taylor Landlord, O'Hanlon's Spring Gold or something from the Vale or Cottage breweries.

A traditional public house with separate dining area. Food served at lunchtime and evenings. Children not admitted.

OPEN *11am–3pm and 5.30–11pm.*

BRADWELL COMMON

The Countryman

Bradwell Boulevard, Bradwell Common, Milton Keynes MK13 8EZ
☎ *(01908) 676346* Dave Keating

A freehouse with eight cask ale pumps. Marston's Pedigree is among the regular brews served.

A one-bar pub built in 1986 in the middle of the estate. Popular with families. Food available. Children's room. Bradwell Boulevard is the main road through Bradwell Common.

OPEN *11am–11pm Mon–Sat; 12–10.30pm Sun.*

CHESHAM

The Black Horse

The Vale, Chesham HP5 3MS
☎ *(01494) 784656* Lyn Hawkes

Tied to Benskins (Carlsberg-Tetley), with four real ales. Regulars include Morland Old Speckled Hen, Black Stallion (5%, brewed specially by Tring Brewery) and Adnams Best Bitter.

A fourteenth-century coaching inn just outside Chesham (with certified ghosts!), mainly operating as a restaurant. Large garden. Children allowed in bar area.

OPEN *12–3pm and 6–11pm Mon–Sat (sometimes all day during summer); 12–10.30pm Sun.*

The Queens Head

120 Church Street, Old Chesham HP5 1JD
☎ *(01494) 783773* Mr Shippey

A freehouse regularly offering Brakspear Bitter and Special, plus Fuller's London Pride. Other brews served include Brakspear and Fuller's seasonal ales.

A traditional family pub, offering English and Thai food in the bar, and a Thai restaurant. Children allowed.

OPEN *11am–2.30pm and 5–11pm Mon–Fri; 11am–3pm and 5–11pm Sat; 12–3pm and 7–10.30pm Sun.*

CUBLINGTON

The Unicorn

High Street, Cublington
☎ *(01296) 681261* Mr and Mrs Ibbotson

Five beers always available including brews from Morland plus Jennings Bitter and Shepherd Neame Spitfire Ale. Approx 100 guests per year including Vale Wychert Ale and Greene King Abbot.

A country pub dating from 1600 with open fires and low beams in the main bar. Bar and restaurant food served at lunchtime and evenings during the week. Car park and garden. Children allowed in the restaurant.

OPEN *12–3pm and 5.30–11pm.*

HADDENHAM

The Rising Sun
9 Thame Road, Haddenham HP17 8EN
☎ *(01844) 291744* Michael Mock

A freehouse with Charles Wells Eagle and IPA always on sale. Guest beers, including Badger Tanglefoot, Wadworth 6X and Morland Old Speckled Hen, change on a daily basis.

A village pub, on the main road from Thame to Aylesbury. Very much a drinker's pub, with bar snacks only. Children allowed until 7.30pm.

OPEN 11am–3pm and 5.30–11pm Mon–Thurs; 11am–11pm Fri–Sat; 12–10.30pm Sun.

HEDGERLEY

The White Horse
Village Lane, Hedgerley, Slough SL2 3UY
☎ (01753) 643225 Mr and Mrs Hobbs

Seven or eight beers always available and dispensed by gravity including brews from Charles Wells and Greene King. Also dozens of guest beers from small breweries only.

Beer festival held every year. No machines, no music, no straight glasses. Bar food at weekends. Car park, garden. Bird sanctuary nearby.

OPEN 11am–2.30pm and 5.30–11pm Mon–Fri; 11am–3pm and 6–11pm Sat; usual Sun hours.

IBSTONE

The Fox
The Common, Ibstone, Nr High Wycombe HP14 3GG
☎ *(01491) 638722* Mrs Banks

Brakspear ales always available plus three guests in summer, two in winter, serving a range of real ales such as Fuller's London Pride or Rebellion. Stocks beers from local breweries whenever possible.

A 300-year-old traditional country inn. Bar and restaurant food available lunchtimes and evenings. Accommodation. Children allowed.

OPEN 12–3pm and 6–11pm (10.30pm Sun).

LITTLE MARLOW

The King's Head
Church Road, Little Marlow SL7 3RZ
☎ *(01628) 484407* Tim Pegrum

Tied to Whitbread with up to six real ales. Fuller's London Pride, Timothy Taylor Landlord and something from Brakspear always on sale. Others, changed every three to four weeks, include Wadworth 6X, Greene King Abbot Ale, Marston's Pedigree and beers from Rebellion, Vale and Eccleshall breweries.

Situated between Marlow and Bourne End, the pub has one large, comfortable bar, a non-smoking dining room, and a function room for 50–80 people. Food is served at lunchtime and evenings Mon–Sat and all day Sun. Children welcome.

OPEN 11am–3pm and 5–11pm Mon–Fri; 11am–11pm Sat; 12–10.30pm Sun.

LITTLE MISSENDEN

The Crown
Little Missenden HP7 0RD
☎ *(01494) 862571* Mr How

A freehouse with four beers on pumps and occasionally one from the wood. Marston's Pedigree, Hook Norton Best and Bateman's brews are always on offer. Other guests, changed twice weekly, include Mordue Workie Ticket or something from Greene King, Brakspear, King and Barnes, Adnams, Rebellion or Vale breweries.

A country pub off the A413 coming from Amersham towards Aylesbury, with one bar and two real fires. Mixed clientele, no juke box or machines. Large garden. Food served at lunchtime only. Children allowed, but not in bar area.

OPEN 11am–2.30pm and 6–11pm Mon–Sat; 12–3pm and 7–10.30pm Sun.

LITTLEWORTH COMMON

The Jolly Woodman
Littleworth Common, Burnham SL1 8PF
☎ *(01753) 644350* Debbie Akehurst

A Whitbread-managed house with no restrictions on the guest beer policy so a good selection is maintained. Brakspear Bitter always available, plus four guests changed twice-weekly, including Rebellion Mutiny and Smuggler, Smiles March Hare, Caledonian Deuchars IPA, Timothy Taylor Landlord, Morland Old Speckled Hen, Wadworth 6X, Marston's Pedigree, Greene King Abbot Ale and seasonal beers.

A traditional seventeenth-century pub in the middle of Burnham Beeches. Lovely walks all around. Beer garden. Food available at lunchtime and evenings. Children allowed, but not at the bar.

OPEN 11am–11pm Mon–Sat; 12–10.30pm Sun.

Derehams Inn

5 Derehams Lane, Loudwater HP14 3ND
☎ *(01494) 530965*
Graham and Margaret Sturgess

Eight beers always available including Fuller's London Pride, Young's Bitter, Brakspear Bitter, Timothy Taylor Landlord and two guest beers rotating constantly.

Small and cosy local freehouse. Bar food on weekdays at lunchtime. Car park, garden. Children allowed in the restaurant area. Less than a mile from M40 junction 3.

OPEN *11.30am–3pm and 5.30–11pm.*

The Prince of Wales

1 Mill Road, Marlow SL7 1PX
☎ *(01628) 482970* Mr WS Sarrell

Tied to Whitbread, with Fuller's London Pride, Brakspear Bitter and Greene King IPA always served. A guest beer changes every three weeks. Brakspear Special, Wadworth 6X, Greene King Abbot and brews from Rebellion, Vale and Hook Norton are regular favourites.

A traditional pub just off the high street, with no juke box, pool, darts or alcopops. Food served at lunchtime and evenings. Separate dining area. Children allowed.

OPEN *11am–11pm Mon–Sat; 12–10.30pm Sun.*

The New Inn

2 Bradwell Road, New Bradwell, Milton Keynes MK13 0EN
☎ *(01908) 312094* Mr Fulker

A Charles Wells tenanted house. Four real ales always available (Adnams Broadside, Morland Old Speckled Hen, Charles Wells Eagle and Bombardier) plus a guest beer, changed at least once a month.

Canalside, family-run traditional pub, with juke box, pool table and beer garden, between Newport Pagnell and Wolverton. Food available in a separate 70-seater restaurant. Children allowed. No restrictions on guests.

OPEN *11.30am–11pm Mon–Sat; 12–10.30pm Sun.*

The Bull Inn

33 Tickford Street, Newport Pagnell MK16 9AE
☎ *(01908) 610325* Terry Fairfield

A freehouse serving up to eight cask ales at any one time, with a minimum of two changed each week. Favourites include Young's Special, Fuller's London Pride, Wadworth 6X and Bateman's ales. Others might be Shepherd Neame Spitfire, Hampshire Pride of Romsey, Jennings Sneck Lifter, Burton Bridge Top Dog Stout and Ridleys ESX Best, to name but a few.

An old-fashioned coaching inn, just like pubs used to be! No music in lounge. Food at lunchtime and evenings. Children allowed in restaurant only, if eating. Take M1, junction 14; pub next door to the Aston Martin Lagonda factory

OPEN *11.30am–2.30pm and 5–11pm Mon–Fri; 11am–11pm Sat; 12–10.30pm Sun.*

The Green Man

92 Silver Street, Newport Pagnell
☎ *(01908) 611914* Alan and Julie Newman

Greene King IPA and Everards Tiger usually available plus one guest beer, such as Marston's Pedigree, Young's Special, Greene King Abbot Ale or Fuller's London Pride.

Good old-fashioned boozer with quiet front bar and games and music in the back bar. No food. No children.

OPEN *12–11pm (10.30pm Sun).*

The Cock Inn

16 High Street, North Crawley, Newport Pagnell MK16 9LH
☎ *(01234) 391222* Terry McLaren

Tied to Charles Wells, serving four real ales at any one time. Adnams Broadside and Charles Wells Eagle always available, plus a guest, changed every couple of months, from somewhere like Everards, Wadworth or Young's.

A very old, oak-beamed pub, built around 1460, next to the church in the village square. A broad cross-section of customers. Two bars and a family room. Food served at lunchtime and evenings, except Sunday evening. Children allowed in family room.

OPEN *11am–3pm and 6–11pm Mon–Sat; 12–4pm and 7–10.30pm Sun.*

The King's Head

188 Wycombe Road, Prestwood HP16 OHJ
☎ *(01494) 868101* Simon Wiles

Greene King ales always available, including Abbot and IPA. Special and guest ales are regularly featured.

An old pub tastefully refurbished, offering a full range of meals from 12–10pm daily. Friendly service to tables or at the bar. Large car park. Children tolerated. Garden and barbecue. Take the A4128 from High Wycombe.

OPEN *11am–11pm Mon–Sat; 12–10.30pm Sun.*

Rose & Crown

Hollybush Hill, Stoke Poges SL2 4PW
☎ *(01753) 662148* Mr Holloran

A Morland tied house serving Morland beers plus Adnams Broadside.

A traditional village pub with food served at lunchtimes. Well-behaved children allowed.

OPEN *11am–3pm and 5.30–11pm (10.30pm Sun).*

Vaults Bar

The Bull Hotel, 64 High Street, Stony Stratford, Milton Keynes MK11 1AQ
☎ *(01908) 567104* Paul Wareing

Fuller's London Pride, Young's Bitter, Eldridge Pope Royal Oak, Wadworth 6X and Adnams Bitter usually available. One guest beer is also available from a very varied list. Timothy Taylor Landlord is the one repeat beer.

Simple, characterful bar in imposing Georgian coaching inn, prominently located in the High Street. Food available 12–10pm. Car park. Children welcome although there are no special facilities.

OPEN *12–11pm.*

The Tatling Arms

Oxford Road, Tatling End SL9 7AT
☎ *(01753) 883100* Joe Cullan

A freehouse off the old A40 Oxford Road, formerly called The Stag and Griffin. Four real ales on offer, two (Fuller's London Pride and Rebellion IPA) always available, two as guests, changed monthly. Brakspear and Rebellion are favoured breweries.

A small 300-year-old listed building with a mixed clientele. Vehicles in the car park range from Rolls Royces to Transits. Food served all day. Children allowed.

OPEN *11am–11pm Mon–Sat; 12–10.30pm Sun.*

The Cock & Rabbit

The Lee, Great Missenden HP16 9LZ
☎ *(01494) 837540*

A freehouse, with four to five real ales always available. Permanent fixtures are Cock and Rabbit Bitter (brewed by Morland), Fuller's London Pride and Morland Old Speckled Hen. Other guests are changed seasonally.

A classic English pub with an Italian flavour. Restaurant, dining area and garden lounge. Food served lunchtimes and evenings, seven days a week. Children allowed.

OPEN *12–2.30pm and 6–11pm Mon–Sat; 12–3pm and 7–10.30pm Sun.*

The Old Swan

Swan Lane, Swan Bottom, The Lee, Great Missenden HP16 9NU
☎ *(01494) 837239* Sean Michaelson-Yeats

A freehouse, with something from Adnams and Brakspear always available, plus a guest beer.

A traditional sixteenth-century inn in the Chiltern Hills. Off the beaten track, it lies between Tring, Chesham, Great Missenden and Wendover. Food served at lunchtime and evenings, with fresh fish a speciality. Restaurant area. Large garden. Children allowed.

OPEN *12–3pm and 6–11pm Sun–Fri; all day Sat; closed Mon except bank holidays.*

The Lone Tree

Bletchley Road, Thornborough MK18 2DZ
☎ *(01280) 812334* PB Taverner

Five beers available (over 850 served so far) produced by breweries stretching from Orkney to Cornwall, Norfolk to Wales. Plus one real cider.

Small roadside pub with a large choice of food available at lunchtime and evenings. Car park and garden. Supervised children allowed.

OPEN *11.30am–3pm and 6–11pm Mon–Sat; 12–3pm and 6.30–10.30pm Sun.*

WENDOVER

The Red Lion Hotel

9 The High Street, Wendover HP22 6DU
☎ *(01296) 622266* Phil Hills

Young's Special and Brakspear Pale Ale usually available, plus one monthly changing guest purchased through the Beer Seller. This might be Adnams Best, Wadworth 6X or something similar.

A sixteenth-century coaching inn situated in beautiful Chilterns countryside, ideal for walkers. One bar, open fires, outside seating. Very busy restaurant serving fresh food all day every day, plus separate bar food available at lunchtimes and evenings. Children allowed. Accommodation.

7 am for breakfast; 11am–11pm.

WHEELER END

The Chequers

Bullocks Farm Lane, Wheeler End,
High Wycombe HP14 3NH
☎ *(01494) 883070* Ron Henry

A Fuller's tied house with London Pride and ESB, and Brakspear Bitter always available, plus one guest pump serving a Fuller's seasonal ale.

A very old, beer pub. Beamed, inglenook fireplace, beer garden. Food served at lunchtime only. Supervised children allowed. Live music every Tuesday and Saturday evening.

11am–11pm Mon–Sat; 12–10.30pm Sun.

WING

The Cock Inn

26 High Street, Wing, Nr Leighton Buzzard
LU7 0NR
☎ *(01296) 688214*
Alberto Marcucci and Stuart Mosley

Four weekly changing guest beers regularly available from a number of different breweries.

Privately-owned, fine English country pub with good home-cooked food available every lunchtime and evening in a separate restaurant and at the bar. Car park. Children welcome, high chairs available.

11.30am–3pm and 6–11pm Mon–Sat;
12–3pm and 7–10.30pm Sun.

YOU TELL US

★ *The Grapes*, 36 Market Square, Aylesbury
★ *The Greyhound*, West Edge, Marsh Gibbon
★ *The King's Arms*, 1 King Street, Chesham
★ *Prince Albert*, Moors End, Frieth
★ *The Red Lion*, Chenies
★ *The Rose & Crown*, Desborough Road, High Wycombe
★ *The Rose & Crown*, Vicarage Lane, Ivinghoe
★ *The Stag & Griffin*, Oxford Road, Tatling End

Places Featured:

Boxworth
Brandon Creek
Cambridge
Castle Camps
Dogsthorpe
Ely
Glinton
Graveley
Hinxton
Holywell
Huntingdon
Keyston
Leighton Bromswold

March
Madingley
Milton
Needingworth
Newton
Old Weston
Peterborough
St Ives
Six Mile Bottom
Stow cum Quay
Thriplow
Whittlesey
Wisbech
Woodston

THE BREWERIES

CITY OF CAMBRIDGE BREWERY LTD

19 Cheddars Lane, Cambridge CB5 8LD
☎ *(01223) 353939*

 JET BLACK 3.7% ABV
Smooth and dark.
BOAT HOUSE BITTER 3.8% ABV
Refreshing.
HOBSON'S CHOICE 4.1% ABV
Pale and hoppy.
BLEND '42' 4.4% ABV
Golden-coloured and rounded blend of beers.
ATOMSPLITTER 4.7% ABV
Full-bodied and hoppy.
DARWIN'S DOWNFALL 5.0% ABV
Blended beer with crisp, hoppy fruit flavours.
PARKER'S PORTER 5.3% ABV
Good fruity hoppiness.
BRAMLING TRADITIONAL 5.5% ABV
Fruity.

ELGOOD AND SONS LTD

North Brink Brewery, Wisbech PE13 1LN
☎ *(01945) 583160*

 BLACK DOG MILD 3.6% ABV
Malty, dark mild with good balance.
CAMBRIDGE BITTER 3.8% ABV
Malt fruit flavours with dry finish.
PAGEANT ALE 4.3% ABV
Rounded and balanced with a bittersweet flavour.
OLD BLACK SHUCK 4.5% ABV
November ale.
GOLDEN NEWT 4.6% ABV
Dry and hoppy.
BARLEYMEAD 4.8% ABV
September ale.
GREYHOUND STRONG BITTER 5.2% ABV
Bittersweet flavour.
REINBEER 5.9% ABV
December ale.
WENCESLAS 7.5% ABV
December ale.
Plus seasonal brews.

THE FENLAND BREWERY

Unit 4, Prospect Way, Chatteris PE16 6TY
☎ *(01354) 696776*

 **TELL TALE PALE ALE 3.6% ABV**
FBB 4.0% ABV
SMOKESTACK LIGHTNING 4.2% ABV
FRACT ALE 4.5% ABV
SPARKLING WIT 4.5% ABV
DOCTOR'S ORDERS 5.0% ABV
RUDOLPH'S ROCKET FUEL 5.5% ABV

MILTON BREWERY CAMBRIDGE LTD

Unit 111, Norman Industrial Estate, Cambridge Road, Milton CB4 6AT
☎ *(01223) 226198*

 MINOTAUR 3.3% ABV
Dark mild with rich chocolate malt flavour.
JUPITER 3.5% ABV
A spring/summer session beer.
NEPTUNE 3.8% ABV
Crisp, nutty, autumn/winter brew.
PEGASUS 4.1% ABV
Hoppy with balancing long fruity, malt finish.
PYRAMID 4.4% ABV
Hoppiness with citrus orange flavour and good bitterness.
ELECTRA 4.5% ABV
Golden, malty sweetness and powerful bitter finish.
CYCLOPS 5.3% ABV
Rounded malt and fruit flavours.
MAMMON 7.0% ABV
Dark winter warmer for December.

OAKHAM ALES

80 Westgate, Peterborough PE1 1RD
☎ *(01733) 358300*

 JEFFREY HUDSON BITTER 3.8% ABV
WHITE DWARF 4.3% ABV
Slightly cloudy wheat beer
FIVE LEAVES LEFT 4.5% ABV
Autumn/winter brew.
BISHOP'S FAREWELL 4.6% ABV
Golden and refreshing.
HELTER SKELTER 5.0% ABV
Seasonal.
MOMPESSONS GOLD 5.0% ABV
Seasonal. Golden, light and full-flavoured.
OLD TOSSPOT 5.2% ABV
Seasonal: brewed Sept–May.
BLACK HOLE PORTER 5.5% ABV
Black, sweet and rich.

PAYNE BREWERIES

Unit 1 Eco Site, St Mary's Road, Ramsey PE17 1SL
☎ *(01487) 710800*

 BULLSEYE 3.8% ABV
Amber-coloured, balanced, smooth and
quenching.
FENLAND GOLD 4.2% ABV
Gold-coloured, honeyed fruit flavour and
delicate hoppiness.
RAMSEY PRIDE 5.0% ABV
Malty, full-bodied and fruity. Good dry finish.
STRONG OLD NOLL 8.0% ABV
Good hop and barley flavours.
RAMSEY RUIN 13.0% ABV
Powerful, hop flavour and some sweetness.
Plus seasonal and occasional brews.

ROCKINGHAM ALES

25 Wansford Road, Elton PE8 6RZ
☎ *(01832) 280722*

 **FINESHADE 3.8% ABV**
ELTON PALE ALE 3.9% ABV
FOREST GOLD 3.9% ABV
HOP DEVIL 3.9% ABV
A1 AMBER ALE 4.0% ABV
FRUITS OF THE FOREST 4.1% ABV
OLD HERBACEOUS 4.5% ABV
Winter brew.

THE PUBS

BOXWORTH

The Golden Ball

High Street, Boxworth CB3 8LY
☎ *(01954) 267397* Hilary Paddock

Beers available include Adnams
Broadside and Greene King IPA. Guests
include Old Speckled Hen, Ruddles County,
Potton Village Bike and many more.

Typical country pub in good walking area.
Bar and restaurant food at lunchtime and
evenings, with interesting and upmarket fare.
Meeting room, car park. Large garden with
separate entrance. Children allowed. Ten
miles from Cambridge, six miles from St Ives.

OPEN *11.30am–2.30pm and 6.30–11pm.*

BRANDON CREEK

The Ship

Brandon Creek, Downham Market PE38 0PP
☎ *(01353) 676228* Mr A Hook

A regularly changing range of guest
beers which often features something
from Adnams, Iceni, Mauldons, Fenland or
Kings Head.

Situated by the River Ouse, this is a food-
oriented pub offering special weekend
carveries on Saturday evening and Sunday
lunchtime in winter, Sunday lunchtime in
summer. Regular menu available 12–2pm and
6.30–9pm at other times. Car park. Children
welcome, but no special facilities.

OPEN *May–Sept: 11am–11pm Mon–Sat;*
12–10.30pm Sun. Phone for winter opening
times.

CAMBRIDGE

Ancient Druids

Napier Street, Cambridge CB1 1HR
☎ *(01223) 576324*

There are plans to expand the range of
beers brewed here. They have recently
begun producing a dark mild of about 3.3%.
Plus a range of guest beers.

There is a history of brewing on the
premises. Charles Wells originally set up
business here and the present managers took
over and restarted production in 1993.
This big, bright pub enjoys a laid-back
atmosphere, with a wide variety of customers
including students and shoppers. Background
music. Bar food available all day until 10pm.
Children allowed.

 ELLIES SB 6.0% ABV

OPEN *11am–11pm.*

Cambridge Blue
85–7 Gwydir Street, Cambridge CB1 2LG
☎ *(01223) 361382*
Chris and Debbie Lloyd

At least six beers always available, focusing on Cambridgeshire breweries. Favourites include City of Cambridge Hobson's Choice and other ales in their range, plus beers from the Milton brewery, such as Pegasus. Stocks a range of East Anglian beers – always open to suggestions.

Terraced side-street pub, totally non-smoking, with large garden and two bars. Healthy bar food at lunchtimes and evenings, seven days a week. Children allowed in conservatory area until 9pm. Off Mill Road on the city side of railway bridge.

12–2.30pm (3.30pm Sat) and 6–11pm.

The Elm Tree
42 Orchard Street, Cambridge CB1 1JT
☎ *(01223) 363005* John Simons

A Charles Wells tenancy with Bombardier and Eagle IPA always on offer. Two guest beers, such as Adnams Best or Marston's Pedigree, are changed regularly.

A traditional one-bar pub off the city centre, near Grafton shopping centre, with large-screen TV and lots of table games (including chess). Rolls only served. No children allowed.

12–2.30pm and 4 or 5–11.30pm Mon–Thurs; 11am–11pm Fri–Sat; 12–10.30pm Sun.

The Free Press
Prospect Row, Cambridge CB1 1DU
☎ *(01223) 368337* Chris and Debbie Lloyd

A Greene King tied house with Abbot, IPA and XX Dark Mild always available.

A famous East Anglian real ale house, the first pub in Cambridge to stock real ales when the revival began. Healthy bar food available 12–2pm Monday to Friday and 12–2.30pm at weekends. Food also available evenings 6–9pm. Totally non-smoking. Located near Grafton Shopping Centre.

12–2.30pm Mon–Fri; 12–3pm Sat–Sun; 6–11pm Mon–Sat; 7–10.30pm Sun.

Live and Let Live
40 Mawson Road, Cambridge CB1 2EA
☎ *(01223) 460261* Margaret Holliday

Seven beers available. The landlord deals mainly with Everards but also Adnams and B&T. The guest list (20 per year) includes Exmoor Stag, Felinfoel Double Dragon, Morland Old Speckled Hen, Shepherd Neame Bishops Finger, Badger Tanglefoot, Bateman Lincolnshire Yellow Belly and Victory Ale.

Situated in central Cambridge, off Mill Road, popular with students and business people alike. Wooden furniture and walls plus real gas lighting. Bar food available at lunchtime and evenings. Street parking. Children allowed in restaurant section.

12–2.30pm and 6–11pm.

St Radegund
129 King Street, Cambridge CB1 1LD
☎ *(01223) 311794* Terry Kavanagh

One of the few freehouses in Cambridge, where Bateman XB, Fuller's London Pride and Shepherd Neame Spitfire are always available. Occasional guest beers also served.

The smallest pub in Cambridge. CAMRA-listed from 1991–99 and Pub of the Year 1993–94. No juke box, no games machines. Background jazz music. Filled rolls only. Children not allowed. Opposite the Wesley church in King Street.

4.30–11pm Mon–Fri; 12–11pm Sat; 6–10.30pm Sun.

Tap & Spile
14 Mill Lane, Cambridge CB2 1RX
☎ *(01223) 357026* Peter Snellgrover

Approx 300 beers per year (nine at any one time) including brews from Adnams, Bateman, Black Sheep, Hadrian, Thwaites, Ushers, Nethergate and many other independent breweries.

Traditional alehouse with oak floors and exposed brickwork in picturesque setting right next to the river (perhaps the biggest beer garden in England?). Punting station nearby. Bar food at lunchtime.

11am–11pm Mon–Sat; 12–3pm and 7–10.30pm Sun.

Wrestlers
337 Newmarket Road, Cambridge CB5 8JE
☎ *(01223) 566553* Tom Goode

A house tied to Charles Wells, with Eagle IPA and Bombardier always served, plus two guest beers changed fortnightly. Favoured breweries include Lees, Archers, Morland, Caledonian and Adnams.

The pub specialises in Thai food. Children allowed.

OPEN *12–3pm and 5–11pm Mon–Sat; closed Sun.*

CASTLE CAMPS

The Cock Inn
High Street, Castle Camps, Cambridge CB1 6SN
☎ *(01799) 584207* Mr Puell

A freehouse always serving Greene King IPA plus a guest beer, which may be Fuller's London Pride, something from Nethergate or Shepherd Neame Spitfire. Changed weekly.

An olde-worlde drinkers' pub. Snacks available. Children allowed.

OPEN *12–2pm and 7–11pm Sun–Fri; 11am–11pm Sat.*

DOGSTHORPE

The Blue Bell Inn
St Pauls Road, Dogsthorpe, Peterborough PE1 3RZ
☎ *(01733) 554890* Mr PR and Mrs TL Smith

Elgoods Black Dog Mild, Cambridge Bitter and Greyhound usually available with a weekly changing guest beer such as Bateman XXXB and beers from Hook Norton, Adnams and Burton Bridge.

Good old-fashioned character to this listed, sixteenth-century, Elgoods tied house. Food served 11am–2pm Mon–Fri; but not bank holidays. Car park. Children permitted in small lobby room and garden. Located on the junction of Welland Road/ St Pauls Road, near to Dogsthorpe fire H.Q.

OPEN *11am–2.30pm and 6–11pm Mon–Fri; 11.30am–3pm and 6–11pm Sat; 12–3pm and 7–10.30pm Sun.*

ELY

The Fountain
1 Silver Street, Ely CB7 4JF
☎ *(01353) 663122* John Borland

A freehouse with Adnams Best and Broadside plus Fuller's London Pride as permanent fixtures. A guest beer, changed frequently, could well be Charles Wells Bombardier.

A modern, one-bar pub. No food. Children allowed until 9pm.

OPEN *5–11.30pm Mon–Fri; 12–2pm and 6–11.30pm Sat; 12–2pm and 7–11pm Sun.*

GLINTON

The Blue Bell
10 High Street, Glinton, Peterborough PE6 7LS
☎ *(01733) 252285* Mr Mills

Tied to Greene King brewery and permanently serving IPA and Abbot Ale. Other guests from various breweries available.

A village pub with separate dining area. Food served at lunchtime and evenings. Children allowed.

OPEN *12–3pm Mon–Thurs; 11am–11pm Fri–Sat; 12–10.30pm Sun.*

GRAVELEY

The Three Horseshoes
23 High Street, Graveley, Huntingdon PE18 9PL
☎ *(01480) 830992* Alfred Barrett

A freehouse with three pumps serving a variety of guest beers, which change weekly, mainly from independent breweries such as Marston's, Adnams and others.

A very old country inn, with no juke box or pool tables. Non-smoking restaurant. Food at lunchtime and evening. Children allowed.

OPEN *11am–3pm and 6–11pm Mon–Sat; 12–2pm and 7–11pm Sun.*

HINXTON

The Red Lion
32 High Street, Hinxton, Cambridge CB10 1QX
☎ *(01799) 530601* Linda Crawford

A freehouse with Adnams Best and Woodforde's Wherry Best always on sale. There is also one guest.

A sixteenth-century pub half a mile south of junction 9 off the M11, with one bar and a non-smoking restaurant. Food served at lunchtime and evenings. Children allowed.

OPEN *11am–2.30pm and 6–11pm Mon–Sat; 12–2.30pm and 7–10.30pm Sun.*

HOLYWELL

The Ferryboat Inn
Holywell PE17 3TG
☎ *(01480) 463227* Joules Bonnett

Tied to Greene King, with IPA and Abbot always available. Guest beers, mainly available in the summer months, include Timothy Taylor Landlord and Morland Old Speckled Hen.

A remote pub in a rural setting down a country lane and overlooking the River Great Ouse. Ring for directions, if needed! Large bar and eating area with function room. Emphasis on food, which is served at lunchtime and evenings. Children welcome.

OPEN *12–3pm and 6–11pm Mon–Fri; 11am to 11pm Sat; 12–10.30pm Sun. Summer hours may vary – ring for details.*

The Old Bridge Hotel

1 High Street, Huntingdon PE18 6TQ
☎ *(01480) 452681* Martin Lee

Adnams Best and City of Cambridge Hobson's Choice are always available, along with a guest beer.

A smart townhouse hotel that includes a busy and welcoming bar. Restaurant meals and snacks served every day, with full afternoon teas. Well-behaved children allowed. Occasional live entertainment.

OPEN *11am–11pm Mon–Sat; 12–10.30pm Sun.*

The Pheasant

Keyston, Huntingdon PE18 0RE
☎ *(01832) 710241* Clive Dixon

Adnams Best always available, plus three guests from a changing selection, with brews from Potton and City of Cambridge appearing regularly.

A thatched inn in a quiet village, with oak beams and large open fires. Quality food served in the pub, and in the small restaurant. Food available lunchtimes and evenings. Car park. Children welcome.

OPEN *12–3pm and 6–11pm.*

The Green Man

37 The Avenue, Leighton Bromswold,
Nr Huntingdon PE18 0SH
☎ *(01480) 890238* Mr Hanagan

Timothy Taylor Landlord, Nethergate Bitter, Badger Tanglefoot and Fuller's London Pride always available plus two guest beers (150 per year) perhaps from Wadworth, Adnams, Nene Valley, Young's, Robinson's, Everards or Goddards breweries.

Seventeenth-century, detached public house with a collection of water jugs and memorabilia. Bar food available at lunchtime and evenings. Car park, garden, children's room. One mile off the A14.

OPEN *12–3pm and 7–11pm; closed Mon.*

The Three Horseshoes

Madingley CB3 8AB
☎ *(01954) 210221* Richard Stokes

Adnams Best is a permanent feature, with two guests also served, City of Cambridge being a regular.

A thatched inn with a bar and large garden. Imaginative food served in the bar, garden and conservatory-restaurant. Meals available 12–2pm and 6.30–9.30pm daily. Car park. Children welcome.

OPEN *11.30am–2.30pm and 6–11pm Mon–Sat; 12–3pm and 7–10.30pm Sun.*

The Rose & Crown

41 St Peters Road, March PE15 9NA
☎ *(01354) 652879* Mr D Evans

Up to six beers from a menu that changes on a daily basis. Caledonian Deuchars IPA and Marston's Pedigree are usually popular.

Olde-worlde pub. Non-smoking lounge bar. Bar snacks Thurs–Sat. No children.

OPEN *12–2.30pm and 7–11pm Mon–Fri (closed Wed lunchtime); 12–3pm and 7–11pm Sat–Sun.*

The Waggon & Horses

39 High Street, Milton CB4 6DF
☎ *(01223) 860313*
Nick and Mandy Winnington

Elgood's Cambridge Bitter, Black Dog Mild, Golden Newt and Greyhound Strong Bitter permanently available, plus one guest ale from a varied range.

Imposing 1930s mock-Tudor building set back from the main road. Large child-friendly garden to rear. Note hat collection and eclectic pictures on walls. Bar billiards and darts. Children allowed in pub under supervision (9pm curfew), as are animals on a lead. Car park.

OPEN *12–2.30pm and 5–11pm Mon–Fri; 12–4pm and 6–11pm Sat; 12–3pm and 7–10.30pm Sun.*

The Queen's Head

30 High Street, Needingworth, Nr Huntingdon PE17 2SA
☎ *(01480) 463946* Mr and Mrs Vann

Six beers always available including Smiles Best, Woodforde's Wherry Best and Hop Back Summer Lightning. Approximately 100 guests per year including Nene Valley Old Black Bob, the Reindeer range, Timothy Taylor Landlord, Parish Somerby Premium, Butterknowle Conciliation, Hook Norton Best, Chiltern Beechwood, Sarah Hughes Dark Ruby Mild and brews from Wild's brewery.

Friendly pub. Bar snacks served 12–8pm. Car park and garden. Children allowed in lounge bar. Close to St Ives.

OPEN *12–11pm.*

NEWTON

Queen's Head

Newton, Nr Cambridge CB2 5PG
☎ *(01223) 870436* Mr David Short

Has specialised in Adnams beers for the past 30 years. Best Bitter and Broadside always available plus Old Ale in winter and Tally Ho at Christmas.

A typical early eighteenth-century pub beside the village green. Bar food at lunchtime and evenings. Car park, children's room, various bar games. Three miles from M11 junction 10; less than two miles off the A10 at Harston.

OPEN *11.30am–2.30pm and 6–11pm Mon–Sat; 12–2.30pm and 7–10.30pm Sun.*

OLD WESTON

The Swan

Main Road, Old Weston, Huntingdon PE17 5LL
☎ *(01832) 293400* Jim Taylor

Greene King Abbot, Adnams Best and Broadside are always available in this free house, along with two guest beers each week. Hook Norton Old Hooky is regularly featured.

A restaurant/pub, with a fish and chip night each Wednesday. Children allowed.

OPEN *6.30–11.30pm Mon–Fri; 11am–11pm Sat; 12–10.30pm Sun.*

PETERBOROUGH

Bogart's Bar and Grill

17 North Street, Peterborough PE1 2RA
☎ *(01733) 349995*

A house beer brewed by Eldridge Pope plus six guest beers always available from a varied selection (300+ per year) usually ranging in strength from a mild at 3.0% to 5.5% ABV. The pub hosts a regional beer festival at the start of each month, featuring brewers from a specific part of the United Kingdom. Real cider also available.

B ogart's was built at the turn of the century and now has a wide-ranging clientele of all ages. The horseshoe-shaped bar is decorated with film posters and Humphrey Bogart features prominently. There is background music but no juke box or pool table. Bar food available at lunchtime. Car park opposite and beer garden. Children not allowed. Located off the main Lincoln Road.

OPEN *11am–11pm Mon–Sat; closed Sun.*

Charters Cafe Bar

Town Bridge, Peterborough PE1 1DG
☎ *(01733) 315700* Paul Hook

Oakham JHB plus Fuller's London Pride and Everards Tiger always available. Also up to eight (400 per year) guest beers from every independent brewery possible.

A floating connected Dutch barge moored in the centre of town. CAMRA Pub of the Year 1994. Bar food available at lunchtime and evenings, restaurant meals Thurs–Sat evenings only. Parking and garden. Children allowed. Town Bridge crosses the River Nene in central Peterborough.

OPEN *12–11pm.*

ST IVES

The Royal Oak

13 Crown Street, St Ives PE17 4EB
☎ *(01480) 462586* Miss M Pilson

Marston's Pedigree always on sale. Six guests, changed weekly, might include something from breweries such as Smiles or Maclays.

A n old-style pub with one bar, in a Grade II listed building. Food served from 12–2pm. Children allowed until 7pm.

OPEN *11am–11pm Mon–Sat; 12–10.30pm Sun.*

SIX MILE BOTTOM

Green Man Inn

London Road, Six Mile Bottom CB8 UUF
☎ *(01638) 570373* James Ramselle

Greene King IPA and Adnams Best bitter usually available. One guest beer is served, such as Nethergate Umbel Ale.

C ountry inn with dining room, garden, barbecue and petanque court. Food served daily 12.30–2pm and 6.30–9pm. Car park. Located on the A1304 near Newmarket.

OPEN *11.30am–11pm.*

STOW CUM QUY

Prince Albert

Newmarket Road, Stow cum Quy CB5 9AQ
☎ *(01223) 811294* Mr and Mrs Henderson

Five beers always available including Greene King IPA. Guests might include Ash Vine Bitter, Stormforce Ten, Worzel Wallop and Shardlow Reverend Eaton's Ale.

L ively roadside pub built in 1830. Bar and restaurant food served at lunchtime and weekend evenings. Private functions catered for. Car park and garden. Children allowed. Just off A14 on the Newmarket road (A1303).

OPEN *11am–3.30pm and 5–11pm Mon–Fri; all day Sat–Sun.*

White Swan

Main Street, Stow cum Quy CB5 9AB
☎ *(01223) 811821* Mr A Cocker

Among those beers always available are Greene King IPA, Adnams Best, Shepherd Neame Spitfire and Woodforde's Wherry Best plus a guest beer changed fortnightly. Regulars include Everards Tiger, Fuller's London Pride and something from Charles Wells.

A freehouse and restaurant with one small public bar. No smoking. Food served at lunchtime and Tue–Sun evenings. Children allowed but no facilities for them.

OPEN *11am–3pm and 6–11pm Tue–Sat; 12–3pm and 7–10.30pm Sun.*

THRIPLOW

The Green Man

2 Lower Street, Thriplow SG8 7RJ
☎ *(01763) 208855* DS and RJ Ward

Adnams Best Bitter, Hook Norton Best and Timothy Taylor Landlord always available plus two or three guests beers (30 per year) from Felinfoel, Nethergate, Bateman, Black Sheep or Morland breweries.

Open-plan, two-bar pub by the village green with small non-smoking dining area. Formerly Charles Wells. Bar and restaurant food available at lunchtime and evenings (not Sunday). Car park and garden. Children not allowed. Turn off the A505 near the Imperial War Museum, Duxford.

OPEN *12–3pm Mon–Sat; 12–3pm and 7–10.30pm Sun.*

WHITTLESEY

The Boat Inn

2 Ramsey Road, Whittlesey, Nr Peterborough PE7 1DR
☎ *(01733) 202488*

Elgood's Cambridge Bitter and Pageant Ale always available plus Black Dog Mild in May. Guest beers (12 per year) have included Morrells Graduate and Crouch Vale Millennium Gold.

A seventeenth-century pub on a site mentioned in the Domesday Book. Large informal bar, plus small restaurant featuring the bow of a boat as the bar. Resident ghost! Bar and restaurant food at lunchtime and evenings. Car park and garden. Children allowed. Ask for directions on reaching Whittlesey.

OPEN *11.30am–2.30pm and 6.30–11pm.*

WISBECH

The Rose Tavern

53 North Brink, Wisbech PE13 1JX
☎ *(01945) 588335*

Everards Beacon and Morrells ales always available, plus guest beers.

A 200-year-old listed building forming a comfortable, one-roomed pub on the banks of the river. The closest pub to Elgood's Brewery. Outdoor area, wheelchair access, traditional pub games, accommodation.

OPEN *12–3pm and 5.30–11pm.*

WOODSTON

Palmerston Arms

82 Oundle Road, Woodston, Peterborough PE2 9PA
☎ *(01733) 565865* Mrs P Patterson

A freehouse always offering Hop Back Summer Lightning and Bateman XB, with regular guest beers including Shepherd Neame Spitfire, Church End Vicar's Ruin and RCH Pitchfork.

A traditional pub with lounge and public bar. All beers straight from the barrel from cellar. No food. No children.

OPEN *12–11pm (10.30pm Sun). Closed bank holiday Mondays.*

YOU TELL US

★ *Chequers*, 71 Main Road, Little Gransden
★ *The Golden Pheasant*, 1 Main Street, Etton
★ *Hand & Heart*, 12 Highbury Street, Peterborough
★ *Pig & Abbot*, High Street, Abingdon Piggots
★ *The Plough*, St Peters Street, Duxford

Places Featured:

Appleton Thorn
Aston
Chester
Frodsham
Great Sutton
Handforth
Heaton Norris
Higher Hurdsfield
Langley

Macclesfield
Mobberley
Nantwich
Penketh
Stalybridge
Strines
Tushingham
Warrington
Whitchurch

THE BREWERIES

BEARTOWN BREWERY

Unit 9, Varey Road, Eaton Bank Industrial Estate, Congleton CW12 1UW
☎ *(01260) 299964*

 AMBEARDEXTROUS 3.8% ABV
Copper-coloured and quenching.

BEAR ASS 4.0% ABV
Aromatic, with smooth, dry malty flavour.

KODIAK GOLD 4.0% ABV
Refreshing, straw-coloured with smooth, rounded finish.

BEARSKINFUL 4.2% ABV
Golden, dry sharp flavour, with a hoppy, rich malt aftertaste.

POLAR ECLIPSE 4.8% ABV
Rich dark oatmeal stout.

BLACK BEAR 5.0% ABV
Smooth, dark ruby mild.

BRUINS RUIN 5.0% ABV
Golden, smooth and full-flavoured.

WHEAT BEER 5.0% ABV
Crisp, refreshing award winner.

BURTONWOOD BREWERY PLC

Bold Lane, Burtonwood, Warrington WA5 4PJ
☎ *(01925) 225131*

MILD 3.0% ABV
Dark and mellow with malt.

BITTER 3.7% ABV
Rich, smooth malt flavour. Hoppy aroma.

TOP HAT 4.8% ABV
Rich flavour with dry hop character

COACH HOUSE BREWING CO. LTD

Wharf Street, Howley, Warrington WA1 2DQ
☎ *(01925) 232800*

COACHMAN'S BEST BITTER 3.7% ABV
Smooth, rich malt flavour, with some fruit.

GUNPOWDER STRONG MILD 3.8% ABV
Full flavour, with slight bitter aftertaste.

HONEYPOT BITTER 3.8% ABV

OSTLERS SUMMER PALE ALE 4.0% ABV

SQUIRES GOLD SPRING ALE 4.2% ABV

DICK TURPIN 4.2% ABV
Golden and smooth with good hoppiness.

FLINTLOCK PALE ALE 4.4% ABV

INNKEEPER'S SPECIAL RESERVE 4.5% ABV
Crisp and malty with balancing hops.

GINGERNUT PREMIUM 5.0% ABV

POSTHORN PREMIUM 5.0% ABV
Rich, smooth and complex.

TAVERNERS AUTUMN ALE 5.0% ABV
Plus seasonal brews.

FREDERIC ROBINSON LTD

Unicorn Brewery, Stockport SK1 1JJ
☎ *(0161) 480 6571*

HATTERS MILD 3.3% ABV
Fresh, with malt throughout.

OLD STOCKPORT BITTER 3.5% ABV
Golden, with a hoppy flavour.

XB 4.0% ABV
Malt flavour with hoppy bitterness.

BEST BITTER 4.2% ABV
Light in colour with a bitter hop taste and aroma.

FREDERIC'S 5.0% ABV
Smooth and well-balanced, gold in colour.

OLD TOM 8.5% ABV
Superb, mellow winter warmer.

STORM BREWING CO.

15 Larkhill Crescent, Macclesfield
☎ *(0161) 908 5032*

 BEAUFORTS 3.8% ABV
ALE FORCE 4.2% ABV
WINDGATHER 4.5% ABV
STORM DAMAGE 4.7% ABV

WEETWOOD ALES LTD

The Brewery, Weetwood, Tarporley CW6 0NQ
☎ *(01829) 752377*

BEST BITTER 3.8% ABV
Sharp with a hoppy finish.
EASTGATE ALE 4.2% ABV
Golden, with fruity hoppiness.
OLD DOG BITTER 4.5% ABV
Deep colour, smooth and rich.
OASTHOUSE GOLD 5.0% ABV
Pale and hoppy with a dry finish.

THE PUBS

APPLETON THORN

Appleton Thorn Village Hall

Stretton Road, Appleton Thorn, Nr Warrington WA4 4RT
☎ *(01925) 268370* Mrs Karen Howard

Seven real ales always available, always different (over 1,500 served in last three years).

A charitable village club operated voluntarily by local residents. Membership not required for entry, though new members always welcome (£4 per year). Car park, garden, playing field, bowling green, pool and darts. Children welcome. From M6 Jct 20 or M56 Jct 10, follow signs for Appleton Thorn. Hall is 100m west of village church. 1995 CAMRA national club of the year.

8.30–11pm Thurs–Sat; 1–3pm and 8.30–10.30pm Sun. Open lunchtimes on first and third Sunday of each month.

ASTON

Bhurtpore Inn

Wrenbury Road, Aston, Nr Nantwich CW5 8DQ
☎ *(01270) 780917* Simon and Nicky George

Hanby Drawwell always available plus nine guest beers (over 800 per year) which may include a brew from Tomlinson's, Burton Bridge, Weetwood, Adnams, Slaters (Eccleshall), Bateman, Black Sheep and Rudgate. Also real cider and 180 bottled Belgian beers plus three Belgian beers on draught.

The family has been connected with this comfortable, traditional, award-winning pub since 1849. Fresh bar and restaurant food at lunchtime and evenings. Car park, garden. Children allowed in pub at lunchtime and in early evening. Located just west of the A530, midway between Nantwich and Whitchurch.

12–2.30pm and 6.30–11pm Mon–Sat; 12–3pm and 7–10.30pm Sun.

The George & Dragon Hotel

Liverpool Road, Chester CH2 1AA
☎ *(01244) 380714* Tony Chester

A huge range of real ales always available in this freehouse. Castle Eden Ale is a permanent fixture. Regular guests, changed weekly, include Wadworth 6X, Titanic White Star, Timothy Taylor Landlord, Morland Old Speckled Hen, Fuller's London Pride and Greene King Abbot Ale.

A pub with a traditional atmosphere. Separate dining area and background music. Hotel accommodation. Food served at lunchtime and evenings. Children not allowed.

OPEN *11am–11pm Mon–Sat; 12–10.30pm Sun.*

The Mill Hotel

Milton Street, Chester CH1 3NF
☎ *(01244) 350035*

CAMRA Pub of the Year 1996 and Millennium Pub of the Year 2000, offering 15 real ales, including three permanently available, Weetwood Best, Coach House Mill Premium and Cains Traditional Bitter. Guests change daily (approx. 900 served every year) and always include a mild and either a stout or a porter. Requests welcome!

Hotel bar and restaurant on the site of a once-working mill. Bar and restaurant food available at lunchtime and evenings. Canalside patio, restaurant boat lunch and dinner cruises. Accommodation available (expansion to 130 rooms during 2000). Non-smoking area. Sky Sports on TV (with sound turned down). Families most welcome. Ample car parking. Visit our website at: www.millhotel.com

OPEN *11am–11pm Mon–Sat; 12–10.30pm Sun.*

The Union Vaults

44 Egerton Street, Chester CH1 3ND
☎ *(01244) 322170* Miss Lee

Former Greenalls pub offering Plassey Bitter from Wrexham plus two guests, which are changed weekly.

A little local alehouse, five minutes from Chester train station, this is a drinker's pub with one bar. No food. Children allowed.

OPEN *11am–11pm Mon–Sat; 12–10.30pm Sun.*

Netherton Hall

Chester Road, Frodsham WA6 6UL
☎ *(01928) 732342* Mr Rowland

A freehouse with a Jennings brew a permanent fixture plus four guest beers rotated every other day. Regulars include beers from Weetwood, Burtonwood, Phoenix and Hanby.

A typical Cheshire country pub on the main road, with one large bar, half of which is smoking and half non-smoking. Food served at lunchtime and evenings, and all day Friday and Saturday. Well-behaved children allowed.

OPEN *11am–11pm Mon–Sat; 12–10.30pm Sun.*

Rowland's Bar

31 Church Street, Frodsham WA6 6PN
☎ *(01928) 733361* Matt and Nick Rowland

Weetwood Best Bitter always available plus four from around 250 guest beers per year, mostly from independent breweries such as Oak, Coach House, Cains, Hanby and Dyffryn Clwyd.

One-room public bar with restaurant above. Bar and restaurant food at lunchtime and evenings. Restaurant closed Saturday lunchtime and all day Sunday. Parking. Children allowed in restaurant. In the main shopping area, close to British Rail station.

OPEN *11am–11pm.*

The White Swan Inn

Old Chester Road, Great Sutton CH66 3NZ
☎ *(0151) 339 9284* Denise Hardy

Tied to the Burtonwood Brewery, offering five different brews a week, the Burtonwood range plus guests such as Shepherd Neame Bishops Finger and Jennings Sneck Lifter.

A community local, off the main road (not signposted), with Sky TV and pub grub served at lunchtime and evenings. No children allowed.

OPEN *11am–11pm Mon–Sat; 12–10.30pm Sun.*

HANDFORTH

The Railway

Station Road, Handforth, Wilmslow
☎ *(01625) 523472* Linda Cook

Robinson's Best Bitter and Hatters Mild usually available with one other Robinson's beer such as Frederics, Old Tom (in winter) and occasionally Hartleys XB.

Friendly, traditional locals' pub. Non-smoking area. Food served 12–2pm Mon–Sat. Car park. Children are welcome at lunchtimes although there are no special facilities. Opposite Handforth railway station.

OPEN *11.45am–3.30pm and 5.30–11pm Mon–Sat; 12–3pm and 7–10.30pm Sun.*

HEATON NORRIS

The Crown Inn

154 Heaton Lane, Heaton Norris, Stockport SK4 1AR
☎ *(0161) 429 0549* Graham Mascord

Ten guest pumps serve a varied and interesting choice of real ales. Breweries featured may include Bank Top, Hanby, Hart, Hartington, Rudgate, Marston Moor, Phoenix, Wye Valley, Eccleshall, Salopian, Hampshire, or any of the independent brewers in the UK. Micro-breweries also favoured. Annual beer festival. A range of 15 malt whiskies also available, plus real cider.

Very cosy, old-fashioned boozer, with the focus on real ale for the real ale lover. Bar menu available lunchtimes, cold snacks served evenings.

OPEN *12–3pm and 6–11pm Mon–Wed; 12–3pm and 5–11pm Thur–Fri; 12–11pm Sat; 12–3pm and 7–10.30pm Sun.*

HIGHER HURDSFIELD

George & Dragon

61 Rainow Road, Higher Hurdsfield, Macclesfield SK10 2PD
☎ *(01625) 424300* D Molly Harrison

Fuller's London Pride and a beer from Storm Brewing Co. usually available.

Traditional part-seventeenth-century pub with food served 12–2pm Mon–Fri and Sun. Car park. Children welcome, but no special facilities.

OPEN *12–3pm and 7–11pm Mon–Sat; 12–3pm and 7.30–10.30pm Sun.*

LANGLEY

Leathers Smithy

Langley, Nr Macclesfield SK11 0NE
☎ *(01260) 252313*

Morland Old Speckled Hen and Timothy Taylor Landlord always available, plus alternating guests.

A former smithy (originally run by William Leather), built in the sixteenth century in beautiful surroundings on the edge of Macclesfield Forest overlooking the Ridge Gate Reservoir (fishing possible). Food available at lunchtime and evenings. Also 80 different whiskies. Car park, garden, family/function room.

OPEN *12–3pm and 7–11pm Mon–Thurs and Sat; 12–3pm and 5.30–11pm Fri; 12–10.30pm Sun.*

MACCLESFIELD

Waters Green Tavern

96 Waters Green, Macclesfield SK11 6LH
☎ *(01625) 422653* Mr MacDermott

Up to four beers available. Regular guests might come from Exmoor, Whim and Lloyds breweries.

A traditional pub with food served at lunchtime only. Children not allowed.

OPEN *11.30am–3pm and 5.30–11pm Mon–Sat; 7–11pm Sun.*

MOBBERLEY

The Roebuck Inn

Mill Lane, Mobberley WA16 7XH
☎ *(01565) 872757* Dave Robinson

A freehouse with Timothy Taylor Landlord and Greene King Abbot Ale always available, plus regular guests, changed weekly, that may include Hydes' Anvil Bitter, Shepherd Neame Spitfire or Elgood's Pageant Ale.

A friendly country inn with a contemporary twist, recently refurbished. Fresh food served at lunchtime and evenings. Children allowed.

OPEN *12–3pm and 5.30–11pm Mon–Fri; 12–11pm Sat; 12–10.30pm Sun.*

NANTWICH

The Black Lion

29 Welsh Row, Nantwich CW5 5ED
☎ *(01270) 628711* Jill Llewellyn

A three-pump freehouse with Weetwood Old Dog and Best Bitter plus Titanic Premium always available.

A traditional two-bar pub. Food at lunchtime and evenings. No children.

OPEN *11am–11pm Mon–Sat; 12–10.30pm Sun.*

Wilbraham Arms
58 Welsh Row, Nantwich CW5 5EJ
☎ *(01270) 626419*

 Marston's Pedigree and JW Lees Best Bitter always available.

Close to the town centre, near canal, with traditional Georgian frontage, bar and dining area. Bar food available at lunchtime and evenings. Small car park, accommodation. Children allowed in dining room.

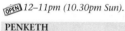 *12–11pm (10.30pm Sun).*

The Ferry Tavern
Station Road, Penketh, Warrington WA5 2UJ
☎ *(01925) 791117 Mr T Maxwell*

Ruddles County usually available with one guest beer, perhaps Phoenix Wobbly Bob, Greene King Abbot Ale, Morland Old Speckled Hen or something from Black Sheep. Guest beers are chosen by customer request.

Built in the eleventh century, the Ferry Tavern has been an alehouse for 300 years and stands in a unique position on an island between the river Mersey and the St Helens canal. Bar food is served 12–2pm and 6–7.30pm, full menu 6–9pm. Car park. Children welcome.

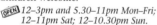 *12–3pm and 5.30–11pm Mon–Fri; 12–11pm Sat; 12–10.30pm Sun.*

The Buffet Bar
Stalybridge Railway Station, Stalybridge SK15 1RF
☎ *(0161) 303 0007*

Seven or eight real ales available. Wadworth 6X is a permanent fixture plus a constantly changing range of guest beers from independent breweries.

A unique and authentic buffet bar built in 1855 with a real fire, real ale, and real people! Bar food available at most times. Parking. Children allowed. On platform one at Stalybridge railway station.

11am–11pm Mon–Sat; 12–10.30pm Sun.

Q Inn
3 Market Street, Stalybridge SK15 2AL
☎ *(0161) 303 9157 David Conner*

Beers from Marston and Thwaites always available. Guest beers (200 per year) from Gibbs Mew, Phoenix, Hull, Hart, Bateman, Fuller's, Wadworth and Exmoor breweries also served.

The pub with the shortest name in Britain forms part of the Stalybridge Eight – eight pubs in the town offering 37 different beers. Brick walls and a flagstone floor. Quiz night on Monday, Cocktail bar on Friday. No food. Next to the railway station.

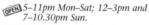 *5–11pm Mon–Sat; 12–3pm and 7–10.30pm Sun.*

The White House
1 Water Street, Stalybridge SK15 2AG
☎ *(0161) 303 2288 Mr Connor*

A freehouse with a good range of real ales always available. Exmoor Gold, Greene King Abbot, a Marston's brew and a Timothy Taylor brew are permanent fixtures, plus four guests such as Morland Old Speckled Hen or Moorhouse's Pendle Witches Brew.

A traditional town-centre working-man's pub. Snacks only. Children allowed until 8pm.

 All day, every day.

The Sportsman's Arms
105 Strines Road, Strines SK12 3AE
☎ *(0161) 427 2888*

Cains Mild and Bitter always available, plus a weekly alternating guest from any independent brewery.

An old, two-roomed pub with a lounge/dining room. Home-cooked food is available at lunchtime and evenings. Car park, garden. On the B6101.

12–3pm and 5.15–11pm Mon–Fri; all day Sat and Sun.

TUSHINGHAM

The Blue Bell Inn

Tushingham, Nr Whitchurch
☎ *(01948) 662172* Patrick and Lydia Gage

Hanby Drawwell Bitter always available plus one or two others (20 per year), perhaps including beers from Plassey, Joule, Four Rivers, Cains and Felinfoel breweries.

Dating from 1667, this claims to be Cheshire's oldest pub, with an American landlord and Russian landlady. Friendly and welcoming. No games machines or loud music. Sunday papers and comfortable settee. Bar and restaurant food available at lunchtime and evenings. Car park and garden. Children and dogs always very welcome. Four miles north of Whitchurch on the A41 Chester road.

OPEN *12–3pm and 6–11pm Mon–Sat; 7–11pm Sun.*

WARRINGTON

The Old Town House

Buttermarket Street, Warrington WA1 2NL
☎ *(01925) 242787* Roy Baxter

A five-pump freehouse, always serving Marston's Pedigree and Morland Old Speckled Hen.

A country town pub with one bar, situated in the main street leading into the town centre. Food served at lunchtime only. Children allowed.

OPEN *11am–11pm Mon–Sat; 12–10.30pm Sun.*

WHITCHURCH

Willeymoor Lock Tavern

Tarporley Road, Nr Whitchurch SY13 4HF
☎ *(01948) 663274* Mrs Elsie Gilkes

Four guest beers served in summer, two in winter. These may include beers from Beartown, Hanby Ales, Kitchen, Cottage, Weetwood, Coach House, Wood, Springhead or Wychwood breweries.

Situated next to a working lock on the Llangollen Canal, this pub was formerly a lock-keeper's cottage. Food served lunchtimes and evenings. Children welcome: there is a large garden with a play area. Car park. Situated two miles north of Whitchurch on A49. Pub found at end of driveway, pub sign on the road.

OPEN *12–2.30pm (2pm winter) and 6–11pm Mon–Sat; 12–2.30pm (2pm winter) and 7–10.30pm Sun.*

Places Featured:

Altarnun
Blisland
Boscastle
Charlestown
Crackington Haven
Crantock
Edmonton
Falmouth
Golant
Gorran Haven
Gunnislake
Hayle
Helston
Launceston
Lerryn
Lostwithiel
Nancenoy

Penzance
Polperro
Porthallow
Porthleven
Portreath
Quintrell Downs
St Austell
St Cleer
Stratton
Trebarwith Strand
Tregrehan
Tresparrett
Trevaunance Cove
Truro
Widemouth Bay
Zelah

THE BREWERIES

BLACKAWTON BREWERY
Woodside Stables, Carkeel, Saltash PL12 6PH
☎ *(01752) 848777*

BITTER 3.8% ABV
Well-hopped. A popular session beer.
DEVON GOLD 4.1% ABV
Summer brew. European style. Light and fresh.
44 SPECIAL 4.5% ABV
Full-bodied with rich nutty flavour.
EXHIBITION 4.7% ABV
Pale, soft and fruity.
HEADSTRONG 5.2% ABV
Rich and powerful with fruit flavour. Deceptively smooth.
Plus occasional brews.

KELTEK BREWERY
Unit 3a Restormel Industrial Estate, Liddicoat Road, Lostwithiel PL22 0HG
☎ *(01208) 871199*

4 K MILD 3.8% ABV
GOLDEN LANCE 3.8% ABV
KELTEK MAGIC 4.2% ABV
KELTIK KING 5.1% ABV
Plus monthly and seasonal brews.

ST AUSTELL BREWERY CO. LTD
63 Trevarthian Road, St Austell PL25 4BY
☎ *(01726) 74444*

BOSUN'S BITTER 3.1% ABV
Well-balanced, sweeter light flavour.
XXXX MILD 3.6% ABV
Dark and distinctive, with malt flavour.
TINNERS ALE 3.7% ABV
Well-balanced hops and malt throughout.
DAYLIGHT ROBBERY 4.2% ABV
HICKS SPECIAL DRAUGHT 5.0% ABV
Powerful and distinctive.
Plus seasonal brews

SHARP'S BREWERY
Rock, Wadebridge PL27 6NU
☎ *(01208) 862121*

CORNISH COASTER 3.6% ABV
DOOM BAR BITTER 4.0% ABV
EDEN ALE 4.4% ABV
OWN 4.4% ABV
WILL'S RESOLVE 4.6% ABV
SPECIAL ALE 5.2% ABV

SKINNER'S BREWING CO.
Riverside View, Newham, Truro TR1 2SU
☎ *(01872) 271885*

COASTLINER 3.4% ABV
Quenching and well-hopped.
SPRIGGAN ALE 3.8% ABV
Quenching, with flavour of hops.
BETTY STOGS BITTER 4.0% ABV
Light-coloured, with hops throughout.
CORNISH KNOCKER 4.5% ABV
Gold in colour and refreshing.
FIGGY'S BREW 4.5% ABV
Rich and well-rounded.
WHO PUT THE LIGHTS OUT? 5.0% ABV
Beauty of Hops Gold Award winner 1999

VENTONWYN BREWING CO. LTD
Unit 2b, Grampound Ind Est., Truro TR2 4TB
☎ *(01726) 884367*

LEVANT GOLDEN 4.0% ABV
Refreshing and fruity with delicate hoppiness
OLD PENDEEN 4.0% ABV
Rounded and hoppy with refreshing bitter finish.
CORNISH GLORY 4.2% ABV
Smooth and balanced with hoppy finish.

ALTARNUN

The Rising Sun

Altarnun, Nr Launceston PL15 7SN
☎ *(01566) 86332* Mr and Mrs Manson

Up to six beers available, including brews from Sharp's, Hoskins & Oldfield, Cotleigh, Skinner's, Butcombe, Otter and Exe Valley. Continually changing.

Sixteenth-century, single-bar pub with open fires and slate/hardwood floor. Bar food available at lunchtime and evenings. Ample parking. Children allowed. One mile off the A30, seven miles west of Launceston.

OPEN *11am–3pm and 5.30–11pm Mon–Fri; 11am–11pm Sat; 12–10.30pm Sun. Open all day, every day, during summer season.*

BLISLAND

Blisland Inn

The Green, Blisland, nr Bodmin PL30 4JF
☎ *(01208) 850739* Mr Marshall

Six pumps with guests changing every couple of days. Skinner's Cornish Ales are regulars.

Country-style freehouse, with lounge, public bar and family room. Separate dining area for bar food served at lunchtime and evenings. Children allowed in family room.

OPEN *11.30am–3.30pm and 6–11pm Mon–Thurs; 11am–11pm Fri–Sat; 12–10.30pm Sun.*

BOSCASTLE

The Cobweb Inn

Boscastle PL35 0HE
☎ *(01840) 250278* AI and AP Bright

St Austell Tinners and Greene King Abbot usually available, plus three or four guest beers perhaps from Sharp's, Skinner's, St Austell, Exmoor, Cotleigh, Wadworth or Bateman.

Atmospheric, seventeenth-century freehouse, close to the harbour. Food served lunchtimes and evenings. Car park. Children permitted in family room, restaurant and outside seating, but not in bar area. The pub is across the road from the car park at the bottom of the village.

OPEN *11am–11pm Mon–Fri; 11am–midnight Sat; 12–10.30pm Sun.*

CHARLESTOWN

Rashleigh Arms

Charlestown Road, Charlestown, St Austell PL25 3NJ
☎ *(01726) 73635* Glen Price

A 14-pump freehouse, Wadworth 6X and Sharp's Doom Bar among those always available. Two guests are changed twice a week. Skinner's ales are often featured.

A country pub with family room, TV and juke box, plus entertainment in winter. Food served at lunchtimes and evenings. Children allowed.

OPEN *11am–11pm Mon–Sat; 12–10.30pm Sun.*

CRACKINGTON HAVEN

Coombe Barton Inn

Crackington Haven, Bude EX23 0JG
☎ *(01840) 230345* Mr Cooper

A freehouse offering eight beers including four guests. Sharp's Doom Bar and Dartmoor Best are always available. Regular guests come from St Austell and Sharp's breweries.

A seaside family-run pub on the sea front, with separate dining area and family room. Six rooms available for bed and breakfast. Food at lunchtime and evenings. Children allowed in family room.

OPEN *Summer: 11am–11pm Mon–Sat; 12–10.30pm Sun; winter: 11am–3pm and 6–11pm.*

CRANTOCK

Old Albion

Langurroc Road, Crantock, Newquay TR8 5RB
☎ *(01637) 830243*
Mr Andrew Brown and Miss S. Moses

Sharp's and St Austell beers always available. Three guests, changed frequently, might include Cotleigh brews, Morland Old Speckled Hen, Exmoor Gold and Fuller's London Pride.

A country pub, which used to be used for smuggling beer, situated next to the church in Crantock. Homemade food served at lunchtime and evenings in bar area. Children allowed in family room.

OPEN *12–11pm.*

EDMONTON

The Quarryman

Edmonton, Wadebridge PL27 7JA
☎ *(01208) 816444* Terrence de-Villiers Kuun

A four-pump freehouse, with guest beers changed every two or three days. Favourites include Skinner's and Sharp's brews plus Cottage Golden Arrow.

An old Cornish inn with separate restaurant and bar food. Food served at lunchtime and evenings. Well-behaved children allowed.

OPEN *11am–11pm Mon–Sat; 12–10.30pm Sun.*

FALMOUTH

The Quayside Inn

41 Arwenack Street, Falmouth TR11 3JQ
☎ *(01326) 312113*
Howard Graves and Julie Marshall

Up to 15 beers always available. Sharp's Special, Skinner's Cornish Knocker, Marston's Pedigree, Wadworth 6X, Ringwood Old Thumper and Morland Old Speckled Hen permanently served, plus a range of guests from breweries such as Bateman, Shepherd Neame and Fuller's.

Twice-yearly beer festivals at this quayside pub overlooking the harbour. Two bars – comfy upstairs lounge and downstairs real ale bar. Food available all day, every day in summer, and at lunchtimes and evenings in winter (skillet house with food cooked in skillets). Also sells 200 whiskies including 179 single malts. Parking and garden. Children very welcome – children's menu. On Custom House Quay.

OPEN *Both bars all day in summer. Alehouse all day in winter.*

GOLANT

The Fisherman's Arms

Fore Street, Golant, Fowey PL23 1LN
☎ *(01726) 832453* Michael Moran

An Ushers pub with Best and Founders Ale always served.

A village pub on the banks of the River Fowey. Food at lunchtime and evening. Children allowed.

OPEN *12–3pm and 6–11pm Mon–Fri; 11am–11pm Sat; 12–10.30am Sun.*

GORRAN HAVEN

Llawnroc Inn

33 Chute Lane, Gorran Haven, St Austell PL26 6NU
☎ *(01726) 843461*
Alan Freeman and Don Reece.

A Sharp's beer is regularly available.

Relaxing, family-run hotel with beautiful sea views situated in an old fishing village. Food served 12–2.30pm and 6–9.30pm in summer and 12–2pm and 7–9pm in winter. Car park. Children welcome. From St Austell continue past Heligan Gardens and after Gorran Haven, turn right.

OPEN *12–11pm Mon–Sat (10.30pm Sun) in summer. 12–3pm and 6.30–11pm Mon–Sat, 12–3pm and 7–10.30pm Sun in winter.*

GUNNISLAKE

Rising Sun Inn

Calstock Road, Gunnislake PL18 9BX
☎ *(01822) 832201* Jan and Roger English

A freehouse with Sharp's Cornish Coaster, Skinner's Betty Stogs Bitter and Sutton XSB always available, plus a range of guest beers.

Seventeenth-century olde-worlde freehouse on the outskirts of Gunnislake. Home-cooked food served lunchtimes and evenings Wed–Sat and lunchtime Sun. Beautiful gardens. Well-behaved children welcome.

OPEN *12–2.30pm and 5–11pm Mon–Sat; 12–3pm and 7–10.30pm Sun.*

HAYLE

Bird in Hand

Trelissick Road, Hayle TR27 4HY
☎ *(01736) 753974* Mr Miller

A freehouse and brewpub serving a range of own brews, plus two guest beers, perhaps including Greene King Abbot or Shepherd Neame Spitfire.

An old coach house with one bar. Live music. Food at lunchtime and evenings (summer only). Children allowed.

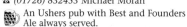 **PARADISE 3.8–4.0% ABV**
A light session bitter.
MILLER'S 4.2–4.4% ABV
A medium light bitter.
SPECKLED PARROT 5.5–6.5% ABV
A dark ale.

OPEN *11am–11pm Mon–Sat; 12–10.30pm Sun.*

The Blue Anchor

50 Coinagehall Street, Helston TR13 8EX
☎ *(01326) 562821*

One of only four pubs in Britain which has brewed continuously for centuries and still produces its famous Spingo ales, from a Victorian word for strong beer.

This thatched town pub was originally a monks' rest home in the fifteenth century. Brewing continued on the premises after the Reformation and the Blue Anchor is now believed to be the oldest brewpub in Britain. Bar snacks and meals are available at lunchtime. Garden, children's room, skittle alley, function room. Accommodation available.

MIDDLE 5.0% ABV
BEST 5.3% ABV
SPECIAL 6.6% ABV
CHRISTMAS AND EASTER SPECIAL 7.6% ABV

11am–11pm Mon–Sat; 12–10.30pm Sun.

The Eliot Arms

Tregadillet, Launceston
☎ *(01566) 772051*

Sharp's Doom Bar and Special regularly available.

Ivy-clad pub with softly lit rooms, open fires, slate floors, high-backed settles and fine Victorian furniture and artifacts. Food served 12–2pm and 7–9.30pm. Car park. Children welcome.

11am–3pm and 6–11pm Mon–Sat; 12–3pm and 7–10.30pm Sun.

The Ship

Lerryn, Nr Lostwithiel PL22 0PT
☎ *(01208) 872374 Mr Packer*

Four beers available including Sharp's brews and guests such as Exmoor Gold, Morland Old Speckled Hen, Fuller's London Pride and Otter Ale.

A pub since the early 1600s, with a wood burner in the bar and slate floors. Bar and restaurant food available at lunchtime and evenings. Set in a quiet riverside village three miles south of Lostwithiel. Car park, garden, accommodation. Children allowed.

11.30am–3pm and 6–11pm Mon–Sat; 12–3pm and 7–10.30pm Sun.

The Royal Oak Inn

Duke Street, Lostwithiel PL22 0AG
☎ *(01208) 872552 Mr and Mrs Hine*

Marston's Pedigree, Sharp's Own and Fuller's London Pride always available. Orkney Skullsplitter, the Blue Anchor Spingos, Woodforde's Headcracker, Exmoor Gold, Ash Vine Bitter, Badger Tanglefoot and Best are among the guest beers (50 per year).

A popular thirteenth-century inn catering for all tastes. Bar and restaurant food at lunchtime and evenings. Car park, garden, children's room. Spacious accommodation. Located just off the A390 going into Lostwithiel.

11am–11pm.

Trengilly Wartha Inn

Nancenoy, Constantine, Nr Falmouth TR11 5RP
☎ *(01326) 340332*
Nigel Logan and Michael MacGuire

Sharp's Cornish Coaster always available, plus a couple of constantly rotating guests which may include brews from Skinner's, Keltek, St Austell or Exmoor.

A country freehouse and restaurant in six acres of valley gardens and meadows. Bar and restaurant food at lunchtime and evenings. Car park, garden and children's room. Eight bedrooms. Just south of Constantine – follow the signs.

11am–2.30pm and 6.30–11pm.

Globe & Ale House

Queen Street, Penzance TR18 4BJ
☎ *(01736) 364098 Jenny Flewitt*

Tied to Greenalls, Skinner's Cornish Knocker and Sharp's Own always available. The three guest beers may be from Bateman or Titanic. Four real ales are straight from the barrel.

An alehouse with live music once a week and quiz nights. Food served lunchtimes and evenings, but no separate dining area. No children.

11am–11pm Mon–Sat; 12–10.30pm Sun.

Mounts Bay Inn

Promenade, Wherry Town, Penzance TR18
☎ *(01736) 363027* Christopher Kent

Skinner's beers usually available, plus guest brews which often include ales from the Sharp's range.

A warm welcome awaits in this characterful olde-worlde pub. Food served lunchtimes and evenings. Local authority car park situated opposite the pub. Children welcome if eating. Small side terrace with seating.

[OPEN] *11am–11pm Mon–Sat; 12–10.30pm Sun.*

POLPERRO

The Blue Peter Inn

The Quay, Polperro, Nr Looe PL13 2QZ
☎ *(01503) 272743* Terry Bicknell

St Austell HSD and Tinners Ale, plus Sharp's Doom Bar Bitter always available. Also guest beers (up to 100 per year) changing almost daily, with the emphasis on minor breweries from all over the country. Plus draught local scrumpy.

Small, atmospheric, traditional pub with beamed ceilings and log fires. No games machines or juke box – the house plays the music; primarily blues and jazz. Live music on Saturday nights and Sunday afternoons. No food, so bring your own rolls and sandwiches. Family room. Children not allowed in the bar. At the end of the fish quay.

[OPEN] *11am–11pm Mon–Sat; 12–10.30pm Sun all year.*

The Old Mill House

Mill Hill, Polperro PL13 2RP
☎ *(01503) 272362* Suzanne Doughty

Sharp's Eden Ale and St Austell HSD always available.

White-painted, cottage-style pub with a nautical theme. Food available 12–2.30pm and from 7pm in the evening. Car parking for residents only. Toys available in the children's room. Garden.

[OPEN] *Summer: 11am–11pm (10.30pm Sun); Winter: 12–11pm (10.30pm Sun).*

PORTHALLOW

The Five Pilchards

Porthallow, St Keverne, Helston TR12 6PP
☎ *(01326) 280256* Brandon Flynn

A four-pump freehouse with Greene King Abbot Ale and Sharp's Own always available. Two guests, changed fortnightly, might include favourites Skinner's or Sharp's.

An old Cornish seafaring pub with separate dining area. Food served lunchtimes and evenings. Children allowed.

[OPEN] *12–2.30pm and 6–11pm.*

PORTHLEVEN

Atlantic Inn

Peverell Terrace, Porthleven, Helston TR13 9DZ
☎ *(01326) 562439* Valerie Moore

A freehouse with Skinner's Figgy's Brew always available. Guest beers include Wadworth 6X.

A traditional seaside pub in a village location (signposted), with live entertainment every Saturday. Food served lunchtimes and evenings in lounge bar. Children allowed.

[OPEN] *11am–11pm Mon–Sat; 12–10.30pm Sun.*

PORTREATH

Basset Arms

Tregea Terrace, Portreath TR16 4NS
☎ *(01209) 842277* Craig Moss and Don Reece

Sharp's Doom Bar and Marston's Pedigree regularly available.

Warm and friendly pub situated directly opposite Portreath Bay. Food served 12–2pm and 6.30–9.30pm. Car park. Children's play area.

[OPEN] *Summer: 11–30am–11pm Mon–Sat and 12–10.30pm Sun; Winter: 11.30am–2.30pm and 6–11pm Mon–Sat, 12–2.30pm and 7–10.30pm Sun.*

QUINTRELL DOWNS

The Two Clomes

East Road, Quintrell Downs, Nr Newquay TR8 4PD
☎ *(01637) 871163* Frank and Lynn Cheshire

Approx 100 guest beers per year, three or four at any one time. Beers from Exmoor, Otter, St Austell, Fuller's, Cains and Four Rivers breweries all favoured.

A converted and extended old miner's cottage built from Cornish stone with a beer garden and 48-seater restaurant. Open log fires in winter. Bar food available at lunchtime and evenings. Car park. Take the A392 from Newquay to Quintrell Downs, straight on at the roundabout, then second right.

[OPEN] *12–3pm and 7–11pm (10.30pm Sun).*

ST AUSTELL

The Barley Sheaf

Gorran, St Austell PL26 6HN
☎ *(01726) 843330* Andy Thomson

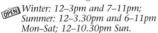 Sharps Doom Bar and Skinners Betty Stogs usually available with two guest beers often also from Sharps or Skinners.

Olde-worlde nineteenth-century country pub featured in Wycliffe, the Cornish detective series and Michael Aspel's Strange But True. Food served every day 12–2pm and 7–9pm. Car park. Children permitted in the skittle alley. Situated four miles west of The Lost Gardens of Heligan.

OPEN Winter: 12–3pm and 7–11pm; Summer: 12–3.30pm and 6–11pm Mon–Sat; 12–10.30pm Sun.

ST CLEER

The Stag Inn

Fore Street, St Cleer, Liskeard PL14 5DA
☎ *(01579) 342305* Alann Eberlein

A seven-pump freehouse, Sharp's Doom Bar and Special plus Greene King Abbot always available. A guest beer, changed weekly, might well be Skinner's Betty Stogs.

An old pub with TV and non-smoking dining area. Food at lunchtime and evenings. Well-behaved children allowed.

OPEN 11am–11pm Mon–Sat; 12–10.30pm Sun.

STRATTON

King's Arms

Howell's Road, Stratton, Bude EX23 9BX
☎ *(01288) 352396* Steven Peake

A freehouse with four pumps, two serving guest beers. Permanently available are Sharp's Own, Doom Bar Bitter and Exmoor Ale. Favourite guests, changed weekly, include Shepherd Neame Spitfire, Everards Beacon Bitter and Exmoor Gold.

A traditional pub with TV and sports coverage. Food at lunchtime and evenings. Children allowed.

OPEN 12–2pm and 6.30–11pm Mon–Thurs; 11am–11pm Fri–Sat; 12–10.30pm Sun.

TREBARWITH STRAND

Mill House

Trebarwith Strand, Nr Tintagel PL34 0HD
☎ *(01840) 770932* Roy and Jenny Vickers

Seven beers available including Sharp's Cornish Coaster, Doom Bar Bitter and Own. Also St Austell Tinners Ale and HSD plus a guest beer changed each month.

A seventeenth-century mill with seven acres of woodland and a trout stream. Bar and restaurant food available at lunchtime and evenings. Car park, garden and patio, accommodation. Children welcome. Head for Trebarwith from Tintagel.

OPEN 11am–11pm.

TREGREHAN

The Britannia Inn

Tregrehan Par, Tregrehan PL24 2SL
☎ *(01726) 812889* Richard Rogers

This seven-pump freehouse serves Sharp's Own, Fuller's London Pride, Morland Old Speckled Hen and Greene Abbot Ale. A guest beer is changed twice weekly. Regulars include Marston's Pedigree and Fuller's ESB.

An eating house with two separate bars; one tends towards the young, the other towards eating. Food served at lunchtime and evenings. Children allowed in the dining area

OPEN 11am–11pm Mon–Sat; 12–10.30pm Sun.

TRESPARRETT

The Horseshoe Inn

Tresparrett, Camelford PL32 9ST
☎ *(01840) 261240* Mr Kirby

Sutton's Knickerdroppa Glory and Hospice (brewed especially for The Horseshoe Inn by Sutton Brewery) always available, plus up to four more including others from Sutton's.

A one-bar country pub situated in walking country. Separate dining area, outside seating, food served lunchtime and evening. Six darts teams and two pool teams. Children allowed. Located off the A39

OPEN 12–3pm and 6.30–11pm (10.30pm Sun).

TREVAUNANCE COVE

Driftwood Spars Hotel and Driftwood Brewery

Quay Road, Trevaunance Cove, St Agnes TR5 0RT
☎ *(01872) 552428* Jill and Gordon Treleaven

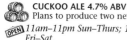 Home brew Cuckoo Ale permanently available, plus Sharp's Own and a Hicks or Skinner's ale. One guest also usually available which is regularly from Skinner's but could also be from any independent brewery.

Built in 1660 as a tin mining chandlery/warehouse, this three-bar pub is situated a stone's throw from the sea, with attractive sea views. Food available all day in summer with Sunday carveries. Children and dogs allowed. Accommodation. Once you are in Trevaunance Cove, bear right at the church, go down a steep hill and turn sharp left.

CUCKOO ALE 4.7% ABV
Plans to produce two new brews shortly.
11am–11pm Sun–Thurs; 11am–midnight Fri–Sat.

TRURO

The Old Ale House

7 Quay Street, Truro TR1 2HD
☎ *(01872) 271122* Mark and Bev Jones

A house ale brewed by the local Skinner's brewery, Kiddlywink, is permanently available, plus a range of guest ales served straight from the barrel. Regulars include Wadworth 6X, Sharp's Own, Exmoor Stag and Gold, Cotleigh Tawny and Old Buzzard, Fuller's London Pride and Shepherd Neame Spitfire.

An olde-worlde pub in the town centre with old furniture and free peanuts. *The Good Pub Guide* Beer Pub of the Year 2000. Bar food available at lunchtime and evenings with skillets and hands of bread a speciality. Live music twice a week. Children welcome.

11am–11pm Mon–Sat; 12–10.30pm Sun.

WIDEMOUTH BAY

The Bayview Inn

Marine Drive, Widemouth Bay, Bude EX23 0AW
☎ *(01288) 361273*
M Gooder (Licensee)/D Kitchener (Manager)

A freehouse with Sharp's Own and Sharp's Doom Bar always available, as is Skinner's Kitch's Klassic (exclusive to this pub). One constantly changing guest also served, usually from Skinner's (Betty Stogs, Cornish Knocker, Skilliwidden), but also from Otter, Exmoor, Cotleigh, Cottage or St Austell. Cask-conditioned cider also available.

A traditional old-style seaside pub decorated with the pump clips of beers past! Two bars, garden, children's play area, large car park. Food available at lunchtimes from 12–2.30pm and evenings from 6–9.30pm. Dining and family room. Accommodation with stunning views of the sea. Children allowed.

June–Sept 11am–11pm (10.30pm Sun); Oct–May 12–3pm and 6–11pm (10.30pm Sun).

ZELAH

Hawkins Arms

High Road, Zelah, Truro TR4 9HU
☎ *(01872) 540339* Peggy Lomas

A freehouse with seven pumps. Guests change regularly.

A one-bar country-style pub. Food served at lunchtime and evenings. Children allowed.

11am–3pm and 6–11pm Mon–Sat; 12–3pm and 7–10.30pm Sun.

YOU TELL US

★ *London Inn*, Kilkhampton, Bude
★ *The Smuggler's Den*, Trebellan

Places Featured:

Allonby
Ambleside
Appleby
Barngates
Broughton in Furness
Carlisle
Cartmel
Cockermouth
Coniston
Dent
Elterwater
Foxfield
Grasmere
Great Corby
Great Langdale

Hayton
Hesket Newmarket
Holmes Green
Ings
Ireby
Kendal
Kirkby Lonsdale
Kirksanton
Lanercost
Nether Wasdale
Strawberry Bank
Tirril
Troutbeck
Wasdale Head
Winton

THE BREWERIES

DENT BREWERY

Hollins, Cowgill, Dent LA10 5DQ
☎ *(01539) 625326*

BITTER 3.7% ABV
Lightly hopped, and slightly sweet.
AVIATOR 4.0% ABV
Full, rounded hop flavour.
RAMSBOTTOM STRONG ALE 4.5% ABV
Medium-dark, caramel flavour, hop balance.
KAMIKAZE 5.0% ABV
Very pale, good hop flavour and creamy
maltiness.
T'OWD TUP 6.0% ABV
Powerful stout. Roast barley, bite and softness.
Plus monthly brews.

DERWENT BREWERY

Station Road Industrial Estate, Carlisle
CA5 4AG
☎ *(01697) 331522*

CARLISLE STATE BITTER 3.7% ABV
PARSON'S PLEDGE 4.0% ABV
TEACHERS PET 4.3% ABV
WHITWELL & MARK PALE ALE 4.4% ABV
BILL MONK 4.5% ABV
Plus occasional brews.

HESKET NEWMARKET BREWERY

Old Crown Barn, Hesket Newmarket CA7 8JG
☎ *(01697) 478066*

GREAT COCKUP PORTER 2.8% ABV
Dark, smooth and malty.
BLENCATHRA BITTER 3.1% ABV
Ruby-coloured and hoppy.
WEDDING ALE 3.5% ABV
Pale, fruity bitter.
SKIDDAW SPECIAL BITTER 3.7% ABV
Gold-coloured and full-flavoured.
HESKET SHOW ALE 3.9% ABV
Occasional pale ale.
PIGS MIGHT FLY 4.0% ABV
First brewed to mark brewery 10th anniversary.
MEDIEVAL ALE 4.3% ABV
Brewed without hops.
DORIS'S 90TH BIRTHDAY ALE 4.3% ABV
Full-flavoured, with fruit throughout.
DORIS'S EXTRA STRONG FESTIVAL ALE 4.9% ABV
Stronger version of Doris's 90th Birthday Ale.
KERN KNOTT'S CRACK-ING STOUT 5.0% ABV
CATBELLS PALE ALE 5.1% ABV
Refreshing, easy quaffing brew.
OLD CARROCK STRONG ALE 5.6% ABV
Rich, smooth and strong.
AYALA'S ANGEL 7.0% ABV
Stout/barley wine, Christmas brew.
Plus seasonal and occasional brews.

JENNINGS BROS PLC

The Castle Brewery, Cockermouth CA13 9NE
☎ *(01900) 823214*

 DARK MILD 3.1% ABV
Sweetness, with malt flavour.
BITTER 3.6% ABV
Dark bitter. Nutty and mellow, with malt.
CUMBERLAND ALE 4.0% ABV
Gold-coloured, rich and smooth.
CROSS BUTTOCK ALE 4.5% ABV
Malty autumn ale.
COCKER HOOP 4.8% ABV
A well-hopped premium bitter.
SNECK LIFTER 5.1% ABV
Strong, slightly sweet and warming.
LA'AL COCKLE WARMER 6.5% ABV
Smooth, Christmas brew.

LAKELAND BREWING CO.

Sepulchre Lane, Kendal LA9 4NJ
☎ *(01539) 734528*

 LAKELAND TERRIER 3.8% ABV
A summer brew.
AMAZON 4.0% ABV
GREAT NORTHERN 5.0% ABV
Winter brew.
DAMSON ALE 5.5% ABV
Seasonal brew.

THE PUBS

ALLONBY

Ship Hotel

Main Street, Allonby CA15 6PZ
☎ *(01900) 881017* Peter and Carole Yates

 Yates Bitter and Premium always available plus guests changed each week including Orkney Dark Island.

Overlooking Solway Firth, a 300-year-old hotel with considerable history. Bar and restaurant food served at lunchtime and evenings. Car park, accommodation. Dogs welcome.

12–3pm and 7–11pm (10.30pm Sun). Winter lunchtime hours may vary.

AMBLESIDE

Queens Hotel

Market Place, Ambleside LA22 9BU
☎ *(015394) 32206* Mr Bessey

A freehouse with Jennings Bitter always available. Two constantly changing guests from a mixture of nationals and independents, with Coniston Bluebird and Old Man Ale, Black Sheep and Yates Bitter regularly offered.

A centrally situated, Victorian-style pub, with two traditional bars. Food available 12–9.30pm daily. Smoking and non-smoking areas, and à la carte restaurant. Children welcome.

11am–11pm Mon–Sat; 12–10.30pm Sun.

APPLEBY

The Royal Oak Inn

Bongate, Appleby CA16 6UB
☎ *(017683) 51463* Ed McCauley

Yates Bitter is among those beers permanently available plus up to seven guests (50 per year) including Holt's Bitter and ales from Maclay, Harviestoun, Wadworth, Hexhamshire, Hesket Newmarket, Timothy Taylor and Black Sheep breweries.

A long white-washed building, roughly 400 years old with lots of character. Bar and restaurant food available at lunchtime and evenings. Two dining rooms, one non-smoking. Parking and terrace. Children allowed. Accommodation. CAMRA Cumbria Pub of the Year 1993. On entering Appleby from Brough on the A66, the inn is at the foot of a hill, on the right.

11am–11pm Mon–Sat; 12–10.30pm Sun.

BARNGATES

The Drunken Duck Inn

Barngates, Ambleside LA22 0NG
☎ *(015394) 36347* Stephanie Barton

The home of the Barngates brewery, with Cracker Ale, Tag Lag, Chester's Strong & Ugly plus Jennings Bitter.

Delightful 400-year-old inn, set in beautiful countryside and oozing olde-worlde charm. Tempting restaurant and modern, stylish accommodation. Amusing story behind the pub name – ask the landlady! Food available 12–2.30pm and 6–9pm. Car park. Children are welcome, but there are no special facilities.

 CRACKER ALE 3.9% ABV
Delicate quenching hoppiness with balancing malt.
TAG LAG 4.4% ABV
Pale and fruity with good bitterness.
CHESTER'S STRONG & UGLY 4.9% ABV
Rounded and flavoursome.

11.30am–11pm Mon–Sat; 12–10.30pm Sun.

BROUGHTON IN FURNESS

The Manor Arms

The Square, Broughton in Furness LA20 6HY
☎ *(01229) 716286* David Varty

Seven well-kept real ales available including 160 guest beers per year from small breweries. New brews, winter warmers – you name it, they have served it!

Eighteenth-century traditional family-run freehouse with a welcoming atmosphere. Regular CAMRA pub of the year award-winner. Bar snacks available all day. Parking and outside seats overlooking a picturesque market square. Luxurious accommodation. Children allowed.

12–11pm (10.30pm Sun).

Fox & Pheasant

Armathwaite, Carlisle CA4 9PY
☎ *(01697) 472400* Mr A Glass

A maximum of four real ales are offered in this freehouse, two in winter and one rotating. Something from Hesket Newmarket (usually Doris' 90th Birthday Ale) is always available. Regular guests, changed weekly, include Ridleys Nobody's Fool and Jennings Cumberland, with a varied selection of others, mostly from local Cumbrian breweries.

A seventeenth-century coaching inn, overlooking the River Eden, in a small village. Log fires, eight bedrooms, outside seating. Food served at lunchtime and evenings in a separate dining area. Children allowed.

OPEN *11am–11pm Mon–Sat; 12–10.30pm Sun.*

Cavendish Arms

Cavendish Street, Cartmel LA11 6QA
☎ *(01539) 536240* Tom Murray

Four beers always available from a range of more than 300 per year. Favourite guest beers include Timothy Taylor Landlord, Castle Eden, Banner Bitter, Hop Back Summer Lightning, Fuller's ESB and Shepherd Neame Spitfire.

A coaching inn, 500 years old, offering bar and restaurant food at lunchtime and evenings. Car park, dining room, non-smoking room, accommodation. Children allowed until 8.30pm.

OPEN *11am–11pm Mon–Sat; 12–10pm Sun.*

The Bitter End

15 Kirkgate, Cockermouth CA13 9PJ
☎ *(01900) 828993* Susan Askey

Bitter End Cockersnoot is always available in this freehouse and brewpub, along with four guests, changed weekly, which often include Yates Bitter, Coniston Bluebird, Isle of Skye Red Cuillin or Hesket Newmarket Doris' 90th Birthday Ale. Other home brews when available.

A very traditional pub with background music, non-smoking area at lunchtimes. Food served at lunchtime and evenings. Children allowed.

COCKERSNOOT 3.8% ABV
A golden, clean, refreshing beer.
CUDDY LUGS 4.3% ABV
Strong hop aroma with a dry aftertaste.
SKINNER'S OLD STRONG 5.5%
A rich amber beer, sweet and fruity.

OPEN *11.30am–2.30pm and 6–11pm Mon–Thurs; 11.30am–3pm and 6–11pm Fri–Sat; 11.30am–3pm and 7–10.30pm Sun.*

The Bush

Main Street, Cockermouth CA13 9JS
☎ *(01900) 822064* Maureen Williamson

A Jennings house with 12 hand pumps. The full Jennings range is always on offer. Two or three guests, changed weekly, include a wide selection of beers, bought through Flying Firkin.

A very homely pub with open fires. Food served at lunchtime only. Children allowed.

OPEN *11am–11pm Mon–Sat; 12–10.30pm Sun.*

The Black Bull

Yewdale Road, Coniston LA21 8DU
☎ *(01539) 441335* Ronald Edward Bradley

A seven-pump freehouse and brewpub, with the Coniston Brewery at the rear of the pub. Always available are Coniston Bluebird and Old Man Ale. Specials include Coniston Opium and Blacksmith's Ale. Guests are rotated on two pumps and changed fortnightly: regulars are Moorhouse's Black Cat, also Saxons Scrumpy Cider. Other guests are all from small independent and micro-breweries.

A sixteenth-century coaching inn in the centre of Coniston, with oak beams and log fire. No juke box or fruit machines. Outside seating area. Separate restaurant. Food served all day. Children allowed.

BLUEBIRD BITTER 3.6% ABV
A session ale. Champion Best Bitter 1998. Also available as bottle-conditioned at 4.0%.
OPIUM 4.0%
A seasonal autumn brew. Dark amber, malty ale.
OLD MAN ALE 4.4% ABV
Dark and ruby-coloured.
BLACKSMITH'S ALE 5.0% ABV
A seasonal Christmas brew. Winter warmer.

OPEN *11am–11pm Mon–Sat; 12–10.30pm Sun.*

The Sun Hotel

Coniston LA21 8HQ
☎ *(01539) 441248*
Alan Piper (Manager Keith Brady)

Timothy Taylor Landlord, Ruddles County, Coniston Bluebird and Black Sheep Bitter permanently available, plus one guest ale which may be Dent Aviator or something from Crouch Vale. Smaller breweries supported whenever possible.

Under new ownership from April 2000, this is a sixteenth-century pub with a nineteenth-century hotel attached to it. One bar, beer garden, seating at front. Extensive bar menu served lunchtimes and evenings, snacks all day. Children and dogs welcome. Situated on the hill leading up to the Old Man of Coniston, 100 yards above Coniston village, turn left at the bridge.

OPEN *11am–11pm (10.30pm Sun).*

DENT

The George & Dragon
Main Street, Dent LA10 5QL
☎ *(01539) 625256* Mrs Dorothy Goad

Owned by Dent Brewery, with Dent beers always available.

A country pub, with accommodation. Food served lunchtimes and evenings, separate dining area. Children and dogs allowed. Ten miles from junction 37 of the M6.

Summer: 11am–11pm; closed afternoons in winter.

The Sun Inn
Main Street, Dent LA10 5QL
☎ *(01539) 625208* Martin Stafford

Owned by Dent Brewery. Five Dent brews always available.

A traditional country pub in the cobbled main street. Friendly atmosphere, large beer garden, pool room, non-smoking dining area. Food served lunchtimes throughout the year and evenings (summertime only). Children allowed till 9pm.

Winter: 12–2pm and 7–11pm Mon–Fri; 11am–11pm Sat; 12–10.30pm Sun. Summer: 11am–11pm Mon–Sat; 12–10.30pm Sun.

ELTERWATER

Britannia Inn
Elterwater, Ambleside LA22 9HP
☎ *(01539) 437210* Judy Fry

A freehouse with Jennings Bitter, Coniston Bluebird and Dent Aviator always on the menu, plus two guests changed frequently.

A country inn with quiz nights on Sundays. Food served lunchtimes and evenings. Separate dining area. Accommodation. Children and dogs allowed.

11am–11pm Mon–Sat; 12–10.30pm Sun.

FOXFIELD

The Prince of Wales
Foxfield, Broughton in Furness LA20 6BX
☎ *(01229) 716238* Stuart Johnson

The home of the Foxfield Brewery. Four hand pumps dispense a constantly changing range of beers – over 1000 different ales sold in the last four years. There is usually a mild and something from Tigertops or Foxfield breweries available. Set up by Stuart and Lynda Johnson of the Tigertops brewery in Wakefield, both breweries brew experimental and varied beer styles. The range in pub and brewery is constantly changing.

A 'no-frills' real ale house, for real ale lovers. No food. No children. Car park. Located opposite Foxfield railway station.

5–11pm Wed–Thurs; 12–11pm Fri–Sat; 12–10.30pm Sun; closed Mon–Tues.

GRASMERE

The Travellers Rest Inn
Grasmere, LA22 9RR
☎ *(01539) 435604* Graham Sweeney

A pub owned by a family of dedicated beer sellers, with five real ales offered at any one time. Always available are Jennings House Bitter, Snecklifter and Mild. Regular guests, changed every six weeks, include Jennings Cumberland and Marston's Pedigree.

A sixteenth-century inn. One bar, beer garden, bed and breakfast (ensuite accommodation). Food served from 12–3pm and 6–9pm (winter); 12–9pm (summer). Smoking dining area and non-smoking restaurant. Children allowed. Half a mile north of Grasmere village.

11am–11pm Mon–Sat; 12–10.30pm Sun.

GREAT CORBY

The Corby Bridge Inn
Great Corby, Carlisle CA4 8LL
☎ *(01228) 560221* Barbara Griffiths

Thwaites Bitter and Mild always available plus a rotating guest, changed at least twice a week, often including Nethergate Old Growler, Charles Wells Bombardier, Fuller's London Pride, Timothy Taylor Landlord, Badger Tanglefoot or a Wychwood brew.

A freehouse built in 1838. Originally a railway hotel. Grade II listed. Approximately four miles from junction 43 of M6. One bar, pool and darts room and non-smoking dining area. Large garden, games area, accommodation. Food served all day Tues–Sun and Bank Holiday Mondays. Well-behaved children welcome.

12–11pm (10.30pm Sun).

GREAT LANGDALE

Old Dungeon Ghyll Hotel
Great Langdale, Ambleside LA22 9JY
☎ *(01539) 437272* Neil and Jane Walmsley

Seven real ales and scrumpy available in this freehouse. Yates Bitter and Jennings Cumberland Ale always present. Three guests are changed regularly, one barrel at a time. Black Sheep Special is popular.

An interesting National Trust-owned, listed building with real fire. Food served at lunchtime (12–2pm) and evenings (6–9pm). Children allowed.

11am–11pm Mon–Sat; 12–10.30pm Sun.

HAYTON

Stone Inn

Hayton, Nr Carlisle CA4 9HR
☎ *(01228) 670498*
Johnnie and Susan Tranter

Four beers from Jennings and Thwaites permanently available plus occasional guest beers, as available.

A traditional village pub. Toasted sandwiches available all day, though the focus is on beer rather than food. There are function facilities, and coach parties can be catered for if booked in advance. The pub has a car park, and is situated seven minutes east of M6 junction 43, just off the A69.

OPEN *11am–3pm and 5.30–11pm.*

HESKET NEWMARKET

The Old Crown

Hesket Newmarket, Caldbeck, Wigton CA7 8JG
☎ *(01697) 478288* Kim Matthews

A freehouse, but concentrating on the Hesket Newmarket brews, with the brewery situated close by Old Carrock Strong Ale, Skiddaw Special, Catbells Pale Ale, Doris' 90th Birthday Ale, Pigs Might Fly, Kern Knott's Crack(ing) Stout, Blencathra Bitter and Great Cockup Porter are always on the menu. A guest is changed once a month. Regulars include Coniston Bluebird and Timothy Taylor Landlord.

A small, old-fashioned pub, with two bars. Food served at lunchtime and evenings. Children allowed. On the edge of the Lake District National Park, the only pub in the village.

OPEN *5.30–11pm Mon; 12–2.30pm and 5.30–11pm Tues–Sat; 12–2.30pm and 7–10.30pm Sun.*

HOLMES GREEN

Black Dog Inn

Broughton Road, Holmes Green, Dalton-in-Furness LA15 8JP
☎ *(01229) 462561* Jack Taylor

A freehouse with Coniston Bluebird and Butterknowle Bitter always available. Five guests might include favourites such as Wye Valley Hereford Pale Ale or York Yorkshire Terrier.

An old country inn half a mile from South Lakes Wildlife Park. Dining area. Food served all day. Children allowed.

OPEN *11am–11pm Mon–Sat; 12–10.30pm Sun.*

INGS

The Watermill Inn

Ings, Nr Staveley, Kendal LA8 9PY
☎ *(01539) 821309* AF and B Coulthwaite

JW Lees Moonraker is among those beers always available, plus up to 15 guest beers (500 per year) which may come from the Hop Back, Cotleigh, Ridleys, Shepherd Neame, Exmoor, Ash Vine, Summerskills, Black Sheep, Coach House, Yates and Wadworth breweries.

Formerly a wood mill, now a traditional, family-run pub full of character with log fires, brasses and beams and a relaxing atmosphere. Two bars. No juke box or games machines. Many times winner of Westmorland Pub of the Year. Bar food at lunchtime and evenings. Car park, garden, seats and tables by the river. Disabled toilets. Children allowed. Accommodation. From the M6, junction 36, follow the A591 towards Windermere. One mile past the second turning for Staveley. Turn left after the garage, before the church.

OPEN *12–2.30pm and 6–11pm Mon–Sat; 12–3pm and 7–10.30pm Sun.*

IREBY

The Lion

The Square, Ireby, Carlisle CA5 1EA
☎ *(01697) 371460*
Peter Boulton and Karen Spencer

A four-pump freehouse offering Bateman XB, Titanic Premium and Marston's Pedigree, plus one guest, usually from Yates or Hesket Newmarket.

This freehouse was the area's first Irish pub in the late 1980s. Café bar, with traditional oak panels, open fire and wooden floor. Back bar/games room for pool and darts. Food served at lunchtimes, and at lunchtimes and evenings at weekends. Children allowed.

OPEN *5.30–11pm Mon–Fri; 12–3pm and 6–11pm Sat; 12–3pm and 7–10.30pm Sun.*

KENDAL

Ring o' Bells

39 Kirkland, Kendal LA9 5AF
☎ *(01539) 720326* Tony Bibby

One weekly-changing guest always served from a range of 11, including Bateman XB, Jennings Cumberland, Marston's Pedigree, Brains SA and Adnams Broadside.

An unspoilt seventeenth-century pub in the grounds of the parish church. Bar food available at lunchtime and evenings. Parking. Children allowed. Accommodation. Take M6 junction 36, then follow the A590 and A591 to the A6 in Kendal.

OPEN *12–3pm and 6–11pm Mon–Sat; usual hours Sun.*

KIRKBY LONSDALE

The Snooty Fox
Main Street, Kirkby Lonsdale LA6 2AH
☎ *(01524) 271308* Richard Parker

A freehouse, with Timothy Taylor Landlord regularly available, plus a wide range of guest cask ales.

A seventeenth-century inn, with two bars, stonework and beams. Nine en-suite bedrooms. Food at lunchtime and evenings. Children allowed.

11am–11pm Mon–Sat; 12–10.30pm Sun.

KIRKSANTON

King William IV
Kirksanton, Nr Millom LA18 4NN
☎ *(01229) 772009*
Roger and Sandra Singleton

A freehouse with Jennings Cumberland Ale (@ £1.50) always available. Up to four guests are changed weekly. Regulars include Marston's Pedigree, Fuller's London Pride, the Slaters ales (Eccleshall) or something from Wye Valley, Coniston or Rooster's breweries.

A 200-year-old country pub with oak beams and real fires. Four letting rooms available for bed and breakfast. Non-smoking dining area. Food at lunchtime and evenings. Children allowed. On the main road from Millom to Whitehaven.

12–3pm and 7–11pm.

LANERCOST

Abbey Bridge Inn
Lanercost, Brampton CA8 2HG
☎ *(016977) 2224* Phillip Sayers

Yates Bitter always available plus a couple of guests (100+ per year) including Wadworth 6X, Bateman XXXB, Shepherd Neame, Greene King, Fuller's, Burton Bridge, Black Sheep, Charles Wells, Jennings and Exmoor ales.

Family-run country hotel and bar in a converted seventeenth-century forge retaining original beams and character. Bar and restaurant food available at lunchtime and evenings. Car park, garden, children allowed. Accommodation. CAMRA Cumbria Pub of the Year 1992 plus merit award 1995. Situated close to Lanercost Priory on the riverbank.

12–2.30pm and 7–11pm.

NETHER WASDALE

The Screes Hotel
Nether Wasdale, Seascale CA20 1ET
☎ *(01946) 726262* DH Simpson

A freehouse, with Yates, Jennings and Black Sheep brews always available. Four guests, changed weekly, come from independents such as Dent.

An eighteenth-century pub with split-level bar, separate dining area, small function room and five letting rooms. Magnificent views of the fells. Food served at lunchtime and evenings. Children allowed. Can be tricky to find. Ring for directions, if necessary.

May–Sept: 11am–11pm Mon–Sat; 12–10.30pm Sun. Winter: 12–3pm and 6–11pm.

STRAWBERRY BANK

The Mason's Arms
Strawberry Bank, Cartmel Fell LA11 6NW
☎ *(01539) 568486* Mrs Stevenson

A brewpub, home of The Strawberry Bank Brewery. Five real ales always available, including Barnsley, Cumberland and Blackpool brews. Other guests are from all over the country, e.g. Young's, Okells and Yates. Good selection of fruit beers and bottle-conditioned beers. Hoegarden and Budvar also available. The Strawberry Bank Brewery's one home brew is a bottle-conditioned beer which is always on offer.

A rural freehouse set in the middle of nowhere! Slate floor and open fires. Terrace with 12 tables overlooking the valley. Self-catering studio apartments available. Homemade food served at lunchtime and evenings, with a good vegetarian and vegan selection. Children allowed.

DAMSON BEER 7% ABV

11.30am–3pm and 6–11pm Mon–Fri; all day Sat–Sun.

TIRRIL

The Queen's Head

Tirril CA10 2JF
☎ *(01768) 863219* Chris Thomlinson

 Offers two house beers, with a third being planned for the near future. Also has two guest pumps.

A 300-year-old pub, once owned by William Wordsworth, situated on the B5320, with stone walls and beams. Two bars. The small village of Tirril once boasted two breweries, one being at this inn. It was closed in 1899, and reopened 100 years later in October 1999 by the present landlord, in an outhouse at the rear of the pub. The pub itself is a Cask Marque winner. Food served at lunchtime and evenings, with a separate dining area available. Cumbrian Beer and Sausage Festival held annually on second weekend of August. Children allowed.

JOHN BEWSHER'S BEST BITTER 3.8% ABV
CHARLES GOUGH OLD FAITHFUL 4.0% ABV
THOMAS SLEE'S ACADEMY ALE 4.2% ABV

12–3pm and 6–11pm Mon–Fri; 12–11pm Sat; 12–10.30pm Sun.

TROUTBECK

The Queen's Head Hotel

Troutbeck LA23 1PW
☎ *(01539) 432174* Mark Stewerdson

A freehouse with four guests, which change every few days, and which might include Coniston Bluebird, Old Man Ale, Burton Bridge Amazon or Great Northern.

A food-oriented pub and hotel, with nine rooms and seating area outside. Food served at lunchtime and evenings. Children allowed.

11am–11pm (10.30pm Sun).

WASDALE HEAD

Wasdale Head Inn

Wasdale Head, Nr Gosforth CA20 1EX
☎ *(01946) 726229* Howard Christie

Jennings Cumberland and Cocker Hoop are always on offer in this freehouse. Local ales served regularly, up to nine at any one time, including brews from Jennings, Hesket Newmarket, Dent, Derwent, Coniston and Foxfield. The pub's own micro-brewery is due to open during 2000.

A traditional pub with a beer garden, set in the Lake District National Park. Food served at lunchtime and evenings. Children allowed (if on a lead!). Visit our website at: www.wasdale.com

11am–11pm Mon–Sat; 12–10.30pm Sun.

WINTON

The Bay Horse Inn

Winton, Kirkby Stephen CA17 4HS
☎ *(01768) 371451* Derek Parvin

A freehouse offering four real ales, two rotated, and all hand-pulled from the cask. Black Sheep Bitter is always on offer. Varied guests, changed twice weekly, may include Coniston Bluebird or perhaps a Harviestoun brew .

A pub dating from the late 1600s, off the A685, two miles north of Kirkby Stephen. Lounge bar, panelled walls, beams, two open fires, flag floors. Public and lounge bars with central servery. Modern 50-seater dining area. Food served at lunchtime and evenings. Children allowed.

12–2pm and 7–11pm Mon–Sun (closed Tues lunchtimes). More flexible in summer.

YOU TELL US

★ *The Slip Inn*, Barras, Kirkby Stephen

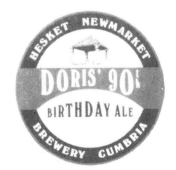

Places Featured:

Bradwell
Buxworth
Chesterfield
Cromford
Dale Abbey
Derby
Fenny Bentley
Hope
Horsley Woodhouse
Ilkeston
Ingleby
Kirk Ireton
Kniveton
Makeney
Marsh Lane

Melbourne
Old Tupton
Over Haddon
Rowarth
Shardlow
Smalley
Staveley
Swinscoe
Ticknall
Tideswell
Wardlow Mires
Whaley
Whitehough
Woolley Moor

THE BREWERIES

TOWNES BREWERY
Speedwell Inn, Lowgates, Chesterfield S43 3TT
☎ *(01246) 472252*

SUNSHINE 3.6% ABV
Pale and spicy with full-flavoured finish.
GOLDEN BUD 3.8% ABV
BEST LOCKOFORD BITTER 4.0% ABV
Plus monthly brews.

WHIM ALES
Whim Farm, Hartington, Buxton SK17 0AX
☎ *(01298) 84991*

ARBOR LIGHT 3.6% ABV
Pale and easy drinking.
MAGIC MUSHROOM MILD 3.8% ABV
Very dark and flavoursome.
HARTINGTON BITTER 4.0% ABV
Pale and refreshing.
HARTINGTON IPA 4.5% ABV
Light and well-balanced.
Plus occasional brews.

THE PUBS

BRADWELL

Valley Lodge
Church Street, Bradwell, Hope Valley S33 9HJ
☎ *(01433) 620427* Angela Davies

A freehouse serving up to eight brews.
Guests are changed weekly, and may
include Adnams and many other interesting
beers.

A large village pub in walking country
with three bar areas and a games room.
Outside seating. Food served at lunchtime
and evenings. No children.

*7–11pm Mon–Fri; 12–3pm and 7–11pm
Sat; 12–3pm and 7–10.30pm Sun.*

BUXWORTH

Navigation Inn
*Bugsworth Canal Basin, Buxworth, High Peak
SK23 7NE*
☎ *(01663) 732072* Alan Hall

A freehouse with Timothy Taylor
Landlord and Marston's Pedigree always
on the menu, plus regularly changing guest
beers, including Abbeydale, Moonshine,
Greene King Abbot, and many others.

A 200-year-old stone inn on the site of a
recently restored canal basin. Full of
interesting memorabilia and canalwares.
Separate restaurant, play area, pets' corner,
games room and stone-floored snug. Website:
www.navigationinn.co.uk

11am–11pm Mon–Sat; 12–10.30pm Sun.

The Derby Tup

4 Sheffield Road, Wittington Moor, Chesterfield S41 8LS
☎ *(01246) 454316* Mr Williams

Ten beers always available with Kelham Island Fat Cat and Marston's Pedigree among them. Guests come from Cotleigh, Robinson's, Timothy Taylor, Exmoor, Bateman etc.

Old and original, beamed with three rooms and open fires. Bar food available at lunchtime and evenings. Parking nearby, children allowed.

OPEN *11.30am–3pm and 5–11pm Mon–Sat; 12–4pm and 7–10.30pm Sun.*

The Market

95 New Square, Chesterfield S40 1AH
☎ *(01246) 273641* Keith Toone

Tied to Punch Retail, with Marston's Pedigree and Greene King Abbot always available. Five guests may include Black Sheep Special, Hop Back Summer Lightning or Ushers Founders Ale.

A one-bar, market pub, with dining area in bar. Food served at lunchtime only. No children.

OPEN *11am–11pm Mon–Sat; 12–3pm and 7–10.30pm Sun*

The Royal Oak

43 Chatsworth Road, Brampton, Chesterfield S40 2AH
☎ *(01246) 277854* Mrs A Younger

A freehouse with Marston's Pedigree and Ruddles (Morland) always available, plus two guests from local breweries, changed weekly. Other beers featured include Morland Old Speckled Hen, Charles Wells Bombadier and many more (500 per year).

A traditional local pub with timbers and open fire. Friendly staff and regulars of all ages. Live music three times a week, pool and darts. Beer festivals and annual music festival. No food. Car park, patio and children's play area.

OPEN *11am–11pm Mon–Sat; 12–10.30pm Sun.*

The Rutland Arms

23 Stephenson Place, Chesterfield S40 1XL
☎ *(01246) 205857* Paul Young

Tied to Whitbread, serving four ales straight from the barrel and five on pumps. Castle Eden, Marston's Pedigree and Greene King Abbot are always on offer plus guests, changed every ten days, which often include Morland Old Speckled Hen, Bateman XXXB or Black Sheep Best.

Predominantly wooden interior, close to Chesterfield's famous crooked spire church. Non-smoking dining area away from the bar. Food served 11am–9pm Mon–Thurs and 11am–7pm Fri–Sun. No children.

OPEN *11am–11pm Mon–Sat; 12–10.30pm Sun.*

The Boat Inn

Scarthin, Cromford, Matlock DE4 3QF
☎ *(01629) 823282* Mr Gridley

A freehouse with Mansfield Bitter and Marston's Pedigree always available plus all sorts of guests from a good mix of national and independent brewers. Charles Wells Bombardier and Shepherd Neame Spitfire are regularly featured.

A village pub built about 1772, near the market square. Two bars, log fires, beer garden. Bar snacks at lunchtime and evenings plus Sunday lunches. Children allowed.

OPEN *11.30am–3pm and 6–11pm.*

The Carpenters Arms

Dale Abbey, Ilkeston DE7 4PP
☎ *(0115) 932 5277* John Heraty

Tied to Allied Domecq, with Marston's Pedigree always on the menu. Two guests, changed weekly, may include Wadworth 6X, Greene King Abbot, Morland Old Speckled Hen or Ruddles County (Morland).

A village pub in picturesque walking country, with children's play area, family room and large car park. Food served at lunchtimes and evenings. Children not allowed in bar. Three miles from junction 25 of the M1.

OPEN *12–3pm and 6–11pm (10.30pm Sun).*

DERBY

The Alexandra Hotel

203 Siddals Road, Derby DE1 2QE
☎ *(01332) 293993* Mark Robins

Bateman XB, Hook Norton Best Bitter and Timothy Taylor Landlord always available plus six guest beers (600 per year) with the emphasis firmly on new and rare micro-breweries. Also traditional cider.

Built as a coffee and chop house in 1865. Now trading as a comfortable award-winning pub decorated with a railway and brewery theme. Bar food at lunchtimes and evenings. Car park and garden. Three minutes' walk from Derby Midland Railway Station.

OPEN *11am–11pm Mon–Sat; 12–3pm and 7–10.30pm Sun.*

The Brunswick Inn

1 Railway Terrace, Derby DE1 2RU
☎ *(01332) 290677*

Fourteen pumps serve beer from all around the country, notably Marston's Pedigree and Timothy Taylor Landlord, plus five or six ales from the on-site brewery.

Built in 1841–2 as the first purpose-built railwaymen's pub in the world. The birthplace of the Railway Institute, an educational establishment for railway workers. It fell into dereliction in the early 1970s and trading ceased in April 1974. The Derbyshire Historic Buildings Trust started restoration work in 1981. The trust sold it to Trevor Harris, a local businessman, in May 1987. The pub reopened in October 1987 and the installation of the brewing plant followed in 1991. The first beer was produced on June 11 that year. Bar and restaurant food is available at lunchtime and on request in the evening. Parking, garden, children's room, non-smoking room, function room.

RECESSION ALE 3.3% ABV
MILD 3.7% ABV
TRIPLE HOP 4.0% ABV
SECOND BREW 4.2% ABV
RAILWAY PORTER 4.3% ABV
OLD ACCIDENTAL 5.0% ABV

OPEN *11am–11pm Mon–Sat; 12–10.30pm Sun.*

The Crompton Tavern

46 Crompton Street, Derby DE1 1NX
☎ *(01332) 733629* Mr and Mrs Bailey

Marston's Pedigree and Timothy Taylor Landlord always available plus four guest beers (200 per year) perhaps from Fuller's, Coach House, Kelham Island, Banks & Taylor or Burton Bridge breweries. A porter or stout is normally available.

A small pub just outside the city centre. Popular with locals and students. Cobs and sandwiches available daily. Car park and garden. Children now allowed.

OPEN *11am–11pm Mon–Sat; 12–10.30pm Sun.*

The Falstaff Public House & Brewing Company

74 Silver Hill Road, Derby DE23 6UJ
☎ *(01332) 342902* Adrian Parkes

Between four and six real ales are always on offer. Greene King Abbot Ale is served straight from the barrel, plus two permanent Falstaff brews. Guests from Burton Bridge and Wye Valley also featured.

A 125-year-old former coaching house with one main bar serving three rooms. Outside seating. Sandwiches available. Children allowed. From the city, take the Normanton road, turn right at painted island and take the first available right, then right at the T-junction. Visit the website at: www.thefalstaff.co.uk for further information.

SUMMER ALE 3.7% ABV
A full pale malt session beer, late hopped with fuggles to give that citrussy aroma of hot summer days.

SOCIETY ALE 4.1% ABV

HIT & MISS 4.5% ABV
A rich amber beer full of maris Otter pale malt with a taste of crystal malt for depth and just a hint of late hopping.

FESTIVAL ALE 4.8% ABV
A stronger sweeter version of Hit & Miss.

FALSTAFF'S FOLLY 5.8% ABV
A strong, well-balanced beer, fully fermented to leave a clean flavour of malt.

OPEN *12–11pm (10.30pm Sun).*

The Flowerpot

25 King Street, Derby DE1 3DZ
☎ *(012332) 204955* S Manners

Marston's Pedigree and Timothy Taylor Landlord always available plus at least seven guest beers (500+ per year) from all over the United Kingdom.

A traditional friendly town pub with parts of the building dating from the late seventeenth century. Age range of regulars is 18 to 95. Ground-level cellar bar has a unique 'beer wall', through which customers can see ale being cared for and dispensed. Home-made bar food served at lunchtime through to evening. Garden area. Function suite with capacity for up to 250 people. Wheelchair access to all areas. Children welcome till 7.30pm. Car park 30 yards away. Situated on the A6 just off the inner ring road, 300 yards north of the Cathedral.

OPEN *11am–11pm Mon–Sat; 12–10.30pm Sun.*

The Friargate

114 Friargate, Derby DE1 1EX
☎ *(01332) 297065* Roger Myring

A freehouse serving Marston's Pedigree straight from the barrel plus up to eight others. Regulars come from Rooster's, Whim and Oakham breweries.

A quiet town pub with one main bar. Acoustic music on Wednesdays. Food served at lunchtime (not Sun). No children.

OPEN *11am–11pm Mon–Sat; 12–3pm and 7–10.30pm Sun.*

The Rowditch Inn

246 Uttoxeter New Road, Derby DE22 3LL
☎ *(01332) 343123* Mr Birkin

A freehouse with six real ales available including Mansfield Riding Bitter, Old Bailey and Marston's Pedigree. Three rotating guests change on a daily basis.

A traditional beer house with one bar, non-smoking area, snug and beer garden. No food, no children. On the main road.

OPEN *7–11pm Mon–Sun and most lunchtimes (not Weds).*

The Smithfield

Meadow Road, Derby DE45 1NN
☎ *(01332) 370429* Mr Stevenson

A freehouse with Whim Arbor Light, Oakham JHB and Bishops Farewell always available. Six guest beers, changed two or three times a week, might include Whim IPA and Marston's Pedigree.

Traditional, friendly atmosphere. Lounge with open fire and pub games plus a family room. Food served 12–2pm only. Children allowed. Ring for directions.

OPEN *11am–11pm Mon–Sat; 12–10.30pm Sun.*

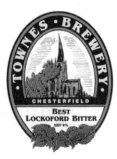

The Bentley Brook Inn & Fenny's Restaurant

Fenny Bentley, Ashbourne DE6 1LF
☎ *(01335) 350278* Mrs Jeanne Allingham

Home to the Leatherbritches Brewery with Bespoke and Belter permanently available, and also Marston's Pedigree and Mansfield. Plus an additional, changing Leatherbritches ale.

A traditional, family-run, busy country inn with a lovely setting of large gardens, five acres of wild flower meadows, trout stream and woods. Food served 12–9.30pm. Car park. Childrens facilities.

GOLDINGS 3.6% ABV
BELTER 4.0% ABV
Light, golden with flowery hoppiness.
HAIRY HELMET 4.7% ABV
BESPOKE 5.0% ABV
Ruby-coloured and smooth.
Plus occasional brews.

OPEN *All day, every day.*

The Coach & Horses

Fenny Bentley DE6 1LB
☎ *(01335) 350246*
John and Matthew Dawson

A family-run freehouse offering a continually changing range of award-winning cask ales. Marston's Pedigree always available, plus three guests, which may include Abbeydale's Moonshine, Coniston Bluebird or Timothy Taylor Landlord.

A traditional seventeenth-century coaching inn with background music and beer garden. Food served every day at lunchtime and evenings. Children welcome.

OPEN *11am–3pm and 5–11pm Mon–Fri; 11am–11pm Sat; 12–10.30pm Sun.*

The Woodroffe Arms Hotel

1 Castleton Road, Hope, Hope Valley S33 6SB
☎ *(01433) 620351* Barry Thomson

Marston's Pedigree permanently available.

Attractive one-bar pub with traditional log fires, conservatory restaurant, outside seating and patio with swings for children. Food available every lunchtime and evening with £3.50 specials available Mon–Sat lunchtimes. Children allowed.

OPEN *11.30am–11pm Mon–Sat; 12–10.30pm Sun.*

HORSLEY WOODHOUSE

Old Oak Inn
*176 Main Street, Horsley Woodhouse, Ilkeston
DE7 6AW*
☎ *(01332) 780672* Mr Hyde

A freehouse with Marston's Pedigree and something from Mansfield always available. Two or three guest beers are offered each week (300 to date). Favourites include Everards Tiger and Morland Old Speckled Hen.

A village pub with background music and beer garden. No food. Children allowed.

5.30–11pm Mon–Fri; 11am–11pm Sat; 12–10.30pm Sun.

ILKESTON

The Dewdrop Inn
Station Street, Ilkeston DE7 5TE
☎ *(01159) 329684* Danny Meakin

Timothy Taylor Landlord and Whim Hartington IPA usually available, with guest beers from Mallard, Abbeydale, Brewsters, Shardlow, Wye Valley, RCH, Hardys & Hansons, Castle Rock, Springhead and Burton Bridge breweries often served.

Unspoilt Victorian pub with real fire in lounge. Dart board in public bar. Beer garden with pergola and outside skittle alley. Food served 11.30–2.30pm Mon–Fri. Family room. Located two-and-a-half miles off Junction 26 of the M1 – follow signs for Ilkeston, turn off near railway bridge.

11.30am–2.30pm and 7–11pm Mon–Fri; 7–11pm Sat; 12–4.30pm and 7–10.30pm Sun.

Spring Cottage
1 Fulwood Street, Ilkeston DE7 8AZ
☎ *(0115) 932 3153* Mr Wootton

Tied to Punch Taverns, with two guests changed daily, that may include Wadworth 6X, Morland Old Speckled Hen, Marston's Pedigree, Greene King Abbot Ale or Shepherd Neame Spitfire.

A traditional town pub with two bars and background music. Children's room. The lounge doubles as a dining area. Food at lunchtime and evenings. Children allowed. Near the main shopping area on one-way system.

11am–3pm and 6–11pm Mon–Thur; 11am–4pm and 6–11pm Fri; 11am–5pm and 7–11pm Sat; 12–3pm and 7–10.30pm Sun.

INGLEBY

John Thompson Inn
Ingleby, Melbourne DE73 1HW
☎ *(01332) 862469* John Thompson

Home of the John Thompson Brewery, which re-introduced brewing to Derbyshire in 1977. John Thompson Special plus the seasonal ale is permanently available.

Converted fifteenth-century oak-beamed farmhouse, with a collection of paintings and antiques. Food served from the carvery lunchtimes only. Car park. Children's room and large garden.

**JOHN THOMPSON SPECIAL 4.2% ABV
JOHN THOMPSON PORTER 4.5% ABV**
Available in winter.
JOHN THOMPSON SUMMER GOLD 4.5% ABV
Available in summer.

10.30am–2.30pm Mon–Sat; 12–2pm and 7–10.30pm Sun.

KIRK IRETON

The Barley Mow Inn
Kirk Ireton, Ashbourne DE6 3JP
☎ *(01335) 370306* Mary Short

Marston's Pedigree, Hook Norton Best Bitter and Old Hooky always available plus five guest beers, many from local breweries.

Seventeenth-century village inn with unspoilt interior. Beers served straight from the barrel. Rolls available at lunchtime. Children are permitted inside the pub at lunchtime, but there are no special facilities. Garden area at front. Car park. Accommodation.

12–2pm and 7–11pm (10.30pm Sun).

KNIVETON

The Red Lion
Winksworth Road, Kniveton, Ashbourne DE6 1JH
☎ *(01335) 345554* Angela Tegram

This freehouse always has something from Burton Bridge and Blanchfield on the menu. A guest beer, changed every few days, is also offered. Black Sheep Special is popular.

A small village pub with separate dining area. Background music only. Food served at lunchtime and evenings. Children allowed.

12–2pm and 7–11pm Mon–Fri; 11am–11pm Sat; 12–10.30pm Sun

The Holly Bush Inn

Holly Bush Lane, Makeney, Milford
☎ *(01332) 841729* JJK Bilbie

Marston's Pedigree and Ruddles County (Morland) always available plus four (200+ per year) guests that may include Morland Old Speckled Hen, Exmoor Gold, Fuller's ESB, Marston's Owd Roger, Greene King Abbot, Timothy Taylor Landlord and brews from Bateman. Also scrumpy cider.

A Grade II listed twelfth-century coaching inn with flagstone floors and open fires. Bar food at lunchtime, barbecues in summer. Car park and children's room. Private parties welcome. Just off the main A6 at Milford, opposite the Makeney Hotel.

12–3pm and 6–11pm Mon–Fri; 12–11pm Sat–Sun.

The George Inn

46 Lightwood Road, Marsh Lane, Eckington
☎ *(01246) 433178* Martyn and Christa

A regularly changing guest beer available perhaps from Everards, Robinson's, Young's, Bateman and others, all 4.2% ABV or above and served in over-sized glasses.

Village freehouse with taproom and lounge, each with real fire and free of any machines or music. Outside seating at front and small garden to rear. No food. Car park. Children welcome during the day. Dogs welcome.

1–4pm and 7–11pm Mon–Sat; 12–3pm and 7–10.30pm Sun.

The Railway Hotel

222 Station Road, Melbourne DE73 1BQ
☎ *(01332) 862566* Lucy Kelly

A freehouse with two rotating guest beers, changed weekly. Favourites include Marston's Pedigree.

A small pub within a family-run hotel with seven bedrooms and a restaurant. Food served at lunchtime and evenings. Children allowed.

12–3pm and 6–11pm Mon–Thurs; 11am–11pm Fri–Sat; 12–10.30am Sun.

The Royal Oak Inn

Derby Road, Old Tupton, Chesterfield S42 6LA
☎ *(01246) 862180* John Angus

Morland Old Speckled Hen always available plus four guests, changed weekly, often including Ruddles County (Morland), Ushers Founders Ale or Tomintoul Witches Cauldron.

A 100-year-old pub with three rooms. Food at lunchtime and evenings. No children.

12–3pm and 5–11pm Mon–Thur; 11am–11pm Fri–Sat; 12–3pm and 7–10.30pm Sun.

Lathkil Hotel

Over Hadden DE45 1JE
☎ *(01629) 812501* Robert Grigor-Taylor

A freehouse featuring Charles Wells Bombadier plus guests, changed weekly, which may include Timothy Taylor Landlord or Black Sheep Bitter.

A pub with stunning views over the Dales. Occasional TV for sporting events. Food at lunchtime and evenings. Dining area evenings only. Children allowed lunchtimes only.

May–Sept: 11.30am–3pm and 6–11pm Mon–Fri; 11.30am–11pm Sat; 12–10.30pm Sun. Winter opening hours vary – check with hotel.

Little Mill Inn

Rowarth, High Peak SK22 1EB
☎ *(01663) 743178* Mr Barnes

A freehouse always offering Banks's Bitter, Marston's Pedigree, Camerons Strongarm and Hardys and Hansons Kimberley Best. A guest beer, changed weekly, may well be Hartleys SB (Robinson's).

An old-style pub in the middle of nowhere with a waterwheel at the side. Twelve bars, live music twice a week, quiz and bingo nights. Upstairs restaurant area. Food served all day. Children allowed. Isolated, but fully signposted.

11am–1pm Mon–Sat; 12–10.30pm Sun.

SHARDLOW

The Old Crown
Cavendish Bridge, Nr Shardlow DE72 2HL
☎ *(01332) 792392*
PM Horton and GR Morton Harrison

Marston's Pedigree always available plus three guest beers (400 per year) which may include Bateman XXXB, Otter Ale, something from the Shardlow brewery, Eldridge Pope Royal Oak, Shepherd Neame Spitfire or Brewery on Sea Black Rock.

A small inn by the River Trent serving bar food at lunchtime. Car park and garden. Children allowed in the bar at lunchtime for food. Accommodation. Turn left on the A6 before the river bridge, before Shardlow from the M1.

11.30am–3pm and 5–11pm Mon–Sat; 12–3pm and 7–10.30pm Sun.

SMALLEY

The Bell Inn
Main Road, Smalley, Ilkeston DE7 6EF
☎ *(01332) 880635* Vincent Fletcher

A freehouse often featuring Mallard brews, Marston's Pedigree and Ruddles County (Morland). Guests, changed every two to three weeks, may include something from Rooster's brewery.

A two-roomed, Victorian-style pub. Food at lunchtime and evenings. No children.

11.30am–2.30pm and 6–11pm (10.30pm Sun).

STAVELEY

Speedwell Inn
Lowgate, Staveley, Chesterfield S43 3TT
☎ *(01246) 472252* Alan Wood

A freehouse whose owners run the Townes Brewery on the premises. At least four Townes brews, such as Sunshine and Golden Bud always available, plus occasional guests.

A traditional pub, refurbished in 1998, with occasional live music. Non-smoking area. No food. No children. Local CAMRA Pub of the Season for Winter 1999 and Pub of the Year 2000.

6–11pm Mon–Thurs; 5–11pm Fri; 12–11pm Sat; 12–10.30pm Sun.

SWINSCOE

The Dog and Partridge Country Inn
Swinscoe, Ashbourne DE6 2HS
☎ *(01335) 343183* Mr MJ Stelfox

Morland Old Speckled Hen and Ruddles County usually available, plus one or two guest beers such as Charles Wells Bombardier, Hartington Best Bitter, Marston's Pedigree, Burton Bridge Best Bitter or Top Dog.

Seventeenth-century inn, with olde-worlde beamed bar and log fire in winter. Restaurant and garden. Bar and restaurant food available all day, including breakfasts. Car park. Indoor and outdoor children's play areas, highchairs and special children's menu.

7.30am–11pm.

TICKNALL

The Staff of Life
7 High Street, Ticknall DE73 1JH
☎ *(01332) 862479* Mr Nix

Marston's Pedigree, Everards Tiger, East Street Cream, Timothy Taylor Landlord and Fuller's ESB available plus five guests (200 per year) which may include Exmoor Gold, Hook Norton Old Hooky, Hop Back Summer Lightning, Mauldons Black Adder, Ringwood Old Thumper, Uley Old Spot and Temperance Relief.

A fifteenth-century beamed former bakehouse. Bar and restaurant food at lunchtime and evenings, home-cooked British foods a speciality. Car park, garden and children's room. Now also offers accommodation. At the south end of the village at the intersection between the Ashby-de-la-Zouch and Swadlincote roads.

11.30am–2.30pm and 6–11pm Mon–Sat; 12–2.30pm and 7–10.20pm Sun.

TIDESWELL

The George Hotel
Commercial Road, Tideswell, Buxton SK17 8NU
☎ *(01298) 871382* Mr Norris

A pub tied to Hardys & Hansons' Kimberley Brewery, so with Kimberley Best and Classic always available. Also four guest beers, changed every six to eight weeks, including Hardys and Hansons seasonal ales.

A coaching house dating back to 1730, with separate dining area. Food served at lunchtime and evenings. Children allowed.

11am–3pm and 7–11pm Mon–Sat; 12–3pm and 7–10.30pm Sun.

WARDLOW MIRES

Three Stags' Heads

Wardlow Mires, Tideswell SK17 8RW
☎ *(01298) 872268* Mr and Mrs Fuller

Springhead Bitter, Kelham Island Fat Cat Pale Ale and Pale Rider plus Hoskins & Oldfield Old Navigation Ale always available. Also a guest (ten per year) such as Springhead Leveller, Uley Old Spot, Hoskins & Oldfield Ginger Tom, Christmas Noggin or Wheat Beer. Also farmhouse cider and a selection of bottled beers.

A small seventeenth-century Peak District farmhouse pub with stone-flagged bar and its own pottery workshop. Unspoilt, with no frills, no piped muzak, no games machines. Live folk/Irish music at weekends. Bar food at lunchtime and evenings. Car park. Children allowed. On the A623 at the junction with the B6465.

OPEN *7–11pm Mon–Fri; 12–11pm Sat–Sun and bank holidays.*

WHALEY

Shepherd's Arms

7 Old Road, Whaley, High Peak SK23 7HR
☎ *(01663) 732384* Mr Hollingsworth

A Marston's tenancy, where Banks's Mild, Marston's Bitter and Pedigree are always available. Two guest beers, changed twice a week.

Old-fashioned, traditional, family-orientated pub, with large beer garden. No food. Children allowed. Families and dogs allowed.

OPEN *Summer: 11am–11pm Mon–Sat; 12–10.30pm Sun. Winter: 11am–11pm Mon–Fri; 11.30am–4pm and 7–11pm Sat–Sun.*

WHITEHOUGH

The Oddfellows Arms

Whitehead Lane, Whitehough, Chinley, High Peak SK23 6EJ
☎ *(01663) 750306* Changed hands May 1999.

Tied to Marston's, so always offers Marston's Bitter and Pedigree.

A one-bar country pub. Food at weekends only. Children allowed.

OPEN *5–11pm Mon–Fri; all day Sat–Sun.*

WOOLLEY MOOR

The White Horse Inn

Badger Lane, Woolley Moor, Alfreton DE55 6FG
☎ *(01246) 590319* Bill and Jill Taylor

A freehouse with four guests which often include Everards Beacon, Bateman Salem Porter and Shepherd Neame Spitfire.

A two-bar pub with non-smoking areas in main lounge, and conservatory for dining. Adventure playground, football goalposts, outside seating on two patios with 25 tables, disabled facilities. Barbecue in summer. Food served at lunchtime and evenings. Walkers welcome. Children allowed.

OPEN *11am–2.30pm and 6–11pm Mon–Sat; 12–10.30pm Sun.*

YOU TELL US

★ *The Bull's Head Inn*, Foolow
★ *The Grouse Inn*, Longshaw
★ *The Thorn Tree*, 48 Jackson Road, Matlock

Places Featured:

Barnstaple
Blackawton
Branscombe
Brendon
Broadhempston
Buckfastleigh
Chittlehampton
Coleford
Combeinteignhead
Combe Martin
Crediton
Dartmouth
Doddiscombsleigh
Egg Buckland
Exeter
Exmouth
Georgeham
Halwell
Hatherleigh
Holbeton
Horndon
Horsebridge
Iddlesleigh
Kingsbridge
Lapford

Mortehoe
Newton Abbot
Newton St Cyres
North Tawton
Okehampton
Ossaborough
Pilton
Plymouth
Plymstock
Princetown
Ringmore
Shaldon
Silverton
Slapton
Stokenham
Tavistock
Teignmouth
Topsham
Torquay
Tuckenhay
West Down
West Pusehill
Wimple
Winkleigh
Yarde Down

THE BREWERIES

BARUM BREWERY

c/o Reform Inn, Reform Road, Pilton, Barnstaple EX31 1PD
☎ *(01271) 329994*

BSE 3.5% ABV
GOLD 4.0% ABV
ORIGINAL 4.4% ABV
DARK STAR 4.8% ABV
BREAKFAST 5.0% ABV
Hoppy bitterness throughout.
BARUMBURG 5.1% ABV
Real lager.
TECHNICAL HITCH 5.3% ABV
CHALLENGER 5.6% ABV
BARNSTABLASTA 6.6% ABV
Christmas brew.

THE BRANSCOMBE VALE BREWERY

Great Seaside Farm, Branscombe EX12 3DP
☎ *(01297) 680511*

BRANOC 3.8% ABV
Golden and malty with a light hop finish.
ANNIVERSARY ALE 4.6% ABV
Light-coloured with clean, crisp hoppy flavour.
OWN LABEL 4.6% ABV
House beer, may be sold under different names.
HELLS BELLES 4.8% ABV
Oct–Mar. Smooth, mellow and hoppy.
SUMMA THAT 5.0% ABV
Golden, light and hoppy throughout.
YO HO HO 6.0% ABV
From November onwards. Fruity, and flavour packed.
Plus occasional brews.

CLEARWATER BREWERY

*2 Devon Units, Hatchmoor Industrial Estate,
Torrington EX38 7HP*
☎ *(01805) 625242*

 CAVALIER 4.0% ABV
BEGGARS TIPPLE 4.2% ABV
RAMBLER'S SPECIAL 4.5% ABV
OLIVER'S NECTAR 5.2% ABV
Plus occasional brews.

THE JOLLYBOAT BREWERY

4 Buttgarden Street, Bideford EX39 2AU
☎ *(01237) 424343*

 BUCCANNEER 3.7% ABV
Nut-brown colour and hoppy
throughout.
MAINBRACE BITTER 4.2% ABV
Light chestnut colour, late hopped for aroma.
PLUNDER 4.8% ABV
Dark red with Carribean flavours. Fuggles hop.
PRIVATEER 4.8% ABV
Full-flavoured and hoppy. Mixed hop.
CONTRABAND 5.8% ABV
Christmastide feasting ale/porter. Cascade hop.
Plus occasional brews.

OTTER BREWERY

Mathayes Farm, Luppit, Honiton EX14 0SA
☎ *(01404) 891285*

 BITTER 3.6% ABV
Pale brown. Hoppy, fruity aroma.
BRIGHT 4.3% ABV
Light and delicate with long malty finish.
ALE 4.5% ABV
Well-balanced. Malty and well-hopped.
OTTER CLAUS 5.0% ABV
Christmas beer.
HEAD 5.8% ABV
Smooth, strong and malty.

PRINCETOWN BREWERIES LTD

Tavistock Road, Princetown PL20 6QF
☎ *(01822) 890789*

 DARTMOOR IPA/ BEST 4.0% ABV
Pale, refreshing and hoppy.
JAIL ALE 4.8% ABV
Plus occasional brews.

SCATTER ROCK BREWERY

*Unit 5, Gidley's Meadow, Christow, Exeter
EX6 7QB*
☎ *(01647) 252120*

 SCATTY BITTER 3.8% ABV
TEIGN VALLEY TIPPLE 4.0% ABV
SKYLARK 4.2% ABV
DEVONIAN 4.5% ABV
GOLDEN VALLEY 4.6% ABV
*Plus the Tor Collection: two brews each month,
named after local Tors.*

SUMMERSKILLS BREWERY

*Unit 15, Pomphlett Farm Industrial Estate,
Broxton Drive, Billacombe, Plymouth PL9 7BG*
☎ *(01752) 481283*

 CELLAR VEE/BBB 3.7% ABV
Well-balanced.
BEST BITTER 4.3% ABV
Pale, with malty flavour and honey hints.
TAMAR 4.3% ABV
MENACING DENNIS 4.5% ABV
Occasional. Robust and clean flavour.
WHISTLEBELLY VENGEANCE 4.7% ABV
Dark ruby colour. Hop, dark malt and liquorice
flavour.
NINJABEER 5.0% ABV
Winter ale. Rich and golden, with soft malt,
hops and toffee flavour.
TURKEY'S DELIGHT 5.1% ABV
Christmas ale.
INDIANA'S BONES 5.6% ABV
Rich, dark winter warmer.

TEIGNWORTHY BREWERY,

*The Maltings, Teign Road, Newton Abbot
TQ12 4AA*
☎ *(01626) 332066*

 REEL ALE 4.0% ABV
Hoppy, dry session beer.
SPRING TIDE 4.3% ABV
Sweeter, darker brew, with hops throughout.
OLD MOGGIE 4.4% ABV
One of the brewery owners has a Morris Minor!
BEACHCOMBER 4.5% ABV
Thirst-quenching and well-balanced.
MALTSTERS ALE 5.0% ABV
Seasonal brew.
CHRISTMAS CRACKER 6.0% ABV
Seasonal brew.
Plus occasional brews.

BARNSTAPLE

The Check Inn

Castle Street, Barnstaple EX31 1DR
☎ *(01271) 375964* Doug Watkins

🍺 Four hand pumps, soon to be six, offer a constantly changing range of beers, direct from independent breweries around the UK.

A true freehouse with one bar, a friendly, local atmosphere and the usual pub games. Music (mainly blues/rock) on alternate Fri–Sat evenings. Food served lunchtimes and evenings Mon–Fri, all day Sat–Sun. Car park. Children welcome. Bed and breakfast accommodation available.

OPEN *11am–11pm Mon–Sat; 12–10.30pm Sun.*

The Corner House

108 Boutport Street, Barnstaple EX31 1SY
☎ *(01271) 343528* Christine Billett

🍺 A freehouse with two guests, changed every two days, often include Greene King Abbot, Young's Special or something from Wye Valley.

An old-fashioned drinking pub in the town centre, with separate lounge room. Rolls only. Children allowed in the separate lounge room.

OPEN *11am–3pm and 5–11pm Mon–Thurs; 11am–11pm Fri–Sat; 11am–3pm and 5–10.30pm Sun.*

BLACKAWTON

The George Inn

Main Street, Blackawton, Totnes TQ9 7BG
☎ *(01803) 712342* Mr O'Dowell

🍺 Princetown Dartmoor IPA is always on sale in this freehouse. Guest beers change every two days, and often include Orkney Dark Island, Teignworthy's Strawberry and Cream, something from Scatter Rock, or Ash Vine Black Bess Porter.

An old village pub with eating area in the lounge bar. Four en-suite bed and breakfast rooms. Live bands every so often. Food at lunchtime and evenings (summer), evenings only (winter). Children allowed.

OPEN *Winter: 12–2.30pm Fri–Sun (closed Mon–Thurs lunchtimes); 7–11pm Mon–Sat; 7–10.30pm Sun. Summer: 12–2.30pm Tues–Sun (closed Mon lunchtimes); 7–11pm Mon–Sat; 7–10.30pm Sun.*

BRANSCOMBE

The Fountain Head

Branscombe EX12 3AG
☎ *(01297) 680359* Mrs Luxton

🍺 Branscombe Vale Branoc, Olde Stoker and Summa That often available. Guests (60 per year) include Hook Norton Old Hooky, Crouch Vale Millennium Gold and Freeminer Speculation Ale.

A fourteenth-century pub at the top of the village with flagstone floors, log fires and wood panelling. The lounge bar was formerly the village blacksmith's. Food at lunchtime and evenings. Car park, outside seating, non-smoking area and children's room. Self-catering accommodation.

OPEN *11.30am–2.30pm and 6.30–11pm Mon–Sat; 12–2.30pm and 7–10.30pm Sun.*

BRENDON

The Rockford Inn

Brendon, Nr Lynton EX35 6PT
☎ *(01598) 741214* Barrie Jon Marden

🍺 Regularly changing beers often include Cotleigh Barn Owl and Tawny, Cottage and Clearwater beers or Fuller's London Pride.

Seventeenth-century riverside inn, in quiet village at the heart of Exmoor. Food served 12–2pm and 7–9pm. Cream teas all day in season. Small beer garden and accommodation. Car park. Children's room.

OPEN *11am–11pm daily during the summer season; 12–3pm and 6–11pm daily out of season.*

BROADHEMPSTON

Coppa Dolla Inn

Broadhempston, Totnes TQ9 6BD
☎ *(01803) 812455* Robert Burke

🍺 A freehouse with Marston's Pedigree, Wadworth 6X and Morland Old Speckled Hen always on sale.

A country pub with restaurant area. Food at lunchtime and evenings. Children allowed. Easy to find, once you're in Broadhempston.

OPEN *11.30am–3pm and 6.30–11pm (10.30pm Sun).*

BUCKFASTLEIGH

The White Hart

2 Plymouth Road, Buckfastleigh TQ11 0DA
☎ *(01364) 642337* Louise Mann

A freehouse with Teignworthy Beachcomber and a house ale always on the menu. One guest, changed every two days, might well be Greene King Abbot.

An olde-worlde pub, Grade II listed, with flagstone floors and log fires. One bar, background music. Partitioned dining area and family room. Food served at lunchtime and evenings. Children allowed.

11am–11pm Mon–Sat; 12–10.30pm Sun (closes 6pm Mon).

CHITTLEHAMPTON

The Bell Inn

The Square, Chittlehampton, Umberleigh EX37 9QL
☎ *(01769) 540368* Mark Jones

A freehouse serving six real ales. Regulars include beers from Badger, Barum and Greene King (especially Abbot).

A traditional, one-bar local opposite the church, with a large garden. Home-made food lunchtimes and evenings. Families welcome at this child-friendly pub.

11am–3pm and 6–11pm Mon–Fri and Sun; 11am–11pm Sat.

COLEFORD

New Inn

Coleford, Crediton EX17 5BZ
☎ *(01363) 84242* Mr PS Butt

A freehouse with Otter Ale, Badger Best and Wadworth 6X permanently available, plus one guest.

A thirteenth-century thatched pub, with lots of oak beams. Restaurant and bar meals available. Food served lunchtimes and evenings. Six luxury bedrooms. Well-behaved children allowed.

12–2.30pm and 6–11pm Mon–Sat; 7–10.30pm Sun.

COMBEINTEIGNHEAD

The Wild Goose

Combeinteignhead, Newton Abbot TQ12 4RA
☎ *(01626) 872241*
Rowland and Thelma Honeywill

A freehouse offering 30 different real ales a month. Regularly featured are Otter Bright, Princetown Jail Ale, Teignworthy Springtide, Skinner's Betty Stogs and Exe Valley Devon Glory, plus ales from other independent West Country brewers.

An old, traditional, country village pub with dining area. Jazz every Monday. Food at lunchtime and evenings. Well-behaved children only (not really a children's pub). Down country lanes, is signposted.

11.30am–2.30pm and 6.30–11pm Mon–Sat; 12–3pm and 7–10.30pm Sun.

COMBE MARTIN

The Castle Inn

High Street, Combe Martin EX34 0HS
☎ *(01271) 883706* Chris Franks

Four real ales are available at this freehouse, from a list of more than 500 guests.

A village pub, with one bar and a big screen TV. A restaurant opened May 1999. Food served at lunchtime and evenings. Large car park and garden. Children allowed.

12–11pm Mon–Sat; 12–10.30pm Sun.

CREDITON

The Crediton Inn

28A Mill Street, Crediton EX17 1EZ
☎ *(01363) 772882* Diane Heggadon

A freehouse with Sharp's Doom Bar Bitter always available, plus two guests changed every two days. Examples include Branscombe Vale Branoc and Teinworthy Reel Ale.

A friendly local, with skittle alley and function room. Bar meals and snacks. No children.

11am–11pm Mon–Sat; 12–2pm and 7–10.30pm Sun.

DARTMOUTH

The Cherub Inn

13 Higher Street, Dartmouth TQ6 9RB
☎ *(01803) 832571* Alan Jones

A freehouse with Wadworth 6X, Morland Old Speckled Hen and Old Cherub Real Ale among the beers always offered. One guest, changed once a month, might be Everards Beacon or something from Cains, Jennings or Brains.

A 600-year-old pub, very small with beams and open fire. Air-conditioned cellar. Bar food at lunchtime, à la carte restaurant in the evenings. Over-10s only in the restaurant, no under-14s in the bar. See our website at: www.the-cherub.co.uk

OPEN *11am–11pm Mon–Sat; 12–10.30pm Sun.*

DODDISCOMBSLEIGH

The Nobody Inn

Doddiscombsleigh, Nr Exeter EX6 7DS
☎ *(01647) 252394* Nick Borst-Smith

Nobody's House Ale always available plus two guest beers (40 per year) which may include Ballard's Wassail, Titanic Anniversary, Rebellion Mutiny, Exmoor Stag and Exe Valley Devon Glory.

A sixteenth-century inn with beams and inglenook fireplaces. Bar and restaurant food available at lunchtime and evenings. Speciality cheeses. Car park and garden. Children allowed in the restaurant. Accommodation unsuitable for children under 14. Three miles southwest of Exeter racecourse.

OPEN *12–2.30pm and 6–11pm.*

EGG BUCKLAND

Prince Maurice

3 Church Hill, Egg Buckland, Plymouth PL6 5RJ
☎ *(01752) 771515* Rick and Anne Dodds

Ten real ales always available, including Badger Tanglefoot, Summerskills Best and Indiana's Bones, plus many various guest beers.

Small, seventeenth-century freehouse with two bars and log fires. CAMRA Pub of the Year 1994 and 1995. Weekday lunchtime bar snacks. Car park, patio.

OPEN *11am–3pm and 7–11pm Mon–Thurs (6–11pm Fri); all day Sat; 12–3pm and 7–10.30pm Sun.*

EXETER

Double Locks Hotel

Canal Bank, Exeter EX2 6LT
☎ *(01392) 256947* Tony Stearman

Smiles Golden, Best and Heritage, Adnams Broadside, Everards Old Original, Branscombe Branoc, Greene King Abbot Ale plus up to six guest beers.

Recently acquired by Smiles, the pub is located in a 250-year-old building situated by twin locks on the oldest ship canal in the country. Bar food is available all day. Car park, large garden, volleyball, barbecue in summer and children's room. Located on the south-west edge of the city, through the Marsh Barton Trading Estate.

OPEN *11am–11pm Mon–Sat; 12–10.30pm Sun.*

Great Western Hotel

St David's Station Approach, Exeter EX4 4NU
☎ *(01392) 274039* Trevor Crouchen

Fuller's London Pride is always available. Guest beers, changed weekly, may include favourites such as Orkney Dark Island and Morland Old Speckled Hen.

A traditional freehouse within a hotel. Staff pride themselves on looking after their customers. Thirty bedrooms with en-suite facilities. Background music. Live music on bank holidays. Food served all day. Children allowed.

OPEN *11am–11pm Mon–Sat; 12–10.30pm Sun.*

The Hole Inn the Wall

Little Castle Street, Exeter EX14 3PX
☎ *(01392) 273341* Mr Kerrigan

A pub tied to Eldridge Pope, in a back street near the law courts, with five pumps serving real ale. Hardy Country and Royal Oak always on offer.

A two-storey pub with eight pool tables, pub bar at very top. Quiz night on Tuesday. Food at lunchtime only (12–2pm). No children; over-18s only.

OPEN *11am–11pm Mon–Sat; 7–10.30pm Sun and bank holidays.*

The Well House Tavern

Cathedral Yard, Exeter EX1 1HB
☎ *(01392) 495365*
Tracy Cherry and Ian Scanes

Five guest beers available which may include Morland Old Speckled Hen, Guernsey Sunbeam Bitter and Oakhill Best.

There is live music and a quiz night at this popular pub on alternate Sundays. Bar food is available at lunchtime and evenings. Facing Exeter Cathedral, with a Roman cellar.

OPEN *11am–11pm Mon–Sat; 7–11pm Sun.*

EXMOUTH

The Grove
The Esplanade, Exmouth EX15 2AZ
☎ *(01395) 272101 Mr Doble*

A freehouse with Fuller's London Pride always available. A guest beer is changed monthly. Regulars include Otter Ale and Morland Old Speckled Hen.

A quiet, family-run pub with one bar. Live bands on Fridays. Food at lunchtime and evenings. Children allowed.

OPEN *11am–11pm Mon–Sat; 12–10.30pm Sun.*

GEORGEHAM

The Rock Inn
Rock Hill, Georgeham EX33 1JW
☎ *(01271) 890322 Mr and Mrs Scutts*

Ruddles and Wadworth brews always available plus Morland Old Speckled Hen. Also a couple of guest beers often including ales from Cotleigh, St Austell, Barum and Fuller's breweries.

A 400-year-old inn one mile from the sea. CAMRA North Devon Pub of the Year 1994–96. Bar food available at lunchtime and evenings. Car park, garden, conservatory and children's room. Accommodation.

OPEN *11am–3pm; all day Sat–Sun.*

HALWELL

Old Inn
Halwell, nr Totnes TQ9 7JA
☎ *(01803) 712329 Mr Crowther*

A freehouse with RCH East Street Cream always on offer. There is also one guest, changed weekly.

A food and beer pub, with dining area and background music. Food at lunchtime and evenings. Children allowed.

OPEN *11am–3pm and 6–11pm Mon–Sat; 12–3pm and 6–10.30pm Sun.*

HATHERLEIGH

Tally Ho Country Inn
14 Market Street, Hatherleigh EX20 3JN
☎ *(01837) 810306*

Offers a range of six popular brews which are produced in the micro-brewery on the premises.

Although the present brewery only started brewing in 1990, its history goes back over 200 years. Records show that it was producing ales in 1790, when it was known as The New Inn Brewery. It was destroyed by fire in 1806 but was brewing again in 1824. The brewery finally closed down in the early 1900s, when it could no longer compete with the larger breweries of the time. The new brewery is situated at the back of The Tally Ho Country Inn in what used to be the town bakery and can produce 260 gallons of real ale a week. The pub itself has background music. Bar and restaurant food available at lunchtime and evenings. Car park, garden, accommodation. Children allowed.

MARKET ALE 3.7% ABV
TARKA'S TIPPLE 4.0% ABV
NUTTERS ALE 4.6% ABV
MIDNIGHT MADNESS 5.0% ABV
THURGIA 6.0% ABV
Plus seasonal ales such as Master Jack's Mild (3.5% ABV) and Jollop (6.6% ABV).

OPEN *11am–2.30pm and 6–11pm.*

HOLBETON

Mildmay Colours
Holbeton, Plymouth PL8 1NA
☎ *(01752) 830248 Louise Price*

Mildmay Colours Best and SP (Skinner's) always on the menu in this freehouse. Two guests, changed fortnightly, may include Skinner's Cornish Knocker or Bunces Danish Dynamite.

A traditional country pub with upstairs dining and bar area. Occasional rock and jazz bands. Food at lunchtime and evenings. Children allowed.

OPEN *11am–11pm Mon–Sat; 12–10.30pm Sun.*

HORNDON

The Elephant's Nest

Horndon, Nr Mary Tavy PL19 9NQ
☎ *(01822) 810273* Nick Hamer

Palmer's IPA and St Austell HSD always available plus two guest beers (150 per year) including those from Exe Valley, Wye Valley, Cotleigh, Exmoor, Hook Norton, Summerskills and Ash Vine breweries. Also draught cider.

This sixteenth-century Dartmoor inn with a large garden and log fires has a collection of 'Elephant's Nests' written in different languages on the beams in chalk. Bar food at lunchtime and evenings. Car park and children's room. The garden is home to rabbits, ducks and chickens. Travel along the A386 into Mary Tavy. Take the road signposted Horndon for just under two miles.

11.30am–2.30pm and 6.30–11pm Mon–Sat; 12–2.30pm and 7–10.30pm Sun.

HORSEBRIDGE

The Royal Inn

Horsebridge TL19 8PJ
☎ *(01822) 870214* Catherine Eaton

A freehouse with Wadworth 6X and a Sharp's brew always available. Two guests also offered.

An old pub with open fires, patio and beer garden. Food at lunchtime and evenings. Children allowed at lunchtime only.

12–3pm and 7–11pm (10.30pm Sun).

IDDESLEIGH

Duke of York

Iddesleigh EX19 8BG
☎ *(01837) 810253* J Stewart

A freehouse, with all real ales served straight from the barrel; no pumps used. Adnams Broadside and Cotleigh Tawny are always available, plus numerous guest beers which change daily. Wye Valley brews are a favourite.

A pub in a rural setting (ring for directions!). No TV, occasional live music. Separate dining area. Food served all day. Children allowed.

11am–11pm Mon–Sat; 12–10.30pm Sun.

KINGSBRIDGE

The Ship & Plough

The Promenade, Kingsbridge TQ7 1JD
☎ *(01548) 852485* Jackie Blewitt

A brewpub, home of Blewitts Brewery with the full range of own brews always available, plus Wadworth 6X. Plans to start a cask-conditioned lager.

A large pub, with beams and open fires, situated in the Sorley Tunnel. The tunnel itself is open to the public (admission charge) and has a children's play area, shop, restaurant and a workshop in which pottery and metalwork are demonstrated. There is also a glass viewing area in which people can watch the brewing process. The pub itself has live music on Thursdays. Food available. Children allowed in family room.

BLEWITTS BEST 4.0% ABV
Fruity.
BLEWITTS WAGES 4.5% ABV
Made with barley and maize.
BLEWITTS HEAD OFF 5.0% ABV
A fruity, sweet flavour

11am–11pm Mon–Sat; 12–10.30pm Sun.

LAPFORD

The Old Malt Scoop Inn

Lapford, Nr Crediton EX17 6PZ
☎ *(01363) 83330* John and Pam Berry

Adnams Broadside and Marston's Pedigree always available, plus 52 guest beers each year, to include Sharp's Doom Bar, Shepherd Neame Spitfire, Charles Wells Bombadier and many more. Also traditional cider.

This sixteenth-century freehouse is open for morning coffee, bar snacks, meals and cream teas. There are inglenook fireplaces, beamed ceiling, panelled walls, skittle alley, beer garden, patio areas and car park. Children are allowed in the sun lounge and one of the bars. Lapford is on the A377 between Crediton and Barnstaple. Follow brown tourist signs near village. The inn is at the centre of the village, opposite the church.

11am–11pm May–Sept; 12–3pm and 6–11pm Oct–end April.

The Chichester Arms

Chapel Hill, Mortehoe, Woolacombe EX34 7DU
☎ *(01271) 870411* David and Jane Pugh

Ushers Best Bitter, Badger Tanglefoot, Barum Original and Gold regularly available, plus a guest beer perhaps from Cains, Robinson's, Cotleigh, Shepherd Neame, Brakspear, Fuller's, Young's, Banks's, Timothy Taylor, Jennings, Exmoor, Thwaites or others.

Mortehoe's original village inn, built as a vicarage in 1620. Converted in 1820, it is basically unchanged since and is still partly gas lit, although it does also have its own electricity generator. Commended for the best pub food in Devon for the past two years. Food served 12–2pm and 6–9pm every day. Children's room and garden. Car park.

OPEN *Winter: 11.30am–3pm and 6–11pm Mon–Sat; 12–3pm and 7–10.30pm Sun. Summer: 11am–11pm Mon–Sat; 12–10.30pm Sun.*

Dartmouth Inn

63 East Street, Newton Abbot TQ12 2JP
☎ *(01626) 353451*
Malcolm and Brenda Charles

Guest beers (300 per year) may include RCH East Street Cream, Sarah Hughes Dark Ruby Mild, Teignworthy Springtide and Sutton Knickerdroppa Glory.

This 450-year-old pub is reputed to be the oldest inn in Newton Abbot. Beautiful beer garden, a previous Bloom of Britain winner. The pub has also won the regional CAMRA Pub of the Year award on several occasions. Five minutes' walk from the station.

OPEN *11am–11pm Mon–Sat; 12–10.30pm Sun.*

The Golden Lion

4 Market Street, Newton Abbot EX39 1PW
☎ *(01626) 367062* Ali Snell

A freehouse always offering Teignworthy Reel Ale. Two guests may include favourites such as Badger Tanglefoot, Fuller's London Pride or something from Scatter Rock.

An olde-worlde one-bar pub, with juke box. Food at lunchtime only. No children. In a back alley, can be hard to find.

OPEN *11am–2.30pm and 5.30–11pm Mon–Fri; 11am–4pm and 6–11pm Sat; 11am–3pm and 7–10.30pm Sun.*

The Beer Engine

Sweetham, Newton St Cyres, Nr Exeter EX5 5AX
☎ *(01392) 851282* Fax *(01392) 851876*
Peter and Jill Hawksley

Rail Ale, Piston Bitter and Sleeper Heavy brewed on the premises and always available. Seasonals and specials brewed occasionally.

The brewery was established along with a cellar bar in the basement of a former station hotel in 1983. It has now expanded to produce three brews and supplies a couple of local pubs and wholesalers. Home-made food available at lunchtime and evenings. Car park, garden. Children allowed.

RETURN TICKET 3.4% ABV
An occasional beer.

RAIL ALE 3.8% ABV
Amber-coloured, malty nose and flavour of fruit.

PISTON BITTER 4.3% ABV
Sweetness throughout, with some bitterness in the finish.

GOLDEN ARROW 4.6% ABV
An occasional beer.

PORTER 4.7% ABV
An occasional beer.

SLEEPER HEAVY 5.4% ABV
Red, with fruit, sweetness and some bitterness.

WHISTLEMAS 6.7% ABV
A Christmas brew.

OPEN *11am–11pm Mon–Sat; 12–10.30pm Sun.*

Fountain Inn

Exeter Street, North Tawton EX20 2HB
☎ *(01837) 82551* Lesley Whitehouse

A freehouse, recently taken over. Shepherd Neame Spitfire, St Austell Hicks and Tinners always available.

A large, lively and friendly pub. Separate dining area. Food at lunchtime and evenings. Well-behaved children allowed.

OPEN *11.30am–2.30pm and 5.30–11pm Mon–Fri (closed Mon lunch); 11.30am–4pm and 6–11pm Sat; 12–4pm and 7–10.30pm Sun.*

Railway Inn

Whiddon Down Road, North Tawton EX20 2BE
☎ *(01837) 82789* Claire Speak

A freehouse with Wadworth 6X always available. Regular guests include Jollyboat Mainbrace, Teignworthy Beachcomber and Reel Ale, Adnams Broadside and Badger Best.

An old country inn, on the main road but slightly hidden, with one bar and dining area. Bar snacks and evening meals. Children allowed.

OPEN *12–3pm (not Mon) and 6–11pm Mon–Sat; 12–3pm and 7–10.30pm Sun.*

Plymouth Inn

26 West Street, Okehampton EX20 1HH
☎ *(01837) 53633* Geoff and Jill Hoather

🐾 A freehouse, with beers served straight from the barrel. Accent on beers from the West Country, though others are often featured.

A country-style town pub with restaurant, beer garden and function room. Mini beer festivals and occasional folk bands. Food at lunchtime and evenings. Children allowed; function room doubles as children's room.

OPEN *12–3pm and 7–11pm Mon–Fri; 12–11pm Sat and bank holidays; 12–10.30pm Sun.*

The Old Mill

Ossaborough, Woolacombe EX34 7HJ
☎ *(01271) 870237* D Huxtable

🐾 Brains Buckley's Reverend James usually available plus one guest beer from Brains or Barum brewery.

Once a mill, this seventeenth-century country pub has plenty of olde-worlde charm and retains many decorative features. Food is served 12–2pm and 6–9pm. Children welcome, outdoor play area. Car park. Take the first right-hand turning out of Woolacombe.

OPEN *Winter: 12–3pm and 6–11pm (10.30pm Sun); Summer 11am–11pm (10.30pm Sun).*

The Reform Inn

Reform Street, Pilton, Barnstaple EX31 9PD
☎ *(01271) 323164* Mark Kilminster

🐾 Barum Original, Breakfast and Technical Hitch usually served, with the other Barum beers regularly available.

The Reform Inn offers a pool table, darts, shove ha'penny and two computer terminals for games and access to the internet. Rolls/baguettes and toasted sandwiches available. The Barum Brewery is situated behind the pub, but is separately owned. Children welcome.

OPEN *11.30am–11.30pm (10.30pm Sun).*

The Clifton

35 Clifton Street, Greenbank, Plymouth PL4 8JB
☎ *(01752) 266563* Mr Rosevear

🐾 A freehouse with Clifton Classic (house beer) and Summerskills Indiana's Bones always on offer. Two guests are changed weekly; regulars include Badger Tanglefoot, Greene King Abbot and Timothy Taylor Landlord.

A locals' pub, with one bar and Sky TV for football. No food. No children. Not far from the railway station.

OPEN *5–11pm Mon–Thurs; 11am–11pm Fri–Sat; 12–10.30pm Sun.*

The Library

15 Wyndham Street East, Plymouth EX17 6AL
☎ *(01752) 266042* Douglas Russell

🐾 A freehouse with Cornish Rebellion and Sutton XSB always available, plus two guest beers.

A student-style pub (juke box (free on Student Night – Tuesday), one long bar. Big-screen TV/Sky. Live acts or karaoke Wednesdays. Pool room. Food: burgers, hot dogs, chips. No children after 7pm.

OPEN *11am–11pm Mon and Wed–Sat; 12–5pm and 7–11pm Tues; 12–10.30pm Sun.*

The Tap & Spile

20 Looe Street, Plymouth PL4 0DA
☎ *(01752) 662485* Jackie Grey

🐾 Tied to Century Inns and offering eight real ales, changed every two or three days. Morland Old Speckled Hen, Coach House Dick Turpin and St George's Ale plus Greene King Abbot regularly featured.

A town-centre pub with exposed brickwork and lots of bric-a-brac. Background music. Raised area at top of pub for eating. Food served at lunchtimes. Children allowed.

OPEN *11am–3pm and 5–11.30pm Mon–Fri; 11am–11pm Sat; 12–10.30pm Sun.*

Thistle Park Tavern

32 Commercial Road, Plymouth PL4 0LE
☎ *(01752) 204890*

 Next door to the Sutton Brewery, so serves the full range of Sutton brews.

Brewing began in November 1993. Polished wooden floors, maritime relics and oil paintings by a local artist. Bar food and a range of South African cuisine served at lunchtime and evenings. Parking, patio. Further information available on website: www.quintin@xsb42.force9.co.uk.

DARTMOOR PRIDE 3.8% ABV
XSB 4.2% ABV
HOPNOSIS 4.5% ABV
EDDYSTONE LIGHT 5.0% ABV
KNICKADROPPA GLORY 5.5% ABV

11am–11pm Mon–Sat; 12–10.30pm Sun.

The Boringdon Arms

13 Boringdon Terrace, Turnchapel, Nr Plymstock PL9 9TQ
☎ *(01752) 402053*

 Butcombe Bitter, RCH Pitchfork and Summerskills Best among the beers always available plus up to five guests beers (250 per year) from Orkney (north), Burts (south), Skinner's (west), Scott's (east) and all points in between.

An ex-quarrymaster's house with a good atmosphere. No juke box. Live music on Saturday nights. CAMRA's first Plymouth Pub of the Year, and Plymouth CAMRA's Pub of the Year for 1999/2000. Bar food available at lunchtime and evenings. Conservatory and beer garden in the old quarry to the rear of the pub. Bi-monthly beer festivals. Accommodation. Located at the centre of the village, four miles south-east of Plymouth, on south coast footpath. Signposted from the A379. Website: www.bori.co.uk

11am–11pm Mon–Sat; 12–10.30pm Sun.

The Two Bridges Hotel

Two Bridges, Princetown, Yelverton PL20 6SW
☎ *(01822) 890581* Philip Davis

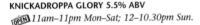 A freehouse and brewery home of the Princetown Brewery, with home brews always on offer plus seasonal specials.

A sixteenth-century country house hotel. Piano player three times a week, occasional jazz band. Restaurant seats 70. Food served 11am–9pm. Children allowed.

DARTMOOR IPA 4% ABV
JAIL ALE 4.8% ABV

11am–11pm Mon–Sat; 12–10.30pm Sun.

The Journey's End

Ringmore, Nr Kingsbridge TQ7 4HL
☎ *(01548) 810205*

 Up to ten brews available including Exmoor Ale and Otter Ale, Badger Tanglefoot, Shepherd Neame Spitfire, Adnams Broadside and Crown Buckley Reverend James Original. Also guests (50 per year) changed weekly including Archers Golden, Greene King Abbot and brews from Fuller's, Cains and Wye Valley.

An eleventh-century thatched inn with flagstone floors and open fires. Bar and restaurant food served at lunchtime and evenings. Conservatory, car park, garden, non-smoking dining room. Accommodation. No children in the bar.

11.30am–3pm and 6–11pm Mon–Sat; 12–10.30pm Sun.

The Clifford Arms

34 Fore Street, Shaldon, Teignmouth TQ14 0DE
☎ *(01626) 872311* Mr Balster

A freehouse with Blackawton Headstrong and Greene King Abbot always on sale. Regular guests include Fuller's London Pride and Shepherd Neame Spitfire.

A one-bar pub with garden, juke box and live music. Food at lunchtime and evenings. Children allowed in certain areas.

11am–2.30pm and 5–11pm Mon–Fri; 11am–11pm Sat; 11am–2.30pm and 5–11pm Sun.

Silverton Inn

Fore Street, Silverton, Nr Exeter EX5 4HP
☎ *(01392) 860196*

Exe Valley Dob's Best Bitter always available, plus three guests, changed weekly, from a wide range of breweries. Greene King Abbot is a favourite.

Traditional, cosy wooden pub between Exeter and Tiverton with easy access to sea coasts and shopping towns. Separate upstairs restaurant. Food available at lunchtime and evenings. Recently converted, well-equipped luxury rooms are now available. Nearby parking, beer garden. Children allowed in restaurant. Killerton House, a National Trust property, is nearby.

11.30am–3pm and 5.30–11pm.

The Tower Inn

Slapton, Nr Kingsbridge TQ7 2PN
☎ *(01548) 580216* Mr and Mrs Dickman

Exmoor Ale and Badger Tanglefoot always available plus three or four guests (20+ per year) which may include Gibbs Mew Bishop's Tipple, Blackawton Headstrong, Palmers IPA, Timothy Taylor Landlord and Eldridge Pope Royal Oak.

A fourteenth-century inn offering accommodation and a superb garden. Bar and restaurant food available at lunchtime and evenings. Car park and children's room. Hidden in the centre of the village at the foot of the old ruined tower.

12–3pm and 6–11pm.

The Tradesman's Arms

Stokenham, Kingsbridge TQ7 2SZ
☎ *(01548) 580313*
John and Elizabeth Sharman

Adnams Southwold and Broadside usually available plus a guest beer from Fuller's or local breweries such as Blewitts.

Welcoming, picturesque country pub, well known locally for its imaginative and interesting food. Good range of malt whiskies. Food served 12–1.30pm and 6.30–9.30pm. Children welcome at lunchtime only. Car park. Situated 100 yards off the A379, Kingsbridge to Dartmouth road.

12–2.30pm Wed–Fri and Sun; 6.30–11pm Tues–Sat; closed at other times, except bank hoildays.

The Halfway House

Grenofen, Tavistock PL19 9ER
☎ *(01822) 612960* Peter Jones

A freehouse with Sharp's Doom Bar Ale always available. Two guests are changed weekly and may include beers from Skinner's, Sutton and Sharp's.

A country inn on the A386. Public bar. Background music. Separate dining and lounge bar. Food served every lunchtime and evening. Children allowed. En-suite accommodation available.

11.30am–3pm and 5–11pm Mon–Sat; 12–4pm and 6–10.30pm Sun.

The Blue Anchor

Teign Street, Teignmouth TQ14 8EG
☎ *(01626) 772741* Paul Fellows

A freehouse serving Adnams Broadside, Marston's Pedigree and Teignworthy Reel Ale. Three guests, changed two or three times a week, include favourites such as Greene King Abbot, Fuller's ESB or something from Bateman or Branscombe Vale.

A small, very boozy, locals' pub. Old, with log fire. Rolls only. No children.

11am–11pm Mon–Sat; 12–10.30pm Sun.

The Golden Lion

85 Bitton Park Road, Teignmouth TQ14 9BY
☎ *(01626) 776442*

At least two guest beers (approx 50 per year) usually available from regional brewers such as Blackawton, Teignworthy, Exe Valley and Oak Hill.

This is a locals' pub on the main road just out of the town with a public and lounge bar. Darts and pool are played. Bar food is available at lunchtime and evenings. Small car park. Children not allowed.

12–4pm and 6–11pm (10.30pm Sun).

Bridge Inn

Bridge Hill, Topsham, Nr Exeter EX3 0QQ
☎ *(01392) 873862*
Mr N Cheffers and Mrs CA Cheffers-Heard

Nine or ten real ales usually available, which may include Branscombe Vale's Yo Ho Ho, Hells Belles, Anniversary Ale and Branoc, Moor's Old Freddy Walker, Exe Valley's Winter Glow and Mr Sheppard's Crook, Badger Tanglefoot and Adnams Broadside. Brews from local breweries are particularly popular.

This is a sixteenth-century pub overlooking the River Clyst has been in the same family since 1897 through four generations. Simple bar food at lunchtime. Car park and children's room. Two miles from M5 junction 30. Topsham is signposted from the exit. In Topsham, follow the yellow signpost (A376) to Exmouth. For further information visit the website at www.cheffers.co.uk

12–2pm and 6–10.30pm (11pm Fri–Sat).

TORQUAY

Chelston Manor Hotel

Old Mill Road, Torquay TQ2 6HW
☎ *(01803) 605142* Simon Breed

A freehouse with Wadworth 6X always available, plus guest beers such as Marston's Pedigree and Morland Old Speckled Hen, Fuller's London Pride, Young's Special, Fuggles IPA, Brains IPA and brews from Brakspear.

Olde-worlde converted manor house with accommodation. Large bar with three separate areas, pool table, children's room, large beer garden. Food served at lunchtime and evenings in the bar, or in the à la carte restaurant

OPEN *12–3pm and 6–11pm (10.30pm Sun).*

Crown & Sceptre

2 Petitor Road, St Marychurch, Torquay TQ1 4QA
☎ *(01803) 328290* Mr R Wheeler

Marston's Pedigree and Ruddles County always on sale. A guest beer, changed weekly, might come from a local brewery such as Teignworthy.

A traditional pub with two bars, children's room and garden. Live music. Food at lunchtimes only. Children allowed.

OPEN *11am–3pm and 5.30–11pm Mon–Fri; 11am–4pm and 6.30–11pm Sat; 12–3pm and 7–10.30pm Sun.*

TUCKENHAY

Maltsters Arms

Bow Creek, Tuckenhay TQ9 7EQ
☎ *(01803) 832350*
Quentin and Denise Thwaites

A freehouse with Blackawton beers and Princetown Dartmoor IPA usually available. One or two guests, changed every two days, may include Otter Ale or something from Wye Valley or Thwaites. Young's Millennium bottle-conditioned ale also served.

A traditional country pub with separate eating area overlooking the river. Bed and breakfast, with themed bedrooms. Barbecues on the river bank. Regular live music. Food at lunchtime and evenings. Children allowed in certain areas. In the middle of nowhere. If you manage to find Tuckenhay, you'll find the pub.

OPEN *All day every day during summer holidays. 11am–3pm and 6–11pm Mon–Fri; 11am–11pm Sat; 12–10.30pm Sun at other times.*

WEST DOWN

The Crown Inn

The Square, West Down
☎ *(01271) 862790* Russ Trueman

Barum Original usually available plus one guest beer. This might be another Barum beer, Wadworth 6X, Greene King Abbot Ale, Marston's Pedigree or local ales of interest.

A small seventeenth-century village pub with open fire, non-smoking area and delightful garden. Food served in separate restaurant 12–2pm and 6–10pm. Children welcome. Car park. Follow the brown tourist signs between Braunton and Ilfracombe and Lynton Cross and Mullacott Cross.

OPEN *12–3pm and 6–11pm Mon–Sat; 12–4pm and 7–10.30pm Sun.*

WEST PUSEHILL

Pig on the Hill

West Pusehill, Westward Ho!, Bideford EX39 5AH
☎ *(01237) 477615*

Home to the Country Life Brewery, with the four house beers rotated on the pumps.

Friendly country inn in rural setting with food available each session. Garden, terrace and children's play area. Games room and giant TV. Petanque club and holiday cottages.

OLD APPLEDORE 3.7% ABV
Dark red colour and quenching.
WALLOP 4.4% ABV
Pale, easy-quaffing, summer brew.
GOLDEN PIG 4.7% ABV
Gold-coloured and well-rounded.
COUNTRY BUMPKIN 5.7% ABV
Dark, with malty sweetness.

OPEN *12–3pm and 6–11pm Mon–Sat; 12–3pm and 7–10.30pm Sun.*

WHIMPLE

New Fountain Inn

Church Road, Whimple, Exeter EX5 2TA
☎ *(01404) 822350* Paul Mallett

A freehouse with Teignworthy beers and Branscombe Vale Branoc usually on the menu. Guest beers (one from the barrel) come from local independent breweries.

A family-run village inn split into two tiers, the top one used for eating. Food served at lunchtime and evenings. Children and dogs welcome. There are plans to open a heritage centre on the site.

OPEN *12–2.30pm and 6–11pm Mon–Sat; 12–2.30pm and 7–11pm Sun.*

WINKLEIGH

The Kings Arms

Fore Street, Winkleigh EX19 8HQ
☎ *(01837) 83384* Steve and Ann Kinsey

 Princetown Best Bitter usually available plus two guest beers which may be from local breweries or any independent brand in the country, such as St Austell HSD, Princetown Jail Ale or Fuller's London Pride.

Traditional, thatched country pub in pretty village. Award-winning bar food served 12–2pm and 6.30–9pm (restaurant from 7pm). Bar food only on Sunday nights. No food on Mondays. Children welcome, but no special facilities. Follow signs 'To the village'.

OPEN 11am–3pm and 6–11pm Mon–Fri; 11am–11pm Sat; 12–3pm and 7–10.30pm Sun.

YARDE DOWN

Poltimore Arms

Yarde Down, South Molton EX36 3HA
☎ *(01598) 710381* Richard Austen

A freehouse with real ales served straight from the barrel. Cotleigh Tawny Ale is always available, and guests, changed weekly, may include Marston's Pedigree, Morland Old Speckled Hen or Greene King Abbot Ale.

Dates back to 1600. Has its own generator for electricity. Food served; a very large menu. Children allowed. In the middle of nowhere; best to ring for directions.

OPEN 12–2.30pm and 6.30–11pm Mon–Sat; 12–2.30pm and 7–10.30pm Sun.

YOU TELL US

★ *The Little Mutton Monster*, 240 James Street, Plymouth
★ *The London Hotel*, West Street, Ashburton
★ *The Manor Inn*, Lower Ashton
★ *Nog Inn*, Sidmouth Junction, Feniton
★ *The Prince of Wales*, Tavistock Road, Princetown, Yelverton
★ *The Welcome Inn*, Haven Banks, Exeter

THE BREWERIES

THE BADGER BREWERY

Blandford St Mary, Blandford Forum DT11 9LS
☎ *(01258) 452141*

IPA 3.6% ABV
Well-hopped and refreshing.
BEST BITTER 4.0% ABV
Fruity with refreshing, hoppy finish.
CHAMPION 4.6% ABV
Golden with delicate hop and citrus flavours.
DEACON (for Gibbs Mew) 4.8% ABV
Pale and rounded.
TANGLEFOOT 5.1% ABV
Pale, full fruit, with bittersweet finish.
BISHOPS TIPPLE (for Gibbs Mew) 6.5% ABV

GOLDFINCH BREWERY

47 High East Street, Dorchester DT1 1HU
☎ *(01305) 264020*

TOM BROWN'S BITTER 4.0% ABV
Hoppy throughout.
FLASHMAN'S CLOUT 4.5% ABV
Balanced and flavoursome.
MIDNIGHT SUN 4.5% ABV
Replaces Flashman's Clout during the summer.
MIDNIGHT BLINDER 5.0% ABV
Sweet malt with balancing hoppiness.
Plus occasional brews.

JC AND RH PALMER

*The Old Brewery, West Bay Road, Bridport
DT6 4JA*
☎ *(01308) 422396*

BRIDPORT BITTER 3.2% ABV
Refreshing, with hops and bitterness
throughout.
DORSET GOLD 3.7% ABV
Golden with delicate fruity hoppiness.
BEST BITTER 4.2% ABV
Well-balanced and good hop character.
TALLY HO! 5.5% ABV
Nutty and distinctive.
200 5.0% ABV
Smooth, full-flavoured and complex.

POOLE BREWERY

68 High Street, Poole BH15 1DA
☎ *(01202) 682345*

BEST BITTER or DOLPHIN 3.8% ABV
BEDROCK BITTER 4.2% ABV
Occasional.
HOLES BAY HOG 4.5% ABV
BOSUN 4.6% ABV
DOUBLE BARREL 5.5% ABV
Occasional.

THE QUAY BREWERY

Brewers Quay, Hope Square, Weymouth DT4 8TR
☎ *(01305) 777515*

 **WEYMOUTH HARBOUR MASTER 3.6% ABV**
Rounded and easy-drinking.
SUMMER KNIGHT 3.8% ABV
Award-winning wheat beer. Available May–Oct
WEYMOUTH SPECIAL PALE ALE 4.0% ABV
Gold and well-balanced.
WEYMOUTH JD 1742 4.2% ABV
Quenching bittersweet flavour.
BOMBSHELL BITTER 4.5% ABV
Sweet and malty.
QUAY STEAM BEER 4.5% ABV
Aromatic and full-flavoured. American hops.
OLD ROTT 5.0% ABV
SILENT KNIGHT 5.9% ABV
Dark wheat beer.
Plus occasional beers.

THOMAS HARDY BREWING LTD

Weymouth Avenue, Dorchester DT1 1QT
☎ *(01305) 250255*

POPE'S TRADITIONAL 3.8% ABV
HARDY COUNTRY 4.2% ABV
Well-balanced with clean bitterness in the finish.
ROYAL OAK 5.0% ABV
Warming, excellent balance and smooth finish.
For Morrell's:
OXFORD BITTER 3.7% ABV
VARSITY 4.3% ABV
GRADUATE 5.2% ABV

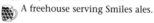
THE PUBS

BENVILLE

The Talbot Arms

Benville, Dorchester DT2 0NN
☎ *(01935) 83381* Mr Skelcher

A freehouse serving Smiles ales.

A country pub/restaurant with beer garden. Food served at lunchtime and evenings. Children allowed.

OPEN *12–2.30pm and 7–11pm (10.30pm Sun).*

BOURNEMOUTH

The Goat & Tricycle

27–9 West Hill Road, Bournemouth BH2 5PF
☎ *(01202) 314220* Sandra Gillard

Wadworth 6X, Henry's Original IPA and Farmer's Glory always available, plus four or five regularly changing guests including Morland Old Speckled Hen or brews from Bateman and Hop Back.

A traditional pub with family area and courtyard. No juke box, background music only. No children in the bar. Food served lunchtimes and evenings.

OPEN *12–3pm daily; 5.30–11pm Mon–Fri; 6–11pm Sat; 7–10.30pm Sun.*

Moon in the Square

4–8 Exeter Road, Bournemouth BH2 5AL
☎ *(01202) 314940*
Sue and Martin Groundwater

Four guest real ales always available, with Shepherd Neame Spitfire a regular feature.

A traditional, Wetherspoons pub, recently refurbished, with no smoking at the bar. Food served all day. No children.

OPEN *All day, every day.*

BURTON BRADSTOCK

The Dove Inn

Southover, Burton Bradstock, Bridport DT6 4RD
☎ *(01308) 897897* Neil Walker

Branscombe Vale Branoc, Otter Ale, Morland Old Speckled Hen are among the brews usually available, plus one regularly changing guest, usually from a local or micro-brewery.

A listed building with thatched roof. Recently refurbished to convert three cottages into one building. One bar, restaurant area, large garden terrace, car park. Food served lunchtimes and evenings. Children allowed. Signposted from Burton Bradstock.

OPEN *All day, every day.*

CATTISTOCK

The Fox & Hounds

Duck Street, Cattistock
☎ *(01300) 320444* Anne Hinton

 Lots of guest beers, two at any one time. These may include Fuller's London Pride, Charles Wells Bombadier and ales from Oakhill and Cottage breweries.

A fifteenth-century village inn with large fires, flagstones and a separate restaurant. Relaxing atmosphere. Bar and restaurant food available at lunchtime and evenings. Parking, garden and play area opposite. Campsite nearby. Accommodation. On the A37, look out for the sign for Cattistock, just past the Clay Pigeon Cafe from Yeovil or the sign on the road from Dorchester.

🍺 *12–2.30pm and 7–11pm.*

CHETNOLE

The Chetnole Inn

Chetnole, Sherborne DT9 6NU
☎ *(01935) 872337*

A freehouse. Branscombe Vale Branoc Ale always available, plus guests often from the Butcombe or Otter breweries.

A two-bar village pub with background music and occasional small live bands. Beer garden and dining area. Food served at lunchtime and evenings. Children allowed in garden and dining area. Opposite the church.

🍺 *11am–2.30pm and 6–11pm Mon–Sat; 12–3pm and 7–10.30pm Sun.*

CHILD OKEFORD

Saxon Inn

Gold Hill, Child Okeford DT11 8HD
☎ *(01258) 860310*
Hilary and Roger Pendleton

Three real ales regularly available, always including something from Butcombe. One guest beer, perhaps Shepherd Neame Spitfire or Fuller's London Pride.

A friendly old village pub with two cosy bars and log fires. Food served every lunchtime, and evenings except Tuesday and Sunday. Varied menu. Pleasant garden with a variety of animals, including two friendly New Zealand Kune Kune pigs. Families welcome.

🍺 *11.30am–2.30pm and 7–11pm Mon–Fri; 11.30am–3pm and 7–11pm Sat; 12–3.30pm and 7–10.30pm Sun.*

CORFE MULLEN

Coventry Arms

Mill Street, Corfe Mullen BH21 3RH
☎ *(01258) 857284* Mrs Nikki

Owned by Greenalls, serving local beers straight from the barrel, including Ringwood Best and Old Thumper plus other guests as available.

An old-style, one-bar country pub with food served at lunchtime and evenings in a separate dining area. Children allowed. Located on the main A31.

🍺 *11am–3pm and 5.30–11pm Mon–Fri; all day Sat–Sun.*

CRANBORNE

The Sheaf of Arrows

The Square, Cranborne BH21 5PR
☎ *(01725) 517456*
Carol Driver and Vicky Donaghue

Ringwood Best Bitter regularly available plus four constantly changing guest beers. Fuller's London Pride may reappear, but different beers are usually served each time.

Small, friendly village local with lots of passing trade. Open fires in both bars. Garden, pool table, Sky Sports and skittle alley. Home-cooked food served 10–11.30am (breakfast), 12–2pm and 7–9pm daily. No children.

🍺 *10am–2.30pm and 6–11pm Mon–Sat; 12–2.30pm and 7–10.30pm Sun.*

DORCHESTER

Blue Raddle

Church Street, Dorchester DT1 1JN
Arthur and Lesley Ash

Sharp's Cornish Coaster, Greene King Abbot Ale, Otter Bitter and Raddle Tupping Bitter regularly available, plus two or three guest beers (over 300 in the last five years), perhaps from Hop Back, Tisbury, Oakhill, RCH, Cottage or Sharp's.

Small, market-town pub. Food served 12–2pm Mon–Sat. No children.

🍺 *11.30am–3pm and 7–11pm Mon–Sat; 12–3pm and 7–10.30pm Sun.*

HINTON ST MARY

The White Horse

Hinton St Mary, Sturminster Newton DT10 1NA
☎ *(01258) 472723* Mr Thomas

A freehouse serving a wide range of real ales (8–10 per week) on a rotating basis including Ringwood Best and True Glory plus brews from Tisbury and Cottage Breweries. One light beer (under 3.9% ABV) and one heavy (over 4% ABV) always available. On Fridays one real ale is selected for a special offer at £1 per pint.

A busy nineteenth-century pub. Public bar, lounge bar and beer garden. Restaurant area in the lounge with à la carte menu and specials plus Sunday Roasts. Food served at lunchtime and evenings. Children allowed.

OPEN *11.15am–3pm and 6.15–11pm Mon–Sat; 12–3pm and 7–11pm Sun.*

HURN

Avon Causeway Hotel

Hurn, Christchurch BH25 6AS
☎ *(01202) 482714* Keith Perks

Up to five real ales available, including Rockingham Forest Gold and a Ringwood ale such as Best or Old Thumper, plus guests.

A quaint country hotel, ten minutes from Bournemouth. Formerly Hurn railway station, the pub is decorated with lots of railway bric-a-brac. Food served at lunchtime and evenings in a separate large lounge. Murder mystery nights are a feature, and make use of an old Victorian carriage. Beer garden with large children's play area. Inside, children are allowed in dining area only.

OPEN *All day, every day.*

LOWER BURTON

Sun Inn

Lower Burton, Nr Dorchester DT2 7RX
☎ *(01305) 250445* Robin Maddex

Three constantly changing beers available, some directly from the cask.

A traditional coaching inn with the motto 'Good Beer and Good Cheer'. Garden and disabled facilities. Carvery and bar menu served every lunchtime and evening. Car park. Children's menu and high chairs available. Situated half a mile from Dorchester town centre on the Sherbourne road.

OPEN *11am–3pm and 5.30–11pm Mon–Sat; 12–3pm and 6.30–10.30pm Sun.*

LYME REGIS

The Nag's Head

Silver Street, Lyme Regis DT7 3HS
☎ *(01297) 442312* Mrs Hamon

A freehouse with up to four ales available, perhaps including Ward's Best and Ringwood Best.

A traditional one-bar pub with background music and beer garden. Separate dining area. Food served every lunchtime and Mon, Wed, Fri and Sat evenings. Children allowed in the bar or restaurant when eating.

OPEN *11am–3pm and 6–11pm Mon; all day Tues–Sun (10.30pm Sun).*

NORTH WOOTTON

The Three Elms

North Wootton, Nr Sherborne DT9 5JW
☎ *(01935) 812881* Mr and Mrs Manning

Fuller's London Pride, Shepherd Neame Spitfire Ale, Hop Back Summer Lightning, Smiles and Butcombe brews always available. Plus two or three guests (160 per year) to include Oakhill Somer Ale, Black Sheep Special, RCH Pitchfork, Smiles Mayfly and Bateman's Strawberry Fields.

A busy roadside pub with a large garden and car park. Contains a collection of 1000+ diecast model cars and lorries in display cabinets around the walls. Bar and restaurant food available at lunchtime and evenings. Children allowed. Accommodation. Situated on the A3030 Sherborne to Sturminster Newton road, two miles from Sherborne.

OPEN *11am–2.30pm Mon–Sat, 12–3pm Sun; 6.30–11pm Mon–Thurs, 6–11pm Fri–Sat, 7–10.30pm Sun.*

PARKSTONE

Branksome Railway Hotel

429 Poole Road, Parkstone, Poole BH12 1DQ
☎ *(01202) 769555*
Terry Kirby and Bill Whiteley

A Whitbread pub with a guest beer policy. Hampshire Strong's Best always available, plus two weekly changing guests from Cottage, Hop Back, Brains, Fuller's, Jennings and many more.

Victorian pub, built in 1894, recently refurbished. Two bars, games including pool and darts. Bar snacks available. Themed dining evenings featuring local guests chefs. B&B in large, comfortable en-suite accommodation. Located on the A35.

OPEN *All day, every day.*

The Brace of Pheasants

Plush DT2 7RQ
☎ *(01300) 348357* Mr Knights

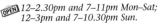 A freehouse with Fuller's London Pride always available, plus one or two weekly rotated guests, including Hop Back Summer Lightning or something from Butcombe, Smiles or Tisbury breweries.

A sixteenth-century thatched village inn. Non-smoking family room, non-smoking restaurant area, large garden. Bar meals and snacks and à la carte restaurant food served lunchtimes and evenings. Children allowed in the garden and family room only. Situated off B3142 Dorchester/Sherborne road.

12–2.30pm and 7–11pm Mon–Sat; 12–3pm and 7–10.30pm Sun.

POOLE

The Bermuda Triangle

Parr Street, Lower Parkstone, Poole BH14 0JY
☎ *(01202) 748087* Mrs G Crane

Three real ales constantly changing. These may include Timothy Taylor Landlord, Fuller's ESB and London Pride, Adnams Broadside, Hop Back Summer Lightning, Greene King Abbot Ale, Ringwood Old Thumper and Fortyniner. Also Young's, Wychwood, Hampshire, Smiles and Shepherd Neame brews.

An interesting theme pub. German lagers on draught and at least 30 bottled beers from all around the world. Good music, great atmosphere. Bar food at lunchtime. Car park. Near Ashley Cross.

11.30am–3pm and 5.30–11pm.

The Blue Boar

29 Market Close, Poole BH15 1NE
☎ *(01202) 682247* Fax *(01202) 661875*
Mr and Mrs Kellawar

A freehouse with five real ales available. Cottage Southern Bitter is a permanent feature, and the two constantly changing guests are from independent breweries.

An unusual three-storey pub in a restored eighteenth-century listed mansion. Cellar bar with live music twice a week, pub games (shove ha'penny, darts), children's certificate while meals are served (lunchtimes). Comfortable lounge bar on ground floor. Conference facility with bar on first floor. E-mail: blue.board@saqnet.co.uk

11am–3pm and 5–11pm Mon–Sat; 12–4pm and 7–10.30pm Sun.

The Brewhouse

68 High Street, Poole BH15 1DA
☎ *(01202) 685288* David Rawlins

The only tied house for the Poole Brewery, situated at the rear of the premises. Range of Poole ales are pumped directly to pub from brewery. Low-price policy (£1.26–£1.36 per pint). Seasonal Poole ales also served, plus trial brews for other independent breweries.

A welcoming pub with a varied clientele. Pool table and darts team. Pub has narrow frontage on High Street, so could easily be missed.

All day, every day.

Sandacres Free House

3 Banks Road, Sandbanks, Poole BH13 7PW
☎ *(01202) 707244* Peter Fay

Ringwood Best, Gales HSB, Ringwood Fortyniner and Greene King Abbot always available, plus two guests (in high season), from breweries such as Wadworth, Smiles and Hampshire. Tries to support small and local breweries, and micro-breweries.

A modern-style waterside pub in Poole Harbour with lovely views. One large bar, children's area, outside seating. Disabled facilities with no steps. Food served at lunchtimes and evenings. Children allowed until 9pm.

11am–3pm and 6–11pm Mon–Sat; 12–3pm and 7–10.30pm Sun.

PULHAM

Halsey Arms

Pulham, Dorchester DT2 7DZ
☎ *(01258) 817344* Mrs Dunn

A freehouse serving Ringwood Best plus weekly changing guests including bitters from breweries such as Adnams, Bath and Fuller's.

A local's pub with dining area and occasional live entertainment. Food served at lunchtime and evenings. Children allowed.

11.30am–2.30pm and 6–11pm Mon–Sat; 12–3pm and 7–10.30pm Sun.

SHERBORNE

The Digby Tap

Cooks Lane, Sherborne DT9 3NS
☎ *(01935) 813148* Peter LeFevre

Twenty different beers served each week from a range of 100 per year. Brews from the Smiles, Teignworthy, Ringwood, Exmoor, Oakhill, Otter and Cottage breweries, plus many other regional producers.

A traditional, local, one-bar pub with flagstone floors. Bar snacks available at lunchtime (not on Sundays). Children are allowed at lunchtime only. Just 100 yards from the abbey, towards the railway station.

OPEN 11am–2.30pm and 5.30–11pm Mon–Sat; 12–2.30pm and 7–10.30pm Sun.

SHROTON/IWERNE COURTNEY

The Cricketers

Shroton/Iwerne Courtney, Nr Blandford Forum DT11 8QD
☎ *(01258) 860421* Robert and Sarah Pillow

Greene King IPA and Abbot Ale and Shepherd Neame Spitfire usually available with a guest beer of the month which may include Fuller's London Pride, Timothy Taylor Landlord or many others.

Friendly pub, well-known locally for its good food. Good walking country nearby. Food served lunchtimes and evenings. Car park and roadside parking. Children welcome – playground opposite the pub. Located just off the A350 between Blandford and Shaftbury.

OPEN 11.30am–2.30pm and 7–11pm Mon–Sat; 12–3pm and 7–10.30pm Sun.

SPYWAY

The Spyway Inn

Spyway, Askerswell, Dorchester DT2 9EP
☎ *(01308) 485250*
Mr A Dodds and Mrs LS Nugent

Greene King IPA and Abbot Ale plus Branscombe Vale Branoc and an Adnams beer usually available with one other Greene King brew.

Old smugglers' lookout, situated in glorious Dorset countryside. Atmospheric bars with oak beams, high-backed settles and vast collection of china cups. Good walks from the pub. Terrace and garden. Food served 12–2pm and 7–9pm Tues–Sat; 12–2pm Sun. Large car park. Separate dining room for families.

OPEN 11am–3pm and 6–11pm Tues–Sat; 12–3pm and 7–10.30pm Sun.

STOURTON CAUNDLE

Trooper

Stourton Caundle, Stourminster Newton DT10 2JW
☎ *(01963) 362405* Mr Skeats

A freehouse. Cottage Champflower and Oakhill Bitter always available plus two monthly changing guests including perhaps Hampshire King Alfred's Bitter and Exmoor brews.

A very small pub with two bars and a countryside and rural museum. Snacks served at lunchtime. Children allowed at lunchtime only. Situated off the main road, can be difficult to find.

OPEN 12–2.30pm and 7–11pm (closed Monday lunchtimes except on bank holidays).

TARRANT MONKTON

The Langton Arms

Tarrant Monkton, Nr Blandford DT11 8RX
☎ *(01258) 830225* Barbara Cassins

A freehouse serving 30 different guest ales every month through four real ale pumps. A fifth pump permanently serves The Langton's Best, brewed by Ringwood Brewery.

An attractive seventeenth-century thatched inn with a separate restaurant (evenings only). Bar food available lunchtime and evenings. Car park, garden, children's room and play area. Accommodation. Less than two miles off the A354 Blandford to Salisbury road, five miles north of Blandford.

OPEN All day, every day.

TRENT

The Rose & Crown

Trent, Nr Sherborne DT9 4SL
☎ *(01935) 850776* Mr and Mrs Crawford

Butcombe Best and Shepherd Neame Spitfire always available plus two guest beers (24 per year) including Wadworth 6X, Charles Wells Bombardier, Otter Ale plus brews from Smiles, Hook Norton, Morland and Sam Smith.

A fifteenth-century part-thatched freehouse opposite Trent church. Bar and restaurant food available at lunchtime and evenings. Car park, garden, children's room and playground. Less than two miles north of the A30 between Sherborne and Yeovil.

OPEN 12–2.30pm and 7–11pm Mon–Sat; 12–3pm and 7–10.30pm Sun.

VERWOOD

Albion Inn

Station Road, Verwood BH31 7LB
☎ *(01202) 825267* Rex Neville

An Enterprise Inns pub, with Ringwood Best Bitter always available.

A traditional two-bar layout. Was previously a railway-owned pub. Food served at lunchtime and evenings. Children allowed.

OPEN All day, every day.

WESTBOURNE

The Porterhouse

113 Poole Road, Westbourne BH4 9BG
☎ *(01202) 768586* Ray Rutter

Ringwood Best, True Glory, Fortyniner and Old Thumper always available, plus regular guests changed every few days such as Fuller's London Pride, Everards Mild, Hop Back Summer Lightning or Hogs Back Hop Garden Gold

A traditional one-bar pub on the main road. Food served at lunchtime only. No children under 14.

OPEN All day, every day.

WEYMOUTH

King's Arms

15 Trinity Road, Weymouth DT4 8TJ
☎ *(01305) 770055* Martin Taylor

Wadworth 6X and Ringwood Best and Fortyniner always available, plus one regular guest from the Quay Brewery, perhaps Weymouth JD.

An olde-worlde quayside pub owned by Greenalls with separate dining area. Two bars, pool table. Food served every lunchtime and Wed–Sat evenings. Children allowed.

OPEN All day, every day.

The Weatherbury Freehouse

7 Carlton Road North, Weymouth DT4 7PX
☎ *(01305) 786040* Mr and Mrs Cromack

Four beers (200 per year) which may include Townes IPA, Badger Tanglefoot, Wild's Redhead and Fuller's London Pride.

A busy town local in a residential position. Bar and restaurant food available at lunchtime and evenings. Car park, patio and dining area (where children are allowed). Dart board and pool table. Accommodation. Coming in to Weymouth, turn right off the Dorchester road.

OPEN 12–11pm (10.30pm Sun).

WINKTON

The Lamb Inn

Burley Road, Winkton BH23 7AN
☎ *(01425) 672427* Mr and Mrs J Haywood

Four real ale pumps, one serving Fuller's London Pride, the others with a range of ales such as Ringwood Best Bitter.

Situated in the heart of the New Forest, this pub has a lounge and public bar. Bar and restaurant food available at lunchtime and evenings. Car park and garden. Children are allowed in the restaurant and garden.

OPEN 11am–3pm and 5–11pm Mon–Sat; 12–3pm and 7–10.30pm Sun.

WYKE REGIS

The Wyke Smugglers

76 Portland Road, Wyke Regis, Weymouth DT4 9AB
☎ *(01305) 760010* Mick Nellville

Ringwood Old Thumper always available plus two real ales served as guests which change weekly.

A local drinker's pub, sport orientated. No food. No children.

OPEN 11am–2.30pm and 6–11.30pm.

YOU TELL US

- ★ *The Queens Arms Inn*, Corton Denham, Sherborne
- ★ *The Ship*, High Street, Christchurch
- ★ *Tom Brown's*, 47 High East Street, Dorchester
- ★ *The Volunteer Inn*, 31 Broad Street, Lyme Regis

Places Featured:

Billy Row
Consett
Croxdale
Darlington
Durham
Forest in Teesdale
Framwellgate Moor
Great Lumley
Hartlepool

Kirk Merrington
Middlestone Village
Newton Aycliffe
No Place
North Bitchburn
Rookhope
Shadforth
Tantobie

THE BREWERIES

CAMERONS BREWERY CO

Lion Brewery, Hartlepool TS24 7QS
☎ *(01429) 266666*

 CREAMY BITTER 3.6% ABV
Smooth and full-flavoured.
STRONGARM 4.0% ABV
An individual brew, very smooth.

CASTLE EDEN BREWERY

Castle Eden, Hartlepool TS27 4SX
☎ *(01429) 836007 (Brewery tours)*

 BITTER 3.9% ABV
BANNER 4.0% ABV
Well-balanced and fruity.
ALE 4.2% ABV
Smooth malt with hoppy aftertaste.
CONCILIATION 4.2% ABV
Fruity with good hoppy bitterness.
NIMMO'S XXXX 4.4% ABV
*Plus Knights seasonal beers: Spring, Summer,
Autumn and Winter.*

DARWIN BREWERY,

Unit 5, Castle Close, Crook DL15 8LU
☎ *(01388) 763200*

 DARWIN BITTER 3.6% ABV
Light, refreshing and fruity. Good
hoppiness.
SIDDELEYS PURGE 3.8% ABV
Clean and hoppy with good fruitiness.
DURHAM LIGHT 4.0% ABV
Light colour with good bitter hoppiness.
EVOLUTION ALE 4.0% ABV
Good hoppiness.
HODGE'S ORIGINAL 4.0% ABV
Balanced.
PENSHAWS PINT 4.2% ABV
Balanced, malty fruit flavour. Hoppy finish.
RICHMOND ALE 4.5% ABV
Rounded and smooth.
FOUNDRY ALE 4.5% ABV
Plenty of flavours and long finish.
PROF'S PINT 4.8% ABV
Refreshing, smooth and well-balanced.
SAINTS SINNER 5.0% ABV
Dark with powerful roast flavour.
KILLER BEE 6.0% ABV
Powerful honeyed flavour.
IMPERIAL STOUT 7.0% ABV
Smooth and powerful.
EXTINCTION ALE 8.3% ABV
Smooth, fruity, lingering flavours.

THE DURHAM BREWERY

Unit 5a, Bowburn North Industrial Est.,
Bowburn DH6 5PF
☎ *(0191) 377 1991*

 FROSTBITE 3.6% ABV
Winter ale.

SUNSTROKE 3.6% ABV
Summer ale.

GREEN GODDESS 3.8% ABV
Refreshing and spicy.

MAGUS 3.8% ABV
Pale, well-hopped lager-style beer.

NEWCASTLE GOLD 3.9% ABV
Light and golden.

BLACK VELVET 4.0% ABV
A weaker version of Black Friar.

WHITE GOLD 4.0% ABV
Pale, refreshing with citrus fruit flavours.

WHITE VELVET 4.2% ABV
Light, malty smoothness with flavour of fruit.

CELTIC GOLD 4.3% ABV

MELCHIOR'S GOLD 4.5% ABV
Christmas brew.

REAL ALE 4.5% ABV

BLACK FRIAR 4.5% ABV
Smooth porter.

CANNY LAD 4.5% ABV
Complex and malty with good bitterness.

INVINCIBLE 4.5% ABV
A strong version of Magus.

WHITE SAPPHIRE 4.5% ABV
Quenching, light and easy drinking.

WHITE BISHOP 4.8% ABV
Easy drinking and fruity with lager malt.

PAGAN 4.8% ABV
Golden, with some bitterness.

CUTHBERT'S ALE 5.0% ABV
Quenching, golden and fruity.

BLACK BISHOP 5.5% ABV
Black stout with powerful roast malt flavour.

SANCTUARY 6.0% ABV
Rounded, old ale.

Plus seasonal brews.

TRIMDON CASK ALES

Unit 2c, T G Industrial Estate, Trimdon Grange
TS29 6PA
☎ *(01429) 880967*

BUSTY BITTER 4.3% ABV
TILLEY BITTER 4.3% ABV
HARVEY BITTER 4.9% ABV
PITPROP 6.2% ABV

BILLY ROW

Dun Cow Inn (Cow Tail)

Old White Lea, Billy Row, Crook
Steve Parkin

One or two Darwin beers regularly available from a changing selection which may include Richmond Ale.

Established in 1740, this pub is only open four nights a week and has a unique atmosphere. 'A bit of a good crack.' The current licensee has been here since 1960. Car park. Well-behaved children welcome.

OPEN *8–11pm Wed, Fri, Sat; 8–10.30pm Sun.*

CONSETT

The Grey Horse

115 Sherburn Terrace, Consett DH8 6NE
☎ *(01207) 502585* Mr and Mrs Conroy

Home of the Derwent Rose Brewery, with home beers brewed and always available on the premises, plus up to four other ales.

A brewpub with bar snacks available. No children.

MUTTON CLOG 3.8% ABV
Hoppy, bittersweet beer.

STEEL TOWN 3.8 % ABV
Hop flavours and bitter aftertaste.

RED DUST 4.2% ABV
Ruby coloured, with malt and fruit flavours. Bittersweet in the finish.

SWORDMAKER 4.5% ABV
Fruit and malt flavours, with bitter hop finish.

COAST 2 COAST 5.0% ABV
Balanced, hoppy bitter.

DERWENT DEEP 5.0% ABV
Deep-coloured, with roast barley flavour, and hops in the finish.

OPEN *11am–11pm Mon–Sat; 12–10.30pm Sun.*

CROXDALE

The Daleside Arms

Front Street, Croxdale, Durham DH6 5HY
☎ *(01388) 814165* Mr Patterson

A freehouse with Black Sheep Special and Mordue Workie Ticket always available. Four guest beers, which change weekly, include other favourites from Mordue, Black Sheep and Border breweries.

A village pub in a country setting, with en suite accommodation and two bars (a pub/lounge and restaurant). Food served in the evenings in the restaurant. Children allowed.

OPEN *2–11pm Mon–Fri; all day Sat–Sun.*

Number Twenty 2

Coniscliffe Road, Darlington DL3 7RG
☎ *(01325) 354590* Mr Wilkinson

Ten ales including Hambleton Nightmare, White Boar and Old Raby always available plus guests (500 per year) such as Dent Ramsbottom, Hadrian Gladiator and Butterknowle's Conciliation.

Traditional town-centre freehouse. Food available at lunchtime and evenings. Parking nearby, children allowed.

OPEN *11am–11pm.*

The Railway Tavern

8 High Northgate, Darlington DL1 1UN
☎ *(01325) 464963* Mr Greenhow

Tied to Whitbread, this pub offers Wadworth 6X and Greene King Abbot on a regular basis. Guests include beers from Durham, Black Sheep, Mordue, Northumberland and Timothy Taylor breweries.

This small local pub was probably the first railway pub in the world, since the land on which it stands is owned by the Pease family, who founded Darlington Railway. On the main road through Darlington, the pub has two bars, a pool room with darts, and features live music on Fridays and occasionally on Sunday afternoons. Bar snacks at lunchtime and evenings. Children allowed if supervised.

OPEN *12–11pm.*

The Tap & Spile

99 Bondgate, Darlington DL3 7JY
☎ *(01325) 381679* Stella Bowden

Eight guests (100 per year) at any one time continually changing with brews from Marston's, Greene King, Butterknowle, Durham, Hadrian, Hambleton, Lees, Robinson's, Adnams, Bateman, Burtonwood, Exmoor, Jennings, Hardington, Morland, Nethergate, Steam Packet, Ridleys, Titanic, Ushers, Oak, Belhaven and Harviestoun.

A traditional town-centre alehouse where the policy is to offer one beer a month at a discounted price (£1.19–£1.24), sponsored by the brewer. Food available at lunchtime. Parking, children's room and non-smoking room.

OPEN *11.30am–11pm Mon–Sat; 12–10.30pm Sun.*

Ye Old Elm Tree

12 Crossgate, Durham DH1 4PS
☎ *(0191) 386 4621* Mr Dave Cruddace

Ward's Waggle Dance and four others. Regular guests, two rotating every two weeks, may include Fuller's London Pride, Morland Old Speckled Hen or Bateman XXXB.

An alehouse dating from 1601, situated in the centre of Durham city, off Framwellgate Bridge. Two guest rooms, beer garden and patio. The bar is built round an elm tree. Quiz and folk nights held. Light snacks at lunchtime and evenings. Children allowed.

OPEN *12–3pm and 6–11pm Mon–Fri; 11am–11pm Sat; 12–4pm and 7–10.30pm Sun.*

The High Force Hotel

Forest in Teesdale DL12 0XH
☎ *(01833) 622222* Gary Wilson

Home of the High Force brewery with three own brews always available.

A country hotel, which is easy to find, serving food at lunchtime and evenings. Children allowed.

TEESDALE BITTER 3.8% ABV
FOREST XB 4.2% ABV
CAULDRON SNOUT 5.6% ABV

OPEN *11am–11pm Mon–Sat; 12–10.30pm Sun. Opening hours subject to seasonal variation.*

Tap & Spile

27 Front Street, Framwellgate Moor, Durham DH1 5EE
☎ *(0191) 386 5451* Jean McPoland

Up to nine beers available. Marston's Pedigree and Fuller's London Pride are usually among them.

A traditional pub with a family room, non-smoking room, and games room for darts and billiards. Pet-friendly. Snacks served all day. Children allowed. Two miles north of Durham city centre, on the old A1.

OPEN *11.30am–3pm and 6–11pm Mon–Sat; 12–3pm and 7–10.30pm Sun.*

The Old England

*Front Street, Great Lumley, Nr Chester le Street
DL3 4JB*
☎ *(0191) 388 5257* Mr Barkess

Three or four different ales a week are available in this freehouse, with a good mix of nationals and micro-breweries from all over the country. Regular guests include Hop Back Summer Lightning and brews from Caledonian and Wychwood.

A pub/restaurant set off the road, with a 200-seat lounge, 150-seat bar, separate dining area, darts, dominoes, pool. Food served mostly during evenings, lunchtime at weekends. Children allowed in dining area.

11am–11pm Mon–Sat; 12–10.30pm Sun.

Tavern

56 Church Street, Hartlepool TS24 7DX
☎ *(01429) 222400* Chris Sewell

Camerons Strongarm and three guest beers regularly available such as Orkney Dark Island or something from the Jennings range.

Traditional town-centre one-bar pub with upstairs, open-plan dining area. Home-cooked food served 11am–2pm and 5–8pm Mon–Sat, 12–4pm Sun. Children welcome until 8pm and they eat half price. Situated close to the railway station.

11am–3pm and 5–11pm Mon–Fri; 11am–11pm Sat; 12–3pm and 7–10.30pm Sun.

The Half Moon Inn

Crowther Place, Kirk Merrington, Nr Spennymoor DL16 7JL
☎ *(01388) 811598* Mrs Crooks

Something from Durham Brewery always available in this freehouse. Favourite guest beers might come from the Kitchen Brewery, or include Elgood's Black Dog and Hart's Squirrels Hoards. Anything and everything has been tried.

A traditional pub on the village green, with one room, games area and car park. Bar meals at lunchtime and evening. Children allowed up to 8pm.

All day, every day.

The Ship Inn

Low Row, Middlestone Village, Bishop Auckland DL14 8AB
☎ *(01388) 810904* Mr Freeman

A freehouse with three real ales always available. Ales from local breweries, such as Castle Eden's Nimmo are popular.

A well-appointed traditional pub with a small bar and lounge. Built into the hillside in walking country and offers panoramic views. Restaurant on first-floor balcony doubles as a function room. Food served from 5.30–9.30pm, and Saturday and Sunday lunchtimes. Children allowed if parents are eating.

5–11pm Mon–Fri; 12–3pm and 5–11pm Sat; 12–3pm and 7–10.30pm Sun.

The Blacksmith's Arms

Preston-le-Skerne, Newton Aycliffe DL5 6JH
☎ *(01325) 314873* Pat Cook

Three local beers are rotated each week (100 per year). Favourites come from Hambleton, Barnsley and a range of micro-brewers.

A country pub in the middle of farmland, in an isolated position two miles from Newton Aycliffe. Two bars, a one-acre beer garden, rabbits and a plant nursery. Ice creams served. Food available at lunchtime and evenings, outdoors in summer. Children allowed.

All day, every day in summer. 12–3pm and 6.30–11pm in winter.

Beamish Mary Inn

No Place, Nr Stanley DH9 0QH
☎ *(0191) 370 0237* Graham Ford

Black Sheep Special and Bitter and Jennings Cumberland Ale always available, plus three guests often including No Place, a beer brewed specially by Big Lamp Brewery. Others come from Border and other small local breweries.

Over 100 years old, this pub is a throwback from the Beamish Museum housing many interesting artefacts. Live music four nights a week in the converted stables of the old barn. Food served 12–2pm and 7–9.30pm in a separate restaurant area. B&B. Children allowed.

12–3pm and 6–11pm Mon–Thurs; all day Fri–Sun.

NORTH BITCHBURN

Famous Red Lion
*North Bitchburn Terrace, Barnard Castle
DL15 8AL*
☎ *(01388) 763561* Mr Kyte

A freehouse with Black Sheep Special, Marston's Pedigree and Greene King Abbot always available. There is also a guest beer; Morland Old Speckled Hen is a favourite, but many others also served.

An easy-to-find, typical, olde-worlde inn with one bar and a small patio. Food served at lunchtime and evenings. Separate dining room. Children allowed.

11am–11pm Mon–Sat; 12–10.30pm Sun.

ROOKHOPE

The Rookhope Inn
Rookhope, Nr Stanhope DL13 2BG
☎ *(01388) 517215* Stephen Thompson

A freehouse offering a constantly changing choice of beers. A Hexhamshire and a Hadrian (Four Rivers) brew are always available, with Four Rivers Moondance and Hexhamshire Devil's Water particularly popular. Also Butterknowle Conciliation and Fuller's London Pride. No nationals; other guests are sourced as special offers through wholesalers or direct from small breweries.

A seventeenth-century pub with open fires and real beams. Three rooms (games/lounge/restaurant). Prior booking required for restaurant; soup and sandwiches served in bar and lounge. Children allowed in games room and restaurant.

7–11pm daily; 12–3pm Sat–Sun (and weekdays by arrangement).

SHADFORTH

The Plough Inn
South Side, Shadforth, Durham DH6 1LL
☎ *(0191) 372 0375* Jane Barber

A freehouse with a varied and ever-changing range of beers, which change once or twice a week. Regular guests, which now number in the hundreds, come mainly from independents and micro-breweries. You name it, they've probably served it.

A small, traditional country pub, with one bar and lounge. No food. Children allowed.

6.30–11pm Mon–Fri; 11am–11pm Sat; 12–10.30pm Sun.

TANTOBIE

The Highlander
White-le-Head, Tantobie, Nr Stanley DH9 9SN
☎ *(01207) 232416* Mr CD Wright

Up to 100 beers per year changed weekly including something from Thwaites, Timothy Taylor, Black Sheep and Marston's, plus beers from many other smaller breweries as available.

One bar has games and music (pool, darts, etc). Also a small lounge and dining area. Hot food available on weekday evenings and weekend afternoons. Car park, beer garden, children's room and function room. Occasional accommodation. Ring to check. One mile off the A692 between Tantobie and Flint Hill.

7.30–11pm Mon–Fri; 12.30–3pm and 7.30–11pm Sat–Sun.

YOU TELL US

★ *Dun Cow*, 43 Front Street, Sedgefield
★ *The Malt Shovel*, Lower Wharn, Bishop Auckland
★ *Tap & Spile*, 13 Cockton Hill Road, Bishop Auckland
★ *Traders*, Blue Post Yard, Stockton-on-Tees

Places Featured:

Basildon
Billericay
Birdbrook
Black Notely
Brentwood
Brightlingsea
Burnham-on-Crouch
Chelmsford
Colchester
Coxtie Green
Epping
Feering
Fyfield
Gestingthorpe
Hatfield Broad Oak
Herongate Tye
Horndon on the Hill
Hutton
Leigh-on-Sea
Little Clacton
Little Oakley
Littlebury
Maldon
Manningtree

Mill Green
Moreton
Navestock Heath
Orsett
Pebmarsh
Pleshey
Quendon
Radwinter
Ridgewell
Rochford
South Fambridge
Southend-on-Sea
Southminster
Stanford Rivers
Stock
Stow Maries
Tendring
Thornwood Common
Tillingham
Toot Hill
Wendens Ambo
Witham
Woodham Ferrers
Woodham Water

THE BREWERIES

CROUCH VALE BREWERY LTD

12 Redhills Road, South Woodham Ferrers,
Chelmsford CM3 5UP
☎ *(01245) 322744*

 BEST DARK ALE 3.6% ABV
Easy-drinking mild.
WOODHAM IPA 3.6% ABV
Golden, with hoppy, fruity finish.
BEST BITTER 4.0% ABV
Malt and fruit, some hops. Bitter finish.
MILLENNIUM GOLD 4.2% ABV
Sharp fruit and hops. Malty bitter
ESSEX PORTER 4.9% ABV
Rounded, roast barley flavour.
STRONG ANGLIAN SPECIAL 5.0% ABV
Tawny. Clean-tasting bitter with dry aftertaste.
FINE PALE ALE 5.9% ABV
Occasional, dangerously drinkable, pale beer.
WILLIE WARMER 6.4% ABV
Winter only, barley wine.
Plus occasional brews.

MIGHTY OAK BREWING CO.

9 Prospect Way, Hutton Industrial Estate,
Brentwood CM13 1XA
☎ *(01277) 263007*

 BARRACKWOOD IPA 3.6% ABV
Occasional. Light amber. Good hoppy
bitterness.
OSCAR WILDE 3.7% ABV
Mellow and nutty dark mild. Seasonal.
RUBY TUESDAY 3.9% ABV
Chocolate flavour with ruby hue and bitter finish.
BURNTWOOD BITTER 4.0% ABV
Copper-coloured, deep hops and rounded malt.
BRASS MONKEY 4.1% ABV
Excellent session beer. Brewed Nov–Mar.
ALE DANCER 4.2% ABV
Smooth and mellow. Brewed April–June.
MILLENNIUM RINGER 4.2% ABV
Complex combination of malt and hop flavours.
SAFFRON GOLD 4.3% ABV
Clean, refreshing bitterness. Brewed July–Oct.
SIMPLY THE BEST 4.4% ABV
Clean and fragrant with distinctive bitterness.
ESSEX COUNTY ALE 4.6% ABV
Good hoppy bitterness and balancing malt.
BITTER 4.8% ABV
Full-flavoured and well-rounded.
TWENTY THIRST CENTURY ALE 5.5% ABV
Burnished gold colour with powerful bitterness.
Plus monthly special brews.

TD RIDLEY AND SONS LTD
Hartford End Brewery, Chelmsford CM3 1JZ
☎ *(01371) 820316*

IPA 3.5% ABV
Flavour of hops, with some malt.
MILD 3.5% ABV
Dark-coloured, with a fruity and rich malty flavour.
ESX BEST 4.3% ABV
Strong, well-hopped flavour.
WITCHFINDER PORTER 4.3% ABV
Based on traditional porter recipe.
SPECTACULAR 4.6% ABV
Very light-coloured, easy-quaffing ale.
RUMPUS 4.5% ABV
Ruby, with smooth nutty character.
SANTA'S SECRET 4.8% ABV
Dark, full-bodied, fruity bitter.
Plus monthly specials and occasional brews.

BASILDON

Moon on the Square
1–15 Market Square, Basildon SS14 1DF
☎ *(01268) 520360* Ian and Carol Durham

A Wetherspoon's pub. Eight guests, changed weekly, from a list that includes Shepherd Neame Spitfire, Adnams Clipper, Arundel Old Knuckler, Eldridge Pope's Royal Oak, Spinnaker and Hop Back brews amongst other independents.

A busy market pub with one large bar. A mixed clientele of business customers and lunchtime shoppers. Food served all day. No children.

OPEN *10am–11pm Mon–Sat; 12–10.30pm Sun.*

BILLERICAY

The Coach & Horses
36 Chapel Street, Billericay CM12 9LU
☎ *(01277) 622873* Mr J Childs

Greene King IPA and Abbot always available, plus two guest beers, one of which is changed each week, the other every fortnight. Guests include Ushers St George and the Dragon and Greene King Triumph. Tries to stock independent breweries' beers whenever possible.

A town pub with one bar. Friendly locals but clientele tend to be business lunchers during the day, regulars in the evening. Food available Mon–Sat lunchtime. Beer garden. No children. Next to Waitrose.

OPEN *All day Mon–Sat; 12–3.30pm and 7–10.30pm Sun.*

BIRDBROOK

The Plough
The Street, Birdbrook CO9 4BJ
☎ *(01440) 785336* Stuart Walton

Fuller's London Pride, Adnams Best and Greene King IPA always available, plus two rotating guests changing weekly. These might include Morland Old Speckled Hen and Adnams Broadside plus beers from smaller breweries such as Mighty Oak when possible.

A sixteenth-century thatched freehouse with a very low beamed ceiling. Two interlinking bars, safe beer garden. Food served every lunchtime and evening except Sunday evenings. Children allowed. Follow signs to Birdbrook from A1017.

OPEN *11.30am–3pm and 6–11pm (10.30pm Sun).*

The Vine Inn

105 The Street, Black Notely, Nr Braintree CM7 8LJ
☎ *(01376) 324269* Arthur Hodges

One Adnams brew and Ridleys IPA always available plus three guests changed three or four times a week. Of 192 beers served last year, regulars included Kelham Island Pale Rider and Nethergate Old Growler and Augustinian.

A country freehouse dating from 1640 with an old barn end, stone floor and a minstrel's gallery which is used as a small restaurant and for beer festivals. Food served at lunchtime and evenings. Children allowed. A couple of mile outside Braintree on the Notely Road

12–2pm and 6.30–11pm Mon–Fri; all day Sat–Sun.

The Swan

123 High Street, Brentwood CM14 4RX
☎ *(01277) 211848* Nick Parade

Young's Special, Fuller's London Pride, Mighty Oak Burntwood Bitter, Shepherd Neame Spitfire, Wadworth 6X, Gales HSB and Greene King Abbot always available, plus four weekly changing guests such as Adnams Best, Shepherd Neame or Bateman brews

A thirteenth-century pub with a friendly atmosphere. Mainly a locals' pub with quiet background music. Food served 12–9pm. No children.

All day, every day.

The Famous Railway Tavern

58 Station Road, Brightlingsea CO7 0DT
☎ *(01206) 302581* David English

Crouch Vale Best, a dark mild and a real cider always available, plus up to five guests from local breweries such as Tolly Cobbold amongst others. Gravity-fed in winter.

A friendly, traditional pub with real fire and floorboards. No fruit machines or juke box in the public bar. Garden, children's room. Table football, shove ha'penny, darts, cribbage, dominoes. Campsite opposite, 11 pubs within walking distance. Buskers' afternoon held once a month between October and April.

🛢 **CRAB & WINKLE MILD 3.7% ABV**
🛢 **STRONGER EEL ALE 5.0% ABV**
Seasonal. Other seasonals planned.

5–11pm Mon–Thurs; 3–11pm Fri; 12–11pm Sat; 12–3pm and 7–10.30pm Sun.

The Anchor Hotel

The Quay, Burnham-on-Crouch CM0 8AT
☎ *(01621) 782117* Mr Veal

Greene King IPA and Adnams and Crouch Vale brews usually available, plus three guests from breweries such as Titanic or Ridleys. Seasonal ales also stocked.

A locals' pub with a broad clientele in a small seaside town with seating on the sea wall. Two bars, dining area. Food available at lunchtime and evenings. Children allowed.

All day, every day.

The Queen's Head

30 Lower Anchor Street, Chelmsford CM2 0AS
☎ *(01245) 265181* Mike Collins

One of two local Crouch Vale-owned houses. Crouch Vale Best and seasonal ales always available, plus guests (300 a year), always including a mild, stout or porter. Guests come from a range of independent breweries such as Elgood's Buffy's, RCH, Titanic and Green Jack.

A traditional alehouse a mile from the cricket ground. Built in 1895 but totally refurbished – one bar with real fires, courtyard and beer garden. Pub games, no music. Food available Mon–Sat lunchtimes only, with home-made pies and locally produced beer sausages a speciality. No children.

11am–3pm and 5.30–11pm Mon–Thurs; all day Fri–Sun.

The White Horse

25 Townfield Road, Chelmsford CM1 1QT
☎ *(01245) 269556* John Stewart (Manager)

Up to nine cask-conditioned ales served at this pub managed by Wessex Taverns. Morland Old Speckled Hen, Marston's Pedigree, Young's Bitter and Special, Greene King IPA and Wadworth 6X usually available, plus guests.

Large comfortable one-bar pub with a plethora of traditional pub games. Bar food available at lunchtime and evenings. Specialises in gourmet sausages cooked over a griddle. Turn right from the rear of the railway station.

All day, every day.

Odd One Out
28 Mersea Road, Colchester CO2 7ET
☎ *(01206) 578140* John Parrick

Tolly Original, Archers Best and a dark ale always available plus up to four guest beers which may include Nethergate Bitter, Tolly Mild, Mauldons Moletrap, Crouch Vale SAS, Swale Kentish Pride. Also up to three traditional ciders.

Friendly pub about 100 yards up the Mersea Road from St Botolph's roundabout. A traditional drinker's alehouse with garden. Also has a good range of whiskies.

OPEN *4.30–11pm Mon–Thurs; 11am–11pm Fri–Sat; 12–10.30pm Sun.*

The Tap & Spile
123 Crouch Street, Colchester CO3 3HA
☎ *(01206) 573572* Mr and Mrs Mathieson

Adnams Bitter, Marston's Pedigree and Nethergate Bitter always available plus up to five others including Morland Old Speckled Hen, Greene King Abbot Ale, Charles Wells Bombardier, Shepherd Neame ales, Thwaites Mild, Ushers Founders Ale, Everards Tiger, Black Sheep Best and many more.

Traditional English alehouse with no carpets, video machines or juke box. Soft background music. Bar food served at lunchtime. Outside patio. Children allowed. Just outside the town centre, opposite the Essex County Hospital, on Lexden Road.

OPEN *11am–2.30pm and 5.30–11pm Mon–Fri; all day Sat; 12–3pm and 7–10.30pm Sun.*

The White Horse
173 Coxtie Green Road, Coxtie Green, Brentwood CM14 5PX
☎ *(01277) 372410* Mr Hastings

Ridleys Rumpus, Fuller's London Pride and Adnams Bitter always available, plus three rotating guests such as Wolf Brewery's Coyote, Hop Back Summer Lightning, Timothy Taylor Landlord or Crouch Vale, Ash Vine or Mighty Oak brews. Over 100 guest beers served every year. Beer festival held each July with 30–40 real ales.

A semi-rural pub, with public bar and lounge. Darts, large garden. Barbecues in summer, some children's facilities in the garden. Food served at lunchtime Mon–Sat and evenings Thurs–Sat. Children allowed. Situated off the A128 towards Ongar.

OPEN *All day, every day.*

The Moletrap
Tawney Common, Epping CM16 7PU
☎ *(01992) 522394* Mr and Mrs Kirtley

A freehouse with Fuller's London Pride always available plus ever-changing guests from all over the country with the emphasis on independent and micro-breweries.

A 250-year-old listed building which has recently been enlarged. Outside seating. Food served at lunchtime and evenings. Children allowed. Down a rural country lane, but five minutes from Epping.

OPEN *Winter: 12–3pm and 7–11pm. Summer: 11.30am–3pm and 6–11pm.*

The Sun Inn
3 Feering Hill, Feering, Nr Kelvedon CO5 9NH
☎ *(01376) 570442* Mr and Mrs Scicluna

Five ever-changing beers (up to 20 per week). The emphasis is firmly on the more unusual micro-breweries.

A heavily timbered former mansion, richly decorated with carved beams and open fires. Bar and restaurant food is available at lunchtime and evenings. Car park and garden. Two beer festivals every year – Easter and August bank holiday. Small functions (up to 28 persons) catered for. Turn off the Kelveden bypass when coming from the north or south.

OPEN *11am–3pm and 6–11pm Mon–Sat; 12–3pm and 7–10.30pm Sun.*

The Queen's Head
Queen Street, Fyfield, Ongar CM5 0RY
☎ *(01277) 899231* Nick Thain

Badger Best, Adnams Best and Broadside available plus three constantly changing guests from a range of independent and micro-breweries.

A friendly freehouse, reputed to be 500 years old and run by the same family for 25 years. Food served at lunchtime and evenings (not Sat evening). Children allowed.

OPEN *11am–3pm and 6–11pm; all day Sat; 12–3pm and 7–10.30pm Sun.*

GESTINGTHORPE

The Pheasant

Audley End, Gestingthorpe CO9 3AX
☎ *(01787) 461196*

Greene King IPA, Adnams Best and Broadside always available with a guest beer in summer.

This recently refurbished multi-roomed, 400-year-old freehouse has exposed timbers, open fires and a warm friendly atmosphere. There are three bars, including a dining area. Food is available at lunchtime and evenings, except Sunday and Monday. Car park, garden. Children allowed. Well signposted, the only pub in the village.

12–3pm and 6–11pm Mon–Sat; 7–10.30pm Sun.

HATFIELD BROAD OAK

The Cock Inn

High Street, Hatfield Broad Oak CM22 7HF
☎ *(01279) 718273*
Miss Holcroft and Mr Sulway

Adnams Best and Fuller's London Pride always available, plus four guests changing twice-weekly. Independent brews always included.

A traditional country freehouse with open fires, non-smoking area, private function room, car park, disabled access and outside seating. Food served at lunchtime and evenings. Children allowed.

12–2.30pm and 6–11pm Mon–Sat; all day most Sundays.

HERONGATE TYE

The Old Dog Inn

Billericay Road, Herongate Tye, Brentwood CM13 3SD
☎ *(01277) 810337* Sheila Murphy

Ridleys IPA and Rumpus plus something from Mauldons, Nethergate, Adnams and Crouch Vale. Also two or three regularly changing guests, such as Fuller's London Pride or Shepherd Neame Spitfire.

A sixteenth-century family-owned and -run Essex weatherboard pub. One bar, garden, background music only. Food served at lunchtime and evenings in a separate dining area. Children allowed. Located off the A128 Brentwood/Tilbury Road.

11am–3pm and 6–11pm (10.30pm Sun).

HORNDON ON THE HILL

The Bell Inn

High Road, Horndon On The Hill SS17 8LD
☎ *(01375) 642463* John Vereker

Green King IPA usually available, with regularly changing guest beers such as Hop Back Summer Lightning, Crouch Vale Millennium Gold and SAS, Young's Special, Shepherd Neame Spitfire, Slaters Top Totty and Mighty Oak Burntwood.

Attractive 400-year-old village inn. Courtyard filled with hanging baskets in summer. Award-winning restaurant and bar food available lunchtimes and evenings (except bank holiday Mondays). Car park. Children welcome in the restaurant and bar eating area.

11am–2.30pm and 5.30–11pm Mon–Fri; 11am–3pm and 6–11pm Sat; 12–4pm and 7–10.30pm Sun.

HUTTON

Chequers

213 Rayleigh Road, Hutton, Brentwood CM13 1PJ
☎ *(01277) 224980* Peter Waters

Greene King IPA always available plus a range of guest ales served on one pump. Tends towards the lighter brews.

A seventeenth-century coaching house. Two cosy bars, beer garden, main road location. Bar snacks available at lunchtime. Children allowed. Situated on the main road A129.

All day, every day.

LEIGH-ON-SEA

The Broker Free House

213–17 Leigh Road, Leigh-on-Sea SS9 1JA
☎ *(01702) 471932* Alan Gloyne

Shepherd Neame Spitfire and Tolly Original always available, plus two guests which regularly include Fuller's London Pride, Young's Bitter and beers from Mighty Oak, Wherry, Harveys, Mansfield, Bateman and Cottage breweries. Often serves 14 different beers over 10 days.

A family-run, welcoming freehouse, catering for 18–96 year olds! One big bar, beer garden, children's licence and dedicated children's area. Sunday night is live music or quiz night. Food served at lunchtime and evenings (not Sundays). Children allowed. Website: www.brokerfreehouse.co.uk

11am–3pm and 6–11pm (opens 5.30pm Sat).

The Elms

1060 London Road, Leigh-on-Sea SS9 3ND
☎ *(01702) 474687*
Theo and Leanne Korakianitis

Shepherd Neame Spitfire available, plus more than 100 guests every year such as Ringwood Old Thumper and Exmoor Beast. Twice-yearly beer festival.

A Wetherspoon's pub. Modern bar with an old-looking exterior. Outside seating. Non-smoking area. Food served 11am–10pm. No children.

All day, every day.

The Apple Tree

The Street, Little Clacton CO16 9LS
☎ *(01255) 861026* Mrs Clarke

Charles Wells IPA always available plus three others (60+ per year) including Nethergate Old Growler, Morland Old Speckled Hen, Wadworth 6X, Adnams Broadside, Hook Norton Old Hooky, Brakspear Special, Everards Tiger and Gales HSB.

A well-run family pub with live entertainment every Saturday. Bar and restaurant food available at lunchtime and evenings. Car park and garden. Children allowed in the restaurant. Follow the 'old' road into Clacton (i.e. not the bypass).

11am–11pm Mon–Fri; 11am–midnight Sat; 12–3pm and 7–10.30pm Sun.

Ye Olde Cherry Tree Inn

Clacton Road, Little Oakley, Harwich CO12 5JH
☎ *(01255) 880333* Steve and Julie Chandler

Adnams Best and Broadside, Charles Wells Eagle IPA and Fuller's London Pride always available, plus one rotating guest changing weekly.

A traditional country pub, recently refurbished, with traditional pub games. One bar, beer garden and children's play area. Friendly, family atmosphere, overlooking the sea. Food served at lunchtime and evenings. A la carte restaurant open Thursday, Friday and Saturday evenings. Cask Marque winner. Children allowed.

11am–2.30pm and 5–11pm Mon–Fri; all day (subject to trade) Sat–Sun.

The Queen's Head

High Street, Littlebury, Nr Saffron Walden CB11 4TD
☎ *(01799) 522251* Mr and Mrs Collins

A Greene King tied house with IPA and Abbot permanently available, plus two seasonal Greene King ales alternating on a guest basis.

A sixteenth-century coaching inn with exposed beams, a snug and two open fires. Bar and restaurant food available at lunchtime and evenings. Non-smoking area, car park, garden. Accommodation. Children allowed. On the B1383, between Newport and junction 9 of the M11.

12–11pm (10.30pm Sun).

The White Horse

26 High Street, Maldon CM9 5PJ
☎ *(01621) 851708* Mr RJ Wood

A Shepherd Neame tied house. So, Bishop's Finger, Spitfire, Master Brew X, Master Brew XX always available plus one rotating guest.

A typical high-street pub with pub grub served at lunchtime. Children allowed.

All day, every day.

Manningtree Station Buffet

Station Road, Lawford, Manningtree CO11 2LH
☎ *(01206) 391114* Richard and Debbie Rowley

Adnams Best, Shepherd Neame Spitfire plus one Crouch Vale beer and one Fuller's beer always available.

A station buffet, built in 1846. Food served all day in a 24-seater restaurant. Restaurant menu in evenings, pies and breakfast until 2.30pm. Children allowed.

5.30am–11pm Mon–Fri; 7am–11pm Sat; 8am–3pm Sun.

The Viper

Mill Green Road, Mill Green, Nr Ingatestone CM4 0PT
☎ *(01277) 352010* Mr FW and Mr RDM Beard

Four real ales always available which will include Ridleys IPA, one from Mighty Oak Brewery and one other from around the country, changed weekly. A mild or stout is always available.

A small, traditional, unspoilt country pub with award-winning garden. Bar food available at lunchtime. Car park. Children allowed in garden only. Take the Ivy Barn road off the A12. Turn off at Margaretting. Two miles north-west of Ingatestone.

12–3pm and 6–11pm Mon–Sat; 12–3pm and 7–10.30pm Sun.

MORETON

The Nag's Head

Church Road, Moreton, Nr Ongar CM5 0LF
☎ *(01277) 890239* Richard Keep

Adnams Best and Fuller's London Pride always available plus one rotating guest, perhaps Greene King Abbot, Morland Old Speckled Hen or a Young's brew.

A country freehouse with B&B. Food served at lunchtimes and evenings in a separate dining area. Children allowed.

11.30am–3pm and 6–11pm Mon–Fri; all day Sat–Sun.

NAVESTOCK HEATH

The Plough Inn

Sabines Road, Navestock Heath RM4 1HD
☎ *(01277) 372296*

Marston's Pedigree and Fuller's London Pride among the beers always available in a varied selection of eight real ales (100+ per year) chosen from all across the land.

A one-bar public house with a small dining room and family room. Background music, no juke box, machines or pool table. Bar snacks and meals are available at lunchtime and evenings (except Sunday and Monday). Car park, two gardens, children allowed. The pub is difficult to find, so ring for directions.

11am–11pm Mon–Sat; 12–10.30pm Sun.

ORSETT

The Foxhound

High Road, Orsett RM16 3ER
☎ *(01375) 891295* Jackie Firman

Although this is a tied house, one pump offers a regularly changing guest beer, perhaps from Elgood's, Fuller's, O'Hanlon's, Everards, Charles Wells, York, Millennium, Hampshire, Phoenix or Shepherd Neame, among others.

Traditional, two-bar country pub with local pictures and memorabilia covering the walls. Saloon lounge bar with open fire and 'tree'. Bar and restaurant food available every lunchtime and Saturday evenings. Traditional roasts on Sundays. Darts and pub games in public bar. Dogs welcome. Patio. Large car park. Well-behaved children welcome in the restaurant.

11am–3.30pm and 6–11pm Mon–Fri; 11am–11pm Sat; 12–3.30pm and 7–10.30pm Sun.

PEBMARSH

The King's Head

The Street, Pebmarsh, Nr Halstead CO9 2NH
☎ *(01787) 269306* Ian Miller

Greene King IPA always available plus three guest beers including Timothy Taylor Landlord, Fuller's London Pride, Woodforde's, Mauldons, Ridleys, Enville and Rooster's brews.

An oak-beamed freehouse built in 1740. Bar snacks and meals available at lunchtime and evenings. Barbecues in season. Car park, garden, barn with skittle alley, children's room. One mile off the Halstead to Sudbury road.

12–2pm and 7–11pm.

PLESHEY

The White Horse

The Street, Pleshey, Chelmsford CM3 1HA
☎ *(01245) 237281* John Thorburn

Nethergate Umbel Ale, Tolly Original, Crouch Vale Millennium Gold, Mighty Oak Burntwood and Barrackwood IPA plus Ridleys IPA regularly available, plus other guests from breweries such as Cottage and Elgood's. No national beers served.

A village pub in very picturesque historic village. One bar and two eating areas, large garden, play area, car park. Food served at lunchtime and evenings during the week and all day at weekends. Children allowed.

11am–3pm and 7–11pm Mon–Fri; all day Sat–Sun.

QUENDON

The Cricketer's Arms

Rickling Green, Quendon, Saffron Walden CB11 3YG
☎ *(01799) 543210* Tim Proctor

A freehouse. with three guest ales always available from a list including Adnams Extra, Fuller's ESB, one best bitter and one dark mild. The focus is on stronger brews. Also a selection of Belgian beers.

A heavily timbered building dating from 1590, ten en-suite bedrooms, three dining rooms (one non-smoking). Food served daily at lunchtime and evenings. Children not allowed in the main bar area. Facing the cricket green, just off the B1383 at Quendon. Visit our website at: www.cricketers.demon.co.uk

All day, every day.

The Plough Inn

Radwinter, Nr Saffron Walden CB10 2TL
☎ *(01799) 599222* Tony Birdfield

A freehouse with Adnams Best and Greene King IPA always available, plus two or three rotating guests such as Oakhill Mendip Gold, Jennings Cumberland Ale, Shepherd Neame Spitfire, Timothy Taylor Landlord, Nethergate Golden Gate and Hop Back Summer Lightning.

A seventeenth-century country freehouse with heavy emphasis on food and accommodation. Non-smoking area in the restaurant. Food available at lunchtime and evenings. Children and dogs welcome. From the junction of B1053 and B1054, four miles east of Saffron Walden.

12–3pm and 6.30–11pm (10.30pm Sun).

The White Horse

Mill Road, Ridgewell CO9 4SG
☎ *(01440) 785532* Robin Briggs

A freehouse serving a constantly changing range of real ales, which may include Ridleys IPA, Fuller's London Pride or brews from Shepherd Neame, Belhaven, Cottage or other smaller breweries.

A rural village pub with games room, pool table and darts. Single bar covered in old pennies (4,200 in all). Large restaurant, beer garden and car park. Food served at lunchtime and evenings. Children allowed. Located on the old A604 between Halstead and Haverhill.

11am–3pm and 6–11pm (10.30pm Sun).

The Golden Lion

35 North Street, Rochford SS4 1AB
☎ *(01702) 545487* Sue Williams

Greene King Abbot Ale and Fuller's London Pride always available, plus three or four guests ales which constantly change. Emphasis on unusual brews from smaller breweries.

A sixteenth-century traditional-style freehouse with one bar with beams and brasses and a small beer garden. Regular live music and quiz nights. Bar snacks served at lunchtime. Well-behaved children and dogs welcome.

12–11pm.

The Anchor Hotel

Fambridge Road, South Fambridge, Rochford SS4 3LY
☎ *(01702) 203535* Mr Cracknell

Greene King Abbot is one of two beers always available, plus two rotating guests such as Shepherd Neame Bishops Finger, Smiles Heritage, Ringwood Fortyniner, Morland Old Speckled Hen, Crouch Vale SAS or Young's Special.

A traditional country freehouse with two bars and a restaurant. Four minutes' walk from the sea wall of River Crouch. Good views. Food available at lunchtime and evenings. Children allowed.

11am–3pm and 6–11pm.

Cork & Cheese

10 Talza Way, Victoria Plaza, Southend-on-Sea SS2 5BG
☎ *(01702) 616914* John Murray

Nethergate Best always available plus three guests (250 per year) including brews from Concertina, Butterknowle, Rooster's, Woodforde's, Titanic, Hop Back, Wild's and Clark's.

An alehouse with a cosmopolitan trade. Separate dining area for bar and restaurant meals. Food available at lunchtime. Multi-storey car park nearby. Patio in summer. Children allowed in the restaurant. Located on the basement floor of the Victoria Circus shopping centre in Southend.

11am–11pm Mon–Sat; closed Sun.

Last Post

5 Weston Road, Southend-on-Sea SS1 1BZ
☎ *(01702) 431682* Neil Sanderson

Ridleys IPA always available, plus up to five daily-changing guests such as Morland Old Speckled Hen or Hop Back Summer Lightning. Anything and everything from brewers of real ale considered.

A busy two-bar operation with disabled access and toilets. No music, a real drinker's pub. Two non-smoking areas. Food served all day every day. No children. Opposite the railway station.

10am–11pm.

SOUTHMINSTER

The Station Arms

39 Station Road, Southminster CM0 7EW
☎ *(01621) 772225* Martin Park

Crouch Vale Best and Fuller's London Pride always available, plus three guest beers from a range of small indpendent brewers.

A welcoming, one-bar, Essex weatherboard pub with open fire and traditional pub furniture. 1997–98 CAMRA East Anglia Pub of the Year. Pub games played. Restaurant and courtyard to the rear. Bar and restaurant food served Mon–Thurs evenings only. Street parking. Children allowed in the restaurant. Three beer festivals held each year, with 30 real ales at each. Just 200 yards from Southminster railway station.

OPEN *12–2.30pm and 6–11pm Mon–Fri; 12–11pm Sat; 12–4pm and 7–10.30pm Sun.*

STANFORD RIVERS

The Woodman

155 London Road, Stanford Rivers, Ongar
☎ *(01277) 362019* Peter Benefield

Shepherd Neame Master Brew, Spitfire and Bishop's Finger regularly available.

Wooden-clad, fourteenth-century inn set in three acres. Food served all day. Car park. Children's play area.

OPEN *11am–11pm Mon–Sat; 12–10.30pm Sun.*

STOCK

The Hoop

21 High Street, Stock CM4 9BD
☎ *(01277) 841137* Albert and David Kitchen

Up to ten beers available. Brews from Adnams, Crouch Vale, Wadworth and Charles Wells always served. Guests from Bateman, Archers, Ringwood, Hop Back, Jennings, Exmoor, Fuller's, Marston's, Nethergate, Rooster's and Shepherd Neame.

The pub has been adapted from some late fifteenth-century beamed cottages. There is an extensive beer garden to the rear. Bar food available all day. Barbecues at weekends in summer, weather permitting. Parking. Children not allowed. Take the B1007 from the A12 Chelmsford bypass, then take the Galleywood-Billericay turn off.

OPEN *11am–11pm.*

STOW MARIES

The Prince of Wales

Woodham Road, Stow Maries CM3 6SA
☎ *(01621) 828971* Robert Walster

Fuller's Chiswick always available plus any four guests (too many to count) including a mild and a stout/porter from small independent and the better regional brewers.

A traditional Essex weatherboard pub with real fires and Victorian bakehouse. Bar food available at lunchtime and evenings. Car park, garden and family room. Under two miles from South Woodham Ferrers on the road to Cold Norton.

OPEN *11am–11pm Mon–Sat; 12–10.30pm Sun.*

TENDRING

The Cherry Tree

Crow Lane, Tendring CO16 9AP
☎ *(01255) 830340* Mr Whitnell

Greene King IPA, Abbot and Adnams Best always avaiable, plus a regularly changing guest.

An olde-worlde pub and restaurant. One bar, big garden. Food served at lunchtime and evenings. Well-behaved children allowed.

OPEN *11am–3pm and 6–11pm Mon–Sat; all day Sun.*

THORNWOOD COMMON

The Carpenter's Arms

Carpenter's Arms Lane, Thornwood Common, Epping CM16 6LS
☎ *(01992) 574208* Martin Gale

Crouch Vale Best Bitter and SAS, Adnams Broadside and McMullen AK always available, plus two constantly changing guests, perhaps from Wye Valley, Woodforde's or Mighty Oak. One dark mild always available.

A traditional country pub. Three bars, two beer gardens, pub games, live music, Essex Pub of the Year 1998–99. Food served 12–2 pm. Children allowed.

OPEN *11am–3pm and 6–11pm Mon–Thurs; all day Fri–Sun.*

TILLINGHAM

Cap and Feathers

8 South Street, Tillingham CM70 7TH
☎ *(01621) 779212* Tony Burdfield

Crouch Vale Woodham IPA, Best Bitter, Dark Ale and Millennium Gold always available plus a guest (400 per year) which might include Morland Old Speckled Hen, Titanic Best, Buffy's Polly's Folly and Clark's Burglar Bill.

Dates from 1427, an old weatherboard building. Unspoilt, with a relaxed atmosphere. Bar food available at lunchtime and evenings. Car park, garden, non-smoking family room. Accommodation. Between Southminster and Bradwell.

OPEN 11.30am–3pm and 6–11pm Mon–Sat; 12–3pm and 7–10.30pm Sun.

TOOT HILL

The Green Man and Courtyard Restaurant

Toot Hill, Nr Ongar CM5 9SD
☎ *(01992) 522255* Mr J Roads

Crouch Vale Best always available plus two guests changing twice weekly including, perhaps, an Adnams brews or Fuller's London Pride. No strong bitters over 4.3% ABV.

A country freehouse with two restaurants, one bar, courtyard and beer garden. Food served at lunchtime and evenings. Children aged 11+ allowed.

OPEN 11am–3pm and 6–11pm (10.30pm Sun).

WENDENS AMBO

The Bell

Royston Road, Wendens Ambo CB11 4JY
☎ *(01799) 540382* Geoff and Bernie Bates

Adnams Bitter and Highgate Dark Mild always available plus a couple of guests (50 per year), including beers from Crouch Vale, City of Cambridge, Wolf, and other small breweries.

Built in 1576, beamed with open fires in winter. Background music only. Bar food available at lunchtime and evenings (not Monday). Car park, garden, children's play area.

OPEN 11.30am–2.30pm and 6–11pm Mon–Sat; 12–3pm and 7–10.30pm Sun.

WITHAM

The Woolpack

7 Church Street, Witham CM8 2JP
☎ *(01376) 511195* Mrs Hazel Hadgraft

Greene King IPA and Tolly Cobbold Original or Best always available, plus one rotating guest changed fortnightly.

A small community locals' drinking pub. Team orientated (darts, pool, cribbage etc). Sandwiches available at lunchtime. No children.

OPEN All day, every day.

WOODHAM FERRERS

The Bell Inn

Main Road, Woodham Ferrers, Chelmsford CM3 8RF
☎ *(01245) 320443* D L Giles and S Rowe

Ridleys IPA and Adnams Bitter regularly available, plus five guest beers often from Ridleys, Adnams, Mauldons, Crouch Vale or Cottage.

Friendly village pub with cosy bars and open fire in winter. Freshly-cooked food served 12–2.30pm and 7–10pm Mon–Fri, 12–10pm Sat–Sun. Car park. No children.

OPEN 11am–3pm and 6–11pm Mon–Fri; 11am–11pm Sat; 12–10.30pm Sun.

WOODHAM WATER

The Bell

The Street, Woodham Water, Maldon CM9 6RF
☎ *(01245) 223437* Mr Alan Oldfield

A freehouse with Greene King's IPA permanently available, plus two guest pumps serving real ales such as Morland Old Speckled Hen, Fuller's ESB, Hook Norton Old Hooky or Everards Tiger or Triple Gold.

A traditional sixteenth-century village inn with beams, one bar and three adjoining rooms. No music or machines. Beer garden. Food available lunchtimes and evenings in a separate dining room. Children allowed.

OPEN 12–3pm and 7–11pm (10.30pm Sun).

YOU TELL US

★ *The Angel*, 36 Bocking End, Bocking
★ *Boadicea*, St John's Street, Colchester
★ *The George Inn*, The Street, Shalford
★ *The Retreat*, 42 Church Street, Bocking
★ *The Royal Fusiliers*, Aingers Green Road, Aingers Green

Places Featured:

Apperley	France Lynch
Ashleworth	Gloucester
Avening	Ham
Awre	Hanham Mills
Bedminster	Hawkesbury Upton
Birdlip	Kingswood
Bishopston	Lime Street
Blaisdon	Littleton upon Severn
Bledington	Longborough
Bourton-on-the-Hill	Longhope
Bourton-on-the-Water	Lower Apperley
Box	Newland
Bristol	Oakridge Lynch
Broad Campden	Pill
Cheltenham	Pope's Hill
Chipping Campden	Quedgeley
Chipping Sodbury	Sapperton
Churchill	Sheepscombe
Cirencester	Slad
Clearwell	Sling
Cockleford	Snowshill
Coleford	South Woodchester
Cowley	Stow-on-the-Wold
Duntisbourne Abbots	Tewkesbury
Dursley	Uley
Ebrington	Waterley Bottom
Ford	Westbury on Trym
Frampton Cottrell	Whitminster

BERKELEY BREWING CO.

The Brewery, Bucketts Hill, Berkeley GL13 9NZ
☎ *(01453) 511799*

OLD FRIEND 3.8% ABV
Gold-coloured, with well-balanced fruit and hops.
SEVERN UP 4.0% ABV
DICKY PEARCE 4.3% ABV
Plus seasonal brews.

BUTCOMBE BREWERY LTD

Rusling House, Butcombe, Bristol BS40 7XQ
☎ *(01275) 472240*

BITTER 4.0% ABV
A dry, clean-tasting bitter with strong hop flavour.
GOLD 4.7% ABV
Golden and moreish.

DONNINGTON BREWERY

Upper Swell, Stow-on-the-Wold GL54 1EP
☎ *(01451) 830603*

BB 3.6% ABV
Plenty of flavour for gravity.
SBA 4.6% ABV
Smooth and malty.

FREEMINER BREWERY LTD

The Laurels, Sling, Coleford GL16 8JJ
☎ *(01594) 810408*

BITTER 4.0% ABV
STRIP AND AT IT 4.0% ABV
MORSES LEVEL 4.0% ABV
Hoppy with powerful malty balance.
IRON BREW 4.2% ABV
SPECULATION ALE 4.8% ABV
CELESTIAL STEAM GALE 5.0% ABV
GOLD STANDARD 5.0% ABV
SHAKEMANTLE GINGER ALE 5.0% ABV
SLAUGHTER PORTER 5.0% ABV
DEEP SHAFT 6.0% ABV
TRAFALGAR IPA 6.0% ABV

GOFF'S BREWERY LTD

9 Isbourne Way, Winchcombe GL54 5NS
☎ *(01242) 603383*

KNIGHT RIDER 3.6% ABV
Amber, hoppy and refreshing.
JOUSTER 4.0% ABV
Fruity, with hop flavours.
FALLEN KNIGHT 4.4% ABV
Hoppy with bittersweet aftertaste.
WHITE KNIGHT 4.7% ABV
Pale, with hoppiness throughout.

NORTH COTSWOLD BREWERY

Unit 3, Ditchford Farm, Moreton-in-Marsh GL56 9RD
☎ *(01608) 663947*

SOLSTICE 3.7% ABV
Summer brew.
GENESIS 4.0% ABV
FOUR SHIRES 4.2% ABV
Spring brew.

SMILES BREWING CO. LTD

Colston Yard, Colston Street, Bristol BS1 5BD
☎ *(0117) 929 7350*

BA 3.3% ABV
Pale and refreshing.
ORIGINAL 3.8% ABV
GOLDEN BREW 3.8% ABV
Golden pale with thirst-quenching hoppy flavour.
BEST BITTER 4.1% ABV
Well-rounded, hop, fruit and malt flavours.
HERITAGE 5.2% ABV
Dark and rich with roast malt character.
Plus monthly brews.

STANWAY BREWERY

Stanway, Cheltenham GL54 5PQ
☎ *(01386) 584320*

COLTESWOLD GOLD 3.9% ABV
Light refreshing ale only brewed in summer.
LORDS-A-LEAPING 4.5% ABV
Winter ale.
STANNEY BITTER 4.5% ABV
Quenching, with hoppiness throughout.
Plus seasonal brews.

ULEY BREWERY LTD

The Old Brewery, The Street, Uley, Dursley GL11 5TB
☎ *(01453) 860120*

HOGSHEAD BITTER 3.5% ABV
Light in colour and well-hopped.
BEST BITTER 4.0% ABV
Balanced and full-flavoured.
OLD RIC 4.5% ABV
OLD SPOT 5.0% ABV
Flagship ale. Powerful malt flavour with fruit and hops.
PIG'S EAR 5.0% ABV
Smooth IPA.

WICKWAR BREWERY CO.

The Old Cider Mill, Station Road, Wickwar, Wootton-under-Edge GL12 8NB
☎ *(01454) 294168*

COOPERS WPA 3.5% ABV
Quenching, full-flavoured pale ale.
BRAND OAK BITTER 4.0% ABV
Characterful and well-balanced.
OLD ARNOLD 4.6% ABV
OLD MERRYFORD ALE 5.1% ABV
Flavoursome, with hoppy fruit aroma.
Plus seasonal and occasional brews.

THE PUBS

APPERLEY

Coal House Inn

Gabb Lane, Apperley GL19 4DN
☎ *(01452) 780211* Mrs McDonald

Wickwar Brand Oak Bitter always available plus one regularly changing guest ale. Traditional underground cellar.

A country freehouse on the east bank of the River Severn. Home-cooked food served lunchtimes and evenings. 'Portuguese Steak on a Stone' a speciality. Large car parks and riverside garden. Children allowed. Moorings for boats (24 hours). Apperley is signposted on B4213 south of Tewkesbury. Follow signs for Coalhouse Wharf from village centre.

OPEN *April–Sep: 11.30am–2.30pm and 6–11pm; Oct–Mar: 11.30am–2.30pm and 7–11pm; 12–3pm and 7–10.30pm Sun (all year).*

ASHLEWORTH

The Boat Inn

The Quay, Ashleworth GL19 4HZ
☎ *(01452) 700272* Mrs Nicholls

Arkell's 3B, RCH Pitchfork, Oakhill Yeoman 1767 and Wye Valley brews always available plus at least three constantly changing guest beers served straight from the cask including, for example, Exmoor Gold, Oakhill Somer Ale and Black Magic, Arkell's Summer Ale, Smiles Exhibition, brews from Hambleton, Church End, Goff's, Cottage, Sporting Ales and Eccleshall plus various Christmas ales.

A fifteenth-century cottage pub on the banks of the River Severn. Small and friendly, has remained in the same family for 400 years. Bar food available at lunchtime. Car park and garden. Children allowed. Ashleworth is signposted off the A417 north of Gloucester. The Quay is signed from the village.

OPEN *April–Sep: 11am–2.30pm and 6–11pm Mon–Sat; 12–3pm and 7–10.30pm Sun; Oct–Mar: 11am–2.30pm Thurs–Tues, closed Wed lunchtime; 7–11pm Mon–Sat; 12–3pm and 7–10.30pm Sun.*

AVENING

The Bell

29 High Street, Avening, Tetbury GL8 8NF
☎ *(01453) 836422* Melissa Bovey

A freehouse with Wickwar Brand Oak usually available plus two guests such as Berkeley Old Friend or a Smiles or Abbey brew.

A traditional Cotswold pub with log fire, dining area and garden. Food served at lunchtime and evenings. Children allowed. Accommodation.

OPEN *12–3pm and 6.30–11pm Mon–Fri; all day Sat–Sun.*

AWRE

The Red Hart Inn

Awre, Newnham GL14 1EQ
☎ *(01594) 510220* Gerry Bedwell

A freehouse with a Freeminer brew always available, plus two guests changing weekly. Examples include Fuller's London Pride, Wadworth 6X, or something from Goff's or Sporting Ales. The landlord's policy is to support smaller breweries as much as possible.

A beamed hostelry dating from 1483 with one bar area. Non-smoking area. Outside seating in front garden. Bar snacks and à la carte menu available at lunchtime and evenings. Children allowed until 8pm, if well supervised. Accommodation. In the middle of nowhere! Turn off A48 between Newnham and Blakeney.

OPEN *6.30–11pm Mon; 12–3pm and 6.30–11pm Tues–Sat; 12–3pm and 7–10.30pm Sun.*

BEDMINSTER

Robert Fitzharding

24 Cannon Street, Bedminster, Bristol BS3 1BN
☎ *(0117) 966 2757* John Baldwin

A Wetherspoon's pub with Butcombe Bitter always available. Four guest pumps serve a range of 30 guests every quarter. Examples include Coniston Bluebird, Exmoor Beast, Caledonian Deuchars IPA or something from Burton Bridge.

A city suburb pub with non-smoking area. Two beer festivals held each year. Food served all day. No children.

OPEN *All day, every day.*

BIRDLIP

The Golden Heart Inn

Nettleton Bottom, Nr Birdlip GL4 8LA
☎ *(01242) 870261*
Mr D Morgan and Miss C Stevens

Marston's Pedigree, Hook Norton Best and Ruddles brews always available plus four guest beers (400 per year), perhaps from Greene King, Timothy Taylor and many local brewers.

A sixteenth–century pub with stone floors, beams and bric-a-brac. Bar food available at lunchtime and evenings. Car park, garden, children's room and function room. Situated on the A417 between Cheltenham, Gloucester and Cirencester, two miles from Birdlip.

OPEN *10.30am–3pm and 6–11pm Mon–Sat; 12–3pm and 7–10.30pm Sun.*

BISHOPSTON

The Annexe

Seymour Road, Bishopston, Bristol BS7 9EQ
☎ (0117) 949 3931 Mr Morgan

A tied house regularly serving Smiles brews plus Marston's Pedigree. Also a range of guests including Morland Old Speckled Hen, Archers Golden and beers from Bath Ales.

A town pub with disabled access, children's room, garden, darts etc. Bar food available at lunchtime and restaurant food in the evenings. Children allowed until 8.30pm in the conservatory only.

OPEN 11am–2.30pm and 6–11pm Mon–Fri; all day Sat–Sun.

BLAISDON

The Red Hart Inn

Blaisdon, Nr Longhope GL17 0AH
☎ (01452) 830477 Guy Wilkins

Hook Norton Best Bitter regularly available plus three guest beers perhaps from Uley, Wickwar, Berkeley, Freeminer, Goff's, RCH, Timothy Taylor, Wood, Eccleshall, Exmoor, Otter, Hop Back, Adnams, Cotleigh or Greene King.

Traditional English village pub with stone floor, low-beamed ceiling and open fire. Large bar area and separate non-smoking restaurant with food available 12–2pm and 7–9pm Sun–Thurs, 12–2pm and 7–9.30pm Fri–Sat. Barbecue and large garden with children's play area. Car park. Unattended children in the bar are sold as slaves.

OPEN 11.30am–2.30pm and 6–11pm Mon–Sat; 12–3pm and 7–10.30pm Sun.

BLEDINGTON

The Kings Head Inn & Restaurant

The Green, Bledington OX7 6XQ
☎ (01608) 658365
Michael and Annette Royce

Wadworth 6X and a beer from Hook Norton usually available, plus two guest beers which may include Shepherd Neame Spitfire, Timothy Taylor Landlord, Uley Old Spot or Pigs Ear, Wychwood Hobgoblin or Fiddlers Elbow, Smiles Best, Adnams Broadside amongst many others.

Quintessential, fifteenth-century Cotswold stone inn located on the village green with brook and attendant ducks. Retains olde-worlde charm of pews, settles, flagstone floors, beams, antique furnishings and inglenook fireplace. Tasteful accommodation. Food served 12–2pm and 7–9.45pm. Children welcome, under supervision, in the garden room. Large car park. On the B4450.

OPEN 11am–2.30pm and 6–11pm Mon–Sat; 12–3pm and 7–10.30pm Sun.

BOURTON-ON-THE-HILL

The Horse & Groom

Bourton-on-the-Hill, Moreton-in-Marsh GL56 9AQ
☎ (01386) 700413 Linda Balhatchet

A freehouse offering Hook Norton brews plus rotating guests such as Morland Old Speckled Hen.

A village pub on the main road with bar and restaurant area. Food served at lunchtime and evenings. Children allowed.

OPEN 11.30am–3pm and 7–11pm (10.30pm Sun).

BOURTON-ON-THE-WATER

The Kingsbridge Inn

Riverside, Bourton-on-the-Water, Cheltenham GL54 2BS
☎ (01451) 820371 John and Julie Swan

Caledonian 80/- and Deuchars IPA are served, plus two guests. All beers are subject to change. Guests include Morland Old Speckled Hen or Bourton Ale (a summer session ale brewed specially by Smiles).

An olde-worlde riverside pub in the Cotswolds with beer garden and tables out front. Family- and tourist-orientated. One bar with food served at lunchtime and evenings in both smoking and non-smoking dining areas. Three en-suite rooms overlooking the river, recently refurbished. Disabled access and disabled toilet. Children welcome, play area provided.

OPEN All day, every day.

BOX

The Halfway House

Minchinhampton, Box, Stroud GL6 9AE
☎ (01453) 832631

Marston's Best Bitter and Pedigree, Banks's Bitter, and Timothy Taylor Landlord always available, plus one rotating guest – perhaps a Berkeley or Wickwar ale. Under new management.

A prettily situated freehouse with L-shaped bar, 70-seater function room, skittle alley, garden with children's play area and 50-seater restaurant. Food served at lunchtime and evenings. On the edge of Minchinhampton Common.

OPEN 12–3pm and 6–11pm (10.30pm Sun). Sometimes all day in summer.

The Bag O'Nails

141 St Georges Road, Hotwells, Bristol BS1 5UW
☎ *(0117) 940 6776* Gordon Beresford

Fuller's London Pride usually available plus up to five others served on a guest basis (over 300 served in two years). Mainly supplied by smaller, independent breweries. The pub's own web page gives details of beers stocked at any one time (www.cix.co.uk/bagonails/). For a monthly e-mail list of forthcoming beers send e-mail address to gordon@bagonails.cix.co.uk

A small, quiet, gas-lit city-centre pub with one bar. Situated just 25 yards from the Dock. Simples lunches only served 12–2pm. No children.

12–2.30pm and 5–11pm Mon–Thurs; all day Fri–Sun.

The Bell Inn

21 Alfred Place, Kingsdown, Bristol BS2 8HD
☎ *(0117) 907 7563* Anna Luke

A freehouse regularly offering Wickwar Brand Oak Bitter and Olde Merryford Ale. Also RCH Pitchfork plus occasional guests.

A small, one-bar locals' pub. Toasted sandwiches available at lunchtime only. No children. Situated off St Michael's Hill, at the back of the BRI hospital.

12–2.30pm and 5.30–11pm (10.30pm Sun).

Cadbury House

68 Richmond Road, Montpelier, Bristol BS6 5EW
☎ *(0117) 924 7874* Rachel Bickerton

A freehouse serving Wickwar Brand Oak Bitter and Olde Merryford plus Quay Bombshell and one rotating guest. Wickwar Station Porter or other winter ales usually available from October.

A locals' pub in a residential area. Clientele a mix of regulars and students. Large beer garden. Bar meals served 12–6.30pm and traditional Sunday roasts. Children allowed.

All day, every day.

Commercial Rooms

43–5 Corn Street, Bristol BS1 1HT
☎ *(0117) 927 9681* Dana Edwards

A freehouse serving Butcombe Bitter and Gold plus two guests changing constantly.

A town-centre pub with twice-yearly beer festivals in April and October. Food served all day. No children.

10.30am–11pm.

Cornubia

142 Temple Street, Bristol BS1 6EN
☎ *(0117) 925 4415* Nick Luke

A freehouse with no permanent beers, just a constantly changing range of guests. Local brewers generally favoured. Tries to include a dark porter or stout when possible.

A Georgian, listed building with traditional town-centre pub atmosphere. Food available at lunchtime only. Well-behaved children allowed.

11am–11pm Mon–Sat; 12–10.30pm Sun.

Hare On The Hill

41 Thomas Street North, Kingsdown
☎ *(0117) 9081982* John Lansdall

Bath Ales SPA, Gem, Barnstormer, SPA Extra (summer) and Festivity (winter) usually available with one or two guest beers from mostly local or Yorkshire breweries, all above 4.8% ABV.

Popular, Bath Ales award-winning pub. Bar food served lunchtimes and evenings. Sunday roasts 12–3pm. Well-behaved children welcome, but there are no special facilities.

12–2.30pm and 5–11pm Mon–Thurs; 12–11pm Fri–Sat; 12–10.30pm Sun.

The Highbury Vaults

164 St Michael's Hill, Cotham, Bristol BS2 8DE
☎ *(0117) 973 3203* Bradd Francis

Smiles Best, Golden and Heritage always available plus seasonal brews and Brains SA. Also guest beers, changed weekly, including Fuller's London Pride, Greene King Abbot, Adnams Broadside, Uley Old Spot, Hampshire Pendragon, Quay Bombshell, Ridleys Rumpus and Bateman XXXB.

Very traditional pub set in the heart of university land with no music, fruit machines, pool tables etc. Lots of atmosphere for young and old, students and locals. Cheap bar food available at lunchtime and evenings (nothing fried). Heated rear garden. Children allowed in garden.

12–11pm (10.30pm Sun).

The Hope & Anchor

38 Jacobs Wells Road, Clifton, Bristol BS8 1DR
☎ *(0117) 929 2987* Martin Hughes

Six beers always available, changed every few days. Up to 30 brews per year including Fuller's London Pride, Gales HSB, Titanic Best, Felinfoel Double Dragon, Greene King Abbot, Palmers IPA and Badger Tanglefoot.

Friendly one-bar pub with relaxed atmosphere. No TV or games machines. Bar food available at lunchtime and evenings. Children allowed in beer garden. Near The Triangle in Clifton, north of Bristol city centre.

12–11pm (10.30pm Sun).

The Phoenix

15 Wellington Street, St Judes, Bristol BS2
☎ *(0117) 955 8327* Jeffrey Fowler

Up to ten beers always available including those from Oakhill and Wickwar breweries plus Wadworth 6X. Also a selection from 100 guest beers per year. Brews from Young's, Shepherd Neame, Cottage, Bateman, Everards, Ash Vine, Uley, Burton Bridge, Burtonwood, Exmoor and many more.

Small, local one-bar freehouse in Grade II listed building. Snacks available at lunchtime and evenings. Parking, garden, children's room, accommodation. On the edge of Broadmead shopping area.

11.30am–11pm Mon–Sat; 12–3pm and 7–10.30pm Sun.

Smiles Brewery Tap

6–8 Colston Street, Bristol BS1 5BT
☎ *(0117) 921 3668 Stephen J Lovell*

Smiles Original, Best, Heritage, Blonde Ale and seasonal brews available.

A traditional pub atmosphere awaits in this small horseshoe bar with hops adorning the ceiling. Separate non-smoking room and small bar with wood panelling and chequered tiled floor. Hot food served 12–3pm Mon–Sat; sandwiches always available. No children.

11am–11pm Mon–Sat; 7–10.30pm Sun.

The Swan with Two Necks

12 Little Ann Street, St Judes, Bristol BS2 9EB
☎ *(0117) 955 1893* Michael Blake

Six to eight beers always available from a range of hundreds per year. A wide range of regional ales is served, from the British Isles and the Republic of Ireland. The emphasis is on smaller independent breweries.

Basic one-bar pub with open fireplaces, ten minutes from city centre and docks. No music or machines. Bar food available at lunchtime. Parking. Regular beer festivals held. Tricky to find. Coming into Bristol on M32, left at first set of lights, then 3rd left. Website: www.sw2n.co.uk

12–3pm and 5–11pm Mon–Thurs; 12–11pm Fri–Sat; 12–10.30pm Sun.

The Woolpack Inn

Shepherds Way, St Georges, Bristol BA3 6SP
☎ *(01934) 521670* PW Sampson

Four beers always available, 30 per year to include Charles Wells Bombardier and Oakhill Best.

Village freehouse in 200-year-old building. Bar and restaurant food at lunchtime and evenings. Car park, garden, conservatory planned. No children. Off M5, junction 21.

12–2.30pm and 6–11pm Mon–Sat; 12–3pm and 7–10.30pm Sun.

BROAD CAMPDEN

The Bakers Arms

Broad Campden, Chipping Campden GL55 6UR
☎ *(01386) 840515* Sally and Ray Mayo

Timothy Taylor Landlord, Donnington and Hook Norton ales always available, plus two rotating guest ales.

A small, friendly Cotswold country pub with open fire. Bar food available every lunchtime and evening. Car park, garden, patio and children's play area. In a village between Chipping Campden and Blockley.

Winter: 11.30am–2.30pm and 6.30–11pm Mon–Sat; 12–3pm and 7–10.30pm Sun. Summer: 11.30am–3pm and 6–11pm Mon–Sat; 12–3pm and 7–10.30pm Sun.

CHELTENHAM

The Kemble Brewery Inn
27 Fairview Street, Cheltenham GL52 2JF
☎ *(01242) 243446* Dennis Melia

An Archers house with Village, Best and Golden usually available plus one or two guest beers which may include others from Archers or ales from Fuller's, Donnington, Young's or Hook Norton.

This small, friendly local with rear courtyard is one of the few remaining real ale pubs in Cheltenham. Situated behind Fowlers motorcycle shop in the Fairview area. Food served 12–2.30pm Sun–Mon, 6–8.30pm Mon–Fri. Children welcome in courtyard.

OPEN *11.30am–2.30pm and 5.30–11pm Mon–Fri; 11.30am–11pm Sat; 12–4pm and 7–11pm Sun.*

Tailors
4 Cambray Place, Cheltenham GL50 1JS
☎ *(01242) 255453* Mrs Cherri Dandridge

A Wadworth tied house with 6X and IPA always available. Three guest ales, changed fortnightly, might include Badger Tanglefoot or a Shepherd Neame brew.

A town-centre pub with cellar bar and comfortable armchairs. Live music on Thursdays. Two beer gardens. Food served every lunchtime except Sunday. Children allowed.

OPEN *All day, every day.*

CHIPPING CAMPDEN

The Volunteer
Lower High Street, Chipping Campden GL55 6DY
☎ *(01386) 840688* Mrs H Sinclair

North Cotswold's Genesis, Stanway's Stanney Bitter and Hook Norton Best always available, plus three guests from local breweries such as Uley, Wood or Charles Wells.

A country inn with garden. Food served at lunchtime and evenings. Children allowed. Accommodation.

OPEN *11.30am–3pm and 5–11pm Mon–Sat; 12–3pm and 6.30–10.30pm Sun.*

CHIPPING SODBURY

Beaufort Hunt
Broad Street, Chipping Sodbury, Bristol BS37 6AG
☎ *(01454) 312871* Mrs Jarvis

Greene King IPA always available plus two guests including, perhaps, Wickwar Olde Merryford, Fuller's London Pride, Shepherd Neame Bishop's Finger or Everards Tiger.

An olde-style village pub with beer garden. Food available at lunchtime. Children aged 14–18 allowed in lounge bar only if eating. Under 14s not allowed.

OPEN *10.30am–3pm and 5–11pm (10.30pm Sun).*

CHURCHILL

The Crown Inn
The Batch, Skinners Lane, Churchill, Nr Bristol
☎ *(01934) 852995*

Butcombe Bitter, RCH PG Steam and Palmers Best always available straight from the barrel, plus up to five guest beers (100+ per year) to include Palmers Tally Ho, Greene King Abbot, Tomintoul Wild Cat, Otter Bright and Hop Back Summer Lightning.

An old pub with small rooms and flagstone floors. Large fires in winter. Food made and prepared to order when practical. Parking, garden, children's room. Children not allowed in bar area. South of Bristol, just off the A38, not far from M5.

OPEN *11.30am–3pm and 5.30–11pm.*

CIRENCESTER

The Bear Inn
12 Dyer Street, Cirencester GL7 2PF
☎ *(01285) 653472* Serena McBride

A Mole's Brewery tied house. Wadworth 6X always available, plus Mole's Best in summer and a range of seasonal brews.

A town-centre pub, soon to be refurbished in the style of an old coaching inn. Home-cooked food served at lunchtime and evenings in a separate dining area. Children allowed.

OPEN *All day, every day.*

Corinium Hotel
12 Gloucester Street, Cirencester GL7 2DG
☎ *(01285) 659711* Tim McGrath

Hook Norton Best and Old Hooky always available, plus one guest beer.

A sixteenth-century wool merchant's house, now a hotel, bar and restaurant. Wide selection of food served lunchtimes and evenings. Children welcome in restaurant and garden.

OPEN *11am–11pm (10.30pm Sun).*

The Drillman's Arms

84 Gloucester Road, Cirencester GL7 2JY
☎ *(01285) 653892* Richard Elby

A freehouse serving Archers Best and Village plus either Wadworth 6X or Greene King Abbot Ale. Also a rotating guest from local brewers such as Berkeley or Hampshire.

A village pub with log fire and function room. Food served at lunchtime and evenings. Children allowed.

11am–3pm and 5.30–11pm Mon–Fri; all day Sat; 11am–4pm and 7–10.30pm Sun.

CLEARWELL

The Lamb Inn

The Cross, Clearwell, Coleford GL16 8JU
☎ *(01594) 835441* FJ Yates and SY Lewis.

Freeminer Best Bitter usually available, with a range of guest beers which may include Goff's Jouster, Berkeley Old Friend, Bath Ales Gem, Oakhill Best Bitter or beers from Ash Vine, Slater's, Otter, Hampshire, Church End, Wye Valley or Archers.

Nineteenth-century stone-built inn with later additions. No food, machines or music and the beer is served straight from the barrel. Well-behaved children welcome till 8.30pm. Car park. Situated 200 yards from Clearwell Cross on the Newland and Redbrook road.

6–11pm Mon–Thurs; 12–3pm and 6–11pm Fri–Sat and bank holidays; 12–3pm and 7–10.30pm Sun.

COCKLEFORD

Green Dragon Inn

Cockleford, Cowley, Cheltenham GL53 9NW
☎ *(01242) 870271* Steve and Alison Parker

Hook Norton Best Bitter regularly available with two changing guest beers. Morland Old Speckled Hen and Wadworth 6X are popular.

Traditional Cotswold inn with stone-clad floors and roaring log fire in winter. Function room and patio overlooking lake. Accommodation. Food served 12–2.30pm and 6.30–10.30pm Mon–Sat, 12–2pm and 7–9pm Sun. Car park. Children's menu and high chairs available.

11am–11pm Mon–Sat; 12–10.30pm Sun.

COLEFORD

The Angel Hotel

Market Place, Coleford GL16 8AE
☎ *(01594) 833113* Barry C Stoakes

Freeminer Speculation usually available plus three guest beers which regularly include other beers from Freeminer, Timothy Taylor and Hook Norton.

Dating from the sixteenth century and situated in the Forest of Dean, this was once used as a town hall but is now nine-room hotel with real ale bar. Courtyard and beer garden. Separate nightclub attached. Food served lunchtimes and evenings with sandwiches available during the afternoons. Children welcome if dining, until 7pm.

7am (for breakfast) and 10.30am–11pm daily (1am in nightclub).

COWLEY

The Green Dragon

Cockleford, Cowley, Nr Cheltenham GL53 9NW
☎ *(01242) 870271* Pia-Maria Boast

Smiles Best, Brewery Bitter and Exhibition always available plus up to three guest beers (30 per year) which may include Fuller's ESB, Badger Dorset Best and Tanglefoot, Marston's Owd Roger, Hook Norton Best, Cotleigh Old Buzzard, Greene King Abbot, Bateman Victory and Shepherd Neame Spitfire.

A traditional seventeenth-century pub with flagstones, open fires and candles. Bar food served at lunchtime and evenings. Car park and patio. Private function room and bar available for wedding receptions and parties.

11.30am–2.30pm and 6–11pm.

DUNTISBOURNE ABBOTS

Five Mile House

Gloucester Road, Duntisbourne Abbots, Cirencester GL7 7JR
☎ *(01285) 821432* JW Carrier

A freehouse serving Marston's Bitter and Timothy Taylor Landlord plus one guest of 3.8% ABV or less. Archers Village is a popular example.

A traditional country pub with old bar, family room and garden. Food served at lunchtime and evenings in non-smoking restaurant. Children allowed.

12–3pm and 6–11pm (7–10.30pm Sun).

Old Spot Inn

Hill Road, Dursley GL11 4JQ
☎ *(01453) 542870*

Uley Old Ric always available, plus guests (four different ones every week), which may include Goff's Jouster, Abbey Bellringer, Wickwar BOB, Bath Gem, and something from Adnams or Thwaites.

Originally a farm cottage, then a school, built in 1776 on the Cotswold Way, beamed with open fires. Bar snacks available at lunchtime. Live music. Parking, garden. No children.

OPEN *11am–11pm Mon–Sat; 12–3pm and 7–10.30pm Sun.*

The Ebrington Arms

Ebrington, Nr Chipping Campden GL55 6NH
☎ *(01386) 593223* Gareth Richards

Hook Norton Best and Donnington SBA always available plus a guest beer (52 per year), perhaps from Wadworth, Fuller's, Wychwood, Goff's, Uley, or Greene King breweries.

An unspoilt traditional Cotswold village pub. No music or machines. Traditional games. Bar and restaurant food at lunchtime and evenings. Car park and garden. Children in the restaurant only. The owner has a pottery in the courtyard where he makes bowls, jugs and cruet sets used in the restaurant. Accommodation.

OPEN *11am–2.30pm and 6–11pm Mon–Sat; 12–3pm and 7–10.30pm Sun.*

The Plough Inn

Ford, Temple Guiting GL54 5RU
☎ *(01386) 584215* Chris Turner

A Donnington Brewery house always serving BB and SBA.

A thirteenth-century Cotswold stone inn with inglenook fireplace, beams and flagstone floor. Food served at lunchtime and evenings in a separate dining area. Children allowed. Located on the main road between Stow-on-the-Wold and Tewkesbury

OPEN *All day, every day.*

The Rising Sun

43 Ryecroft Road, Frampton Cotterell, Nr Bristol BS17 2HN
☎ *(01454) 772330* Roger Stone

Six beers always available with up to 30 featured per year. Examples include Smiles brews, Phoenix Mayfly, Crown Buckley Rev James Original and Buchanan Original.

Small, friendly, single-bar local. CAMRA Pub of the Year for Avon in 1995. Bar food available at lunchtime. Large patio area.

OPEN *11.30am–3pm and 7–11pm Mon–Sat; 12–3pm and 7–10.30pm Sun.*

The King's Head

France Lynch, Stroud GL6 8LT
☎ *(01453) 882225* Mike Duff

A freehouse serving Hook Norton and Archers brews, plus two guests that change frequently.

A small, traditional, country pub with large garden. No juke box. Live music every Monday evening. Food served at lunchtime and evenings. Children's play area.

OPEN *12–2.30pm and 6–11pm Mon–Fri; 12–4pm and 6–11pm Sat; 12–4pm and 7–10.30pm Sun.*

England's Glory

66–8 London Road, Gloucester GL1 3PB
☎ *(01452) 302948* Sarah Chapel

A Wadworth-managed house with IPA, 6X and Badger Tanglefoot always available. Three guests might include Mayhem's Odda's Light or seasonal Wadworth beers such as Summersault.

A food-oriented pub on the outskirts of town. Disabled access, non-smoking area, beer garden. Food available at lunchtime and evenings. Children allowed in the non-smoking area only.

OPEN *11.30am–2.30pm and 5–11pm Mon–Fri; 12–2.30pm and 6–11pm Sat; 12–3pm and 7–10.30pm Sun.*

The Linden Tree

73–5 Bristol Road, Gloucester GL1 5SN
☎ *(01452) 527869* Simon Cairns

Hook Norton Best, Smiles Exhibition, Wadworth 6X and IPA and Badger Tanglefoot always available plus two guest beers (more than 100 per year) which may include Exmoor Stag, Crown Buckley Rev James Original and Wadworth Old Timer.

A true country pub in the heart of Gloucester, south of the city centre. Large Georgian Grade II listed building. Bar food available at lunchtime and evenings. Parking, skittle alley, function room. Children allowed. Accommodation. Follow the Bristol road from the M5.

OPEN *11am–2.30pm and 5–11pm Mon–Thurs; 11am–11pm Fri–Sat; 12–3pm and 7–10.30pm Sun.*

The Regal

32 St Aldate Street, King's Square, Gloucester GL1 1RP
☎ *(01452) 332344* Neil Marther

A Wetherspoon's pub. Archers Golden, Morland Old Speckled Hen and a Banks's brew always available plus up to ten guests changed on a weekly basis.

A large town pub with non-smoking areas, disabled access and toilets. Beer garden. Food served all day. No children. Regular beer festivals held.

OPEN *All day, every day.*

The Salutation Inn

Ham, Berkeley GL13 9QH
☎ *(01453) 810284* Mrs BS Dailly

Berkeley Old Friend usually available plus a seasonal brew from Berkeley such as Jenner's Cure, Dicky Pearce or Late Starter.

Friendly pub set in pleasant countryside. Situated off the A28 towards Berkeley. Food served 12–2pm and 7–9pm. Children are welcome, but there are no special facilities. Car park.

OPEN *11am–3pm and 7–11pm daily (10.30pm Sun).*

Old Lock & Weir

Hanham Mills, Bristol BS15 3NU
☎ *(0117) 967 3793* Mark Brian

A freehouse usually serving Exmoor Gold and Stag, Marston's Pedigree and Towpath Tippler (a special house brew).

A riverside country pub with dining area and garden. Food available at lunchtime and evenings. Children allowed in dining area and garden only.

OPEN *All day, every day.*

The Beaufort Arms

High Street, Hawkesbury Upton GL9 1AU
☎ *(01454) 238217*

Wickwar BOB., plus two or three guest beers which may include Fuller's London Pride, Timothy Taylor Landlord, Greene King Abbot Ale or beers from Bath Ales, Goff's or Otter.

Traditional Cotswold freehouse with extensive collection of old advertising signs, pub mirrors, bottles and jugs. Dining room and recently added skittle alley. Food served 12–2.30pm and 7–9.30pm every day. Well-behaved children welcome, but no special facilities. Car park.

OPEN *12–3pm and 5.30–11pm Mon–Fri; 12–11pm Sat; 12–10.30pm Sun.*

Dinneywicks Inn

The Chippings, Kingswood, Wotton-under-Edge GL12 8RT
☎ *(01453) 843328* Mrs Thomas

A Wadworth house serving 6X and IPA with other seasonal guests. Also Adnams Broadside.

A recently refurbished village pub with garden and petanque court. Food served at lunchtime and evenings, including traditional Sunday lunch. Children allowed.

OPEN *11.30am–3pm and 6–11pm (all day Sat in winter).*

The Greyhound Inn

Lime Street, Eldersfield GL19 4NX
☎ *(01452) 840381* Matthew and Kate Brown

A freehouse with Wadworth 6X and a Butcombe brew always available, plus a weekly changing guest beer from an independent brewery such as Dorothy Goodbody's (Wye Valley), Ledbury, Wickwar, Smiles or Oakhill.

A rural country inn with two bars and real fires, skittle alley/function room. Large garden with play area. Food served every lunchtime and evening except Mondays. Children allowed. Look for Lime Street on the map, not Eldersfield!

OPEN *11.30am–2.30pm Mon–Sat; 12–3pm Sun; 7–11pm Mon; 6–11pm Tues–Sat; 7–10.30pm Sun.*

GLOUCESTERSHIRE

LITTLETON UPON SEVERN

The White Hart Inn

Littleton upon Severn, Nr Bristol BS12 1NR
☎ *(01454) 412275 Mr and Mrs Berryman*

Smiles Best and Exhibition always available plus two or three guest beers to include Burton Bridge Bitter, Wadworth 6X, Bateman XB, Fuller's London Pride, Shepherd Neame Spitfire Ale and Greene King Abbot.

Near the Severn Bridges and Thornbury Castle. Bar food at lunchtime and evenings. Children not allowed. Leave the M4 at junction 21. Head towards Thornbury, then Elberton village. Signposted from there.

11.30am–3pm and 6–11pm Mon–Fri; 11.30am–11pm Sat; 12–10.30pm Sun.

LONGBOROUGH

The Coach & Horses Inn

Longborough Village, Moreton-in-Marsh GL56 0QJ
☎ *(01451) 830325 Connie Emm*

A Donnington tied house with XXX and Best Bitter served.

Old, original Cotswold locals' inn in lovely village setting with good views from patio. Sandwiches and ploughmans available at lunchtimes, if pre-ordered. Children welcome at lunchtime and early evening.

11am–3pm and 7–11pm (10.30pm Sun).

LONGHOPE

The Glasshouse Inn

May Hill, Longhope GL17 0NN
☎ *(01452) 830529 Mr S Pugh*

A freehouse regularly serving Butcombe brews. Guests served straight from the barrel include ales from Adnams and Hook Norton.

An old-fashioned country pub with garden. Food served at lunchtime and evenings. Well-behaved children allowed.

11.30am–3pm and 6.30–11pm Mon–Sat; 12–3pm and 7–10.30pm Sun.

LOWER APPERLEY

The Farmer's Arms

Ledbury Road, Lower Apperley GL19 4DR
☎ *(01452) 780307 Viv Healey*

Home of the Mayhem Brewery. Odda's Light and Sundowner's Heavy always available plus six other guests, which may include Marston's Pedigree and Wadworth 6X.

An eighteenth-century inn with one bar, oak beams and open fires. The brewery was opened in the grounds in 1992. Bar and restaurant food available at lunchtime and evenings. Car park, garden, children's play area. B4213 Ledbury Road, four miles south of Tewkesbury.

 ODDA'S LIGHT 3.8% ABV
SUNDOWNER'S HEAVY 4.5% ABV

11am–3pm and 6–11pm Mon–Sat; 12–3pm and 7–11pm Sun.

NEWLAND

The Ostrich Inn

Newland, Nr Coleford GL16 8NP
☎ *(01594) 833260 Mr and Mrs Dewe*

Wadworth 6X, Shepherd Neame Spitfire and RCH Old Slug Porter always available plus four guest beers (50 per year) which may include Otter Head, RCH Pitchfork, Moles Tap, Durham Pagan, Uley Pig's Ear, Ridleys Spectacular, Bull Mastiff Best, Marston's Pedigree, Black Sheep Bitter and Exmoor Gold. Also real cider and German lager.

A thirteenth-century inn in the Forest of Dean with beams, log fire, settles and candles. Bar and restaurant food available at lunchtime and evenings. Garden and accommodation. In the village centre, opposite the church.

12–2.20pm and 6.30–11pm Mon–Fri; 12–3pm and 6.30–11pm Sat; 12–3pm and 7–10.30pm Sun.

OAKRIDGE LYNCH

Butchers Arms

Oakridge Lynch, Nr Stroud GL6 7NZ
☎ *(01285) 760371 PJ Coupe*

Archers Best Bitter, Greene King Abbot Ale, Berkeley Old Friend and Marston's Pedigree regularly available plus an occasional guest beer.

Friendly, 200-year-old village pub with log fires, exposed beams and attractive garden. It has been in the same hands for 15 years. Separate restaurant. Food served in the bar each lunchtime and evening (except Sun evening). Restaurant open 7.30–9.30pm Wed–Sat and Sun lunchtimes. Car park. Children welcome in the restaurant and small dedicated room off bar area. Can be difficult to find so ring for directions.

12–3pm and 6–11pm Mon–Sat; 12–3pm and 7–10.30pm Sun.

The Star Inn

13 Bank Place, Pill, Nr Bristol BS20 0AQ
☎ *(01275) 374926* Mrs Fey

Approximately 300 different ales sold in the past eight years. Small regional brews favoured. Butcombe Bitter always available plus two or three from a selection of 50–60 brews per year including Bullmastiff Son of a Bitch, Ringwood Old Thumper, Wychwood Hobgoblin, Gibbs Mew Wake Ale and Moorhouse's Pendle Witches Brew.

Local village pub with a wide range of customers. Parking. Children allowed in bar. Junction 19 off the M5.

OPEN *12–4pm and 7–11pm.*

The Greyhound Inn

The Slad, Pope's Hill, Gloucester GL14 1JX
☎ *(01452) 760344* Mr Pammenter

A freehouse serving Timothy Taylor and Freeminer brews. One twice-weekly changing guest from any brewery in the UK. Examples are Fuller's London Pride, Exmoor Gold, RCH Pitchfork and Cottage brews.

A country pub with non-smoking family room and garden. CAMRA Forest of Dean Pub of the Year 1999. Food served at lunchtime and evenings. Children allowed in the family room only.

OPEN *11am–3pm and 5.30–11pm (12–3pm Sun).*

Little Thatch Hotel

Bristol Road, Quedgeley, Gloucester GL2 4PQ
☎ *(01452) 720687* Mrs J McDougall

Berkeley Old Friend and Dicky Pearce usually available plus one or two guest beers often from Goff's, Oakhill or Robinson's plus others from time to time.

Black and white timber-frame hotel built in 1351 with recent addition. Food served 12–2pm and 7–9.30pm Mon–Fri, 7–10pm Sat and 12–2pm Sun. Car park. Children welcome.

OPEN *12–2.30pm and 6.30–10.30pm Mon–Fri; 7–10.30pm Sat; 12–3.30pm and 7–10.30pm Sun.*

The Daneway

Sapperton, Nr Cirencester GL7 6LN
☎ *(01285) 760297*

Five real ales always available including Wadworth 6X, Archers Best and Daneway Bitter. Guests (30+ per year) might come from the West Berkshire Brewery or Greene King.

Built in 1784, this beamed pub is set in some wonderful Gloucestershire countryside. It features a lounge and public bar, plus small non-smoking family room. No music, machines or pool but traditional pub games. Bar food is available at lunchtime and meals in the evening. Car park, garden, children allowed in family room. Less than two miles off the A419 Stroud–Cirencester road.

OPEN *11am–2.30pm and 6.30–11pm.*

The Butcher's Arms

Sheepscombe, Painswick GL6 7RH
☎ *(01452) 812113*
Johnny and Hilary Johnston

A freehouse with Hook Norton Best, Uley Old Spot and an Archers brew always available.

A sixteenth-century country pub with panoramic views and sheltered gardens. Bar and restaurant food served lunchtimes and evenings. Car park. Children allowed. Situated off A46 north of Painswick (signposted from main road).

OPEN *11.30am–3pm and 6.30–11pm (10.30pm Sun).*

Woolpack Inn

Slad Road, Slad, Stroud GL5 7QD
☎ *(01452) 813429* Dan Chadwick

Wickwar Coopers WPA, Uley Bitter, Old Spot and Pigs Ear regularly available. One or two guest beers are usually served, which may include Blue Anchor Spingo Special or Middle, or Fuller's London Pride.

The haunt of the late Laurie Lee (*Cider with Rosie*) and situated in the beautiful Slad Valley. Food served 12–2.30pm and 7–10pm Mon–Sat, 1–4pm (best to book) and 7–10pm Sun. Car park. Small garden and terrace. Children welcome.

OPEN *11.30am–3pm and 6–11pm Mon–Fri; 11.30am–11pm Sat; 12–10.30pm Sun.*

The Miners Arms

Sling, Coleford GL16 8LH
☎ *(01594) 836632* Mrs Jeynes

 A freehouse serving four Freeminer brews.

Old-fashioned, one-bar locals' pub in tourist area. Nice walking and views. Large garden, juke box and darts. Food served all day. Children allowed. Situated on the main road from Chepstow to Coleford and the Forest of Dean

OPEN *All day, every day.*

The Snowshill Arms

Snowshill, Broadway WR12 7JU
☎ *(01386) 852653* David J Schad

 Donnington SBA and BB usually available.

Rural Donnington-owned, family pub in the heart of the Cotswolds. The open plan bar has a log fire in winter. Food lunchtimes and evenings. Children welcome, with play area in garden for use under parental supervision. Car park.

OPEN *11am–2.30pm and 6–11pm Mon–Sat; 12–3pm and 7–10.30pm Sun.*

The Ram Inn

South Woodchester, Nr Stroud GL55 EL
☎ *(01453) 873329* Mike McAsey

Archers Best Bitter, Wickwar BOB., Cains Dr Duncan and Wychwood Hobgoblin usually available plus three constantly changing guest beers from around the country. Approximately 400 served last year.

This bustling old Cotswold pub was built around 1601. Beautiful village setting, with wonderful views. Food served 12–2.30pm and 6–9.30pm every day. Children welcome. Plenty of outside seating, and real fires in the winter. Car park. Follow brown tourist signs from A46.

OPEN *All day, every day.*

The Golden Ball Inn

Lower Swell, Stow-on-the-Wold GL54 1LF
☎ *(01451) 830247*
Andrew and Angie Knowles

Tied to the nearby Donnington Brewery, so BB and SBA are always available.

A seventeenth-century, Cotswold stone, village local with log fires in winter. Accommodation available. Typical old pub games played (darts, dominoes, cribbage, Aunt Sally). Bar food served at lunchtime and evenings. Car park and garden. Children and pets welcome. On the B4068, one mile from Stow-on-the-Wold.

OPEN *12–2.20pm and 6.30–11pm Mon–Fri; 12–3pm and 6.30–11pm Sat; 12–3pm and 7–10.30pm Sun.*

The Berkeley Arms

8 Church Street, Tewkesbury GL20 5PA
☎ *(01684) 293034* Mr and Mrs J Mather

Wadworth IPA, 6X and Mayhem Odda's Light always available, plus two guests (15 per year) which may include Badger Tanglefoot, Wadworth Old Timer, Morland Old Speckled Hen and Charles Wells Bombardier.

A small, homely fifteenth-century pub. Bar and restaurant food available. Street parking. The restaurant can be hired for functions. Children allowed in the restaurant.

OPEN *11am–3pm and 5–11pm Mon–Thur; all day Fri–Sun.*

The White Bear

Bredon Road, Tewkesbury GL20 5BU
☎ *(01684) 296614* H and G Stone

A freehouse serving Wye Valley Bitter, plus two guests from breweries such as Wood, Hook Norton, RCH, Wyre Piddle and Banks's.

A games-orientated, male-dominated boozer! No food. Children allowed in the garden only.

OPEN *All day, every day.*

ULEY

Old Crown Inn
The Green, Uley, Dursley GL11 8SN
☎ *(01453) 860502* Mrs Morgan

A freehouse with Uley Bitter and Pig's Ear regularly available, plus three weekly changing guests from breweries such as Cotleigh, Greene King, Hook Norton, Hampshire or Hop Back.

A village pub with games room, garden and accommodation. Home-cooked pub food served at lunchtimes and evenings. Children allowed.

11.30am–3pm and 7–11pm (10.30pm Sun).

WATERLEY BOTTOM

The New Inn
Waterley Bottom, North Nibley, Nr Dursley GL11 6EF
☎ *(01453) 543659* Ruby Sainty

Cotleigh Hobby Ale and Tawny, Greene King Abbot plus Smiles Best and Exhibition always available. Also occasional guests (104 per year) to include B&T Dragonslayer and Adnams May Day.

A remote freehouse with two bars, set in a beautiful valley. Bar food available at lunchtime and evenings. Car park, garden and accommodation. CAMRA Gloucestershire Pub of the Year 1992–93. From North Nibley, follow signs for Waterley Bottom.

12–2.30pm and 7–11pm (10.30pm Sun).

WESTBURY ON TRYM

The Post Office Tavern
17 Westbury Hill, Westbury on Trym, Nr Bristol BS9 3AH
☎ *(0117) 940 1233* Steve Fitzgerald

Up to ten beers available from an extensive range including Shepherd Neame Spitfire Ale, Fuller's London Pride and Smiles brews.

Early twentieth-century alehouse full of post office memorabilia. Non-smoking lounge. Bar food lunchtime and evenings. Street parking, small patio. Children allowed with parents for food in early evenings only. On main road in Westbury village.

11.30am–11pm Mon–Sat; 12–3pm and 7–10.30pm Sun.

The Victoria Inn
20 Chock Lane, Westbury on Trym, Bristol BS9 3EX
☎ *(0117) 950 0441* Alastair Deas

A Wadworth tied house with 6X and Henry's IPA and Adnams Broadside always available, plus two weekly changing guests such as Badger Tanglefoot and seasonal brews.

A village pub with garden. Food available at lunchtime and evenings. Children allowed.

12–2.30pm and 5.30–11pm.

WHITMINSTER

The Old Forge
Bristol Road, Whitminster GL2 7NY
☎ *(01452) 741306* Peter Brian

A freehouse serving Exmoor Gold, Exmoor Ale and Uley Bitter plus one rotating guest from breweries such as York or Cotleigh.

An old, traditional pub with dining area and beer garden. Food served at lunchtime and evenings. Children allowed.

11am–3pm and 7–11pm Mon–Fri; all day Sat; 12–3pm and 7–11pm Sun.

YOU TELL US

★ *Adam & Eve*, 8 Townsend Street, Alstone, Cheltenham
★ *Bayshill Inn*, 85 St George's Place, Cheltenham
★ *The Bristol Brewhouse*, Stokes Croft, Bristol
★ *The Cat & Wheel*, Cotham Brow, Bristol
★ *The Prince Albert*, Two Mile Hill Road, Kingswood, Bristol
★ *The Rose & Crown*, High Street, Iron Acton
★ *The Swan*, Pillowell
★ *The Twelve Bells*, 12 Lewis Lane, Cirencester

Places Featured:

Aldershot
Beauworth
Bentworth
Bishops Waltham
Chalton
Charter Alley
Cheriton
Dunbridge
Easton
Fareham
Farnborough
Freefolk Priors
Frogham
Froxfield
Gosport
Hamble
Hartley Wintney
Horndean

Lasham
Linwood
Liss
Little London
Meonstoke
Micheldever
Ovington
Portsmouth
Priors Dean
Ringwood
Rotherwick
Shedfield
Southampton
Southsea
Titchfield
Weyhill
Whitsbury

THE BREWERIES

BALLARD'S BREWERY LTD

*Unit C, The Old Sawmill, Nyewood, Rogate,
Petersfield GU31 5HA*
☎ *(01730) 821362*

 MIDHURST MILD 3.5% ABV
Winter brew, dark and smooth.
TROTTON BITTER 3.6%
Well-flavoured, well-hopped session bitter.
BEST BITTER 4.2% ABV
Nutty and well-balanced, with hops and
bitterness in the finish.
GOLDEN BINE 4.2% ABV
Occasional brew.
ON THE HOP 4.5% ABV
Occasional brew.
WILD 4.7% ABV
Occasional brew.
WHEATSHEAF 5.0% ABV
Occasional brew.
NYEWOOD GOLD 5.0% ABV
Golden, hoppy brew.
WASSAIL 6.0% ABV
Malty and powerful, but not over-sweet.
Plus a powerful Christmas ale.

BECKETT'S BREWERY LTD

*8 Enterprise Court, Rankine Road, Basingstoke
RG24 8GE*
☎ *(01256) 472986*

 OLD TOWN BITTER 3.7% ABV
ORIGINAL BITTER 4.0% ABV
BIER BLONDE 4.3% ABV
Pale with floral hoppiness. May and early July.
LIGHT MILD 4.3% ABV
Amber brown. Smoky and sweeter. May.
OLIVER'S ALE 4.3% ABV
Rounded and malty with delicate hoppiness. Jan.
WHITEWATER 4.3% ABV
Fruity, wheat flavour. Mid-July–late Aug.
AMBER 4.5% ABV
Rounded and hoppy. Late Aug–end Sept.
EXTRA MILD 4.5% ABV
Smoky, bitter flavour. Oct–mid-Nov.
LODDON BITTER 4.5% ABV
Amber and aromatic. Mid-Mar–end Apr.
GOLDEN GRALE 4.5% ABV
COBBETT'S BITTER 4.7% ABV
Hoppy bitterness. Jan–mid-Mar.
PORTER 4.7% ABV
Traditional porter-style ale. Mid-Nov.
ST NICHOLAS 5.3% ABV
Malty, Christmas brew.

THE CHERITON BREWHOUSE

Cheriton, Alresford SO24 0QQ
☎ *(01962) 771166*

 POTS ALE 3.8% ABV
Golden, with hoppiness throughout.
BEST BITTER 4.2% ABV
Pronounced fruit and malt flavour.
DIGGERS GOLD 4.6% ABV
Powerful hoppiness and bitter finish.
FLOWER POWER 5.2% ABV
TURKEY'S REVENGE 5.9% ABV
A Christmas ale.

CLARENCE TAVERN AND OLD CHAPEL BREWERY

1 Clarence Road, Gosport PO12 1BB
☎ *(023) 9252 9726*

OLD CHAPEL 3.8% ABV
BUCKLAND'S BEST 4.1% ABV
INVINCIBLE STOUT 4.5% ABV
WHOLE HEARTED 4.7% ABV
BLAKE'S GOSPORT BEST 5.2% ABV
Plus occasional brews.

GEORGE GALE & CO. LTD

The Brewery, Horndean PO8 0DA
☎ *(023) 9257 1212*

BUTSER BREW 3.4% ABV
A sweet brew, with fruit throughout.
GB 4.0% ABV
Malt flavour with some fruitiness. Bitter.
FESTIVAL MILD 4.8% ABV
Sweet and dark, with fruitiness.
HSB 4.8% ABV
Sweet and malty.
WINTER BREW 4.2% ABV
Smooth and rounded. Available Nov–Feb.

HAMPSHIRE BREWERY LTD

Romsey Industrial Estate, Greatbridge Road, Romsey SO51 0HR
☎ *(01794) 830000*

KING ALFRED'S BITTER 3.8% ABV
Amber, light, refreshing and complex.
LIONHEART 4.2% ABV
Golden and refreshing with subtle hop finish.
IRONSIDE 4.2% ABV
Amber, with crisp hop flavour and bitter finish.
PENDRAGON 4.8% ABV
Excellent balance. Bursting with malt hops.
PRIDE OF ROMSEY 5.0% ABV
Fragrant with distinctive bitterness.
1066 6.0% ABV
Light, powerful pale ale. Clean and subtle.
Plus seasonal brews.

ITCHEN VALLEY BREWERY

Shelf House, New Farm Road, Alresford SO24 9QE
☎ *(01962) 735111*

 GODFATHERS 3.8% ABV
Golden and hoppy with bittersweet flavour.
EASTER BUNNIES 4.0% ABV
Seasonal brew.
FAGIN'S 4.1% ABV
Balanced and hoppy, with citrus fruitiness.
WYKEHAMS GLORY 4.3% ABV
Smooth maltiness throughout.
JUDGE JEFFREYS 4.5% ABV
Copper coloured, rounded with hoppy bitterness.
GOLDEN ALE 4.8% ABV
FATHER CHRISTMAS 5.0% ABV
Seasonal brew
WATT TYLER 5.5% ABV
Seasonal brew.
Plus occasional brews.

PACKHORSE BREWERY

5 Somers Road, Southsea PO5 4PR
☎ *(023) 9275 0450*

SOUTHERN STAR 3.5% ABV
OLD POMPEY 4.8% ABV
RUDOLPH'S REVENGE 7.9% ABV
Seasonal brew.

RINGWOOD BREWERY LTD

138 Christchurch Road, Ringwood BH24 3AP
☎ *(01425) 471177*

BEST BITTER 3.8% ABV
Sweet malt flavour, becoming dry. Bitterness in the finish.
BOONDOGGLE 3.9% ABV
Available May–Sept.
TRUE GLORY 4.3% ABV
Smooth and malty throughout, with some fruit.
XXXX PORTER 4.7% ABV
Full-bodied, winter brew. Fruit, coffee and vanilla flavours.
FORTYNINER 4.9% ABV
Hop and malt flavour with malty finish.
OLD THUMPER 5.6% ABV
Golden with various fruit flavours.

TRIPPLE FFF BREWING CO.

Magpie Works, Unit 3, Station Approach,
Four Marks, Alton GU34 4HN
☎ *(01420) 561422*

BILLERICAY DICKIE 3.8% ABV
Hoppy session brew.
PRESSED RAT AND WARTHOG 3.8% ABV
Dark and malty with hoppy bitterness.
AFTER GLOW 4.0% ABV
Golden with delicate citrus fruit flavours.
MOONDANCE 4.2% ABV
Golden with fruity, hoppy flavour.
DAZED AND CONFUSED 4.6% ABV
Pale and hoppy.
STAIRWAY TO HEAVEN 4.6% ABV
Excellent balance.
LITTLE RED ROOSTER 5.0% ABV
Dark, with chocolate maltiness.
COMFORTABLY NUMB 5.0% ABV
Dark and fruity.

THE PUBS

ALDERSHOT

The Red Lion

Ash Road, Aldershot GU12 4EZ
☎ *(01252) 403503 Mr Freeth*

A freehouse serving a range of up to six weekly changing beers including Timothy Taylor Dark Mild, Oakham Perrywig and many, many more.

A traditional pub with beer garden. No music or pool. Food available Tues–Fri lunchtimes. Well-behaved children allowed.

All day Mon–Sat; 12–4pm and 7–10.30pm Sun.

BEAUWORTH

The Milburys

Beauworth, Alresford SO24 0PB
☎ *(01962) 771248 Mr Larden*

A freehouse with Milbury's Best (house beer) plus Hampshire Pride of Romsey and King Alfred's always available. Two guests change every couple of months.

A country pub with dining area and beer garden. Food available at lunchtime and evenings. Children allowed.

11am–3pm and 6–11pm (10.30pm Sun).

BENTWORTH

The Sun Inn

Bentworth, Nr Alton GU34 5JT
☎ *(01420) 562338 Mary Holmes*

Ringwood Best, Cheriton Pots Ale, Hampshire Sun (house beer) and Bunces Pigswill always available, plus at least four guest ales changed weekly. Regulars include Hogs Back TEA, Timothy Taylor Landlord, Ringwood Old Thumper, Badger Best and Abbey Bellringer.

A pretty seventeenth-century country inn with three connecting rooms. Stone and wooden floors. Food available at lunchtime and evenings. Children allowed.

12–3pm and 6–11pm Mon–Sat; all day Sun.

BISHOPS WALTHAM

The Hampshire Bowman
Dundridge Lane, Bishops Waltham,
Southampton SO32 1GD
☎ *(01489) 892940* Jim Park

A freehouse serving Archers Village and Golden and Ringwood Fortyniner plus guests such as Cheriton Flower Power.

Freehouse in a rural setting with beer garden. Archery next door. Food available at lunchtime and evenings. No children.

12–2pm Mon; 11am–2.30pm Tues–Sat;
12–3pm Sun; 6–11pm Mon–Sat;
7–10.30pm Sun.

CHALTON

The Red Lion
Chalton, Waterlooville PO8 0BG
☎ *(01705) 592246* Mr McGee

A Gales brewery tied house, serving HSB, Butser Bitter and GB plus one rotating guest changed monthly. This might be Marston's Pedigree, Shepherd Neame Spitfire, Charles Wells Bombardier or Wadworth 6X.

Reputed to be the oldest in Hampshire, this country pub with garden overlooks the Downs. Thatched roof, non-smoking dining area. Food available at lunchtime and evenings (not Sunday evenings). Under 14s allowed only if eating.

11am–3pm and 6–11pm Mon–Sat;
12–3pm and 7–10.30pm Sun.

CHARTER ALLEY

The White Hart
White Hart Lane, Charter Alley, Tadley
RG26 5QA
☎ *(01256) 850048* Howard Bradley

A freehouse with Greene King Abbot Ale always available, plus two guest beers. Brews from Otter and Harveys breweries are popular.

A village pub with dining area, skittle alley and garden. Food available at lunchtime and evenings. Children allowed in certain areas.

12–2.30pm Mon–Fri; 12–3pm Sat–Sun;
7–11pm Mon–Sat; 7–10.30pm Sun.

CHERITON

The Flower Pots Inn
Cheriton, Alresford SO24 0QQ
☎ *(01962) 771318*
Paul Tickner and Jo Bartlett

The Cheriton Brewhouse is situated very close to this pub, hence the full range of Cheriton brews are always available, plus occasional Cheriton specials. The two businesses are run separately though, and this is not the 'brewpub' that it is often mistaken for.

The pub is an unspoilt traditional inn on the edge of the village. Bar food is available every lunchtime and Mon–Sat evenings. Car park, garden, small children's room, accommodation. Children not allowed in the pub. CAMRA regional pub of the year 1995.

12–2.30pm and 6–11pm Mon–Sat;
12–3pm and 7–10.30pm Sun.

DUNBRIDGE

The Mill Arms
Barley Hill, Dunbridge, Nr Romsey SO51 0LF
☎ *(01794) 343401* Terry Lewis

A freehouse with up to four real ales changed every few days. These often include something from the Hampshire, Ringwood or Badger breweries.

A quiet country pub in the middle of nowhere! Two open fires, conservatory, restaurant, function room. Accommodation available in six en-suite rooms, some with four-poster beds. Large garden. Food available at lunchtime and evenings. Children and dogs welcome.

11am–3pm and 6–11pm (12–3pm during winter).

EASTON

The Cricketers Inn
Easton, Winchester SO21 1ET
☎ *(01962) 779353* John Sturges

A freehouse with a Ringwood brew and Otter Ale always available. Three weekly changing guests might be Hop Back Summer Lightning or a brew from Cottage or Sharp's.

A traditional village pub with drinking terrace and non-smoking dining area. Food available at lunchtime and evenings. B&B. Children allowed.

11am–3pm and 6–11pm (10.30pm Sun).

Osborne View Hotel

67 Hill Head Road, Fareham PO14 3JP
☎ *(01329) 664623* Ian Reabman

A Hall and Woodhouse (Badger) tied pub. Badger Best and IPA, Tanglefoot and Golden Champion always available plus two guests such as Gribble Blackadder.

A seafront pub on three levels. Non-smoking area, sea views, parking. Food available at lunchtime and evenings. Children and dogs welcome.

OPEN *11am–11pm (10.30pm Sun).*

The Prince of Wales

184 Rectory Road, Farnborough GU14 8AL
☎ *(01252) 5545578*

Brakspear Bitter, Badger Best and Tanglefoot, Fuller's London Pride, Hog's Back TEA and Ringwood Fortyniner always available plus up to four guest beers at any one time, which may include Hop Back Summer Lightning, Cheriton Pots Ale and Gales Festival.

An Edwardian freehouse with antique touches in three small connecting rooms. A busy, traditional pub serving food at lunchtime. Just around the corner from Farnborough North railway station. Children over 14 allowed.

OPEN *11.30am–2.30pm and 5.30–11pm Mon–Sat; 12–3.30pm and 7–10.30pm Sun.*

The Watership Down Inn

Freefolk, Nr Whitchurch RG28 7NJ
☎ *(01256) 892254* Mark and Alison Lodge

Real ale on five pumps with Archers Best, Brakspear IPA and a mild always available plus two constantly changing guests usually from smaller breweries including Ringwood, Otter, Moor, Juwards, Beckett's, Itchen Valley, Oakhill, Tripple FFF and Butts.

Built in 1840, renamed after the Richard Adams novel that was set locally, a one-bar pub with an open fire and pretty garden with many outside tables. Bar and restaurant food available at lunchtime and evenings, plus new non-smoking conservatory that seats 30 diners. Car park, children's play area. Children allowed in the restaurant. On the B3400 between Whitchurch and Overton.

OPEN *11.30am–3.30pm and 6–11pm (10.30pm Sun).*

The Forester's Arms

Abbots Well Road, Frogham, Fordingbridge SP6 2JA
☎ *(01425) 652294* Mr M Harding

A Wadworth tied house with 6X and Henry's IPA always available plus two seasonal or special brews such as Mayhem Odda's Light.

A country inn in the New Forest area. Dartboard, garden children's play area. Food available at lunchtime and evenings in a separate restaurant. Children and dogs welcome.

OPEN *11am–3pm and 6–11pm Mon–Sat; 12–3pm and 7–10.30pm Sun.*

The Trooper Inn

Froxfield, Petersfield GU32 1BD
☎ *(01730) 827293* Mr Matini

A freehouse serving Ringwood Fortyniner and Best plus a couple of weekly changing guests from breweries such as Ballard's.

A country pub with dining area, function room and garden. Food available at lunchtime and evenings. Children allowed.

OPEN *All day, every day.*

Queens Hotel

143 Queens Road, Gosport
☎ *(023) 9258 2645* Sue Lampon

Archers Village, Black Sheep Special and Badger Tanglefoot are usually available, plus a porter served during the winter months. Two or three guest beers are also served from a constantly changing selection of breweries.

Popular town pub with good selection of ales. Snacks and rolls served at lunchtimes only. No children.

OPEN *11.30am–2.30pm and 7–11pm Mon–Fri; 11.30am–11pm Sat; 12–3pm and 7–10.30pm Sun.*

The King & Queen

High Street, Hamble, Southampton SO31 4HA
☎ *(01703) 454247* Ken Smith

A Whitbread house with Fuller's London Pride, Wadworth 6X, and a Brakspear brew always available, plus a changing guest from local breweries such as Cottage or Hampshire.

A sailing pub with log fires and billiards. Separate restaurant serving food at lunchtime and evenings. Children allowed in the restaurant only.

OPEN *11am–11pm (10.30pm Sun).*

HARTLEY WINTNEY

The Wagon & Horses

High Street, Hartley Wintney, Nr Hook
RG27 8NX
☎ *(01252) 842119* Neil Scott

A freehouse with Gales HSB always available, plus two guest beers, often brews from Ringwood but changing all the time.

A typical village pub with secluded garden. Food available at lunchtime. No children.

11am–11pm Mon–Sat; 12–3pm and 7–10.30pm Sun.

HORNDEAN

Ship & Bell Hotel

6 London Road, Horndean, Waterlooville
PO8 0BZ
☎ *(01705) 592107* Allan Clarke

A Gales Brewery house serving Butser, HSB and GB plus seasonal specials and a range of other guests perhaps including Everards Tiger.

A village pub with separate dining area and accommodation. Children allowed if eating.

All day, every day.

LASHAM

The Royal Oak

Lasham, Nr Alton GU34 5SJ
☎ *(01256) 381213* Rob Caithness

Ringwood Best, Fuller's London Pride, Hogs Back TEA and a house ale brewed by Beckett's of Basingstoke, plus guests from independent breweries including Sharp's, Triple FFF and Stonehenge Ales. Cask marque approved.

A cosy, two-bar pub with open fires, beams and brickwork. Quiet, enclosed beer garden. Pool table and dartboard in the village bar. Bar food available at lunchtime and evenings. Car park. Just off the A339, four miles from Alton, six miles from Basingstoke.

11am–2.30pm and 6–11pm Mon–Fri; 11am–3pm and 6–11pm Sat; 12–3pm and 7–10.30pm Sun.

LINWOOD

The Red Shoot Inn & Brewery

Toms Lane, Linwood, Ringwood BH24 3QT
☎ *(01425) 475792*
Mr P Adams and Mr AJ Benson

Wadworth 6X, IPA and Farmers Glory plus Red Shoot's own beers – Forest Gold and Tom's Tipple – usually available. Wadworth seasonal brews also served.

This Wadworth-owned, New Forest pub is home to the Red Shoot Brewery. Food served lunchtimes and evenings. Children welcome. Car park. Signposted from A338 at Ellingham.

 FOREST GOLD 3.8% ABV
TOM'S TIPPLE 4.8% ABV

Winter: 11am–3pm and 6–11pm Mon–Fri; 11am–11pm Sat; 12–10.30pm Sun; Summer: 11am–11pm Mon–Sat; 12–10.30pm Sun.

LISS

The Bluebell

Farnham Road, Liss GU33 6JE
☎ *(01730) 892107* George Doa

A freehouse with Fuller's London Pride always available plus three guests including, perhaps, Hogs Back Triple and Moondance, Ballard's Best, Beckett's Original or Gales GB.

A pub/restaurant, half smoking and half non-smoking. International cuisine served at lunchtime and evenings, with a choice of either à la carte or bar menu. Beer garden. Children allowed.

11.30am–3pm and 5–11pm (10.30pm Sun).

LITTLE LONDON

The Plough Inn

Silchester Road, Little London, Tadley RG26 5EP
☎ *(01256) 850628* Mr Brown

A freehouse with Ringwood Best and True Glory usually available plus a large selection of guest ales.

A country pub with nice gardens and log fires in winter. Hot, filled baguettes served at lunchtime and evening. Children allowed.

12–2.30pm and 6–11pm Mon–Sat; 12–3pm and 7–10.30pm Sun.

MEONSTOKE

The Bucks Head

Bucks Head Hill, Meonstoke, Southampton
SO32 3NA
☎ *(01489) 877313* Stewart McKenzie

A Morland house with Old Speckled Hen and Ruddles Best always available plus two guests from a list including Charles Wells Bombardier and Cheriton Best.

A rural country pub on the banks of the river. Tourist Board recommended with separate restaurant and B&B. Food available at lunchtime and evenings. Well-behaved children and dogs allowed. Situated just off the A32 north of Dropsford

11am–3pm and 6–11pm Mon–Fri; all day Sat–Sun and bank holidays.

MICHELDEVER

Half Moon & Spread Eagle

Winchester Road, Micheldever SO21 3DG
☎ *(01962) 774339*
Belinda and Ray Boughtwood

A Greene King tenancy with Greene King ales always available, plus guests.

A popular rural pub with sixteenth-century walls and original beams. Wide selection of mainly home-cooked food served lunchtimes and evenings daily, plus take-away service. Large garden and patio, children's play area overlooking village cricket green. Car park. Less than a mile off the A33, six miles north of Winchester, 12 miles south of Basingstoke.

12–3pm and 6–11pm Mon–Sat; 12–3pm and 7–10.30pm Sun.

OVINGTON

The Bush Inn

Nr Arlesford, Ovington SO24 0RE
☎ *(01962) 732764* Nick Young

Wadworth 6X and IPA and The Red Shoot brewpub's Pom's Tipple permanently available, plus two guests changing every two weeks. Wadworth Farmer's Glory and Badger Tanglefoot are regular features.

A seventeenth-century up and down pub with lots of little rooms and antique memorabilia. Real fires make it cosy in the winter. One main bar in the middle of the pub. Beer garden. Food available every lunchtime and Mon–Sat evenings. Well-behaved children allowed. Situated off the A31 towards Winchester.

11am–3pm and 6–11pm Mon–Sat; 12–3pm and 7–10.30pm Sun.

PORTSMOUTH

The Connaught Arms

119 Guildford Road, Fratton, Portsmouth
PO1 5EA
☎ *(023) 9264 6455* Mick and Carol Frewing

Three guest beers usually available, perhaps Caledonian Deuchars IPA, Fuller's London Pride, Hopback Summer Lightning, Cheriton Pots Ale, Ringwood Fortyniner or others.

Comfortable pub hidden in the back streets of Fratton famous for its interesting range of pasties. Bar menu available 11.45am–2.15pm Mon–Sat; pasties available every session. Well-behaved children welcome until 7pm. Situated at the junction of Penhale and Guildford roads.

11.30am–2.30pm and 6–11pm Mon–Thurs; 11.30am–11pm Fri–Sat; 12–4pm and 7–10.30pm Sun.

The Dolphin

41 High Street, Portsmouth PO1 2LV
☎ *(023) 9282 3595* Romayne Spooner

Eight real ales on tap including Wadworth 6X, Badger Tanglefoot, Gales HSB and Marston's Pedigree plus something from Ringwood and Fuller's and many other guests on a constantly rotating basis. Local brewers supported whenever possible.

A sixteenth-century coaching inn with wood and flagstone floors. Historic area with good walks nearby. The pub boasts Nelson's signature on a piece of glass in the bar! Bar food available at lunchtime and evenings. Small function room. Children allowed. Directly opposite the cathedral in old Portsmouth.

11am–11pm Mon–Sat; 12–10.30pm Sun.

The Tap

17 London Road, North End, Portsmouth
PO2 0BQ
☎ *(023) 9261 4861*

Up to 11 beers available including Ruddles Best and Ringwood Old Thumper. Guests (100 per year) will include Ringwood Best, Badger Tanglefoot, Gales HSB and brews from the Brewery on Sea. Micro-breweries particularly favoured.

A one-bar drinking pub in the town centre with no juke box or fruit machines. Formerly the brewery tap for the now defunct Southsea Brewery. Bar meals available at lunchtime. Street parking opposite, small yard, disabled toilet. Children not allowed.

10.30am–11pm Mon–Sat; 12–10.30pm Sun.

The Wellington

62 High Street, Portsmouth PO1 2LY
☎ *(023) 9281 8965* Mr Western

Wadworth 6X and Greene King IPA available plus a guest from breweries such as Fuller's.

A traditional community pub with a reputation for good food served at lunchtime and four evenings per week. Use the harbour entrance. Children allowed.

OPEN *11am–11pm (10.30pm Sun).*

Wetherspoons

2 Guildhall Walk, Portsmouth PO1 2DD
☎ *(023) 9229 5112*
Linda Price and Stuart Coxshall

Hop Back Bitter and Bateman Mild always available plus two guests changed daily including, perhaps, Tom Wood Harvest Bitter (High Wood), Hook Norton Generation or Bateman Spring Breeze.

A friendly town pub with non-smoking area. Food served all day. No children.

OPEN *10am–11pm Mon–Sat; 12–10.30pm Sun.*

The Winchester Arms and Buckland Brewery

99 Winchester Road, Portsmouth PO2 7PS
☎ *(023) 9266 2443* Mr Mapleton

Home of the Buckland Brewery with Buckland Best, Blakes of Gosport and Old Chapel permanently available, plus other home brews as and when available. Guests from the Beer Seller, such as Mendip Gold also sometimes featured.

Small, back-street, community village pub: come in a stranger, go home a friend! Piano player Sun evenings. Traditional Sunday roasts and barbecues are the only food available. Children allowed in the non-smoking, snug bar (not main bar).

OLD ANVIL 3.6% ABV
OLD CHAPEL 3.8% ABV
BUCKLAND BEST BITTER 4.2% ABV
INVINCIBLE STOUT 4.5% ABV
WHOLEHEARTED SUMMER 4.7% ABV
WINCHESTER WISE BEER 5.0% ABV
BLAKES OF GOSPORT 5.2% ABV
TRUE BLUE 5.4% ABV
Plus seasonal specials.

OPEN *6–11pm Mon; 12–2pm and 4–11pm Tues–Thurs; 11am–11pm Fri–Sat; 12–4pm and 7–10.30pm Sun.*

The White Horse Inn

Priors Dean, Nr Petersfield GU32 1DA
☎ *(01420) 588387* Mr J Eddleston

Gales Festival Mild, HSB and Butser Brew Bitter, Ballard's Best plus Ringwood Fortyniner always available and guest beers (ten per year) including Wadworth 6X, Bateman Summer Breeze, Gales IPA and Porter, plus a range of one-off brews from Gales.

An olde-world pub untouched for years, with log fires, rocking chairs, antique furniture and a grandfather clock. Bar food available at lunchtime. Car park and garden. Nearby caravan site. Tricky to find. Midway between Petersfield and Alton, five miles from Petersfield, seven miles from Alton.

OPEN *11am–2.30pm and 6–11pm Mon–Fri; 11am–3pm and 6–11pm Sat; 12–3pm and 7–10.30pm Sun.*

Inn on the Furlong

12 Meeting House Lane, Ringwood BH24 1EY
☎ *(01425) 475139* Joyce Perkins

Tied to the Ringwood brewery, so Best, Fortyniner and Old Thumper available, plus a seasonal beer.

An old building with log fire, conservatory and beer garden. Food available at lunchtime. Children allowed.

OPEN *All day Wed/Fri/Sat; closed afternoons Mon/Tue/Thurs.*

The Falcon

The Street, Rotherwick, Hook RG27 9BL
☎ *(01256) 762586* Robert Tilbrook

An Eldridge Pope tied house with Brakspear Bitter plus three guests such as Hampshire Pendragon or Gibbs Mew Bishop's Tipple.

A traditional family pub with restaurant and beer garden. Food available at lunchtime and evenings. Children allowed.

OPEN *All day, every day.*

CHERITON BREWHOUSE

Diggers Gold

4.6% ABV

SHEDFIELD

The Wheatsheaf Inn
Botley Road, Shedfield, Southampton SO32 2JG
☎ *(01329) 833024* Mr Rennie

A freehouse serving Cheriton Pots Ale, Mansfield Four Season, Cotleigh Tawny, and Hop Back Summer Lightning plus two different guests every week.

A country pub with garden. Food available at lunchtime. Children allowed in the garden only.

OPEN *All day, every day.*

SOUTHAMPTON

The Alexandra
6 Belle Vue Road, Southampton SO15 2AY
☎ *(023) 8033 5071* Miss Hiles

A Whitbread house with Wadworth 6X and Fuller's London Pride always available, plus two guests per week, such as Gales HSB, Hop Back Summer Lightning or a Ringwood brew.

A town-centre pub with traditional building. One bar with big TV and juke box. Food available at lunchtime. No children.

OPEN *All day, every day.*

Bevois Castle
63 Onslow Road, Bevois Valley, Southampton SO14 OJL
☎ *(023) 8033 0350* Mr D Bulpitt

Two guest beers from Itchen Valley and Hampshire brewery regularly served.

Small, traditional pub with real fire and shove ha'penny board. Full menu available 11.30am–3pm and 6.30–9.30pm. Hot pies and pasties available all day. No children's facilities. Car park.

OPEN *11am–11pm (10.30pm Sun).*

The Crown Inn
9 Highcrown Street, Southampton SO17 1QE
☎ *(023) 8031 5033* Jackie Hayer

A Whitbread house with Wadworth 6X and Fuller's London Pride always available plus a rotating guest ale, often from Archers.

A city pub and restaurant with food available at lunchtime and evenings. Children allowed in the restaurant only.

OPEN *11am–11pm Mon–Sat; 12–10.30pm Sun.*

The Duke of Wellington
36 Bugle Street, Southampton SO14 2AH
☎ *(023) 8033 9222* Mr Wyle

A Wadworth-managed house offering the range of Wadworth ales, plus Ringwood Best. Guests may include Adnams Southwold.

Built in the twelfth century, this is the oldest pub in Southampton. Food available at lunchtime and evenings in a separate dining area. Function room. Children welcome.

OPEN *All day, every day.*

The Eagle
1 Palmerston Road, Southampton SO14 1LL
☎ *(023) 8033 3825* Tina Austin

A Whitbread house with Wadworth 6X and Fuller's London Pride always available, plus four guests from a range of ales such as Gibbs Mew Bishop's Tipple, Ringwood Porter (winter only), Old Thumper, Fortyniner or Marston's Pedigree.

A traditional town-centre pub with darts and pool. Food available at lunchtime. No children.

OPEN *All day, every day.*

The South Western Arms
36–40 Adelaide Road, Southampton SO17 2HW
☎ *(023) 8032 4542* Simon Woodall

Wadworth 6X, Fuller's London Pride, Gales HSB and Badger Tanglefoot are permanent fixtures, plus three guests such as Greene King Abbot.

A split-level pub with the bar on the ground floor and a games area with TV on the first floor. No food. Children allowed upstairs only.

OPEN *4–11pm Mon–Thurs; all day Fri–Sun.*

The Standing Order
30 High Street, Southampton SO14 3HT
☎ *(023) 8022 2121* Wayne Ellis

A Wetherspoon's pub with Bateman Dark Mild, Shepherd Neame Spitfire and Marston's Pedigree always available, plus about ten different guests per week.

A traditional high-street pub with non-smoking area. Food available all day. No children.

OPEN *10am–11pm Mon–Sat; 12–10.30pm Sun.*

The Stiles

163 University Road, Southampton SO17 1TS
☎ *(023) 8058 1124* Kelvin Jiggle

Gales HSB and a couple of guests always on offer. Something like Brains SA, Ruddles Best or perhaps Fuller's London Pride.

A city-based student pub with food served at lunchtimes only. No children.

OPEN *11am–11pm.*

Waterloo Arms

101 Waterloo Road, Southampton SO15 3BS
☎ *(023) 8022 0022* Paul Osgood

A Hop Back pub serving Summer Lightning, Thunderstorm, GFB, Festive Stout and Best, plus guests rotated weekly on one pump, perhaps King and Barnes Festive, Woodforde's Wherry or something from the Hampshire Brewery.

A local, traditional, village pub with garden. Food available at lunchtime and evenings. Children allowed.

OPEN *All day, every day.*

The Wellington Arms

56 Park Road, Freemantle, Southampton SO15 3DE
☎ *(023) 8022 7356* Charles Oliver

A freehouse with Wadworth 6X, Ringwood Old Thumper and Best, Fuller's London Pride and ESB always available, plus four constantly changing guests. Has served 2,300 real ales (54 different ones in April 1999 alone). Also serves one Belgian and one German brew.

A town pub with garden and à la carte restaurant. Bar or restaurant food served at lunchtime and evenings. Children allowed in the garden.

OPEN *11.30am–3pm Mon–Sat; 12–4pm Sun; 5.30–11pm Mon–Thurs; 5–11pm Fri; 6–11pm Sat; 6.30–10.30pm Sun.*

SOUTHSEA

The Artillery Arms

Hester Road, Southsea PO4 8HB
☎ *(023) 9273 3610* Tom Forsyth

A freehouse with Gales, Hampshire and Cheriton brews always available, plus up to four guest ales.

A traditional pub with garden. Food available at lunchtime and evenings. Children allowed until 9pm (8pm Sat).

OPEN *11am–3pm and 6–11pm Mon–Thurs; all day Fri–Sun.*

The Old Oyster House

291 Lockway Road, Southsea, Portsmouth PO4 8LH
☎ *(023) 9282 7456* Mark and Karen Landon

A constantly changing selection of beers, usually including a mild, is available perhaps from Ash Vine, Hop Back, Packhorse, Teignworthy or Abbey Ales.

Friendly, comfortable and busy pub with separate games bar for pool, darts, table football and big screen Sky Sport. Large garden and patio. No food. Large public car park opposite. Well-behaved children welcome in the games bar. Located at the end of a mile-long cul de sac.

OPEN *4–11pm Mon–Thurs; 12–11pm Fri–Sat; 12–10.30pm Sun.*

Wine Vaults

43–7 Albert Road, Southsea PO5 2SF
☎ *(023) 9286 4712*
Mike Hughes and Jeremy Stevens

Hop Back GFB and Summer Lightning usually available plus up to six other brews, perhaps from Greene King, Itchen Valley, Tisbury, Stonehenge or Ringwood breweries.

Friendly, traditional pub with varied clientele and good atmosphere. Food served 12–9pm daily. Well-behaved over 5s welcome, but there are no special facilities. Located directly opposite Kings Theatre.

OPEN *12–11pm (10.30pm Sun).*

TITCHFIELD

The Wheatsheaf Inn

1 East Street, Titchfield, Fareham PO14 4AD
☎ *(01329) 842965* Adrienne DoNoia

A freehouse serving Fuller's London Pride and Woodforde's Wherry plus two guests changed weekly. Examples may include Hook Norton Best and Exmoor Gold.

A village pub with dining area, open fire, patio and garden. Food available at lunchtime and evenings. Children allowed in the dining area only.

OPEN *12–3pm and 6–11pm Mon–Thurs; all day Fri; 12–3pm and 6–11pm Sat; 12–3pm and 7–10.30pm Sun.*

WEYHILL

Weyhill Fair

Weyhill Road, Weyhill, Nr Andover SP11 0PP
☎ *(01264) 773631* Mr and Mrs Rayner

 Fuller's London Pride, Chiswick and ESB always available plus three guest beers (200 per year) including brews from Shepherd Neame, Adnams and Ringwood.

A friendly local freehouse offering bar food at lunchtime and evenings. Cask Marque award winner. Car park, garden and non-smoking family room. On the A342 west of Andover.

11am–3pm and 6–11pm Mon–Thurs; 11am–3pm and 5–11pm Fri; 11am–3pm and 6–11pm Sat; 12–3pm and 7–10.30pm Sun.

WHITSBURY

The Cartwheel

Whitsbury Road, Whitsbury, Nr Fordingbridge SP6 3PZ
☎ *(01725) 518362 Fax (01725) 518886* Patrick Lewis

Up to six beers always available (120 per year) but brews continually changing. Breweries favoured include Adnams, Shepherd Neame, Bunces, Hop Back, Ringwood and Mole's. Seasonal beers and small breweries preferred.

A relaxed bar with exposed beams and open fire, in good walking country. Bar and restaurant food available at lunchtime and evenings. Car park and garden. Children allowed in the restaurant. Turn west of Salisbury onto the Fordingbridge road at Breamore. Signposted from the A338. E-mail: thecartwheel@lineone.net

11am–2.30pm and 6–11pm; all day Sun in summer.

YOU TELL US

★ *The Axford Arms*, Farleigh Road, Axford
★ *The Eagle Hotel*, City Road, Winchester
★ *Hawkley Inn*, Pococks Lane, Hawkley, Liss
★ *The Newport Inn*, Newport Lane, Brashfield
★ *The Old Gaol House*, 11 Jewry Street, Whitchurch
★ *The Plough*, Ashmansworth
★ *The Raven*, Bedford Street, Portsmouth (brewpub)
★ *The Rampant Cat*, Broad Layings, Woolton Hill
★ *Sir Robert Peel*, Astley Street, Southsea

Places Featured:

Aston Crews
Aymestry
Birtsmorton
Bretforton
Broadway
Bromyard
Dodford
Evesham
Fromes Hill
Hampton Bishop
Hanley-Broadheath
Hanley Castle
Hereford
Kempsey
Kidderminster
Kington
Knightwick

Ledbury
Leominster
Malvern
Much Dewchurch
Norton Canon
Offenham
Ombersley
Pensax
Pershore
Ross-on-Wye
Shatterford
Stourport-on-Severn
Tenbury Wells
Uphampton
Weatheroak
Worcester

THE BREWERIES

BRANDY CASK BREWING CO.
25 Bridge Street, Pershore WR10 1AJ
☎ *(01386)552602*

WHISTLING JOE 3.6% ABV
BRANDY SNAPPER 4.0% ABV
JOE BAKER'S ORIGINAL 4.8% ABV

FROME VALLEY BREWERY
Bishop's Frome WR6 5AS
☎ *(01531) 640321*

PREMIUM BITTER 3.8% ABV
FIFTY NOT OUT 4.0 ABV
Plus occasional brews.

HOBSONS BREWERY & CO.
Newhouse Farm, Tenbury Road, Cleobury
Mortimer, Kidderminster DY14 8RD
☎ *(01299) 270837*

BEST BITTER 3.8% ABV
Excellent, hoppy session bitter.
TOWN CRIER 4.5% ABV
Smooth, mellow sweetness with balancing hops.
OLD HENRY 5.2% ABV
Darker, smooth and flavoursome.
Plus occasional brews.

MALVERN HILLS BREWERY
15 West Malvern Road, North Malvern
WR14 4ND
☎ *(01684) 577336*

BITTER 3.9% ABV
WORCESTERSHIRE WHYM 4.1% ABV
BLACK PEAR 4.4% ABV

MARCHES ALES
Unit 6, Western Close, Southern Avenue
Industrial Estate, Leominster HR6 0QD
☎ *(01568) 611084*

SUNSHINE ALE 3.5% ABV
BEST BITTER 3.8% ABV
Easy drinking.
BLACK HORSE BITTER 3.8% ABV
Specially brewed for the Black Horse, Leominster.
LEMPSTER ORE 3.8% ABV
Hoppy, easy quaffer.
FOREVER AUTUMN 4.2% ABV
Brewed with new season's hops.
GOLD 4.5% ABV
Pale, award-winner.
LORD PROTECTOR 4.7% ABV
Powerful hoppiness.
PRIORY ALE 4.8% ABV
Smooth, ruby ale.
JENNY PIPES BLONDE BIERE 5.2% ABV
Brewed with Saaz hops.
EARL LEOFRIC'S WINTER ALE 7.2% ABV
Winter warmer, available December.

SP SPORTING ALES LTD
Cantilever Lodge, Stoke Prior, Leominster
HR6 0LG
☎ *(01568) 760226*

WINNERS 3.5% ABV
Amber, refreshing and full-flavoured for
gravity.
DOVES DELIGHT 4.0% ABV
Dark amber, rich and well-balanced.
JOUST BOOTIFUL 4.2% ABV
JOUST 'PERFIC' 4.5% ABV
Smooth and creamy.
Plus seasonal brews.

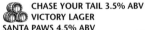

SPINNING DOG BREWERY
88 St Owen Street, Hereford HR1 2QD
☎ *(01432) 274998*

 CHASE YOUR TAIL 3.5% ABV
VICTORY LAGER
SANTA PAWS 4.5% ABV
Seasonal Christmas ale.

ST GEORGE'S BREWERY
The Old Bakehouse, Bush Lane, Callow End, Worcester WR2 4TF
☎ *(01905) 831316*

 PRIDE 3.8% ABV
WAR DRUM 4.1% ABV

WOODBURY BREWERY LTD
Home Farm Cottage, Great Witley, Worcester WR6 6JJ
☎ *(01299) 896219*

WHITE GOOSE 3.8% ABV
Pale, refreshing with clean, hoppy bitterness.
OLD HOUSE 4.3% ABV
Full-bodied, malty with a touch of wheat.
MONUMENTAL 5.0% ABV
A stronger version of Old House.
WITLEY WONOFFS
Occasional brews, seasonal or just for the fun of it!

WOODHAMPTON BREWERY
Aymestrey
☎ *(01568) 770503*

WYE VALLEY BREWERY
69 Owen Street, Hereford, Herefordshire HR1 2JQ
☎ *(01432) 274968*

BITTER 3.5% ABV
HEREFORD PALE ALE 4% ABV
DOROTHY GOODBODY'S WONDERFUL SPRINGTIME BITTER 4% ABV
DOROTHY GOODBODY'S GOLDEN SUMMERTIME ALE 4.2% ABV
BUTTY BACH 4.5% ABV
DOROTHY GOODBODY'S AUTUMN DELIGHT 4.4% ABV
DOROTHY GOODBODY'S WHOLESOME STOUT 4.6% ABV
WINTER TIPPLE 4.7% ABV
TRAVELLER'S BEST 5.0% ABV

WYRE PIDDLE BREWERY
Craycombe Farm, Fladbury, Evesham WR10 2QS
☎ *(01386) 860473*

 PIDDLE IN THE HOLE 3.9% ABV
PIDDLE IN THE WIND 4.2% ABV
Plus occasional and seasonal brews.

THE PUBS

ASTON CREWS

The Ha'Penny
Aston Crews, Nr Ross-on-Wye, Herefordshire HR9 7LW
☎ *(01989) 750203*

Wadworth 6X, Marston's Pedigree and Bitter and Banks's Mild always available plus two guests (20 per year) including Morland Old Speckled Hen, Timothy Taylor Landlord and Adnams Best and others from smaller breweries.

A beautifully restored old pub in glorious countryside. Bar food available at lunchtime and evenings. Car park, garden and games room. Turn off the A40 Ross to Gloucester road at Lea, onto the B4222.

OPEN *12–3pm and 6–11pm.*

The Penny Farthing
Aston Crews, Nr Ross-on-Wye, Herefordshire HR9 7LW
☎ *(01989) 750366 Mr and Mrs Brown*

Marston's Pedigree and Bitter and Wadworth 6X always available plus a guest beer (ten per year) which may be Shepherd Neame Spitfire, Morland Old Speckled Hen or from Robinson's or Hook Norton breweries.

A country inn and restaurant. Bar and restaurant food available at lunchtime and evenings. Car park and garden. Children allowed in the restaurant. Turn off the A40 Ross-on-Wye to Gloucester road at Lea, on to the B4222 (signposted to Newent). The Penny Farthing is one mile down this road.

OPEN *12–3pm and 7–11pm.*

AYMESTRY

The Riverside Inn
Aymestry, Leominster, Herefordshire HL6 9ST
☎ *(01568) 708440 Steve Bowen*

Beers from the nearby Woodhampton Brewery including Red Kite, Kingfisher and Jack Snipe. Also one guest, which could be Timothy Taylor Landlord or Marston's Pedigree.

A rural village pub with one bar, dining area and riverside garden. Limited disabled access, but willing. Food available at lunchtime and evenings. Children over seven permitted.

OPEN *12–3pm and 6.30–11pm (10.30pm Sun).*

BIRTSMORTON

The Farmer's Arms
Birts Street, Birtsmorton, Malvern, Worcestershire WR13 6AP
☎ *(01684) 833308* Julie Moore

Hook Norton Best and Old Hooky always available plus one guest from breweries such as Ledbury, Cottage or Cannon Royall.

A traditional two-bar country freehouse with beer garden. Food available at lunchtime and evenings in a separate dining area at one end of the bar. Children allowed.

11am–3pm and 6–11pm Mon–Sat; 12–4pm and 7–10.30pm Sun.

BRETFORTON

The Fleece Inn
The Cross, Bretforton, Worcesterhire WR11 5JE
☎ *(01386) 831173* Graham Brown

Hook Norton and Uley brews always available, plus guests.

This pub is 650 years old and has been used by the BBC as a film location. Owned by the National Trust, it is also a working museum. Non-smoking family room. East of Evesham, in the middle of the village.

11am–3pm and 6–11pm Sun–Fri; all day Sat.

BROADWAY

The Crown & Trumpet Inn
Church Street, Broadway, Worcestershire WR12 7AE
☎ *(01386) 853202* Andrew Scott

Morland Old Speckled Hen and Wadworth 6X available. In summer, Colteswold Gold (produced especially by Stanway Brewery) is available, and in winter, Stanway Lords-a-Leaping is served.

A seventeenth-century village inn built from Cotswold stone. Food at lunchtimes and evenings. Beer garden. Accommodation. Well-behaved children allowed. Website: www.cotswoldholidays.co.uk

11am–2.30pm and 5–11pm Sun–Fri; all day Sat.

BROMYARD

The Rose & Lion Inn
5 New Road, Bromyard, Herefordshire HR7 4AJ
☎ *(01885) 482381* Mrs Herdman

A Wye Valley tied house always serving Bitter, Hereford Pale Ale, Dorothy Goodbody's and Butty Back beers. One weekly changing guest, sometimes a seasonal Wye Valley ale such as Springtime, or brews such as Coach House Gunpowder Strong Mild.

A two-bar drinking house. Old, traditional building with garden. No food. Children allowed in the garden only.

11am–3pm and 6–11pm Mon–Fri; all day most Sat–Sun.

DODFORD

The Dodford Inn
Whinfield Road, Dodford, Bromsgrove, Worcestershire B61 9BG
☎ *(01527) 832470* Larry Bowen

Three guests available, from breweries such as Titanic, Evesham and Young's. Some 2000 beers served over five years.

A traditional country pub situated in an historic village. Beamed ceilings, very large garden and campsite plus two patios. Food served at lunchtime and evenings. Children allowed.

12–3pm and 6–11pm Mon–Fri; all day Sat; 12–3pm and 6–10.30pm Sun.

EVESHAM

The Green Dragon
17 Oat Street, Evesham, Worcestershire WR11 4PJ
☎ *(01386) 443462*

Home of the Evesham Brewery. Two Asum brews produced and sold, 'Asum' being the local pronunciation of 'Evesham'. Other guest ales also offered.

The brewery is housed in the old bottle store. A Grade II listed pub with a cosy lounge. Bar and restaurant food is served at lunchtime and evenings. Car park, garden, large function room. Children allowed.

ASUM ALE 3.8% ABV
A malty session ale.
ASUM GOLD 5.2% ABV
Fruity, malty and sweet strong ale.

11am–11pm Mon–Thur; 11pm–1am Fri–Sat.

The Queens Head & Fat God's Brewery

Iron Cross, Evesham, Worcestershire WR11 5SH
☎ *(01386) 871012* Andy and Kym Miller

Home to the Fat God's Brewery with the whole range of beers usually available.

Rural brew pub on B4088 Evesham to Alcester road opposite Salford Priors. Food served all day. Children welcome. Car park.

FAT GOD'S BITTER 3.6% ABV
Light-coloured and hoppy.
MORRIS DANCER 3.9% ABV
Red-tinged, smooth and full-flavoured.
FAT GOD'S MILD 4.0% ABV
Dark and nutty.
MERRY MILLERS RUSTY DUSTY 4.0% ABV
Reddish golden brown colour. Hoppy. Available Sept–Oct.
PORTER OF THE VALE 4.1% ABV
Black and packed with smooth roast malt flavour.
MERRY MILLERS SUMMER SENSATION 4.3% ABV
Hoppy seasonal brew. Availble Jul–Aug.
THUNDER & LIGHTNING 4.3% ABV
Balanced, malty full-flavoured bitter.
MERRY MILLERS SPRING CELEBRATION 4.5% ABV
Golden and flavour-packed. Available Mar–June.
MERRY MILLERS WINTER WOBBLER 4.9% ABV
Hoppy, easy-drinking seasonal brew. Available Nov–Feb.

All day, every day.

FROMES HILL

Wheatsheaf Inn

Fromes Hill, Ledbury, Herefordshire HR8 1HT
☎ *(01531) 640888* Mr Mirfin

A brewpub serving Fromes Hill Buckswood Dingle and Overture. Also occasional guests.

A country inn with one bar, dining area and garden. Food served at lunchtime and evenings. Children allowed.

BUCKSWOOD DINGLE 3.6% ABV
EIGHTH OVERTURE 4.2% ABV

All day, every day.

HAMPTON BISHOP

Bunch of Carrots

Hampton Bishop, Hereford, Herefordshire HR1 4JR
☎ *(01432) 870237*
Chris Collins and Mhari Ashworth

Hook Norton Best Bitter and a guest beer, often from local breweries, regularly available.

Traditional country inn with open fires and stone-clad floors, beer garden and function room. Situated two miles from Hereford city centre on the B4224, close to the River Wye. Disabled facilities. Carvery and bar food served lunchtimes and evenings. Car park. Children's menu and play area in the garden.

11am–3pm and 6–11pm Mon–Sat; 12–4pm and 6–10.30pm Sun.

HANLEY-BROADHEATH

The Fox Inn

Hanley-Broadheath, Tenbury Wells, Worcestershire
☎ *(01886) 853219* Keith Williams

Batham Best Bitter and a beer from Hobsons usually available.

Set in lovely countryside, part of this pub dates from the sixteenth century. Food available 12–2.30pm (summer only) and 6–9.30pm in separate reastaurant. Games room. Car park. Outside children's play area. Situated on the B4204 Tenbury Wells to Worcester road.

12–2.30pm and 6–11pm daily (10.30pm Sun).

HANLEY CASTLE

The Three Kings

Church End, Hanley Castle, Worcestershire WR8 0BL
☎ *(01684) 592686* Mrs Sheila Roberts

Thwaites and Butcombe brews available plus three guest beers (more than 150 per year) perhaps from Brandy Cask, Evesham, Mildmay, Fromes Hill, Crouch Vale, Berkeley, Otter, Hop Back, Goff's, Stanway Woods and Belhaven breweries.

A traditional fifteenth-century freehouse that has been in the same family for 87 years. Bar food available at lunchtime and evenings. Parking, garden and children's room. CAMRA pub of the Year 1993. Just off the B4211, Upton-upon-Severn to Malvern road. Take the third turn on the left from Upton.

11am–3pm and 7–11pm Mon–Sat; 12–3pm and 7–10.30pm Sun.

HEREFORD

The Barrels

69 Owen Street, Hereford, Herefordshire HR1 2JQ
☎ *(01432) 274968* Cath Roden

The Wye Valley Brewery is on the premises, so home-brewed ales are served in the pub. Also offers one guest ale, such as O'Hanlon's Red.

A town boozer. One of the last multi-roomed public houses in Hereford. Clientele a mix of old regulars and students. Occasional live music. Outside seating and fishpond. Annual beer festival on August bank holiday weekend, during which over 50 beers and ciders are available. No food. No children.

All day, every day.

Lichfield Vaults

11 Church Street, Hereford, Herefordshire
HR1 2LR
☎ *(01432) 267994* Charles Wenyon

Marston's Pedigree usually available plus up to seven guest ales including, perhaps, Hoskins & Oldfield Ginger Tom, Shepherd Neame Spitfire or a Greene King brew.

A traditional town-centre pub, one bar, patio. Food served at lunchtime only. No children.

OPEN All day Mon–Sat; 7–10.30pm Sun.

The Victory

88 St Owen Street, Hereford, Herefordshire
HR1 2QD
☎ *(01432) 274998*
Mr Kenyon and Miss Brooks

A freehouse and brewery tap with the Spinning Dog Brewery located on the premises. Chase Your Tail always available, plus three guests such as Flannery's Celtic.

A two-bar boozer with a nautical theme. Live music from Thursday to Sunday. Beer Garden. Food served lunchtimes and evenings Mon–Sat and traditional roasts on Sundays 12–5pm. Children allowed. Brewery tours by appointment; views of brewery through glass windows from the bar.

OPEN All day, every day.

Walter de Cantelupe Inn

Main Road, Kempsey, Worcestershire WR5 3NA
☎ *(01905) 820572* Martin Lloyd Morris

A freehouse with Marston's Bitter and Timothy Taylor Landlord among the brews always available, plus one guest from a wide range. Examples include Greene King Abbot, Cannon Royall Arrowhead, Wood Shropshire Lad, Orkney Raven Ale and Felinfoel Double Dragon.

A Tudor village pub with wooden beams and stone floors. One bar, dining area and garden. Food available Tues–Sun lunchtime and evenings. Children allowed during the day only.

OPEN 12–2.30pm and 6–11pm Mon–Sat; 7–10.30pm Sun.

The Boar's Head

39 Worcester Street, Kidderminster, Worcestershire DY10 1EA
☎ *(01562) 862450* Andy Hipkiss

Banks's Bitter and Original, Camerons Strongarm and Marston's Pedigree always available plus three guests such as Fuller's London Pride, Cains Formidable and Brewery Bitter or a selection from Bateman.

A two-bar town-centre pub with stone floors and beamed ceilings. Small beer garden and all-weather bricked courtyard covered with a glass pyramid. Food available Mon–Sat 12–3pm. Children allowed in the courtyard only.

OPEN 12–11pm Mon–Sat; 12–3pm and 7–10.30pm Sun.

The King & Castle

Severn Valley Railway Station,
Comberton Hill, Kidderminster, Worcestershire
☎ *(01562) 747505* Peter Williamson

Batham Best is among the brews always available plus guest beers (250 per year) from Enville, Hobsons, Hanby, Three Tuns, Timothy Taylor, Holt, Holden's, Berrow, Wood, Burton Bridge and Wye Valley breweries.

The pub is a copy of the Victorian railway refreshment rooms, decorated in the 1930s, GWR-style. Bar food available. Car park and garden. Children allowed until 9pm. Located next to Kidderminster railway station.

OPEN 11am–4pm and 5–11pm.

The Queen's Head and Dunn Plowman Brewery

Bridge Street, Kington, Herefordshire HR5 3DW
☎ *(01544) 231106* Michael John Hickey

Home of the Dunn Plowman Brewery with the full range of home brews always available.

A 400-year-old pub in the old market town. Food available all day Tues–Sun. Beer garden. Petanque court. Accommodation. Children allowed.

BREW HOUSE BITTER 3.8% ABV
EARLY RISER 4.0% ABV
KINGTON 5.0%
Traditional Bitter.
Also bottled beers sold to other pubs through James Williams distributors.

OPEN 11.30am–11pm (10.30pm Sun).

KNIGHTWICK

Talbot

Knightwick, Worcester, Worcestershire
☎ *(01886) 821235*

Home of the Teme Valley Brewery, with all own beers usually available, plus Hobsons Bitter.

Attractive, 500-year-old country inn standing by the River Teme. Well known locally for its home-produced food. Food available lunchtimes and evenings. Car park. Children welcome and high chairs are available. Located just off A44 Bromyard to Worcester on B4197 at Knightford Bridge.

T'OTHER 3.5% ABV
THIS 3.7% ABV
THAT 4.1% ABV
WOT 6.0% ABV

11am–11pm Mon–Sat; 12–10.30pm Sun.

LEDBURY

The Horseshoe Inn

The Homend, Ledbury, Herefordshire HR8 1BP
☎ *(01531) 632770* David Tegg

A freehouse with Hobsons Bitter always available. Two guests could well come from Wye Valley.

A small family inn in Ledbury town with one bar and garden. Food available at lunchtime only. Children allowed.

All day, every day.

The Royal Oak Hotel

The Southend, Ledbury, Herefordshire HR8 2EY
☎ *(01531) 632110* Mr Barron

The home of the Ledbury Brewery with the range of Ledbury brews produced and served on the premises. Also Wadworth 6X and seasonal Ledbury ales plus occasional guests such as Morland Old Speckled Hen and Greene King Abbot.

Built in 1420, with the main building added in 1645, this was the original Ledbury inn. Bar and restaurant food served at lunchtime and evenings. Car park and accommodation. Children allowed.

DOGHILL BITTS 3.6% ABV
LEDBURY SB 3.8% ABV
LEDBURY BEST 4.2% ABV
EXHIBITION 5.1% ABV
XB 7.5% ABV

11am–11pm.

LEOMINSTER

The Black Horse Coach House

South Street, Leominster, Herefordshire HR6 8JF
☎ *(01568) 611946* Peter Hoare

A freehouse serving Marches Black Horse (house ale) and Hobsons Town Crier plus two guests such as Fuller's London Pride, Hobsons Best or other micro-brews. Has served 150 beers over the past 12 months.

A town pub in a traditional building. Two bars, restaurant and garden. Food served every lunchtime and Mon–Sat evenings. Children allowed.

11am–2.30pm and 6–11pm Mon–Fri; all day Sat; 12–3pm and 7–10.30pm Sun.

The Grape Vaults

Broad Street, Leominster, Herefordshire HR6 8BS
☎ *(01568) 611404* Mrs Greenwold

A freehouse offering Marston's Pedigree and Best and Banks's Mild plus one rotating guest such as a Marston's special brew or Timothy Taylor Landlord, Morland Old Speckled Hen, Greene King Abbot or Fuller's London Pride.

A small pub in the town centre. Old-fashioned with log fire, no music. Bar snacks available at lunchtime and evenings. Children allowed if eating.

11am–3pm and 5–11pm Mon–Fri; 11am–3.30pm and 6–11pm Sat; 12–4pm and 6.30–10.30pm Sun.

MALVERN

Bolly & Bass Bar

Foley Arms Hotel, Worcester Road, Malvern, Worcestershire
☎ *(01684) 573397* Nigel Thomas

An ever-changing selection of four guest beers usually available, which may include Shepherd Neame Spitfire, Morland Old Speckled Hen, Fuller's London Pride or brews from Malvern Hills, Charles Wells, Hook Norton and many others.

Friendly, cosy, locals' pub, situated in the historic Foley Arms Hotel offering live music on Monday nights. Full bar menu available. Car park. Children very welcome. Situated in middle of Malvern on the A449.

12–2.30pm and 5–11pm Mon–Sat; 12–3pm and 7–10.30pm Sun.

Malvern Hills Hotel

Wynds Point, Malvern, Worcestershire
WR13 6DW
☎ *(01684) 540690*
Oswald John and Karen Elizabeth Dockery

Hobsons Best Bitter, Malvern Hills Black Pear and Timothy Taylor Landlord usually available. Two guest beers, which may include, Fuller's London Pride, Charles Wells Bombardier, Marston's Pedigree or Wood Shropshire Lad are also regularly served.

High on the western slopes of the Malverns at British Camp with 'one of the goodliest vistas in England', offering walks with breathtaking views. Warm, traditional oak-panelled lounge bar with sun terrace. Bar food and separate restaurant food available every lunchtime and evening. Car park. Children welcome but no special facilities. Situated on the A449 at British Camp hill fort (also known as the Herefordshire Beacon) midway between Malvern and Ledbury.

11am–11pm Mon–Sat; 12–10.30pm Sun.

MUCH DEWCHURCH

The Black Swan Inn

Much Dewchurch, Hereford, Herefordshire
HR2 8DJ
☎ *(01981) 540295* A Davies

Beers from breweries such as Timothy Taylor, Badger and Adnams usually available plus one rotating guest such as Reverend James' Shropshire Lad or a beer from Frome Valley or Hook Norton breweries.

A fourteenth-century freehouse with lounge and public bar. Dining area in lounge. Patio. Food available at lunchtime and evenings. Children allowed.

12–3pm and 6–11pm Mon–Fri;
11.30am–3pm and 6–11pm Sat;
12–3pm and 7–10.30pm Sun.

NORTON CANON

Three Horse Shoes Inn

Norton Canon, Hereford, Herefordshire HR4 7BH
☎ *(01544) 318375* Frank Goodwin

Home of the Shoes Brewery, with both beers regularly available.

Two bars and games room, with grassed area for summer use. Situated on the A480. No food. Car park. Children welcome.

NORTON ALE 3.6% ABV
CANON BITTER 4.1% ABV

6–11pm Mon–Thurs; 12–3pm and 6–11pm
Mon–Sat; 12–3pm and 7–10.30pm Sun.

OFFENHAM

The Bridge Inn and Ferry

Offenham, Evesham, Worcestershire WR11 5RS
☎ *(01386) 446565* Morris Allan

Something from Bateman and Caledonian regularly available plus up to six guest beers from breweries around the country.

Independent, historic freehouse on the banks of the River Avon. Large heated patio. Bar and lounge/dining area. Food served 12–2.30pm and 6.30–9pm daily. Car park. Well-behaved children welcome. Follow signs to ferry from main road.

11am–11pm Mon–Sat; 12–10.30pm Sun.

OMBERSLEY

The Crown & Sandys Arms

Main Road, Ombersley, Worcester, Worcestershire
WR9 0EW
☎ *(01905) 620252* Richard Everton

Greene King Abbot Ale, Marston's Pedigree, Adnams Best Bitter and Broadside usually available, plus two guest beers such as Wood Parish Bitter, Hobsons Best Bitter, Wyre Piddle Piddle In The Wind or Cannon Royall Arrowhead.

Seventeenth-century refurbished freehouse with large bar and two busy bistros. Extensive wine list. Food served lunchtimes and evenings Mon–Fri and all day Sat–Sun. Gardens. Car park. Children welcome.

11am–3pm and 5–11pm Mon–Fri;
11am–11pm Sat; 12–10.30pm Sun.

PENSAX

The Bell

Pensax, Abberley, Worcestershire WR6 6AE
☎ *(01299) 896677* John and Trudy Greaves

At least five beers available at any one time. Regulars include Archers Golden, Timothy Taylor Landlord and brews from Hook Norton. Local beers also featured, such as Woodbury White Goose, Enville Bitter and ales from Hobsons and Wood breweries.

Friendly, rural freehouse with various traditional drinking areas and dining room. Large garden, superb views, three real fires in winter. Beer festival held on Whitsuntide weekend. Seasonal home-cooked bar and restaurant food served at lunchtimes and evenings. Families welcome. Located on the B4202 Great Witley to Cleobury Mortimer road, between Abberley and Clows Top.

5–11pm Mon (closed Mon lunchtimes
except bank holidays); 12–2.30pm and
5–11pm Tues–Sat; 12–10.30pm Sun.

The Brandy Cask

25 Bridge Street, Pershore, Worcestershire
WR10 1AJ
☎ *(01386) 552602*

The ales brewed here now supply 30 outlets. Also Ruddles Best and County available plus guest beers.

Town-centre freehouse. Bar and restaurant food is served at lunchtime and evenings. Large riverside garden. Children allowed.

BRANDY SNAPPER 4% ABV
JOHN BAKER'S ORIGINAL 4.8% ABV

[OPEN] *11.30am–2.30pm and 7–11pm.*

The Crown Inn

Gloucester Road, The Lea, Ross-on-Wye,
Herefordshire HR9 7JZ
☎ *(01989) 750407* Mr F and Miss C Ellis

Hook Norton Best, RCH Pitchfork and Fuller's London Pride permanently available, plus two guests often from Wye Valley Brewery. Small, independent breweries favoured.

A splendid fifteenth-century country village pub with a warm welcome always assured. One bar, beer garden. Smoking and non-smoking restaurant. Food available Mon–Sun lunchtimes and Tues–Sat evenings. Children allowed. Situated on the A40 from Ross-on-Wye to Gloucester.

[OPEN] *11am–11pm.*

The Crown & Sceptre

Market Place, Ross-on-Wye, Herefordshire
HR9 5NX
☎ *(01989) 562765* Mr M Roberts

A Whitbread pub serving Archers Best, Shepherd Neame Spitfire and Greene King Abbot Ale plus two changing guests such as Young's Special, Brains SA or Gales HSB.

A town pub with a friendly atmosphere and mixed clientele. One bar, patio and garden. Bar food served at lunchtimes and evenings. Well-behaved children allowed.

[OPEN] *All day, every day.*

The Red Lion Inn

Bridgnorth Road, Shatterford, Nr Kidderminster
DY12 1SU
☎ *(01299) 861221* Richard Tweedie

Banks's Mild and Bitter plus Batham Bitter usually available. Two guest beers are also served, often from Wood, Wye Valley, Marston's and Cannon Royall breweries.

Truly rural pub, well known locally for its food. Non-smoking areas and restaurant. Food every lunchtime and evening, including traditional Sunday roasts. Two car parks: one in Worcestershire, the other in Shropshire! Children welcome, with special children's menu available.

[OPEN] *11.30am–2.30pm and 6.30–11pm*
Mon–Sat; 12–3pm and 7–10.30pm Sun.

The Rising Sun

50 Lombard Street, Stourport-on-Severn,
Worcestershire DY13 8DU
☎ *(01299) 822530* Robert Hallard

Banks's Original, Bitter and Hanson's Mild plus Marston's Pedigree always available, plus one guest such as Goddards Inspiration. Seasonal and celebration ales served whenever available.

A 200-year-old canalside pub. One bar, small dining area and patio. Food available at lunchtime and evenings. Children allowed in the dining room and patio only.

[OPEN] *All day, every day.*

The Wheatsheaf

39 High Street, Stourport-on-Severn,
Worcestershire DY13 8BS
☎ *(01299) 822613* Mr M Webb

Banks's Mild, Bitter and Hansons Bitter usually available.

A games-orientated house in the town centre, with relaxing lounge and cosy bar. Food served 10.30am–3pm Mon–Sat and 12–2pm Sun. Children welcome until 9.30pm. Car park.

[OPEN] *10.30am–11pm.*

TENBURY WELLS

The Ship Inn
Teme Street, Tenbury Wells, Worcestershire
WR15 8AE
☎ *(01584) 810269* Michael Hoar

A freehouse with Hobsons Best always available plus a guest such as Morland Old Speckled Hen or Shepherd Neame Bishop's Finger.

A seventeenth-century, market town pub with beamed ceilings and two separate non-smoking dining areas. Food available at lunchtime and evenings. Beer garden. Children allowed.

11am–3pm and 7–11pm (10.30pm Sun).

UPHAMPTON

The Fruiterer's Arms
Uphampton, Ombersley, Worcestershire
WR9 0JW
☎ *(01905) 621161*

Cannon Royall brews produced and served on the premises plus a guest beer.

Brewing began in this converted cider house in July 1993. The maximum output is now 16 barrels per week and there are plans for expansion. The pub has two bars and a log fire in winter. Bar food is served at lunchtime. Car park. Children allowed.

FRUITERER'S MILD 3.7% ABV
Replaces Millward's Musket Mild.
ARROWHEAD 3.9% ABV
Beer with strong hoppiness in the finish.
BUCKSHOT 4.5% ABV
Rich and malty, leaving a round and hoppy aftertaste.
Plus winter ales, changed annually.

12.30–2.30pm and 7–11pm; 12–3pm Sat and Sun.

WEATHEROAK

The Coach & Horses
Weatheroak Hill, Weatheroak,
Worcestershire B48 7EA
☎ *(01564) 823386* Philip Meads

Home of the Weatheroak Brewery, with full range of own brews and Black Sheep Bitter and Morland Old Speckled Hen always available. Plus at least one guest. Beer festivals held twice a year.

A country pub with 100-seater restaurant, large garden, children's play area, lounge and public bars. Food available every lunchtime and Mon Sat evenings. Well-behaved children allowed. Located close to junction 3 of M42. Take the A435 to Birmingham, turn off at signs for Weatheroak.

LIGHT OAK 3.6% ABV
Light-coloured bitter.
WEATHEROAK ALE 4.1% ABV
Light-coloured bitter.
REDWOOD 4.8% ABV
Bitter.
TTT 5.1% ABV
Darker, full-tasting.

11.30am–2.30pm and 5.30–11pm Mon–Thurs; 11am–11pm Fri–Sat; 12–10.30pm Sun.

WORCESTER

The Dragon Inn
The Tything, Worcester, Worcestershire
☎ *(01905) 25845* RM Appleton

Cannon Royall Fruiterer's Mild usually available plus five or six guest beers. The new licensee has offered 200 different beers during his first nine months, from Abbeydale, Beowulf, Buffy's, Cains, Church End, Durham, Mighty Oak, Iceni, Six Bells and Teme Valley, to mention just a few.

Late Georgian, Grade II listed alehouse with L-shaped bar and outside drinking area. No food. Well-behaved children welcome, but no special facilities. Situated a three-minute walk from Foregate Street Station, away from the city centre.

12–11pm (10.30pm Sun).

The Postal Order
18 Foregate Street, Worcester,
Worcestershire WR1 1DN
☎ *(01905) 22373* Tom Dunkley

Bank's Mild, Greene King Abbot Ale, Shepherd Neame Spitfire and two selected from Wyre Piddle Brewery always available. Up to six guest real ales purchased through East West.

An open-plan Wetherspoon's freehouse converted from an old telephone exchange (originally a sorting office). Separate non-smoking area, no music. Food available all day. No children. Situated opposite the cinema.

11am–11pm Mon–Sat; 12–10.30pm Sun.

YOU TELL US

★ *The Chase Inn*, Bishops Frome
★ *Greyhound Inn*, 30 Rock Hill, Eldersfield, Bromsgrove
★ *The Halfway House*, Droitwich Road, Bastondford, Fernhill Heath
★ *Old Fogey*, 37 High Street, Kington
★ *The Plume of Feathers*, Feathers Pitch, Castlemorton
★ *The Swan Inn*, Letton
★ *Tap & Spile*, 35 St Nicholas Street, Worcester

Places Featured:

Aldbury
Amwell
Arrington
Ashwell
Astwick
Ayot St Lawrence
Baldock
Barley
Benington
Bishop's Stortford
Bricket Wood
Chenies Village
Datchworth
Flaunden
Great Gaddesden

Harpenden
Hertford
Ickleford
King's Langley
Much Hadham
Old Knebworth
St Albans
Sawbridgeworth
Tonwell
Tring
Tyttenhanger Green
Waltham Cross
Wareside
Whitwell
Wild Hill

THE BREWERIES

DARK HORSE BREWING CO. LTD
*Adams Yard, Maidenhead Street, Hertford
SG14 1DR*
☎ *(01992) 509800*

ALE 3.6% ABV
Light and refreshing with some maltiness.
MOONRUNNER MILD 3.8% ABV
SUNRUNNER 4.1% ABV
Pale with fruitiness, bitterness in the finish.
FALLEN ANGEL 4.2% ABV
Pale, extremely drinkable ginger beer.
BLACK WIDOW 4.4% ABV
Ruby-coloured stout (occasional).
WHITE HORSE (ON A CLOUDY DAY) 4.6% ABV
Continental-style, cloudy, white beer.
DEATH WISH 5.0% ABV
Full-bodied and distinctive.

GREEN TYE BREWERY
Green Tye SG10 6JP
☎ *(01279) 841041*

SHOT IN THE DARK 3.6% ABV
Dark ruby colour and hoppy flavour. Available October.
IPA 3.7% ABV
Refreshing, pert hoppiness and dry finish.
SNOWDROP 3.9% ABV
Quenching, balanced hop flavour, with some sweetness.
MAD MORRIS 4.2% ABV
Golden and quenching with citrus fruit tanginess.
WHEELBARROW 4.3% ABV
Balanced hop, malt and fruit flavours. Easy drinker.
TREADMINER'S ALE 4.3% ABV
Porter-style bitter.
COAL PORTER 4.5% ABV
Flavour-packed porter. Winter brew.
TUMBLEDOWN DICK 5.3% ABV
Strong and hoppy.

MCMULLEN & SONS LTD
*The Hertford Brewery, 26 Old Cross, Hertford
SG14 1RD*
☎ *(01992) 584911*

ORIGINAL AK 3.7% ABV
Light, well-balanced with good hoppiness.
COUNTRY BEST BITTER 4.3% ABV
Hoppy, fruity aroma and flavour.
GLADSTONE 4.3% ABV
Smooth, with finely rounded bitterness.
STRONGHART 7.0% ABV
Powerful, complex, sweet and dark.
Plus seasonal beers.

THE TRING BREWERY CO. LTD

81–2 Akeman Street, Tring HP23 6AF
☎ *(01442) 890721*

SIDE POCKET FOR A TOAD 3.6% ABV
Pale and refreshing with hoppy citrus flavour.
MOTHER HAGGY'S FINEST SUMMER ALE 3.7% ABV
Quenching, golden, fruity summer brew.
JACK O' LEGS 4.2% ABV
Copper-coloured, fruity with good hoppiness.
CUCKOO'S COMING 4.5% ABV
Golden, seasonal brew.
REAP THE RYE 4.7% ABV
Powerfully malty, seasonal brew.
COLLEY'S BLACK DOG 5.2% ABV
Dark, nutty malt flavour. Very drinkable.
SANTA'S LITTLE HELPER 5.7% ABV
Warming winter ale.
Plus seasonal brews.

DARK RUBY

THE PUBS

ALDBURY

The Greyhound

19 Stocks Road, Aldbury, Tring HP23 5RT
☎ *(01442) 851228* Craig Parker

A Badger Brewery pub serving Dorset Best and Tanglefoot plus two guests such as Greene King Abbot, Wadworth 6X or Mauldons Black Adder.

A country pub with courtyard garden and non-smoking conservatory. Dining area. B&B. Food available at lunchtime and evenings. Children allowed.

From 9am for coffee, all-day licence.

AMWELL

Elephant & Castle

Amwell Lane, Amwell, Wheathampstead AL4 8EA
☎ *(01582) 832175*

Amwell Ale brewed specially for the pub is always available plus up to seven other real ales (80 per year) selected from anywhere and everywhere. Strengths generally vary from 3.7% to 5.2% ABV.

This pub is 475 years old, with three bars on different levels. There is a 200ft well in the middle of the bar. No music or machines, with the emphasis on good beer and good conversation. Bar meals available at lunchtime and evenings. Car park, two gardens (one for adults only), dining area. Children not allowed in bar. The pub is difficult to find. Ask in Wheathampstead or ring for directions.

11am–3pm and 5.30–11pm Mon–Fri; all day Sat–Sun.

ARRINGTON

Hardwicke Arms Hotel

96 Ermine Street, Arrington, Nr Royston SG8 0AM
☎ *(01223) 208802* Mr J R Julius

Morrells Oxford Blue and Greene King IPA regularly available, plus two guest beers perhaps from Wychwood, Shepherd Neame, Brains, Hook Norton, Thwaites, Tisbury or Young's.

Thirteenth-century coaching inn. Food served 11.30–2pm and 6.30–9.15pm. Car park. Children welcome in the garden.

11.30am 2.15pm and 6.30–11pm Mon–Sat; 12–2.15pm and 7–10.30pm Sun.

ASHWELL

The Bushel & Strike

Mill Street, Ashwell
☎ *(01462) 742394*
Mrs J Grommann and Mr N Burton

Charles Wells Eagle and Bombardier usually available plus three guest beers which may include Adnams Broadside or Morland Old Speckled Hen.

A Charles Wells two-bar house with large restaurant, patio, barbecue and small garden. Food served 12–2.30pm Mon–Sun, 7–9pm Mon–Sat. Car park. Special children's menu. From Ashwell village, turn left by the Indian take-away and continue to the car park. The pub is opposite the church tower.

11.30am–3pm and 6–11pm Mon–Sat; 12–10.30pm Sun.

ASTWICK

Tudor Oakes Lodge

Taylors Road, Astwick, Nr Hitchin SG5 4AZ
☎ *(01462) 834133* Mr Welek

A freehouse serving Mauldons White Adder, Shepherd Neame Spitfire and Wolf Hare of the Dog plus other guests including Oakham Old Tosspot.

A fifteenth-century building with hotel and restaurant, one bar and courtyard. Food available at lunchtime and evenings. Children allowed. Situated off the A1.

All day, every day.

AYOT ST LAWRENCE

The Brocket Arms

Ayot St Lawrence AL6 9RT
☎ *(01438) 820250* Tony Wingfield-Digby

Greene King IPA and Abbot Ale, Brakspear Special, Adnams Broadside and Wadworth 6X always available plus a guest beer, changing weekly, from any independent brewery.

A traditional, oak-beamed pub with a walled garden and accommodation. Bar and restaurant food served at lunchtime and evenings (except Sunday and Monday nights). Parking. For access from the A1 or M1, head for Wheathampstead (B653 and A6129). Then take directions to Shaw's Corner at Ayot St Lawrence.

11am–11pm.

BALDOCK

The Old White Horse

1 Station Road, Baldock SG7 5BS
☎ *(01462) 893168* Vincent Walker

A Whitbread tied house with Fuller's London Pride, Timothy Taylor Landlord, Wadworth 6X and a Burton brew usually available, plus other occasional guests.

A town pub with restaurant specialising in Caribbean and English food. Restaurant open from 7pm. Beer garden. Children allowed.

11am–3pm Mon–Thurs; all day Fri–Sun.

BARLEY

The Fox & Hounds

Barley SG8 8HU
☎ *(01763) 848459*

Morland Old Speckled Hen, Adnams Bitter and IPA always available.

Parts of the heavily beamed pub date back to 1450. Formerly known as The Waggon & Horses, there is an inglenook fireplace and original beams. Bar and restaurant food is available. Non-smoking area in dining room. Bar billiards, games tables, darts etc. Car park, garden, children's room (occasionally used for other functions), disabled toilets, baby-changing facilities. Well-behaved children welcome.

12–2.30pm and 6–11pm Mon–Sat; 12–3pm and 7.30–10.30pm Sun.

BENINGTON

The Lordship Arms

42 Whempstead Road, Benington
☎ *(01438) 869665*

Young's Special, Fuller's ESB and London Pride always available, plus three guest beers (150 per year). The pub specialises in ales from small independent and micro-breweries. Also draught cider.

A cosy village freehouse with a display of telephone memorabilia. Bar snacks available weekday lunchtimes. Home-cooked roast lunches served on Sundays (booking advisable). Curry night on Wednesdays. Car park and garden. Children not allowed. Take the A602 exit off the A1(M), follow the A602 then turn left. Signposted Aston, Benington.

12–3pm and 6–11pm Mon–Sat; 12–3pm and 7–10.30pm Sun.

The Cock Inn

High Street, Huttfield Broadoak, Bishop's Stortford CM22 7HF
☎ *(01279) 718273* Miss Holcroft

Adnams Best, Greene King IPA and Fuller's London Pride always available plus three guests (up to 150 per year) including Everards Tiger and brews from Robinson's, Oakhill, Marston's and Wadworth.

A sixteenth-century coaching inn, beamed with log fires. Bar and restaurant food available at lunchtime and evenings. Non-smoking room, car park, function room. Children allowed. Easy to find.

OPEN *12–3pm and 5–11pm Mon–Sat; 12–10.30pm Sun.*

The Half Moon

31 North Street, Bishop's Stortford CM23 2LD
☎ *(01279) 834500* Rohan Wong

Adnams Broadside and a mild always available plus up to five others, often including brews from Adnams, Jennings or Batemans.

A town pub with children's room and beer garden. Food available at lunchtimes only. Children allowed in children's room.

OPEN *All day Mon–Sat; 12–3pm and 7–10.309pm Sun.*

Moor Mill

Smug Oak Lane, Bricket Wood, Nr St Albans AL2 3TY
☎ *(01727) 875557* Mr and Mrs Muir

A selection of ten real ales available from breweries such as Brakspear, Wadworth, Greene King and Gales. Seasonal guests also available (50 per year).

An eighteenth-century converted corn mill sitting astride the River Ver. Bar and restaurant food available at lunchtime and evenings. Occasional pig roasts and barbecues. Car park, garden and meeting room. Children allowed.

OPEN *11am–11pm Mon–Sat; 12–3pm and 7.30–10.30pm Sun.*

Red Lion

Chenies Village, Rickmansworth WD3 6ED
☎ *(01923) 282722* Mike Norris

Wadworth 6X, Vale Notley Ale and Lion Pride, especially brewed by Rebellion, usually available.

Small country pub serving slightly different food, situated off the A404. Food served 12–2pm and 7–10pm, 12–2pm and 7–9.30pm Sun. Car park. No children.

OPEN *11am–2.30pm and 5.30–11pm Mon–Sat; 12–2.30pm and 7–10.30pm Sun.*

Tilbury (The Inn off the Green)

1 Watton Road, Datchworth SG3 6TB
☎ *(01438) 812496* Ian Miller

Hides Bitter and Hop Pit Bitter brewed and available on the premises plus two or three rotating guests from independent brewers.

A seventeenth-century, two-bar village pub and micro-brewery. Bar and restaurant food available. Large garden and car park. Well-behaved children allowed. On the Datchworth crossroads, on the road from Woolmer Green to Watton.

HIDES BITTER (4.0% ABV)
HOP PIT BITTER (4.5% ABV)

OPEN *11am–3pm and 5–11pm Mon–Wed; all day Thurs–Sun.*

The Bricklayers Arms

Hog Pits Bottom, Flaunden HP3 0PH
☎ *(01442) 833322* Peter Frazer

A freehouse regularly serving Fuller's London Pride, Marston's Pedigree or a beer from Beechwood or Chiltern breweries plus four guests from independent breweries such as Nethergate Old Growler or Rebellion Smuggler.

An old English country pub. One bar with three areas. Garden and restaurant area. Food available at lunchtime and evenings. Children allowed.

OPEN *11.30am–2.30pm and 6–11pm Mon–Fri; all day Sat–Sun.*

GREAT GADDESDEN

The Cock & Bottle
Great Gaddesden, Hemel Hempstead HP1 3BU
☎ *(01442) 255381* Gary Gadfton

A freehouse with Fuller's ESB always available plus five guests regularly including Wadworth 6X, Morland Old Speckled Hen, Greene King Abbot, Fuller's London Pride, Hop Back Summer Lightning, Ringwood Old Thumper or Shepherd Neame Spitfire. Seasonal and celebration beers served when available.

A traditional, old-style pub with two bars, beams and fireplace. Beer garden. Food available at lunchtime and evenings. Children allowed.

11.30am–3pm and 5.30–11pm Mon–Sat; 12–4pm and 7–10.30pm Sun.

HARPENDEN

The Oak Tree
15 Leyton Green, Harpenden AL5 2TG
☎ *(01582) 763850* Mr Needham

McMullen AK, Fuller's London Pride and Everards Tiger always available plus three guests changed twice-monthly, such as Timothy Taylor Landlord or a Bateman brew.

A one-bar town freehouse with beer garden. A leaflet is available listing the beers of the month. Food available at lunchtime. No children.

All day, every day.

HERTFORD

The Prince of Wales
244 Hertingfordbury Road, Hertford SG14 2LG
☎ *(01992) 581149* Andrew Thomas

A freehouse with Fuller's London Pride, Greene King IPA, McMullen AK and Wadworth 6X always available.

A one-bar country pub with garden. Food available at lunchtime only, but restaurant planned for August 1999. Children allowed.

All day, every day.

The White Horse
33 Castle Street, Hertford SG14 1HH
☎ *(01992) 501950* Mike Mills-Roberts

Fuller's London Pride, ESB and seasonal brews, plus Adnams Southwold Bitter usually available. Up to six guest beers of all types may be served, from micro-breweries around the country.

Classic fifteenth-century alehouse, well known for its selection of real ales. Food served 12–2.30pm Mon–Sun, 6–10pm Mon–Thurs. Children welcome in the upstairs non-smoking lounges. Street parking.

11.30am–2.30pm and 5.30–11pm Mon–Fri; 11.30am–11pm Sat–Sun.

ICKLEFORD

The Cricketers
107 Arlesey Road, Ickleford, Hitchin SG5 5TH
☎ *(01462) 432629* John Wallace

Freehouse serving an Adnams bitter and Everards Tiger and Beacon plus guests.

A one-bar traditional country pub. Food available at lunchtime. Children allowed.

11am–3.30pm and 5–11pm Mon–Thurs; all day Fri–Sun.

The Plume of Feathers
Upper Green, Ickleford, Hitchin SG5 3YD
☎ *(01462) 432729* Teresa Thompson

A Whitbread house with Fuller's London Pride and Wadworth 6X always available plus one rotating guest from a wide range of smaller breweries such as Mauldons or Timothy Taylor. Recent beers served include Adnams Regatta, Tomintoul Highland Heir and Archers Golden.

A village pub with dining area and garden. Food available at lunchtime and evenings. Well-behaved children allowed.

11am–3pm and 6–11pm Mon–Fri; all day most Sat and Sun.

KING'S LANGLEY

The Unicorn
Gallows Hill, Kings Langley WD4 8LV
☎ *(01923) 262287* Terry Ashcroft

An Adnams brew is usually available plus two guests from a range of constantly changing ales. Examples have included Bateman Hill Billy, Nethergate Golden Gate, Beartown Bearskin Full and Rebellion Blonde Bombshell.

An upmarket family pub with function room (seats 80 people). Large beer patio. Food served at lunchtime and evenings in a separate dining area. Children allowed if eating.

11.30am–3pm and 5–11pm Mon–Thurs; all day Fri–Sun.

MUCH HADHAM

The Prince of Wales
Green Tye, Much Hadham SG10 6JP
☎ *(01279) 842517* Gary Whelan

A freehouse with the Green Tye Brewery to the rear of the premises. Green Tye beers always available, plus a McMullen ale.

A country pub with beer garden. Food available at lunchtime only. Children allowed.

12–2.45pm and 5.30–11pm Mon–Fri; all day Sat–Sun and bank holidays.

OLD KNEBWORTH

The Lytton Arms

Park Lane, Old Knebworth SG3 6QB
☎ *(01438) 812312* Steven Nye

Fuller's London Pride, Woodforde's Wherry and Young's Special are among those ales always available plus up to six guest beers (200 per year) from Adnams, Nethergate, Cotleigh, Exmoor, B&T, Brewery on Sea, Morland and Elgood's etc. Note also the Belgian beers and malt whiskies.

A traditional freehouse on the edge of Knebworth Park, built in 1837. Beamed with open fires. Bar food available at lunchtime and evenings. Car park, garden and children's room. Located halfway between Knebworth and Codicote.

11am–3pm and 5–11pm Mon–Thurs; 11am–11pm Fri–Sat; 12–10.30pm Sun.

ST ALBANS

The Blacksmith's Arms

56 St Peter's Street, St Albans AL1 3HG
☎ *(01727) 855761* Sue and Noel Keane

Marston's Pedigree and Wadworth 6X always available plus a continuous cycle of guests including Hoskins Maypole, Gibbs Mew The Bishop's Tipple, Brakspear Bee Sting and Hoskins and Oldfield Ginger Tom.

A Hogshead pub with one bar. No music. Food served 12–9pm Sun–Thurs, 12–7pm Fri–Sat. Background music. Large garden. No children. Located on the main road.

All day, every day.

The Duke of Marlborough

110 Holywell Hill, St Albans AL1 1DH
☎ *(01727) 858982* Eamonn Murphy

Greene King IPA and Young's Special usually available with one guest beer.

Situated on the main road through St Albans, near the park and Abbey railway station. Big screen TV for sport. Food served 12–3pm daily. Children welcome in beer garden, function and pool rooms. Car park.

All day, every day.

The Farmer's Boy

134 London Road, St Albans AL1 1PQ
☎ *(01727) 766702* Viv Davies

Home of the Verulam Brewery. All own brews available plus Adnams Best and occasionally brews from the Dark Horse Brewery.

A town pub with garden. Food served all day, every day. Children allowed.

SPECIAL 3.8% ABV
A light mild.
IPA 4.0% ABV
A true bitter.
FARMER'S JOY 4.5% ABV
A darker ale.
Plus a cask-conditioned lager 'VB' at 3.8%.

All day, every day.

The Lower Red Lion

34–6 Fishpool Street, St Albans AL3 4RX
☎ *(01727) 855669* Mrs Turner

Fuller's London Pride, Oakham JHB and regularly Black Sheep Special plus five guests (500 per year) from all over the country. Two beer festivals held each year (May bank holiday and August bank holiday).

A city two-bar traditional coaching house in the conservation area of St Albans with a wide-ranging clientele. No music or games machines. Bar food is available 12–2.30pm Mon–Sat. Car park and garden.

12–2.30pm and 5.20–11pm Mon–Fri; 12–11pm Sat; 12–3pm and 7–10.30pm Sun.

SAWBRIDGEWORTH

The Gate Public House

81 London Road, Sawbridgeworth CM21 9JJ
☎ *(01279) 722313* Gary and Tom Barnet

Nine hand pumps serving a constantly changing range of guest ales, including Fuller's London Pride, Charles Wells Bombadier or something from Adnams. There are plans to open the Sawbridgeworth Brewery on the premises, in which case house brews will be available.

A traditional pub with two bars, darts and pool. Food available at lunchtime. Children allowed.

11.30am–2.30pm and 5.30–11pm Mon–Thur; all day Fri–Sat; 12–3pm and 7–10.30pm Sun.

TONWELL

The Robin Hood

14 Ware Road, Tonwell, Ware SG12 0HN
☎ *(01920) 463352* Mr Harding

Dark Horse brews always available, plus three guests often including Hampshire Brewery's Lion Heart, Nethergate Swift or Shepherd Neame Spitfire.

A 300-year-old, traditional village pub. One bar and non-smoking restaurant. B&B. Food available at lunchtime and evenings. Children allowed in the restaurant only.

OPEN *12–2.30pm and 5.30–11pm Mon–Fri; 12–3pm and 5.30–11pm Sat; 12–3pm and 7–10.30pm Sun.*

TRING

The King's Arms

King Street, Tring HP23 6BE
☎ *(01442) 823318*
Victoria North and John Francis

A freehouse. Wadworth 6X always available plus guests from a wide-ranging list including Adnams Bitter, Brakspear Special or Bee Sting, Hop Back Summer Lightning and local Tring brewery ales.

A town pub with a distinctive covered and heated beer garden. Home-cooked food available at lunchtime and evenings. Non-smoking area. Children allowed at lunchtime only.

OPEN *12–2.30pm and 7–11pm Mon–Sat; 12–4pm and 7–10.30pm Sun.*

TYTTENHANGER GREEN

The Plough

Tyttenhanger Green, Nr St Albans AL4 0RW
☎ *(01727) 857777* Mike Barrowman

Marston's Pedigree, Morland Old Speckled Hen, Wadworth 6X, Fuller's London Pride and ESB, Greene King IPA and Abbot Ale, Tring Ridgeway and Timothy Taylor Landlord always available, plus numerous unusual and interesting guest beers.

These purveyors to the multitude of murky beers and watery spirits specialise in incompetent staff, greasy food and exhorbitant prices in a terrible atmosphere. Ideal for discreet liaisons. Bar food available at lunchtime. Car park and garden.

OPEN *Various and flexible without notice.*

WALTHAM CROSS

The Vault

160 High Street, Waltham Cross EN8 7AB
☎ *(01992) 631600* Mr P Laville

A freehouse with no permanent beers but a regularly changing selection that might include Crouch Vale SAS, Clark's Burglar Bill or a Brewery on Sea brew. Microbreweries favoured.

A family- and food-orientated pub with separate dining area. Food available at lunchtime and early evenings. Upstairs non-smoking conservatory planned for 2000. Live bands every Thursday. Beer garden. Children allowed.

OPEN *All day, every day.*

WARESIDE

Chequers Inn

Wareside, Ware SG12 7QY
☎ *(01920) 467010* Mrs Julie Cook

A freehouse with Dark Horse brewery's Chequers Ale and Adnams Best and Broadside usually available plus three regularly changing guests such as Marston's Pedigree, Fuller's London Pride, Shepherd Neame Spitfire or Wadworth 6X.

A tiny old village pub, parts of the building date from the thirteenth century and parts from the seventeenth century. Food available at lunchtime and evenings in a 36-seater restaurant. Bench seating outside, hog roast on bank holidays. Live band on Sundays. Children allowed. Less than three miles outside Ware

OPEN *12–3pm and 6–11pm Mon–Fri; all day Sat–Sun.*

WHITWELL

Maidens Head

67 High Street, Whitwell, Nr Hitchin SG4 8AH
☎ *(01438) 871392* Mike Jones

A McMullen tied house with AK Original and Country Best available plus two guests, perhaps including Shepherd Neame Spitfire, Everards Tiger or Wadworth 6X.

A two-bar village pub, timbered building with garden seating. Food available at lunchtime and evenings Tues–Sat. No children.

OPEN *11.30am–3pm and 5–11pm Mon–Fri; 11.30am–4pm and 6–11pm Sat; 12–3pm and 7–10.30pm Sun.*

The Woodman

45 Wildhill Lane, Wild Hill, Hatfield AL9 6EA
☎ *(01707) 642618* Graham Craig

McMullen ales, Greene King Abbot and
IPA available plus three guests from
independent breweries such as Rooster's,
Hampshire, Mighty Oak or York.

A country pub with garden. Sandwiches available at lunchtime (no food on bank holidays). No children.

*OPEN 11.30am–2.30pm and 5.30–11pm
Mon–Sat; 12–2.30pm and 7–10.30pm Sun.*

Places Featured:

Arreton
Brightstone
Cowes
Newport
Niton
Northwood

Sandown
Totland Bay
Ventnor
Wroxhall
Yarmouth

THE BREWERIES

GODDARDS BREWERY

Barnsley Farm, Bullen Road, Ryde PO33 1QF
☎ *(01983) 611011*

LIBERTY LAGER 4.0% ABV
Refreshing and moreish.
ALE OF WIGHT 4.0% ABV
Pale, refreshing and fruity.
SPECIAL BITTER 4.0% ABV
Well-balanced with good hoppiness.
IRON HORSE 4.8% ABV
Dark, with liquorice/chocolate flavour.
FUGGLE DEE DUM 4.8% ABV
Golden, full-bodied and spicily aromatic.
DUCK'S FOLLY 5.2% ABV
Light colour, strong and hoppy.
INSPIRATION ALE 5.2% ABV
Floral and exotic.
WINTER WARMER 5.2% ABV
Dark and smooth.

VENTNOR BREWERY LTD

119 High Street, Ventnor
☎ *(01983) 856161*

GOLDEN BITTER 4.0% ABV
Light and fruity.
SUNFIRE 4.3% ABV
OYSTER STOUT 4.5% ABV
KANGAROO BITTER 4.8% ABV
Smooth, with malt and fruit sweetness.
WIGHT SPIRIT 5.0% ABV
SANDROCK 5.6% ABV
Plus seasonal brews.

THE PUBS

ARRETON

The White Lion

Main Road, Arreton, Newport PO30 3AA
☎ *(01983) 528479*
Kelly Baron and Paul Hastett

A freehouse with Wadworth 6X, Best and IPA always available plus a guest ale, perhaps from the Badger Brewery.

An old coaching inn in a picturesque country village. One bar, non-smoking restaurant, garden with patio and aviary. Food available at lunchtime and evenings. Children allowed in a designated area.

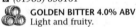 *12–3pm and 6–11pm (10.30pm Sun).*

BRIGHTSTONE

The Countryman

Limerstone Road, Brightstone
☎ *(01983) 740616* Mr R Frost

Badger IPA, Dorset Best and Tanglefoot usually available, plus one guest beer, frequently from Ringwood or Goddards breweries.

Situated in a countryside setting in the south west of the island, with panoramic views of the coast and sea. Well known locally for food. Car park. Families welcome. Functions room. From Brightstone, the pub is about 400 yards along Shorewell Road.

11am–3pm and 5.30–11pm.

COWES

The Anchor Inn

High Street, Cowes PO31 7SA
☎ *(01983) 292823* Andy Taylor

Wadworth 6X and Fuller's London Pride always available plus four guests, usually from local or independent breweries. Goddard Fuggle Dee Dum and Inspiration Ale and Badger Tanglefoot are popular.

A high-street pub built in 1704. Three bars, garden. Stable bar with music Fri–Sat. Food available at lunchtime and evenings. Children allowed in the garden and middle eating area.

All day, every day.

The Ship & Castle

21 Castle Street, East Cowes PO32 6RB
☎ *(01983) 280967* Mrs Malcolm

Morland Old Speckled Hen and Marston's Pedigree always available plus guests such as Badger Brewery ales or local brews from Ventnor Brewery. The preference is for independent beers.

A tiny pub with a friendly, traditional atmosphere. No pool or music. No food but the restaurant across the road delivers food to the pub! Well-behaved children allowed.

All day, every day.

The Blacksmith's Arms

Calbourne Road, Newport PO30 5SS
☎ *(01983) 529263* Edgar Nieghorn

A freehouse with five real ale pumps serving a range of constantly changing ales. Examples include Fuller's London Pride, Hop Back Summer Lightning, Nethergate Augustinian and Bunces Sign of Spring.

A countryside pub with small restaurant, garden and play area. Food available at lunchtime and evenings. Children allowed.

OPEN *All day, every day in summer (tourist season); 11am–3pm and 6–11pm (10.30pm Sun) at other times.*

The Buddle

St Catherine's Road, Niton PO38 2N3
☎ *(01983) 730243* John Bourne

Six beers available, always including Adnams Best, something from Goddards and one of the local Ventnor Brewery range. From Easter to October a locally made cider is also featured.

A sixteenth-century, stone-built pub with oak beams, flagstone floors and open fires. Food available at lunchtime and evenings. Car park, dining room and garden. Children allowed. Near St Catherine's Lighthouse.

OPEN *11am–11pm Mon–Sat; 12–10.30pm Sun.*

Traveller's Joy

85 Pallance Road, Northwood, Cowes PO31 8LS
☎ *(01983) 298024* Mr and Mrs D Smith

Locally brewed Goddards Special Bitter and Ringwood Old Thumper are among the beers on offer, plus a wide range of guest ales from all around the country.

Multiple winner of the local branch of CAMRA's Real Ale Pub of the Year. Food is available at lunchtime and evenings and a traditional roast lunch is served on Sundays. There is a large car park and a garden with a patio, swings and children's play area in addition to two children's rooms. On the main Cowes to Yarmouth road.

OPEN *11am–2.30pm and 5–11pm Mon–Thurs; 11am–11pm Fri–Sat; 12–10.30pm Sun.*

Old Comical

15 St Johns Road, Sandown PO36 8ES
☎ *(01983) 403848* Rosemary Morris

Ushers Best and seasonal brews, Badger Bishops Tipple and Greene King Abbot Ale usually available.

Traditional, two-bar town pub with large garden. Barbecues on Sunday evenings in summer. Live music Friday evenings. Bar food served 12–3pm daily. Children welcome. Car park.

OPEN *11am–11pm (10.30pm Sun).*

Highdown Inn

Highdown Lane, Totland Bay PO39 0HY
☎ *01983 752450*
Miss S White and Mr MK Ballantyne

Ushers Best Bitter, Founders and a seasonal brew usually available.

Ideal rambler's pub, nestling at the foot of Tennyson Down, only half a mile from Alum Bay and the Needles. Wide selection of home cooked food, including children's theme menu, served 12–3pm and 6–9pm every day. Car park. Large garden with adventure playground. En-suite accommodation. Follow Alum Bay old road for Freshwater Bay.

OPEN *Winter: 11am–3pm and 6–11pm; Summer: all day, every day.*

The Volunteer Inn

30 Victoria Street, Ventnor PO38 1ES
☎ *(01983) 852537* Tim Saul

A freehouse with a good range of regularly changing ales. Regulars include Badger Best, Tanglewood, and the locally produced Ventnor Golden Bitter. Six real ales on hand pump always available.

This award-winning freehouse is the smallest pub on the island, and a haven for adult drinkers. Traditional wooden floors, lively conversation and gourmet pickled eggs, but no chips, children, fruit machines or juke box. Annual October beerfest with over 24 real ales. Muddy boots and (cat-proof) dogs welcome. Visit our website at: www.thevolunteer.demon.co.uk

OPEN *All day, every day.*

WROXALL

The Star Inn

Clarence Road, Wroxall, Nr Ventnor PO38 3BY
☎ *(01983) 854701* Mr and Mrs Boocock

Six guest beers available (15 per year), including Eldridge Pope Royal Oak, Mansfield Old Baily and Wadworth 6X.

The Star Inn offers the weary traveller hot and wholesome food and seven real ales. Destroyed by fire in 1980 but since rebuilt. Food available at lunchtime and evenings. Car park and garden. Children allowed. Wroxhall lies in the south of the island, two miles north of Ventnor on the B3327.

OPEN *11am–3pm and 7–11pm.*

YARMOUTH

The Wheatsheaf

Bridge Road, Yarmouth PO41 0PH
☎ *(01983) 760456* Mrs Keen

Goddards Fuggle Dee Dum, Wadworth 6X, Morland Old Speckled Hen and a Brakspear bitter usually available.

A traditional, food-oriented pub with two bar areas, separate eating area, two family areas, conservatory and garden. An extensive menu is available at lunchtime and evenings. Children allowed. Near the ferry.

OPEN *All day, every day.*

YOU TELL US

★ *The Cask & Cucumber*, Ryde
★ *The Central Tap*, High Street, Ventnor

GODDARDS FUGGLE DEE-DUM

SPREADING A LITTLE HOPPINESS

Places Featured:

Ashford
Aylesford
Badlesmere
Barfreston
Borden
Bossingham
Boughton Monchelsea
Burham
Canterbury
Charing
Chatham
Chiddingstone Causeway
Dartford
East Malling
Elham
Fairseat
Farningham
Faversham
Folkestone
Gillingham
Gravesend
Great Chart

Halstead
Harvel
Luddesdown
Marden
Margate
Marsh Green
Ramsgate
Ringlestone
Rochester
St Mary-in-the-Marsh
Sittingbourne
Smarden
Snargate
Southborough
Southfleet
Stone Street
Tonbridge
Upnor
West Malling
Whitstable
Worth

THE BREWERIES

ALES OF KENT BREWERY
Unit 30, Lordswood Industrial Estate, Revenge Road, Chatham ME5 8UD
☎ *(01634) 669296*

OLD MA WEASEL 3.6% ABV
WEALDON WONDER 3.7% ABV
STERLING AG 4.0% ABV
DEFIANCE 4.1% ABV
STILTMAN 4.3% ABV
SMUGGLERS GLORY 4.8% ABV
BRAINSTORM 8.0% ABV

THE FLAGSHIP BREWERY
The Historic Dockyard, Chatham ME4 4TZ
☎ *(01634) 832828*

VICTORY MILD
CAPSTAN 3.8% ABV
DESTROYER 4.0% ABV
SPRING TIDE 4.0% ABV
SPANKER 4.2% ABV
ENSIGN 4.2% ABV
FRIGGIN' IN THE RIGGIN' 4.7% ABV
CROWS NEST 4.8% ABV
FUTTOCK 5.2% ABV
OLD SEA DOG STOUT 5.5% ABV
Seasonal.
GANG PLANK 5.8% ABV
NELSONS BLOOD 6.0% ABV
Seasonal.

P & DJ GOACHER

Unit 8, Tovil Green Business Park, Tovil,
Maidstone ME15 6TA
☎ *(01622) 682112*

 REAL MILD ALE 3.4% ABV
Malt taste, slightly bitter.
FINE LIGHT ALE 3.7% ABV
Light with hops and some balancing malt.
BEST DARK ALE 4.1% ABV
Darker bitter brew with malt flavours.
CROWN IMPERIAL STOUT 4.5% ABV
GOLD STAR 5.1% ABV
Pale ale.
OLD 1066 ALE 6.7% ABV
Powerful, dark winter ale.

KENT GARDEN BREWERY

Davington Mill, Bysing Wood Road, Faversham
ME13 7UB
☎ *(01795) 532211*

CORN ROSE 3.6% ABV
HAPPY MAJOR 4.0% ABV
KENT GARDEN BITTER 4.5% ABV
BLUE ROCKET 4.5% ABV
GOLDEN BLOOM 5.0% ABV

LARKINS BREWERY LTD

Larkins Farm, Chiddingstone, Edenbridge
TN8 7BB
☎ *(01892) 870328*

TRADITIONAL ALE 3.4% ABV
Malty with balancing hoppiness.
CHIDDINGSTONE BITTER 4.0% ABV
BEST BITTER 4.4% ABV
PORTER 5.2% ABV

SHEPHERD NEAME LTD

17 Court Street, Faversham ME13 7AX
☎ *(01795) 532206*

MASTER BREW BITTER 3.7% ABV
Well-hopped and slightly sweet
throughout.
BEST BITTER 4.1% ABV
Rich malt flavour with good hoppiness.
EARLY BIRD 4.3% ABV
Spring ale.
LATE RED 4.5% ABV
Autumn ale.
GOLDINGS 4.7% ABV
Summer ale.
SPITFIRE ALE 4.7% ABV
Well-rounded, commemorative ale.
BISHOP'S FINGER 5.2% ABV
Smooth, well-rounded and complex.

THE SWALE BREWERY CO. LTD

Unit 1, D2 Trading Estate, Castle Road,
Sittingbourne ME10 3RH
☎ *(01795) 426871*

KENTISH PRIDE 3.8% ABV
AMERICAN BLONDE 4.0% ABV
KENTISH POCKET 4.0% ABV
SUMMER BLONDE 4.0% ABV
INDIAN SUMMER PALE ALE 4.2% ABV
GUILDED LILY 5.0% ABV

THE PUBS

ASHFORD

Hooden Horse on the Hill
Silver Hill Road, Ashford TN24 0NY
☎ *(01233) 662226*

Seven beers always available including Hop Back Summer Lightning, Hook Norton Old Hooky and Goacher's Light. Also some 200+ guest beers per year, which may include Greene King Abbot Ale and Hop Back Wheat Beer. Micro-breweries are well represented.

The oldest and busiest pub in Ashford, beamed and candlelit with hops in the ceiling. One bar, friendly staff, background music only. Food available at lunchtime and evenings. Car park and garden. Children allowed. Off the Hythe Road, near the ambulance station.

12–10.30pm.

AYLESFORD

The Little Gem
19 High Street, Aylesford ME20 7AX
☎ *(01622) 717510* Harvey Tox

Fuller's London Pride and ESB always available plus three or four guest beers weekly, which may include Charles Wells Bombardier, Gales HSB or Morland Old Speckled Hen.

Reputedly the smallest pub in Kent. A former bakery, the building dates back to 1106 in the reign of Henry I. The pub also has a small gallery which seats 12 people. Bar food available at lunchtime Mon–Sat and evenings Mon–Thurs. Next door to the post office.

11am–3pm and 6–11pm Mon–Fri; 11am–11pm Sat; 12–10.30pm Sun.

BADLESMERE

The Red Lion
Ashford Road, Badlesmere, Faversham ME13 0NX
☎ *(01233) 740320* Moira Anderson

A freehouse with Shepherd Neame Master Brew, Fuller's London Pride, Greene King Abbot and a mild always available. Two rotating guest taps serve, perhaps, Timothy Taylor Landlord, Hop Back Summer Lightning or Tomintoul Nessie's Monster Mash.

A sixteenth-century village local. Large garden housing pigs and sheep! Food available at lunchtime and evenings. Children allowed.

12–3pm Mon–Thurs; all day Fri–Sun.

BARFRESTON

Yew Tree Inn
Barfreston, Nr Dover CT15 7JH
☎ *(01304) 831619* Mrs P White

Greene King Mild and IPA, Otter Ale, Black Sheep Best, Timothy Taylor Landlord, Mauldons Black Adder and Thatcher's cider always available plus at least one guest (40 per year) including Wyre Piddle Piddle in the Wind, Bateman XB and Dark Mild, Fuller's ESB, Gales HSB, and Wadworth 6X.

An unspoilt traditional village freehouse with three bars. The main bar has a wooden floor and pine-scrubbed tables. Bar food available from 12–2.30pm and 7–9pm. Car park, children's room and terrace at the back overlooking open countryside. B&B. Approximately eight miles south of Canterbury, two miles off the main A2 towards Dover, signposted Barfreston.

11am–11pm (10.30pm Sun).

BORDEN

The Plough & Harrow
Oad Street, Borden, Sittingbourne ME9 8LB
☎ *(01795) 843351* David Budden

Greene King IPA, Young's Best and Shepherd Neame Master Brew always available, plus a range of guest ales. Examples include Young's Special and Shepherd Neame Early Bird and Spitfire.

A small country pub with two bars and a garden with children's area. Food available at lunchtime daily and evenings Fri–Sat. Children allowed.

All day, every day.

BOSSINGHAM

The Hop Pocket
The Street, Bossingham, Canterbury CT4 6DY
☎ *(01227) 709866* Mr M Austen

A freehouse specialising in local real ales. Two Shepherd Neame brews always available plus their seasonal beers rotated on a guest basis: Early Bird (spring), Golding (summer), Late Red (autumn), Spitfire (winter). Other guests from independent breweries across the country include Timothy Taylor Landlord, Harveys Sussex Best and Hook Norton Old Hooky.

A village pub with a family atmosphere. Victorian building, decorated with hops. Conservatory, garden and meadow with pond and children's area. Extensive menu available at lunchtime and evenings. Children allowed. Parties catered for.

12–3pm and 7–11pm (10.30 Sun).

BOUGHTON MONCHELSEA

The Red House

Hermitage Lane, Boughton Monchelsea
ME17 4DA
☎ *(01622) 743986* Mr and Mrs Richardson

Six beers available at any one time (150 per year). Otter Bitter and Everards Tiger always available, plus guests such as Ringwood Fortyniner, Wolf in Sheep's Clothing, Burton Bridge Porter, Green King Triumph, Blackawton 44 Special, King & Barnes Festive and Butcombe Bitter. Guests change constantly.

A country freehouse with pool room and two other bars, one with an open log fire. Also a conservatory/children's room, a large garden and camp site. Bar food available at lunchtime and evenings. South off the B2163 at Marlpit, take the Wierton Road, then left down East Hall Hill. OS783488. Website: www.the-redhouse.co.uk

12–3pm and 7–11pm Mon–Fri; 12–11pm Sat; 12–10.30pm Sun. Closed Tues lunch.

BURHAM

The Toastmaster's Inn

65–7 Church Street, Burham, Rochester
ME1 3SB
☎ *(01634) 861299* Mr Nik Frangoulis

A freehouse serving Greene King IPA, Abbot and Triumph, Young's Bitter and Shepherd Neame Spitfire. One guest ale from a range including Marston's Pedigree and King and Barnes Sussex Bitter.

A country pub with back bar, snug and restaurant. Tuesday night is bikers' night. Pub food served all day. Children allowed in the restaurant only. Exit J6 of the M20.

All day, every day.

CANTERBURY

Canterbury Tales

12 The Friars, Canterbury CT1 2AS
☎ *(01227) 768594*
Alan Hicks and Matthew Wood

Fuller's London Pride, Adnams Bitter and Greene King IPA always available, plus one guest beer.

A lively city-centre pub used by locals and actors. Food available all day from a varied bar menu. Traditional English food also served in a new restaurant, 'The Secret Garden'. Children allowed. Opposite the Marlowe Theatre.

All day, every day.

Tap & Spile

76 St Dunstan's Street, Canterbury CT2 8BN
☎ *(01227) 463583* Jim Atley

Tap & Spile Premium always available plus six guest ales including Greene King Abbot and Hop Back Summer Lightning.

An olde-worlde traditional pub with two bars and a beer garden. No food. Children allowed in the garden only.

All day, every day.

CHARING

The Bowl Inn

Egg Hill Road, Charing, Ashford TN27 0HG
☎ *(01233) 712256* Alan Paine

A freehouse with Fuller's London Pride always available plus three guests. The whole Fuller's range is often stocked, also brews such as Badger Tanglefoot, Gales HSB, Adnams Best or a Harveys ale.

A traditional country freehouse. One bar with children's designated area. Beer garden. Bar snacks served untl 10pm every day.

5–11pm Mon–Thurs; all day Fri–Sun.

CHATHAM

The Tap & Tin

24 Railway Street, Chatham ME4 4JT
☎ *(01634) 847926* Dave Gould

A range of beers are brewed on the premises by the brewer from the Flagship Brewery. Also one guest ale, often from Greene King.

A lively pub with a largely student clientele. Quiz nights on Tuesday, live music on Thursday and Sunday. No food. Children allowed.

CAULKER'S BITTER 3.7% ABV
A light gold ale, refreshingly dry with hints of fruit and bitter aftertaste.

CAPTIN'S TACKLE 4.2% ABV
Dry, malty ale with subtle roast tones and a bitter finish.

FLOGGIN 4.1% ABV

YARDARM 4.3% ABV
Well-balanced malty ale, slightly nutty with a smooth bitter aftertaste.

11am–11pm Mon–Sat; 12–10.30pm Sun.

CHIDDINGSTONE CAUSEWAY

The Little Brown Jug
*Chiddingstone Causeway, Nr Tonbridge
TN11 8JJ*
☎ *(01892) 870318* Mr and Mrs CR Cannon

Harveys Best always available plus three guest beers (130 per year) including Timothy Taylor Landlord, Brakspear Bitter, Hop Back Summer Lightning, Ringwood Old Thumper, Fuller's London Pride, Morland Old Speckled Hen, Exmoor Gold and Gales HSB. Also brews from Larkins and Adnams.

A friendly, family-owned country pub with no games machines or music. Bar and restaurant food available at lunchtime and evenings. Car park, garden, conference facilities and accommodation. Children allowed.

OPEN *11.30am–3pm and 6–11pm.*

DARTFORD

Paper Moon
55 High Street, Dartford DA1 1DL
☎ *(01322) 281127* Tuesday Webb

A Wetherspoon's pub with Shepherd Neame Spitfire always available plus a selection of four guest ales from any independent brewery or micro-brewery in the United Kingdom.

A traditional one-bar town pub with non-smoking area. Food served all day. No children.

OPEN *All day, every day.*

EAST MALLING

The Rising Sun
125 Mill Street, East Malling ME19 6BX
☎ *(01732) 843284* Mr Kemp

A freehouse specialising in local ales from breweries such as Goacher's and Shepherd Neame. Up to three guests usually from micro-breweries such as Bateman or Gales.

A locals' pub with two bars and a beer garden. Food available at lunchtime Mon–Fri. No children.

OPEN *All day, every day.*

ELHAM

The Rose & Crown
High Street, Elham, Canterbury CT4 6TD
☎ *(01303) 840226* Denise McNicholas

A freehouse serving a selection of cask ales, with Bateman XB usually available. Other may include Rother Valley Level Best, Ruddles County and Greene King Abbot Ale.

A sixteenth-century village inn. Full à la carte, bar food and fresh fish menus available lunchtimes and evenings in lounge bar or non-smoking restaurant. En-suite accommodation, patio.

OPEN *11am–3pm and 6–11pm Mon–Sat; 12–3pm and 7–10.30pm Sun.*

FAIRSEAT

The Vigo Inn
*Gravesend Road, Fairseat, Nr Sevenoaks
TN15 7JL*
☎ *(01732) 822547* Mrs PJ Ashwell

Young's, Harveys and Flagship brews always available guests list which may include Ridleys ESX Best and Rumpus.

Situated on the North Downs, partly non-smoking. No music or games machines. Bar food is available. Car park. Children allowed in the garden only.

OPEN *12–3pm and 6–11pm Mon–Sat; 12–3pm and 7–10.30pm Sun. Closed Mon lunchtime.*

FARNINGHAM

The Chequers
High Street, Farningham, Dartford DA4 0DT
☎ *(01322) 865222*
Alan Vowls and Karen Jefferies

A freehouse serving Fuller's ESB and London Pride and Timothy Taylor Landlord plus six guest ales including brews from Hop Back, Bateman, Oakham, Greene King and other small breweries

A 300-year-old beamed village pub. Close to the river in the Brands Hatch area. Food served 12–2.30pm. Children allowed.

OPEN *11am–11pm (10.30pm Sun).*

The Elephant Inn

31 The Mall, Faversham ME13 8JN
☎ *(01795) 590157*
Sharon Yates and Aden Brady

Greene King IPA always available plus five alternating guest beers including one cask mild. Ales come from Harveys, Hop Back and Adnams among many others, changed weekly.

Traditional, old-fashioned locals' pub with a friendly atmosphere. Excellent home-made food served every lunchtime and Thurs–Sat evenings in the bar or the non-smoking restaurant. Walled garden, families welcome.

12–11pm Mon–Fri; 11am–11pm Sat; 12–10.30pm Sun.

The Lifeboat

42 North Street, Folkestone CT19 6AD
☎ *(01303) 243958* P O'Reilly

Fuller's London Pride usually available plus three guest beers from a range including Bateman Victory and XXXB and Mansfield Old Bailey.

Largely a locals' pub in a tourist area. One bar and beer garden. Food available at lunchtime and evenings. Children allowed in the garden only.

All day, every day.

Roseneath

79 Arden Street, Gillingham ME7 1HS
☎ *(01634) 852553*
Mr T Robinson and Mrs H Dobson

Up to six beers available, perhaps including Greene King Abbot, Bateman XB, Cotleigh Barn Owl, Belchers Best, Charles Wells Bombardier, Adnams Broadside, B&T Dragonslayer, Coach House Gunpowder Strong Mild, Ward's Waggle Dance and many more.

A friendly pub with perhaps the most adventurous selection of beers in north Kent. Doorstep sandwiches. Crazy bar billiards. Just five minutes from the railway station.

11am–11.30pm Mon–Sat; 12–10.30pm Sun.

The Jolly Drayman

Wellington Street, Gravesend DA12 1JA
☎ *(01474) 352355* Mr Fordred

Everards Tiger always available, plus three guests, ranging from 3.5% to 5.5% ABV in strength.

A country-style pub in a town-centre location. Housed in part of the Wellington Brewery building. Patio and garden. Food available at lunchtime (not Sunday). Barbecues on Friday and Saturday evenings, May–Sept. Children allowed in the garden only.

11.30am–2.30pm and 6–11pm Mon–Thurs; 11.30am–2.30pm and 5.30–11pm Fri; 12–3pm and 7–11pm Sat; 12–3pm and 7–10.30pm Sun.

Somerset Arms

10 Darnley Road, Gravesend DA11 0RU
☎ *(01474) 533837* Mr and Mrs Cerr

Six beers always available from a range of hundreds per year. These may include Exmoor Gold, Timothy Taylor Landlord, Kelham Island Pale Rider, Maclays Broadsword, Ash Vine Hop and Glory and brews from Harviestoun, Hoskins & Oldfield, Youngs and Fullers.

A country-style pub. The Best Town Pub in Kent 1993, and winner of Cask Marque award. Bar food available. Children allowed. Opposite Gravesend railway station.

11am–midnight.

The Hooden Horse

The Street, Great Chart, Ashford TN23 3AN
☎ *(01233) 625583* Mr Jackson

Hook Norton Old Hooky and Morland Old Speckled Hen always available plus a guest pump serving a real ale such as Greene King Abbot.

An old English pub with one bar decorated with hops, and a Mexican restaurant. Beer garden. Food available at lunchtime and evenings. No children.

12–2.30pm and 6–11pm daily.

HALSTEAD

The Rose & Crown

Otford Lane, Halstead, Sevenoaks TN14 7EA
☎ *(01959) 533120* Joy Brushneen

Larkins Traditional and a Harveys brew always available plus three guests (over 100 per year) from independent breweries such as Otter, Gales or Kelham Island.

A rural drinking pub with two bars, pool room and enclosed garden. Food available at lunchtime Mon–Fri. Children allowed in the garden and pool room.

OPEN All day, every day.

HARVEL

Amazon & Tiger

Harvel Street, Harvel, Nr Meopham DA13 0DE
☎ *(01474) 814705* Lesley Whitehouse

The three beers served vary on a weekly basis and may include Greene King IPA and Triumph, Morland Old Speckled Hen, Ruddles Best or beers from Brains among many others.

Typical village pub appealing to all age groups, with sporting and games bias. Occasional Friday night entertainment. Food served every lunchtime. Children welcome. Car park.

OPEN 12–3pm and 6–11pm Mon–Fri; 12–11pm Sat; 12–10.30pm Sun.

LUDDESDOWN

The Cock Inn

Henley Street, Luddesdown DA13 0XB
☎ *(01474) 814208* Mr A Turner

Adnams Bitter always available plus six guest beers (two new ones per day). If it is brewed, it has probably been sold here.

A sixteenth-century traditional two-bar public house set in idyllic countryside. Bar food available until 8pm. Seafood specialities. Car park and garden.

OPEN 12–11pm (10.30pm Sun).

MARDEN

The Stilebridge Inn

Staplehurst Road, Marden, Tonbridge TN12 9BH
☎ *(01622) 831236* Mr and Mrs S Johnson

A freehouse with a constantly changing, varied range of up to seven real ales. Local and micro-breweries favoured.

A traditional country pub with restaurant, three bars and beer garden. Food available at lunchtime and evenings. Children allowed.

OPEN 11–30am–3pm Mon–Sat, 6–11pm Tues–Fri, 6.30–11pm Sat; all day Sun (closed Mon evening).

MARGATE

The Spread Eagle

25 Victoria Road, Margate CT9 1LW
☎ *(01843) 293396* Neil Hall

A freehouse serving Greene King IPA, Fuller's London Pride, Adnams Best and Morland Old Speckled Hen, plus guests.

A traditional Victorian pub with bar and dining areas. Food available daytimes and evenings. Children allowed.

OPEN 11.30am–3pm and 5.30–11pm Mon–Thurs; all day Fri–Sat; 12–3pm and 6–10.30pm Sun.

MARSH GREEN

The Wheatsheaf

Marsh Green, Edenbridge TN8 5QL
☎ *(01732) 864091* Neil Foster

Harveys brews available plus a good selection of guests (approx 150 per year) including, perhaps, Fuller's London Pride, Timothy Taylor Landlord, Gales HSB, Young's Ram Rod, or an Adnams brew.

A traditional village pub with four bars, conservatory and beer garden. Food available at lunchtime and evenings. Children allowed.

OPEN 11am–3pm and 5.30–11pm; all day Sat–Sun.

RAMSGATE

The Artillery Arms

36 Westcliffe Road, Ramsgate CT12 9JJ
☎ *(01843) 853282* Tony Sowden

A freehouse serving only real ales on a constantly rotating basis. No permanent brews but 600 different ones served over 18 months!

A basic beer-drinker's pub with no extras. No food. No children.

OPEN 12–11pm (10.30pm Sun).

The Churchill Tavern

19–22 The Paragon, Ramsgate CT11 9JX
☎ *(01843) 587862* John Williams

Ringwood Old Thumper, Timothy Taylor Landlord, Morland Old Speckled Hen and Fuller's London Pride usually available, plus up to seven guests including Cottage Golden Arrow, Exmoor Gold, Wychwood Dog's Bollocks and many more.

A country-style pub in the town. Two bars in a four-storey building, live music with jazz club, folk and blues club (members club in basement). Annual beer festival. Food available at lunchtime and evenings. Children allowed.

OPEN All day, every day.

RINGLESTONE

Ringlestone Inn

Nr Harrietsham, Maidstone ME17 1NX
☎ *(01622) 859900* Michael Millington-Buck

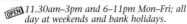 Five beers always available including Shepherd Neame Best and guests (40 per year) from brewers such as Bateman, Adnams, Young's, Hook Norton, Fuller's, Felinfoel, Harveys and Shepherd Neame, plus seasonal variations.

Built as a hospice for monks, a sixteenth-century inn and hotel, beamed with open fires and two bars. Bar and restaurant food. Car parks, garden. Children allowed. Accommodation. From junction 8 of the M20, follow signs to Hollingbourne, drive through Hollingbourne, then at the water tower turn right and straight over at next crossroads.

OPEN *11.30am–3pm and 6–11pm Mon–Fri; all day at weekends and bank holidays.*

ROCHESTER

The Man of Kent

6–8 John Street, Rochester ME1 1YN
☎ *(01634) 818771* Mr and Mrs Sandmann

Five ever-changing beers available at any one time (100 per year) with local breweries such as Goacher's and Flagship favoured. Also Theobald's cask-conditioned cider.

A friendly old-style pub with one L-shaped bar. Games include chess, bar billiards, darts, carpet bowls and shove ha'penny. Bar food is available at lunchtime and evenings. Parking and garden. Off Victoria Street, near the Main Star Hill junction. Near the school.

OPEN *12–11pm (10.30pm Sun).*

The Star Inn

Star Hill, Rochester ME1 1UZ
☎ *(01634) 826811* Vana Bartelow

Fuller's London Pride usually available, plus guests from independents and micro-breweries such as such as Timothy Taylor Landlord or an Adnams ale.

A boozer's pub in the town centre. One bar, old building. No food. No children.

OPEN *All day, every day.*

Who'd Ha Thot It?

9 Baker Street, Rochester ME1 3DN
☎ *(01634) 830144*

Six beers always available including Butchers Brew (brewed specially for the pub), Greene King Abbot, Thomas Hardy Royal Oak, Fuller's London Pride. Guests include Goacher's brews and vary in strength from 3.5% to 5.2% ABV. The landlord tries to favour smaller breweries.

A nineteenth-century pub off the main Maidstone Road, refurbished and with an open fire. There is a games bar and lounge bar, no juke box. Bar food available. Street parking, beer garden. Well-behaved children only.

OPEN *12–11pm (10.30pm Sun).*

ST MARY-IN-THE-MARSH

The Star Inn

St Mary-In-The-Marsh, Romney Marsh TN29 0BX
☎ *(01797) 362139*
Marc and Jenny van Overstreten

Shepherd Neame Spitfire plus a seasonal brew usually available.

Family-run freehouse with large beer garden and views of the church and surrounding countryside. Food served 12–2pm and 7–9pm Mon–Sat, 12.30–2pm Sun. No children's facilities. Car park. Accommodation.

OPEN *11am–3pm and 7–11pm Mon–Sat; 12–3pm and 7–10.30pm Sun.*

SITTINGBOURNE

The Barge

17 Crown Quay Lane, Sittingbourne ME10 3JN
☎ *(01795) 423291* John Aitken

Greene King IPA usually available with a guest beer possibly from Young's, Greene King, Tolly Cobbold, Marston's, Brains, Adnams or Charles Wells.

Friendly, two-bar family pub with restaurant area. Very large garden. Live entertainment on Saturday and Sunday. Food available 11.30am–2pm and 7–9pm Mon–Sat. Children welcome. Car park. Located two minutes off the main High Street, on the edge of Eurolink Industrial Estate.

OPEN *11.30am–11pm (10.30pm Sun).*

The Red Lion

58 High Street, Sittingbourne ME10 4PB
☎ *(01795) 472706* Rod Bailey

Fuller's London Pride and one beer from Swale Brewery usually available, plus four others which may include Wadworth 6X, Greene King Abbot Ale or IPA, Gales HSB, Harveys Best Bitter, Badger Tanglefoot or Charles Wells Bombardier.

A fourteenth-century inn with a wealth of history and a myriad of famous visitors over the centuries. Lovely garden courtyard. Winner of Kent 1999 Town Centre Pub of the Year. Food served daily: snacks and meals at lunchtimes and meals only in the evenings. Children welcome till 6pm, but no special facilities. Small car park at rear.

OPEN *Summer: 11am–3pm and 5–11pm Mon–Thurs; 11am–11pm Fri–Sat; 12–3pm and 7–10.30pm Sun; Winter: 11am–3pm and 6–11pm Mon–Thurs; Fri–Sun as summer.*

The Bell Inn

Bell Lane, Smarden, Nr Ashford TN27 8PW
☎ *(01233) 770283* Ian Turner

Shepherd Neame Best, Fuller's London Pride, Goacher's IPA, Morland Old Speckled Hen and Marston's Pedigree are always available plus a couple of guest beers, perhaps from breweries such as Bateman and Young's.

A fifteenth-century inn, beamed with stone floors and an inglenook fireplace. Three bars (one non-smoking). Bar food available. Car park, garden, children's room, accommodation.

OPEN *11.30am–2.30pm and 6–11pm Mon–Sat; 12–3pm and 7–10.30pm Sun.*

The Bat & Ball

141 London Road, Southborough, Tunbridge Wells TN4 0NA
☎ *(01892) 518085* Sonia Law

A freehouse with five pumps serving a constantly changing range of real ales. These might include Morland Old Speckled Hen, Flagship Nelson's Blood and Destroyer, Fuller's London Pride and brews from Black Sheep, Hook Norton or Larkins.

An old-fashioned two-bar boozer in a village area. Music. Garden. No food. No children.

OPEN *All day, every day.*

The Red Lion

Snargate, Romney Marsh TN29 9UQ
☎ *(01797) 344648* Doris Jemison

Goacher's Light and Tailwagger and a house beer brewed by Rother Valley Brewery usually available, plus five guest beers which may include Bateman XB, Swale Black Marigold Mild, Black Sheep Best Bitter, Woodforde's Wherry or something from Cottage, Kitchen, Ales of Kent or Hart.

Unspoilt, sixteenth-century pub serving real ale drawn straight from the cask. Real fires, traditional pub games and large garden. No food. Car park. Children welcome, but not in main bar.

OPEN *11am–3pm and 7–11pm Mon–Sat (6–11pm in summer) 12–3pm and 7–10.30pm Sun (6–10.30pm in summer)*

The Black Lion

Red Street, Southfleet, Gravesend DA13 9QJ
☎ *(01474) 832153* Dave Pettit

A freehouse serving five real ales, plus guests from local micro-breweries.

A traditional two-bar pub with garden. Food available 12–9pm and 12–3.30pm on Sundays, with traditional pies a speciality. Supervised children welcome.

OPEN *All day, every day.*

The Padwell Arms

Stone Street TN15 0L
☎ *(01732) 761532*

Seven beers always available including Badger Best, Hook Norton Old Hooky and Harveys Best. Also some 300+ guest beers per year mainly from micro-breweries. Definitely no nationals.

A country pub one mile off the A25 between Seal and Borough Green. Features include two real fires and views overlooking apple and pear orchards. Bar food is available at lunchtime. Car park, garden and outside terrace with barbecues in summer. Children allowed under sufferance. Live Blues music on the last Saturday of every month.

OPEN *12–3pm and 6–11pm Mon–Sat; 12–3pm and 7–10.30pm Sun.*

TONBRIDGE

The New Drum

54 Lavender Hill, Tonbridge TN9 2AU
☎ *(01732) 365044* Matt Spencer

Harveys Best, Fuller's London Pride and Larkins Chiddingstone always available, plus a range of guests including Young's Special, Greene King IPA and Abbot, Tisbury Stonehenge and Charles Wells Bombardier.

A traditional local with one bar and garden. Rolls only available. Children allowed.

OPEN All day, every day.

The Royal Oak

Lower Haysden Lane, Tonbridge TN11 9BD
☎ *(01732) 350208* Mr and Mrs Bird

Adnams Bitter always available plus two or three guest beers (100+ per year), perhaps from Bateman, Wychwood, Ash Vine, Crouch Vale or Harviestoun breweries.

Olde-worlde country pub and restaurant. Bar and restaurant food available at lunchtime. Car park and garden. Children allowed. Follow the signs to Haysden Country Park, south of Tonbridge.

OPEN 11am–11pm Mon–Sat; 12–10.30pm Sun.

Wonderful Hooden Horse

59 Pembury Road, Tonbridge TN9 2JB
☎ *(01732) 366080* Michelle Crawford

Greene King IPA always available, plus three guests. Greene King Abbot and Adnams Broadside regularly featured plus customers' choice of guest ales on a weekly basis ('The Ale Spotter's Guide' system).

An old building with great atmosphere. Beer garden. Live music at least once a fortnight. Beer festivals, barbecues and art and craft fairs. Mexican and Mediterranean food available at lunchtime and evenings. Children allowed in the garden and in designated area inside if eating.

OPEN 12–2.30pm and 6–11pm Mon–Thurs; all day Fri–Sun.

UPNOR

The Tudor Rose

29 High Street, Upnor, Rochester ME2 4XG
☎ *(01634) 715305* Mr Rennie

A freehouse serving Young's Bitter and Special plus four guests such as Charles Wells Bombardier, or Hampshire Pendragon.

A 430-year-old pub with one main bar and a small 20-seater restaurant. Food available at lunchtime and evenings. Children allowed. Near Upnor Castle (follow signs for the castle).

OPEN 11.30am–3.30pm and 7–11pm (10.30pm Sun).

WEST MALLING

The Lobster Pot

47 Swan Street, West Malling ME19 6JU
☎ *(01732) 843265* Ed Austin

A freehouse offering six real ales from breweries such as Goacher's, Adnams and Larkins, as well as lesser-known micro-breweries. Local beers are always a feature.

A traditional 300-year-old pub, runner-up in CAMRA Pub of the Year for Kent in 1999. Two bars, restaurant and function room. Food available at lunchtime and evenings. Children allowed in the restaurant only.

OPEN 12–2.30pm and 6–11pm (10.30pm Sun).

WHITSTABLE

The Ship Centurion Arminius

111 High Street, Whitstable CT5 1AY
☎ *(01227) 264740*
Janet, Roland and Armin Birks

One strong bitter always available, such as Cains Formidable, Morland Old Speckled Hen, Nethergate Augustinian, Hop Back Summer Lightning, or Adnams Broadside. Only pub in town to serve cask mild. Examples include Cains Dark Mild and Elgood's Black Dog. Adnams Southwold and Timothy Taylor Landlord are regular features.

A one-bar town freehouse with disabled access and dining area. Home-cooked bar food served lunchtimes and evenings, Hungarian Goulash Soup and German Bratwurst are specialities. Quiz teams and Sky TV. Children with well-behaved parents allowed in 24-seater sun lounge! Cask Marque award winner.

OPEN All day, every day.

WORTH

St Crispin Inn
The Street, Worth, Deal CT14 0DF
☎ *(01304) 612081* Jane O'Brien

A freehouse serving Shepherd Neame Master Brew plus three guests. Examples include Shepherd Neame Early Bird, Rye and Coriander plus Gales HSB.

A sixteenth-century oak-beamed pub. One open bar, patio, large beer garden. Bat and chat pitch. Accommodation. Food served at lunchtime and evenings in a separate 28-seater restaurant. Children allowed.

OPEN *Generally all day, every day in summer. 11am–2.30pm and 5–11pm (10.30pm Sun) at other times.*

YOU TELL US

★ *Golding Hop*, Sheet Hill, Borough, Sevenoaks
★ *The Kings Head*, 38 London Road, Sittingbourne
★ *The Mogul*, Chapel Place, Dover
★ *The Papermaker's Arms*, The Street, Plaxton, Sevenoaks
★ *The Red Lion*, 61 High Street, Bluetown, Sheerness
★ *The Royal Oak*, 2 High Street, Shoreham
★ *Wat Tyler*, 80 High Street, Dartford
★ *The Wheatsheaf*, 74 Herne Bay Road, Whitstable

Places Featured:

Accrington	Darwen
Arkholme	Entwhistle
Bispham Green	Fleetwood
Blackburn	Great Harwood
Blackpool	Haslingden
Burnley	Little Eccleston
Chorley	Lytham
Clayton-le-Moors	Ormskirk
Clitheroe	Preston
Cliviger	Whalley
Colne	Wharles
Croston	Wrightington
Dalton	

THE BREWERIES

MOORHOUSE'S BREWERY LTD

4 Moorhouse's Street, Burnley BB1 5EN
☎ *(01282) 422864*

BLACK CAT MILD 3.4% ABV
Refreshing.
PREMIER BITTER 3.7% ABV
Full-flavoured with good hoppiness.
PRIDE OF PENDLE 4.1% ABV
Smooth and well-rounded.
PENDLE WITCHES BREW 5.1% ABV
Complex, sweet malt and fruit flavour.
OWD ALE 6.0% ABV
Old ales don't get better than this!

THE THREE B'S BREWERY

Hamilton Street, Blackburn BB2 4AJ
☎ *(01254) 208154*

BOBBIN'S BITTER 3.8% ABV
STOKERS SLAK 3.6% ABV
Mild.
TACKLER'S TIPPLE 4.3% ABV
PINCH NOGGIN 4.6% ABV
KNOCKER UP 4.8% ABV
Porter.
SHUTTLE ALE 5.2% ABV
Plus occasional beers.

DANIEL THWAITES BREWERY

Star Brewery, Blackburn BB1 5BU
☎ *(01254) 54431*

BEST MILD 3.3% ABV
Sweet and full-bodied.
BITTER 3.6% ABV
Amber, distinctive and malty.
CHAIRMAN'S 4.2% ABV
Golden, easy-drinking.
DANIEL'S HAMMER 5.0% ABV
Pale and malty with dry hoppy finish.
Plus occasional beers.

THE PUBS

ACCRINGTON

The George Hotel
185 Blackburn Road, Accrington BB5 0AF
☎ *(01254) 383441*

Four beers always available from an ever-changing list that might include Titanic Stout, Cains FA, Passageway St Arnold and Goose Eye Bitter.

A friendly freehouse with an open-plan bar area and separate restaurant in converted stables. Bar and restaurant food available at lunchtime and evenings. Street parking, garden/patio area. Children allowed. Accommodation. Close to the railway and bus stations.

OPEN 12–11pm (10.30pm Sun).

ARKHOLME

The Bay Horse Hotel
Arkholme, Carnforth
☎ *(015242) 21425)* Peter Dawson Jackson

A guest beer usually available, perhaps Greene King Abbot Ale, Morland Old Speckled Hen, Everards Tiger or one of several other regular beers.

Typical, unspoilt country pub. Food served Tues–Sun lunchtimes and every evening. Car park. Children welcome. From junction 35 of the M6, follow the Kirkby Lonsdale sign for 5 miles.

OPEN 11.30am–3pm and 6–11pm (10.30pm Sun).

BISPHAM GREEN

The Eagle & Child
Bispham Green, Nr Ormskirk L40 3SG
☎ *(01257) 462297* Monica Evans

A freehouse with Moorhouse's Black Cat Mild and a Liverpool Brewery brew such as Bury Street Bitter, Blondie or First Gold always available. Also four guests from breweries such as Hanby, Hart or Phoenix. Annual beer festival on May bank holiday with a selection of 50 real ales.

An old-fashioned country pub with flagstone floors, old furniture, bowling green, croquet lawn and beer garden. Food served at lunchtime and evenings. Children allowed.

OPEN 12–3pm and 5.30–11pm Mon–Sat; all day Sun.

BLACKBURN

The Cellar Bar
39–41 King Street, Blackburn
☎ *(01254) 698111* Dan Hook

Two regularly changing beers available often from Moorhouse's, Three B's, Castle Eden, Dent, Jennings or RCH.

Buried underground in the first mayor of Blackburn's family home and the oldest Georgian house in the town, this pub has a cosy, friendly atmosphere, real fire, live music and the biggest beer garden in Blackburn. No food. Car park. Children welcome.

OPEN 11am–11pm Mon–Tues; 11am–1am Wed–Fri; 7pm–1am Sat; 7–10.30pm Sun.

The Postal Order
15 Darwen Street, Blackburn BB2 2BY
☎ *(01254) 676400* George and Beryl Little

A Wetherspoon's pub serving several guest ales. Thwaites Mild is a regular feature, and other guests might include Exmoor Fox, Gales GB and Cotleigh Barn Owl.

A large, traditional town pub near the Cathedral. One long bar with two separate areas. Non-smoking dining area. Food served all day. No children.

OPEN All day, every day.

BLACKPOOL

The Shovels
Common Edge Road, Blackpool FY4 5DH
☎ *(01253) 762702* Steve Norris

Two regulars and four guest beers usually available from breweries such as Hart or Eccleshall. Micro-breweries favoured whenever possible.

A steak 'n' ale pub in a suburban location. One bar, real fire, front patio, disabled access/toilet. Dining area, non-smoking conservatory. Food served every day (12–9.30pm). Children allowed, but not near bar area. Situated just off the M55.

OPEN All day, every day.

BURNLEY

The Sparrowhawk Hotel

Church Street, Burnley BB11 2DN
☎ *(01282) 421551* Mr Baker

A freehouse specialising in real ales. Moorhouse's Premier and Pendle Witches Brew always available plus Ruffled Feathers (brewed especially for The Sparrowhawk by Moorhouse's) or a Hart Brewery ale.

A country-style inn in the town centre. Two bars, restaurant and accommodation. Food served at lunchtime and evenings. Children allowed.

OPEN *11am–3pm and 6–11pm Mon–Fri; all day Sat–Sun.*

CHORLEY

Malt 'n' Hops

50–2 Friday Street, Chorley PR6 0AH
☎ *(01257) 260967*

Timothy Taylor Landlord and Moorhouse's Pendle Witches Brew always available plus four guest beers (at least one changed every day) perhaps including something from Lloyds Country Beers, Batham, Cains and many other breweries.

A Victorian-style, one-bar pub ideal for trainspotters. Bar food available at lunchtime. Parking. Children allowed. Just 200 yards behind the Manchester to Preston railway station.

OPEN *All day, every day.*

CLAYTON-LE-MOORS

The Albion

243 Whalley Road, Clayton-le-Moors, Accrington BB5 5HD
☎ *(01254) 238585* John Burke

Porter Dark Mild, Bitter, Porter and Sunshine always available plus seasonal ales such as Ginger Beer, Floral Dance, Young Tom and others.

A traditional real ale pub. One bar, darts, beer garden. Mooring spot for barges on the Liverpool to Leeds canal. Sandwiches only. Children allowed in the garden only.

OPEN *5–11pm Mon–Tues; all day Wed–Sun.*

CLITHEROE

The New Inn

Parson Lane, Clitheroe BB7 2JN
☎ *(01200) 423312* Mr and Mrs Lees

A Whitbread house with a guest beer policy serving Fuller's London Pride, Marston's Pedigree and a Moorhouse's brew plus a guest, changed weekly, from smaller breweries if possible. Beers featured have included Greene King Abbot, Gales HSB and Wadworth 6X.

An old English pub with one bar and an open fire. Four adjoining rooms, plus a non-smoking room. No music or games, but folk club on Friday nights. Children allowed in designated area. No food.

OPEN *All day, every day.*

CLIVIGER

Queens

412 Burnley Road, Cliviger, Nr Burnley
☎ *(01282) 436712* Alec Heap

Three guest beers usually available from a wide range of micro-breweries.

Simple alehouse. No pool table, juke box or bandits. No food. Children welcome, but there are no special facilities.

OPEN *1–11pm Mon–Sat; 12–10.30pm Sun.*

COLNE

The Hare & Hounds Inn

Black Lane Ends, Colne BB8 7EP
☎ *(01282) 863070* Paul Smith

A freehouse serving Timothy Taylor Golden Best, Dark Mild and Landlord on a regular basis plus various guests such as Black Sheep Bitter or Riggwelter.

A country pub. One bar, real fires, stone and wood floors and beams. Food available all day. Children allowed.

OPEN *All day, every day.*

CROSTON

The Black Horse

Westhead Road, Croston, Nr Chorley PR5 7RQ
☎ *(01772) 600338* Mr S Welsh

At least four regular and guest ales (650 per year) from breweries such as Cains, Hydes, Mansfield, Hanby, Lloyds, Tom Wood, Banks, Timothy Taylor, Coach House, Sutton and Bushy's. Emphasis on micro-breweries and unusual brews.

A family-run traditional village freehouse. Bar and restaurant food is served at lunchtime and evenings. Car park, garden, children's play area, bowling green, French boules pitch. Children allowed in the restaurant. In the village of Croston, close to Chorley and midway between Preston and Southport.

OPEN *All day, every day.*

DALTON

The Beacon Inn
Beacon Lane, Dalton WN8 7RR
☎ *(01695) 632607* Kevin Balke

Jennings Mild, Bitter and Cumberland regularly available plus a guest beer which may include Fuller's London Pride or something from Castle Eden.

Acquired by Jennings in 1999, this country pub is much used by ramblers as it is situated by Ashurst Beacon Point. Also handy for Beacon Golf Club. Food served 12–2pm Tues–Sat, 12–5pm Sun. Car park. Large beer garden. Children welcome.

OPEN *12–11pm (10.30pm Sun).*

DARWEN

Greenfield Inn
Lower Barn Street, Darwen BB3 2HQ
☎ *(01254) 703945* John Howard

A freehouse with Thwaites Mild and Bitter plus Timothy Taylor Landlord always available. Also three guests including, perhaps, Shepherd Neame Spitfire, Greene King Abbot, Moorhouse's Pendle Witches Brew or special Porter's ales.

A traditional one-room pub with beer garden. Food served at lunchtime and evenings. Children allowed. Situated on the outskirts of Blackburn.

OPEN *12–3.30pm and 5–11pm Mon, Wed, Thur; 5.30–11pm Tues; all day Sat–Sun.*

ENTWHISTLE

The Strawbury Duck
Overshores Road, Entwhistle, Bolton BL7 0LU
☎ *(01204) 852013* Greg and Angie Brown

Moorhouse's Pendle Witches, Timothy Taylor Landlord, Black Sheep Special and a house ale called Duck Best (3.5% ABV) permanently available, plus a wide variety of guests served on three pumps. Regulars include Morland Old Speckled Hen, Marston's Pedigree or ales from Brains or Caledonian including seasonals.

A 300-year-old pub situated next to Entwhistle Railway Station. One bar, several dining areas, pool room, non-smoking room, beer garden, accommodation. Food served 12–2.30pm and 6.30–9.30pm Mon–Thurs, all day Fri–Sun. Children welcome, with special menu and crayons available.

OPEN *11am 11pm Mon Sat; 12 10.30pm Sun.*

FLEETWOOD

Wyre Lounge Bar
Marine Hall, The Esplanade, Fleetwood FY7 6HF
☎ *(01253) 771141*

Eight beers always available including Moorhouse's brews. Also 200+ guest beers per year which may come from Young's, Charles Wells, Banks's and Timothy Taylor.

Part of the Marine Hall Sports Complex in Fleetwood. Food available at lunchtime. CAMRA Pub of the Year. Car park, garden, function room. No children.

OPEN *11am–4.30pm and 7–11pm Mon–Sat; 12–4pm and 7–10.30pm Sun.*

GREAT HARWOOD

The Dog & Otter
Cliffe Lane, Great Harwood, Blackburn BB6 7PG
☎ *(01254) 885760* Alberto Rodriguez

A Jennings-managed house with Jennings Bitter and Cumberland Ale always available, plus one rotating guest ale, perhaps Fuller's London Pride or a Marston's brew.

A pub/restaurant with one bar and outside tables. Old-style building with extension. Food served at lunchtime and evenings Mon–Sat, all day Sun. Children allowed.

OPEN *11.30am–3pm and 5.30–11pm (10.30pm Sun).*

The Royal Hotel
Station Road, Great Harwood, Blackburn BB6 7BA
☎ *(01254) 883541* Mr Hughes

A freehouse with five guest ales constantly changing. Moorhouse's Premier, Charles Wells Bombardier, Cains Bitter, Tomintoul Wild Cat and Culloden, RCH East Street Cream or a Burtonwood brew regularly featured.

A Victorian pub/hotel. One bar, dining area, garden, accommodation. Food available at lunchtime and evenings. Children allowed.

OPEN *12–2pm and 7–11pm (10.30pm Sun).*

Black Cat Mild
3.2% ALCOHOL V/V
ORIGINAL GRAVITY 1034°
MOORHOUSE'S
BREWERS OF REAL ALE

The Griffin Inn

84 Hud Rake, Haslingden, Rossendale BB4 5AF
☎ *(01706) 214021* David Porter

Home of the Porter Brewing Company. A brewpub with Dark Mild, Bitter, Porter, Sunshine and Rossendale Ale brewed and served on the premises.

A traditional no-frills alehouse and local community pub on the northern edge of town. No music or TV. No food. No children.

DARK MILD 3.3% ABV
BITTER 3.8% ABV
ROSSENDALE ALE 4.2% ABV
PORTER 5.0% ABV
SUNSHINE 5.3% ABV
Plus occasional and seasonal brews.
OPEN *All day, every day.*

The Cartford Hotel

Cartford Lane, Little Eccleston, Preston PR3 0YP
☎ *(01995) 670166. Fax (01995) 671785*
Andrew Mellodew

The Hart Brewery operates from the premises producing a range of 16 beers for sale in the hotel and some local freehouses. Fuller's London Pride and Timothy Taylor Landlord are also regularly available plus a range of over 3,000 other beers so far served on a guest basis.

An award-winning, 400-year-old family pub. One large bar, large garden with children's play area. Quiet eating area with food available at lunchtime and evenings. Children allowed. Brewery tours by appointment. Car park. Games room. Accommodation.

SECOND COMING 3.8% ABV
Easter special. Light and sweet.
GOLD BEACH 3.8% ABV
A true summer session ale, light and hoppy.
GOLDEN SQUIRREL 3.9% ABV
A summer ale blending Squirrels Hoard and Gold Beach.
DISHY DEBBIE 4.0% ABV
A year-round session beer. Light and golden with a citrus flavour.
SQUIRRELS HOARD 4.0% ABV
Award-winning session beer. Intense nut taste.
AMBASSADOR 4.2% ABV
A relatively dry beer, red in colour.
NO BALLS 4.5% ABV
Christmas ale. Light and refreshing.
NEMESIS 4.5 % ABV
Golden premier bitter. Also known as The Goddess.
CRIMIN ALE PORTER 4.7% ABV
A true porter brewed once a year.
VAL.(ADDICTION) (4.8% ABV)
Dark, sweet, easy-drinking beer.
AMADEUS 5.0% ABV
Dark, rich winter warmer.
COBBLESTONE 5.0% ABV
A stout-style beer.
EXCALIBUR 5.0% ABV
A light lager-style beer with citrus taste and sweet finish.
OLD RAM 5.0% ABV
Bronze, full-bodied beer. Brewed more in the winter than summer.
CESTRIAN HART 5.2% ABV
Dark and sweet.
STEAMIN' JACK 5.5% ABV
A version of Nemesis.

OPEN *12–3pm and 6.30–11pm Mon–Sat; all day Sun.*

LYTHAM

The Taps
Henry Street, Lytham FY8 5LE
☎ *(01253) 736226* Ian Rigg

A Whitbread house with an extensive guest beer policy. Hook Norton Old Hooky, Wychwood The Dog's Bollocks, Orkney Dark Island and Moorhouse's Pendle Witches Brew regularly available, plus beers from breweries such as Black Sheep.

A town pub with yard, viewing cellar. Disabled facilities and toilets. Food served at lunchtime only. Children allowed only if dining.

All day, every day.

ORMSKIRK

The Queen's Head
30 Moor Street, Ormskirk L39 2AQ
☎ *(01695) 574380* Gerry Fleming

Up to four guest ales are available including Fuller's London Pride, Shepherd Neame Bishop's Finger and Spitfire, Black Sheep Special or Wychwood The Dog's Bollocks.

A traditional one-bar pub with beer garden. Annual themed beer festival. Food served 12–2pm Mon–Sat. Well-behaved children allowed.

All day, every day.

PRESTON

The Stanley Arms
Lancaster Road, Preston PR1 1DA
☎ *(01772) 254004. Fax (01772) 562092*
Ian Reid (Manager)

One guest beer always available, changing regularly.

A traditional pub in a Grade II listed building. The downstairs bar area has recently unergone a minor refurbishment. Food available 11am–9.30pm Mon–Thurs, 11am–5pm Fri–Sat, and 12–5pm Sun.

All day, every day.

WHALLEY

The Swan Hotel
62 King Street, Whalley BB7 9SN
☎ *(01254) 822195* CD White Acma

Swan Ale brewed by Mansfield and a Thwaites and Black Sheep beer usually available.

A small, friendly, family run hotel. Food served 12–9pm Mon–Thurs, 12–8pm Fri–Sat, and 12–7pm Sun. Children welcome. Car park.

11am–11pm Mon–Sat; 12–10.30pm Sun.

WHARLES

The Eagle & Child Inn
Church Road, Wharles, Nr Kirkham
☎ *(01772) 690312* Brian Tatham

Two guest beers regularly available perhaps from Mansfield, Clark's, Wadworth or Eccleshall.

Relaxed atmosphere and lovely antiques in this thatched country inn. No food. Car park. Well-behaved children welcome, subject to licensing regulations.

7–11pm Mon–Sat; 12–4pm and 7–10.30pm Sun.

WRIGHTINGTON

Hinds Head
Mossy Lea Road, Wrightington, Nr Wigan WN6 9RN
☎ *(01257) 421168* Mr Ferro

Two guest ales always available such as Morland Old Speckled Hen.

A big traditional pub with restaurant, beer garden and bowling green. Food available. Children allowed.

11am–2.30pm Tues–Thurs; 5.30–11pm Mon–Thurs; all day Fri–Sun.

YOU TELL US

★ *The Blue Anchor,* South Road, Bretherton, Preston
★ *Lane Ends Hotel,* Weeton Road, Wesham, Preston
★ *The Mayfield,* 22 County Road, Ormskirk
★ *The Old Black Bull,* 35 Friargate, Preston
★ *The Prince Albert,* 109 Wigan Road, Westhead
★ *The Saddle Inn,* Bartle
★ *The Tap & Spile,* Fylde Road, Ashton-on-Ribble, Preston

THE BREWERIES

BELVOIR BREWERY LTD
*Woodhill, Nottingham Lane, Old Dalby
LE14 3LX*
☎ *(01664) 823455*

 WHIPPLING 3.6% ABV
Light, refreshing and hoppy.
STAR BITTER 3.9% ABV
Citrus fruit and hoppy flavour.
BEAVER 4.3% ABV
Smooth, balanced with malt flavour and bitter
finish.
PEACOCK'S GLORY 4.7% ABV
Golden, fruity and hoppy.
Plus occasional brews.

BREWSTERS BREWING CO. LTD
Penn Lane, Stathern, Melton Mowbray LE14 4JA
☎ *(01949) 81868*

 HOPHEAD 3.6% ABV
MARQUIS 3.8% ABV
MONTY'S MILD 4.0% ABV
BITTER 4.2% ABV
SERENDIPITY II 4.3% ABV
Seasonal brew.
CLAUDIA 4.5% ABV
Seasonal brew.
VPA 4.5% ABV
FRAU BRAU 5.0% ABV
Seasonal brew.
BREWSTERS STOCKING 5.5% ABV
Seasonal brew.
DOMEHEAD 5.6% ABV
Seasonal brew.

EVERARDS BREWERY LTD
Castle Acres, Narborough LE9 5BY
☎ *(0116) 2014100*

 BEACON BITTER 3.8% ABV
Award-winning, fresh, clean taste.
TIGER BEST BITTER 4.2% ABV
Good body, dry hopped and long bitter finish.
OLD ORIGINAL 5.2% ABV
Copper-brown, smooth, malty and sweetish.
Plus seasonal beers.

THE GRAINSTORE BREWERY
*Davis's Brewing Co. Ltd, Station Approach,
Oakham LE15 6QW*
☎ *(01572) 770065* (Brewery tours)

COOKING 3.6 ABV
Golden and well-balanced.
TRIPLE B 4.2% ABV
Malty sweetness with balancing hop flavours.
TEN FIFTY 5.0 ABV
Easy-drinking sweet maltiness, with bitter finish.
LAZY SUMMER 4.0% ABV
STEAMIN' COUNTRY 4.0% ABV
STEAMIN' BILLY 4.3% ABV
GOLD 4.5% ABV
Seasonal brew.
SPRINGTIME 4.5% ABV
Seasonal brew.
THREE KINGS 4.5% ABV
Seasonal brew.
HARVEST IPA 5.0% ABV
Seasonal brew.
WINTER NIP 7.1% ABV
Seasonal brew.

TOM HOSKINS BREWERY PLC
*Beaumanor Brewery, 133 Beaumanor Road,
Leicester LE4 5QE*
☎ *(0116) 2661122*

BITTER 3.7% ABV
Powerful bitterness throughout.
TOM'S GOLD 4.4% ABV
Malty throughout.
CHURCHILL'S PRIDE 4.9% ABV
Sweet and malty.
OLD NIGEL 6.0% ABV
Winter brew.
Plus monthly changing brews.

HOSKINS & OLDFIELD BREWERY LTD

North Mills, Frog Island, Leicester LE3 5DH
☎ *(0116) 2510532*

 HOB BEST MILD 3.5% ABV
Dark, balanced, traditional mild.

BRIGADIER 3.6% ABV
Light, easy-drinking session beer.

HOB BITTER 4.0% ABV
Pale, with hop flavour.

LITTLE MATTY 4.0% ABV
Dark and full-flavoured.

WHITE DOLPHIN 4.0% ABV
Pale, tart wheat beer.

IPA 4.2% ABV
Traditional pale ale.

TOM KELLY STOUT 4.2% ABV
Dark and malty with hoppy bitterness.

SUPREME 4.4% ABV
Golden and refreshing.

PORTER 4.8% ABV
Dark, traditional-style porter.

EXS 5.0% ABV
Golden and well-balanced.

SHENANIGANS
Lager style.

TOM KELLY'S CHRISTMAS PUDDING PORTER 5.0% ABV
Available December.

'04' ALE 5.2% ABV
Well-rounded.

GINGER TOM 5.2% ABV
Red, ginger beer.

RECKLESS RASPBERRY 5.5% ABV
Raspberry-flavoured wheat beer.

OLD NAVIGATION 7.0% ABV
Dark, classic winter warmer.

CHRISTMAS NOGGIN 10.0% ABV
Smooth, sweet and rounded.

Plus occasional brews.

SHARDLOW BREWING CO. LTD

Old Stables, British Waterways Yard, Cavendish Bridge DE72 2HL
☎ *(01332) 799188*

CHANCELLOR'S REVENGE 3.6% ABV
BEST BITTER 3.9% ABV
GOLDEN HOP 4.1% ABV
NARROW BOAT 4.3% ABV
OLD STABLE 4.4% ABV
CAVENDISH GOLD 4.5% ABV
REVEREND EATON'S ALE 4.5% ABV
PLATINUM BLONDE 5.0% ABV
WHISTLE STOP 5.0 ABV
Plus occasional brews.

THE PUBS

BARROWDEN

The Exeter Arms

Main Street, Barrowden, Oakham, Rutland LE15 8EQ
☎ *(01572) 747247* Mr Peter Blencowe

A freehouse and home of the Blencowe Brewing Company. A full range of brews is always available (and only sold here). Also various guests such as Fuller's London Pride, Wyre Piddle Piddle in the Wind or Bateman XB. The aim is only to repeat the guest beers a maximum of three times a year.

A very traditional country pub, situated off the beaten track. One bar, huge garden. Brewery tours by appointment only. Food available every lunchtime and Tues–Sat evenings. Accommodation consists of two twin rooms and one double. Children allowed. Ring for directions.

BARROWDEN BOYS 3.6% ABV
A year-round session bitter

BEACH BOYS 3.8% ABV
Brewed mainly in summer

LOVER BOYS 3.8% ABV
Valentine's Day special

YOUNG BOYS 4.1% ABV

BIG BOYS 4.5% ABV

DANNY BOY 4.5% ABV
An autumn-winter stout

STRONG BOYS 5% ABV
Brewed mainly in Autumn and Winter

🍺 *11am–2.30pm and 6–11pm (10.30pm Sun).*

FRISBY ON THE WREAKE

The Bell Inn

2 Main Street, Frisby on the Wreake LE7 2NJ
☎ *(01664) 434237* Mr Simpson

A freehouse with Marston's Pedigree, Greene King Abbot and IPA among the beers permanently available plus occasional guests.

A 250-year-old village pub. One bar serves two rooms. Outside seating and conservatory. Food served at lunchtime and evenings. Children allowed in the conservatory only.

🍺 *12–2.30pm and 6–11pm (10.30pm Sun).*

GLOOSTON

The Old Barn Inn

Andrews Lane, Glooston, Nr Market Harborough LE16 7ST
☎ *(01858) 545215* Charles Edmondson-Jones

Four beers (30 per year) always available from brewers such as Adnams, Hook Norton, Fuller's, Wadworth, Oakhill, Nene Valley, Ridley, Bateman, Thwaites, Leatherbritches, Mauldons, Cotleigh, Greene King and Tolly Cobbold.

A sixteenth-century village pub in rural location with a log fire, no juke box or games machines. Bar and restaurant food available in evenings and Sunday lunchtime. Car park. Catering for parties, receptions and meetings. Well-behaved children and dogs welcome. Accommodation. On an old Roman road between Hallaton and Tur Langton.

OPEN *12–2.30pm Tues–Sun; 7–11pm Mon–Sat.*

HOSE

The Rose & Crown

43 Bolton Lane, Hose LE14 4JE
☎ *(01949) 860424* Brian Morley

Greene King Abbot and IPA are permanently available, plus three other real ales, changing constantly.

Not easy to find at the back of the village, this modernised open-plan bar is now under new ownership. Olde-worlde lounge with open fire, attractive bar with darts and pool plus background music. Beamed restaurant open Thurs–Sun is available for functions. Large car park and gardens.

OPEN *12–2.30pm and 7–11pm (5–11pm Fri); closed some lunchtimes in winter.*

KIRBY MUXLOE

The Royal Oak

Main Street, Kirby Muxloe, Leicester LE9 2AN
☎ *(0116) 239 3166* Mr Jackson

An Everards house with Tiger, Beacon and Old Original always available. Also two guest pumps serving beers such as Greene King Abbot Ale, Nethergate Old Growler or an Adnams brew.

A food-oriented village pub. Modern building with traditional decor. Function facilities. Disabled access. Garden. Food available at lunchtime and evenings. Children allowed.

OPEN *11am–3pm and 5.30–11pm (10.30pm Sun).*

LEICESTER

The Hat & Beaver

60 Highcross Street, Leicester LE1 4NN
☎ *(0116) 2622157* Mr A Cartwright

Hardys & Hansons tied house serving Mild, Best Bitter and Kimberley Classic.

Traditional town-centre pub. Rolls served at lunchtime. Children welcome in beer garden only.

OPEN *12–11pm (10.30pm Sun).*

The North Bridge Tavern

Frog Island, Leicester LE3 5AG
☎ *(0116) 251 2508* Rod Woodward

A freehouse with Marston's Pedigree always available plus one guest, often from a small local brewery such as Tom Hoskins.

A food-oriented town pub. One bar, function room. Non-smoking dining area. Traditional building with disabled access. Food available all day. Children allowed.

OPEN *All day, every day.*

Rainbow & Dove Tap House

185 Charles Street, Leicester LE1 1LA
☎ *(0116) 255 5916* Nicola Turner

Up to nine real ales available including Banks's Bitter, Camerons Strong Arm and Marston's Pedigree plus two guests often including Timothy Taylor Landlord, Hop Back Summer Lightning, Fuller's ESB, Badger Tanglefoot, Wychwood The Dog's Bollocks or Orkney Dark Island.

A traditional town alehouse with one bar and function room. Food served at lunchtime and evenings. No children.

OPEN *All day, every day.*

Tom Hoskins

133 Beaumanor Road, Leicester LE4 5QE
☎ *(0116) 261 1008* Mr Watson

The Hoskins Brewery operates from the back of this pub, so Hoskins Bitter, Churchill's Pride and Tom's Gold are always available, plus seasonal specials.

A traditional community pub with garden and the oldest cottage tower brewery in Britain. Disabled access. Function room. Pub food available at lunchtime. Children allowed in the function room only.

OPEN *All day Mon–Sat; 12–3pm and 7–10.30pm Sun.*

The Vaults

1 Wellington Street, Leicester LE1 6HH
☎ *(0116) 255 5506* Mr Spencer

A freehouse offering 15 to 18 constantly changing real ales from micro- and smaller breweries. More than 1,300 beers served in the past three years.

A traditional pub with cellar bar. One bar area. Music on Sundays with an admission charge. No food. No children.

5–11pm Mon–Thurs; 12–11pm Fri–Sat; 12–3pm and 7–10.30pm Sun.

The Albion Inn

Canal Bank, Loughborough LE11 1QA
☎ *(01509) 213952* Mr Hartley

Samuel Smith OBB and Mansfield Riding Mild always available plus guests such as Shepherd Neame Spitfire and Early Bird, Black Sheep Special or brews from Morland.

A traditional two-bar pub with garden, situated on the canal bank. Disabled access. Food available at lunchtime and evenings. No children.

11am–3pm and 6–11pm (10.30pm Sun).

The Swan in the Rushes

21 The Rushes, Loughborough
☎ *(01509) 217014* Ian Perkins

Timothy Taylor Landlord, Archers Golden and Marston's Pedigree always available plus six guest beers (1000 per year) at any one time, to include absolutely anything.

A cosmopolitan town-centre alehouse, smart yet down to earth, with a friendly atmosphere. Home-cooked bar food is available at lunchtime and evenings. Car park and accommodation. Children allowed. On the A6, behind Sainsbury's.

11am–11pm Mon–Sat; 12–10.30pm Sun.

Tap & Mallet

36 Nottingham Road, Loughborough LE11 1EU
☎ *(01509) 210028* Steve Booth

Marston's Pedigree permanently available, plus six guest beers often from Abbeydale, Brewsters, Cannon Royall, Church End, Buffy's, Durham, Mallard, Rooster's, Salopian, Six Bells, Stonehenge, West Berkshire, Woodforde's, Oldershaw, Cottage or Broadstone. Many other breweries used but on a less frequent basis.

The pub features a good selection of well-kept beers, plus a pets' corner, children's play area and large garden. No food.

11.30am–11pm Mon–Sat; 12–10.30pm Sun.

The Nevill Arms

Medbourne, Market Harborough LE16 8EE
☎ *(01858) 565288* Mrs Hall

A freehouse with Adnams Bitter always available plus two guests changing twice-monthly. Fuller's London Pride and Timothy Taylor Landlord are popular but beers from many other breweries are also stocked.

A traditional, two-bar country pub. Outside seating on benches near a brook. Accommodation. Bar food served at lunchtime and evenings. Well-behaved children allowed.

12–2.30pm and 6–11pm Mon–Sat; 12–3pm and 7–10.30pm Sun.

The Cow & Plough

Stoughton Farm Park, Gartree Road, Oadby LE2 5JB
☎ *(0116) 272 0852*

HOB Bitter (Hoskins & Oldfield), Fuller's London Pride and Steaming Billy Bitter and Mild always available, plus rotating guest beers (150 per year) mainly from micro-breweries.

A converted barn on a leisure park, open as part of the park during the day and as a pub from 5pm daily. The vaults are full of brewing memorabilia with a Victorian bar at the back. Adjoining car park, garden, children's room. CAMRA East Midlands Pub of the Year 1995 and 1998. Signposted on the A6 as Farmworld.

5–9pm.

The Crown Inn

Debdale Hill, Old Dalby, Nr Melton Mowbray LE14 3LF
☎ *(01664) 823134* Ms Lynn Busby

A range of ales is available, some served straight from the cask behind the bar, including Marston's Pedigree, Charles Wells Bombadier and something from Banks's. Regular guests are featured, often from the local Belvoir brewery.

Built in 1590, a pub with six small rooms, oak beams, open fires, antique furniture and prints. Large patio and terrace with orchard at bottom of the garden. Beer served from cellar near back door. Bar and restaurant food served at lunchtime and evenings. Car park, petanque pitch. Take the A46 Nottingham to Leicester road. Turn off at Willougby Hotel, left for Upper Broughton, right for Old Dalby.

12–3pm and 6–11pm.

SADDINGTON

The Queens Head

Main Street, Saddington
☎ *(0116) 2402536* Steve Cross

Everards Beacon and Tiger plus Adnams Southwold Bitter usually available. Also one guest beer, supplied through Everards.

A nicely situated, award-winning country inn and restaurant. Food served 12–2pm and 6.30–10pm, but not on Sunday evenings. Large car park. No children. Siutated near to Fleckney.

OPEN *11am–3pm and 5.30–11pm (10.30pm Sun).*

SHAWELL.

White Swan Inn

Main Street, Shawell, Nr Lutterworth LE17 6AG
☎ *(01788) 860357* Mike and Susan Walker

Marston's Pedigree, Adnams Southwold, Banks's Original and Camerons Creamy regularly available.

B uilt in the main street of a small hamlet in around 1700, it retains many original features. Local skittles in the bar. Restaurant and seating to the front of the pub. Food served 12–2.30pm and 7–9.30pm Tues–Fri, 7–9.30pm Sat, 12–2.30pm Sun. Car park. Children welcome.

OPEN *12–2.30pm and 7–11pm Tues–Fri; 7–11pm Sat; 12–2.30pm Sun.*

SHEARSBY

Chandler's Arms

Village Green, Shearsby, Nr Lutterworth LE17 6PL
☎ *(0116) 247 8384* Mr Ward

Fuller's London Pride and Marston's Pedigree and Bitter always available plus four guests. Beers featured include Greene King Abbot, Wadworth 6X, Exmoor Gold or brews from Timothy Taylor or Jennings.

A seventeenth-century red-brick pub overlooking the village green, with a three-tier prize-winning garden. Two lounges. AA recommended. International cuisine served at lunchtime and evenings. Children allowed.

OPEN *12–2.30pm and 6.30–11pm (10.30pm Sun).*

SOMERBY

The Old Brewery Inn

High Street, Somerby, Leicester LE14 2PZ
☎ *(01664) 454777* Barrie Parish

Home of the Parish Brewery. Robin a Tiptoe, Cropped Oak and Coat o'Red always available plus a good range of Parish bitters such as Somerby Premium, Poachers Ale and Special. Other celebration ales, as appropriate, for instance Life Sentence, which was brewed for the landlady's wedding!

T hree bars, restaurant, function room and beer garden. Disabled access. Brewery visits permitted if quiet or pre-arranged. Food served at lunchtime and evenings Tues–Sun. Children allowed.

JOHN O'GAUNT:
ROBIN A TIPTOE 3.9% ABV
CROPPED OAK 4.4% ABV
COAT O'RED
PARISH:
MILD 3.5% ABV
SPECIAL BITTER 3.8% ABV
FARM GOLD 4% ABV
SOMERBY PREMIUM 4% ABV
PORTER 4.8% ABV
POACHERS ALE 6% ABV
BAZ'S BONCE BLOWER 11% ABV
BAZ'S SUPER BREW 23% ABV

OPEN *11.30am–3pm and 6–11pm Mon–Fri; all day Sat–Sun.*

The Stilton Cheese Inn

High Street, Somerby LE14 2PZ
☎ *(01664) 454394* Jeff Evans

Marston's Pedigree and Grainstore 1050 (a local beer brewed in Rutland) permanently available, plus one or two constantly changing guests. Over 1000 beers served in five years.

A sixteenth-century stone building with beams, two rooms and upstairs restaurant. Decorated with hops and hunting prints. Food available 12–2pm and 6–9pm daily. Children allowed in the restaurant and small bar. Small patio with seating for 20.

OPEN *12–3pm and 6–11pm.*

SUTTON BASSETT

The Queen's Head

Sutton Bassett, Market Harborough LE16 8HP
☎ *(01858) 463530* Mario Cancelliere

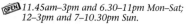 A freehouse with up to eight real ales including Timothy Taylor Landlord and Adnams Bitter plus a selection of guests including Fuller's London Pride and Morland Old Speckled Hen.

A friendly country pub with traditional decor, real fires, front and back bars. Disabled facilities on ground floor. Patio and petanque court. Food served at lunchtime and evenings (pub food in the bar and Italian food in restaurant upstairs). Large parties and functions catered for. Children allowed. Prettily situated with views of the Welland valley.

OPEN *11.45am–3pm and 6.30–11pm Mon–Sat; 12–3pm and 7–10.30pm Sun.*

WALCOTE

The Black Horse

Lutterworth Road, Walcote LE17 4JU
☎ *(01455) 552684* Mrs Tinker

HOB Bitter (Hoskins & Oldfield), Timothy Taylor Landlord, Greene King Abbot and Oakham Jeffrey Hudson Bitter always available plus two guest beers (75 per year) always from independent breweries.

A one-bar village pub. Bar and restaurant food available at lunchtime and evenings. Authentic Thai cooking. Car park, garden and children's room. One mile east of M1 junction 20.

OPEN *7–11pm Mon–Thurs; 12–2pm and 5.30–11pm Fri; 6.30–11pm Sat; 12–3.30pm and 6.30–10.30pm Sun.*

Places Featured:

Allington
Aslackby
Aubourn
Barnack
Boston
Caythorpe
Dyke
Frognall
Gainsborough
Grainthorpe
Grantham

Harmston
Laughterton
Lincoln
Louth
North Kelsey
Rothwell
Scamblesby
Spalding
Whaplode St Catherine
Woolsthorpe-by-Belvoir

THE BREWERIES

GEORGE BATEMAN & SON LTD

Salem Bridge Brewery, Mill Lane, Wainfleet, Skegness PE24 4JE
☎ *(01754) 880317*

 DARK MILD 3.0% ABV
Dark and fruity, some roast malt, hoppy finish.
XB 3.7% ABV
Distinctive, refreshing dry bitterness.
VALIANT 4.3% ABV
Golden, complex, well-balanced. Clean finish.
SALEM PORTER 4.7% ABV
Dry, nutty, rich malt and superb hop flavours.
XXXB 4.8% ABV
Multi-faceted malt and fruit character.
For 2001 the Jolly's Follies monthly brews will be replaced by the Good Hones Tails range.
Plus a seasonal and special selection.

BIGFOOT BREWERY

New Farm, Blyton Carr, Gainsborough DN21 3EN
☎ *(01427) 811922*

 BLYTON BEST 3.6% ABV
GENESIS 3.8% ABV
GAINSBOROUGH GOLD 4.5% ABV
EXTRA 4.9% ABV
Plus seasonal and occasional brews.

DARK TRIBE BREWERY

25 Doncaster Road, Gunness, Scunthorpe DN15 8TG
☎ *(01724) 782324*

DIXIE'S MILD 3.6% ABV
Dark, tasty award-winner.
FULL AHEAD 3.8% ABV
Dry-hopped bitter.
GUNESS STOUT 4.1% ABV
Traditional dark stout. Occasional brew.
FUTTOCKS 4.2% ABV
Easy-quaffing and hoppy.
DIXIE'S BOLLARDS 4.5% ABV
Ginger beer.
DR GRIFFIN'S MERMAID 4.5% ABV
Dark bitter.
OLD GAFFER 4.5% ABV
Traditional bitter.
AEGIR ALE 4.7% ABV
Flavour-packed.
GALLEON 4.7% ABV
Popular award-winner.
TWIN SCREW 5.1% ABV
Powerful, occasional brew.
SIXTEEN BELLS 6.5% ABV
Easy-drinking for gravity. Occasional brew.
Plus other occasional brews.

HIGHWOOD BREWERY LTD

Melton Highwood, Barnetby DN38 6AA
☎ *(01652) 680020*

 TOM WOOD BEST BITTER 3.5% ABV
Well-hopped and refreshing.
TOM WOOD SHEPHERD'S DELIGHT 4.0% ABV
Easy-quaffing and full-flavoured.
TOM WOOD BARN DANCE 4.2% ABV
Seasonal brew.
TOM WOOD LINCOLNSHIRE LEGEND 4.2% ABV
Good, hoppy bitterness throughout.
TOM WOOD HARVEST 4.3% ABV
Soft and well-balanced.
TOM WOOD SUMMER DAYS 4.4% ABV
Seasonal brew.
TOM WOOD OLD TIMBER 4.5% ABV
Smooth and full-flavoured.
TOM WOOD BOMBER COUNTY 4.8% ABV
Red, with good hoppy flavour.

NEWBY WYKE BREWERY

13 Calder Close, Grantham NG31 7QT
☎ *(01476) 402167*

SIDEWINDER 3.8% ABV
SUMMER SESSION BITTER 3.8% ABV
Seasonal brew.
BARDIA 4.0% ABV
Seasonal brew.
BRUTUS 4.0% ABV
LORD ANLASTER 4.0% ABV
Summer brew for Willoughby Arms, Little
Bytham.
SKIPPER EDDIES ALE 4.0% ABV
SLINGSHOT 4.2% ABV
Seasonal brew.
SLIPWAY 4.2% ABV
Seasonal brew.
BITTER 4.4% ABV
Seasonal brew.
RED SQUALL 4.4% ABV
Seasonal brew.
STAMFORD GOLD 4.4% ABV
Occasional brew for the Green Man, Stamford.
BLACK SQUALL PORTER 4.6% ABV
Seasonal brew.
LORD WILLOUGHBY 4.8% ABV
Winter brew for Willoughby Arms, Little
Bytham.
WHITE SQUALL 4.8% ABV
KINGSTON AMBER 5.2% ABV
Seasonal wheat beer.
DISTANT GROUNDS 5.2% ABV
Seasonal IPA.
WHITE SEA 5.2% ABV
Seasonal brew.
HOMEWARD BOUND 6.0% ABV
Seasonal brew.

OLDERSHAW BREWERY

12 Harrowby Hall Estate, Grantham NG31 9HB
☎ *(01476) 572135*

HARROWBY BITTER 3.6% ABV
Occasional brew.
HIGH DYKE 3.9% ABV
Gold-coloured with good hoppiness.
SUNNYDAZE 4.0% ABV
Bright, quenching, summer wheat beer.
VETERAN ALE 4.1% ABV
Traditional, gently bitter brew.
NEWTON'S DROP 4.1% ABV
Golden and hoppy.
ERMINE ALE 4.2% ABV
Pale and refreshing hoppiness.
CASKADE 4.2% ABV
Pale golden brew.
AHTANUM GOLD 4.3% ABV
Gold-coloured and hoppy. New Zealand hops.
GRANTHAM STOUT 4.3% ABV
Dark and moreish occasional brew.
REGAL BLONDE 4.4% ABV
Cask-conditioned lager.
TOPERS TIPPLE 4.5% ABV
Autumn/winter brew.
OLD BOY 4.8% ABV
Golden chestnut colour with good balance.
YULETIDE 5.2% ABV
Powerful flavours. Christmas brew.
Plus seasonal brews.

THE PUBS

ALLINGTON

The Welby Arms

The Green, Allington, Grantham NG32 2EA
☎ *(01400) 281361* Mr Dyer

Timothy Taylor Landlord is one of three brews always available, plus three guests perhaps including Wadworth 6X, Phoenix Wobbly Bob or Greene King Abbot.

A traditional village pub with log fires and terrace. Disabled access. Baguettes or soup available at lunchtime in the bar, plus restaurant food at both lunchtime and evenings. Well-behaved children allowed.

OPEN *12–2.30pm and 6–11pm (10.30pm Sun).*

ASLACKBY

Robin Hood & Little John

Aslackby, Sleaford NG34 0HL
☎ *(01778) 440681* Mike Wickens

A freehouse with Greene King Abbot always available, plus one guest pump serving a real ale such as, perhaps, Adnams Broadside or a Wood or Oldershaw ale.

A traditional country pub, one bar, function room, restaurant. Food available at lunchtime and evenings. Children's garden with sheep next door, children allowed in designated area only.

OPEN *11am–3pm and 5.30–11pm (10.30pm Sun).*

AUBOURN

The Royal Oak

Royal Oak Lane, Aubourn LN5 9DT
☎ *(01522) 788291*

Bateman XB and XXXB and Samuel Smith OBB always available plus three guest beers from breweries stretching from the Orkneys to Cornwall.

A traditional village pub with character. Bar food available at lunchtime and evenings. Car park and garden. Children welcome at lunchtime and evenings in the function room until 8.30pm. South of Lincoln, off the A46.

OPEN *12–2.30pm and 7–11pm (10.30pm Sun).*

BARNACK

The Millstone Inn

Millstone Lane, Barnack, Nr Stamford PE9 3ET
☎ *(01780) 740296* Aubrey Sinclair-Ball

Everards Old Original and Tiger plus Adnams Southwold usually available. A regularly changing guest beer is supplied through Everards.

The inn was built in 1672 of Barnack rag stone which was quarried nearby. The interior is olde-worlde with beamed ceilings. Walled courtyard. Food served 11.30am–2pm Mon–Sun and 6.30–9pm Mon–Sat. Children welcome. Car park.

OPEN *11.30am–2.30pm and 5.30–11pm Mon–Sat; 12–4pm and 7–10.30pm Sun.*

BOSTON

The Carpenter's Arms

Witham Street, Boston PE21 6PU
☎ *(01205) 362840* John Blakeborough

A Bateman house with XB always available plus two changing guests which are often other Bateman brews but also sometimes Marston's Pedigree, Morland Old Speckled Hen or Fuller's London Pride. A wider selection of real ales is available in the summer than during the winter.

A traditional one-bar town pub. Games room, real fires, outside seating. No food. Well-behaved children allowed.

OPEN *11am–3pm and 7–11pm Mon–Thurs; all day Fri–Sun.*

The Eagle

144 West Street, Boston PE21 8RE
☎ *(01205) 361116* Mr Andy Watson

Timothy Taylor Landlord, Adnams Broadside and Bank's Bitter always available, plus up to three guests such as Exmoor Gold, Hop Back Summer Lightning or Bateman special brews. May operate up to eight real ales during beer festivals.

A traditional local on the outskirts of Boston town centre. Two bars, real fires, garden. Regular annual beer festival held at the end of July, plus several others during the year. Kitchen under refurbishment but food will be available again from the middle of 2000. Children allowed in the garden only.

OPEN *11am–2.30pm and 5–11pm Mon–Thurs; all day Fri–Sun.*

CAYTHORPE

The Red Lion Inn
62 High Street, Caythorpe, Grantham NG32 3DN
☎ *(01400) 272632* Ann Roberts

A freehouse serving Adnams Best plus up to three guests from every possible brewery. Glentworth and Slaters (Eccleshall) brews are particular favourites.

A seventeenth-century traditional country inn with two gardens and two bars. No music or games machines. Disabled access. Food available at lunchtime and evenings in a separate restaurant. Children allowed in the restaurant and one of the bars only.

OPEN 11am–2.30pm and 6–11pm (10.30pm Sun).

DYKE

The Wishing Well Inn
Main Street, Dyke, Bourne PE10 0AF
☎ *(01778) 422970* Mr B F Creaser

Everards Beacon and Tiger and Greene King Abbot usually available plus two constantly changing beers from micro-breweries around the country. Over 2500 different beers sold to date.

A attractive country inn with accommodation and a large restaurant. Food served 12–2pm and 6.30–9.30pm daily. Children welcome. Large car park. One mile north of Bourne, off A15. Look for signs.

OPEN 11am–2.30pm and 6–11pm (10.30pm Sun).

FROGNALL

The Goat
155 Spalding Road, Frognall, Deeping St James, Nr Peterborough PE6 8SA
☎ *(01778) 347629* Peter Wilkins

Adnams Bitter plus up to five guest beers from micro-breweries and brewpubs. Over the past five years, more than 1400 different guests have been served, from more than 300 breweries.

A country pub dating from 1640. Bar and restaurant food at lunchtime and evenings. Functions catered for. Car park, large beer garden with play equipment and children's room. Cask Marque winner. On the old A16 between Market Deeping and Spalding.

OPEN 11am 2.30pm (3pm Sat) and 6–11pm Mon–Sat; 12–3pm and 6–10.30pm Sun.

GAINSBOROUGH

The Eight Jolly Brewers
Ship Court, Caskgate Street, Gainsborough DN21 2DL
☎ *(01427) 677128* Alex Craig

Timothy Taylor Landlord and Black Sheep Best always available plus a varied range of guest ales. No national beers served, micro-breweries favoured. Examples include Highwood Lincolnshire Legend and Glentworth Little Gem.

A 300-year-old town-centre freehouse with two bars in a traditional building. Small outdoor area and patio. Sandwiches available at lunchtime only. No children. Located near the Guildhall.

OPEN 11am–11pm Mon–Sat; 12–10.30pm Sun.

GRAINTHORPE

The Black Horse Inn
Mill Lane, Grainthorpe, Louth LN11 78U
☎ *(01472) 388229* Mrs Donaghue

A freehouse serving Bateman ales plus a guest such as Timothy Taylor Landlord. Micro-brewery on premises, so own ales served in pub.

A cosy country village pub with a real ale theme. Open fires, beer garden with children's area. Food served every evening and at lunchtime at weekends and during the summer. Children allowed, if eating.

MOLLY'S MILD 3.6% ABV
DANNIE BOY BITTER 4.0% ABV

OPEN 7–11pm and lunchtime at weekends and during the summer.

GRANTHAM

The Blue Bull
64 Westgate, Grantham NG31 6LA
☎ *(01476) 70929*

Bateman XB and Wadworth 6X always available plus three guest beers (100 per year) perhaps from Enville, Hampshire, Greene King, Clark's, Rooster's and Kelham Island.

CAMRA Lincolnshire Pub of the Year 1995. Dates from the 1850s. Bar and restaurant food available at lunchtime and evenings. Car park. Children allowed in the restaurant. Three minutes from the main line BR railway station.

OPEN 11am–3pm and 7–11pm.

The Thorold Arms

High Street, Harmston, Lincoln LN5 9SN
☎ *(01522) 720358* Mr Duffield

The tiny Duffield Brewery operates from the cellar of this freehouse and a home brew is usually available. Also something from Greene King and perhaps a celebration or seasonal ale from an independent brewery.

A rural pub with traditional decor and two log fires. Disabled access and toilets. Food available at lunchtime and evenings in a separate dining area. No children.

BITTER 3.6% ABV
SPECIAL 4.3% ABV
MULLEY'S IRISH STOUT 4.4% ABV
EXTRA SPECIAL BITTER 4.8% ABV

11am–3pm and 6–11pm (10.30pm Sun).

The Friendship Inn

Main Road, Laugherton, Lincoln LN21 2JZ
☎ *(01427) 718681* Diane Humphries

A freehouse with Marston's Pedigree and Mansfield Friendship Bitter always available plus guests, which may well be something from Brewsters, Slaters (Eccleshall) or another micro-brewery.

A traditional, friendly one-bar village pub. Log fires, garden, disabled access. Food available at lunchtime and evenings (except Sun evening) in a designated dining area. Children allowed.

11.30am–2.30pm and 6–11pm Mon–Sat; 12–3pm and 7–10.30pm Sun.

The Golden Eagle

21 High Street, Lincoln LN5 8BD
☎ *(01522) 521058* Mr and Mrs Fairclough

A freehouse with Everards Beacon, Bateman XB and Timothy Taylor Landlord always available plus one mild and one real cider. Three guest ales, rotating continually.

A locals' pub with two bars, one with no music or games machines, half a mile from the city centre. No food. Car park and garden. Children not allowed in the pub.

11am–3pm and 5.30–11pm Mon–Thur; all day Fri–Sun.

The Portland Arms

50 Portland Street, Lincoln
☎ *(01522) 513912*
Lisa Nicholson and David Spiers

Bateman XXXB and Highgate Dark Mild usually available plus a changing selection of ales from various breweries.

Relaxed, games-orientated pub with music and TV. New beer garden. Fresh rolls daily. Children welcome in beer garden. Car park.

11am–11pm Mon–Sat; 12–10.30pm Sun.

Sippers Freehouse

26 Melville Street, Lincoln LN5 7HW
☎ *(01522) 527612* Philip Tulley

Morland Old Speckled Hen, Marston's Pedigree and two regularly changing guest beers (mostly from micro-breweries) usually available.

Traditional city-centre pub. Food served lunchtime and evenings Mon–Fri, lunchtime only Sat. No food Sun. No children.

11am–2pm and 5–11pm Mon–Thurs; 11am–2pm and 4–11pm Fri; 11am–2pm and 7–11pm Sat; 7–10.30pm Sun.

The Tap & Spile

21 Hungate, Lincoln LN1 1ES
☎ *(01522) 534015* Mr and Mrs Cay

Eight beers always available but the range changes daily. Approx 150 brews per year including Charles Wells Fargo, Thwaites Craftsman and Greene King IPA.

Formerly the White Horse, a city-centre pub with stone and wood floors, bare brick and plaster walls. Bar food available at lunchtime. Pay and display car park opposite. Children not allowed. At the top of the high street turn left, then 200 yards on the left near the police station.

11am–11pm Mon–Sat; 12–3pm and 7–10.30pm Sun.

The Victoria

6 Union Road, Lincoln LN1 3BJ
☎ *(01522) 536048* Mr Renshaw

Up to ten beers always available including Everards Tiger and Old Original, Timothy Taylor Landlord, Bateman XB and Oldershaw Regal Blonde. Plus four guests (up to 1,000 per year) including Orkney Raven Ale, Brains Bitter, Exmoor Gold, Hop Back Summer Lightning and Adnams brews.

A traditional, two-bar Victorian terraced pub with a small patio, in the city by the west gate of the castle. Bar food available at lunchtime. Regular beer festivals and brewery feature nights.

11am–11pm Mon–Sat; 12–10.30pm Sun.

LOUTH

The Woodman Inn

134 Eastgate, Louth LN11 9AA
☎ *(01507) 602100* Dave Kilgour

Greene King Abbot always available plus two guests. Among those recently featured are Wadworth 6X, Charles Wells Bombardier and brews from Cotleigh and Abbeydale. Other specials from microbreweries stocked when possible.

Situated on the edge of town, this pub has a film theme. Two bars, one a live rock and blues music venue. Food available at lunchtime only. Children allowed.

11am–4pm and 7–11pm Mon–Fri; all day Sat; 12–3.30pm and 7–10.30pm Sun.

NORTH KELSEY

The Butchers Arms

Middle Street, North Kelsey, Market Rasen LN7 6EH
☎ *(01652) 678002* Steve Cooper

A freehouse predominantly serving Tom Wood Highwood beers, plus one constantly changing guest.

A small, old-style village pub. One bar. No music or games. Outside seating. Sandwiches, salads and ploughmans available at weekends. Children allowed.

4–11pm Mon–Fri; 12–11pm Sat–Sun.

ROTHWELL

The Nickerson Arms

Hillrise, Rothwell LN7 6AZ
☎ *(01472) 371300* Peter Wright

Mansfield Old Bailey, Marston's Pedigree and Charles Wells Bombardier always available, plus guests.

A 400-year-old haunted pub, formerly a blacksmiths, with oak beams, real fires and candles. Bar and restaurant food available at lunchtime and evenings. Car park, garden, children's room and function room. Free sausage and chips on Tuesday nights, from 7–9pm. Three miles off the A46 between Grimsby and Caistor.

12–3pm and 7–11pm Mon–Sat; 12–4pm and 7–10.30pm Sun.

SCAMBLESBY

The Green Man

Old Main Road, Scamblesby, Louth LN11 9XG
☎ *(01507) 343282*
Michael Jones and Margaret Barnard

A freehouse with three pumps serving a constantly changing range of real ales. Charles Wells Bombardier and Highwood Tom Wood Best are popular. Independent breweries favoured.

A country pub with lounge and public bar. Food available at lunchtime and evenings. Children allowed.

12–2pm and 7–11pm (in summer, closed Tues–Wed lunch).

SPALDING

The Lincolnshire Poacher

11 Double Street, Spalding PE11 2AA
☎ *(01775) 766490* Pauline Broderick

A Tom Hoskins tied house with Hoskins Bitter and Churchill's Pride always available. Three guest pumps serve a range of real ales including Morland Old Speckled Hen.

A food-oriented pub, situated near the river, with two bars, garden and non-smoking dining area. Disabled access. Food available at lunchtime only. Children allowed.

11am–3pm and 5–11pm (10.30pm Sun).

WHAPLODE ST CATHERINE

Blue Bell Inn & Brewery

Cranesgate South, Whaplode St Catherine, Holbeach PE12 6SN
☎ *(01406) 540300* Mr Pilkington

Olde Honesty is brewed on the premises and permanently available, plus one guest, usually from another micro-brewery.

A pub and restaurant with one main bar and a separate smoking room. Pool and darts. Beer garden with occasional barbecues in summer. Separate restaurant open evenings only. Children allowed. Situated in the middle of nowhere, so do ring for directions.

OLDE HONESTY 4.1% ABV
Award-winning, East Anglian ale.

7–11pm Mon–Fri; 12–4pm and 7–11pm Sat–Sun.

WOOLSTHORPE-BY-BELVOIR

The Chequers

Main Street, Woolsthorpe-by-Belvoir, Grantham
NG32 1LV
☎ *(01476) 870701* Mr Potter

A freehouse with Marston's Bitter and Pedigree always served, plus two guest ales available seasonally, such as Timothy Taylor Landlord or Greene King Abbot plus beers from local breweries such as Brewsters.

A country pub with olde-worlde decor. Five-acre garden and private cricket field. Accommodation. Restaurant food available at lunchtime and evenings. Children allowed.

12–3pm and 7–11pm (10.30pm Sun).

YOU TELL US

★ *Ebrington Arms,* Main Street, Kirkby on Bain, Woodhall Spa, Lincolnshire
★ *New Inn,* Hill Road, Springthorpe, Gainsborough

Places Featured:

LONDON CENTRAL
EC1: Clerkenwell
EC1: Islington
EC2: Barbican
EC3: Aldgate
EC4: Fleet Street
EC4: St Paul's
WC1: Bloomsbury/Holborn
WC2: Bloomsbury
WC2: Covent Garden

LONDON EAST
E1: Spitalfields
E2: Bethnal Green
E3: Bow
E5: Clapton
E7: Forest Gate
E11: Leytonstone
E14: Limehouse
E15: Stratford
E17: Walthamstow

LONDON NORTH
N1: Hoxton
N2: East Finchley
N8: Crouch End
N9: Lower Edmonton
N16: Stoke Newington
N17: Tottenham
N21: Winchmore Hill

LONDON NORTHWEST
NW1: Euston
NW2: Cricklewood
NW8: St John's Wood

LONDON SOUTHEAST
SE1: Borough
SE5: Camberwell
SE8: Deptford
SE13: Lewisham
SE20: Penge
SE25: South Norwood

LONDON SOUTHWEST
SW1: Haymarket
SW1: Whitehall
SW2: Brixton
SW3: Chelsea
SW4: Clapham
SW6: Fulham
SW6: Walham Green
SW7: Chelsea
SW8: Stockwell
SW9: Brixton
SW12: Balham
SW18: Wandsworth

LONDON WEST
W1: Marylebone
W1: Regent Street
W1: Soho
W2: Lancaster Gate
W2: Paddington
W4: Strand-on-the-Green
W5: Ealing
W6: Hammersmith
W7: Hanwell
W9: Maida Vale

THE BREWERIES

FULLER, SMITH & TURNER PLC

Griffin Brewery, Chiswick Lane South, Chiswick W4 2QB
☎ *(020) 8996 2000*

 CHISWICK BITTER 3.5% ABV
Quenching, with flowery hop character.
SUMMER ALE 3.9% ABV
Seasonal. Lager-style beer.
LONDON PRIDE 4.1% ABV
Smooth and rounded, with excellent balance.
ORGANIC HONEY DEW 4.3% ABV
Seasonal. Golden smooth and honeyed sweetness.
RED FOX 4.3% ABV
Seasonal. Tawny, mellow and well-rounded.
OLD WINTER ALE 4.8% ABV
Seasonal. Amber, sweet and nutty.
ESB 5.5% ABV
Powerful, rounded and well-balanced.
GOLDEN PRIDE 8.5% ABV
Rare in cask form.

HAGGARDS BREWERY

577 King's Road SW6 2EH
☎ *(020) 7384 2246*

 HORNY ALE/IMPERIAL ALE 4.3% ABV
Light, balanced, easy-drinking, with bittersweet finish.

O'HANLON'S BREWING CO.

114 Randall Road, Vauxhall SE11 5JR
☎ *(020) 7793 0803*

FIREFLY 3.7% ABV
WHEATBEER 4.0% ABV
BLAKELEY'S BEST NO.1 4.2% ABV
DRY STOUT 4.2% ABV
MYRICA ALE 4.5% ABV
PORT STOUT 4.8% ABV
Plus seasonal brews.

PITFIELD BREWERY

The Beer Shop, 14 Pitfield Street, Hoxton N1 6EY
☎ *(020) 7739 3701*

ORIGINAL BITTER 3.7% ABV
EAST KENT GOLDINGS 4.2% ABV
ECO WARRIOR 4.5% ABV
HOXTON HEAVY 4.8% ABV
BLACK EAGLE 5.0% ABV
Plus seasonal and occasional brews.
Certified organic brewery.

SOHO BREWING CO.

41 Earlham Street, Covent Garden WC2
☎ *(020) 7240 0606*

PALE 4.5% ABV
RED 4.6% ABV
HONEY BEER 5.0%
Summer brew. Pilsner-style with honey.
SPECIAL 5.0% ABV
WHEAT 5.0% ABV

YOUNG & CO. BREWERY

The Ram Brewery, Wandsworth SW18 4JD
☎ *(020) 8875 7000*

BITTER 3.7% ABV
Pale and bitter throughout.
TRIPLE 'A' 4.0% ABV
Light, easy-quaffer.
DIRTY DICK'S 4.1% ABV
Seasonal beer.
SPECIAL 4.6% ABV
Excellent malt and hop balance.
WAGGLE DANCE 5.0% ABV
Golden, smooth, honeyed flavour.
WINTER WARMER 5.0% ABV
Rich, smooth and sweet seasonal brew.

LONDON CENTRAL

EC1: CLERKENWELL

The Jerusalem Tavern
55 Britton Street, Clerkenwell EC1M 5NA
☎ *(020) 7490 4281*
Bruce Patterson (Manager)

A St Peter's Brewery tied house serving the range of St Peter's brews such as Best Bitter, Strong Bitter, Wheat Beer, Golden Ale, Fruit Beer (elderberry), Summer Ale and Winter Ale.

A small, old-fashioned pub with no music or machines. Outside seating. Food available at lunchtime from 12–2.30pm and toasted sandwiches in the evenings. Children allowed.

9am (for coffee)–11pm Mon–Fri; closed Sat–Sun.

The Leopard
33 Seward Street, Clerkenwell EC1V 3PA
☎ *(020) 7253 3587* Malcolm Jones

A freehouse with Gibbs Mew (Ushers) Salisbury always available, plus three guests such as Greene King Abbot and brews from O'Hanlon's, Nethergate, Eccleshall and Cottage. Guests changed daily.

A one-bar pub, a mixture of modern and traditional, with wooden floors, conservatory, dining area, disabled facilities and small outside seating area. Food available from 12.30–9pm. Children allowed in conservatory.

11am–11pm Mon–Fri; closed Sat–Sun.

EC1: ISLINGTON

O'Hanlon's
8 Tysoe Street, Islington
☎ *(020) 7278 7630* Patrick Mulligan

Popular home of the O'Hanlon's Brewery serving own beers plus Harveys Best Bitter and five guest beers perhaps from Iceni, Crouch Vale or Ringwood.

Food served 12–3pm and 6–9pm. Children welcome until early evening.

11am–11pm Mon–Sat; 12–10.30pm Sun.

EC2: BARBICAN

Crowders Well
185 Fore Street, Barbican EC2Y 5EJ
☎ *(020) 7628 8574* John Lowe

A Greene King pub with a range of Greene King ales always available.

An old, traditional city-centre pub. Food available at lunchtime only. No children.

All day Mon–Fri; closed Sat–Sun.

EC3: ALDGATE

The Hoop & Grapes
47 Aldgate High Street EC3
☎ *(020) 7265 5171* Hugh Ede

Fuller's London Pride permanently available, plus three guests usually including something like Timothy Taylor Landlord, Brakspear Special and Best, Badger Best, Adnams Southwold and Extra, Charles Wells Bombardier, Eagle or IPA, Shepherd Neame Spitfire, Hook Norton Old Hooky or Wychwood Hobgoblin or Special. An average of 50 different beers served every year.

A 400-year-old 'olde-worlde' pub located inside the square mile. Bar food served every lunchtime 12–3pm, with table service available. No children. Situated outside Aldgate Tube Station.

11am–10pm Mon–Wed; 11am–11pm Thurs–Fri; closed weekends.

EC4: FLEET STREET

The Old Bank of England
194 Fleet Street EC4 2LT
☎ *(020) 7430 2255* Natasha Percival

The Fuller's flagship alehouse with London Pride, Chiswick and ESB always available plus a guest seasonal Fuller's beer and one other real ale such as Timothy Taylor Landlord. Guests changed monthly.

An impressive old pub which was once annexed to the law courts. Styled in brass and wood. Two seperate rooms for dining (smoking and non-smoking) in which food is available 12–8pm. Full bar menu, but the pub is famous for its pies. Children allowed

11am–11pm Mon–Fri; closed Sat–Sun.

EC4: HOLBORN

The Hogshead

78 Ludgate Circus EC4
☎ *(020) 7329 8517* Mike Wren

Marston's Pedigree, Morland Old Speckled Hen, Fuller's London Pride and a beer from Adnams and Brakspear are usually available plus up to four guests. Guests might be from Bateman or any independent brewery.

A modern-style pub which retains an authentic feel. Previously known as The Old King Lud. Food available all day Mon–Thurs. No children.

11.30am–11pm Mon–Fri; closed weekends.

St Bride's Tavern

1 Bridewell Place EC4
☎ *(020) 7353 1614* Carol Partridge

Greene King IPA and Abbot permanently available and one guest pump which regularly features Everards Tiger.

A traditional City of London pub. Food available lunchtimes only. Children allowed

11am–11pm Mon–Fri; closed weekends.

EC4: ST PAUL'S

Williamson's Tavern

1 Groveland Court EC4
☎ *(020) 7248 6280* Russ McGilvrey

Adnams bitters are usually available with up to six guest ales from breweries like Brakspear. Fewer guests available during the winter months.

A very old three-bar pub situated off Bow Lane. Food available 11.30am–3pm and 5–9pm. Well-behaved children allowed.

11.30am–11pm Mon–Fri; closed weekends.

WC1: BLOOMSBURY/HOLBORN

The King's Arms

11a Northington Street, Bloomsbury WC1N 2JF
☎ *(020) 7405 9107* Clive Gilbert

Greene King IPA, Marston's Pedigree and Wadworth 6X usually available, plus occasional guests but no very strong ales.

An office workers' pub in the midst of a legal and media professional area. Food available at lunchtime only. No children.

11am–11pm Mon–Fri; closed Sat–Sun.

The Oarsman

2 New Oxford Street WC1A 1EE
☎ *(020) 7404 5009* Leigh Sullivan-Plews

Two real ales always available. Charles Wells Bombardier is a regular feature but other, more unusual, ales from independent breweries are also served as available.

A small one-bar pub with outside seating. Home-made food available all day. Children allowed.

12–11pm Mon–Fri; private hire only at weekends.

The University Tavern

18 Store Street WC1
☎ *(020) 7436 4697* Paul Davies

A freehouse with Greene King IPA and Adnams Broadside permanently available, plus one rotating guest. This may feature an Adnams seasonal ale like Regatta, or a light beer, or an interesting ale from an independent brewery.

A two-bar pub situated next door to England & Wales College of Law, so very student-orientated. Bare and basic, with wooden floors. Food available 12–4pm. No children. Situated off Tottenham Court Road.

11am–11pm Mon–Fri; 12–6pm Sat; closed Sun.

The Yorkshire Grey

2–6 Theobald's Road, Holborn WC1X 8PN
☎ *(020) 7405 2519* Marianne & Chris Bee

A Scottish & Newcastle tied pub which is home to the Yorkshire Grey Brewery in the cellar. Barristers and QC are brewed and served on the premises. One other pump used for occasional specials. Also guests changed every three weeks.

Traditional city pub with wooden floors and beams. One bar on ground-floor level and function room for hire. Hot and cold food available 11am–11pm. Brewery tours.

BARRISTERS BITTER% ABV
QC BITTER 4.5% ABV

11am–11pm Mon–Fri; closed Sat–Sun unless pre-booked.

WC2: BLOOMSBURY

The Museum Tavern

49 Great Russell Street WC2A
☎ *(020) 7242 8987* Tony Williamson (Manager)

Greene King Abbott Ale is usually available, plus one rotating guest ale, changed fortnightly.

A very old and traditional pub; the front and back bars are listed buildings. Food available all day. Outside seating area. No children. Situated opposite the British Museum.

11am–11pm Mon–Sat; 12–10.30pm Sun and bank holidays.

WC2: COVENT GARDEN

The Crown

43 Monmouth Street WC2H 9DD
☎ *(020) 7836 5861* Mr Brocklebank

An Adnams ale is usually available plus up to four guest ales. Morland Old Speckled Hen and Marston's Pedigree are regular features.

An old, traditional two-bar pub. Generally quiet, with background music and a mixed clientele; a very local pub for the West End. Food available all day. No children. Situated near Seven Dials.

OPEN *11am–11pm Mon–Sat; closed Sun.*

The Round House

1 Garrick Street, Covent Garden WC2E 9AR
☎ *(020) 7836 9838* Ollie McClorey

Greene King Abbot and IPA and Marston's Pedigree usually available, plus a minimum of two guests per week from independent and micro-breweries far and wide.

A small, one-bar real ale house with no juke box or machines. Food available all day. Children allowed at weekends only.

OPEN *11am–11pm Mon–Sat; 12–10.30pm Sun.*

The Round Table

26 St Martin's Court WC2N 4AL
☎ *(020) 7836 6436* Nathan Donnelly

Greene King IPA permanently on offer, with up to three constantly changing guest ales. Any beer from any independent or micro-brewery could be on – they try them all!

A lively pub with a friendly atmosphere located just off Charing Cross Road. Full menu available 11am–11pm daily. Children allowed until 7pm. Separate function room available.

OPEN *11am–11pm Mon–Sat; 12–10.30pm Sun.*

LONDON EAST

E1: SPITALFIELDS

Pride of Spitalfield

3 Heneage Street, Spitalfields E1 5LJ
☎ *(020) 7247 8933* Ann Butler

Crouch Vale IPA, Fuller's London Pride and ESB are available, plus a weekly changing guest beer.

Friendly, small and comfortable side-street pub, attracting good mixed clientele. Home-made food served at lunchtime. Children welcome. Turn left out of Algate East tube station (Whitechapel Art Gallery end), left again then take the third side street on the left.

OPEN *11am–11pm Mon–Sat; 12–10.30pm Sun.*

E2: BETHNAL GREEN

The Approach Tavern

47 Approach Road, Bethnal Green E2 9LY
☎ *(020) 8980 2321* Caroline Apperley

A freehouse with Morland Old Speckled Hen, Fuller's London Pride, Wadworth 6X and Marston's Pedigree always available. Guests stocked occasionally.

A friendly pub with good atmosphere, decorated with photographs. Gallery, beer garden. Famous local chef who featured in Time Out's top 100 chefs and in Marie Claire – food available 1–2.30pm and 7–10pm Tues–Sun. Children and dogs on lead welcome.

OPEN *12pm–close.*

E3: BOW

The Coborn Arms

8 Coborn Road, Bow E3 2DA
☎ *(020) 8980 3793* Colin Shipley

Young's Ordinary and Special always available.

A busy one-bar locals' pub. Food available at lunchtime and evenings. No children.

OPEN *11am–11pm Mon–Sat; 12–10.30pm Sun.*

E5: CLAPTON

The Anchor & Hope

15 High Hill Ferry, Clapton E5 9HG
☎ *(020) 8806 1730* Mr Heath

A Fuller's pub serving ESB and London Pride.

A small, single-bar pub by the river. No food. Children allowed outside only.

OPEN *11am–3pm and 5.30–11pm (10.30pm Sun).*

E7: FOREST GATE

The Old Spotted Dog

212 Upton Lane, Forest Gate E7 9NP
☎ *(020) 8472 1794* Ray Saunders

Marston's Pedigree and Morland Old Speckled Hen always available, plus two guests, changing weekly.

A Tudor pub with two large bars, restaurant, family room and children's play area. Bar snacks available at lunchtime, restaurant food available every evening 7–10pm. Children allowed.

OPEN *11am–11pm Mon–Sat; 12–10.30pm Sun.*

E11: LEYTONSTONE

The Birkbeck Tavern
45 Langthorne Road, Leytonstone E11 4HL
☎ *(020) 839 2584* Mr Delaney

A freehouse with a house brew (Rita's Special 4%) named after the landlady among the beers always available. Two guests such as Barnsley Bitter or brews from Nethergate and Mighty Oak. Guests changed at least twice a week.

A friendly back-street community pub in a late Victorian building. Two bars, function room and garden. Sandwiches only available. Children allowed in the garden. Near Leyton tube on the Central Line.

All day, every day

E14: LIMEHOUSE

The Oporto Tavern
43 West India Dock Road, Limehouse E14 8EZ
☎ *(020) 8987 1530* Steve Baldwin

Three guest beers. Wadworth 6X, Greene King IPA and a Brains brew regularly available. Other guests changed monthly.

A traditional male-dominated boozer set in a Victorian building retaining some original features. One bar, TV, darts, pool, and racing club. Hot food, including specials, and baguettes available 12–3pm. Children allowed in the paved area at front with bench seating.

All day, every day.

E15: STRATFORD

The Golden Grove
146–8 The Grove, Stratford E15 1NS
☎ *(020) 8519 0750* Sue Guyatt

Greene King Abbot Ale and Shepherd Neame Spitfire always available plus three guests such as Hop Back Summer Lightning.

A large Wetherspoon's pub with one bar, non-smoking dining area, no music, disabled access and beer garden. Food available all day. No children.

All day, every day.

King Edward VII
47 Broadway, Stratford E15 4BQ
☎ *(020) 8221 9841* Paul Taylor

Fuller's London Pride and two guest beers usually available, which may include Shepherd Neame Bishop's Finger, Morland Old Speckled Hen, Badger Tanglefoot, Adnams Best, Wychwood Dog's Bollocks, Hop Back Summer Lightning or Timothy Taylor Landlord.

Original, three-bar London tavern with lots of wood, beams and mirrors. Air-conditioned. Prize quiz nights Sunday and Wednesday. Food served 12–7pm every day. No children.

12–11pm (10.30pm Sun).

E17: WALTHAMSTOW

The Village
31 Orford Road, Walthamstow E17 9NL
☎ *(020) 8521 9982* Gary Leader

Guest ales always available on two hand pumps. Favourites include Adnams Broadside, King and Barnes Sussex, Young's IPA, Sharp's Cornish Coaster, Wolf Golden Jackal and Oakham JHB. Beers changed daily during the winter, two or three times a week in the summer.

A newly refurbished residential pub with one bar and one snug. Large garden. Food available Mon–Fri lunchtimes and some evenings. Children allowed in the snug and the garden. Located near the railway station.

11am–11pm (10.30pm Sun).

LONDON NORTH

N1: HOXTON

The Wenlock Arms
26 Wenlock Road, Hoxton N1 7TA
☎ *(020) 7608 3406* Steven Barnes

A freehouse with Adnams Best and Broadside and Mighty Oak brews regularly available. Plus up to six other guests usually including something from the nearby Pitfield Brewery. Guest beers changed every couple of days.

A one-bar town pub. Sandwiches only available. No children.

12–11pm (10.30pm Sun).

N2: EAST FINCHLEY

Madden's Ale House

130 High Road, East Finchley N2 7ED

 Greene King Abbot, Wadworth 6X, Fuller's London Pride and Adnams Broadside always available plus up to eight guests (300 per year) including Ridleys Witchfinder Porter, Gibbs Mew Bishop's Tipple, Ringwood Old Thumper and Fortyniner etc. Also country wines.

A converted shop on the High Road, not far from East Finchley tube. Bar food available at lunchtime. Children allowed.

11am–11pm Mon–Fri; 12–10.30pm Sun.

N8: CROUCH END

The Hogshead

33–5 Crouch End Hill, Crouch End N8 8DH
☎ *(020) 8342 8465* Clare Gardner

Wadworth 6X, Marston's Pedigree, Fuller's London Pride and an Adnams brew always available, plus up to nine guests, regularly including Young's Special.

A town pub with one bar. Disabled access, background music, fruit machines, internet games. Food available 12–9pm. No children.

All day, every day.

N9: LOWER EDMONTON

The Lamb Inn

52–4 Church Street, Lower Edmonton N9 9PA
☎ *(020) 8887 0128*
Dave and Brenda Andrews

A freehouse with Greene King IPA and Fuller's London Pride among the brews always available, plus up to five guests including, perhaps, Greene King Abbot Ale and Fuller's ESB.

A modern community pub with one large bar, non-smoking dining area and disabled access. Food available all day. Children allowed.

All day, every day.

N16: STOKE NEWINGTON

The Rochester Castle

145 Stoke Newington High Street, Stoke Newington N16 0NY
☎ *(020) 7249 6016* Richard Scrivens

Greene King Abbot and Shepherd Neame Spitfire always available plus six guests each week, rotated on three hand pumps. Regulars include Hop Back Summer Lightning and Fuller's London Pride.

A huge Wetherspoon's pub with one big bar, patio, disabled access and facilities. No music. Board games – chess, backgammon etc. Non-smoking dining area. Food available all day. No children.

All day, every day.

N17: TOTTENHAM

The New Moon

413 Lordship Lane, Tottenham N17 6AG
☎ *(020) 8801 3496* Tom Connelly

A freehouse with Wyre Piddle Piddle in the Wind permanently available, plus three guests stocked to customer order. Customers tick a list of suggested ales each month and the ones with the most ticks win! Badger Tanglefoot is popular.

A large town pub with three bars, dining area, patio, disabled access and facilities. Food available lunchtimes and evenings. Children allowed.

All day, every day.

N21: WINCHMORE HILL

The Orange Tree

18 Highfield Road, Winchmore Hill N21 3HD
☎ *(0208) 360 4853*

Greene King IPA, Abbot and Ruddles Best Bitter usually available with a guest frequently from B&T Brewery or Adnams.

Comfortable, traditional one-bar house with pub games and beer garden. Food served 12–2pm daily. Children welcome in beer garden. No car park but plenty of parking nearby. Located off Green Lanes, enter through Carpenter Gardens.

12–11pm (10.30pm Sun).

LONDON NORTHWEST

NW1: EUSTON

Head Of Steam
1 Eversholt Street, Euston NW1 1DN
☎ *(020) 7388 2221* John Craig-Tyler

Nine real ales always available. Shepherd Neame Master Brew, Hop Back Summer Lightning and brews from O'Hanlon's, Cottage, B&T and Brakspear, including one mild, usually featured. Three other brews also served, perhaps from Arundel, Phoenix, Black Sheep, Eccleshall or Barnsley breweries. Monthly beer festivals feature up to 24 different beers.

Victorian-style freehouse with polished floors, featuring regular exhibitions of railway paintings. Food served 12–2.30pm and 5–8pm Mon–Fri, 12–3pm Sat. Children's certificate. Situated outside Euston train/underground station, to the left-hand side of the bus terminal.

11am–11pm Mon–Sat; 12–10.30pm Sun.

NW2: CRICKLEWOOD

The Beaten Docket
55–6 Cricklewood Broadway, Cricklewood NW2 3ET
☎ *(020) 8450 2972* Nick Hand

Shepherd Neame Spitfire and Greene King Abbot always available, plus two constantly changing guests.

A two-bar pub with dining area and patio. Music, but no games. Food available all day. No children.

All day, every day.

NW8: ST JOHN'S WOOD

The Clifton Hotel
96 Clifton Hill, St John's Wood NW8 9JT
☎ *(020) 7624 5233* Sheila Hale

Adnams Best and Marston's Pedigree always available, plus two weekly changing guests such as Timothy Taylor Landlord.

A converted house in St John's Wood with a garden at the front and a patio at the back. A mainly business clientele (average age 25–35ish). Food available 12–3.30pm and 6.30–10pm Mon–Fri and all day Sat–Sun, with traditional roasts on Sun. Children allowed if eating, but not at the bar. Situated off Abbey Road.

All day, every day.

LONDON SOUTHEAST

SE1: BOROUGH

Blue Eyed Maid
173 Borough High Street, Borough SE1 1HR
☎ *(020) 7378 8259* Alex Kecojevic

Fuller's London Pride and Young's Special usually available, with one or two guest beers.

A modern, glitzy, glamour-type bar with a good selection of wine and food. Food available all day in the bar and in a separate restaurant. Children allowed in restaurant only.

11am–11pm Mon–Fri; closed weekends.

The George Inn
77 Borough High Street, Borough SE1 1NH
☎ *(020) 7407 2056* George Cunningham

Fuller's London Pride, Morland Old Speckled Hen and Greene King Abbot among the brews always available, plus at least one guest (often seasonal).

A famous galleried sixteenth-century pub, owned by the National Trust. Large courtyard, one bar, servery, courtyard and function room. Food available Mon–Fri lunchtime and Mon–Sat evenings in restaurant. Children allowed.

All day, every day.

The Glove Tavern
8 Bedale Street, Borough SE1 9AL
☎ *(020) 7407 0043*

An Adnams and Young's brew always available, plus four guests such as Greene King Abbot, Morland Old Speckled Hen and Marston's Pedigree.

A traditional town pub with one bar. Background music, bar billiards, game machines. Disabled access. No food. No children.

11am–11pm Mon–Fri; closed Sat–Sun but available for private hire.

The Market Porter
9 Stoney Street, Borough SE1 9AA
☎ *(020) 7407 2495* Tony Hedigan

Harveys Best and Fuller's London Pride always available, plus between five and 15 guests which vary each week.

An old, traditional pub within Borough Market. Food available at lunchtime. Children welcome in the restaurant. Function room available seven days per week for private functions, meetings, etc.

11am–11pm Mon–Sat; 12–10.30pm Sun.

Fox in the Hill

149 Denmark Hill, Camberwell SE5 8EH
☎ *(020) 7738 4756* Mark Gardner

🍺 Shepherd Neame Spitfire and Hop Back Summer Lightning among the brews always available plus a wide range of guests.

A large, modern Wetherspoon's pub with one bar, non-smoking dining area, garden and disabled facilities. Food available all day. Children allowed in the non-smoking area only.

All day, every day.

Hermit's Cave

28 Camberwell Church Street, Camberwell SE5 8QU
☎ *(020) 7703 3188*

🍺 Twelve beers available including Morland Old Speckled Hen, Marston's Pedigree, Gales HSB, Fuller's London Pride and Adnams Best. Micro-brewers provide the guest beers.

Built in 1902, this beamed pub serves bar food at lunchtime and evenings. Street parking. Children not allowed.

11am–11pm Mon–Sat; 12–10.30pm Sun.

The Dog & Bell

116 Prince Street, Deptford SE8 3JD
☎ *(020) 8692 5664*

🍺 Five beers always available. Brews might include Fuller's London Pride and ESB, Shepherd Neame Spitfire, Nethergate Bitter and something from Larkins or Archers.

Built in 1850 and recently extended. Bar food available. Street parking, garden. Children aged 14 and over allowed. Tucked away, not far from the railway station.

11am–11pm Mon–Sat; 12–5pm and 7–10.30pm Sun.

The Watch House

198–204 Lewisham High Street, Lewisham SE13 6JP
☎ *(020) 8318 3136* Steve Asprey

🍺 Shepherd Neame Spitfire and Hop Back Summer Lightning among the brews always available plus up to five guests from breweries such as Bateman, Ash Vine, JW Lees, Nethergate and Cotleigh.

A town-centre pub with a mature clientele. No music. Patio, non-smoking area, disabled facilities. Food available all day. No children.

All day, every day.

Moon & Stars

164–6 High Street, Penge SE20 7QS
☎ *(020) 8776 5680* Lenny Bignall

🍺 Shepherd Neame Spitfire, Greene King IPA and Abbot and Hop Back Summer Lightning among the beers always available, plus up to six guests.

A large Wetherspoon's pub. Disabled facilities. Non-smoking dining area, beer garden. Food available all day. No children.

All day, every day.

The Alliance

91 High Street, South Norwood SE25 6EA
☎ *(020) 8653 3604* Mr Goodridge

🍺 Wadworth 6X and Marston's Pedigree always available, plus one guest such as Timothy Taylor Landlord, Hook Norton Old Hooky, Hop Back Summer Lightning or Cotleigh Barn Owl.

A traditional country-style pub with leaded windows. Bar snacks available at lunchtime. No children's room.

11am–11pm Mon–Sat; 12–10.30pm Sun.

Portmanor

Portland Road, South Norwood, SE25 4UF
☎ *(020) 8655 1308* Joan Brendan Kelly

🍺 Fuller's London Pride, Greene King Abbot Ale and up to five guest beers regularly available, perhaps from Hogs Back, Flagship or Ales of Kent.

Popular pub with a good atmosphere. Food served 11–3pm and 5–9.30pm. No children.

11am–11pm Mon–Sat; 12–10.30pm Sun.

The Captain's Cabin

4–7 Norris Street, Haymarket SW1Y 4RJ
☎ *(020) 7930 4767* Mervyn and Julie Wood

🍺 Greene King IPA and Abbot usually available plus two constantly changing guests.

Two bars with a central staircase and open balcony characterise this newly refurbished pub. Food served all day. Cash-back facilities available! Top bar available for private hire. No children.

11am–11pm Mon–Sat; 12–10.30pm Sun.

Lord Moon of the Mall

16–18 Whitehall, Trafalgar Square SW1A 2DY
☎ *(020) 7839 7014* James Langan

Fuller's London Pride and Shepherd Neame Spitfire always available, plus four guests such as Ridleys Rumpus, Hop Back Summer Lightning, Everards Tiger, Exmoor Gold, Smiles Golden and Batemans XXXB.

A city pub with high ceilings, arches and oak fittings. Non-smoking area, disabled facilities. Food available all day. No children.

All day, every day.

The Crown & Sceptre

2a Streatham Hill, Brixton SW2 4AH
☎ *(020) 8671 0843*

Shepherd Neame Spitfire among the brews always available plus two guests such as Hop Back Summer Lightning and ales from Adnams or Cotleigh.

One big bar, non-smoking dining area, front and rear patios. Food available all day. Children allowed in the garden only.

All day, every day.

The Crown

153 Dovehouse Street, Chelsea SW3 6LB
☎ *(020) 7352 9505*
Alan Carroll, Karen Moore and Sean Stewart

Adnams Best Bitter, Fuller's London Pride plus a guest beer usually available.

Traditional London pub, due to undergo a refurbishment. Food served 12–2pm Mon–Sun. After refurbishment, evening food may be available. Well-behaved over 14s welcome until 7pm. Situated 100 yards off Fulham Road, between the Brompton and Royal Marsden hospitals.

11am–11pm Mon–Sat; 12–10.30pm Sun.

The Bread & Roses

68 Clapham Manor Street, Clapham SW4 6DZ
☎ *(020) 8498 1779* Peter Dawson

A freehouse with Adnams Best and Workers Ale (a house ale brewed by Smiles) always available, plus two guests, perhaps Adnams Regatta, Old Ale or Broadside, Oakhill Mendip Gold or O'Hanlon's Red Ale.

A bright, modern town pub. Bar and function room, front and rear garden, disabled access and toilets. Food available at lunchtime and evenings. Children allowed during the day in the non-smoking area only.

11am–11pm Mon–Sat; 12–10.30pm Sun.

The White Horse

1 Parsons Green, Fulham SW6 4UL
☎ *(020) 7736 2115 Fax (020) 7610 6091*
Mark Dorber and David Nichol

Harveys Sussex, Adnams Extra and Highgate Mild always available plus guests including Adnams Tally Ho, Barley Mow, Old and Summer Ale, Archers Golden, Bateman Strawberry Fields and Salem Porter, Cains Traditional, Formidable, Stout and Mild, also Rooster's, Lees, Robinson's, Shepherd Neame and Young's. Hoegaarden and Starompramen on draught, plus 55 classic bottled beers from around the world.

A large, comfortable Victorian pub overlooking Parsons Green, with a big reputation for good cask and bottled beers. Recently refurbished to a high standard, the pub now features the non-smoking 'Coach House' restaurant. Brunch is also served on Saturdays, 11am–4pm, and on Sundays. Regular beer festivals, including an Old Ale Festival (last Saturday of November), a Wheat Beer Festival (May) and the 'Beauty of the Hops' competition (June). Elegant function room for private dinner parties, tastings and presentations. Parking, terrace/garden. Children allowed. Just 100 yards from Parsons Green tube station.

All day, every day.

The Imperial

577 King's Road SW6 2EH
☎ *(020) 7736 8549* Andrew and Tim Haggard

Charles Wells Bombardier and Haggards Imperial usually available. The pub lease belongs to the owners of Haggards Brewery and this is the sole outlet for the beer.

A bright, airy, modern town pub with covered rear garden. Lively atmosphere. Food served every lunchtime and weekday evenings. Traditional roasts on Sundays. No children. Situated on the junction with Cambria Street.

11am–11pm Mon–Sat; 12–10.30pm Sun.

SW7: CHELSEA

The Anglesea Arms

15 Selwood Terrace, Chelsea SW7 3GG
☎ *(020) 7373 7960* Andrew Ford

Six real ales permantly available, including Adnams Best and Broadside, Brakspear Special and Bitter, and Fuller's London Pride. Guests beers are rotated on the remaining pump. Belgian beers, Budvar and Hoegaarden always available.

A lively, easy-to-find, 200-year-old pub with a traditional atmosphere – no background music or juke box. Food available lunchtimes and evenings in wood-panelled dining room. Terraced garden area at front. Cask Marque winner. Children over 14 allowed. Just off the Fulham Road.

OPEN *11am–11pm Mon–Sat; 12–4pm and 7–10.30pm Sun.*

SW8: STOCKWELL

The Priory Arms

83 Lansdowne Way, Stockwell SW8 2PB
☎ *(020) 7622 1884* Gary Morris

Adnams Bitter and Broadside, and Harveys Best Bitter always available, plus three guests, mainly from smaller regional breweries and especially micro-breweries.

South West London CAMRA Pub of the Year 1992, 1994, 1996 and 1998. Bar food available at lunchtimes, with traditional roasts on Sundays. Near Stockwell tube station.

OPEN *11am–11pm Mon–Sat; 12–10.30pm Sun.*

SW9: BRIXTON

The Beehive

409 Brixton Road, Brixton SW9 7DG
☎ *(020) 7738 3643* Peter Martin

Shepherd Neame Spitfire permanently available, plus three guests such as Hop Back Summer Lightning, Greene King Abbot or Strawberry Blonde.

One bar, non-smoking dining area, disabled access. Food available all day. No children.

OPEN *All day, every day.*

SW12: BALHAM

Moon Under Water

194 Balham High Road, Balham SW12 9BP
☎ *(020) 8673 0535* James Glover

Hop Back Summer Lightning and Shepherd Neame Spitfire permanently available, plus two guest beers.

Friendly, Wetherspoon's local. No music. Large non-smoking area. Food served all day, every day. No children.

OPEN *11am–11pm Mon–Sat; 12–10.30pm Sun.*

SW18: WANDSWORTH

The Spotted Dog

72 Garratt Lane, Wandsworth SW18 4DJ
☎ *(020) 8875 9531* Colin Daniels

Fuller's London Pride and ESB and Greene King IPA and Abbot always available, plus two guests such as Jennings Cocker Hoop, Fuller's Summer Ale and Greene King Centenary. Beers changed weekly.

A traditional one-bar town pub with food available 12–4pm. Disabled facilities. Patio. Children allowed if dining.

OPEN *All day, every day.*

LONDON WEST

W1: MARYLEBONE

The Carpenters Arms

12 Seymour Place, Marylebone W1 5WF
☎ *(020) 7723 1050* Tim Saward

Fuller's London Pride and Young's Bitter usually available plus guest beers such as Hop Back Summer Lightning, Everards Tiger, Wadworth 6X or something from Harveys, Hardys & Hansons or Oakhill.

A charming traditional tavern with a warm welcome. Small and intimate one-bar house which is a great favourite with locals, business people and tourists alike. Food served all day every day. No children.

OPEN *11am–11pm Mon–Sat; 12–10.30pm Sun.*

W1: REGENT STREET

Ain't Nothin' But ... Blues Bar

20 Kingly Street W1R 5LB
☎ *(020) 7287 0514* K Hillier

Adnams Best and Broadside usually available, plus a guest beer that changes every few days, such as Fuller's London Pride, Young's Waggle Dance, Charles Wells Bombardier, Morland Old Speckled Hen, Everards Tiger or something from Badger Brewery.

London's only blues bar venue. Good old-fashioned drinkers' bar with mixed clientele. Open late with live music every night. Food served during opening hours. No children. Situated between Regent Street and Carnaby Street behind Hamley's Toy Shop.

OPEN *6pm–1am Mon–Thurs; 6pm–3am Fri–Sat; 7.30pm–midnight Sun.*

W1: SOHO

The Argyll Arms

18 Argyll Street, Soho W1 1AA
☎ *(020) 7734 6117* Mike Tayara

Seven beers always available including Wadworth 6X and an ever-changing selection that might feature Everards Daredevil, Hop Back Summer Lightning, Felinfoel Double Dragon, Charles Wells Bombardier and brews from Jennings, Ringwood, Tomintoul etc.

A 300-year-old pub just off Oxford Circus owned by the Duke of Argyll. Air-conditioned. Bar and restaurant food available at lunchtime and evenings. Function room, non-smoking area. Children allowed in play area.

OPEN 11am–11pm Mon–Sat; 12–10.30pm Sun.

The Blue Posts

18 Kingley Street, Soho W1R 5LB
☎ *(020) 7734 1170* Trevor Mayer

Fuller's London Pride and Wadworth 6X always available, plus one fortnightly changing guest such as Morland Old Speckled Hen.

A traditional English tavern with two bars, wooden floors, beams, dining area, juke box and front patio. Food served 11am–3pm daily. No children. Located behind Hamley's.

OPEN 11am–11pm Mon–Sat; closed Sun.

W2: LANCASTER GATE

Archery Tavern

4 Bathurst Street, Lancaster Gate W2 2SD
☎ *(020) 7402 4916* Tony O'Neil

A Hall & Woodhouse tied pub with Badger Dorset Best, Tanglefoot and IPA always available, plus two guests such as Gribble Black Adder II or Golden Champion Ale.

A one-bar traditional pub. Fruit machines, quiz machine, darts. Food available 12–10pm. Well-behaved children allowed.

OPEN All day, every day.

W2: PADDINGTON

Fountain's Abbey

109 Praed Street, Paddington W2 1RL
☎ *(020) 7723 2364* David Harrison

Greene King Abbot Ale and Morland Old Speckled Hen permanently available, plus one rotating guest ale. Approximately six different guests served every month. Plans for a beer festival (the pub's first) in autumn 2000.

A large, Victorian-style ale house with outside seating and food available all day. Children allowed. Function room for hire.

OPEN 11am–11pm Mon–Sat; 12–10.30pm Sun.

W4: STRAND ON THE GREEN

The Bell & Crown

11–13 Thames Road, Strand on the Green W4
☎ *(020) 8994 4164* Frank McBrearty

A Fuller's tied house with London Pride, Chiswick and ESB permanently on offer. Fuller's seasonal ales served as available.

Backing on to the Thames, this pub has a 40-seater non-smoking dining area and outside seating. Food available 12–10pm daily. Children allowed, under supervision.

OPEN 11am–11pm Mon–Sat; 12–10.30pm Sun.

W5: EALING

The Red Lion

13 St Mary's Road, Ealing W5 5RA
☎ *(020) 8567 2541* Paul Carter

Fuller's Chiswick, London Pride and ESB plus a seasonal brew usually available.

Small, traditional one-bar Fuller's locals' pub. No music or machines. Large patio garden. Food served 12–2.30pm and 6–9pm. Children allowed in garden only. Situated opposite Ealing Studios.

OPEN 11am–11pm Mon–Sat; 12–10.30pm Sun.

W6: HAMMERSMITH

The Cross Keys

57 Black Lion Lane, Hammersmith W6 9BG
☎ *(020) 8748 3541*
Adam and Jackie Pattinson

Fuller's Chiswick, London Pride and ESB usually available.

A traditional pub with back garden open in summer. Food served 12–2.30pm Mon–Fri and Sun. Children welcome before 9pm.

OPEN 11am–11pm (10.30pm Sun).

W7: HANWELL

The Dolphin

13 Lower Boston Road, Hanwell W7 3TX
☎ *(020) 8810 1617* John Connoly

Marston's Pedigree, Morland Old Speckled Hen, Fuller's London Pride, Wadworth 6X or Gales HSB and a Brakspear brew usually available. A guest beer such as Badger Tanglefoot or Bishops Tipple often available too.

Olde-worlde character pub with wooden floors, lovely beer garden and restaurant. Food served 12–2.30pm and 6–9pm Tues–Sun. Kitchen closed Sun evening and Monday. Children welcome, with separate children's menu available. Small car park. Located off one-way system to Uxbridge Road or follow Boston Road to end.

OPEN 12–11pm (10.30pm Sun).

The Truscott Arms

55 Shirland Road, Maida Vale W9 2JD
☎ *(020) 7286 0310* Barbara Slack

Fuller's London Pride, Greene King IPA and Abbot usually available, plus other Fuller's beers.

L ocal community pub with one large centre bar. Secluded rear beer garden. Food served 12–3pm and 6–9pm Mon–Sat, plus 12–3pm Sun for traditional roasts and summer barbecues (weather permitting). Children are welcome until 7pm. Located 200 yards south of Warwick Avenue tube station.

OPEN *11am–11pm Mon–Sat; 12–10.30pm Sun.*

Warrington Hotel

93 Warrington Crescent, Maida Vale W9 1EH
☎ *(020) 7286 2929* J Brandon

Brakspear Special, Young's Special, Fuller's London Pride and ESB usually available, plus one or two guest beers perhaps from Rebellion or Kitchen.

A splendid example of a Victorian public house with art nouveau stained glass, marble bar and fireplace. A family-owned freehouse which has been a popular meeting place for many years. Thai food served in the bar 12–2.30pm and in the upstairs restaurant 6–11pm. No children.

OPEN *11am–11pm Mon–Sat; 12–10.30pm Sun.*

★ *The Clifton Arms*, 21 Clifton Road, SE25
★ *The Cock & Woolpack*, 6 Finch Lane, EC3
★ *Crystal Palace Tavern*, 105 Tanner's Hill, SE8
★ *The Flask*, 77 Highgate West Hill, Highgate
★ *The George*, High Street, Wanstead, E11
★ *The Hedgehog & Hogshead*, 259 Upper Street, Highbury Corner, N1
★ *Kings Ford*, 250 Chingford Mount Road, Chingford, E4
★ *Parisa Café Bar*, 146 Putney High Street, SW15 (brewpub)
★ *The Prince Albert*, 49 Hare Street, Woolwich, SE18
★ *The Prince Arthur*, 95 Forest Road, Dalston, E8
★ *The Railway*, Crouch End Broadway, N4
★ *The Shipwright's Arms*, 88 Tookley Street, Borough SE1
★ *The Spread Eagle*, 141 Albert Street, Camden Town, NW1
★ *Tally Ho*, 749 High Road, North Finchley
★ *The Tap & Spile*, 29 Crouch Hill, N4
★ *The Tappit Hen*, 295 Holloway Road, N7
★ *The Wheatsheaf*, 6 Stoney Street, Borough, SE1
★ *The William IV*, 816 High Road, Leyton, E10

Places Featured:

Barking
Barnet
Bexleyheath
Brentford
Bromley
Carshalton
Croydon
Farnborough
Feltham
Hampton
Harefield
Heathrow
Hounslow
Ilford

Isleworth
Kingston-upon-Thames
North Cheam
Petts Wood
Purley
Richmond
Romford
Staines
Stanmore
Surbiton
Twickenham
Uxbridge
Woodford Green

BARKING

The Britannia

1 Church Road, Barking, Essex IG11 8PR
☎ *(020) 8594 1305* Mrs Pells

A Young's pub with Special and Bitter always available, plus a winter warmer from October and various specials in summer.

An old-fashioned community alehouse with public bar, saloon/lounge bar and snug. Patio. Food available at lunchtime and evenings. No children. Can be extremely difficult to find – ring if need be.

OPEN *11am–3pm and 5–11.30pm Mon–Fri; all day Sat–Sun.*

BARNET

Moon Under Water

148 High Street, Barnet, Hertfordshire EN5 5XP
☎ *(020) 8441 9476* Gareth Fleming

A Wetherspoon's pub with Greene King IPA and Abbot plus Shepherd Neame Spitfire always available. Also three guests such as Hop Back Summer Lightning which are changed on a weekly basis.

An olde-worlde town pub with one large bar, a non-smoking dining area and big beer garden. Food available from 11am–10pm. No children.

OPEN *All day, every day.*

BEXLEYHEATH

Robin Hood & Little John

78 Lion Road, Bexleyheath, Kent DA6 8PF
☎ *(020) 8303 1128* Mr Johnson

A freehouse with Shepherd Neame Spitfire and Golding, Burtonwood Bitter, plus Flagship Destroyer & Futtock, Timothy Taylor Landlord and others regularly available. The least popular brew is dropped each month to try something different. Up to eight pumps in operation.

A one-bar, village-type pub with wood panel walls and old Singer sewing machine tables. Beer garden. Food available at lunchtime only, Mon–Sat. No children.

OPEN *11am–3.30pm and 6–11pm; 7–11pm weekends.*

Wrong Un

234–6 The Broadway, Bexleyheath
☎ *(0208) 298 0439* Timothy Shepherd

Hop Back Summer Lightning and Greene King Abbot Ale regularly available plus four or five guest beers such as Shepherd Neame Spitfire, Bateman XXXB, Brains SA, Hook Norton Old Hooky, Hop Back Thunderstorm or something from Ash Vine or Marston's.

Light, spacious pub with relaxed atmosphere and large non-smoking area. Extensive menu available 10am–10pm Mon–Sat, 12–10.30pm Sun. Disabled facilities. Car park. No children.

OPEN *10am–11pm Mon–Sat; 12–10.30pm Sun.*

BRENTFORD

The Magpie & Crown
128 High Street, Brentford, Middlesex TW8 8EW
☎ *(020) 8560 5658* Charlie and Steve Bolton

A freehouse with four pumps serving a range of ales such as Brakspear Bitter, Greene King IPA, something from Cottage and many, many more.

A mock-Tudor pub. One bar. No food. No children.

[OPEN] *11am–11pm (10.30pm Sun).*

BROMLEY

The Red Lion
10 North Road, Bromley, Kent BR1 3LG
☎ *(020) 8460 2691* Mr and Mrs Humphrey

Beers from Beards and Harveys, plus Greene King Abbot always available with two guest pumps regularly serving Shepherd Neame Golding among others. Guests changed twice weekly

A locals' pub, with food available at lunchtime and evenings. Children allowed.

[OPEN] *All day, every day.*

CARSHALTON

The Racehorse
17 West Street, Carshalton, Surrey SM5 2PT
☎ *(020) 8647 6818* Julian Norton

A freehouse with King and Barnes Sussex among the brews always on sale, plus usually three guests such as Fuller's London Pride and ESB and beers from Gales and Morland. Guests changed every few days.

A locals' pub with two bars, dining area, disabled access and patio. Food available at lunchtime and evenings (not Sunday pm).

[OPEN] *11am–11pm Mon–Sat; 12–4pm and 7–10.30pm Sun.*

CROYDON

Claret Free House
5 Bingham Corner, Lower Addiscombe Road, Croydon CR0 7AA
☎ *(020) 8656 7452* M Callaghan

Palmers IPA, Shepherd Neame Spitfire plus a Cottage brew usually available. One regularly changing guest is also served.

Small, friendly and comfortable community pub. No food. No children. Adjacent to new Tramlink station.

[OPEN] *11.30am–11pm Mon–Sat; 12–10.30pm Sun.*

FARNBOROUGH

The Woodman
50 High Street, Farnborough BR6 7BA
☎ *(01689) 852663* Sharon Pritchard

Shepherd Neame Master Brew, Spitfire, Bishop's Finger and a seasonal brew usually available.

A village pub in a quiet location, with a large garden, grapevine canopy and many hanging baskets, window boxes and tubs. Food served 12–2pm and 7–9pm Mon–Sat and lunchtime roasts every Sunday. Children welcome. Car park. Located just off the A21, three miles from Bromley, sign posted 'Farnborough Village'.

[OPEN] *All day, every day.*

FELTHAM

Moon on the Square
30 The Centre, Feltham, Middlesex TW13 4AU
☎ *(020) 8893 1293* Phil Cripps

Fuller's London Pride and Marston's Pedigree always available, plus four guests changing all the time, from breweries such as Brakspear, Cotleigh, Hook Norton and Exmoor.

One big bar plus non-smoking dining area in which food is available all day. No children.

[OPEN] *All day, every day.*

HAMPTON

The White Hart
70 High Street, Hampton, Middlesex TW12 2SW
☎ *(020) 8979 5352* Mrs Macintosh

Greene King Abbot is among those beers always available plus six guest beers (hundreds per year) including ales from Ringwood, Pilgrim, Nethergate, Hop Back, Archers, Hogs Back, Brakspear, Gales, Shepherd Neame, Charles Wells, Titanic, Woodforde's and Harviestoun breweries.

Mock-Tudor pub in an historical area with a log fire in winter and large patio area. No darts or pool. Home-made bar food served at lunchtime and a Thai restaurant in the evenings. Car park, garden and function room with bar. Close to Hampton BR station. Easy access from the M3 and A316. On main bus routes from Richmond, Heathrow and Wimbledon.

[OPEN] *11am–3pm and 5–11pm Mon–Fri; 11.30am–11pm Sat–Sun.*

HAREFIELD

The Plough

Hill End Road, Harefield, Middlesex UB9 6LQ
☎ *(01895) 822129 Mr and Mrs Knight*

Ruddles Best, Fuller's London Pride and Brakspear ales always available plus up to six guests including Chiltern Beechwood and Black Sheep Bitter. Half a mile past the main entrance to Harefield Hospital.

A country-style family pub. Bar food available at lunchtime. Car park and garden. Children allowed.

11am–3pm and 5.30–11pm Mon–Sat; 12–3pm and 7–10.30pm Sun.

HEATHROW

The Tap & Spile

Upper Concourse, Terminal One, Heathrow Airport, Middlesex UB5 4PX
☎ *(020) 8897 8418 John Heaphy*

Marston's Pedigree always available plus up to nine guest beers (50 per year) including Rooster's Bitter, Charles Wells Eagle, Brains SA, Nethergate IPA and Adnams Best.

Cosy and relaxing refuge with a 1930s feel overlooking the anarchy of the check-in area. Bar food available at lunchtime and evenings. Car park and children's room. On the catering balcony at departure level in terminal one.

9–11am for breakfast, then 11am–11pm.

HOUNSLOW

Moon Under Water

84–6 Staines Road, Hounslow, Middlesex TW3 3LF
☎ *(020) 8572 7506 Gary Hancock*

Fuller's London Pride and Shepherd Neame Spitfire always available plus two guests such as Hop Back Summer Lightning.

A Wetherspoon's pub with non-smoking area, beer garden, patio, disabled facilities. Food available all day from 11am–10pm. No children.

All day, every day.

ILFORD

The Rose & Crown

16 Ilford Hill, Ilford, Essex IG1 2DA
☎ *(020) 8478 7104 Neil Smith*

Marston's Pedigree and Adnams Best always available along with a monthly selection which might include Shepherd Neame Spitfire or a special brew. Five guest pumps, two changed daily.

A town pub just off the high street with beams and log fires. One bar with dining area and a small terrace. Food available 12–2.30pm Mon–Fri. Children allowed if eating.

12–11pm Mon–Sat; 10am–12.30pm Sun.

ISLEWORTH

The Red Lion

94 Linkfield Road, Isleworth, Middlesex TW7 6QJ
☎ *(020) 8560 1457 Nicky Redding*

A freehouse with up to seven beers available each week. These regularly include Cottage Golden Arrow and other Cottage brews. Guests changed every two days.

A large, friendly, locals' pub in a back street near the station, with live music and a relaxed atmosphere. Two bars and a large garden with BBQs on weekdays and all day Friday, sometimes weekends. Food available 12–3pm Mon–Fri. Children allowed in the garden only.

11am–11pm.

KINGSTON-UPON-THAMES

The Canbury Arms

49 Canbury Park Road, Kingston-upon-Thames, Surrey
☎ *(020) 8288 1882 Paul Adams*

Four real ales usually available which may include Wadworth 6X, Morland Old Speckled Hen, Marston's Pedigree or Greene King Abbot Ale. Over 400 beers from 65 independent/micro-breweries served so far. Regularly changing real cider and annual Easter cider festival.

Back-street pub with mock Tudor interior. Large screen TV for sport. Extensive reference library. Live music on Friday and Saturday evenings, quiz nights on Sunday. Beer garden with patio and small menagerie. Dog the size of a Shetland pony! No food. Car park with secure motorcycle parking. No children.

All permitted hours.

The Fighting Cocks

56 London Road, Kingston-upon-Thames, Surrey KT2 6QA
☎ *(020) 8546 5174 Natalie Salt*

Wadworth 6X among the brews always available plus two guests such as Marston's Pedigree.

A town pub with wooden floors and panelled walls. Two bars and courtyard. No food. Children allowed.

11am–11pm.

The Kelly Arms

Alfred Road, off Villiers Road, Kingston-upon-Thames, Surrey KT1 2UB
☎ *(020) 8296 9815* Vanessa McConnon

Three real ales always available, with Daleside Shrimpers, Harveys Best and Wickwar BOB regularly featured.

A back-street locals' pub with a friendly atmosphere. One big bar. Pool table, Tornado football table, darts, pinball, cable TV. Garden with BBQ. Food available all day, every day. Children allowed if eating or in garden. Functions catered for.

OPEN *11am–11pm Mon–Sat; 12–10.30pm Sun.*

The Willoughby Arms

Willoughby Road, Kingston-upon-Thames, Surrey, KT2 6LN
☎ *(020) 8546 4236* Rick Robinson

Timothy Taylor Landlord, Fuller's London Pride and Marstons Pedigree permanently available, plus one guest ale which is sold at £1.50 per pint on Sunday lunchtimes. The landlord here is the National Secretary of the Society of Preservation of Beers from the Wood. Two annual beer festivals held on St George' s Day and either Hallowe'en or Bonfire Night.

A recently refurbished Victorian corner local. Rolls available at lunchtime, barbecues on Sundays (weather permitting). Children allowed in the large garden which has a pond and waterfall. Large screen TV, bric a brac. Quiz night Sundays. Can be difficult to find, so ring if you get lost.

OPEN *10.30am–11pm Mon–Sat; 12–10.30pm Sun.*

NORTH CHEAM

Wetherspoons

552–6 London Road, North Cheam, Surrey SM3 9AA
☎ *(020) 8644 1808* Dean Kelly

A Wetherspoon's pub with Fuller's London Pride always available plus two guests such as Shepherd Neame Spitfire. Guests changed every three days.

One large bar and non-smoking dining area. Food available all day. Disabled facilities. No children.

OPEN *All day, every day.*

PETTS WOOD

Sovereign of the Seas

109 Queensway, Petts Wood, Orpington, Kent BR5 1DG
☎ *(01689) 891606* Robert Barfoot

A Wetherspoon's pub with Shepherd Neame Spitfire among the brews always available. Two guests might include Hop Back Summer Lightning, or Timothy Taylor Landlord. Guests changed weekly.

A community pub with one big bar, a non-smoking dining area and disabled facilities. Outside patios in summer. Food available all day. No children.

OPEN *All day, every day.*

PURLEY

Foxley Hatch

8–9 Russell Hill Road, Purley CR8 2LE
☎ *(020) 8763 9307*
Jan Bordiak and Helen Mason

Greene King Abbot plus two guest beers from around the country. Three or four festivals are also held each year offering up to 20 beers at a time.

Friendly, locals' pub free of music and television. Non-smoking area and easy access for the disabled. Food served all day, every day. No children.

OPEN *11am–11pm Mon–Sat; 12–10.30pm Sun.*

RICHMOND

The Triple Crown

15 Kew Foot Road, Richmond, Surrey TW9 2SS

Fuller's London Pride and Timothy Taylor Landlord regularly available. Four guest beers are also served totalling over 200 during the last six years.

Traditional, one-bar house. Food served 12–2.30pm. Children welcome.

OPEN *11am–11pm Mon–Sat; 12–10.30pm Sun.*

ROMFORD

The Moon & Stars

103 South Street, Romford, Essex RM1 1NX
☎ *(01708) 730117* Sarah Saye

A Wetherspoon's pub with Greene King Abbot and Shepherd Neame Spitfire among the beers always available. Four guest ales change on a weekly basis.

Large bar, non-smoking dining area, outside seating, disabled facilities. Food available all day. Children allowed outside only.

OPEN *All day, every day.*

STAINES

The Angel Hotel
Angel Mews, High Street, Staines, Middlesex
TW18 4EE
☎ *(01784) 452509* John Othick

A freehouse with two beers from Hogs Back and two from Ushers always available, varying according to the season.

A town pub and restaurant with patio and 12 bedrooms. Food available all day.

OPEN *All day, every day.*

The George
2–8 High Street, Staines, Middlesex TW18 4EE
☎ *(01784) 462181* Jim Conlin

Fuller's London Pride and Greene King Abbot among the beers always available plus four guests such as Marston's Pedigree, Shepherd Neame Spitfire and Morland Old Speckled Hen. Always a good selection of brews from all over the UK. Guests changed monthly

A large, two-level Wetherspoon's pub. No music, non-smoking dining areas upstairs and down, disabled access and toilets. Food available all day. No children.

OPEN *All day, every day.*

The Hobgoblin
14–16 Church Street, Staines, Middlesex
TW18 4EP
☎ *(01784) 452012* Del Woolsgrove

Wychwood Special, Shires XXX and Hobgoblin always available. Three guests could include Marston's Pedigree, Charles Wells Bombardier and beers from Hampshire and Rebellion breweries.

A town-centre, regulars' pub, frequented by the 23–35 age group in evenings, with an older clientele at lunchtimes. An old building with wooden floors and beams, one bar and courtyard. Food available 12–2.30pm. Children allowed in courtyard if open.

OPEN *12–11pm Mon–Sat (10.30pm Sun).*

STANMORE

The Malthouse
7 Stanmore Hill, Stanmore, Middlesex HA7 3DP
☎ *(020) 8420 7265* Charles Begley

A freehouse serving a range of four constantly changing real ales. Favourites include Wadworth 6X and beers from breweries such as Rebellion, Slaters, Ringwood, Cottage and Greene King.

A modern pub decorated in an old-style. Late licence. Garden, disabled access. Food available lunchtimes only. Children allowed.

OPEN *11am–11pm Mon–Tues; 11am–midnight Wed–Thurs; 11am–1am Fri–Sat; 11am–10.30pm Sun.*

SURBITON

Coronation Hall
St Mark's Hill, Surbiton, Surrey KT6 4TB
☎ *(020) 8390 6164* Emma Wales

A Wetherspoon's pub with Shepherd Neame Spitfire and Fuller's London Pride always available. Three guest pumps changed twice a week, which might include Hop Back Summer Lightning.

Large bar area, non-smoking dining area and disabled facilities. Food available all day. No children.

OPEN *All day, every day.*

The Lamb Inn

73 Brighton Road, Surbiton KT6 5NF
☎ *(020) 8390 9229* Ian Stewart

Greene King IPA, Marston's Pedigree and Young's Special permanently available plus one guest changed every two or three days. A good choice of regional ales is offered, from the Isle of Wight to the Isle of Man.

A true old-fashioned community locals' pub. Darts, bar games and a friendly welcoming atmosphere. Large beer garden with grassed area for children. Bar food available every lunchtime. Children allowed in the garden only. From J10 of M25, take left turn towards Kingston; eventually you come to Brighton Road.

OPEN *11am–11pm Mon–Sat; 12–10.30pm Sun.*

TWICKENHAM

Hogshead
33–5 York Street, Twickenham, Middlesex
☎ *(020) 8891 3940* Chanon de Valois

Fuller's London Pride, Wadworth 6X, Marston's Pedigree, Adnams Best Bitter, Greene King Abbot and a Brakspear brew usually available plus two to four guest beers. Something from the Rebellion Brewery is often featured.

A cosy, traditional pub with a contemporary feel. Food served all day, every day. No children.

OPEN *11am–11pm Mon–Sat; 12–10.30pm Sun.*

UXBRIDGE

The Load of Hay

Villier Street, Uxbridge, Middlesex UB8 2PU
☎ *(01895) 234676* Heather Winsbottom

A freehouse with Buckley's Best always available plus three guests from breweries such as Wye Valley, Everards, Rebellion and Cottage – a different one appears each week. Local breweries, micros and small independents favoured.

Situated on the outskirts of town, near the university. University clientele during the daytime, and locals in the evenings. Two bars. Beer garden. Food available every lunchtime and Mon–Sat evenings. Children allowed in the smaller bar area and the garden. In a secluded location – ring for directions if necessary.

11am–3pm and 5.30–11pm Mon–Fri; 11am–3pm and 7–close Sat–Sun.

WOODFORD GREEN

The Cricketers

299–301 High Road, Woodford Green, Essex IG8 9EG
☎ *(020) 8504 2734* Mr and Mrs Woolridge

Owned by McMullen, so AK Original, Gladstone and Country Best Bitter always served, with specials and seasonals when available.

A semi-rural pub with lounge and public bars and beer garden. Food available 12–2pm Mon–Sat, with OAP specials Mon–Thurs. Children allowed till 7.30pm. Situated near the statue of Winston Churchill.

11am–3.30pm and 5.30–11pm Mon–Thurs; all day Fri–Sun.

YOU TELL US

★ *The Albany*, Station Yard, Twickenham
★ *The Beaconsfield Arms*, 63 West End Road, Southall
★ *The Brewery at the Hog & Stump*, 88 London Road, Kingston-upon-Thames
★ *The Cricketer's Arms*, 21 Southbridge Place, Croydon
★ *The Cricketers*, 93 Chislehurst Road, Orpington
★ *The Eel Pie Pub*, 11 Church Street, Twickenham, Middlesex
★ *The Five Bells*, Church Road, Chelsfield, Orpington
★ *The George*, 17 George Street, Croydon
★ *The Greyhound*, 82 Kew Green, Kew
★ *Hedgehog & Hogshead*, 2 High Street, Sutton
★ *The Royal Standard*, 39 Nuxley Road, Upper Belvedere
★ *The Two Brewers*, 19 Wood Street, Kingston-upon-Thames
★ *The Windsor Castle*, 378 Carshalton Road, Carshalton

Places Featured:

Ashton-under-Lyne
Atherton
Bolton
Bury
Castleton
Cheetham
Delph
Failsworth
Hawkshaw
Heywood

Hindley
Hyde
Manchester
Nangreaves
Oldham
Rochdale
Salford
Stalybridge (*see* Cheshire)
Uppermill
Wigan

THE BREWERIES

BANK TOP BREWERY

*Unit 1, Back Lane, Vernon Street, Bolton
BL1 2LD*
☎ *(01204) 528865*

 BRIDGE BITTER 3.8% ABV
FRED'S CAP 4.0% ABV
GOLD DIGGER 4.0% ABV
HAKER 4.2% ABV
SAMUEL CROMPTON'S ALE 4.2% ABV
CLIFFHANGER 4.5% ABV
SANTA'S CLAWS 5.0% ABV
Christmas brew.
SATANIC MILLS 5.0% ABV
SMOKESTACK LIGHTNIN' 5.0% ABV
Plus seasonal brews.

BRIDGEWATER ALES LTD

42 Chapel Street, Salford M3 6AF
☎ *(0161) 831 9090*

NAVIGATOR 3.7% ABV
ASH BLONDE 3.9% ABV
BARTON ALE 4.3% ABV
OLD PINT POT PORTER 4.4% ABV
SSB 4.9% ABV
BLONDIE SPECIAL 5.2% ABV
DELPH PORTER 5.2% ABV

CHESHIRE CAT ALES

*Old Market Tavern, Old Market Place,
Altringham W14 4DN*
☎ *(0161) 927 7062*

POESJE'S BOLLEKES 4.1% ABV

J W LEES & CO.

*Greengate Brewery, Middleton Junction,
Manchester M24 2AX*
☎ *(0161) 643 2487*

 GB MILD 3.5% ABV
Smooth and sweet, with a malt flavour
and a dry finish.
BITTER 4.0% ABV
Refreshing maltiness, with a bitter finish.
MOONRAKER 7.5% ABV
Rounded sweetness, with balancing bitterness.
*Plus a changing brew every two months between
4.0% ABV and 5.0% ABV.*

JOSEPH HOLT PLC

*Derby Brewery, Empire Street, Cheetham,
Manchester M3 1JD*
☎ *(0161) 834 3285*

 MILD 3.2% ABV
Malty with good hoppiness.
BITTER 4.0% ABV
Powerful, hoppy and bitter throughout.

PHOENIX BREWERY

*Oak Brewing Co., Green Lane, Heywood, Greater
Manchester OL10 2EP*
☎ *(01706) 627009*

BANTAM BITTER 3.5% ABV
OAK BEST BITTER 3.9% ABV
HOPWOOD BITTER 4.3% ABV
OLD OAK ALE 4.5% ABV
THIRSTY MOON 4.6% ABV
BONNEVILLE 4.8% ABV
DOUBLE DAGGER 5.0% ABV
WOBBLY BOB 6.0% ABV
Plus seasonal brews.

ASHTON-UNDER-LYNE

The Station

*2 Warrington Street, Ashton-under-Lyne
OL6 6XB*
☎ *(0161) 330 6776 Susan Watson*

Marston's Pedigree and Station Bitter (a special brew) among the beers always available, plus up to six guests, perhaps including Timothy Taylor Landlord and Hydes' Anvil Bitter.

A traditional Victorian freehouse filled with railway memorabilia. Beer garden, happy hours on weekdays from 3–8pm, 4–8pm (Sat) and 12–5pm (Sun). Entertainment on Friday and Saturday nights. Food served at lunchtime and evenings. Children allowed.

OPEN *12–11pm (10.30pm Sun).*

The Witchwood

152 Old Street, Ashton-under-Lyne OL6 7SF
☎ *(0161) 344 0321 Pauline Town*

Marston's Pedigree and Moorhouse's Pendle Witches Brew among the beers always available, plus four guests from a range of 15 independent brewers.

A real ale bar and live music venue six days a week. Two bars, beer garden. Food available. No children.

OPEN *12–11pm (10.30pm Sun).*

ATHERTON

The Pendle Witch

2–4 Warburton Place, Atherton, Manchester M46 0EQ
☎ *(01942) 884537 Joan Houghton*

Tied to Moorhouse's with Premier and Pendle Witches Brew always available plus a couple of others, perhaps Moorhouse's seasonal ales or specials such as Bursting Bitter, Black Witch, Black Panther, Thunder Struck, Black Cat or Easter Ale.

A 100-year-old cottage pub. Light snacks only available. Beer garden. Children allowed inside in the afternoons, or in the garden. Situated off Market Street.

OPEN *All day, every day.*

BOLTON

The Clifton Arms

94 Newport Street, Bolton BL3 6AB
☎ *(01204) 392738 Peter Morris*

Moorhouse's Bitter and Jennings Bitter among the beers always available, plus a good range (up to four new ones per week) available on a guest basis. Regular breweries featured are Black Sheep, Broughton and Caledonian. Three beer festivals held each year with 20 different beers served over 14 days.

A traditional local situated opposite the railway station. Food available during the daytime only. No children.

OPEN *11am–11pm Mon–Sat; 7–10.30pm Sun.*

The Hen & Chickens

Deansgate, Bolton BL1 1EX
☎ *(01204) 389836 Anthony Coyne*

Three constantly changing guests are served, such as Wadworth 6X, Timothy Taylor Landlord, Robinson's Best, Marston's Pedigree or Young's Special.

A traditional pub situated near the post office. Home-made food served at lunchtime only. Children allowed at lunchtime only.

OPEN *11.30am–11pm Mon–Sat; 7–10.30pm Sun.*

Howcroft Inn

36 Pool Street, Bolton BL1 2JU
☎ *(01204) 526814 Clive Knightingale*

Timothy Taylor Landlord always available plus three guests, often from Bank Top Brewery, such as Samuel Crompton's Ale and Gold Digger or from Hart, Phoenix or Moorhouse's. Micro-breweries favoured.

A traditional pub with a broad clientele. Beer garden and bowling green. Food served every lunchtime, including Sundays. Children allowed.

OPEN *12–11pm.*

BURY

Dusty Miller

87 Crostons Road, Bury BL8 1AL
☎ *(0161) 764 1124* Sue Johnson

A Moorhouse's pub with Premier, Pendle Witches Brew and Black Cat Mild always available. Three guests served including, perhaps, Everards Old Original, Ridleys Rumpus, Charles Wells Eagle IPA, Gales Anniversary, Mansfield Old Baily, Cotleigh Old Buzzard or a Crown Buckley brew.

A traditional local pub. No food. No car park. Children allowed in the conservatory only. Located between Walshaw and Bury.

OPEN *2–11pm Mon–Thurs; 12–11pm Fri–Sun.*

CASTLETON

Midland Beer Company

826 Manchester Road, Castleton, Rochdale OL11 3AW
☎ *(01706) 750873* Mr Welsby

A freehouse with Thwaites Bitter plus two guests such as Timothy Taylor Best and Landlord, Mallard IPA or a Cottage Brewery ale.

A traditional pub in an old bank building with beer garden. Food available. Children allowed. Opposite Castleton railway station.

OPEN *All day, every day.*

CHEETHAM

The Queen's Arms

Honey Street, Cheetham M8 8RG
☎ *(0161) 834 4239*

Eight beers always available, usually including Timothy Taylor Landlord and Phoenix Bantam. Others change constantly. Also a wide range of Belgian beers.

A traditional town pub built in the 1800s and subsequently extended. Bar food available at lunchtime and until 8pm. Street parking, children's play area and garden.

OPEN *12–11pm (10.30pm Sun)*

DELPH

Royal Oak Inn

Broad Lane Heights, Delph, Saddleworth OL3 5TX
☎ *(01457) 874460* Michael and Sheila Fancy

A freehouse with Moorhouse's Black Cat Mild and Bitter always available plus four guest ales often including Fuller's London Pride or brews from Black Sheep or Jennings.

Built in 1767 this is an unspoilt pub with low beams, open fires and dining area. Situated in a remote setting off the Delph–Denshaw road, with good views over Saddleworth Moor. Food available Fri–Sun only. Children allowed.

OPEN *7–11pm Mon–Fri (closed lunchtime); 12–3pm and 7–11pm Sat–Sun.*

FAILSWORTH

The Millgate

Ashton Road West, Failsworth M35 0ES
☎ *(0161) 681 8284* David McConvile

A freehouse with Joseph Holt Bitter and Willy Booth's Best (a house beer supplied by Bridgewater Ales) plus two guests such as Liverpool Blondie.

A family-oriented pub with log fires, restaurant, beer garden and children's play area. Food available. Children allowed.

OPEN *11am–11pm (10.30pm Sun).*

HAWKSHAW

The Red Lion Hotel

81 Ramsbottom Road, Hawkshaw, Bury BL8 4JS
☎ *(01204) 856600* Carl Owen

A Jennings brewery house with a range of Jennings brews always available. Two guest pumps, often serving a Bank Top beer.

A traditional pub and restaurant. Bar and restaurant food available. Children allowed.

OPEN *12–3pm and 6–11pm Mon–Sat; all day Sun.*

HEYWOOD

The Wishing Well

89 York Street, Heywood OL10 4NS
☎ *(01706) 620923* Mr TM Huck

A freehouse with Moorhouse's Pendle Witches Brew and Premier, Phoenix Hopwood, Jennings Cumberland and Timothy Taylor Landlord usually available, plus two rotating guests from a vast range of independent and micro-breweries.

A traditional pub with dining area. Food available at lunchtime and evenings. Children allowed.

OPEN *All day, every day.*

HINDLEY

The Edington Arms
186 Ladies Lane, Hindley
☎ *(01942) 259229*

Holt Mild and Bitter always available plus up to nine guests (200 per year).

An old coaching house with two large, comfortable rooms. No food. Parking and garden. Children allowed. A CAMRA pub of the year. Function room upstairs. Next to Hindley railway station.

All day, every day.

HYDE

The Sportsman
58 Mottram Road, Hyde SK14 2NN
☎ *(0161) 368 5000* Geoff Oliver

A freehouse with Plassey Bitter and Hartington Bitter always available, plus two guests from an ever-changing list including Timothy Taylor Landlord, Whim Magic Mushroom Mild or a Robinson's brew.

A traditional alehouse with open fires. Bar food available at lunchtime. Well-supervised children allowed. Near the railway station at Newton St Hyde Central.

All day, every day.

MANCHESTER

The Beerhouse
Angel Street, Manchester
☎ *(0161) 839 7019*

Moorhouse's Pendle Witches Brew and Burtonwood Bitter always available plus up to ten other real ales (up to 300 per year) from a wide range of breweries.

A popular, recently refurbished traditional alehouse off the Rochdale Road, just beyond Mill Street. Bar food is available at lunchtime and Wednesday to Friday evenings. Garden, bar billiards, family room, function room. Children over 14 years allowed before 7pm.

11am–11pm Mon–Sat; 12–10.30pm Sun.

The Lass o'Gowrie
36 Charles Street, Manchester M1 7DB
☎ *(0161) 273 6932* Joe Fylan

Two house brews always available plus three guests from a range of 150 per year to include Morland Old Speckled Hen, Timothy Taylor Landlord and Marston's Pedigree.

A Victorian tiled pub with an open view to the cellar and gas lighting. Bar food available at lunchtime. Close to BBC North. Parking nearby. Children allowed.

11am–11pm Mon–Sat; 12–10.30pm Sun.

Marble Arch Inn
73 Rochdale Road, Manchester M4 4HY
☎ *(0161) 832 5914* Mr Dade

Home of the Marble Brewery, with a range of up to ten beers produced and served on the premises.

A Victorian pub dating from 1880, with mosaic floor, brick ceiling with ornate frieze made of marble. The micro-brewery was installed in December 1998. No food. No children.

DADES BITTER 3.8% ABV
SPOOKY MARBLE 3.8% ABV
Hallowe'en brew.
MARBLE BITTER 4% ABV
LIBERTY IPA 4.6% ABV
SUMMER MARBLE 4.7% ABV
McKENNA'S REVENGE PORTER 5% ABV
TOTALLY MARBLED 5.9% ABV
GINGER MARBLE 6% ABV
Summer brew.
DOBBER 6.5% ABV
WEE STAR 8.6% ABV
Christmas special.

All day Mon–Sat; closed Sun.

Sand Bar
120 Grosvenor Street, All Saints, Manchester M1 7HL
☎ *(0161) 273 3141* Rob Loyeau

A freehouse with Phoenix Bantam and Charles Wells Bombardier always available, plus three guests from breweries such as Abbeydale, Goose Eye, Kelham Island, Eccleshall, Burton Bridge and Phoenix. Also selling the biggest range of bottled beers in Manchester (70 in total, mainly German and Belgian).

A city café bar in an old Georgian building. One main bar and benches outside. Food available 12–3pm Mon–Fri. Children allowed. Located off the A34 by the University.

11am–11pm Mon–Fri; 12.30–11pm Sat; 5–10.30pm Sun.

NANGREAVES

The Lord Raglan

Walmersley Old Road, Nangreaves, Bury
BL9 6SP
☎ *(0161) 764 6680* Brendan Leyden

The home of the Leyden Brewing Company with the full range of ales brewed on the premises and permanently available. Will occasionally swap one of the home brews with another local micro-brewery. Two annual beer festivals held end June/early July and September.

A Victorian two-bar pub and restaurant. Food available lunchtimes and evenings Mon–Sat and all day Sun. Beer garden. Car park. Children allowed. Brewery visits by arrangement. Take the M66 to J1 Burnley, left and left at first lights. The pub is 1½ miles on the left.

NANNY FLYER 3.8% ABV
A very drinkable session bitter with an initial dryness, a hint of citrus followed by a strong malty finish.

BLACK BEARD 3.9% ABV
A very drinkable dark creamy beer brewed using oats and roasted malt.

LIGHT BRIGADE 4.2% ABV
Gold in colour with a complex fruit and hop taste.

RAGLAN SLEEVE 4.6% ABV
A dark amber beer with a good balance of chocolate malt bitterness and hops.

HEAVY BRIGADE 4.7% ABV
A traditional strong bitter, pale in colour with malt and a touch of bitterness coming through in the finish.
Plus seasonals.

12–2.30pm and 7–11pm Mon–Fri; 12–3pm and 7–11pm Sat; 12–10.30pm Sun.

OLDHAM

Hark to Topper

Bow Street, Oldham OL1 1SJ
☎ *(0161) 624 7950* Harry Hurn

A Samuel Smiths pub with two hand pumps, always serving the brewery's ale.

A small, refurbished country-style pub located near the town centre. Open fires. Food available at lunchtime and evenings. Children allowed.

All day, every day.

ROCHDALE

Cask and Feather

1 Oldham Road, Rochdale OL16 1UA
☎ *(01706) 711476* Jackie Grimes

Home of the Thomas McGuinness Brewery, so beers from the range of own brews always available on five hand pumps.

A small brewery founded in 1991 by Thomas McGuinness, who died in early 1993. Expansion plans are in hand. An old-style castle-fronted pub dating from 1814 and close to the town centre. Bar and restaurant food available at lunchtime and evenings. Parking. Children allowed. Located on the main road near the station.

FEATHER PLUCKER MILD 3.4% ABV
Dark in colour, rich maltiness throughout.

BEST BITTER 3.8% ABV
Well-hopped and quenching, with some fruitiness.

SPECIAL RESERVE BITTER 4.0% ABV
Malt flavour, with sweetness and some fruitiness.

JUNCTION BITTER 4.2% ABV
Strong malt flavours.

AUTUMN GLORY 4.6% ABV
Seasonal brew.

WINTER'S REVENGE 4.6% ABV
Seasonal brew.

SUMMER TIPPLE 4.6% ABV
Seasonal brew.

CHRISTMAS CHEER 4.6% ABV
Seasonal brew.

TOMMY TODD PORTER 5.0% ABV
A warming winter brew.

All day, every day.

Cemetery Inn

470 Bury Road, Rochdale OL11 5EU
☎ *(01706) 645635* Kevin Robinson

A freehouse serving Timothy Taylor Best, Landlord and Dark Mild and a Moorhouse's brew plus three guests from breweries such as Phoenix, Wye Valley or Rooster's.

A Victorian pub with log fires, dating from 1865. Food currently available at weekends and for functions only. Children allowed.

All day, every day.

SALFORD

The Crescent

20 The Crescent, Salford M5 4PF
☎ *(0161) 736 5600* Mrs J Davies

Crescent Bitter (house beer) always available plus up to ten others (150 per year) primarily from local breweries, including Oak, Moorhouse's, Titanic and Marston's. Other guests from all around the country. Occasional beer festivals.

A sprawling pub with a comfortable atmosphere, frequented by students and locals alike. Bar food available at lunchtime. Car park. Traditional pub games. Opposite Salford University. The nearest station is Salford Crescent, on the main A6.

12–11pm Mon–Fri; 7.30–11pm Sat; 12–3pm and 7.30–10.30pm Sun.

The Old Pint Pot

2 Adelphi Street, Salford M3 6EN
☎ *(0161) 939 1514* Thomas and Peter Morrison

A freehouse with small micro-brewery producing Bridgewater. Plus two guest ales such as Liverpool's Blondie or Greene King Abbot.

A riverside pub in a converted convent, with a largely student clientele. Food available. Children allowed. Beer garden. Situated next to Salford University, below road level.

BRIDGEWATER % ABV varies

All day, every day.

UPPERMILL

The Church Inn and Belfry Function Suite

Church Lane, Off Church Road, Uppermill, Saddleworth
☎ *(01457) 820902 or 872415*
Julian Paul Taylor

Home of the Saddleworth Brewery with all brews usually available, plus occasional guest beers.

Country freehouse set in a beautiful, historic location with panoramic views and lovely patio area. Peacocks, horses, ducks, geese, cats, dogs and hens too. Caters for all age groups. Log fires in winter. Non-smoking room. Food served lunchtimes and evenings Mon–Fri and all day Sat–Sun. Children welcome. Car park. Situated in Uppermill village, turn into New Street and continue to Church Road. Pub will be found near the church.

SADDLEWORTH MORE 3.8% ABV
Amber-coloured, full-bodied session beer.
AYRTONS ALE 4.1% ABV
Fruity, strawberry blonde, not too bitter.
HOPSMACKER 4.1% ABV
A clean, pure, refreshing bitter, brewed using five different hops.
BERT CORNER 4.1% ABV
Very pale, smooth bitter – a real winner with the ladies.
BOOMTOWN BITTER 4.1% ABV
Smooth golden bitter. A celebration ale brewed to commemorate 150 years of Oldham Borough Council.
SADDLEWORTH MORE GOLD 4.6%
Amber, full-bodied bitter, much stronger version of Saddleworth More.
SHAFTBENDER 5.4% ABV
A black porter/stout bitter, extremely smooth. Nicknamed The Truth Drug – don't expect to drink too much of this and keep secrets!
CHRISTMAS CAROL 7.4% ABV
Seasonal. Liquid Christmas pudding.
Plus seasonal brews.

12–11pm (10.30pm Sun).

WIGAN

The Beer Engine

69 Poolstock Road, Wigan WN3 5DF
☎ *(01942) 321820* John Moran

Moorhouse's Pendle Witches Brew and Ruddles brews always available plus up to five guest beers (186 per year) with the emphasis on supporting the smaller brewer.

Food available on Saturday and Sunday. Function room with a capacity of 250 for hire. Three full-size snooker tables. Crown green bowling alley. Annual beer, pie and music festival in September. Twice winner of CAMRA Pub of the Year. Children allowed. Well known in Wigan, five minutes' walk from the railway station and town centre.

11am–11pm Mon–Sat; 12–10.30pm Sun.

Moon Under Water

Market Place, Wigan WN1 1PE
☎ *(01942) 323437* Paul Hammonds

A Wetherspoon's pub with Cains Mild among the beers always available, plus two guests often from East–West Ales, perhaps Brakspear Bee Sting. Two annual beer festivals.

A quiet town-centre pub with no music. Food available. No children.

OPEN All day, every day.

The Orwell

Wigan Pier, Wallgate, Wigan WN3 4EU
☎ *(01942) 323034* Dean McDonald

A freehouse. Three guest beers always available from micro-breweries whenever possible. Coach House, Titanic and Rooster's brews are recent examples.

A tourists' pub on the edge of town on the pier. Styled as a traditional Victorian cotton warehouse. Three bars, non-smoking dining area, baby changing facilities, disabled toilets, passenger lift to all floors. Benches outside. Food available lunchtimes only. Children allowed.

OPEN All day, every day.

The Tudor House Hotel

New Market Street, Wigan
☎ *(01942) 700296* Mr Miller

A freehouse with Moorhouse's Pendle Witches Brew among the beers always available plus up to four guests including Everards Tiger, Hop Back Summer Lightning, Wychwood Hobgoblin, O'Hanlon's Summer Gold and Phoenix Wobbly Bob.

A predominantly student pub with open fires, a beer garden and accommodation. Food available at lunchtime and evenings, children allowed during the day.

OPEN All day, every day.

YOU TELL US

★ *The Albion*, 600 Whitworth Road, Rochdale
★ *The Crown*, Heaton Lane, Standish
★ *The Hind's Head*, Manchester Road, Heaton Chapel
★ *The Malt & Hops*, Bradshawgate, Bolton
★ *Mash & Air*, 40 Chorlton Street, Manchester (brewpub)
★ *The Railway*, 131 High Street, Golborne
★ *The Swan Inn*, The Square, Dobcross
★ *Tandle Hill Tavern*, Thornham Lane, Middleton, Manchester

Places Featured:

Bebington
Birkenhead
Formby
Irby

Liverpool
Rainhill
St Helens
Southport

THE BREWERIES

ROBERT CAIN & CO. LTD
The Robert Cain Brewery, Stanhope Street,
Liverpool L8 5XJ
☎ *(0151) 709 8734*

DARK MILD 3.2% ABV
Very dark and distinctive.
BREWERY BITTER 3.5% ABV
Light with malt flavours.
TRADITIONAL BITTER 4.0% ABV
Occasional brew.
SUPERIOR STOUT 4.8% ABV
FORMIDABLE 5.0% ABV
Pale, well-rounded and balanced with malt and hop flavours.
Plus seasonal brews.

THE LIVERPOOL BREWING CO.
21–3 Berry Street, Liverpool L1 9DF
☎ *(0151) 709 5055*

BERRY STREET MILD 3.4% ABV
YOUNG STALLION 3.6% ABV
RED 3.8% ABV
BLONDIE 4.1% ABV
FIRST GOLD 4.2% ABV
BITTER 4.3% ABV
ROCKET 4.3% ABV
CELEBRATION 4.8% ABV

THE PASSAGEWAY BREWING CO.
Unit G8, Queen's Dock Commercial Centre,
Norfolk Street, Liverpool L1 0BG
☎ *(0151) 708 0730*

REDEMPTION 4.0% ABV
Amber and smooth, with slight toffee flavour.
GENUINE BLONDE WHEAT BEER 4.2% ABV
Pale with citrus fruit flavour.
SUMMER BALTIC ALE 4.2% ABV
Light, refreshing session ale.
BALTIC EXTRA BITTER 4.5% ABV
Brewed for the Baltic Fleet, Liverpool.
ST ARNOLD 5.0% ABV
Dark, continental-style brew.
Plus monthly brews.

THE PUBS

BEBINGTON

Traveller's Rest Hotel
169 Mount Road, Bebington, Wirral L63 8PJ
☎ *(0151) 608 2988* Alan Irving

Greene King Abbot and Cains Traditional always available, plus two guests from breweries such as Timothy Taylor, Enville, Wye Valley, Hart, Cumberland and Morland.

A rural village pub bordering fields with a view of Wales. Open fires, non-smoking lounge. Food available. No children.

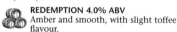 *All day, every day.*

BIRKENHEAD

The Crown & Cushion
60 Market Street, Birkenhead L41 5BT
☎ *(0151) 647 8870* Linda Chesters

Three guest ales available, perhaps Highgate Dark Mild, Morland Old Speckled Hen or a Cains brew.

A traditional town-centre pub. No food. Children allowed until 7pm.

All day, every day.

The Crown Hotel
128 Conway Street, Birkenhead L41 6JE
☎ *(0151) 647 0589* Kevin Oates

Ten cask ales usually available, with regulars being Cains Traditional Bitter and Mild.

A typical old alehouse under new management. Bar food available. Parking, darts/meeting room, beer garden. Children allowed. Head for Birkenhead town centre, not far from the Birkenhead tunnel (Europa Park).

11.30am–11pm Mon–Sat; 12–3pm and 7–10.30pm Sun.

The Dispensary

20 Chester Street, Birkenhead CH41 5DQ
☎ *(0151) 649 8259* Dean Hornby

A Cains tied house, with Traditional and Dark Mild always available, plus a selection of seasonal and special ales with at least one new one each month.

A modern, refurbished building with raised glass ceiling. Formerly a chemist, hence the new name. Used to be known as The Chester Arms. Food available at lunchtime only. Children allowed only if eating.

OPEN *All day, every day.*

The Old Colonial

167 Bridge Street, Birkenhead CH41 1AY
☎ *(0151) 650 1110* Jayne Loftus

Cains Traditional Bitter, Mild and Doctor Duncans IPA, plus seasonal brews usually available.

A friendly, traditional pub. Cask Marque award winner. Food served 12–3pm and 5–7pm Mon–Fri; 12–3pm Sat–Sun. Car park. Children welcome until 7pm, but no special facilities.

OPEN *12–11pm (10.30pm Sun).*

Freshfield Hotel

Massams Lane, Formby L37 7BD
☎ *(01704) 874871* Les Nuttall

Moorhouse's Black Cat Mild, Fuller's London Pride, Marston's Pedigree, Wadworth 6X and Castle Eden Ale usually available, plus five guest beers, often Jennings Cumberland or Bitter, Moorhouse's Pendle Witches Brew, Yates Premium, Timothy Taylor Landlord, Robinson's Best or something from Dent.

A traditional pub with polished wooden floor and log fire. Beer garden and separate music/conference room at rear. Food served 12–2pm Mon–Fri. Car park. No children.

OPEN *12–11pm (10.30pm Sun).*

Shippons Inn

Thingwall Road, Irby, Wirral CH61 3UA
☎ *(0151) 648 0449* Stephen Thompson

A freehouse serving Banks's Mild and Bitter, Cameron Strongarm and Marston's Pedigree, plus two guests, maybe a Banks's seasonal ale or a brew from Bateman, Jennings or Shepherd Neame among others.

A rustic pub with beams and stone floor. Food available 12–2.30pm. No children.

OPEN *All day, every day.*

The Brewery

21–3 Berry Street, Liverpool L1 9DF
☎ *(0151) 709 5055*

Home of the Liverpool Brewing Company. At least six beers available from the six-barrel plant. Plus occasional seasonal brews

The Brewery, previously called The Black Horse & Rainbow, was renamed when it was sold in 1996. It is still a student-based brewpub, serving real ales brewed on the premises. Bar food available.

YOUNG STALLION 3.6% ABV
RED 3.8% ABV
BLONDIE 4.1% ABV
FIRST GOLD 4.2% ABV
ROCKET 4.3% ABV
CELEBRATION 4.8% ABV

OPEN *12pm–2am.*

The Brewery Tap

Stanhope Street, Liverpool L8 5XJ
☎ *(0151) 709 2129* John Wright

Tied to the Robert Cain brewery, so Cains Bitter, Dark Mild and Formidable Ale (FA) always available, plus seasonal and special brews such as Sundowner and Dr Duncans. Also four guests, perhaps Timothy Taylor Landlord, Bateman XB and XXXB, Derwent Bitter or Exmoor Gold and Stag.

Built in 1869, winner of CAMRA's New Heritage Award 1994. Food available. Children allowed if eating.

OPEN *All day, every day.*

The Cambridge Pub

28 Picton Road, Liverpool L15 4LH
☎ *(0151) 280 5126* Joan Adali

A freehouse with Chester's Mild among the brews always available, plus two twice-monthly changing guests.

A modern pub with music. No food. No children.

OPEN *All day, every day.*

Coopers Bar

Lime Street, Liverpool L1 1JD
☎ *(0151) 709 0076* Karen Lee

A good range of real ales available.

A modern pub refurbished in summer 1999. Serving food. No children.

OPEN *7am (for breakfast) –11pm.*

Everyman Bistro

9–11 Hope Street, Liverpool L1 9BH
☎ *(0151) 708 9545* Jeff Hale

A freehouse with Marston's Pedigree, Timothy Taylor Landlord and a Cains beer always available, plus two guests such as Rooster's Yankee and Ringo or a Hanby Ales brew.

A traditional pub with restaurant. Food served all day. Children allowed.

OPEN *12pm–12am Mon–Sat; closed Sun.*

The Ship & Mitre

133 Dale Street, Liverpool L2 2JH
☎ *(0151) 236 0859* David Stevenson

Hydes' Anvil Bitter and Dark Mild always available, plus something from Rooster's and Passageway. Up to eight guests also served (650 different ales per year), plus beers from Belgium, Germany and the Czech Republic on draught.

A town-centre pub, popular with students and council staff. Four-times winner of CAMRA Merseyside Pub of the Year. Good value food served lunchtimes Mon–Fri. The pub has a starred entry in the book *Good Pub Food*. Pay and display car park opposite. Children not allowed. Near the Mersey tunnel entrance, five minutes' walk from Lime Street station and Moorfields station.

OPEN *11.30am–11pm Mon–Fri; 12.30–11pm Sat; 2.30–10.30pm Sun.*

The Swan Inn

86 Wood Street, Liverpool L1 4DQ
☎ *(0151) 709 5281* Clive Briggs

A freehouse with Marston's Pedigree, Phoenix Wobbly Bob and a Cains brew always available, plus three constantly changing guests from breweries such as Hanby Ales, Durham, Cottage, Wye Valley (Dorothy Goodbody's) or Belhaven.

A traditional back-street pub with wooden floors. Food served in separate dining area. No children. Located off Berry Street at the back of Bold Street

OPEN *All day, every day.*

Ye Cracke

13 Rice Street, Liverpool L1 9BB
☎ *(0151) 709 4171* Del Pritchard

Oak Best, Phoenix Wobbly Bob, a Cains brew and a Marston's brew always available, plus two guests from independent and micro-breweries whenever possible. Examples include Tomintoul brews, Phoenix Sticky Wicket, Cottage IPA, Brakspear Bee Sting and Rebellion Red October.

A traditional local with beer garden. Food available. Children allowed in the garden only. Located in a back street off Hope Street.

OPEN *All day, every day.*

The Manor Farm

Mill Lane, Rainhill, Prescot L35 6NE
☎ *(0151) 430 0335* Brian Maguire

A Burtonwood tied house always serving Burtonwood brews. Two other guests from a range including Wyre Piddle Piddle in the Hole.

A traditional seventeenth-century pub with restaurant and beer garden. No juke boxes. Food available. Children allowed.

OPEN *All day, every day.*

Beechams Bar & Brewery

Water Street, St Helens
☎ *(01744) 623420* Robert Barrett

Home to the Beecham Brewery with all beers usually available plus Thwaites Bitter, Daniels Hammer and Chairmans Bitter. A new brewer will be brewing his own recipe beers every four/six weeks. Six-week brewery courses available.

Situated under Beecham's clock, this is a traditional real ale house. Currently only sandwiches available; renovations taking place during the summer of 2000 will lead to a more comprehensive menu being introduced. Nearby public car park. No children.

 BELL TOWER 4.7% ABV
CRYSTAL WHEAT 5.0% ABV

OPEN *12–11pm Mon–Sat; closed Sun.*

Barons Bar in The Scarisbrick Hotel

Lord Street, Southport PR8 1NZ
☎ *(01704) 543000* Sharon Morgan

A freehouse always serving Morland Old Speckled Hen plus brews such as Cains' Traditional, Fuller's London Pride, Timothy Taylor Landlord and Shepherd Neame Bishop's Finger on a guest basis.

A recently refurbished pub with open fire. Bar snacks only in the pub, but there is a restaurant in the adjoining hotel. Children not allowed in the bar.

OPEN *All day, every day.*

Blakes Hotel and Pizza Pub

19 Queens Road, Southport PR9 9HN
☎ *(01704) 500811* Philip Ball

Marston's Bitter, Adnams Best, Fuller's London Pride, Moorhouse's Black Cat Mild and Pendle Witches Brew and Timothy Taylor Landlord always available, plus three constantly rotating guests including, perhaps, Banks's Bitter, another Moorhouse's ale or a Bateman brew.

A family-run freehouse just outside the town centre, anxious to promote the real ale cause, with an extended bar. Music. Pizzas served from 5–11pm. Children allowed. Car park and accommodation. Look behind the fire station.

4–11pm Mon–Fri; 12–11pm Sat–Sun.

Wetherspoons

93 Lord Street, Southport PR8 1RH
☎ *(01704) 530217* Donna Pagett

A Wetherspoon's pub. Regular guest beers served on two pumps include Cotleigh Osprey, Hop Back Summer Lightning and brews from Burton Bridge, Spinnaker (Brewery on Sea), Hook Norton, Everards, Ash Vine and Banks and Taylor.

An old-fashioned, quiet, drinker's pub. Food available. No children.

All day, every day.

Places Featured:

Attleborough
Blickling
Burnham Thorpe
Burston
Cantley
Coltishall
Colton
Downham Market
Erpingham
Fakenham
Foulden
Gorleston
Great Yarmouth
Gressenhall
Happisburgh
Hilborough
Hingham
Hockwold
Kenninghall
King's Lynn
Larling
Little Dunham
Lynford

Mundford
Northwold
Norwich
Pulham St Mary
Reedham
Reepham
Ringstead
Sheringham
Stiffkey
Stowbridge
Swanton Morley
Thornham
Toft Monks
Walsingham
Warham
West Rudham
West Somerton
Whinburgh
Winterton-on-Sea
Wiveton
Woodbastwick
Wreningham
Wymondham

THE BREWERIES

BUFFY'S BREWERY

Mardle Hall, Rectory Road, Tivetshall St Mary MR15 2DD
☎ *(01379) 676523*

NORFOLK TERRIER 3.6% ABV
Light and quenching with good hop character.
BITTER 3.9% ABV
Easy-drinking, well-hopped brew.
MILD 4.2% ABV
Smooth, dark mild.
POLLY'S FOLLY 4.3% ABV
Traditional bitter.
HOPLEAF 4.5% ABV
Pale beer brewed with lager malt and yeast.
IPA 4.6% ABV
Superb, genuine IPA.
NORWEGIAN BLUE 4.9% ABV
Balanced, tawny brew with citrus fruit flavour.
POLLY'S EXTRA FOLLY 4.9% ABV
Stronger version of Polly's Folly.
ALE 5.5% ABV
Well-rounded and hoppy.
FESTIVAL 9X 9.0% ABV
Powerful malt and fruit flavour.

CHALK HILL BREWERY

Rosary Road, Thorpe Hamlet, Norwich NR1 4DA
☎ *(01603) 477077*

TAP BITTER 3.6% ABV
CHB 4.2% ABV
DREADNOUGHT 4.9% ABV
FLINTKNAPPER'S MILD 5.0% ABV
OLD TACKLE 5.6% ABV

HUMPTY DUMPTY BREWERY

Stables Brewhouse, 17 The Havaker, Reedham NR13 3HG
☎ *(01493) 701818*

 MILD 3.5% ABV
Flavoursome mild.
NORD ATLANTIC 3.7% ABV
Red-coloured, easy quaffer.
LITTLE SHARPIE 3.8% ABV
Pale and quenching.
CHOPPER 4.0% ABV
LEMON GINGER 4.0% ABV
TENDER BEHIND 4.0% ABV
Spicy wheat beer.
HUMPTY DUMPTY 4.1% ABV
Easy-drinking, hoppy brew.
OPS ON TRAIN 4.1% ABV
Dry-hopped, gold-coloured beer.
BRIEF ENCOUNTER 4.3% ABV
CLAUD HAMILTON 4.3% ABV
Oyster stout.
STOKER 4.5% ABV
Pale ale.
BUTT JUMPER 4.8% ABV
Sweet malt flavour.
SPARK ARREST 4.8% ABV
Malt predominates in this award-winning brew.
RAILWAY SLEEPER 5.0% ABV
Good hoppy bitterness throughout.
GOBBLER 5.5% ABV
Powerful, with lots of flavour.

THE ICENI BREWERY

3 Foulden Road, Ickburgh IP26 5GJ
☎ *(01842) 878922*

 BOADICEA 3.8% ABV
Full-flavoured and hoppy with some fruit.
CELTIC QUEEN 4.0% ABV
Flavoursome easy drinker.
FINE SOFT DAY 4.0% ABV
Maple syrup and hops give bittersweet flavour.
FEN TIGER 4.2% ABV
Malty with coriander.
FOUR GRAINS 4.2% ABV
Rounded, fruity flavour.
CU CHULAINN 4.3% ABV
Full-bodied with slight toffee sweetness.
DEIRDRE OF THE SORROWS 4.4% ABV
Amber and complex.
ROISIN DUBH 4.4% ABV
Dark and sweet.
KIWI 4.5% ABV
Smooth and easy-drinking, with kiwi fruit.
ICENI GOLD 5.0% ABV
Golden and refreshing.
WINTER LIGHTNING 5.0% ABV
Light, smooth and refreshing.

OLD CHIMNEYS BREWERY

The Street, Market Weston, Diss IP22 2NZ
☎ *(01359) 221411*

MILITARY MILD 3.4% ABV
SWALLOWTAIL IPA 3.6% ABV
Plus seasonal and occasional brews.

REEPHAM BREWERY

Unit 1, Collers Way, Reepham NR10 4SW
☎ *(01603) 871091*

GRANARY BITTER 3.8% ABV
RAPIER PALE ALE 4.3% ABV
NORFOLK WHEATEN 4.5% ABV
VELVET STOUT 4.5% ABV
Plus seasonal brews.

WOLF BREWERY

10 Maurice Gaymer Road, Attleborough NR17 2QZ
☎ *(01953) 457775*

WOLF IN SHEEPS CLOTHING 3.8% ABV
Smooth and malty.
GOLDEN JACKAL 3.7% ABV
BEST BITTER 3.9% ABV
Rounded with good hoppiness.
COYOTE 4.3% ABV
Golden with floral hoppiness.
GRANNY WOULDN'T LIKE IT 4.8% ABV
Complex, malty flavour.
WOILD MOILD 4.8% ABV
Dark, smooth and fruity.
TIMBER WOLF 5.8% ABV
Plus occasional brews.

WOODFORDE'S NORFOLK ALES

Broadland Brewery, Woodbastwick, Norwich NR13 6SW
☎ *(01603) 720353*

MARDLER'S 3.5% ABV
Light, mid-coloured mild.
KETT'S REBELLION 3.6% ABV
Balanced, easy drinker.
WHERRY 3.8% ABV
Superb, well-hopped session ale.
GREAT EASTERN ALE 4.3% ABV
Golden with malt flavour.
NELSON'S REVENGE 4.5% ABV
Flavoursome throughout.
NORFOLK NOG 4.6% ABV
Smooth chocolate malt flavour.
NORKIE 5.0% ABV
Pale and malty. Brewed with lager malt.
HEADCRACKER 7.0% ABV
Fruity and easy to drink for gravity.

THE PUBS

ATTLEBOROUGH

The Griffin Hotel
Attleborough NR17 2AH
☎ *(01953) 452149* Richard Ashbourne

Wolf Best, Coyote and Granny Wouldn't Like It plus Greene King Abbot always available. Also one hand pump serving a guest ale from a range of small breweries.

A sixteenth-century freehouse in the centre of town. Beams, log fires, dining area, accommodation. Food available at lunchtime and evenings. Children allowed.

OPEN *10.30am–3.30pm and 5.30–11pm.*

BLICKLING

The Buckinghamshire Arms
Blickling, Nr Aylsham NR11 6NF
☎ *(01263) 732133* Mark Stubley

Woodforde's Wherry and Blickling (house beer from Woodforde's) plus Adnams brews usually available.

An olde-English, food-oriented freehouse with small bar, log fires and beer garden. Food available at lunchtime and evenings in separate restaurant. Children allowed.

OPEN *11.30am–3pm and 6–11pm.*

BURNHAM THORPE

The Lord Nelson
Walsingham Road, Burnham Thorpe, King's Lynn PE31 8HN
☎ *(01328) 738241* Miss L Stafford

A Greene King house with Abbot, IPA and XX Mild always available, plus Woodforde's Wherry.

A 355-year-old village pub in the birthplace of Nelson. Log fires, beer garden. Food available at lunchtime and evenings. Children allowed.

OPEN *11am–3pm and 6–11pm Mon–Sat; 12–3pm and 7–10.30pm Sun.*

BURSTON

The Crown Inn
Crown Green, Burston, Diss
☎ *(01379) 741257* Valerie Whitehead

Adnams Bitter and three or four guest beers usually available, perhaps from Hampshire, Hop Back, Iceni, Old Chimneys, Burton Bridge, Fenland, Cottage, York, Smiles or other breweries.

A 300-year-old village pub with inglenook fireplace and lots of beams. Food served every lunchtime and evening. Bowling green. Car park. Well-behaved children welcome.

OPEN *12–2.30pm and 6–11pm Mon–Sat; 12–3pm and 7–10.30pm Sun.*

CANTLEY

The Cock Tavern
Manor Road, Cantley NR13 3JQ
☎ *(01493) 700895* Mr and Mrs Johnson

Samuel Smith OBB always available plus four guest beers (100+ per year) including Wild's Wild Blonde, Nethergate Old Growler, Burton Bridge, Woodforde's and Nene Valley brews.

A traditional country pub not far from Norwich with many separate areas, a beamed ceiling and two open fires. Bar food is available at lunchtime and evenings. Car park, garden and children's room. Caravan Club campsite nearby. Turn right off the A47 (Norwich to Yarmouth road) near Acle, then signposted Cantley. Approx four miles from the turn.

OPEN *11am–3.30pm and 6–11pm Mon–Fri; 7–11pm Sat; 12–10.30pm Sun.*

COLTISHALL

The Red Lion
77 Church Street, Coltishall NR12 7DW
☎ *(01603) 737402* Mrs Melanie Bird

Adnams Southwold Bitter and Greene King Abbot Ale usually available plus a guest, often from Woodforde's, who also brew Weaselpis, the house beer.

Olde-worlde, 350-year-old pub full of nooks and crannies, with oak beams and log fires. Food served lunchtimes and evenings Mon–Fri and all day Sat–Sun and bank holidays. Car park. Large beer garden with children's play area. An indoor, soft play area is planned.

OPEN *11am–3pm and 5–11pm Mon–Fri; 11am–11pm Sat and bank holidays; 12–10.30pm Sun.*

COLTON

The Ugly Bug Inn
High House Farm Lane, Colton, Norwich
☎ *(01603) 880794* Peter William Crowland

Iceni Ugly Bug Ale, Greene King Abbot Ale and four guest beers usually available, perhaps from Fuller's, Woodforde's, Elgood's, Shepherd Neame, Buffy's, Iceni or Bateman.

Farm building conversion with informal atmosphere. Restaurant, grounds and lakes of three acres. Food served 12–2pm and 7–9.30pm daily. Patio dining in summer. Ample parking. Children welcome, provided they are supervised if near the deep lakes.

OPEN *12–3pm and 5.30–11pm Mon–Sat; 12–3pm and 7–10.30pm Sun.*

DOWNHAM MARKET

The Crown Hotel
Bridge Street, Downham Market PE38 9DH
☎ *(01366) 382322* Mrs N Hayes

A freehouse with Bateman XB and Charles Wells Bombardier always available, plus a guest which might be Wyre Piddle Piddle in the Wind, Sheperd Neame Spitfire or Charles Wells Summer Solstice.

An olde-worlde pub with open fires. Food available at lunchtime and evenings in two restaurants. No children.

11am–2.30pm and 5–11pm Mon–Thurs; all day Fri–Sat; 12–3pm and 7–10.30pm Sun.

ERPINGHAM

The Spread Eagle
Erpingham, Norwich NR11 7QA
☎ *(01263) 761591* Billie Carder

Woodforde's Wherry, Adnams Regatta and Greene King Abbot always on offer. Also two guests which could be something like Morland Old Speckled Hen or another Woodforde's brew such as Headcracker.

A traditional pub with open fires, non-smoking dining area, pool room and beer garden. Food available at lunchtime and evenings, with roasts on Sundays (booking advisable). Well-behaved children and dogs welcome.

11am–3pm and 6.30–11pm Mon–Sat; 12–3pm and 7–10.30pm Sun.

FAKENHAM

The Bull
Bridge Street, Fakenham NR21 9AG
☎ *(01325) 862560* Graham Blanchfield

Home of Blanchfields Brewery. At least three beers brewed and served on the premises. Other seasonal ales as available.

A nineteenth-century pub with two small bar rooms and a dining area. Food available at lunchtime only. Children allowed. Brewery viewing by arrangement.

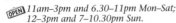

BLACK BULL MILD 3.6% ABV
A traditional dark mild.
BULL BEST BITTER 3.9% ABV
Hoppy bitter.
THE WHITE BULL 4.4% ABV
A seasonal wheat beer available in summer only.
RAGING BULL 4.9% ABV
Strong malty flavoured bitter. Also available in bottles.

11am–3pm and 7–11pm Mon–Wed; 11am–11pm Thurs–Sat; 12–10.30pm Sun.

FOULDEN

The White Hart Inn
White Hart Street, Foulden, Thetford IP26 5AW
☎ *(01366) 328638* Sylvia Chisholm

A freehouse serving Greene King IPA, Mild, XS and Abbot plus two guests such as Shepherd Neame Spitfire or other customer requests.

A traditional pub with dining area, fires and beer garden. Live music on Friday or Saturday. Biker-friendly. Food available at lunchtime and evenings. Children allowed.

11am–3.30pm and 6–11pm.

GORLESTON

The Cliff Hotel
Gorleston NR31 6DH
☎ *(01493) 662179*
Rodney Scott and Vaughan Cutter

Fuller's London Pride, Greene King IPA, Woodforde's Wherry and Marston's Pedigree usually available.

Hotel with two bars and two restaurants overlooking Gorleston beach and harbour. Food served 12–2.30pm and 7–9.30pm every day. Children welcome in gardens or hotel only, not in the bars. Two car parks.

11am–11pm.

GREAT YARMOUTH

The Mariner's Tavern
69 Howard Street South, Great Yarmouth NE30 1LN
☎ *(01493) 332299* Mr Munro

Fuller's London Pride, Highgate Dark, Greene King Abbot and beers from Adnams always available. One guest changed each weekend. Recent brews have included Thwaites Bloomin Ale and Greene King Triumph.

A small traditional pub with log fires. Snacks only. Children allowed. Ring for directions.

11am–3pm and 7–11pm Mon–Sat; closed Sun.

ICENI GOLD

A.B.V. 5.0%

ICENI BREWERY NORFOLK

The Red Herring

24–5 Havelock Road, Great Yarmouth
NR30 3HQ
☎ *(01493) 853384*
Audrey and Graham Bould

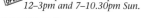 A freehouse with Adnams Best and Elgood's Black Dog Mild always available. Four constantly changing guests such as Greene King Triumph, Woodforde's Wherry, Buffy's Bitter, Mauldons White Adder and Suffolk Pride or Nethergate and Green Jack brews.

An old-fashioned, country-style pub in a town location. Home-made bar food available. Children allowed. Ring for directions.

11am–3pm and 6–11pm Mon–Sat;
12–3pm and 7–10.30pm Sun.

GRESSENHALL

The Swan

The Green, Gressenhall, Dereham NR20 4DU
☎ *(01632) 860340* Mr Mansfield

Greene King IPA always available, plus two guests such as Marston's Pedigree or Young's Bitter.

A family-oriented country pub with dining area, log fires and beer garden. Food available at lunchtime and evenings. Children allowed.

12–2.30pm and 6–11pm Mon–Sat;
12–3pm and 7–10.30pm Sun.

HAPPISBURGH

Hill House

Happisburgh NR12 0PW
☎ *(01692) 650004* Clive and Sue Stockton

Buffy's Hill House Elementary Ale, Shepherd Neame Spitfire and two guest beers regularly available, perhaps from Church End, Black Sheep, Wolf, Adnams, Concertina or Ossett.

Coastal coaching inn known for its Sherlock Holmes connection. Restaurant and large garden. Food served 12–2.30pm and 7–9.30pm daily. 'Kids' Bar' open during school holidays. Car park.

Winter: 12–3pm and 7–11pm (10.30pm Sun). Summer: 12–11pm (10.30pm Sun).

HILBOROUGH

The Swan

Hilborough, Thetford IP26 5BW
☎ *(01760) 756380* Mr Wallis

Greene King Abbot and IPA, Bateman Mild and an Adnams beer always available, plus a guest which changes once a fortnight and may well be a Greene King seasonal or special brew.

An olde-worlde pub with log fires, beer garden and accommodation. Smallholding with animals. Food available at lunchtime and evenings. Children allowed.

11am–3.30pm and 6–11pm.

HINGHAM

The White Hart Hotel

3 Market Place, Hingham, Norwich NR9 4AF
☎ *(01953) 850214* Fax *(01953) 851950*
Les and Carol Foster

Greene King IPA and Abbot always available plus two guests.

The only pub in Hingham, this is a family-oriented pub and restaurant with beer garden and accommodation. Food available at lunchtime and evenings. Children allowed.

12–11pm Mon–Sat; 12–5pm and
7–10.30pm Sun.

HOCKWOLD

The Red Lion

Main Street, Hockwold IP26 4NB
☎ *(01842) 828875* Mrs Miles

Greene King IPA always available plus two guests which change fortnightly. A beer festival is held each August bank holiday.

A village pub and restaurant. Children allowed.

12–2.30pm and 6–11pm Sun–Fri;
12–11pm Sat.

KENNINGHALL

The Red Lion

East Church Street, Kenninghall, Diss NR16 2EP
☎ *(01953) 887849* Mandy and Bruce Berry

A freehouse with Greene King IPA, Abbot, Triumph and Mild always available, plus two guests such as Fuller's London Pride or brews from local breweries such as Wolf or Elgood's.

A one-bar village pub with beams, open fires, bare stone floors and floorboards. The snug is part of a listed building. Bar food available at lunchtimes and evenings every day, and the restaurant is open all day. Beer garden. Children allowed, but not in the bar area. Bed and breakfast accommodation available.

12–3pm and 6.30–11pm Mon–Thurs;
12–11pm Fri–Sat; 12–10.30pm Sun.

KING'S LYNN

Stuart House Hotel

35 Goodwins Road, King's Lynn PE30 5QX
☎ *(01553) 772169* David Armes

Adnams Best Bitter and Broadside plus Woodforde's Wherry and Greene King IPA usually available. One guest beer is also served, such as Timothy Taylor Landlord, Fuller's London Pride, Woodforde's Nelson's Revenge, Oakham JHB or Mompessons Gold.

A family-run hotel, quietly situated within its own grounds in the centre of King's Lynn. Cosy bar with a real fire in winter and doors that open on to the garden in summer. Regular entertainment. Bar menu and à la carte restaurant. Food served 7–9.30pm daily. Car park. Well-behaved children welcome until 8.30pm. Pets' corner in garden.

OPEN *6–11pm Mon–Sat; 12–3pm and 6–10.30pm Sun.*

LARLING

The Angel Inn

Larling, Norwich NR16 2QU
☎ *(01953) 717963* Mr Stammers

Adnams Southwold Bitter and three guest beers usually available, perhaps from Iceni, Woodforde's, Wolf, Mauldons, Orkney or Cottage.

A 400-year-old village pub with quarry-tiled, beamed public bar, real fire and local atmosphere. Live music Thursday evening. Two dining rooms. En-suite accommodation. Food served lunchtimes and evenings. Car park. Children welcome in the lounge and picnic area. Small, fenced play area outside.

OPEN *10am–11pm Mon–Sat; 12–10.30pm Sun.*

LITTLE DUNHAM

The Black Swan

The Street, Little Dunham, King's Lynn PE32 2DG
☎ *(01760) 722200* Mr Budd

A freehouse with two constantly changing real ales always available.

A country pub with log fires, restaurant and beer garden. Food available lunchtimes and evenings. Children allowed. Located off the A47.

OPEN *12–2pm and 7–11pm Mon–Fri; 12–11pm Sat; 12–10.30pm Sun.*

LYNFORD

Lynford Hall

Lynford, Thetford IP26 5HW
☎ *(01842) 878351* Peter Scopes

Adnams Best and Woodforde's Wherry available.

Pub located within Lynford Hall, a stately home and tourist attraction open to the public. Separate restaurant and beer garden. Food available. Children allowed.

OPEN *11am–11pm.*

MUNDFORD

The Crown Hotel

Crown Street, Mundford, Nr Thetford IP26 5HQ
☎ *(01362) 637647* Barry Walker

Seven beers always available including Samuel Smith OBB, Woodforde's Norfolk Wherry and Marston's Pedigree plus more than 100 guests per year including all Iceni brews, Morland Old Speckled Hen, Woodforde's Nelson's Revenge and Mauldons brews.

A sixteenth-century beamed pub with open fires in winter. Bar and restaurant food available at lunchtime and evenings. Pool and darts, car park, garden, function room, accommodation. Children allowed.

OPEN *11am–11pm Mon–Sat; 12–10.30pm Sun.*

NORTHWOLD

The Crown Inn

High Street, Northwold, Thetford IP26 5LA
☎ *(01366) 727317* Rona Bryan

A freehouse. Greene King IPA and Abbot always available plus two local beers available as guests. Breweries favoured include Iceni, Nethergate and Burton Bridge.

A village pub with log fires and beer garden. Food available at lunchtime and evenings. Children allowed.

OPEN *12–3pm and 6–11pm Mon–Fri; all day Sat; 12–3pm and 7–10.30pm Sun.*

NORWICH

Alexandra Tavern

Stafford Street, Norwich NR2 3BB
☎ *(01603) 627772* JL Little

A freehouse with Chalk Hill Best, Flintknapper's Mild, IPA and Dreadnought, Marston's Pedigree and Adnams Best always available. Guests on two hand pumps tend to be local brews such as Green Jack Summer Dream.

A traditional local with log fires in winter. Snacks only. Children allowed until 7pm.

OPEN *All day, every day.*

Billy Bluelight

27 Hall Road, Norwich NR1 3MQ
☎ *(01603) 623768*
Paul Unstead and Rosie Marie Law

Woodforde's Mild, Bluelight, Wherry, Great Eastern, Nelson's Revenge, Norkie, Norfolk Nog and Headcracker usually available, plus four guest beers which may include other Woodforde's brews, Hop Back Summer Lightning or Thunderstorm, Shepherd Neame Bishop's Finger or beers from Smiles, Bateman, Wychwood or Morrells.

Themed 1930s/1940s-style pub. No fruit machine, juke box or pool table. Beer garden with petanque, piste and full-size skittle alley in the functions room. Food served lunchtimes and evenings Mon–Fri, lunchtimes only Sat–Sun. Children welcome until 9pm each day. Located on the junction of Queens and Hall roads.

OPEN *11am–11pm Mon–Sat; 12–10.30pm Sun.*

Coach & Horses

82 Thorpe Road, Norwich NR1 1BA
☎ *(01603) 477077* Bob Cameron

Up to nine beers available at any one time including Chalk Hill Tap, Best, Dreadnought and Old Tackle plus Timothy Taylor Landlord. Guests include Hop Back Summer Lightning, Cheriton Digger's Gold, Otter Bright and Coach House Gunpowder Mild.

Busy old-style pub with open fires. Bar food available at lunchtime and evenings. Children allowed.

OPEN *11am–11pm Mon–Sat; 12–10.30pm Sun.*

Eaton Cottage

75 Mount Pleasant, Norwich NR2 2DQ
☎ *(01603) 453048* Mr M Howard

Marston's Pedigree, Adnams Best and Wolf Old Etonian always available. Four other guests such as Adnams Regatta, Woodforde's Broadsman, Morland Old Speckled Hen, Elgood's Golden Newt and Fuller's London Pride.

A basic traditional corner freehouse. No food. No children.

OPEN *11am–11pm (10.30pm Sun).*

The Fat Cat

49 West End Street, Norwich NR2 4NA
☎ *(01603) 624364*

Up to 25 beers available at any one time. Regulars include Adnams Best, Woodforde's Nelson's Revenge, Kelham Island Pale Rider, Greene King Abbot and a guest list that now runs into thousands.

A traditional Victorian pub decorated with breweriana and pub signs. Bar food available at lunchtime. Street parking. Children not allowed.

OPEN *12–11pm Mon–Fri; 11am–11pm Sat; 12–10.30pm Sun.*

The Jubilee

26 St Leonards Road, Norwich NR11 4BL
☎ *(01603) 618734*
Tim Wood and Teresa Santos

Wadworth 6X, Fuller's London Pride, Greene King Abbot, Jubilee Ale and Triumph always available, plus three other guests including, perhaps, Hop Back Summer Lightning.

A traditional freehouse with beer garden and adults' games room. Food available at lunchtime only. Children allowed until 5pm.

OPEN *All day, every day.*

The Mustard Pot

101 Thorpe Road, Norwich NR1 1TR
☎ *(01603) 432393* Jason Bates

An Adnams house with Best, Broadside and Extra always available, plus Regatta when in season. A range of guest ales such as Charles Wells Summer Solstice or Fuller's London Pride is also served.

A drinkers' pub with beer garden and food available at lunchtime and evenings. No children.

OPEN *All day, every day.*

The Old White Lion

73 Oak Street, Norwich NR3 3AR
☎ *(01603) 620630* Nick Ray (Manager)

Greene King IPA, Woodforde's Wherry, Fuller's London Pride and Adnams Southwold always available, plus around eight guest beers every week.

A 450-year-old pub with old beams, slate floors, and lots of wood and brass. Colourfully decorated with flowers on the outside. Candles every evening. Food available 12–10.30pm – phone orders taken. On the inner ring road going anti-clockwise, first left before river on the east side.

OPEN *11am–11pm Mon–Sat; 12–10.30pm Sun.*

The Ribs of Beef

24 Wensum Street, Norwich NR3 1HY
☎ *(01603) 619517* Julia Cawdron

A freehouse serving 11 cask ales such as Marston's Pedigree, Woodforde's Wherry and Headcracker, Fuller's London Pride and Adnams brews, plus two guests changing twice-weekly. These might be something like Brakspear Bee Sting or Adnams Regatta.

A popular local situated near the river with private jetty. Food available at lunchtime and evenings. Children allowed. Website: www.ribsofbeef.co.uk

OPEN *All day, every day.*

Rosary Tavern

95 Rosary Road, Norwich
☎ *(01603) 666287* Ian Bushell

Seven real ales always available. Adnams Best and Bateman XB on permanently plus five constantly changing guests. Also sells real Norfolk cider.

A traditional pub with a friendly atmosphere. Bar food available at lunchtime, with roasts on Sun, and Mon–Sat evening. Car park, beer garden and function room. Easy to find, near the yacht and railway station, and the football ground.

OPEN *11.30am–11pm Mon–Sat; 12–10.30pm Sun.*

St Andrew's Tavern

4 St Andrews Street, Norwich NR2 4AF
☎ *(01603) 614858*
Jenny Watt and Alan Allred

An Adnams house serving nine cask ales, including the full range of Adnams brews. A cask mild is always available, and guests may come from Ushers, Jennings, Bateman, Fuller's, Elgood's, Badger, Robinson's or Charles Wells.

A friendly, traditional city-centre pub. Good value food available at lunchtimes, including home-cooked specials. Terrace garden and cellar bar. Children not allowed. At the junction of Duke Street and St John Maddermarket opposite St Andrews car park.

OPEN *All day, every day.*

Seamus O'Rourke's

92 Pottergate, Norwich NR2 1DZ
☎ *(01603) 626627* Phil Adams

A freehouse with Adnams Best and O'Rourke's Revenge (house beer) always available, plus up to eight guests including Charles Wells Bombardier, Wolf Coyote, Iceni Fine Soft Day, Scott's Blues and Boater or a Burton Bridge beer.

Irish sports themed pub with open fires and food available at lunchtime. No children.

OPEN *All day, every day (except Christmas Day 12–3.30pm).*

The Steam Packet

39 Crown Road, Norwich NR1 3DT
☎ *(01603) 441545* Nicola Maton

An Adnams house with Best permanently available, plus guests served on three pumps. Other Adnams ales such as Broadside and Millennium, and seasonal ales like Regatta are featured, plus a few beers from other breweries, such as Fuller's London Pride.

A 200-year-old traditional local. The pub has a 'bring your own food' policy – cutlery and condiments are provided. Children welcome. Separate room available for booking.

OPEN *Summer: 11am–11pm Mon–Sat; 12–10.30pm Sun. Winter: closed Sun lunchtime.*

The Trafford Arms

61 Grove Road, Norwich NR1 3RL
☎ *(01603) 628466* Chris and Glynis Higgins

Adnams Bitter, Woodforde's Mardler's and Barley Boy house bitter brewed by Woodforde's, usually available. A mild is always served and guest beers may include Sarah Hughes Ruby Mild, Burton Bridge Porter, Bateman Dark Mild, Elgood's Black Dog Mild, Timothy Taylor Landlord or brews from Mauldons, Rooster's or Reepham.

A welcoming community pub, just out of the city centre. Cosmopolitan collection of customers from all walks of life. No loud music, just a cacophony of chatting voices. Food served lunchtimes only (or evenings by arrangement). Limited parking. No children. Situated very close to Sainsburys on Queens Road.

OPEN *11am–11pm Mon–Sat; 12–10.30pm Sun.*

The York Tavern

1 Leicester Street, Norwich NR22 2AS
☎ *(01603) 620918* Mr Verret

Adnams ales usually available, plus guests such as Wadworth 6X, Marston's Pedigree or Morland Old Speckled Hen.

An old-fashioned London-style pub with open fires, restaurant and beer garden. Food available at lunchtime and evenings. Children allowed in the restaurant only.

OPEN *11am–11pm.*

PULHAM ST MARY

The King's Head

The Street, Pulham St Mary IP21 4RD
☎ *(01379) 676318* Graham Scott

Adnams Best always available plus three guests (150 per year) including Marston's Pedigree, Wadworth 6X, Shepherd Neame Spitfire, Woodforde's Wherry Best and brews from Buffy's, Brains, Robinson's and Scott's.

Built in the 1600s, this pub has an old oak timber frame with exposed beams. Bar and restaurant food available at lunchtime and evenings. Non-smoking dining area, bowling green, paddock, car park, garden, children's area, accommodation. Off the A140 to Harlesdon, on the B1134.

11.30am–3pm and 5.30–11pm Mon–Fri; all day Sat–Sun.

REEDHAM

The Railway Tavern

17 The Havaker, Reedham NR13 3HG
☎ *(01493) 700340*
Mrs Cathy Swan and Mr Ivor Cuders

Woodforde's and Adnams ales always available plus many guest beers including those from Scott's, Chalk Hill and Elgood's breweries. Four beer festivals held so far.

A listed Victorian railway hotel freehouse. CAMRA award. No fruit machines. Bar and restaurant food is available at lunchtime and evenings. Car park, garden and children's room. Take the A47 south of Acle, then six miles on the B1140. By rail from Norwich, Gt Yarmouth or Lowestoft.

12–3pm and 6.30–11pm Mon–Thurs; all day Fri–Sat; normal Sun hours.

REEPHAM

The Crown

Ollands Road, Reepham, Norwich NR10 4EJ
☎ *(01603) 870964* Mr Good

Marston's Pedigree and Greene King Abbot among the beers always available.

A village pub with dining area and beer garden. Food available at lunchtime and evenings. Children allowed.

12–3pm and 7–11pm Mon–Sat; 12–5pm and 7–10.30pm Sun.

The Old Brewery House Hotel

Market Place, Reepham, Norwich NR10 4JJ
☎ *(01603) 870881* Sarah Gardener

A freehouse with Greene King Abbot, Adnams beers and a house bitter always available, plus one changing guest which will be something like Morland Old Speckled Hen, Adnams Regatta or another local brew.

An olde-worlde pub with beams, log fires, restaurant, beer garden and accommodation. Food available at lunchtime and evenings. Children allowed.

11am–11pm.

RINGSTEAD

The Gin Trap Inn

Ringstead, Nr Hunstanton PO36 5JU
☎ *(01485) 525264*
Brian and Margaret Harmes

A freehouse with a house beer brewed by Woodforde's called Gin Trap always available, plus Norfolk Nog, Greene King Abbot and an Adnams ale. One other guest served.

A 350-year-old traditional English pub. Dining area, beer garden, self-catering accommodation. Food available at lunchtime and evenings. Children allowed. Ring for directions.

11.30am–2.30pm and 6.30–11pm Mon–Sat; 12–2.30pm and 6.45–10.30pm Sun.

SHERINGHAM

The Windham Arms

15 Wyndham Street, Sheringham NR26 8BA
☎ *(01263) 822609* Mr Thomas

Woodforde's Wherry and Mardler's Ale and Greene King Abbot and IPA always available, plus a wide selection of guest ales served on three hand pumps (never the same beer twice). An annual beer festival is held on the first weekend in July with 20 different guest beers on offer.

A large pub with restaurant, log fires, beer garden. Food available at lunchtime and evenings. Children allowed.

All day, every day.

The Red Lion

*44 Wells Road, Stiffkey, Wells-next-the-Sea
NR23 1AJ*
☎ *(01328) 830552* Matthew Rees

A freehouse with Woodforde's Wherry, Adnams Best and Greene King Abbot always available, plus two guests, perhaps seasonal Woodforde's ales such as Great Eastern in Summer or Norfolk Nog in Winter, or Elgood's Black Dog Mild, Wolf Best, or something from Nethergate, Green Jack or other local breweries.

An old, rustic pub with tiled floor, log fires and beer garden. Food available at lunchtime and evenings. Children and dogs welcome. Located on the main A149.

OPEN *11am–3pm and 6–11pm.*

The Heron

Station Road, Stowbridge, King's Lynn PE34 3PH
☎ *(01366) 384147* Nick and Brenda Frost

A freehouse with Greene King IPA and Abbot plus Adnams Best always available. Also three guests including, perhaps, Woodforde's Wherry, Charles Wells Bombardier or Morland Old Speckled Hen.

A 150-year-old traditional pub with log fires, beer garden and accommodation. Food available at lunchtime and evenings. Children allowed. Situated between two rivers, ring for directions if necessary.

OPEN *11am–2pm and 7–11pm Mon–Thurs and Sat; 11am–2pm and 5–11pm Fri; 12–4pm and 7–10pm Sun.*

The Angel Inn

Greengate, Swanton Morley, Norwich NR20 4LX
☎ *(01362) 637407* David Ashford

A freehouse with Samuel Smith Old Brewery Bitter always available. Two guests such as Greene King Abbot.

A country village pub dating from 1609 with log fires, beer garden and bowling green. No food. Children allowed.

OPEN *12–11pm Mon–Sat; 12–3pm and 7–10.30pm Sun.*

Darby's Freehouse

*1 Elsing Road, Swanton Morley, Dereham
NR20 4JU*
☎ *(01362) 637647*
John Carrick and Louise Battle

A Greene King tied house with IPA and Abbot always available, plus Greene King seasonals rotating on two other pumps.

A genuine, family-owned and -run freehouse converted from two derelict farm cottages. Traditional English and Thai cuisine available at lunchtime and evenings. Attached to a nearby farmhouse that offers accommodation and camping. Car park, garden and children's room and playground. Take the B1147 from Dereham to Bawdeswell, turn right on to Elsing Road at Swanton Morley.

OPEN *11.30am–3pm and 6–11pm Mon–Fri; 11am–11pm Sat; 12–10.30pm Sun.*

The Lifeboat Inn

Ship Lane, Thornham, Hunstanton PE36 6LT
☎ *(01485) 512236* Mr and Mrs Coker

Adnams, Greene King and Woodforde's ales always available plus a couple of guest beers, mainly from small independents including Tolly Cobbold.

A sixteenth-century smugglers' alehouse with wood beams, hanging paraffin lamps and open fires overlooking salt marshes. Bar and restaurant food available at lunchtime and evenings. Car park, garden and accommodation. Children allowed. Turn first left when entering the village from Hunstanton.

OPEN *All day, every day.*

Toft Lion

Toft Monks, Nr Beccles NR34 0EP
☎ *(01502) 677702* Jan and Giles Mortimer

Adnams Bitter and Broadside regularly available. Two weekly changing guest beers, often from local breweries, are also served.

The Toft Lion has been a pub since 1650 and offers home-cooked food, log fires, beer garden and en-suite accommodation. Dogs and well-behaved children welcome.

OPEN *11.30am–2.30pm and 5–11pm (10.30pm Sun).*

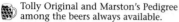

WALSINGHAM

The Bull Inn

Common Place, Shire Hall Plain, Walsingham
NR22 6BP
☎ *(01328) 820333* Philip Horan

Tolly Original and Marston's Pedigree among the beers always available.

A 600-year-old olde-worlde pub with open fires, restaurant, beer garden and accommodation. Food available at lunchtime and evenings. Children allowed.

11am–3pm and 6–11pm Mon–Sat;
12–3pm and 7–10.30pm Sun.

WARHAM

The Three Horseshoes

Bridge Street, Warham, Wells-next-the-Sea
NR23 1NL
☎ *(01328) 710547* Mr Salmon

Woodforde's Wherry and Greene King IPA always available plus a guest (changed each week) such as Greene King Abbot, Morland Old Speckled Hen, Woodforde's Nelson's Revenge and Wadworth 6X.

Traditional cottage pub in the centre of the village with gas lighting and open fires. Bar food available at lunchtime and evenings. Car park, garden, function room, non-smoking room, accommodation. Children allowed.

11.30am–2.30pm and 6–11pm Mon–Sat;
12–3pm and 6–10.30pm Sun.

WEST RUDHAM

The Duke's Head

West Rudham, King's Lynn PE31 8RW
☎ *(01485) 528540* Mr Feltham

A freehouse with a good selection of Woodforde's and Shepherd Neame ales always available.

A fifteenth-century coaching inn. Food oriented with separate dining area and food available at lunchtime and evenings. Children allowed.

11am–3pm and 7–11pm Mon–Sat;
12–2.30pm and 7–10.30pm Sun.

WEST SOMERTON

The Lion

West Somerton, Great Yarmouth
☎ *(01493) 393289*
Mr G I Milroy and S M Milroy

Greene King IPA and Abbot usually available plus two guest beers, often Hampshire Lionheart and a Mauldons ale.

Traditional country pub with children's room. Food served 11.30am–3pm and 6–9.30pm. Car park.

11.30am–3.30pm and 6–11pm Mon–Sat;
12–3.30pm and 6–10.30pm Sun.

WHINBURGH

The Mustard Pot

Dereham Road, Whinburgh, Dereham NR19
☎ *(01362) 692179* Judith Mitchell

A freehouse with Adnams Bitter permanently available, plus guest ales served on four pumps, from local independent breweries such as Wolf and Iceni.

An old pub with beams, log fires and a beer garden. Food available 12–2pm and 5–8pm Mon–Sat and 12–4pm Sun, when traditional roasts are served, in addition to the usual menu. Tea and coffee served all day.

11am–11pm Mon–Sat; 12–10.30pm Sun.

WINTERTON-ON-SEA

The Fisherman's Return

The Lane, Winterton-on-Sea, Great Yarmouth
NR29 4BN
☎ *(01493) 393305* Kate and John Findlay

A freehouse with Woodforde's Wherry, Great Eastern and Norfolk Nog always available, plus two guests changing at least twice a week. These will include something like Mauldons Cuckoo, Buffy's Mild, Cottage Our Ken or Woodforde's Nelson's Revenge.

A 300-year-old brick and flint pub with open fires and beer garden. Food available at lunchtime and evenings. No children.

11am–2.30pm and 6.30–11pm Mon–Fri;
all day Sat–Sun.

WIVETON

The Wiveton Bell

The Green, Wiveton, Blakeney NR25 7TL
☎ *(01263) 40101* Dennis Clark

A freehouse with a range of beers brewed especially for the pub by the Cambridge Brewery: Standard (3.8% ABV), Swift (4.2% ABV – summer), Swallow (5.3% ABV – winter). Other special brews served as guests plus occasional guests from other breweries.

A classic car themed pub. 1997 and 1998 North Norfolk Tourism Award winner for food and drink. Dining area, children's playhouse, beer garden, accommodation. Food available at lunchtime and evenings.

11am–3pm and 6–11pm.

WOODBASTWICK

The Fur & Feather Inn

Woodbastwick, Norwich NR13 6HQ
☎ *(01603) 720003* John and Jean Marjoram

The Woodforde's brewery tap, situtated next door to the brewery. Therefore the pub specialises in the range of Woodforde's ales: Wherry, Kett's Rebellion, Wherry Best, Mardler's, Great Eastern, Nelson's Revenge, Norkie, Norfolk Nog and Headcracker.

A thatched pub/restaurant with beer garden. Food available at lunchtime and evenings. Children allowed.

12–2.30pm and 6–11pm Mon–Sat; 12–3pm and 7–10.30pm Sun.

WRENINGHAM

Bird in Hand

Church Road, Wreningham NR16 1BH
☎ *(01508) 489438* Mrs Carol Turner

A freehouse with Woodforde's Wherry, Fuller's London Pride and an Adnams brew always available, plus one guest, perhaps Greene King Abbot.

A traditional pub with wood burners, restaurant and beer garden. Food available at lunchtime and evenings. Children allowed if eating. Ring for directions.

11.30am–3pm and 6–11pm Mon–Sat; 12–3pm and 6–10.30pm Sun.

WYMONDHAM

The Feathers Inn

Town Green, Wymondham NR18 0PN
☎ *(01953) 605675* Eddie Aldours

Adnams Best, Marston's Pedigree and Greene King Abbot among the brews always available, plus two guests such as Fuller's London Pride, Adnams Regatta, Elgood's Greyhound, Brakspear Bee Sting or Adnams Broadside.

A town freehouse with open fires and beer garden. Food available at lunchtime and evenings. Children allowed.

11am–2.30pm and 7–11pm Mon–Sat; 12–2.30pm and 7–10.30pm Sun.

YOU TELL US

★ *Dock Tavern*, Dock Tavern Lane, Gorleston, Great Yarmouth
★ *The Greyhound*, The Street, Tibenham
★ *The Short Blue*, 47 High Street, Gorleston-on-Sea
★ *The White Horse*, Brandon
★ *The White Horse*, 17 Chapel Road, Upton
★ *The Windmill Inn*, Water End, Great Cressingham

Places Featured:

Ashby St Ledgers
Barnwell
Brackley
Corby
Daventry
Eastcote
Finedon
Fotheringhay
Gayton
Geddington
Great Brington
Great Houghton
Grendon
Higham Ferrers
Holcot
Kettering

Litchborough
Little Brington
Little Harrowden
Marston St Lawrence
Mears Ashby
Milton Keynes
Northampton
Orlingbury
Ravensthorpe
Southwick
Sudborough
Sulgrave
Towcester
Wellingborough
Woodford
Woodnewton

THE BREWERIES

FROG ISLAND BREWERY
The Maltings, Westbridge, St James Road, Northampton
☎ *(01604) 587772*

FUGGLED FROG 3.5% ABV
May brew.
BEST BITTER 3.8% ABV
Golden, quenching and well-hopped. Malty finish.
SHOEMAKER 4.2% ABV
Malty with delicate hoppiness and bitter finish.
FIRE-BELLIED TOAD 4.4% ABV
Pale gold, single hop award winner.
HEAD IN THE CLOUDS 4.5% ABV
August brew.
NATTERJACK 4.8% ABV
Sweet and malty, pale and dangerously drinkable.
CROAK & STAGGER 5.6% ABV
Winter brew.
Plus monthly special brews, usually around 5.0% ABV.

THE PUBS

ASHBY ST LEDGERS

The Olde Coach House Inn
Ashby St Ledgers, Nr Rugby CV23 8UN
☎ *(01788) 890349 Mr and Mrs McCabe*

St Ledger Ale (house brew) and Everards Old Original always available plus five guest ales (200 per year) including Jennings Cumberland, Mansfield Red Admiral, Hop Back Summer Lightning, Hook Norton Haymaker, Frog Island Natterjack and Adnams Broadside.

An olde-English converted farmhouse in the middle of an historic village. Lots of family tables and small intimate nooks and crannies. Large secure garden for children and plenty of parking space. Bar and restaurant food available at lunchtime and evenings. Car park. Accommodation. Three miles from M1 junction 18, close to M6 and M40 and adjacent to A5. Daventry three miles to the south, Rugby four miles to the north.

12–2.30pm and 6–11pm Mon–Fri; 12–11pm Sat; 12–2.30pm and 7–10.30pm Sun.

The Montagu Arms

Barnwell, Oundle, Peterborough PE8 5PH
☎ *(01832) 273726* Ian Simmons

Adnams Southwold and Broadside served with one or two guest beers such as Ash Vine Hop & Glory, Hop Back Summer Lightning or Shepherd Neame Spitfire.

A traditional country inn built in 1601 and retaining many original features. Heavily beamed bar area and more modern non-smoking restaurant. Food served 12–2.30pm and 7–10pm Mon–Sun. Free children's facilities include log swings, activity centre and crazy golf. Car park. Accommodation. To be found just past the bridge.

OPEN *12–3pm and 6–11.30pm Mon–Fri;*
12–11.30pm Sat; 12–10.30pm Sun.

The Greyhound Inn

Milton Malsor, Brackley, Borthampton NN7 3AP
☎ *(01604) 858449* Mr and Mrs Rush

At least six beers always available, with Morland Old Speckled Hen among them.

A fifteenth-century inn, cosy atmosphere wth real fires. Large beer garden. Food available. Children allowed. Situated on the main road into the village.

OPEN *All day, every day.*

Knight's Lodge

Towerhill Road, Corby NN18 0TH
☎ *(01536) 742602* Fred Hope

An Everards house with Tiger, Beacon and Old Original always available. Two other guests including, perhaps, Morland Old Speckled Hen, Wadworth Farmers Glory or Perfick, Nethergate Old Growler, Everards Equinox, Charles Wells Fargo or Wood Shropshire Lad.

A traditional seventeenth-century inn linked to Rockingham Castle by a network of tunnels. Food available in dining area Fri–Sun. Garden. Children allowed in the dining area if eating, and in the garden.

OPEN *12–3pm and 6–11pm Mon–Thurs;*
12–4pm and 6–11pm Fri–Sat;
12–3.30pm and 6–10.30pm Sun.

The Eastcote Arms

6 Gayton Road, Eastcote, Towcester NN12 8NG
☎ *(01327) 830731* John and Wendy Hadley

Fuller's London Pride, Adnams Southwold and Greene King IPA always available, plus one guest, constantly changing. An annual beer festival takes place over the Whitsun bank holiday.

A 330-year-old freehouse with dining area and beer garden. Food served at lunchtime and Thurs–Sat evenings. Children allowed in the dining area only. Ring for directions.

OPEN *6–11pm only Mon; 12–2.30pm and*
6–11pm Tues–Sat; 12–3pm and
7–10.30pm Sun.

The Bell Inn

Bell Hill, Finedon, Nr Wellingborough NN9 5ND
☎ *(01933) 680332* Denise Willmott

A freehouse with Fuller's London Pride always available, plus three guests perhaps from Woodforde's, Cottage, York or Frog Island.

An ancient pub, apparently dating from 1042. Food served at lunchtime and evenings in dining area. Children allowed.

OPEN *11.30am–3pm and 5.30–11pm Mon–Sat;*
12–3pm and 7–10.30pm Sun.

The Falcon Inn

Fotheringham, Oundle, Peterborough PE8 5HZ
☎ *(01832) 226254* Ray Smikle

Adnams Best Bitter and Old, and Greene King IPA always available, plus one weekly changing guest.

A pub and restaurant in a historic village. Emphasis on good food, served in the pub and restaurant at lunchtimes and evenings. Darts and dominoes, function room, car park. Children allowed.

OPEN *12–3pm and 6–11pm.*

GAYTON

Eykyn Arms

20 High Street, Gayton, Northampton NN7 3HD
☎ *(01604) 858361* Robert Pattle

Charles Wells Eagle, Shepherd Neame Spitfire and a Hook Norton brew usually available. One guest beer is served which may be Fuller's London Pride or another beer from Shepherd Neame.

Traditional freehouse with accommodation. Snacks served by prior arrangement. Car park. Children welcome, but no special facilities.

11.30am–2pm and 7–11pm; closed Monday lunchtime.

GEDDINGTON

The Star Inn

2 Bridge Street, Geddington, Kettering NN14 1AD
☎ *(01536) 742386*
Ann Carey and Peter Smart

A freehouse with Marston's Pedigree among the brews always available, plus four guests such as Wadworth 6X, Greene King Abbot, Charles Wells Bombardier and others from local breweries.

A traditional pub. Food available in separate smoking and non-smoking dining areas. Children allowed. Located off the A43 between Kettering and Corby, near the ancient monument.

All day, every day.

GREAT BRINGTON

The Fox & Hounds

Althorp Coaching Inn, Great Brington, Northampton NN7 4JA
☎ *(01604) 770651* Peter Cramples

A freehouse with 11 real ales always available. Greene King IPA and Abbot are permanent features, and there is usually something from Adnams. Other guests are from all over the country.

A sixteenth-century coaching inn with log fires, exposed beams and stone/wood floors. Dining area and beer garden. Food served at lunchtime and dinner, 'Rosette Standard' cooking. Children and dogs allowed. Walkers and horses welcome. Take the A428 from Northampton past Althorp House, then first left turn before railway bridge.

11am–11pm Mon–Sat; 12–10.30pm Sun (summer opening hours phone for winter hours).

GREAT HOUGHTON

The Old Cherry Tree

Cherry Tree Lane, Great Houghton, Northampton NN4 7AT
☎ *(01604) 761399* Mr Carr

A Charles Wells house with Bombardier and Eagle always available, plus one other guest such as Adnams Broadside

A pub and restaurant. Children allowed in the restaurant only. Located off the A428 from Northampton to Bedford. Three miles out of Northampton. Turn right into the village, then first left.

12–3pm and 6–11.30pm (10.30pm Sun).

GRENDON

The Half Moon

42 Main Road, Grendon
☎ *(01933) 663263* Frederick Maffre

Charles Wells Eagle, IPA and one guest beer usually available.

A 300-year-old thatched pub with low ceilings and original beams. Beer garden. Food served lunchtimes and evenings Mon–Sat and Sun lunchtimes only. Car park. Children's menu.

12–2.30pm and 6–11pm Mon–Fri; 12–2.30pm and 6.30–11pm Sat; 12–2.30pm and 7–10.30pm Sun.

HIGHAM FERRERS

The Green Dragon

College Street, Higham Ferrers, Rushden NN10 8DZ
☎ *(01933) 312088* Graham Sharp

A freehouse with Fuller's London Pride and Shepherd Neame Spitfire always available. Guests are numerous and varied and come mostly from small local breweries.

A seventeenth-century coaching inn with open fires, restaurant, beer garden, accommodation. Food served lunchtimes and evenings. Children allowed.

All day, every day.

The Griffin Inn

*High Street, Higham Ferrers, Rushden
NN10 8BW*
☎ *(01933) 312612* Ray Gilbert

Charles Wells Eagle, Greene King Abbot, Fuller's London Pride and Wadworth 6X always available, plus a range of guests constantly changing but often including Marston's Pedigree and Morland Old Speckled Hen.

A luxurious seventeenth-century freehouse with leather Chesterfield, inglenook fireplace and conservatory. Patio. Food served at lunchtime and evenings in a 50-seater restaurant. Children allowed in the restaurant only.

11am–3pm and 5.30–11pm.

HOLCOT

The White Swan Inn

Main Street, Holcot, Northampton NN6 9SP
☎ *(01604) 781263* David Hodgson

A freehouse with Greene King IPA and a Hook Norton brew always available plus one guest beer.

A thatched country pub with two bars, games room and garden. B&B. Food available at lunchtime and evenings. Families welcome.

12–2.30pm and 5.30–11pm Mon–Fri; all day Sat–Sun.

KETTERING

Park House/The Milestone Restaurant

Kettering Venture Park, Kettering NN15 6XE
☎ *(01536) 523377* Rachel Early

Banks's Bitter and Original and Marston's Pedigree always available.

A traditional pub and restaurant. Children allowed.

11am–11pm.

LITCHBOROUGH

The Old Red Lion

*Banbury Road, Litchborough, Towcester
NN12 8HF*
☎ *(01327) 830250* Mr and Mrs O'Shey

Banks's Bitter and a Marston's ale always available.

A small, 300-year-old pub with log fires and beer garden. Food available Tues–Sat, lunchtime and evenings. Children allowed.

11.30am–2.30pm and 6.30–11pm Mon–Sat; 12–3pm and 7–10.30pm Sun.

LITTLE BRINGTON

The Saracen's Head

Little Brington, Northampton NN7 4HS
☎ *(01604) 770640*
Colin Boyson and Derek Lowd

A freehouse with Fuller's London Pride always available, plus guests on three pumps. Beers featured recently include Frog Island Best, Shepherd Neame Spitfire and a Hook Norton brew.

The only pub in Little Brington. Open fires and beer garden. Food available in two restaurants. Children allowed in the restaurants and garden only.

12–2.30pm and 5.30–11pm Mon–Fri; 12–3pm and 5.30–11pm Sat; 12–3pm and 7–10.30pm Sun.

LITTLE HARROWDEN

The Lamb Inn

Orlingbury Road, Little Harrowden, Wellingborough NN9 5BH
☎ *(01933) 673300* John Bevis

A Charles Wells house with Eagle and Bombardier always available, as well as Adnams Broadside, Badger Dorset Best and one guest, regularly changing. Marston's Pedigree, Morland Old Speckled Hen, Charles Wells Summer Solstice and Young's ales are all popular.

A traditional seventeenth-century Northampton inn. Skittles table. Garden. Food available in separate dining area, Children allowed in the garden or in the dining area if eating.

11am–2.30pm and 7–11pm Mon–Sat; 12–3pm and 7–10.30pm Sun.

MARSTON ST LAWRENCE

Marston Inn

Marston St Lawrence, Banbury OX17 2DB
☎ *(01295) 711906*
Ms Claire Ellis and Mr Paul Parker

Hook Norton tied house with a different guest beer served each month, such as Gales HSB, Shepherd Neame Spitfire, Badger Tanglefoot, Fuller's ESB or Caledonian 80/-, among the popular ones.

Fifteenth-century, 'roses-round-the-door' village pub. Converted from three cottages, the pub features oak beams, real fire, two dining rooms (one non-smoking), cosy bar, lounge and gardens. Traditional pub games. Food served 12–2pm Tues–Sun and 7–9.30pm Tues–Sat. Car park. Children welcome in garden or if pre-booked for Sunday lunch.

7–11pm Mon; 12–3pm and 7–11pm Tues–Sat; 12–4pm and 7–10.30pm Sun.

The Griffin's Head

*Wilby Road, Mears Ashby, Northampton
NN6 0DX*
☎ *(01604) 812945* Philip Tompkins

Marston's Pedigree, Charles Wells Eagle and Everards Beacon always available, plus two guests including, perhaps, Everards Tiger or an Adnams brew. Also seasonal ales.

A cosy freehouse with log fires, restaurant and beer garden. Food served at lunchtime and evenings. Children allowed if eating. Can be difficult to find (ring for directions).

11.30am–3pm and 5.30–11pm Mon–Fri; 12–3pm and 6–11pm Sat; 11.30am–10.30pm Sun.

The Navigation Inn

Thrupp Wharf, Castlethorpe Road, Cosgrove, Milton Keynes
☎ *(01908) 543156* Mr H Willis

Greene King IPA and Abbot Ale plus two weekly changing guest beers usually available.

Family-run pub set on the Grand Union canal with unspoilt views over open countryside. Restaurant, sun terrace and family garden. Bar food available lunchtimes and evenings Mon–Sat and all day Sun. Restaurant open evenings only Mon–Sat and all day Sun. Children welcome when dining and in the family garden.

12–3pm and 6–11pm Mon–Fri; 12–11pm Sat–Sun.

The Malt Shovel Tavern

121 Bridge Street, Northampton NN1 1QF
☎ *(01604) 234212* Malcolm Mackenzie

A freehouse with five regular ales, including Castle Eden Ale and Frog Island Natterjack, plus up to eight constantly changing guests such as Oakham JHB, Skinner's Cornish Knocker and Timothy Taylor Dark Mild. The pub sold 746 firkins of guest beer during 1999.

A traditional pub with beer garden. Food served at lunchtime and early evenings. Children allowed in the garden only. Located opposite the Carlsberg Brewery.

11–30am–3pm and 5–11pm Mon–Sat; 12–4pm and 7–10.30pm Sun.

Moon On The Square

*6 The Parade, Market Place, Northampton
NN1 2EE*
☎ *(01604) 634062*
Nigel Abbott and Olivia Jenkinson

Marston's Pedigree, Greene King Abbot Ale and Shepherd Neame Spitfire usually available, plus two guest beers from a wide selection supplied by the excellent East West Ales.

Large city-centre pub with disabled access and no music or games tables. Food served all day, every day. No children.

10.30am–11pm Mon–Sat; 12–10.30pm Sun.

The Queen's Arms

11 Isham Road, Orlingbury NN14 1JD
☎ *(01933) 678258* David Myacn

Up to six guest ales available, perhaps including Exmoor Gold, Young's Special or a Burton Bridge brew. The selection changes every week.

A country freehouse and restaurant with beer garden. Food served at lunchtime and evenings. Children allowed. CAMRA pub of the year 1994.

12–2.30pm and 6–11pm Mon–Fri; all day Sat–Sun.

The Chequers

Chequer's Lane, Ravensthorpe NN6 8ER
☎ *(01604) 770379* Gordon Walker

A freehouse with five hand pumps, serving Fuller's London Pride, Greene King Abbot, something from Thwaites and Jennings, plus one guest.

A cosy village pub serving traditional English fare. Restaurant and bar food served lunchtimes and evenings. Beer garden and children's play area – children welcome.

12–3pm and 6–11pm Mon–Fri; all day Sat; 12–3pm and 7–10.30pm Sun.

The Shuckburgh Arms

Main Street, Southwick, Nr Oundle, Peterborough
PE8 5BL
☎ *(01832) 274007* Nicola Stokes

Fuller's London Pride and Marston's Pedigree usually available, plus one constantly changing guest, such as Shepherd Neame Spitfire, Jennings Best, Timothy Taylor Landlord or beers from Bateman and Cains among others.

Small, thatched, family-run freehouse with log fire and beams. Darts and dominoes regularly played. Food served 12–1.30pm Wed–Sun, 6–9pm Wed–Sat, 6–8.30pm Sun in summer only. Large car park. Small family room and children's play equipment in garden. Situated three miles east of Oundle.

OPEN *12–2pm Wed–Sat; 6–11pm Mon–Sat; 12–3pm and 7–10.30pm Sun (6–10.30pm in summer). Closed Mon–Tues lunchtimes.*

The Vane Arms

Main Street, Sudborough NN14 3BX
☎ *(01832) 733223* Tom Tookey

Nine different beers changed regularly (150 per year) including Hoskins & Oldfield Ginger Tom, Hop Back Summer Lightning, Woodforde's Headcracker, Adnams Broadside and Oakham Old Tosspot.

A centuries-old listed thatched village inn. Bar and restaurant food available at lunchtime and evenings. Mexican specials. Car park, garden, games room. Children allowed. Accommodation. Just off the A6116 between Thrapston and Corby.

OPEN *11.30am–3pm and 5.30–11pm.*

The Star Inn

Manor Road, Sulgrave OX17 2SA
☎ *(01295) 760389* Andy Willerton FBII

Hook Norton Best Bitter and Old Hooky usually available plus a guest beer from a micro- or independent brewery.

Idyllic country inn on the South Northants/Oxon borders. Food served 12–2pm and 6.30–9.30pm Mon–Sat, 12–4pm Sun. Car park. Children welcome in garden if supervised, but there are no special facilities. Follow brown signs for Sulgrave Manor.

OPEN *11am–2.30pm and 6–11pm Mon–Sat; 12–5pm Sun.*

★ *The Exeter Arms*, Main Street, Wakerley
★ *The Old Plough Inn*, 82 High Street, Braunston, Daventry

The Plough Inn

Market Square, Towcester NN12 6BT
☎ *(01327) 350738*
Geraldine, Matthew and Bob Goode

A Charles Wells tied house with Eagle permanently available, plus Adnams Broadside.

Cosy, 400-year-old, award-winning pub which has been in the same hands for 30 years. Food served 12–2pm and 6–10pm daily. Car park. Children's eating area.

OPEN *11am–11pm Mon–Sat; 12–10.30pm Sun.*

Red Well

16 Silver Street, Wellingborough NN14 1PA
☎ *(01933) 440845*
Steve Frost and Tina Garner

A freehouse with five guest ales always available, More than 50 different beers have been served in the past three months. Regulars include Hop Back Summer Lightning, Nethergate Old Growler, Morland Old Speckled Hen, Cotleigh Osprey, Ash Vine Frying Tonight and Adnams Regatta. Beer festivals held three times a year.

A new-age pub, no music, no games. Separate non-smoking area, disabled access, garden. Food available all day, every day. Children allowed in the garden only.

OPEN *All day, every day.*

The Dukes Arms

High Street, Woodford, Nr Kettering NN14 4HE
☎ *(01832) 732224* Mr and Mrs Keith Wilson

Fuller's London Pride, Morland Old Speckled Hen, Banks's Best Bitter and Shepherd Neame Spitfire usually available.

Delightful setting for the oldest pub in the village which prides itself on good real ale and down-to-earth food. Garden and restaurant. Food served lunchtimes and evenings. Children welcome, but no special facilities. Car park.

OPEN *12–2.30pm and 7–11pm (10.30pm Sun).*

The White Swan

Main Street, Woodnewton PE8 5EB
☎ *(01780) 470381* Anne Dubbin

Oakham JHB and Fuller's London Pride usually available plus a guest, often from Brewsters, Rockingham or Eccleshall.

Friendly village pub with à la carte restaurant. Boules played in summer. Food served 12–2.30pm and 7–10pm daily. Car park. Children welcome.

OPEN *12–4pm and 7–11pm (10.30pm Sun).*

Places Featured:

Acomb
Allendale
Alnmouth
Alnwick
Ashington
Bedlington
Berwick-upon-Tweed
Blyth
Cramlington

Great Whittington
Haltwhistle
Hedley on the Hill
Hexham
High Horton
Morpeth
Shotley Bridge
Wylam

THE BREWERIES

BORDER BREWERY CO.

The Old Kiln, Brewery Lane, Berwick-upon-Tweed TD15 2AH
☎ *(01289) 303303*

SPECIAL BITTER 3.8% ABV
Light, golden and hoppy.
FESTIVAL ALE 3.9% ABV
Pale, quenching, hoppy bitter. Aug–Sept.
FLOTSAM 4.0% ABV
Bronze colour with refreshing, citrus bitterness.
FARNE ISLAND 4.0% ABV
Refreshing, amber brew.
OLD KILN ALE 4.0% ABV
Fruit, malt and hops combine in this flavoursome ale.
NOGGINS NOG 4.2% ABV
Dark, with powerful chocolate malt flavour.
Y2K 4.3% ABV
Golden, complex and hoppy.
REIVER'S IPA 4.4% ABV
Amber, hoppy award winner.
JETSAM 4.8% ABV
Gold-coloured, crisp and hoppy.
RAMPART 4.8% ABV
Golden, clean and refreshing.
SOB 5.0% ABV
Red and distinctive, with malt flavours.
RUDOLPH'S RUIN 6.4% ABV
Powerful, malt flavours.
Plus Mythic Beers. Different beer, but always 4.3% ABV, every two months and named after Mythic Gods.
Plus seasonal and occasional brews.

HEXAMSHIRE BREWERY

The Brewery, Leafields, Hexham NE45 1SX
☎ *(01434) 606577*

DEVIL'S ELBOW 3.6% ABV
SHIRE BITTER 3.8% ABV
DEVIL'S WATER 4.1% ABV
WHAPWEASEL 4.8% ABV
Plus seasonal:
OLD HUMBUG 5.5% ABV

THE NORTHUMBERLAND BREWERY

Earth Balance, West Sleekburn Farm, Bomarsund, Bedlington NE22 7AD
☎ *(01670) 822122*

CASTLES 3.8% ABV
Hoppy session bitter.
COUNTY 4.0% ABV
Well-balanced, easy-drinking brew.
BALANCE 4.2% ABV
As the name suggests … well-balanced!
SECRET KINGDOM ALE 4.3% ABV
Smooth and rich.
BEST 4.5% ABV
Rounded and full-flavoured.
BOMAR 5.0% ABV
Pale and refreshing.

ACOMB

The Miner's Arms

Main Street, Acomb, Hexham NE46 4PW
☎ *(01434) 603909* Tom Stokoe

A freehouse serving Miners Lamp (brewed especially by the Big Lamp Brewery) and five guests which may include Durham White Velvet, Mansfield Four Seasons, Northumberland Secret Kingdom, or a Yates or Black Sheep brew.

An unspoilt old-style stone pub, dating from 1750. Two bar areas, outside garden and barbecue. Bar meals served at lunchtime and evenings (not Mondays). Children allowed until 9pm.

OPEN *12–3pm and 5–11pm Mon–Fri; all day Sat–Sun.*

ALLENDALE

The King's Head Hotel

Market Place, Allendale, Hexham NE47 9BD
☎ *(01434) 683681* Margaret Taylor

A freehouse with Jennings Cumberland Ale and Greene King Abbot always available, plus three guests such as Timothy Taylor Landlord, Mordue Workie Ticket, Morland Old Speckled Hen, Marston's Pedigree, Northumberland Cat 'n' Sawdust or one of many Durham Brewery ales.

A cosy quiet pub with two bars, fires and a function room. No music or games. Food served at lunchtime and evenings. Children allowed.

OPEN *All day, every day.*

ALNMOUTH

The Schooner Hotel

Northumberland Street, Alnmouth NE66 2RS
☎ *(01665) 830216*
Mrs Eleanor Johnston (Manager)

Schooner Parson's Smyth Ale 3.6% (brewed for the Schooner Hotel by the Four Seasons Brewery) permanently available plus five guests often featuring Marston's Pedigree, Ruddles County, Charles Wells Bombardier, Border Noggins Nog or Mythic Brews, or other ales from Jennings, Border, Orkney or Northumberland breweries.

A hotel with Chase Bar and Long Bar, conservatory and terraced beer garden. Two real ale beer festivals held every year at the Whitsun Bank Holiday and the weekend before the August Bank Holiday. Two restaurants with full menus, one specialising in seafood and local game, plus bar food at lunchtimes and all day at weekends and school holidays. Children allowed.

OPEN *11am–11pm Mon–Sat; 12–10.30pm Sun.*

ALNWICK

The Market Tavern

Fenkle Street, Alnwick NE66 1HW
☎ *(01665) 602759* Ken Hodgson

Young's Waggle Dance is among the beers always available, plus a rotating guest including, perhaps, Morland Old Speckled Hen or Charles Wells Bombardier. Other seasonal guests such as Wye Valley Winter Tipple when appropriate.

A traditional town-centre pub with one bar, restaurant, disabled access and accommodation. Food available at lunchtime and evenings. Children allowed.

OPEN *All day, every day.*

ASHINGTON

Bubbles Wine Bar

58a Station Road, Ashington NE63 9UJ
☎ *(01670) 850800* David Langdown

A freehouse with three pumps serving a range of real ales. Too many to list; all breweries stocked as and when available.

A town-centre pub for all ages. One bar, back yard area, entertainment and discos. Food served at lunchtime only. Children allowed.

OPEN *11am–3pm and 6–11pm Mon–Thurs; all day Fri–Sat; 7–10.30pm Sun.*

BEDLINGTON

The Northumberland Arms

112 Front Street East, Bedlington
☎ *(01670) 822754* Mrs Mary Morris

Three regularly changing guest beers served, such as Timothy Taylor Landlord, Fuller's ESB or London Pride, Charles Wells Bombardier, Shepherd Neame Spitfire or Bishop's Finger, Black Sheep Bitter or Special and Bateman XXXB.

Friendly pub with interesting beer range. Food served 11.30am–2.30pm Thurs–Sat.

OPEN *7–11pm Mon–Tues; 11am–11pm Wed–Sat; 12–10.30pm Sun.*

BERWICK-UPON-TWEED

Barrels Ale House

Bridge Street, Berwick-upon-Tweed TD15 1ES
☎ *(01289) 308013* Mark Dixon

A freehouse with a house beer (Barrels Best) brewed especially by the Border Brewery, plus three guests, often including another Border ale plus beers from other smaller brewers such as The Kitchen Brewery.

A traditional two-bar pub, one up, one down. Dining area, real fires. Renowned music and comedy venue in basement. Food served at lunchtime and evenings. Children allowed in certain areas.

OPEN *All day, every day.*

BLYTH

The Joiners Arms
Coomassie Road, Blyth
☎ *(01670) 352852* Mrs Ann Holland

Northumberland Secret Kingdom plus a guest beer usually available.

Small, friendly, one-bar pub with entertainment on Thursday, Saturday and Sunday evenings. Seating area at side of pub. Sandwiches and toasties available. Car park. Children welcome.

OPEN *12–11pm (10.30pm Sun).*

CRAMLINGTON

The Plough
Middle Farm, Cramlington NE23 9DN
☎ *(01670) 737633* Sir John Fitzgerald

Four pumps serving a range of cask ales such as Fuller's London Pride and any of the Black Sheep brews.

A two-bar village freehouse with dining area, beer garden and conservatory. Food served every lunchtime, including traditional Sunday roasts. Children allowed only if eating.

OPEN *11am–3pm and 6–11pm Mon–Wed; all day Thurs–Sun.*

GREAT WHITTINGTON

The Queens Head Inn
Great Whittington, Newcastle upon Tyne NE19 2HP
☎ *(01434) 672267* Ian J Scott

Queens Head Bitter (brewed by Nick Stafford), Hambleton Best Bitter and Black Sheep Bitter usually available plus one guest. Hambleton Stud, Black Sheep Special, Northumberland Secret Kingdom and Durham Magus feature frequently.

A fifteenth-century coaching inn which has recently been refurbished and now incorporates a restaurant. Comfortable bar with open fires. Food served Tues–Sat. Car park. Well-behaved children welcome. Situated four miles north of Corbridge, off the Military Road (B6318) towards Newcastle.

OPEN *12–2.30pm and 6–11pm Tues–Sat; 12–3pm and 7–10.30pm Sun.*

HALTWHISTLE

The Black Bull
Market Square, Haltwhistle NE49 0BL
☎ *(01434) 320463* Mr Sandford

Jennings Cumberland Ale always available plus a good range of guests on five additional pumps, plus extra barrels at weekends. Plans for micro-brewing in the near future.

A small, quiet freehouse with one main bar and a small side room. No music or machines. No food. Children allowed at lunchtime only in the smaller area.

OPEN *7–11pm Mon–Wed; 12–3pm and 7–11pm Thurs–Fri; 12–4pm and 7–11pm Sat; 12–3pm and 7–10.30pm Sun.*

HEDLEY ON THE HILL

The Feathers Inn
Hedley on the Hill, Stocksfield NE43 7SW
☎ *(01661) 843607* Marina Atkinson

Mordue Workie Ticket among the beers always available, plus a range of guests from local breweries such as Big Lamp and Northumberland whenever possible. Otherwise Fuller's London Pride and Chiswick or beers from Yates or Barnsley breweries.

A traditional, attractive pub with log fires, beams and stone walls. No music or games. Outside tables. Food served Tues–Sun evenings and lunchtime at weekends. Children allowed.

OPEN *6–11pm Mon–Fri; 12–3pm and 6–11pm Sat; 12–3pm and 7–10.30pm Sun.*

HEXHAM

The Dipton Mill Inn
Dipton Mill Road, Hexham NE46 1YA
☎ *(01434) 606577* Mr Brooker

A freehouse not far from the Hexhamshire brewery, so Hexhamshire beers such as Devil's Elbow, Shire Bitter, Devil's Water and Whapweasel usually available.

An old-fashioned country pub with real fires. No music or games. One bar, garden, disabled access. Food served at lunchtime and evenings. Children allowed.

OPEN *12–2.30pm and 6–11pm Mon–Sat; 12–4.30pm and 7–10.30pm Sun.*

HIGH HORTON

The Three Horseshoes
Hathery Lane, High Horton, Blyth NE24 4HF
☎ *(01670) 822410* Malolm Farmer

A freehouse serving a good range of real ales from breweries such as Shepherd Neame, Bateman, Greene King, Fuller's, Adnams or Morland.

A large open-plan country pub. Dining room, garden, children's area. Disabled access. Food served at lunchtime and evenings. Children allowed.

All day, every day.

MORPETH

Tap & Spile
Manchester Street, Morpeth NE61 1BH
☎ *(01670) 513894* Mrs Boyle

Beers from breweries such as Cumberland, Adnams, Black Sheep, Jennings, Bateman and Fuller's. Also celebration and seasonal ales when available.

An old-fashioned pub with small lounge and bar area. Open fires. Food served at lunchtime. Children allowed in the lounge only.

12–2.30pm and 4.30–11pm Mon–Thurs; all day Fri–Sun.

SHOTLEY BRIDGE

The Manor House Inn
Carterway Heads, Shotley Bridge, Nr Consett DH8 9LX
☎ *(01207) 255268* Mr and Mrs C Brown

Four beers at any one time with an emphasis on a rolling guest ale programme. Beers from all the local brewers (Mordue, Durham, Northumberland, North Yorkshire, Castle Eden) plus a wide range from all over the country, including Hampshire, Morland and many others.

A converted farmhouse, with open log fires in winter. Stunning views over the Derwent Valley. Bar and restaurant food available at lunchtime and evenings. Large car park, garden, accommodation. Children welcome.

11am–3pm and 6–11pm Mon–Sat; 12–3pm and 7–10.30pm Sun; all day Sat and Sun in school summer holidays.

WYLAM

The Boat House
Station Road, Wylam
☎ *(01661) 853431* G N and M Weatherburn

Timothy Taylor Landlord and Border Farne Island Pale Ale usually available, plus five or six guest beers, often from Border, Northumberland, Castle Eden, Kitchen, Marston's or many other independent breweries.

Warm, friendly pub on the south bank of the Tyne, offering a constantly changing selection of eight real ales. Unspoilt bar with real fire. Home-prepared food served lunchtimes and evenings Mon–Thurs, 12–6pm Fri–Sat and 12–5pm Sun. Car park. Children welcome in the beer garden and lounge until 9pm. Continue through Wylam village, the pub is situated just over the bridge.

11am–11pm Mon–Sat; 12–10.30pm Sun.

YOU TELL US

★ *The Angel Inn*, 11 Brewery Bank, Tweedmouth, Berwick-upon-Tweed
★ *The Wallace Arms*, Bowfoot, Featherstone Park, Haltwhistle

Places Featured:

Barnby in the Willows
Basford
Beeston
Carlton on Trent
Caythorpe
Colston Bassett
Dunham on Trent
Kimberley
Mansfield

Newark
Nottingham
Ollerton
Radcliffe on Trent
Retford
Upper Broughton
Upton
Worksop

THE BREWERIES

ALCAZAR BREWING CO.

*At The Fox & Crown, 33 Church Street, Old
Basford, Nottingham NG6 0GA*
☎ *(0115) 942 2002*

ALCAZAR ALE 3.7% ABV
BLACK FOX 3.9% ABV
Mild.
NEW DON MILLENNIUM ALE 4.5% ABV
BRUSH BITTER 4.9% ABV
MAPLE MAGIC 5.0% ABV
Winter brew.
VIXEN'S VICE 5.2% ABV
*Plus the Sherwood Forest selection of occasional
brews.*

BROADSTONE BREWING CO.

PO Box 82, Retford DN22 7ZJ
☎ *(01777) 719797*

BROADSTONE BEST BITTER 3.8% ABV
(UNNAMED) 3.8% ABV
Summer brew.
STONEBRIDGE MILD 4.0% ABV
THE FLETCHER'S ALE 4.2% ABV
CHARTER ALE 4.6% ABV
BROADSTONE GOLD 5.0% ABV
WAR HORSE 5.8 % ABV
Winter brew.

CASTLE ROCK BREWERY

Queens Bridge Road, The Meadows, Nottingham
☎ *(0115) 985 1615*

NOTTINGHAM PALE ALE 3.6% ABV
DAZE (COLLECTION) 3.8% ABV
Summer, winter and Christmas.
HEMLOCK 4.0% ABV
SNOW WHITE 4.2% ABV
BENDIGO 4.5% ABV
Autumn ale.
SALSA 4.5% ABV
Spring ale.
ELSIE MO 4.7% ABV
TRENTSMAN 4.8% ABV
Seasonal.
BLACK JACK STOUT 4.9% ABV
Winter brew.
STAIRWAY 5.2% ABV

CAYTHORPE BREWERY

3 Gonalston Lane, Hoveringham NG14 7JH
☎ *(0115) 966 4376*

DOVER BECK BITTER 4.0% ABV
**OLD NOTTINGHAM EXTRA PALE ALE
4.2% ABV**
BIRTHDAY BREW 4.5% ABV
Plus seasonal and occasional brews.

HARDYS & HANSONS PLC

Kimberley Brewery, Nottingham NG16 2NS
☎ *(0115) 938 3611*

KIMBERLEY BEST MILD 3.1% ABV
Dark red and nutty with good roast malt
flavour.
KIMBERLEY BEST BITTER 3.9% ABV
Golden and well-balanced with pleasing bitter
flavour.
KIMBERLEY CLASSIC 4.8% ABV
Overflowing with malt, fruit and hop flavours.
Plus seasonal brews.

LEADMILL BREWERY

118 Nottingham Road, Selston NG16 6BX
☎ *(01773) 819280*

WILD WEASEL 3.9% ABV
Pale, refreshing and malty.
ARC-LIGHT 4.2% ABV
Dry-hopped, pale and fruity.
ROLLING THUNDER 4.5% ABV
Full-flavoured with some sweetness.
LINEBACKER 4.6% ABV
Flavoursome, with fruity hop finish.
AGENT ORANGE 4.9% ABV
Balanced and hoppy with subtle honey tones.
NIAGARA 5.0% ABV
Malt flavour throughout and dry-hopped.
APOCALYPSE NOW 5.2% ABV
Inviting, well-balanced flavour with some fruit.

MALLARD BREWERY

15 Hartington Avenue, Carlton NG4 3NR
☎ *(0115) 952 1289*

 DUCK AND DIVE 3.7% ABV
WADDLERS MILD 3.7% ABV
BEST BITTER 4.0% ABV
DUCKLING 4.2% ABV
SPITTING FEATHERS 4.4% ABV
DRAKE 4.5% ABV
DUCK DOWN STOUT 4.6% ABV
Black, fruity occasional brew.
OWD DUCK 4.8% ABV
FRIAR DUCK 5.0% ABV
D.A. 5.8% ABV
Complex winter ale.
QUISMAS QUACKER 6.0% ABV
Dark, smoky, coffee-flavoured Christmas ale.

MANSFIELD BREWERY PLC

Littleworth, Mansfield NG18 1AB
☎ *(01623) 625691*

 DARK MILD 3.5% ABV
RIDING TRADITONAL BITTER 3.6% ABV
Refreshing and well-balanced.
CASK ALE 3.9% ABV
Fermented in traditional Yorkshire Squares.
OLD BAILY 4.5% ABV
Full-flavoured, rich and hoppy.

MAYPOLE BREWERY

*North Laithes Farm, Wellow Road, Eakring
NG22 0AN*
☎ *(01623) 871690*

MAYFAIR 3.8% ABV
Available Mar–Oct.
LION'S PRIDE 3.9% ABV
CELEBRATION 4.0% ABV
CENTENARY ALE 4.2% ABV
FLANAGAN'S STOUT 4.4% ABV
Available Mar–Apr.
MAYDAY 4.5% ABV
Available May.
MAE WEST 4.6% ABV
OLD HOMEWRECKER 4.7% ABV
Available Nov–Dec.
POLE AXED 4.8% ABV
Available Oct–Mar.
DONNER & BLITZED 5.1% ABV
Available Dec–Jan.
Plus occasional brews.

SPRINGHEAD BREWERY

*Sutton Workshops, Old Great North Road, Sutton
on Trent, Newark NG23 6QS*
☎ *(01636) 821000*

 HERSBRUCKER WEIZENBIER 3.6% ABV
Wheat beer. Available March to
September.
PURITAN'S PORTER 4.0% ABV
Dark and easy-drinking.
SPRINGHEAD BITTER 4.0% ABV
Refreshing and well-hopped session beer.
ROUNDHEAD'S GOLD 4.2% ABV
Quenching and moreish.
GOODRICH CASTLE 4.4% ABV
Pale ale with rosemary.
THE LEVELLER 4.8% ABV
Rich and rounded.
ROARING MEG 5.5% ABV
Pale and sweet with balancing hoppy, dry
aftertaste.
CROMWELL'S HAT 6.0% ABV
October–March. Herby flavours.

THE PUBS

BARNBY IN THE WILLOWS

The Willow Tree

*Front Street, Barnby in the Willows, Newark
NG24 2SA*
☎ *(01636) 626613* S O'Leary

Timothy Taylor Landlord and two guest
beers available, perhaps from Rudgate,
Eccleshall, Broadstone, Brewsters or Belvoir.

Relaxing village inn with quaint, heavily
beamed bar and restaurant. En-suite
accommodation. Food served 7–9.30pm
Mon–Sun. Car park. Children welcome.

OPEN *7–11pm Mon–Fri; 12–3pm and 7–11pm
Sat; 12–3pm and 7–10.30pm Sun.*

BASFORD

The Lion Inn

Mosley Street, Basford, Nottingham NG7 7FG
☎ *(0115) 970 3506* Simon Ronstance

A freehouse with Lion's Mane (house
brew produced especially by the Castle
Rock brewery) always available, plus
numerous guests such as Charles Wells
Bombardier, Kelham Island Pale Rider, Castle
Rock Elsie Mo, Everards Tiger or Bateman
XXXB. Other seasonal celebration beers on
bank holidays, at Christmas and Easter etc.

A traditional pub with wooden floorboards,
open fires, beer garden and play area. A
broad clientele. Live music (Blues, Blue Grass
or Jazz) four or five times per week. An
extensive menu served at lunchtime only.
Children allowed.

OPEN *All day, every day.*

The Victoria Hotel

*85 Dovecote Lane, Beeston, Nr Nottingham
NG9 1JG*
☎ *(0115) 925 4049*

A constantly changing range of ten beers always available from a list of 500 per year including Woodforde's Wherry, Whim Hartington Bitter, Castle Rock Hemlock, Caledonian IPA and Adnams ales. Also 120 whiskies and extensive wine list.

Refurbished and redecorated Victorian railway pub with high ceilings. Bar and restaurant food is available at lunchtime and evenings. Car park, garden, conference room. Accompanied children allowed in the restaurant and outside. Off Queens Road, behind Beeston railway station.

OPEN *11am–11pm (10.30pm Sun).*

The Great Northern Inn

*Ossington Road, Carlton on Trent, Newark
NG23 6NT*
☎ *(01636) 821348* Ken and Fran Munro

A freehouse with four pumps serving a range of real ales. No permanent beers but guests might include Timothy Taylor Landlord, Marston's Pedigree or a Bateman ale. Local micro-breweries supported whenever possible, including Springhead, Maypole and Brewsters.

A family-oriented pub with two bars, family room, restaurant, outside playground and large car park. CAMRA Pub of the Season for Spring 2000. Food served at lunchtime and evenings, including a children's menu. Traditional roasts available on Sundays. Located 100 yards from the A1, with easy return access to the A1.

OPEN *12–2.30pm and 5–11pm Mon–Thurs; all day Fri–Sun and bank holidays.*

The Black Horse

*29 Main Street, Caythorpe, Nottingham
NG14 7ED*
☎ *(0115) 966 3520* Miss Sharon Andrews

A freehouse and brewpub with a home-brewed ale, Dover Beck, plus brews from Adnams, Timothy Taylor and Black Sheep always available. Other guests include beers from micro-breweries such as Brewsters or Lloyds.

A traditional village pub with two beamed bar areas, garden and function room. Food served at lunchtime and evenings (booking necessary for evenings). No children.

 DOVER BECK BITTER 4% ABV

OPEN *12–2.30pm and 5.30–11pm Tues–Sat (closed Mon lunch); 5.30–11pm Mon–Fri; 6–11pm Sat; 7–10.30pm Sun.*

The Martins Arms Inn

School Lane, Colston Bassett NG12 3FN
☎ *(01949) 81361* Miss L Bryan

Seven beers always available (200 per year), with regulars including Marston's Best and Pedigree, Castle Rock Hemlock, Timothy Taylor Landlord and brews from Black Sheep and Bateman.

This village freehouse was built in 1700 as a farmhouse set in 100 acres owned by the local squire. Now set in one acre with original stables surrounded by National Trust parkland. Antique furniture, prints, old beams, Jacobean fireplace and bar. Bar and restaurant food available at lunchtime and every evening except Sunday. Les Routiers Inn of the Year for Great Britain 2000. Car park, large garden with croquet, children's room. Accommodation. On the A46 Newark to Leicester road.

OPEN *12–3pm and 6–11pm.*

The Bridge Inn

*Main Street, Dunham on Trent, Newark
NG22 0TY*
☎ *(01777) 228385* David Ollerenshaw

A freehouse with three pumps serving a range of ales, with local breweries featured when possible.

A traditional village pub with two bars, non-smoking restaurant and beer garden. Disabled access. Food available at lunchtime and evenings. No children.

OPEN *12–3pm and 5–11pm Mon–Fri; all day Sat–Sun.*

KIMBERLEY

The Nelson & Railway

Station Road, Kimberley NG16 2NR
☎ *(0115) 938 2177* Harry Burton

Three real ales always available including Hardys & Hansons Kimberley Best and Classic. Also an interesting guest from a range of six per year.

Opposite the Hardys & Hansons brewery. A Victorian, family-run village pub with dining area, including non-smoking section. Bar food available at lunchtime and evenings. Car park, garden, skittle alley and games. Accommodation. Children allowed in dining area for meals. One mile north of M1 junction 26.

OPEN *11am–3pm and 5–11pm Mon–Wed; 11am–11pm Thurs–Sat; 12–10.30pm Sun.*

MANSFIELD

The Plough

180 Nottingham Road, Mansfield NG18 4AF
☎ *(01623) 623031* Ms B Stuart

Wadworth 6X and Marston's Pedigree regularly available, plus four guest beers which may include Black Sheep Bitter and Best, Timothy Taylor Landlord, Morland Old Speckled Hen or something from Springhead.

Welcoming, spacious pub situated on the outskirts of Mansfield. Mon: quiz night; Tues: pool night; Thurs: live bands. Also big screen sports. Food served 12–9pm every day (10-ounce steaks from £4.45!). Car park. Restaurant facilities for babies/children and a play area in the safe, family garden.

OPEN *11am–11pm Mon–Sat; 12–10.30pm Sun.*

NEWARK

The Old Malt Shovel

25 North Gate, Newark NG24 1HD
☎ *(01636) 702036* Jose De Sousa Andrade

Timothy Taylor Landlord, Adnams Broadside, Everards Tiger and Malt Shovel Bitter (specially brewed by Rudgate Brewery) usually available plus one or two guest beers. These may be from Brewsters, Cains, Black Sheep, York, Rudgate, Glentworth, Hop Back, Cottage, Morrells, Shepherd Neame, Oakham, Exmoor, Badger or many, many other independent breweries.

Popular, 400-year-old pub situated 200 yards from the River Trent with lovely walks nearby. Home-cooked food available 12–2pm Mon–Sun and 7–9.30pm Wed–Sun, both as bar meals and in a continental-style restaurant (non-smoking). Beer garden. Children welcome in the restaurant. Located midway between North Gate and Castle stations.

OPEN *11.30am–3pm and 6–11pm (10.30pm Sun).*

NOTTINGHAM

Fellows

54 Canal Street, Nottingham NG1 7EH
☎ *(0115) 950 6795* Les Howard

Home of the Fellows, Morton and Clayton Brewhouse Company, with Fellows Bitter and Posthaste always available, plus Timothy Taylor Landlord, Wadworth 6X or a Castle Eden brew. Other guests on four pumps, such as Fuller's London Pride, Burtonwood Top Hat or brews from Cains or local breweries such as Mallard and Castle Rock.

A traditional pub leased from Whitbread with a brewery on the premises. One bar, garden area and restaurant. Food served 12–2.30pm Mon–Fri and 12–6pm Sat–Sun. Children allowed in the restaurant and garden only.

FELLOWS BITTER 3.9% ABV
POSTHASTE
OPEN *All day, every day.*

The Forest Tavern

Mansfield Road, Nottingham NG1 3FT
☎ *(0115) 947 5650*
Amelia Bedford and Max Amos

Castle Rock Hemlock, Woodforde's Wherry, Greene King Abbot and Marston's Pedigree always available. Range of continental bottled beers and draught products also served.

A traditional building on the outside, inside a continental café. Piped music. Night club at the back of premises. Food served until 10.30pm. No children.

OPEN *4–11pm Mon–Thurs; 12–11pm Fri–Sat; 12–10.30pm Sun.*

The Golden Fleece

105 Mansfield Road, Nottingham NG1 3FN
☎ *(0115) 947 2843* Steven Creatorex

Marston's Pedigree and Cains Mild always available plus guests, perhaps from Young's or a micro-brewery.

A nineteenth–century pub with an L-shaped bar and wooden floor. Occasional folk music. Food served 11am–8pm daily. Children allowed if eating.

OPEN *All day, every day.*

The Limelight Bar

Nottingham Playhouse, Wellington Circus,
Nottingham NG1 5AF
☎ *(0115) 941 8467* Ian Quill

Bateman XB, Marston's Pedigree, Fuller's London Pride and Adnams Bitter among those beers always available, plus an ever-changing range of guest beers.

Freshly cooked bar and restaurant food is available from 12–8pm Mon–Sat and 12–2.30pm Sunday. Bookings available on request. Children welcome in the restaurant and outside. Adjacent to Nottingham Playhouse and Nottingham Albert Hall.

11am–11pm Mon–Sat; 12–10.30pm Sun.

Lincolnshire Poacher

161–3 Mansfield Road, Nottingham
NG1 3FR
☎ *(0115) 941 1584* Paul Montgomery

Bateman XB, XXXB and Victory plus Marston's Pedigree at all times. Also up to five guest beers, mostly from small independent brewers such as Kelham Island, Springhead, Shardlow, Highwood etc.

A traditional alehouse. No juke box, no games machines, lots of conversation. Bar food available at lunchtimes and evenings. Parking and garden. Children allowed at the management's discretion. Just north of the city centre on the left-hand side. On the A612 Newark to Southwell road.

11am–3pm and 5–11pm Mon–Thurs;
11am–11pm Fri–Sat; 12–10.30pm Sun.

O'Rourkes Bar

10 Raleigh Street, Nottingham
☎ *(0115) 970 1092* Mrs Rhodes

Adnams Bitter and Greene King Abbot Ale usually available.

Friendly, cosy pub with hand-painted murals. Big screen entertainment, karaoke, pool and quiz nights. Food served 12–2.30pm and 4–7pm Mon–Fri, 12–4pm Sat–Sun. Children permitted only if eating. Car park.

All day, every day.

The Vat & Fiddle

Queensbridge Road, Nottingham NG2 1NB
☎ *(0115) 985 0611* Jerry Divine

The full range of Castle Rock ales brewed and served on the premises. Plus guest ales such as Archers Golden, Whim Hartington IPA, Everards Tiger or Belvoir Star Bitter also available. Micro-breweries favoured.

An old-fashioned alehouse, no machines, TV or music. Small beer garden under construction. Situated on the edge of Nottingham, near the railway station. Food served 12–3pm daily, plus Thurs–Sat 6–8pm. Children allowed if eating.

All day, every day.

Ye Olde Trip to Jerusalem

Brewhouse Yard, Castle Road, Nottingham
NG1 6AD
☎ *(0115) 947 3171* Patrick Dare (Manager)

A Hardys & Hansons tied house with Kimberley Mild, Classic and Best always available, plus Marston's Pedigree. Other seasonal Kimberley ales available as guests.

A three-bar pub built inside raw sandstone caves in the Castle Rock. Two courtyards. No music or juke box. Food served at lunchtime until 3pm during the week, and until 5pm at weekends. No children.

All day, every day.

OLLERTON

The Olde Red Lion

Eakring Road, Nr Ollerton, Wellow NG22 0EG
☎ *(01623) 861000* Vaughan Mitchell

A freehouse with Maypole Lion's Pride and Shepherd Neame Spitfire always available plus three guests, regularly including Charles Wells Bombardier.

A 400-year-old country village pub. No music or games. Food available at lunchtime and evenings in a separate dining area. Beer garden. Children allowed.

11am–3.30pm and 6–11pm Mon–Fri;
11.30am–4pm and 6–11pm Sat; all day
Sun. (Hours may vary during the winter.)

RADCLIFFE ON TRENT

The Royal Oak

Main Road, Radcliffe on Trent NG12 2FD
☎ *(0115) 933 3798*

Up to 14 brews available including Marston's Pedigree, Timothy Taylor Landlord, Morland Old Speckled Hen and Fuller's London Pride. Also guests (200 per year) including Exmoor Gold and Black Sheep Bitter.

An Austrian-style pub with a cosy lounge. No food available at present. Car park. Children not allowed.

11am–11pm Mon–Sat; 12–10.30pm Sun.

RETFORD

Market Hotel
West Carr Road, Ordsall, Nr Retford DN22 7SN
☎ *(01777) 703278* Graham Brunt

Exmoor Gold, Greene King Abbot Ale, Marston's Pedigree and Bitter, Timothy Taylor Landlord, Thwaites Bitter and Marston's Head Brewer's Choice usually available, plus three guest ales from local brewers.

Family-run traditionally decorated pub. Bar food available at lunchtime and evenings. Car park, conservatory restaurant, large banqueting suite. Children allowed. Located two minutes through the subway from the railway station.

11am–3pm Mon–Fri; all day Sat; 12–4pm and 7–10.30pm Sun.

UPPER BROUGHTON

The Golden Fleece
Main Road, Upper Broughton LE14 3BG
☎ *(01664) 822262* Andrew Carnachan

Belvoir Beaver and Marston's Pedigree usually available.

A traditional family pub with beer garden and children's play area, situated on the edge of the Vale of Belvoir. Live jazz on Sundays. Food served all day, every day. Car park.

11am–11pm Mon–Sat; 12–10.30pm Sun.

UPTON

Cross Keys
Main Street, Upton, Nr Newark NG23 5SY
☎ *(01636) 813269* Mr and Mrs Kirrage

Bateman XXXB, Springhead Bitter and Marston's Pedigree always available plus two guest beers (150 per year) which may include Butts Bitter, Wild's Bitter, Enville, Whim, Oakham and Batham brews.

A seventeenth-century listed freehouse and restaurant. Open fires, beams, brasses etc. The former dovecote has been converted into a restaurant, the tap room has carved pews from Newark parish church. Bar food available at lunchtime and evenings. Restaurant open Friday and Saturday evenings and Sunday lunch. Car park, garden, children's area.

11.30am–2.30pm and 5.30–11pm Mon–Sat; 12–2.30pm and 7–10.30pm Sun.

WORKSOP

Mallard
Worksop Railway Station, Station Approach, Worksop S81 7AG
☎ *(01909) 530757* Philip Baynes

No permanent beers here, just two regularly changing guests from micro-breweries only.

A Grade II listed building, part of Worksop Station. Occasional beer festivals are held in the cellar bar. Car park. No food. No children.

2–11pm Mon–Fri; 12–11pm Sat; 12–3pm Sun (closed Sun evening).

Manor Lodge Hotel
Manor Lodge, off Mansfield Road, Worksop S80 3DL
☎ *(01909) 474177* Mr AE Ranshaw

Mansfield, Adnams and Charles Wells brews plus six guest beers (60 per year) from Hardington, Brains, Ridleys, Woodforde's and Burton Bridge breweries etc.

Totally independent, unusual five-storey Elizabethan manor pub/restaurant. Open fires. Bar and restaurant food available at lunchtime and evenings. Car park, garden and children's room. Accommodation. Follow the brown tourist signs down the lane off Mansfield Road.

12–3pm and 5–11pm Mon–Fri; all day Sat–Sun.

YOU TELL US

★ *The Red Lodge*, Fosse Way, Screveton
★ *Tom Hoskins*, Queen's Bridge Road, Nottingham

Places Featured:

Aston
Bampton
Bloxham
Bodicote
Brightwell-cum-Sotwell
Burford
Chadlington
Chalgrove
Charlbury
Childrey
Clifton
Crowell
East Hendred
Faringdon
Fewcott

Fifield
Great Tew
Henley-on-Thames
Long Wittenham
Murcott
North Leigh
Oxford
Ramsden
South Moreton
Stoke Lyne
Thame
Wantage
West Hanney
Witney
Woodcote

THE BREWERIES

THE HOOK NORTON BREWERY CO. LTD

The Brewery, Hook Norton, Banbury OX15 5NY
☎ *(01608) 737210*

 MILD 3.0% ABV
Easy-drinking mild.
BEST BITTER 3.4% ABV
Good well-hopped session bitter.
GENERATION 4.0% ABV
Malty, with good balancing hoppiness.
OLD HOOKY 4.6% ABV
Complex. Rounded and highly drinkable.
DOUBLE STOUT 4.8% ABV
Full-bodied and smooth.
HAYMAKER 5.0% ABV
Smooth and full-bodied.
TWELVE DAYS 5.5% ABV
Nutty, malt flavour. Dec–Jan.
Plus seasonal beers.

OLD LUXTERS

Vineyard, Winery and Brewhouse, Hambledon, Henley-on-Thames RG9 6JW
☎ *(01491) 638330*

BARN ALE BITTER 4.0% ABV
Refreshing, well-hopped session bitter.
BARN ALE SPECIAL 4.5% ABV
Golden and smooth.
Plus occasional brews.

W H BRAKSPEAR & SONS PLC

The Brewery, New Street, Henley-on-Thames RG9 2BU
☎ *(01491) 570200*

 MILD 3.0% ABV
Sweet and full-flavoured.
BITTER 3.4% ABV
Session bitter with hops throughout.
OLD 4.3% ABV
Sweet and rounded.
SPECIAL 4.3% ABV
Malty fruit with excellent hop balance.
Plus seasonal brews.

THE WYCHWOOD BREWERY CO. LTD

Eagle Maltings, The Crofts, Witney OX8 7AZ
☎ *(01993) 702574*

 SHIRES XXX 3.7% ABV
Fruit and malt flavour throughout.
SPECIAL 4.2% ABV
Balanced malt and hop flavour with some fruitiness.
HOBGOBLIN 4.5% ABV
Rich roast malt flavour with some fruit and hops.
BLACK WYCH STOUT 5.0% ABV
Rich, black and smooth.
Plus seasonal and occasional brews.

THE PUBS

ASTON

The Flower Pot Hotel

Ferry Lane, Aston, Henley-on-Thames RG9 3DG
☎ *(01491) 574721*
AR Read and PM Thatcher

Brakspear Mild, Bitter, Special and Old available, plus seasonal brews.

Built around 1890, the Flower Pot has been refurbished to provide modern facilities whilst retaining its Victorian character. Situated in pleasant countryside close to the river and half a mile from Hambledon Lock. Large garden. Bar food served lunchtimes and evenings. Children welcome. Car park.

OPEN *11am–3pm and 6–11pm (10.30pm Sun).*

BAMPTON

The Romany Inn

Bridge Street, Bampton OX18 2HA
☎ *(01993) 850237* Trevor Johnson

Archers Village always available, plus monthly promotions of guest beers.

A seventeenth-century Grade II listed pub with Saxon arches in the cellar. Bar and restaurant food is available at lunchtime and evenings. Car park, garden, picnic tables and children's play area. Accommodation. Bampton is situated on the A4095 Witney to Faringdon road. The pub is in the centre of the village.

OPEN *11am–11pm.*

BLOXHAM

The Red Lion Inn

High Street, Bloxham, Banbury OX15 4LX
☎ *(01295) 720352* Mr and Mrs Cooper

A freehouse with Wadworth 6X and Adnams Best always available, plus two guests such as Morland Old Speckled Hen or something from breweries such as Hampshire, Wychwood or Fuller's. Session bitters are generally popular.

A two-bar village pub with large garden and car park. Food served at lunchtime and evenings. Children very welcome if eating: children's menu and play area. Occasional 'children's days', with bouncy castles, etc.

OPEN *11.30am–2.30pm and 7–11pm Mon–Fri; 12–3pm and 7–11pm Sat–Sun (10.30 Sun).*

BODICOTE

The Plough Inn

Goose Street, Bodicote, Banbury OX15 4BZ
☎ *(01295) 262327* JW Blencowe

Home of the Bodicote Brewery, which was established in 1982 with the range of three brews always available, plus seasonal specials.

A small village pub with separate lounge/diner and saloon. Early Tudor building, 'Cruck' cottage design. Food served at lunchtime and evenings. Children allowed if eating.

BODICOTE BITTER 3.9% ABV
BODICOTE NO.9 4.3% ABV
3 GOSLINGS 4.1% ABV
A summer ale, light in colour.
PORTER 4.5% ABV
A black porter.
XXX 6.0% ABV
A winter ale.

OPEN *11am–3pm and 6–11pm.*

BRIGHTWELL-CUM-SOTWELL

The Red Lion

Brightwell-cum-Sotwell
☎ *(01491) 837373* William Prince

Something from Brakspear, West Berkshire and Hook Norton plus a guest beer often from West Berkshire usually available.

Fifteenth-century thatched freehouse with tables at the front and in the courtyard. Garden and restaurant area. Food served lunchtimes and evenings Tues–Sat, lunchtimes only Sun. Children welcome in the beer garden or restaurant area at lunchtimes only. Car park.

OPEN *6–11pm Mon; 11am–3pm and 6–11pm Tues–Sat; 12–3pm and 7–10.30pm Sun.*

BURFORD

The Lamb Inn

Sheep Street, Burford OX18 4LR
☎ *(01993) 823155* Richard De Wolf

Wadworth 6X, Hook Norton Best Bitter and Badger Dorset Bitter regularly available.

A traditional Cotswold inn with log fires and gleaming copper and brass. Tranquil walled garden with a profusion of cottage-garden flowers. Bar food available Mon–Sat lunchtimes; restaurant open 7–9pm Mon–Sat, 12.30–3pm and 7–9pm Sun. Smaller portions available for children. Residents' car park. Descending Burford High Street, take the first turning on the left.

OPEN *11am–2.30pm and 6–11pm Mon–Sat; 12–2.30pm and 7–10.30pm Sun.*

CHADLINGTON

The Tite Inn
Mill End, Chadlington OX7 3NY
☎ *(01608) 676475* Michael Willis

Archers Village always available plus three guest beers (50 per year) which may include Titanic White Star, Wychwood Dr Thirstys and Nix Wincott That. The emphasis is on smaller breweries.

A sixteenth-century Cotswold stone pub with superb country views. Bar and restaurant food is available at lunchtime and evenings. Car park, garden and garden room. Children allowed. Chadlington is just over two miles south of Chipping Norton off the A361. Website: www.titeinn.com

OPEN *12–3pm and 6.30–11pm Tues–Sun; closed Mon (except bank holidays).*

CHALGROVE

The Red Lion
High Street, Chalgrove, Oxford OX44 7SS
☎ *(01865) 890625* Jonathan Hewitt

A freehouse with Fuller's London Pride and a Brakspear brew always available. Plus guests such as Timothy Taylor Landlord or Fuller's seasonal ales.

A one-bar village pub with separate dining area serving home-made food every lunchtime and evenings except Sundays. Beer garden. Children allowed.

OPEN *12–3pm and 5.30–11pm Mon–Thurs; 12–3pm and 6–11pm Fri–Sat; 12–3pm and 7–10.30pm Sun.*

CHARLBURY

The Rose & Crown
Market Street, Charlbury, Chipping Norton OX7 3PL
☎ *(01608) 810103* Mr T Page

Archers Best and Fuller's London Pride always available plus three guest beers (100 per year) from breweries such as Lichfield, Coach House, Smiles, Butcombe, Marston's, Timothy Taylor, Robinson's, Badger and Hook Norton etc. Range of Belgian bottled beers also available.

A popular one-room Victorian pub with a courtyard. No food. Parking, garden and children's room. Located in the town centre. Website: www.topbeerpub.co.uk

OPEN *12–11pm Mon–Fri; 11am–11pm Sat; 12–10.30pm Sun.*

CHILDREY

Hatchet
Childrey, Nr Wantage
☎ *(01235) 751213* Ian James Shaw

Morland Original Bitter usually available, plus four guest beers often from Adnams, Brains, Brakspear, Charles Wells, Fuller's, Gales, Greene King, Hook Norton, Mansfield, Marston's, Ridleys, Shepherd Neame, Wadworth, Young's, Jennings, Vale, West Berkshire or Butts.

Welcoming one-bar village pub. Food served 12–2pm daily. Car park. Garden play area for children.

OPEN *12–2.30pm and 7–11pm Mon–Fri; 12–3pm and 7–11pm Sat; 12–4pm and 7–11pm Sun.*

CLIFTON

The Duke of Cumberland's Head
Clifton OX15 0PE
☎ *(01869) 338534*

Four beers always available including Hook Norton Best, Adnams Bitter and Wadworth 6X. Guests may include Hampshire King Alfred.

Built in the late 1600s, this thatched Oxfordshire village pub serves bar and restaurant food. Car park, attractive gardens, accommodation. Children allowed.

OPEN *12–3pm and 6.30–11pm.*

CROWELL

The Shepherd's Crook
The Green, Crowell, Nr Chinnor OX9 4RR
☎ *(01844) 351431* Mr Scowen

Hook Norton Best, Bateman XB, Batham Best, Timothy Taylor Landlord and Donnington Best usually available.

A quiet, one-bar country pub, no music or games. Beer garden. Food served 12–2.30pm and 7–9.30pm. Fish is a speciality. Bookings taken. Children allowed.

OPEN *11.30am–3pm and 5–11pm Mon–Fri; all day Sat–Sun.*

EAST HENDRED

Eyston Arms
High Street, East Hendred, Wantage OX12 8JY
☎ *(01235) 833320* Alan Strong

Wadworth 6X is a permanent feature, plus a guest beer which may be from Cotleigh, West Berkshire or Isle of Skye breweries.

Traditional, beamed village pub with darts, dominoes and Aunt Sally. Car park. No food. No children.

OPEN *7–11pm Mon–Thurs; 12–3pm and 7–11pm Fri–Sat; 12–10.30pm Sun.*

The Bell

Market Place, Faringdon SN7 7HP
☎ *(01367) 240534* Howard and Sue Roberts

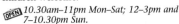 Wadworth 6X and IPA always available.

A thirteenth-century coaching inn, located in the centre of town, with cobbled courtyard recently fully refurbished. Well-known for its floral displays in summer at the back of the hotel. À la carte restaurant and bar food is available at lunchtime and evenings. Eight en suite bedrooms, car park, children welcome.

(OPEN) *10.30am–11pm Mon–Sat; 12–3pm and 7–10.30pm Sun.*

The White Lion

Fewcott, Bicester OX6 9NZ
☎ *(01869) 346639* Paul and Carol King

 Four regularly changing beers which may include brews from Hook Norton, Wadworth, Bateman, Ash Vine, Archers, Rectory, Moor or Holt.

Cotswold stone, country village pub with large beer garden. No food. Car park. Children welcome.

(OPEN) *7–11.30pm Mon–Fri; 12–11.30pm Sat; 12–4pm and 7–10.30pm Sun.*

Merrymouth Inn

Stow Road, Fifield OX7 6HR
☎ *(01993) 831652* Mr Andrew Flaherty

A freehouse with Hook Norton Best and one regularly changing guest ale always available.

An old-style, one-bar pub and restaurant with garden. Large non-smoking areas. Accommodation. Food available 12–2pm and 6.30–9pm. Children allowed.

(OPEN) *11.30am–2.30pm and 6–11pm Mon–Sat; 12–2.30pm and 7–10.30pm Sun.*

The Falkland Arms

Great Tew OX7 4DB
☎ *(01608) 683653* Tim and Ann Newman

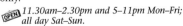 Eight beers available at any one time from a range of about 350 per year. Badger Tanglefoot, Hook Norton Best and Wadworth 6X all favoured. Smaller brewers and some regionals preferred. Also country wines and draught cider.

A traditional seventeenth-century Oxfordshire village inn with a vast inglenook fireplace and smooth flagstones. High-backed settles, oak panelling and beams and sparkling brasses. Bar food every lunchtime and food served in a small dining room from 7–8pm Mon–Sat, booking essential. Parking and garden. Live folk music on Sundays. Accommodation. Filled clay pipes and snuff for sale. Off the B4022, five miles east of Chipping Norton.

(OPEN) *11.30am–2.30pm and 6–11pm Mon–Sat; 12–3pm and 7–10.30pm Sun. Open all day Sat–Sun and bank holidays from Easter–October.*

Bird in Hand

61 Greys Road, Henley-on-Thames RG9 1SB
☎ *(01491) 575775* Graham Steward

A freehouse with Brakspear Mild and Bitter and Fuller's London Pride always available, plus guests on two hand pumps. Examples include Timothy Taylor Landlord, Coniston Bluebird or Mordue Workie Ticket.

An old-fashioned one-bar pub. No music, fruit machines or pool table, not even a till! Large garden. Food served at lunchtime only.

(OPEN) *11.30am–2.30pm and 5–11pm Mon–Fri; all day Sat–Sun.*

Machine Man Inn

Long Wittenham, Abingdon OX14 4QP
☎ *(01865) 407835* Chris Lundsay

A freehouse with West Berkshire Good Old Boy, York Yorkshire Terrier and Rebellion Smuggler always available, plus various guests from breweries such as Crouch Vale.

A three-bar village pub with dining area and interconnected bars. Patio. Accommodation. Food served at lunchtime and evenings. Children allowed.

(OPEN) *12–3pm and 6–11pm (closed Sat lunchtime).*

MURCOTT

The Nut Tree Inn
Murcott, Kidlington OX5 2RE
☎ *(01865) 331253* Gordon Evans

Wadworth Henry's IPA and 6X plus a guest beer, perhaps from Wychwood, Hook Norton, Black Sheep or Charles Wells.

Quaint, white, thatched pub with duck pond, set in a peaceful hamlet. Noted for good steaks and fresh fish. Food served 12–2pm and 6.30–9.30pm Mon–Sat. No food Sun. Car park. Children welcome in the conservatory or outside.

OPEN 11am–3pm and 6.30–11pm Mon–Sat; 12–3pm and 7–10.30pm Sun.

NORTH LEIGH

The Woodman Inn
New Yatt Road, North Leigh, Nr Witney OX8 6TT
☎ *(01993) 881790* Colin Dickenson

Wadworth 6X, Hook Norton Best and Wychwood Shires always available plus two guest beers (150 per year) from breweries such as Adnams, Shepherd Neame, Timothy Taylor, Cotleigh and Charles Wells. The Oxfordshire beer festival takes place here twice a year.

A local village pub on the edge of town, overlooking the Windrush valley. Bar food served at lunchtime and evenings. Car park and garden. Children allowed. Accommodation. Located off the A4095 Witney to Woodstock road.

OPEN 12–2.30pm and 6–11pm Mon–Fri; 12–3pm and 6–11pm Sat; 12–10.30pm Sun.

OXFORD

Folly Bridge Inn
38 Abingdon Road, Oxford OX1 4PD
☎ *(01865) 790106* Eddy Schofield

A Wadworth house with 6X, IPA, Summer Sault (seasonal) and Farmers Glory always available, plus Badger Tanglefoot. Also up to four guests perhaps including Sharp's Doom Bar or Shepherd Neame Spitfire.

A traditional two-bar English pub on the edge of Oxford. Disabled access, patio. Food served at lunchtime and evenings in an environment as smoke-free as possible (there are big smoke extractors). Children allowed.

OPEN All day, every day.

Turf Tavern
4 Bath Place, Oxford OX1 3SU
☎ *(01865) 243235* Trevor Walter

Morland Old Speckled Hen and Archers Golden among the brews always available plus a good selection of guests (442 served during 1998 from more than 200 different breweries).

One of the oldest pubs in Oxford, this is a small, country-style pub in the city centre. Two bars plus an inside and outside alehouse. Three patios. Food available 12–8pm. Children allowed.

OPEN All day, every day.

Wharf House
14 Butterwyke Place, St Ebbes, Oxford
☎ *(01865) 246752* Tony Flatman

Hook Norton Best Bitter and RCH Pitchfork usually available plus two regularly changing guest beers, perhaps from Hampshire, Rebellion, Vale, York, Holt, Moor or Beowulf.

Small, basic but friendly pub on the edge of the city centre, close to the Thames. Sandwiches available at lunchtime. Small car park. Children welcome in the outside seating area, may be allowed inside during bad weather at lunchtime and early evening. Situated at the junction of Thames and Speedwell streets.

OPEN 11am–3pm and 5.30–11pm Mon–Fri; 11am–11pm Sat; 12–4pm and 7–10.30pm Sun.

RAMSDEN

The Royal Oak
High Street, Ramsden OX7 3AW
☎ *(01993) 868213* John Oldham

Hook Norton Best and Archers Golden always available plus a guest (40 per year) such as Brakspear Special, Banks's Bitter, Caledonian 80/- and Titanic Premium.

A sixteenth-century pub, a former coaching inn, situated in a small village. Bar and restaurant food available. Car park and garden. Ramsden is halfway between Witney and Charlbury off the B4022.

OPEN 11.30am–2.30pm and 6.30–11pm Mon–Sat; 12–3pm and 7–10.30pm Sun.

SOUTH MORETON

The Crown Inn

High Street, South Moreton, Nr Didcot
OX11 9AG
☎ *(01235) 812262* Mr and Mrs Cook

Wadworth IPA and 6X, Badger Tanglefoot and Adnams Best always available plus a guest beer (26 per year) from breweries all over the British Isles.

An attractive village pub. Bar and restaurant food available. Car park and garden. Children allowed. The village is signposted from both Didcot and Wallingford.

OPEN 11am–3pm and 5.30–11pm.

STOKE LYNE

The Peyton Arms

Stoke Lyne, Bicester OX6 9SD
☎ *(01869) 345285* Nigel James

Hook Norton Mild, Best Bitter, Generation, Old Hooky and a seasonal beer usually available.

Friendly, unspoilt pub situated in a small village. All beers are gravity dispensed, Best Bitter from the wood. Large garden. No food. Car park. No children.

OPEN 6.30–11pm Mon–Tues; 12–2.30pm and 6.30–11pm Wed–Fri; 12–3pm and 6–11pm Sat; 12–3pm and 7–10.30pm Sun.

THAME

The Abingdon Arms

21 Cornmarket, Thame OX9 2BL
☎ *(01844) 216116* W Bonner

Wadworth 6X, Hook Norton Bitter and Fuller's London Pride usually available, plus two guest beers which may include Vale Wychert Ale or Notley Ale, Hampshire Lionheart or Fuller's ESB.

A sixteenth-century coaching inn which was extensively rebuilt after a fire in 1991. Separate Sky TV, non-smoking section and log fires. Food served lunchtimes and evenings Mon–Fri and all day Sat–Sun. Children welcome, with nappy-changing facilities and high chairs provided, plus play equipment and sand pit. Car park.

OPEN 11am–11pm (10.30pm Sun).

The Swan Hotel

9 Upper Street, Thame OX9 3ER
☎ *(01244) 261211* Sue Turnbull

One Brakspear and one Hook Norton brew usually available plus two guest beers perhaps from Eccleshall, Castle Rock, Hampshire, Rebellion, Timothy Taylor, Shepherd Neame, Clark's, Wye Valley, Flagship, Wychwood, Kitchen and many more.

A sixteenth-century coaching inn situated in the heart of Thame and retaining many original features. Medieval restaurant, oak-beamed bar, log fire, comfortable Chesterfields and seven en-suite bedrooms. Food served lunchtimes and evenings Sun–Fri and all day Sat. Large, free public car park close by. Children permitted before 8pm away from main bar area, but there are no special facilities.

OPEN 11am–11pm Mon–Sat (10.30pm Sun).

WANTAGE

The Royal Oak Inn

Newbury Street, Wantage OX12 8DF
☎ *(01234) 763129* Paul Hexter

West Berkshire Brewery's Dr Hexter's Healer, Dr Hexter's Wedding Ale, Magg's Magnificent Mild and Wadworth 6X permanently available, plus up to six guests.

Fair deals and no frills at this freehouse. Navy paraphernalia decorates the bar. Bar food only available Friday lunchtime. Accommodation.

OPEN 5.30–11pm Mon–Thurs; 12–2.30pm Fri–Sat; 5.30–11pm Fri; 7–11pm Sat; 12–3pm and 7–10.30pm Sun.

WEST HANNEY

The Lamb Inn

West Hanney OX12 0LA
☎ *(01235) 868917* Peter Hall

A freehouse with Young's Special, Oakham Jeffrey Hudson Bitter and Shepherd Neame Spitfire always available, plus two guests changed four times a week from smaller and micro-breweries generally. The landlord tries to stock special beers and not repeat them.

A traditional freehouse. One bar, split into two, children's play area, garden. No juke box, but live music once a week. Annual beer festival on August bank holiday. Food served at lunchtime and evenings. Children allowed in the back room and garden.

OPEN 11.30am–2.30pm and 6–11pm.

House of Windsor

31 West End, Witney OX8 6NQ
☎ *(01993) 704277*
Prue, Stuart and David Thomas

Wadworth 6X, Wychwood Special and Hook Norton Best always available plus one guest beer from breweries such as Fuller's, Archers, Shepherd Neame, Timothy Taylor and Gales.

No machines, no pool or darts in this friendly pub. Coal fire in winter. Bar and restaurant food is available Wed–Sat evenings and Sat–Sun lunchtimes. Large beer garden. Children allowed. Off the A40 and straight across two mini-roundabouts.

6–11pm Mon–Thurs; 4–11pm Fri; 12–3pm and 6–11pm Sat; 12–4.30pm and 6–10.30pm Sun.

The Highwayman

Exlade Street, Woodcote, Nr Reading RG8 0UE
☎ *(01491) 682020*

Fuller's London Pride, Wadworth 6X and Gibbs Mew Bishop's Tipple among those brews always available plus a couple of guests (30 per year) to include Adnams Broadside, Timothy Taylor Landlord, Hook Norton Old Hooky, Shepherd Neame Spitfire and Rebellion ales.

Rambling seventeenth-century country inn with two-roomed bar, beams and open fire. Bar and restaurant food available at lunchtime and evenings. Car park, garden, accommodation. Children allowed in restaurant. Signposted from the A4074 Reading to Wallingford Road.

11am–3pm and 6–11pm Mon–Sat; 12–3pm and 7–10.30pm Sun.

★ *The George & Dragon,* Shutford, Banbury
★ *The Old Anchor Inn,* St Helen Wharf, Abingdon
★ *The Red Lion,* Peppard Common, Rotherfield Peppard

Places Featured:

Aston on Clun
Bishops Castle
Bouldon
Bridgnorth
Cardington
Clun
Coalbrookdale
Craven Arms
Edgeley
Ellerdine Heath
Ironbridge

Little Stretton
Munslow
Oakengates
Oldwoods
Oswestry
Pontesbury
Shifnal
Shrewsbury
Wellington
Wistanstow

THE BREWERIES

HANBY ALES LTD
*New Brewery, Aston Park, Soulton Road, Wem
SY4 5SD*
☎ *(01939) 232432*

BLACK MAGIC MILD 3.3% ABV
Dry, dark and malty award winner.
DRAWWELL BITTER 3.9% ABV
Light, golden medium-strength beer.
ALL SEASONS ALE 4.2% ABV
Quenching, balanced with good hoppiness.
RAINBOW CHASER 4.3% ABV
Rounded, lagerish style.
SHROPSHIRE STOUT 4.4% ABV
Four malts produce powerful flavours.
WEM SPECIAL 4.4% ABV
Straw-coloured and well-rounded.
CASCADE BITTER 4.5% ABV
Very pale, with clean, refreshing hoppiness.
SCORPIO PORTER 4.5% ABV
Complex coffee and chocolate flavours.
PREMIUM 4.6% ABV
Amber-coloured, rounded and malty.
OLD WEMIAN ALE 4.9% ABV
TAVERNERS ALE 5.3% ABV
Smooth, fruity full-bodied old ale.
CHERRY BOMB BITTER 6.0% ABV
Rich, maraschino cherry taste.
JOY BRINGER BITTER 6.0% ABV
Powerful ginger beer. Too easy to drink.
NUTCRACKER BITTER 6.0% ABV
Full-bodied, balanced and distinctive.
Plus seasonal ales and occasional brews.

SALOPIAN BREWERY
67 Mytton Oak Road, Shrewsbury SY3 8UQ
☎ *(01743) 248414*

SHROPSHIRE GOLD 3.8% ABV
Pale, with refreshing fruit and hop
flavours.
MINSTERLEY ALE 4.5% ABV
Smooth and malty with crisp hoppiness.
CHOIR PORTER 4.5% ABV
Mellow porter.
GINGERSNAP 4.5% ABV
Dark, wheat beer with ginger.
PUZZLE 4.8% ABV
Cloudy, white wheat beer.
JIGSAW 4.8% ABV
Black wheat beer.
GOLDEN THREAD 5.0% ABV
Golden, refreshing and moreish.
IRONBRIDGE STOUT 5.0% ABV
Dark with powerful flavours.
Plus occasional brews.

THE WOOD BREWERY LTD
Wistantow, Craven Arms SY7 8DG
☎ *(01588) 672523*

WOOD'S WALLOP 3.4% ABV
Dark, easy-drinking session bitter.
SAM POWELL ORIGINAL 3.7% ABV
Rounded with hop and grain flavours.
PARISH BITTER 4.0% ABV
Light-coloured, refreshing and hoppy.
SPECIAL BITTER 4.2% ABV
Well-rounded and fruity with good hoppiness.
SHROPSHIRE LAD 4.5% ABV
Complex and full of flavours.
SAM POWELL OLD SAM 4.6% ABV
Copper-coloured, rounded and hoppy.
WONDERFUL 4.8% ABV
Powerful flavours. Excellent winter warmer.
Plus seasonal and occasional beers.

THE PUBS

ASTON ON CLUN

The Kangaroo Inn
Clun Road, Aston on Clun SY7 8EW
☎ *(01588) 660263* Michelle Harding

A freehouse with Charles Wells Bombardier and Roo Brew (a house beer produced by the Six Bells Brewery) always available, plus up to three guests from local or micro-breweries whenever possible. Recent examples have included brews from Burton Bridge, Holden's and Moorhouse's.

A prettily situated olde-worlde pub with scenic views. Friendly atmosphere, cosy fire, beer garden and barbecue. Daily newspapers and 'quiet room' available. Food available in separate dining area at lunchtime and evenings. Monthly quizzes, gourmet nights, live music. Children allowed. Situated on the B4368 towards Clun.

7–11pm Mon–Tues; 12–3pm and 7–11pm Wed–Thurs; all day Fri–Sun.

BISHOPS CASTLE

The Six Bells
Church Street, Bishops Castle SY9 5AA
☎ *(01588) 638930* Neville Richards

A freehouse and brewpub, home of The Six Bells Brewery. Three home brews are permanent fixtures plus seasonal ales such as Spring Forward and Old Recumbent when available. An annual beer festival takes place on the second weekend in July.

A traditional two-bar pub with no music or games. Patio. Food available at lunchtime and Fri–Sat evenings. Brewery tours available. Children allowed.

BIG NEV'S 3.8% ABV
Light-coloured session bitter with hop flavours.
MARATHON ALE 4.0% ABV
A darkish, malty brew.
CLOUD NINE 4.2% ABV
Hoppy with citrus flavours in the finish.
Seasonals:
BREW 101 4.8% ABV
SPRING FORWARD 4.6% ABV
OLD RECUMBANT 5.2% ABV
CASTLE STOUT 4.2% ABV
FESTIVAL PALE ALE 5.2% ABV
7 BELLS 5.5% ABV

5–11pm Mon (closed lunchtime); 12–2.30pm and 5–11pm Tues–Thurs and Sun; all day Fri–Sat.

The Three Tuns Inn
Salop Street, Bishops Castle SY9 5BW
☎ *(01588) 638797* Jan Cross

A freehouse and brewpub with the range of three own brews always available plus seasonals and celebration ales three or four times a year. There is an annual beer festival in July.

An old-fashioned, town-centre brewpub; both the pub and the beer recipe date from 1642. Three bars, dining area, garden/yard. Brewery tours and brewery museum. Food available at lunchtime and evenings. Children allowed. Website: www.thethreetunsinn.co.uk

SEXTON 3.7% ABV
XXX 4.3% ABV
A best bitter.
OFFA'S ALE 4.9% ABV
A strong bitter.
SCROOGE 6.5% ABV
A Christmas winter warmer.

12–3pm and 5–11pm Mon–Thurs; all day Fri–Sun.

BOULDON

The Tally Ho Inn
Bouldon, Nr Craven Arms SY7 9DP
☎ *(01584) 841362* Mr S Arblaster

A freehouse with Church End Brewery ales usually available, plus one guest such as Thwaites Daniels Hammer or Morland Old Speckled Hen.

A traditional one-bar village pub with garden. Bar snacks available evenings only. Children allowed.

11am–3pm and 6–11pm Mon–Fri; all day Sat–Sun.

BRIDGNORTH

The Bear Inn
Northgate, Bridgnorth WV16 4ET
☎ *(01746) 763250* Mrs Gennard

A freehouse with Batham Best and Mild always available plus four guests from a wide-ranging list, such as Holden's Special, Salopian Golden Thread or Shepherd Neame Bishop's Finger.

A two-bar town pub with garden. Food available at lunchtime only. No children.

1pm–3pm and 5pm–12am Mon–Sat; 12–3pm and 7–10.30pm Sun.

CARDINGTON

The Royal Oak

Cardington, Church Stretton SY6 7JZ
☎ *(01694) 771266*
David and Christine Baugh

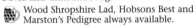 Wood Shropshire Lad, Hobsons Best and Marston's Pedigree always available.

The oldest pub in Shropshire, this is an unspoilt country freehouse, situated in a picturesque hiking/cycling area. One bar, dining room and patio. Food available Tues–Sun lunchtime and Tues–Sat evenings. Children allowed.

Closed Mon, except bank holidays; 12–3pm and 7–11pm Tues–Sun.

CLUN

The White Horse Inn

The Square, Clun SY7 8JA
☎ *(01588) 640305* Bruce Dodgson

Marston's Pedigree usually available with one guest beer that may include something from Salopian, Wye Valley or other micro-breweries or independents.

Set in the beautiful Clun Valley, close to the castle, serving home-made meals in the cosy bar or garden. Food served 12–2pm and 6.30–8.30pm Mon–Sun (except Tues lunch). Children welcome, but no special facilities.

11.30am–2.30pm and 6.30–11pm Mon–Fri; 11.30am–3.30pm and 6.30–11pm Sat; 12–4pm and 6.30–10.30pm Sun.

COALBROOKDALE

The Coalbrookdale Inn

12 Wellington Road, Coalbrookdale, Telford TF8 7DX
☎ *(01952) 433953* Mike Fielding

Fuller's London Pride always available plus up to five guest ales from micro-breweries, both local and across the country.

A traditional village pub with one bar, non-smoking area, air filtration systems and patio. Food served 12–2pm and 6–8pm daily. Children allowed in designated areas.

12–3pm and 6–11pm Mon–Sat; 12–3pm and 7–10.30pm Sun.

CRAVEN ARMS

The Sun Inn and Corvedale Brewery

Corfton, Craven Arms SY7 9DF
☎ *(01584) 861503* Norman and Teresa Pearce

Home brews Norman's Pride and Secret Hop are permanently available plus any special own brews and two guests from micro-breweries such as Six Bells or Lichfield.

A friendly country freehouse with two bars, a quiet lounge and a non-smoking dining area. Food available every lunchtime and evening. Exceptionally good disabled facilities, which have been commended by the Heart of England Tourist Board 'Tourism for All' and British Gas's 'Open to All' award. Children's certificate. Situated on the B4368.

NORMAN'S PRIDE 4.3% ABV
SECRET HOP 4.5% ABV

11am–2.30pm and 6–11pm (10.30pm Sun).

EDGELEY

Olde Vic

1 Chatham Street, Edgeley

Timothy Taylor Landlord always available plus five guest beers (700 per year), all from micro-breweries and independents – no big brewers. Names include Wyre Piddle, Bullmastiff, Wye Valley, Goose Eye and Cotleigh.

Small and cosy pub with beer garden for barbecues. Quiz nights. A CAMRA pub of the year. Bar food served at lunchtime and evenings. Car park. Children welcome. Situated near Stockport railway station.

12–3pm and 5.30–11pm Mon–Thurs; all day Fri–Sun.

ELLERDINE HEATH

The Royal Oak (The Tiddly)

Ellerdine Heath, Telford TF6 6Rl
☎ *(01939) 250300* Barry Colin Malone

Hanby Drawwell, Hobsons Bitter, Wood Shropshire Lad and Shepherd Neame Spitfire usually available, plus a guest from any small independent brewery. Young's Special, Exmoor Gold and Fuller's London Pride make regular appearances.

Lovely country pub in a quiet backwater, yet only a short distance from Telford. Food served during the week 12–3pm and 6–9pm (except Tues), 12–9pm Sat, 12–2.30pm and 7–10.30pm Sun. Children's certificate and play area. Car park. Located halfway between the A53 and A442.

12–11pm Mon–Sat; 12–3pm and 7–10.30pm Sun.

IRONBRIDGE

Ironbridge Brasserie & Wine Bar

29 High Street, Ironbridge, Telford TF8 7AD
☎ *(01952) 432716 Mr Hull*

A freehouse with ales from the local Hobsons brewery always available plus two constantly changing guests. Brains SA is a regular feature, among many others.

A village pub/wine bar/restaurant. One bar, dining area and patio. Food available Fri–Sun lunchtime and Tues–Sun evenings. Children allowed.

OPEN *6.30–11pm Mon–Thurs (closed lunchtimes); 12–2pm and 6.30–11pm Fri–Sun.*

LITTLE STRETTON

The Ragleth Inn

Ludlow Road, Little Stretton, Church Stretton SY6 6RB
☎ *(01694) 722711 D Chillcott*

A freehouse with Hobsons Best always available plus two alternating guests that might include Charles Wells Bombardier, Morland Old Speckled Hen, Shepherd Neame Spitfire, Mole's Best, Hobsons Town Crier or a Tomintoul ale. Large range of malt whiskies also available.

A traditional two-bar country pub with dining area and garden. Limited disabled access. Food available at lunchtime and evenings. Children allowed. Website: www.theraglethinn.co.uk

OPEN *12–2.30pm and 6–11pm; all day Sat–Sun.*

MUNSLOW

The Crown

Munslow, Craven Arms SY7 9ET
☎ *(01584) 841205*
Mr and Mrs Michael Pocock

Formerly a hundred house, this two-bar, traditional freehouse is home to the Munslow brewery. The brewery is visible from inside the pub and the Munslow brews plus a guest beer are usually available.

A ward-winning food served 12–2pm and 7–9.30pm. Car park. Children welcome. Situated on the B4368 between Aston Munslow and Beambridge.

BUTCHERS MILD 3.6% ABV
BUTCHERS BEST BITTER 3.8% ABV
IRONMASTER 4.1% ABV
Brewed for the Golden Ball at Ironbridge.

OPEN *12–2.30pm and 7–11pm (10.30pm Sun).*

OAKENGATES

The Crown Inn

Market Street, Oakengates, Telford TF2 6EA
☎ *(01952) 610888 John Ellis*

A freehouse with Hobsons Best always available plus up to nine guests changing two or three times a week, plus cider. So far, over 1000 ales have been served in four years. Hundreds of breweries featured. Hook Norton, Hanby Ales, Burton Bridge, Wye Valley, Slaters and Lichfield are just a few of the regulars. Only Shropshire beers are sold during the Shropshire Beer Week. Britain's biggest pub-based, hand-pulled beer festivals held twice a year on the first weekends in May and October, featuring 29 hand pulls.

A town-centre pub with three drinking areas, a small yard with picnic tables. Rolls available at lunchtime only. Children allowed in designated areas. Located near the bus and railway stations. Visit our website at: www.oakengates.com

OPEN *12–3pm and 7–11pm Mon–Wed; all day Thurs–Sat; 12–3.30pm and 7–10.30pm Sun.*

OLDWOODS

The Romping Cat

Oldwoods, Shrewsbury SY4 3AS
☎ *(01939) 290273 Mr Simcox*

A freehouse with Fuller's London Pride among the brews always available, plus four guests from breweries such as Adnams, Bateman or Greene King and local breweries such as Salopian.

A traditional rural pub with one bar, no machines or music. Beer garden. No food. No children.

OPEN *11am–3pm Mon, Tues, Thurs (closed Wed and Fri lunchtimes); 7–11pm Mon–Fri; 12.30–3.30pm and 7–11pm Sat; 12–2.30pm and 7–10.30pm Sun.*

OSWESTRY

The Old Mill Inn

Candy, Oswestry SY10 9AZ
☎ *(01691) 657058 Mr and Mrs Atkinson*

Morland Old Speckled Hen always available plus two guests, perhaps an Adnams or Wood brew.

A traditional one-bar country pub with restaurant, garden and children's area. Disabled access. B&B. Food available at lunchtime and evenings. Children allowed.

OPEN *11am–3pm and 6–11pm Mon and Wed–Sat (closed Tues); 12–3pm and 7–10.30pm Sun.*

PONTESBURY

The Horseshoes Inn
Minsterley Road, Pontesbury, Shrewsbury
SY5 0QJ
☎ *(01743) 790278* Mrs Scott

A freehouse with up to four guest ales. Regulars include Fuller's London Pride, but all breweries are featured.

A rural pub with one bar. Food available at lunchtime and evenings. Children allowed if eating. Accommodation.

OPEN *12–3pm and 7–11pm (10.30pm Sun).*

SHIFNAL

The White Hart
High Street, Shifnal TF11 8BH
☎ *(01952) 461161* Andy Koczy

A freehouse with Enville Ale, Chainmaker Mild and Simpkiss Bitter permanently available, plus two guests from micro-breweries whenever possible. Recent examples include Exmoor Gold and Moorhouse's Pendle Witches Brew.

A coaching inn in a traditional timbered building, two bars, beer garden. Food available at lunchtime only. Children allowed.

OPEN *12–3pm and 6–11pm Mon–Thurs; all day Fri–Sun.*

SHREWSBURY

The Dolphin Inn
48 St Michael's Street, Shrewsbury SY1 2EZ
☎ *(01743) 350419* Nigel Morton

A freehouse with Hoskins and Oldfield ales always available, plus four guests from smaller and micro-breweries – no nationals. Phoenix Brewery is regularly supported. There are plans to start brewing.

A pub dedicated to real ales. No lager or beers from national breweries. Traditional decor, wide-ranging, friendly clientele. Coffee available. No food. No children.

OPEN *5–11pm only.*

The Peacock Inn
42 Wenlock Road, Shrewsbury SY2 6JS
☎ *(01743) 355215* C Roberts

Marston's ales are a speciality here, with Pedigree and Owd Roger always available, plus seasonal brews and other guests such as Banks's Mild on one hand pump.

A pub/restaurant with one bar, beer garden, disabled access. Food available at lunchtime and evenings in separate dining area. Children allowed.

OPEN *11.30am–3pm and 6–11pm (10.30pm Sun).*

The Three Fishes
Fish Street, Shrewsbury SY1 1UR
☎ *(01743) 344793* Mr AP Wardrop

Timothy Taylor Landlord, Fuller's London Pride, and Adnams Best Bitter usually available, plus at least one guest beer such as Salopian Golden Thread or Minsterly Ale, Six Bells Big Nev's or Cloud Nine, or beers from Holden's, Hobsons, Hanby, Greene King or Enville.

Old, town-centre, non-smoking pub, serving a variety of real ales and traditional, home-made meals. Food lunchtimes and evenings Mon–Sat; no food Sun. No under 14s.

OPEN *11.30am–3pm and 5–11pm Mon–Thurs; 11.30am–11pm Fri–Sat; 12–3pm and 7–10.30pm Sun.*

WELLINGTON

The Cock Hotel
148 Holyhead Road, Wellington, Telford
TF1 2DL
☎ *(01952) 244954* Peter Arden

A freehouse with four guests, which might include Hobsons Town Crier, Enville White and occasionally Heaven's Gate, a house brew produced for the hotel by the Salopian Brewery.

A traditional pub with two bars, one non-smoking. No food. No children.

OPEN *4–11pm Mon–Wed; 12–11pm Thurs–Sat; 12–3pm and 7–10.30pm Sun.*

WISTANSTOW

The Plough Inn
Wistanstow, Craven Arms SY7 8DG
☎ *(01588) 673251* Kay Edwards

A freehouse with Wood Shropshire Lad and Parish Bitter always available, plus one guest.

A traditional two-bar country pub with restaurant and patio. Food available at lunchtime and evenings. Children allowed.

OPEN *12–3pm and 7–11pm (10.30pm Sun).*

YOU TELL US

★ *All Nations Inn*, Coalport Road, Madeley, Telford (brewpub)
★ *The Castle Vaults Inn*, Castle Gates, Shrewsbury
★ *The Fox & Hounds*, High Street, Stottesdon
★ *The Horseshoe Inn*, Bridges
★ *The King's Arms Hotel*, Church Street, Cleobury Mortimer
★ *The Last Inn*, Wellington Road, Church Aston, Newport
★ *The Mutton & Mermaid*, Shrewsbury
★ *The Old Vaults*, High Street, Ironbridge
★ *The Railway Inn*, Yorton
★ *The Railwayman's Arms*, Hollybush Road, Bridgnorth
★ *The Red Lion*, Bridgnorth Road, Shatterford

Places Featured:

Allerford Crossing	Martock
Ashcott	Nailsea
Barrington	Nether Stowey
Bath	Nettlebridge
Bleadon	North Curry
Bridgwater	Pitminster
Burnham on Sea	Pitney
Chard	Rode
Crewkerne	Shurton
Culmhead	South Cheriton
Frome	Stanton Wick
Hardington Moor	Taunton
Hinton Blewitt	Trudoxhill
Huish Episcopi	Wellington
Kelston	Wellow
Langford Budville	Wells
Langley Marsh	Williton
Langport	Wincanton
Leigh Common	Wiveliscombe
Luxborough	Yeovil

THE BREWERIES

ABBEY ALES LTD
The Abbey Brewery, Lansdown Road, Bath BA1 5EE
☎ *(01225) 444437*

BELLRINGER 4.2% ABV
Golden, hoppy award winner.
TWELFTH NIGHT 5.0% ABV
Christmas brew.

ASH VINE LTD
Unit F, Vallis Trading Estate, Robins Lane, Frome BA11 3DT
☎ *(01373) 300041*

BITTER 3.5% ABV
Hops and bitterness throughout.
CHALLENGER 4.1% ABV
Malty, with a well-hopped, bitter finish.
BLACK BESS PORTER 4.2% ABV
Darker, with fruit flavours and a hoppy finish.
DICK TURPIN 4.3% ABV
Cross between a dark porter and best bitter.
PIGGIN 4.5% ABV
Malty and distinctive.
DECADENCE 4.5% ABV
Malty with some fruitiness.
HOP & GLORY 5.0% ABV
Powerful hoppy flavour with some sweet fruitiness.
Plus a range of seasonal and monthly brews.

BATH ALES LTD
Siston Lane, Webbs Heath, Bristol BS30 5LX
☎ *(0117) 961 5122*

BATH SPA 3.7% ABV
Pale and quenching.
GEM 4.1% ABV
Well-rounded flavours with balancing hops.
BARNSTORMER 4.5% ABV
Roast malt flavour with some fruitiness.
Plus seasonal brews.

BERROW BREWERY
Coast Road, Berrow, Burnham-on-Sea TA8 2QU
☎ *(01278) 751345*

BBBB/4BS 3.9% ABV
CARNIVALE 4.0% ABV
Available late Oct–mid Nov.
MILLENNIUM MASH/MM 4.7% ABV
BERROW PORTER 4.8% ABV
Mellow and fruity.
CHRISTMAS ALE 5.0% ABV
Available Dec–Jan.
TOPSY TURVY 5.9% ABV
Golden, fruity and refreshing.

BUTCOMBE BREWERY LTD
Rusling House, Butcombe, Bristol BS40 7XQ
☎ *(01275) 472240*

BITTER 4.0% ABV
Smooth, rounded and well-hopped.
WILMOT'S PREMIUM ALE 4.8% ABV
Mellow, well-balanced. Hoppy, with fruit flavours.

COTLEIGH BREWERY

Ford Road, Wiveliscombe, Taunton TA4 2RE

HARRIER SPA 3.6% ABV
Pale, with hoppiness throughout.
TAWNY 3.8% ABV
Flavoursome and well-hopped.
BARN OWL 4.5% ABV
Smooth, refreshing with hoppy finish.
OLD BUZZARD 4.8% ABV
Dark, complex winter brew.
Plus occasional and seasonal brews.

COTTAGE BREWING CO.

The Old Cheese Dairy, Lovington, Castle Cary BA7 7PS
☎ *(01963) 240551*

SOUTHERN BITTER 3.8% ABV
WHEELTAPPERS ALE 4.0% ABV
CHAMPFLOWER 4.2% ABV
SOMERSET AND DORSET ALE 4.4% ABV
GOLDEN ARROW 4.5% ABV
OUR KEN 4.5% ABV
GREAT WESTERN REAL ALE 5.4% ABV
NORMAN'S CONQUEST 7.0% ABV
Plus monthly special brews.

EXMOOR ALES LTD

The Brewery, Golden Hill, Wiveliscombe, Taunton TA4 2NY
☎ *(01984) 623798*

ALE 3.8% ABV
Smooth and full-flavoured, with malt throughout.
HOUND DOG 4.0% ABV
Mar–May.
FOX 4.2% ABV
Easy-drinking and flavour-packed.
WILD CAT 4.4% ABV
Sept–Nov.
GOLD 4.5% ABV
Initially sweet, with a hoppy finish.
HART 4.8% ABV
Malty, with balancing hoppiness.
EXMAS 5.0% ABV
Christmas brew.
STAG 5.2% ABV
Well-balanced with lingering finish.
BEAST 6.6% ABV
Dark, with powerful roast malt flavour.
Plus occasional brews.

JUWARDS BREWERY

c/o Fox Brothers & Co. Ltd, Wellington TA21 0AW
☎ *(01823) 667909*

 BITTER 3.8% ABV

Plus occasional brews.

MOOR BEER COMPANY

Whitley Farm, Whitley Lane, Ashcott, Bridgwater TA7 9QW
☎ *(01458) 210050*

WITHY CUTTER 3.8% ABV
AVALON SPRINGTIME 4.0% ABV
MERLINS MAGIC 4.3% ABV
PEAT PORTER 4.5% ABV
SUMMERLAND GOLD 5.0% ABV
OLD FREDDY WALKER 7.3% ABV
Plus occasional brews.

OAKHILL BREWERY

The Old Maltings, Oakhill, Bath BA3 5BX
☎ *(01749) 840134*

BITTER 3.5% ABV
Light and hoppy.
BEST BITTER 4.0% ABV
Malty and refreshing.
BLACK MAGIC STOUT 4.0% ABV
Rich malty flavour with some hoppiness.
CHARIOTEER 4.2% ABV
Distinctive and balanced with fruity aftertaste.
MENDIP GOLD 4.5% ABV
Golden, smooth and rounded.
MENDIP 2K 4.8% ABV
Full-bodied ruby ale. Smooth, fruity hop flavour.
YEOMAN 5.0% ABV
Balanced fruit and hop flavours.

RCH BREWERY

West Hewish, Nr Weston-super-Mare BS24 6RR
☎ *(01934) 834447*

HEWISH IPA 3.6% ABV
Delicate flavours throughout.
PG STEAM 3.9% ABV
Bursting with flavours. Full-bodied for gravity.
PITCHFORK 4.3% ABV
Golden, refreshing and dangerously drinkable.
OLD SLUG PORTER 4.5% ABV
Very dark, traditional porter. Complex flavours.
PUXTON CROSS 4.5% ABV
Single-hop award winner. Occasional brew.
25A 4.7% ABV
Pale and hoppy with good malt character.
EAST STREET CREAM 5.0% ABV
Refreshing, clean flavour, fruity and deceptive.
FIREY LIZ 5.0% ABV
Golden, hoppy, occasional brew.
FIREBOX 6.0% ABV
Powerful bitter with a multitude of flavours.
SANTA FE' 7.3% ABV
Dark, bittersweet Christmas special.

ALLERFORD CROSSING

The Victory Inn
Allerford Crossing, Norton Fitzwarren,
Nr Taunton TA4 1AL
☎ *(01823) 461282* NR Pike

Church End What the Fox's Hat, Cottage Golden Arrow and many many more. Twelve beers always available, 150 per year.

Recently refurbished to enhance the olde-worlde charm and character. Food is available at lunchtime and evenings. Car park, gardens, patio, family room, skittle alley, children's play area. Rooms are available for hire. Take the Norton Fitzwarren road, turn off after Taunton Cider to Allerford.

12–3pm and 6–11pm.

ASHCOTT

Ring o'Bells
High Street, Ashcott, Bridgwater TA7 9PZ
☎ *(01458) 210232* John Foreman

A freehouse with three hand pumps serving a range of constantly changing real ales. The local Moor Beer Company in Ashcott is regularly supported, plus smaller independents and micros, too many to mention.

A medium-sized village pub with three bars, non-smoking dining area and beer garden. Food available at lunchtime and evenings. Children allowed.

12–2.30pm and 7–11pm (10.30pm Sun).

BARRINGTON

The Royal Oak
Barrington, Nr Illminster TA19 0JB
☎ *(01460) 53455* Mr Jarvis

At least five guest beers always available (300 per year) from all corners of the United Kingdom.

A Grade II listed building, sixteenth-century cyder house. Bar and restaurant food served at lunchtime and evenings. Car park, garden and children's room. Follow the National Trust signs for Barrington Court.

12–3pm and 5.30–11pm Mon–Thurs; 12–11pm Fri–Sun (10.30pm Sun).

BATH

Hatchett's
6–7 Queen Street, Bath BA1 1HE
☎ *(01225) 425045* Mr and Mrs Cruxton

Up to five beers always available including a house bitter. The three or four guest beers may include Smiles Exhibition, Shepherd Neame Spitfire, Badger Hard Tackle and Exmoor Gold.

A nineteenth-century pub in Bath city centre with bars upstairs and down. The house bitter is available at £1.50. All beers at reasonable prices. Bar food available at lunchtime. Down a side street in the city centre.

11am–11pm Mon–Sat; 12–10.30pm Sun.

The Hobgoblin
47 St James' Parade, Bath BA8 1UZ
☎ *(01225) 460785* Fidelma Tracey (manager)

A freehouse specialising in Wychwood ales, so Hobgoblin and Wychwood Special always available plus three guests.

A lively town pub with a student clientele. Two bars, tables outside. Food available Mon–Wed 12–2.30pm; Thurs–Fri 12–5pm and Sat 12–4pm. Children allowed.

All day, every day.

The Old Farmhouse
1 Lansdown Road, Bath BA1 5EE
☎ *(01225) 316162* John Bradshaw

Wadworth 6X and IPA, Badger Tanglefoot and beers from Butcombe and Abbey Ales always available, plus occasional guests.

A town pub and restaurant. Two bars, live jazz four nights a week. Patio. Food available. Well-behaved children allowed.

All day, every day.

The Old Green Tree
12 Green Street, Bath BA1 2JZ
☎ *(01225) 448259*
Nick Luke and Sarah le Fèvre

Only stocks draught beer from micro-breweries within a 60-mile radius. Five beers always available including Wickwar Brand Oak Bitter. Others rotated slowly including brews from Uley, Cottage, RCH, Abbey, Bath Ales and Oakhill.

Small oak-lined city-centre pub. No music or machines. Bar food at lunchtime. On a small street in city centre between Milsom Street and the post office.

11am–11pm Mon–Sat; 7–10.30pm Sun.

The Pig & Fiddle

2 Saracen Street, Bath BA1 5BR
☎ *(01225) 460868* Gregory Duckworth

Ash Vine Bitter, Challenger and Hop and Glory among six beers always available. Approximately 100 guest beers per year including Crouch Vale Golden Duck, Fuller's London Pride, Exmoor Stag and Butcombe Bitter.

Very busy town-centre pub but with very relaxed atmosphere. Large outside area including garden. Bar food available at lunchtime. Children not allowed. Opposite the Hilton Hotel.

11.30am–11pm summer; 11.30am–3pm and 5–11pm winter.

BLEADON

The Queen's Arms

Celtic Way, Bleadon, Nr Weston-super-Mare BS24 ONF
☎ *(01934) 812080* Anita and Chris Smith

Palmers IPA and Bridport Bitter, Butcombe Bitter, Badger Tanglefoot and Ringwood Old Thumper always available, plus guest beers.

A friendly sixteenth-century freehouse with flagstone floors and settles, specialising in good food and real ales served straight from the barrel. A good stop for refreshment on the Mendip Walk (last food 9.30pm). Website: www.queensarms.co.uk

11am–2.30pm and 5.30–11pm Mon–Fri; 11am–11pm Sat; 12–10.30pm Sun.

BRIDGWATER

The Fountain Inn

1 West Quay, Bridgwater TA6 3HL
☎ *(01278) 424115*
Gordon Kinnear and Gen Ridgley

Seven real ales always available, including Wadworth 6X and IPA, Badger Tanglefoot and Butcombe Bitter, plus two guests such as Red Shoot Brewery's Forest Gold, Tom's Tipple or seasonal Wadworth ales like Summer Sault.

A traditional one-bar town-centre pub. Background music. Rolls and bar snacks available at lunchtimes only. Several beer festivals held every year, one main festival and then two or three smaller ones throughout the year with up to 18 beers on at a time. No children.

6–11pm Mon–Thurs; 11am–11pm Fri; 11am–3pm and 6–11pm Sat; 12–3pm and 7–10.30pm Sun.

BURNHAM ON SEA

The Royal Clarence Hotel

31 The Esplanade, Burnham on Sea TA8 1BQ
☎ *(01278) 783138*

RCH Pitchfork, PG Steam, East Street Cream and Butcombe Bitter always available plus many other guests, changed throughout the year.

An old coaching hotel under new ownership. Hosts two beer festivals per year and many cabaret attractions. Bar food available all day. Conference facilities. New sports bar with giant TV. Parking, accommodation. Children allowed. Take M5 junction 22, then make for the sea front. The hotel is by the pier.

11am–11pm Mon–Sat; 12–10.30pm Sun. Sports bar has a late licence (1am).

CHARD

The Bell & Crown Inn

Combe Street, Chard TA20 1JP
☎ *(01460) 62470* Marilyn Randall

Otter Bitter and Otter Ale are permanent fixtures, plus three guests, usually from West Country breweries, or seasonal and celebration ales.

A quiet, old-fashioned pub with gas lights. No music. Beer garden. Food available Tues–Sun lunchtime. Children allowed.

11.30am–3pm and 7–11pm (10.30pm Sun).

CREWKERNE

The Crown Inn

34 South Street, Crewkerne TA18 8DB
☎ *(01460) 72464* Trevor Roberts

Ringwood and Exmoor brews usually available.

Welcoming inn dating from 1610. Bar snacks served early evening only. Accommodation. No children.

6.30–11pm Mon–Sat; 12–3pm and 7–10.30pm Sun.

CULMHEAD

Holman Clavel Inn

Culmhead, Taunton TA3 7EA
☎ *(01823) 421432* Cara Lawrence

A freehouse with Butcombe Bitter always available plus three weekly changing guests such as Butcombe Gold, Otter Ale, Church End Vicar's Ruin and What the Fox's Hat, Concertina Bengal Tiger or a Juwards brew.

A fourteenth–century rural pub with garden. Food available at lunchtime and evenings. Children allowed.

12–3pm and 5–11pm (10.30pm Sun).

FROME

The Horse & Groom

East Woodlands, Frome BA11 5LY
☎ *(01373) 462802* Ann-Marie Gould

Greene King IPA, Wadworth 6X and a Butcombe brew always available, plus one guest, changing weekly, which might be Bateman XB or a Brakspear brew.

A two-bar country freehouse with log fires, flag floors, restaurant, conservatory and beer garden. Restaurant and bar food available at lunchtime and evenings. Children allowed in the restaurant only.

11.30am–2.30pm and 6.30–11pm (10.30pm Sun).

HARDINGTON MOOR

The Royal Oak Inn

Moor Lane, Hardington Moor, Yeovil BA22 9NW
☎ *(01935) 862354* 'Hag' Harris

Ales from Butcombe, Brakspear and Branscombe always available plus two guests such as Hook Norton Old Hooky or a Slaters (Eccleshall) brew. Annual themed beer festival held in May each year.

A rural farmhouse freehouse. Two bars, dining area, beer garden, motorcycle-friendly. Food available Tues–Sun lunchtime and evenings. Children allowed.

12–2.30pm and 7–11pm (10.30pm Sun).

HINTON BLEWITT

Ring O'Bells

Hinton Blewitt, Nr Bristol BS39 5AN
☎ *(01761) 452239* Jon Jenssen

Abbey Bellringer and Wadworth 6X usually available with two guest beers, perhaps from Ash Vine, Young's, Fuller's, Butts, Wickwar, Badger or Oakhill.

Traditional country pub with lovely views Food served 12–2pm and 7–10pm. Car park. Children welcome, but no special facilities.

12–3.30pm and 5–11pm (10.30pm Sun).

HUISH EPISCOPI

The Rose & Crown

Huish Episcopi, Langport TA10 9QT
☎ *(01458) 250494* Steve Pittard

A freehouse with a Teignworthy ale always available plus three guests such as Branscombe Vale Summa That, Hop Back Summer Lightning or others from local breweries.

A country pub with central servery and lots of smaller adjoining rooms. Beer garden. Food available at lunchtime and evenings. Children allowed.

11.30am–2.30pm and 5.30–11.30pm Mon–Thurs; all day Fri–Sun.

KELSTON

The Old Crown

Bath Road, Kelston, Nr Bath
☎ *(01225) 423371*

Butcombe Bitter, Smiles Best, and Wadworth 6X always available plus Wadworth Old Timer in winter only.

Traditional old-English pub and restaurant with open fire, original flagstones, candle-light and good atmosphere. Bar food at lunchtime (not Sun), restaurant Thurs–Sat evenings only. Car park and garden. On A43 Bitton to Bath road, three miles outside Bath.

11.30am–2.30pm and 5–11pm Mon–Fri; 11.30am–3pm and 5–11pm Sat; 12–3pm and 7–10.30pm Sun.

LANGFORD BUDVILLE

Martlet Inn

Langford Budville, Wellington TA21 0QZ
☎ *(01823) 400262* Richard Owen

A freehouse with Cotleigh Tawny and Barn Owl and Exmoor Ale always available, plus one guest.

A traditional country pub with dining area and beer garden. Food available at lunchtime and evenings. No juke box or games machines. Children allowed in designated areas.

12–2.30pm Tues–Sat (closed Mon lunchtimes); 7–11pm Mon–Sat; 12–3pm and 7–10.30pm Sun.

LANGLEY MARSH

The Three Horseshoes

*Langley Marsh, Wiveliscombe, Nr Taunton
TA4 2UL*
☎ *(01984) 623763* John Hopkins

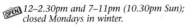 Palmers IPA, Otter Best and Fuller's
London Price always available plus guest
beers which may inclue Harveys Sussex Best
and Timothy Taylor Landlord.

An old, unspoilt, no-nonsense traditional
pub. No juke box or games machines. Bar
and restaurant food is available at lunchtime
and evenings. Car park, garden and
children's room. Children allowed
in the restaurant. Follow the B3227 to
Wiveliscombe, then follow signs to Langley
Marsh.

[OPEN] *12–2.30pm and 7–11pm (10.30pm Sun);
closed Mondays in winter.*

LANGPORT

The Black Swan

North Street, Langport
☎ *(01458) 250355* Chris Pullen

Palmers IPA and Dorset Gold regularly
available, plus a guest beer such as
Badger Tanglefoot, Fuller's London Pride,
Exmoor Stag or Hart, Eldridge Pope Royal
Oak or Hardy County or something from
Cotleigh or Cottage.

Characterful inn with restaurant, skittle
alley and beer garden. Food served
12–2pm and 7–9.30pm every day except
Tuesday. Car park. Children welcome.

[OPEN] *11am–2.30pm and 6–11pm Mon–Fri;
11am–4pm and 6–11pm Sat; 11am–4pm
and 7–10.30pm Sun.*

LEIGH COMMON

Hunters Lodge Inn

Leigh Common, Wincanton BA9 8LD
☎ *(01747) 840439* Mr Bent

A freehouse but with Oakhill Brewery
ales usually available plus a range of
guests from micro-breweries.

A country pub with bars, dining area and
beer garden. Food available at lunchtime
and evenings. Children allowed.

[OPEN] *All day, every day.*

LUXBOROUGH

Royal Oak of Luxborough

*Exmoor National Park, Luxborough, Nr Dunster
TA23 0SH*
☎ *(01984) 640319* Mr K Draper

A freehouse with Cotleigh Tawny and
Exmoor Gold always available plus up
to four guest beers (150 per year) such as
Shepherd Neame Spitfire, Exmoor Beast,
Cottage Golden Arrow and Cotleigh Harrier
SPA, plus brews from Ash Vine, Moor and
Bateman.

An unspoilt rural pub with loads of beams,
flagstones etc. Farmhouse tables. Bar and
restaurant food available at lunchtime and
evenings. Car park and garden. Children
allowed in the restaurant. En suite
accommodation. Off the A396, four miles
south of Dunster.

[OPEN] *11am–2.30pm and 6–11pm.*

MARTOCK

The Nag's Head

East Street, Martock TA12 6NF
☎ *(01935) 823432* Christopher Bell

A freehouse with Otter Bitter among the
brews always available, plus two weekly
changing guests such as Timothy Taylor
Landlord, RCH East Street Cream, Badger
Tanglefoot or other seasonal and celebration
ales.

A local village pub with two bars (lounge
and public), non-smoking dining area,
beer garden, children's play area,
accommodation, disabled access at rear.
Home-made food available at lunchtime and
evenings. Children allowed in the garden
play area only. Can be difficult to find, but
worth it! Phone for directions.

[OPEN] *12–3pm Fri–Sun; 6–11pm daily.*

NAILSEA

The Blue Flame Inn

West End, Nailsea
☎ *(01275) 856910* Mick Davidson

Fuller's London Pride always available
plus two or three guest beers at any
time, including beers from Oakhill, Butcome,
Wickwar and Smiles.

Charming, 200-year-old real country pub
between Nailsea and Clevedon, popular
with locals, joggers, riders and walkers. Three
rooms and a bar, all with real character.
Furnished with mismatched tables and
chairs, as far as you can get from high-street
theme pubs. Large garden with swings,
covered drinking area and a barbecue.
Children allowed everywhere except the
public bar. Car park. No food.

[OPEN] *12–3pm and 6–11pm.*

NETHER STOWEY

The Rose & Crown
St Mary Street, Nether Stowey TA5 1LJ
☎ *(01278) 732265* Malcolm and Gill Bennett

A freehouse with three hand pumps always serving cask ales from breweries such as Cottage, Moor, Oakhill, Cotleigh, Slaters, Ash Vine and Otter.

A traditional fifteenth-century coaching inn. One bar, lounge and beer garden. Food at lunchtime and evenings. Separate restaurant is open Fri–Sun. Children allowed.

OPEN *12–11pm Mon–Sat; 12–5pm and 7–10.30pm Sun.*

NETTLEBRIDGE

Nettlebridge Inn
Nettlebridge, Nr Oakhill
☎ *(01749) 841360* Heather Derrick

Oakhill Best Bitter and Wadworth 6X regularly available.

Olde-worlde, two-bar pub with non-smoking area and lots of hanging baskets in summer. Food served 12–1.45pm and 6–10pm Mon–Sat and 12–10pm Sun. Car park. Children welcome.

OPEN *12–3pm and 6–11pm Mon–Sat; 12–10.30pm Sun.*

NORTH CURRY

The Bird in Hand
1 Queen Street, North Curry, Taunton TA3 6LT
☎ *(01823) 490248* Michael Gage

A freehouse with Badger Tanglefoot and Otter Bitter always available, plus four weekly changing guest pumps perhaps featuring Cotleigh Tawny, RCH Pitchfork, Fuller's London Pride or Exmoor Gold.

A traditional one-bar country pub with log fires and beer garden. Food at lunchtime and evenings. Children at lunchtime only.

OPEN *12–3pm Tues–Sun (closed Mon lunch); 7–11pm daily.*

PITMINSTER

The Queen's Arms
Pitminster, Nr Taunton TA3 7AZ
☎ *(01823) 421529*
Chris and Fay Handscombe

Cotleigh Tawny always available plus up to five guests including Everards Tiger and brews from Ballard's, Teignworthy, Cottage Brewery, etc.

A traditional stone-built pub with a dining room in an attached fourteenth-century restaurant. No background music or games machines. Bar and restaurant food at lunchtime and evenings. Seafood specialities. Car park and garden. Children allowed in the bar until 8pm. Follow the signs for Corfe from Taunton and turn right in Corfe.

OPEN *11am–3pm and 5–11pm.*

PITNEY

Halfway House
Pitney, Nr Langport TA10 9AB
☎ *(01458) 252513* J Litchfield

Up to ten beers available, including brews from Teignworthy, Cotleigh, Butcombe, Otter and Hop Back breweries, plus others.

A real ale pub with flagstone floors and log fires. No music or games machines. Bar food is available at lunchtime and evenings. Car park and garden. Well-behaved children allowed. CAMRA Somerset pub of the year. On the main road between Somerton and Langport (B3151).

OPEN *11.30am–2.30pm and 5.30–11pm.*

RODE

The Bell Inn
13 Frome Road, Rode BA3 6PW
☎ *(01373) 830356* Jeff Simmons

Two guest pumps offering real ales such as Eldridge Pope Royal Oak (Thomas Hardy).

A food-oriented country pub specialising in seafood. Two bars, dining area and beer garden. Food available at lunchtime and evenings. Children allowed.

OPEN *12–3pm and 7–11pm (10.30pm Sun).*

SHURTON

The Shurton Inn
Shurton, Bridgwater TA5 1QE
☎ *(01278) 732695* Dennis Gooden

A freehouse with two Exmoor ales always available, plus one changing guest.

A country pub with one big bar, dining area and beer garden. Food available at lunchtime and evenings. Children allowed.

OPEN *11am–2.30pm and 6–11pm (10.30pm Sun).*

SOUTH CHERITON

The White Horse Inn
South Cheriton, Templecombe BA8 0BL
☎ *(01963) 370394* Miss J Bown

Butcome Bitter and Bath Ales SPA usually available with a guest beer often from Ash Vine or Bath Ales.

Seventeenth-century, two-bar country freehouse set in the Blackmore Vale with beamed bar and open fires. Large beer garden. Two car parks. Well-behaved children welcome. Food served every session.

OPEN *12–3pm and 5.30–11pm Mon–Fri; all day Sat–Sun depending on trade.*

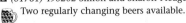

STANTON WICK

Carpenters Arms

Stanton Wick, Nr Pensford BS39 4BX
☎ *(01761) 490202* Simon and Sharon Pledge

Two regularly changing beers available.

Traditional pub with restaurant, situated just off the A368. Accommodation and disabled facilities. Food available in bar and restaurant all day every day. Car park. Children's menu.

OPEN *11am–11pm Mon–Sat; 12–10.30pm Sun.*

TAUNTON

The Eagle Tavern

South Street, Taunton TA1 3AF
☎ *(01823) 275713* Chris Handscombe

Greene King Abbot and a Robinson's brew always available, plus one guest from an independent brewery such as Juwards or Princetown.

A country-style pub in the town, with wooden floors and open fire. Beer garden. Food available at lunchtime and evenings. Children allowed until 8pm.

OPEN *11am–3pm (5pm in summer) and 6–11pm (10.30pm Sun.)*

Perkin Warbeck

22 East Street, Taunton TA1 3LP
☎ *(01823) 335830* Mike Davies

A Wetherspoon's pub with Exmoor Gold among the beers always available, plus two guests such as Wadworth 6X and Stag or Butcombe ales, but beers from any brewery may be stocked if available.

A one-bar town-centre pub. Non-smoking areas, patio. Food avaiable all day, every day. No children.

OPEN *All day, every day.*

Wood Street Inn

Wood Street, Taunton
☎ *(01823) 333011* Shirley Higgins

Three guest beers regularly available often from Cotleigh, Exmoor, Cottage, RCH or Smiles.

Small, friendly family-run pub with live music most weekends. Bar food served all day. Children welcome.

OPEN *11am–11pm Mon–Sat; 12–10.30pm Sun.*

TRUDOXHILL

The White Hart

Trudoxhill, Nr Frome BA11 2DT
☎ *(01373) 836324* Mark Chalkley

This freehouse was once a brewpub, the home of the Ash Vine Brewery, but Ash Vine's expansion forced it to move to bigger premises and become a separate, independent brewery. The close links between the pub and brewery are maintained though, and a good range of Ash Vine ales are always available. One or two guests every week might include Wadworth 6X, Fuller's London Pride, Morland Old Speckled Hen or a Butcombe brew. Occasional themed evenings with beers to suit.

A sixteenth-century county pub. One bar, restaurant, garden and children's play area. Food available 11.30am–9pm daily. Children allowed.

OPEN *All day, every day.*

WELLINGTON

The Cottage Inn

Champford Lane, Wellington TA21 8BH
☎ *(01823) 664650* A and L Sullivan

Greene King Abbot Ale, Fuller's London Pride and beers from Black Sheep and Juwards usually available.

Traditional town-centre pub. Food served 12–2pm daily. Children welcome, but no special facilities. Car park. Directions: in Wellington town centre, go past cinema on the left and take the second turning on the left.

OPEN *11am–3pm and 6–11pm Mon–Sat; 12–3pm and 7–10pm Sun.*

WELLOW

The Fox & Badger

Railway Lane, Wellow, Bath
☎ *(01225) 832293* Eric and Susanne Hobbs

Wadworth 6X and Butcombe Bitter usually available , plus one guest beer perhaps from Ruddles or Bateman.

Sixteenth-century pub set in picturesque countryside, with conservatory, courtyard and skittle alley. Food served each lunchtime and evening. Ample village parking. Children and dogs welcome. See web site www.foxandbadger.co.uk for more details.

OPEN *11.30am– 3pm and 6–11pm Mon–Thurs; 11.30am–11pm Fri–Sun.*

WELLS

The Burcott Inn
Wookey Road, Wookey, Wells BA5 1NJ
☎ *(01749) 673874 Ian and Anne Stead*

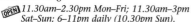 A freehouse with Cottage Southern Bitter always available, plus two guests changing regularly. These may be Timothy Taylor Landlord or Teignworthy Springtide or brews from Cotleigh or Hop Back.

A two-bar country pub with restaurant and garden. Food available at lunchtime and evenings. Children allowed in the garden or inside if eating.

OPEN *11.30am–2.30pm Mon–Fri; 11.30am–3pm Sat–Sun; 6–11pm daily (10.30pm Sun).*

WILLITON

The Egremont Hotel
1 Fore Street, Williton, Taunton TA4 4PX
☎ *(01984) 632500 A Yon*

A freehouse with RCH Pitchfork, Butcombe Gold and an Oakhill brew always available, plus guests such as Hop Back Summer Lightning served straight from the barrel.

A town-centre hotel with two bars, one mainly serving ciders. Restaurant, beer garden, accommodation. Food available in the restaurant at lunchtime and evenings, and bar snacks all day. Children allowed.

OPEN *All day, every day.*

The Forester's Arms Hotel
Long Street, Williton, Taunton TA20 3PX
☎ *(01984) 632508 Mr A Goble*

A freehouse with Cotleigh Tawny and Harrier SPA always available, plus three guests from breweries such as Berrow, Otter or Ash Vine.

A two-bar village pub with dining area, beer garden, accommodation. Food served at lunchtime and evenings. Children allowed, if eating.

OPEN *All day, every day.*

WINCANTON

The Bear Inn
12 Market Place, Wincanton BA9 9LP
☎ *(01963) 32581 Ian Wainwright*

A freehouse with Greene King Abbot always available plus two guests. Regulars include Ringwood Best and Fortyniner, Slaters (Eccleshall) Original and many more.

An old coaching inn with food available at lunchtime and evenings in a separate dining area. Accommodation. Children allowed.

OPEN *All day, every day.*

WIVELISCOMBE

The Bear Inn
10 North Street, Wiveliscombe TA4 2JY
☎ *(01984) 623537 Mr A and Mrs H Harvey*

Butcombe Bitter, Exmoor Gold, Cotleigh Harrier and Tawny regularly available, plus or one two guest beers often from Otter, Teignworthy, Branscombe Vale, Moor or Bath Ales.

Welcoming locals' pub with large, well-laid-out garden and patio. Food served 12–2.30pm and 6–9pm daily. Car park. Family room and large, safe beer garden with children's play equipment.

OPEN *Summer: 11am–11pm Mon–Sat; 12–10.30pm Sun. Winter: 11am–3pm and 6–11pm Mon–Sat; 12–3pm and 7–10.30pm Sun.*

YEOVIL

The Armoury
1 The Park, Yeovil BA20 1DY
☎ *(01935) 471047 Rebecca Keeble*

Wadworth 6X and IPA and a Butcombe brew always available plus two guest ales such as Adnams Broadside.

A traditional real ale house with one environmentally controlled bar. Patio, plans for a skittle alley. Food available at lunchtime and evenings. No children.

OPEN *11am–3pm and 5–11pm Mon–Thurs; all day Fri–Sun.*

YOU TELL US

★ *The Bear & Swan,* South Parade, Chew Magna
★ *The Cooper's Arms Hotel,* Market Street, Highbridge
★ *The Crown,* Keynsham
★ *The King's Head Inn,* Main Street, Higham
★ *The Queens Arms Inn,* Corton Denham
★ *The Ring of Bells,* Pit Hill Lane, Moorlinch, Bridgewater
★ *The Woolpack Inn,* Shepherd's Way, St Georges

Places Featured:

Bignall End
Burston
Burton upon Trent
Eccleshall
Etruria
Fazeley
Great Chatwell
Harriseahead

Ipstones
Leek
Lichfield
Marston
Shraley Brook
Stafford
Stoke-on-Trent
Stone

THE BREWERIES

THE ECCLESHALL BREWERY

The St George Hotel, Castle Street, Eccleshall ST21 6DF
☎ *(01785) 850300*

SLATERS BITTER 3.6% ABV
Balanced easy-quaffer.
TOP NOTCH 3.8% ABV
Summer brew.
SLATERS ORIGINAL 4.0% ABV
Complex and smooth.
TOP TOTTY 4.0% ABV
Well-balanced with good hoppiness.
SLATERS PREMIUM 4.4% ABV
Full-bodied and deceptively smooth.
SLATERS SUPREME 4.7% ABV
Creamy, full-bodied and hoppy.

MARSTON, THOMPSON & EVERARD PLC

The Brewery, Shobnall Road, Burton upon Trent DE14 2BW
☎ *(01283) 531131*

BITTER 3.8% ABV
Well-balanced, easy-drinking brew.
PEDIGREE 4.5% ABV
Smooth and rounded.
OWD RODGER 7.6% ABV
Dark and powerful, with some sweetness.
Plus seasonal brews.

SHRALEY BROOK BREWERY

Knowle Bank Road, Shraley Brook, Audley, Stoke-on-Trent ST7 8DS
☎ *(01782) 723792*

CHARLES FIRST BREW 4.2% ABV
A very light and hoppy bitter.
EXECUTIONER 4.9% ABV
Occasional brew.
GOLDEN SOVEREIGN 5.2% ABV
Occasional brew.

TITANIC BREWERY

Harvey Works, Lingard Street, Burslem, Stoke-on-Trent ST6 1ED
☎ *(01782) 823447*

BEST BITTER 3.5% ABV
Quenching and hoppy.
LIFEBOAT 4.0% ABV
Fruit and bittersweet flavour, with a dry finish.
PREMIUM BITTER 4.1% ABV
Golden, with hoppiness throughout.
STOUT 4.5% ABV
Rich roast malty flavour and some hoppiness.
WHITE STAR 4.8% ABV
Pale, quenching and decepively drinkable.
CAPTAIN SMITH'S STRONG ALE 5.2% ABV
Smooth, rounded roast flavour with good hoppiness.
WRECKAGE 7.2% ABV
Classic winter brew.
Plus monthly brews.

BIGNALL END

The Plough

Ravens Lane, Bignall End, Stoke-on-Trent
☎ *(01782) 720469* Paul Holt

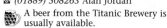 Banks's Bitter permanently available, plus an ever-changing range of guest ales served on four hand pumps.

A traditional roadside pub. Food available lunchtimes and evenings. Children allowed if eating. Car park. Beer garden.

OPEN *12–3.30pm and 7–11pm Mon–Thurs; 12–11pm Fri–Sat; 12–10.30pm Sun.*

BURSTON

The Greyhound Inn

Burston, Stafford ST18 0DR
☎ *(01889) 508263* Alan Jordan

A beer from the Titanic Brewery is usually available.

Traditional seventeenth-century country freehouse in attractive village. Food served lunchtimes and evenings Mon–Sat and all day Sun. Large car park. Children welcome.

OPEN *11.30am–3pm and 6–11pm Mon–Sat; 12–10.30pm Sun.*

BURTON UPON TRENT

The Alfred

Derby Street, Burton upon Trent DE14 2LD
☎ *(01283) 562178* Steve Greenflade

A Burton Bridge Brewery tenancy with Bridge Bitter, Summer Ale, Festival Ale, Burton Porter, Mild and XL Bitter available. Plus one guest, which changes constantly (more than 250 beers served in less than three years). Breweries supported include Leatherbritches and Iceni.

A two-bar town pub with dining area and beer garden. Food served every lunchtime and Mon–Sat evenings. Children allowed.

OPEN *11am–3pm and 6–11pm Mon–Thurs; all day Fri–Sat; 12–3pm and 7–10.30pm Sun.*

Burton Bridge Inn

Bridge Street, Burton upon Trent DE14 1SY
☎ *(01283) 536596* Kevin McDonald

Home of the Burton Bridge Brewery with Bridge Bitter, Porter and Festival Ale always available. Seasonal ales always a feature, for example Summer Ale or Gold Medal Ale. Other guests rotated on two pumps including beers from Timothy Taylor and York breweries.

A one-bar town brewpub. Dining area, patio, brewery tours. Food served lunchtimes. Children allowed.

SUMMER ALE 3.8% ABV
A light golden bitter, brewed during BST.
XL BITTER 4.0% ABV
BRIDGE BITTER 4.2% ABV
Normal brown bitter.
PORTER 4.5% ABV
A dark beer.
SPRING ALE 4.7% ABV
Seasonal.
STAFFORDSHIRE KNOT BROWN ALE 4.8% ABV
Brewed each autumn.
TOP DOG STOUT 5.0% ABV
A winter ale.
HEARTY ALE 5.0% ABV
A Christmas brew.
BATTLE BREW 5.0% ABV
Brewed each July.
FESTIVAL ALE 5.5% ABV
Slightly sweet with a bitter finish.
Plus one new beer each month, always called Gold Medal Ale and at 4.5% ABV, but brewed to varying recipes.

OPEN *11.30am–2.30pm and 5.30–11pm.*

The Roebuck

Station Street, Burton upon Trent DE14 1BT
☎ *(01283) 568660* Ray Ashley

Marston's Pedigree, Greene King Abbot and IPA, and a house brew called Roebuck Bitter always available, plus three guests (approx 700 served over eight years).

Fringe-of-town pub with one open-plan room, small patio, accommodation. Food served 12 noon–11pm. No children.

OPEN *11am–11pm Mon–Sat; 12–3pm and 7–10.30pm Sun.*

Thomas Sykes Inn

Anglesey Road, Burton upon Trent DE14 3PF
☎ *(01283) 510246* Colin Hall

A freehouse with Marston's Pedigree and Owd Rodger usually available plus three guests such as Greene King Abbot or Morland Old Speckled Hen.

A town pub built in an old stable with a cobbled floor. One bar, snug and beer garden. No food. Children allowed.

OPEN *11.30am–2.30pm and 5–11pm Mon–Thurs; all day Fri; 11.30am–2.30pm and 7–11pm Sat; 12–2.30pm and 7–10.30pm Sun.*

ECCLESHALL

The George Hotel

Castle Street, Eccleshall ST21 6DF
☎ *(01785) 850300* Gerard and Moyra Slater

The Eccleshall Brewery is located on the premises, so the Slaters Ales range of up to six beers are brewed and available here plus a variety of guests.

Opened in March 1995 by Gerard and Moyra Slater. The beer is brewed by their son, Andrew. The brewery is a ten-barrel plant. The George is a sixteenth-century coaching inn with olde-worlde beams, log fires, real ales, malt whisky. Bar and restaurant food available. Car park. Accommodation.

OPEN All day, every day.

ETRURIA

The Plough Inn

147 Etruria Road, Stoke-on-Trent
☎ *(01782) 269445* Rob Ward

A Robinson's tied house serving Dark Mild, Best Bitter, Old Stockport Bitter, Hartleys XB and Frederics Premium Ale.

Country-style pub with a collection of valve radios, old TVs, gramophones, telephones, bottled beers and local pictures, plus a preserved classic bus. Beer garden. Well-known locally for good food, which is available 12–2pm Mon–Sat and 7–9pm Mon–Sun. Car park. Children welcome if dining.

OPEN 12–2.30pm and 7–11pm Mon–Sat; 7–10.30pm Sun.

FAZELEY

The Plough & Harrow

Atherstone Street, Fazeley B78 3RF
☎ *(01827) 289596* Paul Kilby

Two brews always available plus two guests such as Morland Old Speckled Hen, Wadworth 6X, Thwaites Daniels Hammer or Fuller's London Pride.

A one-bar village pub. Beer garden. En suite accommodation. New restaurant with food served at lunchtime and evenings. Children allowed.

OPEN 11.30am–3pm and 5.30–11pm Mon–Thurs; all day Fri–Sun.

GREAT CHATWELL

The Red Lion Inn

Great Chatwell, Nr Newport TF10 9BJ
☎ *(01952) 691366* Mrs Paula Smith

Everards Beacon Bitter and Tiger regularly available, plus three guest beers, perhaps from Charles Wells, Robinson's, Wood, Hook Norton, Mansfield, Shepherd Neame, Eccleshall, Lichfield and many others.

Traditional, ivy-clad pub, attracting a mixed clientele. Food served evenings only Mon–Fri, all day at weekends and bank holidays. Car park. Children's play area with animals and birds.

OPEN 6–11pm Mon–Fri; 12–11pm Sat and bank holidays; 12–10.30pm Sun.

HARRISEAHEAD

The Royal Oak

42 High Street, Harriseahead, Stoke-on-Trent ST7 4JT
☎ *(01782) 513362* Barry Reece

A freehouse with Fuller's London Pride and Charles Wells Bombardier often available plus a couple of others from independent and micro-breweries whenever possible. Beers from the Isle of Man are especially favoured.

A traditional village pub with one bar and a lounge. Car park. No food. No children.

OPEN 7–11pm Mon–Fri; 12–3pm and 7–11pm Sat–Sun.

IPSTONES

The Linden Tree

47 Froghall Road, Ipstones, Stoke-on-Trent ST10 2NA
☎ *(01538) 266370* Graham Roberts

A freehouse with guests such as Timothy Taylor Landlord, Whim Hartington IPA and Arbor Light or a Wadworth ale.

A country pub with separate 50-seater non-smoking restaurant. Beer garden. Food served at lunchtime and evenings. Children allowed. E-mail: grlin@ad.com. Website under construction.

OPEN 12–3pm and 6–11pm (10.30pm Sun).

LEEK

Den Engel

23 St Edward Street, Leek ST13 5DR
☎ *(01538) 373751* Geoff and Hilary Turner

Four constantly changing guest beers and small independents and micros are favoured.

Imposing street-corner building, housing impressive continental-style bar. Excellent beer selection. Bar food available Wed–Thurs and Sun evenings, lunchtime and evening Fri and lunchtimes only Sat. A separate restaurant is open Wed–Sat evenings. Ample street parking. Children welcome.

OPEN 5–11pm Mon–Thurs; 12–11pm Fri–Sat; 12–10.30pm Sun.

The Swan Hotel

2 St Edward Street, Leek ST13 5DS
☎ *(01538) 382081* David and Julie Ellerton

Young's Special always available plus three or four rotating guests. Wadworth 6X, Wychwood Hobgoblin and Robinson's Frederics are regular features, plus seasonal specials.

A four-bar town-style pub in moorlands, with an additional bar called JD's attached, which is a young person's modern themed sports bar. Food served at lunchtime and evenings. Children allowed. Function room. Bridal suite. Past winner of CAMRA's pub of the year and pub of the month.

OPEN 11am–3pm and 7–11.30pm.

The Wilkes Head

16 St Edward Street, Leek ST13 5DA
☎ *(01538) 383616*

The Whim Ales flagship pub, with Hartington Bitter and IPA, Magic Mushroom Mild, and Whim Arbor Light always available, plus an ever-changing range of guest ales from around the country. Seasonal ales such as Whim Black Christmas and Old Isaak stocked when available.

An award-winning town pub, famous for its ales. Small and cosy with large beer garden. Children and dogs welcome.

OPEN All day, every day.

LICHFIELD

The Queen's Head

Queen Street, Lichfield WS13 6QD
☎ *(01543) 410932* Roy Harvey

Adnams Best, Timothy Taylor Landlord and Marston's Pedigree always available, plus three guests, which might include Fuller's London Pride, Exmoor Gold or Greene King Abbot.

A traditional, small, back-street pub. No music, small TV, one games machine. Bar food available at lunchtime (12–2.30pm), but the pub is really famous for its selection of cheeses, of which 20 different ones are available all day. Children allowed.

OPEN All day Mon–Sat; 12–3pm and 7–10.30pm Sun.

MARSTON

The Fox Inn

Marston, Nr Church Eaton ST20 0AS
☎ *(01785) 84072*

Eight beers available including Coach House (Joule) Old Priory, Mansfield Old Baily and Charles Wells Eagle. Plus Lloyds and Wood brews and guests from Wychwood, Timothy Taylor etc.

An unadulterated alehouse in the middle of nowhere. Bar and restaurant food available at lunchtime and evenings. Car parking and children's room. Field for tents and caravans. Accommodation.

OPEN 12–3pm and 6–11pm.

SHRALEY BROOK

The Rising Sun

Knowle Bank Road, Shraley Brook, Stoke-on-Trent ST7 8DS
☎ *(01782) 720600* Jill Holland

Home of the Shraley Brook Brewing Company with the range of three home brews avaiable plus guest beers such as Cottage Golden Arrow, RCH Pitchfork and Archers' Golden.

A traditional country pub with three serving rooms, real fires, function room, restaurant, beer garden and a one-acre paddock with Shetland ponies. Plans for brewery tours. Homemade food served at lunchtime and evenings, including real chips! Children allowed.

OPEN 5.30–11pm Mon–Thurs; all day Fri–Sun.

STAFFORD

The Stafford Arms
43 Railway Street, Stafford
☎ *(01785) 253313* Mike Watkins

Six Titanic beers available plus four guests (400 per year) including brews from Orkney, Caledonian, Sutton and many other small independent breweries.

A traditional pub with bar food available at lunchtime and evenings. CAMRA pub of the year 1994. Car park, garden, bar billiards, skittle alley and brewery trips. Children allowed. Just by the railway station.

OPEN *12–11pm Mon–Sat.*

Tap & Spile
Peel Terrace, Stafford ST16 3HE
☎ *(01785) 223563* Mr S Tudeswall

A selection of eight cask ales always available, each changing three times a week so 24 different ales on offer each week. These might well include Timothy Taylor Landlord and Black Sheep Bitter.

A village pub. Non-smoking dining area, beer garden. Food served at lunchtime only. Children allowed.

OPEN *All day, every day.*

STOKE-ON-TRENT

Hogshead
2–6 Percy Street, Hanley, Stoke-on-Trent ST1 1NF
☎ *(01782) 209585* Brett Ritzkowski

A Whitbread house with an extensive range of cask ales always available. Morland Old Speckled Hen and Wadworth 6X on permanently, plus a range of six guests such as Titanic Best or Premium. Each month one beer is featured as Beer of the Month on special offer (buy three get one free).

A town pub in a city-centre location. One bar, disabled access and lift. Non-smoking area. Food available all day. Children allowed before 6pm.

OPEN *All day, every day.*

The Tontine Alehouse
20 Tontine Street, Hanley, Stoke-on-Trent ST1 1AQ
☎ *(01782) 263890* Becky Smith

Marston's Pedigree always available, plus four weekly changing guest ales from independent breweries all over the country.

A one-bar, city-centre pub with beer garden. Food served at lunchtime only. Children allowed, if eating.

OPEN *All day Mon–Sat; closed Sun.*

STONE

The Pheasant Inn
Old Road, Stone ST15 8HS
☎ *(01785) 814603* Mrs Glover

A range of traditional cask ales from independent breweries always available.

A Victorian two-bar pub on the outskirts of town. Recently redecorated dining room and a child-safe beer garden with lockable access though the pub. Darts and traditional pub games. Food available at lunchtime, bookings only for evenings. Children allowed, if accompanied and if eating.

OPEN *All day, every day.*

The Star Inn
Stafford Road, Stone ST15 8QW
☎ *(01785) 813096* Mr Ian Richardson

Banks's Bitter and Original and Marston's Pedigree always available plus two guests such as Cameron Strongarm.

An edge-of-town pub situated by the canal with access to the towpath. Two bars, garden and patio. Food available all day. Children allowed.

OPEN *All day, every day.*

YOU TELL US

★ *The Butcher's Arms,* Reapsmoor
★ *The Crossways,* Nelson Place, Newcastle-under-Lyme
★ *The Plough & Harrow,* High Street, Kinver
★ *The Star,* Market Place, Penkridge
★ *The White Swan,* Coventry Road, Kingsbury, Tamworth

Places Featured:

Bildeston
Boxford
Brandon
Brome
Bungay
Bury St Edmunds
Carlton Colville
Earl Soham
Edwardstone
Felixstowe
Framsden

Freckenham
Gislingham
Hasketon
Ipswich
Kersey
Lavenham
Laxfield
Lowestoft
Pin Mill
Southwold
Swilland

THE BREWERIES

ADNAMS & CO. PLC

Sole Bay Brewery, Southwold IP18 6JW
☎ *(01502) 727200*

BITTER 3.7% ABV
Clean and well-hopped, with fruity flavours.
EXTRA 4.3% ABV
Citrus flavours throughout, with good hoppiness.
REGATTA 4.3% ABV
Seasonal Apr–Aug.
FISHERMAN 4.5% ABV
Seasonal Sep–end Feb.
BROADSIDE 4.7% ABV
Powerful malty brew with balancing hoppiness.
TALLY HO VARIABLE % ABV
Seasonal Dec. Gravity decided on brew day.
Plus seasonal brews.

BARTRAMS BREWERY

8 Thurston Granary, Station Hill, Thurston,
Bury St Edmunds IP31 3QU

MARLD 3.4% ABV
Flavoursome dark mild.
PREMIER 3.7% ABV
Light and hoppy.
RED QUEEN 3.9% ABV
IPA-style brew.
BEES KNEES 4.2% ABV
With honey and coriander.
PIERROT 4.2% ABV
Very light with Tettnang and Saaz hops.
JESTER 4.4% ABV
Full-bodied, easy quaffer.
CAPTAIN BILL BARTRAMS BEST BITTER 4.8% ABV
Full-bodied and strong.
CAPTAINS STOUT
Traditional-style stout also available with cherry or damson.

COX & HOLBROOK

Hillcroft House, High Road, Great Finborough,
Stowmarket IP14 3QA
☎ *(01449) 770682*

OLD MILL BITTER 3.6% ABV
SHELLEY DARK 3.6% ABV
CROWN DARK MILD 3.8% ABV
EAST ANGLIAN PALE ALE 3.8% ABV
STORM WATCH 5.0% ABV
STOWMARKET PORTER 5.0% ABV
PRENTICE 7.0% ABV
Plus occasional brews.

GREEN JACK BREWING CO. LTD

Oulton Broad Brewery, Harbour Road Industrial
Estate, Lowestoft NR32 3LZ
☎ *(01502) 587905*

MILD 3.0% ABV
Occasional.
BITTER 3.5% ABV
CANARY 3.8% ABV
HONEY BUNNY 4.0% ABV
Spring brew.
OLD THUNDERBOX 4.0% ABV
Winter brew.
SUMMER DREAM 4.0% ABV
Summer brew.
GRASSHOPPER 4.2% ABV
ORANGE WHEAT BEER 4.2% ABV
GOLD FISH 4.8% ABV
GONE FISHING 5.0% ABV
NORFOLK WOLF PORTER 5.2% ABV
Occasional.
LURCHER STRONG ALE 5.4% ABV
Occasional.
RIPPER 8.5% ABV
Plus seasonal and occasional brews.

GREENE KING PLC

Westgate Brewery, Bury St Edmunds IP33 1QT
☎ *(01284) 763222*

 XX DARK MILD 3.0% ABV
Sweeter, dark mild.
IPA 3.6% ABV
Hoppy session bitter.
RUDDLES BEST BITTER 3.7% ABV
Transferred from Morland's Abingdon Brewery.
TRIUMPH 4.3% ABV
RUDDLES COUNTY 4.9% ABV
Transferred from Morland's Abingdon Brewery.
ABBOT ALE 5.0% ABV
Rounded and flavoursome.
OLD SPECKLED HEN 5.2% ABV
Transferred from Morland's Abingdon Brewery.

KINGS HEAD BREWERY

132 High Street, Bildeston IP7 7ED
☎ *(01449) 741434*

 BEST BITTER 3.8% ABV
BLONDIE 4.0% ABV
FIRST GOLD 4.3% ABV
Very bitter.
APACHE 4.5% ABV
BILLY 4.8% ABV
DARK VADER 5.4% ABV
Complex, roast character.

MAULDONS

7 Addison Road, Chilton Industrial Estate,
Sudbury CO10 2YW
☎ *(01787) 311055*

 MAYBEE 3.7% ABV
May special brew.
MOLETRAP 3.8% ABV
Rounded easy-quaffer.
BROOMSTICK BITTER 4.0% ABV
Available November.
DICKENS 4.0% ABV
Pale with hoppy fruit flavour and dry finish.
EATONSWILL OLD 4.0% ABV
Dark, old ale.
MID SUMMER GOLD 4.0% ABV
Refreshing summer ale.
MID AUTUMN GOLD 4.2% ABV
Sept–Oct special brew.
PICKWICK BITTER 4.2% ABV
Formerly known as Squires.
CUCKOO 4.3% ABV
Mar–Apr brew.
PLOUGHMAN'S TACKLE 4.3% ABV
Sept–Oct special brew.
GEORGE'S BEST 4.4% ABV
Mar–Apr brew.
THREE LIONS 4.4% ABV
Amber-coloured summer ale.
MID WINTER GOLD 4.5% ABV
Available Nov–Dec.
BLACK SATIN 4.5% ABV
Dark, rounded with good hoppy bitterness.
SUFFOLK PRIDE 4.8% ABV
Powerful hoppiness throughout.
BAH HUMBUG 4.9% ABV
December special brew.

BLACK ADDER 5.3% ABV
Stout.
WHITE ADDER 5.3% ABV
Easy-drinking and well-hopped.
CHRISTMAS RESERVE 6.6% ABV
December special brew.
SUFFOLK COMFORT 6.6% ABV
Superb barley wine.

NETHERGATE BREWERY CO. LTD

11–13 High Street, Clare CO10 8NY
☎ *(01787) 277244*

 IPA 3.5% ABV
Clean hop flavour.
PRIORY MILD 3.5% ABV
UMBEL ALE 3.8% ABV
Distinctive hoppy and coriander flavours.
SUFFOLK COUNTY BEST BITTER 4.0% ABV
Malty and bitter.
AUGUSTINIAN ALE 4.5% ABV
OLD GROWLER 5.0% ABV
Soft, chocolate malt flavours.
UMBEL MAGNA 5.0% ABV
Porter with coriander.
Plus monthly, seasonal brews.

OLD CANNON BREWERY

86 Cannon Street, Bury St Edmunds IP33 1JR
☎ *(01284) 768769*

 BEST BITTER 3.7% ABV
POWDER MONKEY 4.6% ABV
GUNNER'S DAUGHTER 5.5% ABV

ST PETER'S BREWERY CO. LTD

St Peter's Hall, St Peter South Elmham, Bungay
NR35 1NQ
☎ *(01986) 782322*

 BEST BITTER 3.7% ABV
Light, easy-quaffer.
MILD 3.8% ABV
Smooth and delicate traditional mild.
ORGANIC BEST BITTER 4.1% ABV
Refreshing and distinctively hoppy.
EXTRA 4.3% ABV
Hoppy, porter-style beer.
ORGANIC ALE 4.5% ABV
Refreshing, smooth and delicate.
FRUIT BEER (ELDERBERRY) 4.7% ABV
Wheat beer with added elderberry.
FRUIT BEER (GRAPEFRUIT) 4.7% ABV
Refreshing citrus fruit flavour.
GOLDEN ALE 4.7% ABV
Golden, lager-style beer.
SPICED ALE 4.7% ABV
Spicy lemon and ginger flavour.
WHEAT BEER 4.7% ABV
Refreshing, clear and distinctive.
SUFFOLK GOLD 4.9% ABV
Full-bodied bitter ale.
HONEY PORTER 5.1% ABV
Original-style porter with honey.
OLD STYLE PORTER 5.1% ABV
Original porter. Blend of old ale and younger
bitter.
STRONG ALE 5.1% ABV
Smooth, soft and well-rounded.

CREAM STOUT 6.5% ABV
Dark, chocolate cream, bittersweet stout.
SPICED ALE 6.5% ABV
Cinnamon and apple winter brew.
SUMMER ALE 6.5% ABV
Superb balance and easy to drink.
WINTER ALE 6.5% ABV
Balanced winter warmer.

TOLLEMACHE & COBBOLD BREWERY
Cliff Road, Ipswich IP3 0AZ
☎ *(01473) 231723*

MILD 3.2% ABV
Dark with smooth, rich chocolate flavour.
BITTER 3.5% ABV
Hoppy aroma and clean, sharp taste.
ORIGINAL BEST BITTER 3.8% ABV
Full-bodied, with malt and fruit flavours.
COBBOLD'S IPA 4.2% ABV
Golden, hoppy easy-quaffer.
COBNUT SPECIAL 4.2% ABV
Mellow brown ale. September.
SUNSHINE 4.5% ABV
Golden, smooth and hoppy. June–July.
TOLLY OLD STRONG 5.0% ABV
Available Nov–Jan
TOLLYSHOOTER 5.0% ABV
Ruby, balanced and flavoursome.
Plus seasonal and occasional brews.

THE PUBS

BILDESTON

The Kings Head Hotel
132 High Street, Bildeston, Ipswich IP7 7ED
☎ *(01449) 741434/741719*
James Kevin Harrison

Home of The Brettvale Brewery. Kings Head Best Bitter, First Gold, Billy and Old Chimneys Mild regularly available, plus a guest beer often from Old Chimney, Iceni, Buffy's, Wolf, Mighty Oak, Mauldons or Nethergate.

Fifteenth-century timber-framed building with original wattle and daub, situated in a small village. Food served 12–3pm and 7–9.30pm daily. Car park. Children welcome. Accommodation and holiday flat available.

BEST BITTER 3.8 % ABV
FIRST GOLD 4.3 % ABV
BILLY 4.8 % ABV

🍺 *11am–3pm and 5–11pm Mon–Fri; 11am–11pm Sat; 12–10.30pm Sun.*

BOXFORD

White Hart Inn
Broad Street, Boxford CO10 5DX
☎ *(01787) 211071* Marilyn and Barry Hayton

Greene King IPA and Adnams Broadside regularly available, plus two guest beers perhaps from Adnams, Fuller's, Mauldons, Lidstones, Cottage, Wye Valley, Bartrams, Bateman, Charles Wells or Hobgoblin.

Sixteenth-century village pub with garden, separate non-smoking dining-room and home to the local cricket and classic motorcycle clubs. Free quiz night every Sunday. Food served 12–2.30pm and 6–9.30pm Mon–Sat, 12–2.30pm and 7–8.30pm Sun. Children welcome and smaller food portions provided. Website: www.white-hart.co.uk

🍺 *12–3pm and 6–11pm Mon–Sat; 12–3pm and 7–10.30pm Sun.*

BRANDON

The White Horse

White Horse Street, Brandon IP27 0LB
☎ *(01842) 815767* David Marsh

Tolly Cobbold Original, Greene King IPA and Iceni Fine Soft Day usually available plus a variable number of guests, perhaps from Iceni, Mauldons, Wolf, Nethergate, Old Chimneys, Greene King or Tolly Cobbold.

Friendly, family-run freehouse with sporting bias, supporting several darts teams and a successful football team. No food. Car park. Well-behaved children welcome until 8pm. From London Road (by industrial estate), turn into Crown Street. Take the second of two close left turns into White Horse Street.

OPEN *11am–11pm Mon–Sat; 12–10.30pm Sun.*

BROME

Cornwallis

Brome, Eye IP23 8AJ
☎ *(01379) 870326*
Jeffrey Ward and Richard Leslie

St Peter's Best Bitter and a beer from Adnams usually available. A guest such as Fuller's London Pride, Woodforde's Wherry and other St Peter's Brewery beers served.

A former Dower House built in 1561, heavily timbered with a well in the bar. Set in 20 acres of gardens with fine yew topiary, water gardens and ducks. Food served 12–10pm every day, breakfast 7–10am. Children welcome.

OPEN *7am–11pm (10.30pm Sun).*

BUNGAY

The Chequers Inn

23 Bridge Street, Bungay NR35 1HD
☎ *(01986) 893579* Michael and Kim Plunkett

A freehouse with Adnams Best, Fuller's London Pride, Timothy Taylor Landlord and Woodforde's Wherry always available plus five other real ales, changing frequently. More than 1400 different beers served in three years.

A seventeenth-century, two-bar town pub with log fire, large beer garden and patio. Food available Mon–Sat 12–2.30pm. Children allowed. Outside bar facilities available.

OPEN *All day, every day.*

The Green Dragon

29 Broad Street, Bungay NR35 1EE
☎ *(01986) 892681* William and Rob Pickard

Adnams Best plus the four beers from the Green Dragon range brewed and served on the premises.

The pub was bought in 1991 from Brent Walker by William and Rob Pickard. The three-barrel brewery was built and the pub refurbished. Due to increased demand, a second brewery was then built and the capacity expanded to eight barrels. The Green Dragon is a popular pub with a friendly atmosphere. Bar food is available at lunchtime and evenings. Car park, garden, children's room.

MILD 3.4% ABV
CHAUCER ALE 3.7% ABV
BRIDGE STREET BITTER 4.5% ABV
DRAGON 5.5% ABV

OPEN *11am–3pm and 5–11pm Mon–Thurs; 11am–11pm Fri–Sat; 12–3pm and 7–10.30pm Sun.*

BURY ST EDMUNDS

The Old Cannon Brewery

86 Cannon Street, Bury St Edmonds IP33 1JP
☎ *(01284) 768769* Carole and Richard Locker

The full range of Cannon Brewery beers are brewed on the premises and are permanently available in the pub. Also featuring Adnams BB, two guest beers usually from local Suffolk or Norfolk independents and two German Weiss beers.

Half restaurant, half bar, with unique stainless steel brewery sited in the bar. Brewing is done on Mondays, so pub is closed at lunchtime that day. Food available every other lunchtime and every evening. No children. B&B accommodation. Situtated parallel to Northgate Street, off the A14.

OLD CANNON BEST BITTER 3.8% ABV
POWDER MONKEY 4.6% ABV
GUNNER'S DAUGHTER 5.5% ABV

OPEN *12–3pm Tues–Sun; 5–11pm Mon–Sat; 7–10.30pm Sun.*

The Queen's Head
39 Churchgate Street, Bury St Edmunds
IP33 1RG
☎ *(01284) 761554* Alistair Torkington

A freehouse with Adnams Broadside and Nethergate IPA always available, plus guests rotating on one hand pump including, perhaps, Elgood's Black Dog Mild or Timothy Taylor Landlord.

A town-centre pub with a young clientele, particularly in the evenings. One big bar, restaurant, beer garden, conservatory and games room. Food available 12–9pm. Children allowed in the conservatory, garden, games room and restaurant only.

OPEN All day, every day.

The Bell Inn
82 The Street, Carlton Colville, Lowestoft
NR33 8JR
☎ *(01502) 582873*

Green Jack Bitter and Grasshopper always available plus seasonal Green Jack specials such as Gone Fishing and Ripper. Two guests, straight from the barrel, might come from breweries such as Wolf, Woodforde's, Elgood's and Chalk Hill.

A village pub and restaurant with original flagstone floor and open fires. One long bar, disabled access, beer garden. Food available at lunchtime and evenings. Children allowed.

OPEN 11am–3pm and 4–11pm Mon–Thurs; all day Fri–Sun.

The Victoria
Earl Soham, Woodbridge IP13 7RL
☎ *(01728) 685758* Paul Hooper

Home to the Earl Soham Brewery, the full range of own beers is usually available.

A very traditional pub with tiled floors, wooden decor and several interesting pictures of Queen Victoria. No frills, just good beer, food and conversation. Food served lunchtimes and evenings. Car park. Children welcome. Beer garden.

GANNET MILD 3.0% ABV
Dark and flavoursome.
VICTORIA BITTER 3.6% ABV
Tasty with good hop character.
ALBERT ALE 4.6% ABV
Full-bodied and malty.
Plus occasional and seasonal brews.

OPEN 11.30am–3pm and 5.30–11pm Mon–Sat; 12–3pm and 7–10.30pm Sun.

The White Horse Inn
Mill Green, Edwardstone, Sudbury CO10 5PX
☎ *(01787) 211211* Mrs Baker

A freehouse with Greene King IPA plus a frequently changing mild always available (perhaps Elgood's Black Dog). Also two guests from local breweries such as Tolly Cobbold or further afield such as Cottage.

A two-bar village pub with log fires in winter. Beer garden. Caravan and camping club on site for five caravans. Food available at lunchtime and evenings. Children allowed.

OPEN 12–2pm Tues–Sun (closed Mon lunchtime) and 6.30–11pm Mon–Sat (10.30pm Sun).

The Half Moon
303 High Street, Walton, Felixstowe
☎ *(01394) 216009* Patrick Wroe

An Adnams tied house, so Adnams beers always available, plus two guests, such as Fuller's London Pride or Everards Tiger.

Old-fashioned, friendly alehouse. No food, no fruit machine, no music. Darts, cribbage, backgammon. Garden, children's play area, car park.

OPEN 12–2.30pm and 5–11pm Mon–Fri; 12–11pm Sat; 12–3pm and 7–10.30pm Sun.

The Dobermann
The Street, Framsden IP14 6HG
☎ *(01473) 890461* Sue Frankland

Adnams Best and Broadside always available and guests such as Mauldons Moletrap and Woodforde's Dobermann Ale.

A 400-year-old, traditional thatched and beamed Suffolk village pub. Extensive menu of bar food available. Non-smoking area. Car park, garden, accommodation. No children. Easy to find off B1077.

OPEN 12–3pm and 7–11pm (10.30pm Sun).

The Golden Boar

*The Street, Freckenham, Bury St Edmunds
IP28 8HZ*
☎ *(01638) 723000* Alan Strachan

A freehouse with four pumps serving a range of real ales. Adnams Best, Woodforde's Wherry and Nethergate brews are regulars, plus specials and seasonals such as Charles Wells Summer Solstice.

The only pub in Freckenham, this is a restored old-style country village pub with old brickwork and fireplaces, separate dining area and garden. Food available at lunchtime and evenings. Children allowed. There are plans for accommodation.

OPEN *All day Mon–Sat; 12–4pm and 7–10.30pm Sun.*

Six Bells

High Street, Gislingham, Eye IP23 8JD
☎ *(01379) 783349* Mr Buttle

A freehouse with Buttles Bitter (a house ale from Old Chimneys) always available plus two guests changing monthly and not repeating, if possible. Shepherd Neame Spitfire and Brakspear ales are recent examples.

A traditional one-bar village pub with non-smoking dining area and disabled facilities. Food available Tues–Sun lunchtimes and evenings. Children allowed. Function room. Situated near Thornham Walks.

OPEN *12–3pm and 6.30–11pm (10.30pm Sun).*

The Turk's Head Inn

Low Road, Hasketon, Woodbridge IP13 6JG
☎ *(01394) 382584* Tom Thomas

Tolly Cobbold Original, Shooter, Mild and IPA plus Young's Special among the brews always available, plus a range of guests changing fortnightly.

A two-bar country village pub with huge log fires and low beams. Food available at lunchtime and evenings. Decorated with brewery memorabilia and antiques. Beer garden and patio. Camping and caravanning in three acres of meadow. No children.

OPEN *12–3pm Tues–Sun (closed Mon lunchtime) and 6–11pm Mon–Sat (10.30pm Sun).*

The Cricketers

51 Crown Street, Ipswich IP1 3JA
☎ *(01473) 225910* Michael Paddington

A Wetherspoon's pub. Shepherd Neame Spitfire and Woodforde's Wherry among the brews always available plus three guests such as Hop Back Summer Lightning and a range of bottled beers.

A town-centre pub. Large non-smoking area and two beer gardens. Food available all day. Children allowed at weekends only up to 6pm.

OPEN *All day, every day.*

The Fat Cat

288 Spring Road, Ipswich IP4 5NL
☎ *(01473) 726524* John Keetley

A freehouse with up to 18 real ales served straight from the barrel and rotating all the time. Woodforde's Wherry and Adnams brews are regular features.

A spit and sawdust pub with wooden floor, no music or machines. One bar, beer garden. Rolls available at lunchtime. Well-behaved children allowed. On the outskirts of town.

OPEN *All day, every day.*

The Plough

2 Dog's Head Street, Ipswich IP4 1AD
☎ *(01473) 288005* Michelle Stalford

Four real ales always available: Adnams Best Bitter, Morland Old Speckled Hen, Young's Special and Fuller's London Pride.

A traditional alehouse with wooden floors. Bar food available at lunchtime. Children allowed. Next to the old cattle market bus station.

OPEN *12–11.30pm Mon–Wed; 12pm–midnight Thurs–Fri; 12–11pm Sat; 7–10.30pm Sun (closed Sun lunchtime).*

The Tap & Spile

76 St Helens Street, Ipswich
☎ *(01473) 211270*

Eight beers always available (160 per year) from a wide range of ales offered by independent brewers from all parts of the United Kingdom.

A traditional alehouse. Bar food is served at lunchtime (except Sunday). Car park, garden and children's room. Close to Suffolk College and County Hall.

OPEN *11am–3pm and 5–11pm Mon–Wed; 11am–11pm Thur–Sat; 12–3pm and 7–10.30pm Sun.*

KERSEY

The Bell

Kersey
☎ *(01473) 823229* Paul Denton

Three or four beers always available plus brews from a guest list including Shepherd Neame Spitfire, Fuller's London Pride, Adnams Bitter and Greene King Abbot.

Built in 1380, a timber-framed Tudor-style property with log fires and cobbles. Bar and restaurant food available at lunchtime and evenings. Car park, garden, private dining room. Children allowed. Signposted from Hadleigh.

OPEN *11am–3pm and 6.30–11pm Mon–Sat; 12–3pm and 7–10.30pm Sun.*

LAVENHAM

The Angel Hotel

Market Place, Lavenham CO10 9QZ
☎ *(01787) 247388*
Roy and Anne Whitworth and John Barry

Adnams Bitter, Nethergate Suffolk County, Greene King IPA and Abbot usually available, plus one guest beer such as Mauldons White Adder or Woodforde's Wherry.

Family-run inn in the centre of Lavenham, first licensed in 1420 and specialising in beers from East Anglia. Food served 12–2.15pm and 6.45–9.15pm Mon–Sun. Bookings advisable for weekends. Children welcome, high chairs supplied. Car park. Eight en-suite bedrooms.

OPEN *11am–11pm Mon–Sat; 12–10.30pm Sun.*

LAXFIELD

The King's Head Inn

Gorams Mill Lane, Laxfield, Woodbridge IP13 8DW
☎ *(01986) 798395* Michelle Flowley

A freehouse with all beers served straight from the barrel. Adnams Best and Broadside always available plus a selection of guest ales such as Adnams Mild, Extra or seasonals such as Regatta, Greene King IPA and Triumph, and Marston's Pedigree. Celebration ales also sold as available.

Known locally as The Low House, a well-preserved 600-year-old country village pub built in an old tap room. Food served 12–2pm and 7–9pm daily. Beer garden. Music nights on Tuesdays. Carriage rides to nearby Tannington Hall. Separate family room and card room. B&B. Children allowed.

OPEN *11am–3pm and 6–11pm Mon, Wed–Sat; all day Tuesday; 12–3pm and 7–10.30pm Sun.*

LOWESTOFT

The Crown Hotel

High Street, Lowestoft NR32 1HR
☎ *(01502) 500987* Mandy Henderson

A Scott's Brewery house with Blues and Bloater and Hopleaf always available, plus seasonal specials such as Golden Best.

A town pub with wooden floors and winter fires. Food available at lunchtime only. Patio. Children allowed if eating.

OPEN *All day, every day.*

Elizabeth Denes Hotel

6 Corton Road, Lowestoft NR32 4PL
☎ *(01502) 564616*
Colin Cassels Brown and Elizabeth O'Doherty

An Adnams brew plus one guest (depending on the time of year), perhaps from Tolly Cobbold.

Friendly, small hotel with cosy beamed bar, carvery, steakhouse restaurant and 12 en-suite rooms. Food served 12–2.30pm and 6–9.30pm Mon–Sat, plus 12–8pm Sun, carvery. Car park. Children welcome, but no special facilities. Located off the A12 between Lowestoft and Great Yarmouth. On corner at the turn-off to Corton.

OPEN *11am–11pm Mon–Sat; 12–10.30pm Sun.*

The Oak Tavern

73 Crown Street West, Lowestoft NR32 1SQ
☎ *(01502) 537246* Jim and Debbie Baldwin

Woodforde's Oak Tavern Ale and Greene King Abbot Ale usually available plus two guest beers, perhaps from Woodforde's, Buffy's, Wolf, Elgood's, Adnams or Bateman breweries.

Friendly community pub, specialising in real ale and Belgian beers, with a separate pool and darts area, plus Sky Sports wide screen TV. Five minutes from Lowestoft college. Car park. No food. No children.

OPEN *10.30am–11pm.*

The Triangle Tavern

29 St Peter's Street, Lowestoft NR32 1QA
☎ *(01502) 582711* Bob Vipers

Green Jack Bitter, Grasshopper, Gone Fishing and Orange Wheat Beer always available plus other Green Jack brews and a selection of constantly changing guests – up to ten available at any one time. Real cider also served.

Owned by the Green Jack Brewing Company and based in the High Street next to the recently developed Triangle Market Place, a two-bar pub with real fire, fully refurbished in December 1998. Customers are welcome to bring their own food. Live music weekly. Beer festivals held at Easter, Hallowe'en and Christmas. Parking.

OPEN *11am–11pm Mon–Sat; 12–10.30pm Sun.*

Welcome Free House

182 London Road North, Lowestoft NR32 1HB
☎ *(01502) 585500* Gavin Crawford

Adnams Southwold Bitter and Greene King Abbot Ale usually available, plus guest beers such as Marston's Pedigree, Everards Tiger, Charles Wells Eagle or Bombardier, Morland Old Speckled Hen, Brakspear Bitter or Elgood's Greyhound.

A traditional real ale town pub. No food. No children.

10.30am–4pm and 7.30–11pm (10.30pm Sun).

PIN MILL

The Butt & Oyster

Pin Mill, Chelmondiston, Ipswich IP9 1JW
☎ *(01473) 780764* Dick Mainwaring

Tolly Cobbold Mild, Bitter, Original, IPA and Shooter always available plus other specials. One guest ale served straight from the cask, generally from a local brewery.

A sixteenth-century inn with one bar, smoking room and riverside seating area. Food available at lunchtime and evenings. Children allowed.

All day, every day in summer; 11am–3pm and 7–11pm Mon–Fri and all day Sat–Sun in winter.

SOUTHWOLD

The Lord Nelson

East Street, Southwold IP18 6EJ
☎ *(01502) 722079* Mr Illstone

An Adnams house with Best and Broadside always available, plus seasonal ales such as Regatta in summer or celebration ales such as Millennium.

A traditional town pub by the seaside. Beer garden, disabled access. Food available at lunchtime and evenings. Children allowed.

All day, every day.

SWILLAND

The Moon & Mushroom

High Road, Swilland, Ipswich IP6 9LR
☎ *(01473) 785320* Clive John Goodall

Green Jack Bitter and Grasshopper, Nethergate Umbel Ale, Woodforde's Wherry and Norfolk Nog, Wolf Bitter, and Buffy's Hopleaf usually available.

A welcoming atmosphere awaits in this unspoilt pub which supports local micro-breweries. Food served 12–2pm and 6.30–8.15pm Tues–Sat. Children welcome in the garden only.

6–11pm Mon; 11am–2.30pm and 6–11pm Tues–Sat; 12–2.30pm and 7–11pm Sun.

YOU TELL US

- ★ *The Blue Boar Inn*, 28 Oulton Street, Oulton, Lowestoft
- ★ *Fleetwood's*, 25 Abbeygate Street, Bury St Edmunds
- ★ *The Hare & Hounds*, Heath Road, East Bergholt
- ★ *The Lion*, The Street, Theberton
- ★ *The Queen's Head*, Capel St Mary Road, Great Wenham
- ★ *Rose & Crown*, Whiting Street, Bury St Edmunds
- ★ *The White Horse*, Hopton Road, Thelnetham

Places Featured:

Ash
Bletchingley
Churt
Claygate
Coldharbour
Dorking
Englefield Green
Farnham
Godalming
Knaphill
Milford

Newdigate
Puttenham
Redhill
Shackleford
West Byfleet
West Clandon
Windlesham
Woking
Woodstreet Village
Wrecclesham

THE BREWERIES

ALCHEMY BREWING CO.

Lyon Road, Hersham KT12 3PU
☎ *(01932) 703860*

HALCYON DAYS 3.9% ABV
AURUM ALE 4.6% ABV
WINTER LINCTUS 4.5% ABV
Spiced stout, Nov–Feb.
Plus a different beer every two months.

HOGS BACK BREWERY

Manor Farm, The Street, Tongham GU10 1DE
☎ *(01252) 783000*

DARK MILD 3.4% ABV
Traditional easy quaffer. Occasional.
APB 3.5% ABV
Balanced, occasional brew.
HAIR OF THE HOG 3.5% ABV
TRADITIONAL ENGLISH ALE 4.2% ABV
Smooth, well-balanced flavours.
BLACKWATER PORTER 4.4% ABV
Distinctive, occasional brew.
HOP GARDEN GOLD 4.6% ABV
Refreshing with good fruity hoppiness.
RIP SNORTER 5.0% ABV
Balanced and well-rounded.
OTT 6.0% ABV
Powerful, winter brew.
SANTA'S WOBBLE 7.5% ABV
Strong Xmas brew.
A-OVER-T 9.0% ABV
Rich and full-flavoured.
Plus commemorative brews.

THE PILGRIM BREWERY

11c West Street, Reigate RH2 9BL
☎ *(01737) 222651*

SURREY BITTER 3.7% ABV
Hoppy, with a good mixture of flavours.
PORTER 4.0% ABV
Dark with roast malt flavour.
PROGRESS 4.0% ABV
Red and malty.
CRUSADER 4.9% ABV
Gold, with hops and malt throughout.
SPRING BOCK 5.2% ABV
Wheat beer.
Plus seasonal brews.

The Dover Arms

31 Guildford Road, Ash GU12 6BQ
☎ *(01252) 326025* Errol George Faulkner

Marston's Pedigree, Wadworth 6X and, once a month, three beers from Sharp's Brewery. A guest from Hogs Back, Tripple FFF or Hampshire breweries also regularly served.

Rural village pub with pin table, pool and darts. Food served 12–2pm and 7–9pm daily. Car park. Garden. Children welcome.

11.30am–2.30pm and 6–11pm (10.30pm Sun).

BLETCHINGLEY

William IV

Little Common Lane, Bletchingley, Redhill RH1 4QF
☎ *(01883) 743278* Brian Strange

Greene King Abbot, Wadworth 6X and Adnams Best always available plus three monthly changing guests such as a Harveys brew, Marston's Pedigree or Shepherd Neame Spitfire.

An unspoilt Victorian country pub on the edge of the village. Two small bars, dining room and beer garden. Food available at lunchtime and evenings. Children allowed.

11.30am–3pm and 6–11pm Mon–Sat; all day Sun.

CHURT

The Crossways Inn

Churt, Nr Farnham GU10 2JE
☎ *(01428) 714323* Paul Ewens

A freehouse with Cheriton Best, Ringwood Fortyniner and Shepherd Neame The Bishop's Finger always available, plus at least four guests such as Shepherd Neame Spitfire or Hampshire Lionheart. At least ten different beers are served every week, with more from micro-breweries than not. Also real cider from the barrel.

A country village local, winner of Summer Pub of the Year 1999. Two bars, beer garden. Food available at lunchtime only. Well-behaved children allowed. On the main road.

11am–3.30pm and 5–11pm Mon–Thurs; all day Fri–Sat; 12–4pm and 7–10.30pm Sun.

CLAYGATE

The Griffin

58 Common Road, Claygate, Esher KT10 0HW
☎ *(01372) 463799* Tom Harrington

A freehouse with Fuller's London Pride and Badger Dorset Best always available plus two constantly changing guests such as Bateman XB or a Pilgrim ale. Winter warmers on during the colder months. Micro-breweries and smaller independents favoured.

A traditional two-bar village pub with log fires, beer garden and disabled access. Food available Mon–Sat lunchtimes. Children allowed.

All day, every day.

COLDHARBOUR

The Plough Inn

Coldharbour Lane, Coldharbour, Nr Dorking RH5 6HD
☎ *(01306) 711793* Mr and Mrs Abrehart

Nine beers always available from Ringwood, Hogs Back, Timothy Taylor, Adnams and Shepherd Neame. Two beers brewed on the premises under the name of the Leith Hill Brewery. Seasonal brews, guests, topical and special beers. Also a farm cider on hand pump.

A traditional family-run seventeenth-century pub in a beautiful rural setting. Allegedly the highest freehouse in south-east England. Bar and restaurant food served at lunchtime and evenings. Car parking. Children allowed. Accommodation. Just over three miles south-west of Dorking.

CROOKED FURROW 4.2% ABV
Hoppy, light bitter.
TALLYWHACKER 5.6% ABV
Very dark ale. Strong, roasted barley flavour.

11.30am–3pm and 6.30–11pm Mon–Fri; 11am–11pm Sat–Sun.

DORKING

The King's Arms

45 West Street, Dorking RH4 1BU
☎ *(01306) 883361* Mr Yeatman

Fuller's London Pride, Wadworth 6X, Marston's Pedigree and Eldridge Pope Royal Oak (Thomas Hardy) always available. Two guests changing every week from micro-breweries and independents – the smaller and more unusual, the better!

A country-style pub in a town location, this is the oldest building in Dorking. More than 500 years old with oak beams, inglenook fireplace, restaurant and courtyard garden. Food available lunchtimes and evenings. Children allowed.

11am–11pm (10.30pm Sun).

ENGLEFIELD GREEN

The Beehive

34 Middle Hill, Englefield Green, Nr Egham TW20 0JQ
☎ *(01784) 431621* Mr and Mrs McGranaghan

Fuller's London Pride, Hop Back Summer Lightning and Gales HSB and Best always available plus four guest beers, changing weekly, from breweries such as Adnams, Bateman, Everards, Hoskins & Oldfield, Kemptown, Nethergate, Oldbury, Orkney, Thwaites and Young's. Beer festivals at May and August bank holidays.

A country pub now surrounded by expensive houses. Real home-made food available at lunchtime and evenings. Open log fire in winter. Car park and garden. Just off the A30 between Ferrari's and Royal Holloway College.

🍺 *11am–11pm Mon–Sat; 12–10.30pm Sun.*

FARNHAM

The Ball & Wicket

104 Upper Hale Road, Farnham GU9 0PB
☎ *(01252) 735278* Gary Wallace

Home of the Hale and Hearty Brewery, with Upper Ale and Wicket Bitter always available plus Wadworth 6X and B&T Dragonslayer. Seasonals and celebration ales such as the homebrewed Spring Ale.

A country freehouse and brewpub on the village green. No food. Children allowed.

🛢 **UPPER ALE 3.8% ABV**
🛢 **WICKET BITTER 4.3% ABV**
SPRING ALE 5.3% ABV
Seasonal.

🍺 *4–11pm Mon–Fri; 12–11pm Sat; 12–3pm and 7–10.30pm Sun.*

The Duke of Cambridge

East Street, Farnham GU9 7TH
☎ *(01252) 716584 Fax (01252) 716549*
Daniel Burch

A freehouse with seven pumps serving a constantly changing range of real ales from large breweries to micro-breweries. Over 600 different beers have been served in recent years. The aim is variety of choice and the perfect pint every time! Up to 20 single malt whiskies also available.

A family-owned pub dating from the 1830s. Food served every lunchtime and Mon–Thurs and Sat evenings in a separate dining area. Regular music, including jazz on Tuesdays. Hotel-standard B&B. Website: www.dukeofcambridge.co.uk

🍺 *12–3pm and 5.15–11pm Mon–Thurs; 12–11pm Fri–Sat; 12–10pm Sun.*

Exchange

Station Hill, Farnham GU9 8AD
☎ *(01252) 726673*
Mr T Devaney and Ms A Fanning

Greene King IPA and Triumph usually available, with one guest such as Ruddles Best, Wadworth 6X or Bateman XXXB.

T raditional, recently refurbished bar. Garden and patio. Extensive menu, specialising in steaks, available 12–2.30pm and 6.30–9pm daily. Car park. Children welcome, but no special facilities. Located next to Farnham Station.

🍺 *10.30am–3pm and 5.30–11pm Mon–Thurs; all day Fri–Sun.*

The Shepherd & Flock

Moor Park Lane, Farnham GU9 9JB
☎ *(01252) 716675* Steven Hill

A freehouse with Hampshire 1066, Hogs Back TEA, Fuller's London Pride and Gales HSB always available plus three guests, such as Hop Back Summer Lightning, Badger Tanglefoot or Beckett's brews.

S ituated on the outskirts of town, on Europe's biggest inhabited roundabout! A well-known local meeting place, close to the North Downs. Old building with one bar and 50-seater dining room. Food available lunchtimes and evenings. Beer garden. Children allowed in the dining room only.

🍺 *11am–3pm and 5.30–11pm Mon–Thurs; all day Fri–Sun.*

GODALMING

The Anchor Inn

110 Ockford Road, Godalming GU7 1RG
☎ *(01483) 417085* Mr and Mrs Jenkins

Badger Tanglefoot, Hogs Back and Brakspear brews among those always available plus guests (60 per year) from Gales, Hop Back, Ringwood, Titanic, Fuller's, Pilgrim and Wychwood.

A real ale pub with bar billiards and a good mixed clientele. Simple bar food available at lunchtime. Parking and beer garden. On the edge of town on the main road.

🍺 *12–3pm and 5.30–11pm.*

The Old Wharf

5 Wharf Street, Godalming GU7 1NN
☎ *(01483) 419543* John Louden

A wide selection of cask ales available on six hand pumps. Examples have included Fuller's London Pride and Hogs Back TEA.

A traditional town pub. Food available 12–9pm Sun–Thurs; 12–7pm Fri–Sat. Traditional roasts served on Sundays. No children.

🍺 *All day, every day.*

KNAPHILL

The Hooden Takes a Knap

134 High Street, Knaphill GU21 2QH
☎ *(01483) 473374*
Paul Crisp and Elizabeth Williamson

An ever-changing selection of beers from around the country is available, such as brews from Fuller's, Adnams, Greene King, Hop Back, Young's, Brains and Shepherd Neame.

A bistro-style country pub, previously known as The Garibaldi. One small bar, beer garden and BBQ. Food available lunchtimes and evenings in a separate dining area. Mexican food is a speciality, but traditional English, Italian and Indian dishes are also served. Live blues on alternate Thursdays, quiz night on last Sunday of the month, plus regular theme nights. Children allowed. On the crossroads of Knaphill High Street.

12–2.30pm and 5.30–11pm Mon–Thurs; all day Fri–Sun.

MILFORD

The Red Lion

Old Portsmouth Road, Milford, Godalming GU8 5HJ
☎ *(01483) 424342* Lou-Ann Marshall

A Gales house with Butser Bitter, GB and HSB always available plus guests such as Badger Tanglefoot, Everards Tiger, Hampshire Glory and Marston's Pedigree changing fortnightly. Tries not to repeat the beers.

A village pub with skittle alley. Two bars, non-smoking and smoking dining areas, beer garden and children's play area, good disabled access. Food available every lunchtime and Mon–Sat evenings. Children allowed.

11am–2.30pm and 5.30–11pm Mon–Fri; all day Sat–Sun.

NEWDIGATE

Surrey Oaks

Parkgate Road, Newdigate, Dorking RH5 5DZ
☎ *(01306) 631200* Ken Proctor

Adnams Southwold Bitter and Fuller's London Pride usually available, plus two guest pumps. Five or six guest beers served each week and favourites include Timothy Taylor Landlord, Hop Back Summer Lightning, Woodforde's Wherry and something from Hogs Back, Harveys, Pilgrim or Weltons.

Timber-beamed country pub, original parts of which date back to 1570. Two small bars, one with a magnificent inglenook fireplace and stone-flagged floors. Games room and restaurant. Food served lunchtimes and evenings Tues–Sat; lunchtimes only Sun–Mon. Large car park. Children's play area in garden. Situated one mile from Newdigate village on the Charlwood road.

11.30am–2.30pm and 5.30–11pm Mon–Fri; 11.30am–3pm and 6–11pm Sat; 12–3pm and 7–10.30pm Sun.

PUTTENHAM

The Good Intent

62 The Street, Puttenham, Guildford GU3 1AR
☎ *(01483) 810387* William Carpenter

Badger Best always available, plus a selection of guests such as Hogs Back TEA, Hop Back Thunder Storm and Hampshire Pendragon.

A one-bar country pub with food available at lunchtime and evenings. Beer garden. No children.

11am–3pm and 6–11pm Mon–Fri; all day Sat–Sun.

REDHILL

The Hatch

44 Hatchlands Road, Redhill RH1 6AT
☎ *(01737) 764593* Michael McAvee

A Shepherd Neame house with Bishop's Finger, Spitfire and Master Brew always available, plus up to three seasonal or celebration ales such as Goldings or 1698.

A town pub with horseshoe-shaped bar, log-effect fires and oak beams. Beer garden, front patio, pool room. Food availabe 12–2pm and 7–9pm. Children allowed in the garden and pool room only. Situated on the A25.

12–3pm Mon–Sun; 5.30–11pm Mon–Sat; 7–10.30pm Sun.

SHACKLEFORD

The Cyder House

Pepperharrow Lane, Shackleford, Godalming GU8 6AN
☎ *(01483) 810360* Phillip Nisbett

Badger Best, Tanglefoot and Golden Champion always available, plus at least two guest beers.

A light and airy Victorian country pub situated in a pretty village. Extensive blackboard menu offers a range of fine meals and snacks made with fresh seasonal produce. Large patio garden, plenty of parking space. Children and dogs welcome.

11am–3pm and 5.30–11pm Mon–Fri; all day Sat–Sun.

WEST BYFLEET

The Plough Inn

104 High Road, West Byfleet KT14 7QT
☎ *(01932) 353257* Carol Wells

A freehouse with eight pumps serving brews such as Fuller's London Pride and beers from Hogs Back, Hop Back and other independents.

A traditional two-bar village pub with beams and two log fires. Beer garden, car park. Food available Mon–Fri 12–2pm but there are plans for a conservatory which will become an evening restaurant when completed. No children.

11am–3pm and 5–11pm (10.30pm Sun).

WEST CLANDON

The Onslow Arms

The Street, West Clandon, Guildford GU4 7TE
☎ *(01483) 222447* Alan Peck

A freehouse with Fuller's London Pride and brews from Young's, Brakspear and Hogs Back always available plus one rotating guest such as Ringwood Old Thumper, Morland Old Speckled Hen or Greene King Abbot. Also celebration ales as available.

A well-known sixteenth-century coaching inn with four bars and food available at lunchtime and evenings in a restaurant and a carvery bistro. Large car park, disabled access. Garden and patio with arbours. Cocktail lounge. Function rooms. Helipad. Children allowed.

All day, every day.

WINDLESHAM

The Windmill

London Road, Windlesham GU20 6PJ
☎ *(01276) 472281*
Richard and Sandra Hailstone

There may be 13 real ales available at any one time. Hop Back Summer Lightning, Adnams Broadside, Badger (Gibbs Mew) Bishop's Tipple always available plus guests (up to 700 per year) including brews from Ringwood, Hampshire, Archers, Hogs Back, Pilgrim and Rebellion. Always willing to support micro-breweries and will try any new brews. Three beer festivals held each year, with 100 brews at each festival.

Small, friendly pub with two bars and a dining area. No pool tables. Food available. Car park. Large beer garden. Children allowed under parental control. Situated on the main A30.

11am–11pm.

WOKING

Wetherspoons

51 Chertsey Road, Woking GU21 5AJ
☎ *(01483) 722818* Gary Hollis

Hogs Back TEA permanently available, plus a constantly changing range of guest ales on five hand pumps.

A one-bar town pub with no music or TV. Front drinking terrace, disabled access and toilets. Food available all day (11am–10pm) with a non-smoking seating area available. No children.

All day, every day.

WOODSTREET VILLAGE

The Royal Oak

89 Oak Hill, Woodstreet Village, Guildford GU3 3DA
☎ *(01483) 235137* Tony Oliver

A freehouse with Hogs Back TEA always available plus four constantly changing guests. Hop Back Summer Lightning and Cottage Wheeltappers are just two examples from a huge range (850 in less than four years).

A good old-fashioned country pub. One bar, beer garden. Food available Mon–Sat lunchtime. Over 14s only allowed.

11am–3pm and 5–11pm Mon–Fri; 11am–3.30pm and 5–11pm Sat; 12–3.30pm and 7–10.30pm Sun.

The Bat & Ball

Boundstone, Wrecclesham, Farnham GU10 4RA
☎ *(01252) 794564* Andy Bujok

A freehouse with Young's Special, Fuller's London Pride and a Brakspear ale always available, plus four guests including brews such as Archers Golden, Harveys Best, Hop Back Summer Lightning and many, many more.

A traditional country pub with open fires, two bars, restaurant, children's room and play area, beer garden, disabled access. Food available at lunchtime and evenings. Children allowed.

OPEN *12–11pm (10.30pm Sun).*

The Sandrock

Sandrock Hill Road, Wrecclesham, Farnham GU10 4NS
☎ *(01252) 715865* Mr A Baylis

Eight beers available. Batham, Enville and Brakspear brews always on offer plus guests (100 per year) from Holden's, Hampshire, Ballard's, Hogs Back and Cheriton etc.

A small, no-frills pub. Bar food available at lunchtime (except Sunday). Car park and garden. Ten-day beer festival held first two weeks of March. Children allowed. Along the bypass, left at roundabout onto the A325, left into School Hill, over the crossroads into Sandrock Hill Road. Visit our website at: www.sandrockpub.co.uk

OPEN *All day, every day.*

★ *Aitch's Bar-Café*, Angel Court, High Street, Godalming
★ *The Crown*, 38 High Street, Egham
★ *The Feathers*, The Broadway, Laleham
★ *H G Wells' Planets*, Crown Square, Woking
★ *The Hedgehog & Hogshead*, 2 High Street, Sutton
★ *The Moon on the Hill*, 5–9 Hill Road, Sutton
★ *Tap & Spile*, 40 Station Road, Egham
★ *Tap & Spile*, 13 Stoke Fields, Guildford
★ *The Thurlow Arms*, Off Baynards Lane, Baynards
★ *The Whispering Moon*, 25 Ross Parade, Woodcote Road, Wallington

Places Featured:

Amberley	Horsham
Arundel	Hove
Ashurst	Icklesham
Balcombe	Isfield
Battle	Lewes
Beckley	Litlington
Berwick Village	Maplehurst
Bexhill-on-Sea	Midhurst
Bognor Regis	Nutbourne
Brighton	Old Heathfield
Burpham	Oving
Caneheath	Pett
Compton	Portslade
Crawley	Robertsbridge
Eastbourne	Rudgwick
East Grinstead	Rustington
East Hoathly	Rye
Elsted Marsh	St Leonards on Sea
Exceat Bridge	Seaford
Fernhurst	Shoreham
Firle	Sidlescoombe
Fishbourne	Stoughton
Fletching	Tarring
Frant	Telham
Graffham	Thakeham
Gungarden	Ticehurst
Hailsham	Uckfield
Halfway Bridge	West Ashling
Hastings	West Chiltington
Haywards Heath	Worthing
Heathfield	Yapton
Herstmonceux	

THE BREWERIES

ARUNDEL BREWERY

*Ford Airfield Estate, Arundel, West Sussex
BN18 0BE*
☎ *(01903) 733111*

1999 3.5% ABV

CASTLE 3.8% ABV
Well-balanced and malty with some fruitiness.

HAIRY MARY 3.8% ABV
Summer seasonal brew.

CLASSIC 4.5% ABV
Malty with some sweetness.

FOOT SLOGGER 4.4% ABV
Golden seasonal brew.

SUMMER DAZE 4.7% ABV
Seasonal brew.

BLACK BEASTY 4.9% ABV
Seasonal brew.

BULLS EYE 5.0% ABV
Golden seasonal brew.

ARUNDEL GOLD 4.2% ABV
Gold-coloured with good hoppiness.

STRONGHOLD 5.0% ABV
Rounded and full-flavoured.

OLD KNUCKLER 5.5% ABV
All the flavours are here. Winter brew.
Plus seasonal brews.

THE CUCKMERE HAVEN BREWERY

Exceat Bridge, Cuckmere Haven, Seaford,
West Sussex BN25 4AB
☎ *(01323) 892247*

 BEST BITTER 4.1% ABV
SAXON KING STOUT 4.2% ABV
GENTLEMEN'S GOLD 4.5% ABV
GUV'NER 4.7% ABV

DARK STAR BREWING CO.

55–56 Surrey Street, Brighton BN1 3PB
☎ *(01273) 701758*

 ALE TRAIL ROAST MILD 3.5% ABV
PALE ALE 3.7% ABV
OLD ALE 4.2% ABV
PENGUIN STOUT 4.2% ABV
GOLDEN GATE BITTER 4.3% ABV
OLD FAMILIAR 5.0% ABV
SUMMER HAZE 5.0% ABV
DARK STAR 5.0% ABV
CLIFF HANGER PORTER 5.5% ABV
MELTDOWN 6.0% ABV
PAVILION BEAST 6.0% ABV

HARVEY & SONS (LEWES) LTD

The Bridge Wharf Brewery, 6 Cliffe High Street,
Lewes, East Sussex BN7 2AH
☎ *(01273) 480209*

 XX MILD 3.0% ABV
Dark in colour, soft and sweet.
SUSSEX PALE ALE 3.5% ABV
Balanced and well-hopped.
SUSSEX BEST BITTER 4.0% ABV
Hoppiness throughout.
XXXX OLD ALE 4.3% ABV
Full-bodied, nutty seasonal brew.
ARMADA ALE 4.5% ABV
Golden and hoppy, with dryness in the
aftertaste.
Plus seasonal brews.

KING & BARNES LTD

18 Bishopric, Horsham, West Sussex RH12 1QP
☎ *(01403) 270470*

 **MILD 3.5% ABV**
Dark with delicate hoppiness and some
sweetness.
SUSSEX 3.5% ABV
Refreshing hoppiness throughout.
BEST BITTER 4.1% ABV
Refreshing, balanced bitter.
BROADWOOD 4.2% ABV
Malty sweetness with hoppy finish.
FESTIVE 5.0% ABV
Flavoursome and full-bodied.
Plus seasonal and occasional brews.

ROTHER VALLEY BREWING CO.

Station Road, Northiam TN31 6QT
☎ *(01797) 253535*

LIGHTERMAN 3.6% ABV
HOUSE BITTER 3.6% ABV
LEVEL BEST 4.0% ABV
BLUES 5.0% ABV
Winter brew.

SPINNAKER ALES (The Brewery on Sea)

24 Winston Business Centre, Chartwell Road,
Lancing, West Sussex BN15 8TU
☎ *(01903) 851482*

 LANCING SPECIAL DARK 3.5% ABV
Dark and hoppy mild.
SPINNAKER BITTER 3.5% ABV
Light and well-hopped.
SPINNAKER CLASSIC 4.0% ABV
Mellow and malty.
LEAF THIEF 4.2% ABV
RAIN DANCE 4.4% ABV
Light-coloured, refreshing wheat beer.
SPINNAKER BUZZ 4.5% ABV
Golden, with hoppiness and honeyed sweetness.
SPECIAL CREW 5.5% ABV
Pale and deceptively drinkable for gravity.
RIPTIDE 6.5% ABV
Rounded and full-flavoured.
TIDAL WAVE 7.0% ABV
Dark and well-balanced.
Plus seasonal and occasional brews.

WHITE BREWING CO.

The 1066 Country Brewery, Pebsham Farm Ind.
Est., Pebsham Lane, Bexhill
☎ *(01424) 731066*

1066 COUNTRY ALE 4.0% ABV
M2 4.5% ABV
Available upon request.
WHITE CHRISTMAS 4.5% ABV
Seasonal brew.

THE PUBS

AMBERLEY

The Sportsman's Arms

*Crossgates, Amberley, Arundel, West Sussex
BN18 9NR*
☎ *(01798) 831787* Chris Shanaham

A freehouse with Young's Bitter and Special, Fuller's London Pride and a house ale called Miserable Old Bugger (brewed especially by the Brewery on Sea in Lancing). Occasional guests, particularly porters in winter.

An edge-of-village pub with wonderful views across the valley. Three bars, patio area, hexagonal revolving pool table, dining area in conservatory. Home to the Miserable Old Buggers Club. Food served at lunchtime and evenings. Well-behaved children and dogs welcome.

*11am–2.30pm and 6–11pm Mon–Fri;
11am–3pm and 6–11pm Sat; 12–3pm and
7–10.30pm Sun.*

ARUNDEL

Arundel Swan Hotel

27–9 High Street, Arundel, West Sussex
☎ *(01903) 882314* David Vincent

The Arundel Brewery tap, regularly serving Arundel Best, Gold and two seasonal beers plus Fuller's London Pride. A guest beer is also served, perhaps Hop Back Summer Lightning, Shepherd Neame Spitfire, Wadworth 6X or Fuller's ESB.

Restored to its original Victorian splendour, a very popular meeting place for locals and tourists alike. Situated in the heart of Arundel, close to the castle and river. Food served 12–2.30pm and 6.30–9.30pm daily. Car park behind the hotel. No children.

11am–11pm Mon–Sat; 12–10.30pm Sun.

The King's Arms

*36 Tarrant Street, Arundel, West Sussex
BN18 9DN*
☎ *(01903) 882312* Charlie Malcolmson

A freehouse always serving Fuller's London Pride and Young's Special plus two guests such as Hop Back Summer Lightning, Rye and Coriander or Crop Circle, or brews from Harveys or Cottage. Small producers always well-represented.

A small, country style pub dating from 1625, situated out of the town centre. Two bars, patio, table seating at the front. Sandwiches available Mon–Thurs lunchtimes, bar menu Fri–Sun lunchtimes. Children allowed.

*11am–3pm and 5.30–11pm Mon–Fri;
11am–11pm Sat; 12–10.30pm Sun.*

ASHURST

The Fountain Inn

Ashurst, Nr Steyning, West Sussex BN44 3AP
☎ *(01403) 710219*
Mark and Christopher White

Harveys Best and Fuller's London Pride plus a constantly changing range of guests, which may include Harveys Gold or Gales HSB.

An unspoilt sixteenth-century inn with low beams, a flagstone floor and large inglenook fireplace. Picturesque cottage garden and large duck pond. No machines or music. Bar and restaurant food served at lunchtime and evenings (light snacks only Sunday pm and Monday pm). Large car park and garden. Children under 14 not allowed inside the pub. Located on the B2135 north of Steyning.

*11.30am–2.30pm and 6–11pm Mon–Sat;
12–3pm and 7–10.30pm Sun.*

BALCOMBE

The Cowdray Arms

*London Road, Balcombe, Haywards Heath,
West Sussex RH17 6QD*
☎ *(01444) 811280* Gerry McElhatton

Harveys Best Bitter, Greene King Abbot, IPA and Mild always available plus two guests such as Greene King Triumph or Arundel, Bateman, Elgood's or Harveys brews.

A one-bar Victorian pub with high ceilings. Non-smoking dining area, traditional pub games. Garden and car park. Food served at lunchtime and evenings. Children allowed.

*11am–3pm and 5.30–11pm Mon–Sat;
12–3pm and 7–10.30pm Sun.*

BATTLE

The Squirrel Inn

North Trade Road, Battle, East Sussex TN33 9LJ
☎ *(01424) 772717* Mr and Mrs Coundley

Harveys ales always available plus several guests (200 per year) including Rother Valley Level Best and brews from Gales and Mansfield etc. New and seasonal beers ordered as and when available.

An eighteenth-century old drover's pub in beautiful countryside surrounded by fields. Family-run freehouse. Unspoilt public bar with log fires. New restaurant (suitable for functions and weddings). Two large beer gardens, ample parking, purpose-built children's room. Families welcome. Located just outside Battle on the A271.

*11.30am–3pm and 6–11pm Mon–Thurs;
11.30am–11pm Fri–Sat; 12–10.30pm Sun.*

The Rose & Crown

Northiam Road, Beckley, Nr Rye, East Sussex
TN31 6SE
☎ *(01797) 252161* Alice Holland

Harveys Best, Adnams Broadside, Hook Norton Best, Badger IPA, Timothy Taylor Landlord and Fuller's ESB always available plus three constantly changing guests from independent breweries.

An old coaching inn on a site which has been occupied by a pub since the twelfth century. Dining area, large garden, petanque and grumpy landlord! Food available at lunchtime and evenings. Well-behaved children allowed.

OPEN *11.30am–3pm and 5–11pm Mon–Thurs; all day Fri–Sun.*

The Cricketers Arms

Berwick Village, Nr Polegate, East Sussex
BN26 6SP
☎ *(01323) 870469* Peter Brown

A Harveys tied house with Best Bitter and a seasonal brew usually available.

Three-roomed, cottage-style country pub with stone floors, two open fires and picturesque gardens. Situated near the South Downs Way and very popular with walkers and cyclists. Food served each lunchtime and evening. Car park. Children welcome in designated room. Located west of Drusillas roundabout; signposted to Berwick church.

OPEN *11am–3pm and 6–11pm Mon–Sat; 11am–11pm; 12–10.30pm Sun (April–Oct only – closed Sun in winter).*

The Rose & Crown

Turkey Road, Bexhill-on-Sea, East Sussex
TN39 5HH
☎ *(01424) 214625*
Stephen Newman and Sarah Liddy

Greene King Abbot and Martha Greene Bitter always available plus two changing guests.

One bar, dining area, large-screen TV, darts, disabled toilets and beer garden. Food served all day. Under 14s allowed until 9pm in designated area only.

OPEN *All day, every day.*

Old Barn

42 Felpham Road, Bognor Regis, West Sussex
PO22 7DF
☎ *(01243) 821564* Brian Griffith

Ringwood Best Bitter, Greene King IPA, Gales GB, and Hop Back Summer Lightning regularly available, plus one or two guest beers perhaps from Hop Back, Hampshire, Cottage, Gales, Ringwood, Badger, Greene King and others.

Thatched, converted barn on the edge of the village behind Butlin's. Pool, darts and Sky TV. Popular with all ages, locals and Butlin's staff, etc. Food available 11am–7pm. Small car park. Well-behaved children welcome.

OPEN *11am–11pm Mon–Sat; 12–10.30pm Sun.*

The Cobbler's Thumb

10 New England Road, Brighton, East Sussex
BN1 4GG
☎ *(01273) 605636* Stuart McDougal

A freehouse serving Harveys Best and Badger Tanglefoot plus seasonal guests from other breweries.

A traditional locals' pub with wooden floors in the public bar and a lounge with real fire. Four pints for the price of three on a selected brew. Food available weekday lunchtimes and a Sunday roast. Children allowed in the garden or inside until 7pm.

OPEN *11am–11pm Mon–Sat; 12–10.30pm Sun.*

The Evening Star

55–6 Surrey Street, Brighton, East Sussex
BN1 3PB
☎ *(01273) 328931*
Peter Skinner, Matt Wickham and Janine Garrott

The home of the Dark Star Brewing Company. Seven real ales always available including the Skinner's and Dark Star ranges plus a rotating guest list that runs into thousands. Real cider also served.

A brewpub established in 1994 using a unique space-saving full-mash mini-brewing system. Production began in December 1994. In July 1995, Peter Skinner teamed up with brewer Rob Jones, who founded the Pitfield Brewery in 1981 and several other micros. Together, they founded the Dark Star Brewing Company. The Evening Star is a specialist real ale house with wooden floors and church pews. Bar food is available at lunchtime. Children not allowed. Just 150 yards from railway station.

OPEN *11.30am–11pm Mon–Fri; 11am–11pm Sat; 12–10.30pm Sun.*

Hand In Hand

*33 Upper St James's Street, Brighton, East Sussex
BN2 1JN*
☎ *(01273) 699595* Brenda and Bev Robbins

Home of the Kemptown Brewery with all Kemptown brews usually available, plus Badger Best and Tanglefoot.

Cosy, street-corner pub, probably the smallest tower brewery in England. Food served 12–3pm. No children.

BRIGHTON BITTER 3.6% ABV
KEMPTOWN BITTER 4.0% ABV
YE OLDE TROUT 4.5% ABV
STAGGERING IN THE DARK 5.2% ABV
OLD GRUMPY 6.2% ABV
December brew.
Plus seasonal and occasional brews.

OPEN *12–11pm (10.30pm Sun).*

The Lion & Lobster

*24 Sillwood Street, Brighton, East Sussex
BN1 2PS*
☎ *(01273) 776961* Jack Harding

Five guest beers (200 per year) which might include Badger Tanglefoot, Morland Old Speckled Hen, Timothy Taylor Landlord, Harveys Best, Spinnaker Buzz and Hyde's Anvil Bitter.

An Irish family-run pub with a great atmosphere. All ages welcome. Bar and restaurant food available at lunchtime and evenings. Parking and children's room. Located 200 yards from the seafront, in between the Bedford Hotel and Norfolk Hotel.

OPEN *11am–11pm Mon–Sat; 12–3pm and 7–10.30pm Sun.*

The Miller's Arms

*1 Windmill Street, Brighton, East Sussex
BN2 2GN*
☎ *(01273) 380580*
Kim Yallop and Ian Harradine

Five real ales permanently available: Harveys Best, Fuller's London Pride, Young's Special, Adnams Best and Shepherd Neame Spitfire.

Situated upon a hill with panoramic views of Brighton below. A one-bar pub, with no games except darts. Well-maintained beer garden. Members of the CAMRA Ale Trail. Food available at lunchtime. Barbecues held in summer. Children and dogs very welcome.

OPEN *All day, every day.*

Prince Albert

*48 Trafalgar Street, Brighton, East Sussex
BN1 4ED*
☎ *(01273) 730499* Chris Steward

Young's Special and a Harveys brew usually available with two guest beers such as Fuller's London Pride, Morland Old Speckled Hen, Timothy Taylor Landlord or a Bateman or Forge beer.

Large, Grade II listed former Victorian hotel, which was completely refurbished as a pub in 1999. Food served 12–3pm and 5–9pm daily. Children welcome until 5pm. Situated next to Brighton Station, under the Trafalgar Street Bridge.

OPEN *11am–11pm Mon–Sat; 12–10.30pm Sun.*

The Sussex Yeoman

*7 Guildford Road, Brighton, East Sussex
BN1 3LU*
☎ *(01273) 327985* Rosie Dunton

Greene King IPA and Abbot plus a Harveys ale always available. Also occasional seasonal guests.

A trendy pub decorated in orange and blue with a young clientele (25–40) and a relaxed atmosphere. Games nights feature board games, or a pop quiz on Wednesday evenings. Bar snacks and fuller menu available until 9.30pm. No children.

OPEN *12pm–close.*

Tap & Spile

*67 Upper Gloucester Road, Brighton, East Sussex
BN1 3LQ*
☎ *(01273) 329540*

Up to four brews. Shepherd Neame Spitfire, Badger Tanglefoot or beers from Bateman and other smaller breweries are among the regular guests. Seasonals and specials as available.

A quaint 1930s-style alehouse, with church pews, wooden floor and a pool room with quarry tiles. A locals' pub, nice and friendly. No food. No children.

OPEN *12–3pm and 5–11pm Mon–Thurs; all day Fri–Sun.*

BURPHAM

The George & Dragon

Burpham, Nr Arundel, West Sussex BN18 9RR
☎ *(01903) 883131* James Rose

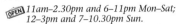 Arundel Best and Harveys Best always available plus five guest beers (100 per year) from breweries such as Woodforde's, Hop Back, Cotleigh, Harviestoun, Ash Vine etc.

Located in a small village two miles from Arundel off the main track, with some of the best views of the Arun valley. Excellent walking all around. Bar and restaurant food available (restaurant evenings and Sunday lunch only). Car park. Children over 12 allowed.

OPEN *11am–2.30pm and 6–11pm Mon–Sat; 12–3pm and 7–10.30pm Sun.*

CANEHEATH

The Old Oak Inn

Caneheath, Arlington, Nr Polegate, East Sussex
☎ *(01323) 482072*

Harveys Best Bitter and Badger Best usually available plus a guest beer, perhaps from Rother Valley, Fuller's, Young's or Charles Wells breweries.

Situated between the South Downs and Michelham Priory, with oak-beamed bar and restaurant, beer garden and barbecue. Food served 12–2pm Mon–Sun and Tues–Sat evenings. Car park. Children welcome, but no special facilities.

OPEN *11am–3pm and 6–11pm Mon–Sat; 12–3pm and 7–11pm Sun.*

COMPTON

The Coach & Horses

Compton, Nr Chichester, West Sussex PO18 9HA
☎ *(01705) 631228* David Butler

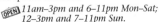 Fuller's ESB always available plus five guest beers (100s per year) from breweries including Cheriton, Adnams, Cottage, Hop Back, Timothy Taylor and Hook Norton.

Situated on the Sussex Downs, a coaching inn built in 1500 with exposed beams and a Victorian extension. Bar and restaurant food is available at lunchtime and evenings. Car parking, garden and skittle alley. Children allowed. Good walking. Take the signed road to Uppark House (B2146).

OPEN *11am–2.30pm and 6–11pm Mon–Sat; 12–3pm and 7–10.30pm Sun.*

CRAWLEY

The Swan Inn

Horsham Road, Crawley, West Sussex RH11 7AY
☎ *(01293) 527447* Jo Harmer

Fuller's London Pride, Greene King Abbot and Wadworth 6X among the brews always on offer, plus two guests, often from Gales (for instance HSB or GB).

An old local with friendly clientele. Live bands. Pool table. Beer garden. No food. Children allowed in the garden, or inside until 6pm.

OPEN *11am–11.30pm Mon–Sat; 12–10.30pm Sun.*

EASTBOURNE

The Lamb Inn

36 High Street, Old Town, Eastbourne, East Sussex BN21 1HH
☎ *(01323) 720545* Mrs Hume

Tied to Harveys Brewery, so Harveys Bitter always available.

An old-style, three-bar pub with seating at the side. Food available at lunchtime and evenings. Children allowed.

OPEN *10.30am–3pm and 5.30–close Mon–Thurs; all day Fri–Sat; 12–4pm and 7–10.30pm Sun.*

The Windsor Tavern

165 Langney Road, Eastbourne, East Sussex BN22 8AH
☎ *(01323) 726206* Shirley Verhulpen

Wadworth 6X and Greene King Abbot always available. Also Hoegaarden Belgian lager.

A quiet country-style pub in the middle of town. Large garden, no juke box or pool table. Food available at lunchtime and evenings. Children allowed in the garden or up to 8pm inside.

OPEN *All day Mon–Sat; 12–3pm and 7–10.30pm Sun.*

EAST GRINSTEAD

The Ship Inn

Ship Street, East Grinstead, West Sussex RH19 4RG
☎ *(01342) 312089* Mr R Connor

A Young's-owned pub, always serving Young's Bitter, Special, Triple A and Winter Warmer (seasonal).

An olde-worlde locals' pub decorated with Guinness memorabilia. Large bar, restaurant and function room. Huge beer garden. Darts, pool, football and golf teams. Three letting bedrooms. Home-made food available Mon–Sat 12–2pm. Situated off the High Street.

OPEN *10am–11pm Mon–Sat; 12–10.30pm Sun.*

EAST HOATHLY

The King's Head

1 High Street, East Hoathly, Lewes, East Sussex BN8 6DR
☎ *(01825) 840238* Robert and Tracie Wallace

A freehouse with Harveys Best always available plus three guests such as Hop Back Summer Lightning, Fuller's London Pride and Morland Old Speckled Hen.

Seventeenth-century pub, formerly a coaching inn, in a conservation village. Character bar, restaurant, function room, enclosed garden. Home-cooked food available at lunchtime and evenings. Children and dogs welcome.

OPEN 11am–4pm daily; 6–11pm Mon–Sat, 7–10.30pm Sun.

ELSTED MARSH

Elsted Inn

Elsted Marsh, West Sussex GU29 0JT
☎ *(01730) 813662*

Most of Ballard's brews usually available plus Fuller's London Pride and a guest beer, changed weekly, usually from Arundel, Cheriton or Hop Back.

Formerly owned by Ballard's, a friendly, old-fashioned Victorian railway pub. Restored inside, with wooden shutters, wood floor, open fires. Very cosy in winter, very cool in summer. No canned music or juke box. Good bar and restaurant food available at lunchtime and evenings. Car park, garden, large pretty terrace. Children and dogs on lead allowed in garden and dining area. Accommodation. Off the A272 between Midhurst and Petersfield, marked Elsted and Harting (and by brown sign for Elsted Inn).

OPEN 11.30am–3pm and 5.30–11pm Mon–Fri (6–11pm Sat); 12–3pm and 6–10.30pm Sun.

EXCEAT BRIDGE

The Golden Galleon

Exceat Bridge, Cuckmere Haven, Seaford, East Sussex BN25 4AB
☎ *(01323) 892247* Stefano Diella

Home of the Cuckmere Haven Brewery, with Cuckmere Haven Best etc always available plus a range of guests (300 per year) including beers from Harveys, Shepherd Neame, Adnams, Timothy Taylor, Forge, 1066, Fuller's and Oakhill.

They have been brewing here since 1994 in small five-barrel tanks. The pub is a prominent black and white timbered building in the Cuckmere valley with beams and open fires in winter. Bar and restaurant food available all day. Car park, garden, conservatory, non-smoking room, function room. Children allowed, but not near the bar. Open all day at weekends in summer. Off the A259 on the River Cuckmere. Two miles from Seaford railway station. Website: www.goldengalleon.co.uk

OPEN 11am–11pm Mon–Sat; 12–10.30pm Sun in summer; 12–4pm Sun in winter.

FERNHURST

The King's Arms

Midhurst Road, Fernhurst, West Sussex GU27 3HA
☎ *(01428) 652005*
Annabel and Michael Hurst

King's Arms Ale (brewed especially by the Brewery on Sea) and Otter Bright always available plus three guests (300 in three years) perhaps including Hogs Back TEA, Timothy Taylor Landlord, Ringwood Fortyniner and RCH Pitchfork.

A seventeenth-century freehouse with oak beams and fireplaces. An L-shaped bar with servery to dining area, plus hay barn for live bands, weddings etc. Surrounded by farmland, customers may come by horse or helicopter. Food available at lunchtime and evenings. Children allowed until 7pm, over 14s thereafter.

OPEN 11.30am–3pm and 5.30–11pm Mon–Sat; 12–3pm only Sun.

FIRLE

The Ram Inn

Firle, Nr Lewes, East Sussex BN8 6NS
☎ *(01273) 858222*
Michael and Keith Wooller and Margaret Sharp

Harveys Best Bitter permanently available, plus two regularly changing guest beers perhaps from Otter or Ringwood breweries.

Simple and unspoilt seventeenth-century coaching inn, situated in attractive village. Log fires during the winter months and large enclosed garden. Regular live folk music. Bar food served 12–2pm and 6–9pm daily; cream teas, soup and ploughmans available 3–5.30pm daily. Car park. Children welcome.

11.30am–11pm Mon–Sat; 12–10.30pm Sun.

FISHBOURNE

The Bull's Head

99 Fishbourne Road, Fishbourne, Nr Chichester, West Sussex PO19 3JP
☎ *(01243) 839895* Roger and Julie Pocock

Gales beers always available plus five guests (150 per year) from traditional family brewers from Adnams to Young's and small independents such as Ash Vine. Repeat favourites include the Kelham Island range, Brewery on Sea brews, Conciliation Ale and Hop Back Summer Lightning.

A converted seventeenth-century farmhouse with a country atmosphere, just one mile from the city centre. Bar and restaurant food available at lunchtime and evenings except Sunday. Car park, garden and children's room. On the A259.

11am–3pm and 5.30–11pm Mon–Fri; 11am–11pm Sat; 12–10.30pm Sun.

FLETCHING

The Griffin Inn

Fletching, Nr Uckfield, East Sussex TN22 3SS
☎ *(01825) 722890*
Nigel and James Pullan and John Gatti

Harveys Best and Badger Tanglefoot usually available, plus two guest beers such as Rother Valley Level Best or a Black Sheep brew.

Sixteenth-century, Grade II listed coaching inn situated in an unspoilt village. Two acres of gardens with lovely views towards Sheffield Park. Restaurant and bar food served every lunchtime and evening. Car park. Children welcome. Eight en-suite rooms.

12–3pm and 6–11pm (10.30pm Sun).

FRANT

Abergavenny Arms

Frant Road, Frant, East Sussex
☎ *(01892) 750233* Simon Wood

Eleven beers available including Rother Valley Level Best, Fuller's London Pride and Harveys brews, plus three rotating guests (250 per year). Regulars include beers from Arundel, Bateman and Exmoor.

Built in the 1430s, a large, two-bar country pub. The lounge bar was used as a courtroom in the eighteenth century, with cells in the cellar. Bar and restaurant food available at lunchtime and evenings. Car park, garden. Children allowed. Easy to find.

11am–3pm and 6–11pm Mon–Fri; 11am–11pm Sat; 12–10.30pm Sun.

GRAFFHAM

The Foresters Arms

Graffham, Petworth, West Sussex GU28 0QA
☎ *(01798) 867202* Lloyd Pocock

Cheriton Pots Ale plus four guest beers available which often include Hop Back Summer Lightning, beers from Harveys and an ever-changing selection from local breweries and micros.

Heavily beamed country freehouse dating from circa 1609. Situated at the foot of the South Downs with big log fires in winter and large garden for the summer. Food served every lunchtime and evening. Car park. Children are permitted in certain areas of the bar and restaurant, but there are no special facilities.

11am–2.30pm and 5.30–11pm Mon–Sat; 12–3pm and 7–10.30pm Sun.

GUNGARDEN

The Ypres Castle Inn

Gungarden, Rye, East Sussex TN31 7HH
☎ *(01797) 223248* Richard Pearce

A freehouse with Harveys Bitter and Mild always available plus up to four guests such as Charles Wells Bombardier, Badger Tanglefoot, Young's Bitter and Coach House Coachman's Best. Local brewers favoured whenever possible.

An old-fashioned weatherboarded pub dating from the seventeenth century. No juke box, games or machines. Non-smoking area, safe garden. Food available at lunchtime and evenings plus Sunday carvery (book for food at weekends). Well-behaved children allowed until 9.30pm, if accompanied. Ring for directions – can be hard to find.

All day, every day.

HAILSHAM

The Bricklayers Arms

1 Ersham Road, Hailsham, East Sussex BN27 3LA
☎ *(01323) 841587* Ray Gosling

Fuller's ESB, Shepherd Neame Bishop's Finger and Greene King Abbot always available straight from the barrel, plus occasional seasonal guests.

Two bars, pool and billiards. Hot snacks available until 8pm. Beer garden. Children allowed in the garden only.

OPEN 11am–3pm and 5–11pm (10.30pm Sun).

HALFWAY BRIDGE

Halfway Bridge Inn

Halfway Bridge, Nr Petworth, West Sussex GU28 9BP
☎ *(01798) 861281* Simon and James Hawkins

Cheriton Pots Ale and Gales HSB always available plus two guests (100 per year) changed each week often from Brewery on Sea, Hampshire or Arundel breweries. Also local cider.

Built in 1710 on the A272 halfway between Midhurst and Petworth, an authentic staging post on the Dover to Winchester road. Four rooms around a central serving area, inglenook fireplace. Bar and restaurant food at lunchtime and evenings. Car park, garden, non-smoking area, traditional games. Children over 10 allowed.

OPEN 11–3pm and 6–11pm Mon–Sat; 12–3pm and 7–11pm Sun.

HASTINGS

The Carlisle

Pelham Street, Hastings, East Sussex TN34 1PE
☎ *(00424) 420193* Mike Ford

A freehouse serving brews from various local breweries, including Old Forge and Arundel, plus seasonal guests.

A bikers' pub but with a mixed clientele. Rock music, bar games. Large function room. Outside seating on concrete mushrooms. Food available at lunchtime and evenings. Children allowed until 7pm.

OPEN All day, every day.

First In Last Out

15 High Street, Hastings, East Sussex TN34 3EY
☎ *(01424) 425079* Mr Bigg

Two beers brewed on the premises and always available. Two guest ales such as Hop Back Rye and Coriander, but always changing. Smaller breweries favoured and normally their stronger brews.

Definitely a real ale house, known locally as FILO, with lots of character and charisma. There are plans to extend and upgrade the brewery so that more beers can be produced, and to alter the pub so that customers can see into the brewery. No pool, music or machines. Food available 12–3pm Tues–Sat in a separate restaurant. Beer garden. Children allowed during the daytime only.

 CROFTERS BEST BITTER 4.0% ABV
CARDINAL SUSSEX PORTER 4.4% ABV

OPEN All day, every day.

HAYWARDS HEATH

The Star

1 The Broadway, Haywards Heath, West Sussex RH16 3AQ
☎ *(01444) 413267* Jason Flexen

Up to 12 beers. Brakspear Bitter, Wadworth 6X, Harveys Sussex and Marston's Pedigree are regularly available, plus guests including Timothy Taylor Landlord, Old Forge, Pett Progress and Hop Back Summer Lightning. Monthly '4 for 3' offers on selected ales. Micro beer festival in April (25 ales) and two-week festival in October (50 ales and ciders).

A large real ale house in the town centre. Recently refurbished. Food served all day, every day. Car park and outside seating. Part of the Hogshead pub group.

OPEN 11am–11pm Mon–Sat; normal hours Sun.

HEATHFIELD

The Prince of Wales

Hailsham Road, Heathfield, East Sussex TN21 8DR
☎ *(01435) 862919* Vivienne and Ted Archer

Regularly changing beers may include Harveys Best, Greene King Abbot Ale and brews from Rother Valley, Old Forge, Morland, Wadworth, Ruddles or Charles Wells, as per customer request.

A freehouse partly dating back to the early nineteenth century, when it was used as a drovers stop-over alehouse. Now enlarged to include two bars, restaurant and conservatory. Food served every day, lunchtime and evenings. Well-behaved children welcome. Car park.

OPEN 11am–3pm and 5–11pm Mon–Tues; 11am–11pm Wed–Sun.

HERSTMONCEUX

The Brewer's Arms

*Gardner Street, Herstmonceux, East Sussex
BN27 4LB*
☎ *(01323) 832226* Barry Dimmack

Greene King IPA and Triumph and a Harveys ale always available plus two or three guests. Examples include Archers Golden and Swale Kentish Pride, but the selection is changing all the time.

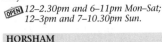

An Elizabethan pub dating from 1580. Low beams, wood panelling, many clocks. Food available at lunchtime (not Tuesday) and evenings in a separate dining area. Garden. Children allowed in the garden only.

12–2.30pm and 6–11pm Mon–Sat; 12–3pm and 7–10.30pm Sun.

HORSHAM

The Foresters Arms

*43 St Leonards Road, Horsham, West Sussex
RH13 6EH*
☎ *(01403) 254458* Jo Mainstone

Three real ales including brews from Shepherd Neame always available.

A small pub with a large garden for outdoor games which is also child- and dog-friendly. Barbecues, quiz nights, happy hours etc. Food only on special occasions (such as BBQs), children in garden only.

12–3.30pm and 6–11pm Mon–Fri; all day at weekends.

The Malt Shovel

*Springfield Road, Horsham, West Sussex
RH12 2PG*
☎ *(01403) 254543* Steve Williams

Gales GB among the beers always available, plus up to six guests including Timothy Taylor Landlord, or something from Cottage or Weltons. A beer festival is held in February or March.

A traditional pub with floorboards, real fires, one bar, patio and car park. Food served until 7pm (9.30pm on Mondays). Children over 14 allowed.

All day, every day.

HOVE

Farm Tavern

13 Farm Road, Hove, East Sussex
☎ *(01273) 325902* Miss AC McKellar

Greene King IPA, Abbot Ale and Triumph usually available. One or two guest beers served such as Fuller's HSB.

Quaint, old-fashioned pub situated near the town centre. Food served 12–5pm daily. No children.

11am–11pm Mon–Sat; 12–10.30pm Sun.

Hedgehog & Hogshead

*100 Goldstone Villas, Hove, East Sussex
BN3 3RU*
☎ *(01273) 733660* Danny Barclay

A freehouse and brewpub with two beers produced on the premises and always available.

One large bar with TV for sport etc. Outside seating. Food available 12–3pm daily, including Sunday roasts. Curry night on Thursdays, live music Fri–Sat evenings. Children allowed in designated licensed area.

BB 4.2% ABV
ORIGINAL 5.2% ABV

All day, every day.

ICKLESHAM

The Queen's Head

*Parsonage Lane, Icklesham, Winchelsea,
East Sussex TN36 4BL*
☎ *(01424) 814552* Ian Mitchell

A freehouse with Greene King IPA and either Old Forge or Brother's Best from the Forge Brewery always available, plus two fortnightly changing guests such as Greene King Abbot, Ringwood Old Thumper and Hop Back Summer Lightning.

A Jacobean pub dating from 1632. Farm implements on ceiling, boules pitch, function room, beer garden overlooking Rye. Food available at lunchtime and evenings. Under 12s allowed until 8.30pm. Situated off the A259.

11am–11pm Mon–Sat; 12–5pm and 7–10.30pm Sun.

ISFIELD

The Laughing Fish

*Station Road, Isfield, Nr Uckfield, East Sussex
TN22 5XB*
☎ *(01825) 750349*
Mick Kirby and Jackie Webber

Harveys Best Bitter, Greene King IPA and Mild plus seasonal variations usually available.

Rural village pub with real fires, pub games and family garden. Food served every lunchtime and evening with plans a-foot to offer food all day. Family room and outside children's play area. Car park.

11.30am–3pm and 5.30–11pm Mon–Fri; 11.30am–11pm Sat; 12–10.30pm Sun (12–4pm and 7–10.30pm Sun in winter).

LEWES

The Black Horse Inn

55 Western Road, Lewes, East Sussex BN7 1RS
☎ *(01273) 473653* Vic Newman

Greene King IPA and Triumph, Archers Golden and a Harveys ale always available, plus two guests from a range of independent brewers.

Built in 1800 as a hotel, this is a quiet, two-bar pub situated on the main road through Lewes. Bar billiards, darts, cribbage, beer garden. Bar snacks available at lunchtime. No children.

11am–2.30pm and 5.30–11pm Mon–Sat; 12–2.30pm and 7–10.30pm Sun.

The Brewer's Arms

91 High Street, Lewes, East Sussex BN7 1XN
☎ *(01273) 475524* Kevin Griffin

A freehouse with Harveys Best always available plus up to four real ales constantly rotating. Harveys seasonals regularly featured, as well as brews such as Fuller's London Pride, Rother Valley Spirit Level or something from Arundel, Brewery on Sea, Northdown, Bateman, Cuckmere, Rector Ales, Larkins, Hampshire and Cottage. Also real ciders.

There has been a pub on this site since 1540. Well-equipped, with two bars, children's room, extractor fans (for smokers), pool and large-screen TV. Bar food available until 7pm, snacks until 11pm. Children welcome, and dogs if on a lead.

All day, every day.

The Elephant & Castle

White Hill, Lewes, East Sussex BN2 2DJ
☎ *(01273) 473797* Dave Whiting

A freehouse with Harveys Best, Morland Old Speckled Hen and Charles Wells Bombardier always available.

An old Sussex pub with one bar and a function room. Meeting place for the Bonfire Society. A themed menu is available at lunchtimes only. Children allowed.

All day, every day.

The Gardener's Arms

46 Cliffe High Street, Lewes, East Sussex BN7 2AN
☎ *(01273) 474808* Chris Nye

A constantly changing range of real ales from independent breweries across the UK is served on up to nine hand pumps.

A traditional pub, little changed in 30 years. Interesting collection of birds. Sandwiches available at lunchtime. Dogs welcome. Country walks nearby.

11am–11pm Mon–Sat; 12–10.30pm Sun.

LITLINGTON

The Plough & Harrow

Litlington, Nr Alfriston, East Sussex BN26 5RE
☎ *(01323) 870631* Roger Taylor

Badger Best and Tanglefoot always available plus four guests from a large list including Wadworth 6X, Charles Wells Bombardier and Eagle IPA, Fuller's London Pride and brews from Harveys and Federation.

A fifteenth-century freehouse with oak beams, two bars and a busy restaurant. Bar and restaurant food available. Car park and garden. Children allowed in the restaurant. Three miles south of the A27, two miles from the nearest village (Alfriston).

11am–2.30pm and 6.30–11pm.

MAPLEHURST

The White Horse Inn

Park Lane, Maplehurst, Horsham, West Sussex RH13 6LL
☎ *(01403) 891208* Simon Johnson

A freehouse with Weltons Dorking Pride and Harveys Best always available, plus four guests, changed weekly, such as Hogs Back TEA, King and Barnes Best, Butcombe Gold, Harveys Armada or Brewery on Sea Spinnaker. Smaller independents and microbreweries favoured.

A traditional three-bar pub with no juke box, machines or piped music. Nonsmoking area, conservatory, garden with good views. Food served at lunchtime and evenings. Children allowed. Situated less than two miles north of the A272 and south of the A281.

12–2.30pm and 6–11pm Mon–Sat; 12–3pm and 7–10.30pm Sun.

MIDHURST

The Crown Inn

Edinburgh Square, Midhurst, West Sussex GU29 9NL
☎ *(01730) 813462* Paul Stevens

Fuller's London Pride and Cheriton Pots available at £1.59 plus up to eight guests (150 per year). Favoured breweries include Cheriton, Hampshire, Ballards, Hogs Back, Tripple F, Oakham, Rooster's, Ringwood, Hop Back, Woodforde's, etc.

A sixteenth-century traditional freehouse hosting occasional beer festivals. Bar and restaurant food served at lunchtime and evenings. Parking, garden, function/games room. Children allowed in the restaurant. Accommodation. Behind and below the church in the old part of the town.

11am–11pm Mon–Sat; 12–10.30pm Sun.

The Rising Sun

*The Street, Nutbourne, Pulborough, West Sussex
RH20 2HE*
☎ *(01798) 812191* Regan Howard

A freehouse serving Fuller's London Pride, Greene King Abbot and King and Barnes Sussex Ale plus a minimum of two guests such as Harveys Sussex and Hogs Back TEA, or something from breweries such as Cottage.

A 400-year-old pub with Victorian frontage in walking country. Two bars, wooden floors, dining area, mixed clientele with very friendly landlord! Food served at lunchtime and evenings. Children allowed.

OPEN *11am–3pm and 6–11pm (10.30pm Sun).*

The Star

*Church Street, Old Heathfield, East Sussex
TN21 9AH*
☎ *(01435) 863570* Mr and Mrs Chappell

Harveys brews and Fuller's London Pride always available plus a guest (50 per year) such as Harviestoun Ptarmigan, Hop Back Summer Lightning, Black Sheep Best; also Daleside Old Legover, Gravesend Shrimpers, NYBC Flying Herbert, Daleside Monkey Wrench and Burton Bridge Hearty Ale etc.

A freehouse built in 1348, licensed in 1388. Original beams and open fires. Famous gardens and views. Bar and restaurant food served at lunchtime and evenings. Car park and garden. Children allowed. At a dead end of a road to the rear of Old Heathfield church.

OPEN *11.30am–3pm and 5.30–11pm.*

The Gribble Inn & Brewery

Oving, Nr Chichester, West Sussex PO20 6BP
☎ *(01243) 786893* Brian and Cyn Elderfield

Gribble Ales all available. Wobbler only from September to March.

The Gribble Inn's brewery is now in its twelfth year and still going strong. Rob Cooper, the head brewer, is constantly developing new beers, using only the best quality hops and malts with no additives or extra sugars, the latest in his range of fine ales and beers being known as Fursty Ferret, a nut-brown beer. This picturesque sixteenth-century inn is a traditional country pub, serving good, wholesome home-cooked food at both lunchtime and evenings, seven days a week. Car park, large garden, no-smoking area, children's room, skittle alley.

EWE BREW 3.8% ABV
GRIBBLE ALE 4.1% ABV
FURSTY FERRET 4.2% ABV
OVING BITTER 4.5% ABV
REG'S TIPPLE 5.0% ABV
BLACK ADDER II 5.8% ABV
PIG'S EAR OLD ALE 6.0% ABV
WOBBLER 7.2% ABV

OPEN *11am–3pm and 5.30–11pm Mon–Sat;
12–3pm and 7–10.30pm Sun.*

The Two Sawyers

*Pett Road, Pett, Nr Hastings, East Sussex
TN35 4HB*
☎ *(01424) 812255* Peter Newmark-Payne

A freehouse with Petts Progress and Forge Bitter from the nearby Old Forge Brewery always available. Two weekly changing guests such as Hop Back Summer Lightning, Greene King Abbot and Gales GB and HSB.

An olde-worlde pub with two bars, restaurant, beer garden, boules pitch and B&B. Live music on Friday nights. Food available at lunchtime and evenings. Children allowed in the dining area only.

OPEN *11.30am–3pm and 6–11pm Mon–Thurs;
all day Fri–Sun.*

The Stanley Arms

47 Wolseley Road, Portslade, East Sussex
BN41 1SS
☎ *(01273) 701590* Pat and Roy Bond

 Three regularly changing beers served.

Traditional, street-corner pub with attractive garden. Barbecues in summer and live blues/rock music most weekends. Sandwiches available. Children welcome in the lounge and garden until 8pm. Situated 400 yards north of Fishersgate station.

1pm–11pm Mon–Thurs; 12–11pm Fri–Sat; 12–10.30pm Sun.

The Seven Stars Inn

High Street, Robertsbridge, East Sussex TN32 5AJ
☎ *(01580) 880333* Ruth McGregor

Harveys Sussex Bitter, Greene King Abbot and IPA and Marston's Pedigree always available, plus up to five guests such as Arundel 1999 and Rother Valley Level Best.

An early-medieval pub, dating from the eleventh century. One bar, pool, video games, car park, beer garden. Food available at lunchtime and evenings. Children and dogs welcome.

All day, every day.

Thurlow Arms

Baynards, Rudgwick, Nr Horsham, West Sussex
RH12 3AD
☎ *(01403) 822459* MR Gibbs

Fuller's London Pride, Hogs Back TEA, Ringwood Best Bitter, Badger Tanglefoot and Dorset Best regularly available.

Large Victorian pub situated on the South Downs Way, with railway memorabilia relating to the closure of Baynards station in 1965. Games room with darts and pool, restaurant, dining rooms and large garden. Food served 12–2pm and 6.15–9.30pm Mon–Fri, 12–2.15pm and 6.15–9.30pm Sat, and 12–2.30pm and 7–9pm Sun. Large car park. Children's play castle and menu.

11–3pm and 6–11pm Mon–Sat; 12–10.30pm Sun.

The Fletcher Arms

Station Road, Rustington, West Sussex
BN16 3AF
☎ *(01903) 784858*
Mr R and Mrs C Dumbleton

Fuller's London Pride, Greene King Abbot Ale, Marston's Pedigree, Ringwood Best and Adnams Broadside permanently available, plus a daily changing guest beer perhaps from Wolf, Ballard's, Wild, Timothy Taylor, Hogs Back, Fuller's, Ringwood, Gales, or many others from around the country.

Large, friendly, 1920s pub, winner of many awards including Cask Marque. Live entertainment, public and saloon bar and olde-worlde barn. Food available 11.30am–2.30pm and 6–9pm Mon–Sat, 12–2.30pm Sun. Large car park. Large garden with pets' corner, swings and bouncy castle. Accommodation.

All day, every day.

The Inkerman Arms

Harbour Road, Rye Harbour, Rye, East Sussex
TN31 7TQ
☎ *(01797) 222464* Mrs May

A freehouse serving a selection of real ales from one of two local brewers (Old Forge or Rother Valley). Guest ales always available.

A traditional harbourside pub with one bar, lounge and dining area. Boules pitch, garden. Full menu available every day, with fish and chips a speciality. Well-behaved children welcome.

12–3pm and 7–11pm Mon–Thurs; all day Fri–Sat; 12–5pm Sun (closed Sun evening).

The Dripping Spring

34 Tower Road, St Leonards on Sea, East Sussex
RN37 6JE
☎ *(01424) 434055* Mr and Mrs Gillitt

Goacher's Light and Fuller's London Pride served, plus ales from local breweries. Other guests from as far afield as possible, preferably 4% ABV and over – more than 1000 guest ales to date.

A small two-bar public house with attractive courtyard to the rear. Sussex CAMRA Pub of the Year 1999–2000. Bar food available at lunchtime. Car parking. Situated in a side street off the A21.

11am–3pm and 5–11pm Mon–Thurs; all day Fri–Sun.

SEAFORD

The Wellington

Steyne Road, Seaford, East Sussex BN25 1HT
☎ *(01323) 890032* Mr Shaw

Fuller's London Pride, Greene King IPA, Abbot and Harveys Best Bitter always available. Also one guest from an independent or micro-brewery, changing daily.

A community pub with two bars and a function roon. Parking nearby. Food available at lunchtime only. Children allowed.

OPEN *All day, every day.*

The White Lion

74 Claremont Road, Seaford, East Sussex
☎ *(01323) 892473* Carole P E Tidy

Harveys Sussex Best Bitter, Old, Porter and Fuller's London Pride regularly available, plus one or two guest beers perhaps from Ruddles, Morland, Shepherd Neame or Harveys.

F riendly, small, family-run hotel by the seafront. Food served every lunchtime and evening. Car park. Large conservatory and separate non-smoking area. Children welcome. En-suite accommodation.

OPEN *11am–11pm Mon–Sat; 12–10.30pm Sun.*

SHOREHAM

The Lazy Toad

88 High Street, Shoreham-by-Sea, West Sussex BN43 5DB
☎ *(01273) 441622* Mr Cederberg

Greene King Abbot, Badger Tanglefoot, Shepherd Neame Spitfire and Gales Festival Mild among the beers always available plus up to three guests.

A small, friendly freehouse with one big bar. Food served only at lunchtime. Children over 14 allowed.

OPEN *All day, every day.*

The Red Lion

Old Shoreham Road, Shoreham-by-Sea, West Sussex BN43 5TE
☎ *(01243) 453171* James and Natalie Parker

Harveys Best Bitter and four or five guest beers regularly available, perhaps from Hop Back, Adnams, Arundel, Fuller's or many more. Annual Easter beer festival features 50–60 beers, live music and barbecue.

W idely considered to be Shoreham's premier country pub, with low beams, inglenook and secluded beer garden. Good atmosphere, full of tales and history. Separate non-smoking eating area. Food served lunchtimes and evenings Mon–Sat, lunchtimes only Sun. Children welcome. The car park is situated some distance from the pub: pass the pub on your left, turn left at mini roundabout then first left again. Follow the road to church and the car park is opposite.

OPEN *11.30am–3pm and 5.30–11pm Mon–Fri; 11.30am–11pm Sat; 12–10.30pm Sun. Jul–Sept: open all day Mon–Fri.*

SIDLESCOOMBE

The Queen's Head

The Green, Sidlescoombe, Battle, East Sussex TN33 0QA
☎ *(01424) 870228* John Cook

Young's Bitter always available plus one guest from an independent brewery. Rother Valley and Pett (Old Forge) brews are popular choices.

A country pub with beams and brasses, on the village green. Beer garden, car park. Bread and cheese available at lunchtime only. Children allowed.

OPEN *10am–2.30pm and 6–11pm.*

STOUGHTON

The Hare & Hounds

Stoughton, West Sussex
☎ *(01705) 631433*

Adnams Broadside, Ringwood Best and Gales HSB always available plus four guest beers (from an endless list) such as Hop Back Summer Lightning, Timothy Taylor Landlord, Fuller's ESB, Brakspear etc.

M ore than 300 years old, a flint-built pub nestling on the Sussex Downs. Bar food available at lunchtime and evenings. Car park and garden. Children allowed. Signposted at Walberton off the B2146.

OPEN *11am–3pm and 6–11pm Mon–Sat; 12–4pm and 7–10.30pm Sun.*

TARRING

The Vine Inn

High Street, Tarring, Worthing, West Sussex
BN14 7NN
☎ *(01903) 202891* Steve and Sheila Culyer

Badger Dorset Best, Champion Ale and Tanglefoot, Ringwood True Glory, Hop Back Summer Lightning and a Harveys ale always available plus two constantly changing guests such as Harveys Old, Gribble Oving Bitter, Fursty Ferret and Black Adder II.

An old-fashioned pub in a listed building dating from 1645. Live entertainment on Mondays, enormous garden and courtyard, car park. Food available at lunchtime, plus Sunday roasts. Children allowed.

12–3pm and 6–11pm Mon–Thurs; 11am–11pm Fri–Sat; 12–10.30pm Sun.

TELHAM

The Black Horse Inn

Hastings Road, Telham, Battle, East Sussex
TN33 0SH
☎ *(01424) 773109* Mr Dunford

A range of Shepherd Neame ales always available.

A one-bar pub with restaurant, beer garden and boules pitch. Music festival held on Spring Bank Holiday every year. Food available at lunchtime and evenings. Children allowed in the restaurant only.

11am–3pm and 5.30–11pm (10.30pm Sun).

THAKEHAM

The White Lion Inn

The Street, Thakeham Village, West Sussex
RH20 3EP
☎ *(01798) 813141* William Newton

A freehouse with Harveys Best and Old Flame and Arundel Best always available.

A two-bar, 500-year-old alehouse with garden. Pub grub available at lunchtime and evenings. Well-behaved children allowed.

11am–4pm and 5.30–11pm Mon–Sat; 12–3.30pm and 6.30–10.30pm Sun.

TICEHURST

The Bull Inn

Dunster Mill Lane, Three Legged Cross,
Nr Ticehurst, East Sussex TN5 7HH
☎ *(01580) 200586* Mrs Josie Wilson-Moir

Up to seven brews always available including Rother Valley Level Best, Morland Old Speckled Hen, King and Barnes Sussex and Harveys ales plus hundreds of guests per year including brews from Adnams, Iceni etc.

Whealden Hall House was built between 1385 and 1425 in good walking country and has been a pub for 100 years. There are two bars with an adjoining restaurant. Food available at lunchtime and evenings (not Sunday and Monday evenings). Car park, garden, children's play area. Coming into Ticehurst from the north on the B2099, turn left beside corner house called Tollgate just before village.

11am–3pm and 6–11pm Mon–Sat; 12–3pm and 7–10.30pm Sun.

UCKFIELD

Alma

Framfield Road, Uckfield, East Sussex
☎ *(01825) 762232* Mrs Joy Hughes

A Harveys house with Mild, IPA, Best Bitter and seasonal brews usually available.

Traditional, family-run (third generation) pub, with Cask Marque award. Food served 12–2pm Mon–Sat. Car park. Separate family and non-smoking rooms.

11am–2.30pm and 6–11pm Mon–Sat; 12–2pm and 7–10.30pm Sun.

WEST ASHLING

The Richmond Arms

Mill Road, West Ashling, West Sussex PO18 8EA
☎ *(01243) 575730* Alan Gurney

Harveys Sussex and Greene King Abbot and IPA always available, plus up to seven guests such as Hop Back Summer Lightning, Hanby Cascade and Fuller's Summer Ale. Seasonal ales always popular.

A comfortable and cosy Victorian pub. Two bars, open fires, skittle alley, pool, darts etc. Terrace garden at the front. Bar food available at lunchtime and evenings. Well-behaved children allowed. Situated half a mile from Funtington.

11am–2.30pm and 5.30–11pm Mon–Fri; all day Sat–Sun.

WEST CHILTINGTON

The Five Bells

Smock Alley, West Chiltington, West Sussex
RH20 2QX
☎ *(01798) 812143*

Five beers always available from an ever-changing range. Favoured brewers include Ballards, Adnams, Bateman, Black Sheep, Brakspear, Bunces, Cheriton, Exmoor, Fuller's, Gales, Greene King, Guernsey, Harveys, Hogs Back, Hook Norton, Jennings, King & Barnes, Mansfield, Palmers, St Austell, Shepherd Neame, Smiles, Samuel Smith, Timothy Taylor and Young's.

An attractive Edwardian-style version of a Sussex farmhouse. Bar and restaurant food available at lunchtime and evenings. Car park, conservatory and beer garden. Well-behaved children allowed. Ask for directions.

11am–3pm and 6–11pm.

WORTHING

The Richard Cobden

2 Cobden Road, Worthing, West Sussex
BN11 4BD
☎ *(01903) 236856* Mike Wilson

Greene King IPA and Wadworth 6X always available plus two guests such as Greene King Abbot.

A typical 1950s street-corner boozer with one bar and a patio. Food served at lunchtimes (not Sunday).

11am–3pm and 5.30–11pm Mon–Thurs; all day Fri–Sat; 12–3pm and 7–10.30pm Sun.

YAPTON

The Lamb Inn

Bilsham Road, Yapton, Arundel, West Sussex
BN18 0JN
☎ *(01243) 551232* John Etherington

Harveys Sussex Ale and Greene King Abbot always available, plus one guest changing fortnightly.

An edge-of-village pub on the road side. Brick floors, large open fire, dining area, car park, garden with children's play area, and petanque/boules. Food served every lunchtime and evening. Children allowed. Located on a minor road between the A259 and Yapton village.

11am–3pm and 5.30–11pm Mon–Thurs; 11am–3pm and 5–11pm Fri; 12–3.30pm and 6–11pm Sat; 12–4.30pm and 6.30–10.30pm Sun. Open all day at weekends during the summer.

The Maypole Inn

Maypole Lane, Yapton, Arundel, West Sussex
BN18 0DP
☎ *(01243) 551417* Keith McManus

A freehouse with Ringwood Best always available plus up to six guests. Hop Back Summer Lightning, Cheriton Pots Ale or something from Skinner's may be featured. Smaller breweries well-represented.

A country pub with public and lounge bars, log fires, skittle alley, small garden. Bar snacks available at lunchtime and Sunday roasts. Children allowed in the public bar only until 8.30pm.

11am–3pm and 5.30–11pm Mon–Fri; all day Sat; 12–3pm and 6–10.30pm Sun.

YOU TELL US

★ *The Cock Robin,* Station Hill, Wadhurst
★ *The Duke of Cumberland,* Henley
★ *The Earl of March,* Lavant Road, Lavant
★ *The Green Man,* The Green, Horsted Keynes, Haywards Heath
★ *Hatter's,* 2–10 Queensway, Bognor Regis
★ *The Horse & Groom,* Singleton
★ *The Linden Tree,* 47 High Street, Lindfield, Haywards Heath
★ *The Ostrich Hotel,* Station Road, Robertsbridge
★ *The Peacock Inn,* Shortbridges, Piltdown
★ *The Sussex Brewery,* Hermitage
★ *Vinols Cross,* 8 Top Road, Sharpthorne
★ *The Wyndham Arms,* Rogate

Places Featured:

Byker	North Shields
Felling	South Shields
Gosforth	Sunderland
Jesmond	Wardley
Low Fell	Washington
Newburn	Westmoor
Newcastle upon Tyne	Whitley Bay
North Hylton	

THE BREWERIES

BIG LAMP BREWERS

*Big Lamp Brewery, Grange Road, Newburn,
Newcastle upon Tyne NE15 8NL*
☎ *(0191) 267 1689*

SUNNY DAZE 3.6% ABV
BITTER 3.9% ABV
DOUBLE M 4.3% ABV
MULLIGAN'S STOUT 4.4% ABV
Seasonal brew.
PRINCE BISHOP ALE 4.8% ABV
PREMIUM 5.2% ABV
EMBERS 5.5% ABV
Winter warmer
OLD GENIE 7.4% ABV
BLACKOUT 11.0% ABV
Plus seasonal brews.

FEDERATION BREWERY

Lancaster Road, Dunston NE11 9JR
☎ *(0191) 460 9023*

BUCHANAN BEST BITTER 3.5% ABV
BUCHANAN ORIGINAL 4.2% ABV
OLD VIC 4.2% ABV
DANGLE YA MAGGOT 5.0% ABV
Seasonal brew.
SALMON LEAP 5.0% ABV
Seasonal brew.
TUMMY TICKLER 5.0% ABV
Seasonal brew.

MORDUE BREWERY

*Unit 21a, West Chirton North Industrial Estate,
Shiremoor NE29 8SF*
☎ *(0191) 296 1879*

SUMMER TYNE 3.6% ABV
Seasonal.
FIVE BRIDGE BITTER 3.8% ABV
SPRING TYNE 4.0% ABV
Seasonal.
GEORDIE PRIDE 4.2% ABV
BLACK MIDDEN STOUT 4.4% ABV
Seasonal.
WORKIE TICKET 4.5% ABV
WALLSEND BROWN ALE 4.6% ABV
Seasonal.
WINTER TYNE 4.7% ABV
Seasonal.
RADGIE GADGIE 4.8% ABV

THE PUBS

BYKER

The Cumberland Arms

*Byker Buildings, Byker, Newcastle upon Tyne
NE6 1LD*
☎ *(0191) 265 6151*

A wide range of constantly changing real ales always available.

An unchanged pub established in 1832 overlooking the Ouseburn Valley. Well known for its live music (traditional and rock). Sandwiches always available. Parking, garden under development. Children allowed in the function room. Over Byker Bridge, then first right, second right, above farm.

OPEN 12–11pm (10.30pm Sun).

The Free Trade Inn

*St Lawrence Road, Byker, Newcastle upon Tyne
NE6 1AP*
☎ *(0191) 265 5764* Richard Grey (Manager)

Mordue Workie Ticket and Geordie Pride, Marston's Pedigree and a Mordue seasonal ale such as Summer Tyne always available plus one guest, usually another Mordue beer such as Five Bridges, Radgie Gadgie or seasonals.

A traditional town pub with a lovely view of the River Tyne. Two beer gardens, one bar. No food. Children allowed during the daytime and early evening only.

OPEN 11am–11pm (10.30pm Sun).

The Ouseburn Tavern

*33 Shields Road, Byker, Newcastle upon Tyne
NE6 1DJ*
☎ *(0191) 276 5120* Peter Bland

Twelve beers always available from a constantly changing range (450 per year) with Bateman Valiant, Charles Wells Eagle and Black Sheep Bitter among them.

Beamed theme pub with open fires and friendly atmosphere. Bar food available at lunchtime and evenings. Car park. Children allowed. Easy to find.

OPEN 12–11pm (10.30pm Sun).

FELLING

The Old Fox

13 Carlisle Street, Felling, Gateshead NE10 0HQ
☎ *(0191) 420 0357* Valerie White

A freehouse with Bateman XB and a Banks's ale always available plus three guests from breweries such as Durham, Northumberland or Adnams. Beers also stocked at customers' request – previous examples have included Marston's Pedigree or Black Sheep Bitter.

A real ale pub in town location, with coal fire, one bar and garden. Bar snacks available at lunchtime. Children allowed if eating, up to 7pm. Bed and breakfast available.

OPEN *12–11pm (10.30pm Sun).*

The Wheatsheaf

26 Carlisle Street, Felling, Gateshead NE10 0HQ
☎ *(0191) 420 0659* Jim Storey

A range of Big Lamp beers such as Bitter, Price Bishop, Premium Ale, Sandgates or Keelman Bitter always available.

An old-fashioned community pub with one bar. Sandwiches and pies available. Children allowed until 7pm.

OPEN *12–11pm (10.30pm Sun).*

GOSFORTH

Gosforth Hotel

High Street, Gosforth
☎ *(0191) 285 6617* John Burtle

Marston's Pedigree is one of eight beers always available. Guests including Bateman XB, Coach House Coachman's Best and Adnams and Burton Bridge brews.

Traditional Victorian alehouse. Bar food available at lunchtime. Car park, accommodation. Children allowed.

OPEN *11am–11pm Mon–Sat; 12–2.30pm and 7–10.30pm Sun.*

JESMOND

Legendary Yorkshire Heroes

Archibold Terrace, Jesmond
☎ *(0191) 281 3010* Colin Colquhoun

Nine beers always available from a rotating list including Black Sheep Bitter and brews from Jennings, Big Lamp and Thwaites.

A lively refurbished modern pub within an office complex. Bar food available on weekday lunchtimes. Four pool tables, big screen sports, live bands Thursday to Saturday. Children allowed at lunchtimes only.

OPEN *11am–11pm Mon–Sat; 12–10.30pm Sun.*

LOW FELL

The Ale Taster

706 Durham Road, Low Fell, Gateshead NE9 6JA
☎ *(0191) 487 0770* Lawrence Gill

Mordue Workie Ticket and Radgie Gadgie always available plus up to six guests such as Timothy Taylor Landlord, Badger Tanglefoot or an Ash Vine brew. Two beer festivals held every year in May and September, serving 30 extra beers.

An old coaching inn with beams and wooden floors, in the town centre. One bar, snug area, large courtyard with children's play area. Food available until 6pm. Children allowed.

OPEN *11am–11pm Mon–Sat; 12–10.30pm Sun.*

NEWBURN

Keelman

Grange Road, Newburn, Newcastle upon Tyne
☎ *(0191) 267 1689* Lee Goulding

Big Lamp Bitter, Prince Bishop Ale, Premium, Summerhill Stout plus other Big Lamp brews regularly available.

Superb conversion of ninteenth-century water board building into a traditional family pub. Situated next to the leisure centre in Newburn Country Park, on the River Tyne. Food served daily 12–3pm and 5–9pm in winter, 12–9pm in summer. Car park. Children's play area.

OPEN *11am–11pm Mon–Sat; 12–10.30pm Sun.*

NEWCASTLE UPON TYNE

The Bodega

125 Westgate Road, Newcastle upon Tyne NE1 4AG
☎ *(0191) 221 1552* Colin Howse

Mordue Workie Ticket, Geordie Pride and Durham Magus among the brews permanently available, plus one guest from breweries such as Border, Shepherd Neame, Black Sheep and Ridleys. Beers changed weekly.

A traditional real ale pub on the outskirts of the town centre. One bar, food available 11am–2.30pm Mon–Sat and 12–2.30pm Sun. No children.

OPEN *11am–11pm Mon–Sat; 12–10.30pm Sun.*

The Head of Steam

2 Neville Street, Newcastle upon Tyne NE1 5EN
☎ *(0191) 232 4379* David Campell

A freehouse with Black Sheep Bitter always available plus up to three guests from a wide range of breweries including, among others, Castle Eden and Hambleton.

A two-bar, city-centre pub with food available all opening hours. No children.

OPEN *3–11pm Mon–Thurs; 12–11pm Fri–Sat; 12–10.30pm Sun.*

The Hotspur

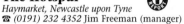

Haymarket, Newcastle upon Tyne
☎ *(0191) 232 4352* Jim Freeman (manager)

Four guests available, changing once or twice a week. Mordue Workie Ticket and Morland Ruddles County are among the most popular ales. A wide range is purchased through the Beer Seller.

A very busy pub, part of the T&J Bernard chain, attracting mainly students and young professionals. Food available all day. Wide selection of wines and whiskies. Beer alley with big screen TV for sport. No children. Located opposite Haymarket Bus Station.

OPEN *11am–11pm Mon–Sat; 12–10.30pm Sun.*

The Tap & Spile

1 Nun Street, Newcastle upon Tyne
☎ *(0191) 232 0026*

Twelve beers always available from a constantly changing range (200 per year) with names such as Durham Canny Lad and Magus, Mordue Workie Ticket and Bateman Yellow Belly.

More than 100 years old, with a ground-floor and basement bar. Bar food available at lunchtime. Children allowed for meals. Live bands in the cellar. Two minutes from the railway station and Greys Monument.

OPEN *11am–11pm Mon–Sat; 12–10.30pm Sun.*

The Tut & Shive

52 Clayton Street West, Newcastle upon Tyne NE1 4EX
☎ *(0191) 261 6998*

A Castle Eden ale always available plus three guests such as Marston's Pedigree or seasonal ales from Marston's.

A friendly town-centre pub with a mixed clientele of young students and business people. Two bars. Hot sandwiches available at lunchtime only. No children. Situated near the railway station.

OPEN *11am–11pm (12–11pm in summer) Mon–Sat; 12–10.30pm Sun.*

The Three Horseshoes

Washington Road, North Hylton, Sunderland SR5 3HZ
☎ *(0191) 536 4183* Frank Jamieson

Three guest ales such as Morland Old Speckled Hen and Charles Wells Bombardier. Annual beer festival held at the end of July.

A traditional country pub with two bars (public and lounge), separate dining area, open fire, pool, darts etc. Food available lunchtimes and evenings. Children allowed. Follow signs for Air Museum, by Nissan entrance.

OPEN *12–3pm and 6.30–11pm (10.30pm Sun).*

Chain Locker

New Quay, North Shields NE29 6LQ
☎ *(0191) 258 0147* Peter McAlister

A freehouse with Mordue Workie Ticket and Radgie Gadgie always available plus four daily changing guests including, perhaps, Mordue Five Bridges and Timothy Taylor Landlord.

A riverside pub by a ferry landing on a fresh fish quay. One bar, styled in a nautical theme, plus separate dining area and beer garden. Food available at lunchtime only. Children allowed.

OPEN *11am–11pm (10.30pm Sun).*

The Garricks Head

Saville Street, North Shields NE30 1NT
☎ *(0191) 296 2064* Ken Ladell

A freehouse with four pumps all serving a range of weekly changing real ales. Morland Old Speckled Hen, Charles Wells Bombardier, Young's Special and Hartleys XB are examples.

A traditional two-bar town pub with function room and restaurant. Food available at lunchtime and evenings. Children allowed in the restaurant only.

OPEN *11am–11pm Mon–Sat; 12–10.30pm Sun.*

The Porthole

11 New Quay, North Shields NE29 6LQ
☎ *(0191) 257 6645* Mike Morgan

Five beers always available from a large list (156+ per year) including Fuller's London Pride and Adnams Broadside.

An old-fashioned friendly pub with a maritime theme, on the banks of the Tyne. Bar food served at lunchtime and evenings. Car park. Children allowed. Near the North Shields ferry landing.

OPEN *11am–11pm Mon–Sat; 12–10.30pm Sun.*

Shiremoor House Farm

Middle Engine Lane, North Shields NE29 8DZ
☎ *(0191) 257 6302* Bill Kerridge

A freehouse with Mordue Workie Ticket always available plus up to five guests such as Moorhouse's Pendle Witches Brew, Jennings Cumberland, Timothy Taylor Landlord, Swale India Summer Pale Ale or Durham Brewery's Celtic. Beers changed two or three times a week.

A converted farmhouse with two bars, stone floors and separate restaurant. CAMRA award winner for best pub conversion. Food available 12–10pm daily. Children allowed.

11am–11pm (10.30pm Sun).

The Tap & Spile

184 Tynemouth Road, North Shields NE30 1EG
☎ *(0191) 257 2523*

Castle Eden Bitter and Nimmo's XXXX always available, plus six guests from a large and varied list. Beers from Harviestoun and Durham breweries usually available.

A real ale bar with a friendly atmosphere. Bar food served at lunchtime. Parking. Opposite the magistrates court in North Shields.

12–11pm Mon–Fri; 11.30am–11pm Sat; 12–10.30pm Sun.

SOUTH SHIELDS

The Dolly Peel

137 Commercial Road, South Shields NE33 1SQ
☎ *(0191) 427 1441* Ken Taylor

A freehouse with Timothy Taylor Landlord, Black Sheep Bitter and something from Mordue always available, plus two guest pumps serving local ales in particular, but also real ales from breweries throughout the UK.

A traditional suburban pub with two bars and outside seating. Named after an eighteenth-century smuggler – details on request! No juke box, no pool table, no darts, no bandits, just good conversation and good beer in pleasant surroundings. Local CAMRA Pub of the Year for last two years. Sandwiches only. No bottled beers. No children.

11am–11pm Mon–Sat; 12–3pm and 6.30–10.30pm Sun.

Holborn Rose & Crown

Hill Street, South Shields NE33 1RN
☎ *(0191) 455 2379* Bob Overton

Two guest beers usually served, often from Morland, Marston's, Bateman, Fuller's, Black Sheep or Mordue breweries.

One-roomed traditional freehouse with beer garden, opposite the old middle docks. Toasted sandwiches available. Children welcome during daytime only.

11am–11pm Mon–Sat; 12–10.30pm Sun.

Riverside

3 Mill Dam, South Shields NE33 1EE
☎ *(0191) 455 2328* TR Mein

Timothy Taylor Landlord and Black Sheep Special regularly available plus two guest beers often from local micro-breweries and from elsewhere around the UK.

Well-decorated, one-roomed pub with background music. Can be very busy at weekends. About half a mile from the town centre, tends to attract people 25 years and older. Sandwiches served at lunchtimes. Car park nearby.

12–11pm Mon–Sat; 12–3pm and 7–10.30pm Sun.

SUNDERLAND

The Tap & Barrel

Nelson Street, Sunderland SR2 8EF
☎ *(0191) 514 2810* Michael Riley

Everards Tiger and Timothy Taylor Landlord among the brews always available, plus four or five guests from a large selection including Banbury Old Vic and Thwaites Bloomin' Ale. Beers changed weekly.

An old-fashioned pub with two bars and a separate dining area. Food available 4–8pm Mon–Fri and 12–4pm Sat–Sun. Children allowed, if eating.

4–11pm Mon–Fri; all day Sat–Sun.

The Tap & Spile

Salem Street, Hendon, Sunderland
☎ *(0191) 232 0026* Janice Faulder

Nine beers always available from a list of 400+ including North Yorkshire Best, Bateman XB, Charles Wells Bombardier and Marston's Pedigree.

Traditional three-bar alehouse with bare boards and exposed brickwork. Bar food available at lunchtime. Function room. Children allowed in eating area.

11am–11pm Mon–Sat; 12–3pm and 7–10.30pm Sun.

WARDLEY

The Green

*White Mare Pool, Wardley, Gateshead
NE10 8YB*
☎ *(0191) 495 0171* Deborah Mackay

A freehouse with six guest ales always available. Timothy Taylor Landlord, Jennings Cumberland, Big Lamp Bitter, Black Sheep Special and Oakham American Blonde are some of the regular features.

A traditional village pub with one bar and one lounge. Patio and restaurant. Disabled facilities. Food available all day, every day. Children allowed in the lounge if eating.

11.30am–11pm Mon–Sat; 12–10.30pm Sun.

WASHINGTON

The Sandpiper

Easby Road, Washington NE38 7NN
☎ *(0191) 416 0038* Lynda Margaret Bewick

Up to six guests such as Marston's Pedigree, Black Sheep Bitter, Fuller's London Pride, something from Daleside or Phoenix Wobbly Bob.

A locals' village community pub with two bars, games area and patio. Charity events held. Food available at lunchtime only. Children allowed until 7pm, if supervised.

11am–11pm (10.30pm Sun).

WESTMOOR

George Stephenson Inn

Great Lime Road, Westmoor, Newcastle upon Tyne NE12 0NJ
☎ *(0191) 268 1073* Richard Costello

Two guests from local independent and micro-breweries such as Mordue, Northumberland and Big Lamp always available.

A community beer drinker's pub with lounge, bar and garden. Adult clientele, no games, live music during week. Food available Mon–Fri lunchtimes. No children.

12–3pm and 5–11pm Mon–Thurs; all day Fri–Sat; 12–4pm and 7–10.30pm Sun.

WHITLEY BAY

The Briar Dene

71 The Links, Whitley Bay NE26 1UE
☎ *(0191) 252 0926* Mrs Gibson

Mordue Workie Ticket and Summertime, Black Sheep Riggwelter and a Yates ale always available, plus five or six guests such as Mordue Radgie Gadgie among others. Six beer festivals held each year with 50–60 brews at each.

A seaside pub with one bar, family room, lounge and children's play area. Food available 11am–2.30pm and 5–10pm. Children allowed in the family room and play room only.

11am–11pm Mon–Sat; 12–10.30pm Sun.

The Fat Ox

278 Whitley Road, Whitley Bay NE26 2TG
☎ *(0191) 251 3852* Mr Carling

Four Rivers Moondance, Black Sheep Bitter and Fox Hat (a house brew produced by the Four Rivers brewery) always available plus three regularly changing guests, perhaps from Rudgate, Ruddles or Morland. Beers not repeated if possible.

A traditional one-bar town-centre pub. Food available at lunchtime only. Children allowed until 3pm. Disabled facilities.

11.30am–11pm Mon–Fri; 11am–11pm Sat; 12–10.30pm Sun.

YOU TELL US

★ *The Archer,* Archbold Terrace, Jesmond
★ *Benton Ale House,* Front Street, Benton, Newcastle upon Tyne
★ *Magnesia Bank,* 1 Camden Street, North Shields
★ *The Melvich Hotel,* Melvich, Sunderland
★ *The Old Cross,* Barmoor Lane, Old Ryton Village, Ryton
★ *The Potter's Wheel,* Sun Street, Sunniside
★ *Shipwrights Arms Hotel,* Rotherfield Road, North Hylton, Sunderland
★ *The Station Hotel,* Hills Street, Gateshead

Places Featured:

Alcester	Kenilworth
Bedworth	Long Lawford
Church Lawford	Rugby
Eathorpe	Shipston-on-Stour
Edgehill	Studley
Great Wolford	Warwick
Hampton Lucy	

THE BREWERIES

COX'S YARD
Bridgefoot, Stratford upon Avon CV37 6YY
☎ *(01789) 404600*

JESTER ALE 3.8% ABV
JUGGLER ALE 4.6% ABV
Plus seasonal ales.

FRANKTON BAGBY BREWERY
The Old Stables, Green Lane, Church Lawford, Rugby CV23 9EF

LITTLE BEAUTY 3.4% ABV
Hoppy, brown mild.
RIBTICKLER 3.8% ABV
Hoppy, with fruit character.
SPRING CHICKEN 3.8% ABV
Balance of hops and citrus fruit flavours.
MIDSUMMER MADNESS 3.9% ABV
Quenching and moreish.
FIRST BORN 4.1% ABV
Light and rounded with good hoppiness.
SQUIRES BREW 4.2% ABV
Good body and balance. Hop character.
RUGBY SPECIAL 4.5% ABV
Good body and balance.
FAT BOB 4.8% ABV
Good body, smooth and fruity.
TOASTMASTER 5.0% ABV
Red in colour, with rounded fruit flavour.
OLD RETAINER 5.8% ABV
Powerful, rounded fruit flavour. Dry finish.
CHRISTMAS PUD 7.0% ABV
Smooth and flavour-packed.

WARWICKSHIRE BEER CO. LTD
Queen Street, Cubbington, Leamington Spa CV32 7NA
☎ *(01926) 450747*

BEST 3.9% ABV
FFIAGRA 4.2% ABV
ST PATRICK'S ALE 4.4% ABV
CASTLE ALE 4.6% ABV
GOLDEN WONDER 4.9% ABV
STELLAR 5.0% ABV
Real lager.
KING MAKER 5.5% ABV
BLACK JACK 6.0% ABV
Winter warmer.
Plus seasonal and occasional brews.

THE PUBS

ALCESTER

Lord Nelson
69 Priory Road, Alcester B49 5EA
☎ *(01789) 762632* Dennis and Brenda Stubbs

Fuller's London Pride and Marston's Pedigree usually available.

Parts of this pub date back 600 years. There is a mature beer garden, a bar with darts and bar billiards and a restaurant area. Food is available 7–9am, 12–2pm and 7–9pm Mon–Sat, with just lunchtime roasts on Sundays. Car park. Children welcome. Accommodation.

12–3pm and 6–11pm Mon–Sat; 12–3pm and 7–10.30pm Sun.

The Three Tuns
34 High Street, Alcester B49 5AB
☎ *(01789) 766550* D Parker

Home of the Bull's Head Brewery, with three ales produced and served on the premises. In addition, up to six guests are available. Everards Tiger, Hobsons Best, Wood Shropshire Lad, Fuller's London Pride, Lichfield Resurrection, North Yorkshire Dizzy Dick, Mildmay Old Horse Whip, Brains SA and Brandy Cask Brandysnapper are all popular brews.

A sixteenth-century public house with open-plan bar, converted back from a wine bar. Beer festivals are held every three months. Occasional live music. Sandwiches only.

BULLHEAD LIGHT 4.5% ABV
GLOBE ALE
GENESIS

11am–11pm Mon–Sat; 12–10.30pm Sun.

The White Swan

All Saints Square, Bedworth
☎ *(02476) 312164* Paul Holden

Charles Wells Eagle, IPA and Bombardier usually served, plus one guest beer such as Morland Old Speckled Hen, Badger Tanglefoot or Adnams Broadside.

Central pub, catering for mixed clientele of all ages. Food served 12–2pm daily. Car parks close by. Children welcome at lunchtime.

OPEN *11am–11pm (10.30pm Sun).*

Old Smithy

Green Lane, Church Lawford, Nr Rugby CU23 9EF
☎ *(02476) 542333* John O'Neill

Frankton Bagby Anvil Ale, plus Greene King IPA and Abbot Ale usually available. A guest beer frequently comes from the Frankton Bagby Brewery which adjoins the pub.

Traditional freehouse situated on the village green. Food served lunchtimes and evenings. Car park. Beer garden and children's play area.

OPEN *11am–3pm and 5.30–11pm Mon–Fri; 11am–11pm Sat; 12–10.30pm Sun.*

Eathorpe Park Hotel

The Fosse, Eathorpe, Leamington Spa CV33 9DQ
☎ *(01926) 632632* Mrs Grinnell

A Church End ale always available plus two guests from breweries such as Hook Norton and Fat God's.

A hotel and restaurant with one bar and accommodation. Disabled access. Bar and restaurant food available at lunchtime and evenings. Children allowed.

OPEN *All day, every day.*

The Castle Inn

Edgehill, Nr Banbury OX15 6DJ
☎ *(01295) 670255* NJ and GA Blann

Hook Norton Best, Generation, Old Hooky and the seasonal brew usually available, plus a guest beer which may be from Shepherd Neame, King & Barnes, Wadworth or Wye Valley.

The inn is situated on the summit of Edgehill near the civil war battle site. Built as a folly in the eighteenth century to commemorate the centenary of the battle, it is a copy of Guy's Tower at Warwick Castle. Food served every session. Car park. Original en-suite bedrooms.

OPEN *11.15am–2.30pm and 6.15–11pm.*

The Fox & Hounds

Great Wolford CV36 5NQ
☎ *(01608) 674220* Mrs Seddon

Hook Norton Best and Shepherd Neame Spitfire always available plus hundreds of guests per year (up to five at any one time) including Wychwood Best, Morland Old Speckled Hen and brews from Eldridge Pope, Smiles and Thwaites.

An atmospheric sixteenth-century pub with stone-flagged floors, Tudor fireplace and dining room. Bar food served at lunchtime and evenings. Car park, terrace, accommodation. Children allowed in the dining room.

OPEN *12–3pm and 7–11pm (10.30pm Sun).*

The Boars Head

Hampton Lucy CV35 8BE
☎ *(01789) 840533* Sally Gilliam

Hook Norton Best Bitter and Shepherd Neame Spitfire usually available, plus one or two guest beers often from Warwickshire, Church End, Frankton Bagby, Timothy Taylor, Fuller's or many others.

Traditional English pub with log fire and great atmosphere. Home-cooked food and nice garden with ample seating. Food served 12–2.15pm and 7–10pm. Car park. Well-behaved children welcome, but no special facilities.

OPEN *11.30am–3pm and 6–11pm Mon–Sat; 12–3pm and 7–10.30pm Sun.*

The Wyandotte Inn

Park Road, Kenilworth
☎ *(01926) 863219* Mrs Jaeger

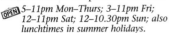 Banks's Bitter plus Marstons' Bitter and Pedigree regularly available.

Street-corner local with split-level single room and log fire in winter. Beer garden. Pool table, monthly quiz and regular musical events. No food. Car park. No children.

OPEN *5–11pm Mon–Thurs; 3–11pm Fri; 12–11pm Sat; 12–10.30pm Sun; also lunchtimes in summer holidays.*

The Sheaf & Sickle

Coventry Road, Long Lawford, Rugby CV23 9DT
☎ *(01788) 544622* Steve Townes

Two guests available from breweries such as Eldridge Pope, Church End, Ash Vine and Judges. Aims not to repeat the beers.

An old village coaching inn with saloon, lounge and restaurant. Beer garden. Food available at lunchtime and evenings. Children allowed.

OPEN *12–2.30pm and 6–11pm Mon–Fri; all day Sat–Sun.*

The Alexandra Arms

72 James Street, Rugby CV21 2SL
☎ *(01788) 578660* Julian Hardy

Marston's Pedigree and Greene King Abbot Ale permanently available, plus two guest beers from a wide selection. Ash Vine, Burton Bridge, Church End and Wye Valley feature regularly.

Award-winning pub with bar billiards, table skittles and pool. Garden. Food available 12–2.30pm and 5–8.30pm. No children. Situated near the main post office.

OPEN *11.30am–3pm and 5–11pm Mon–Thurs; 11.30am–11pm Fri–Sat; 12–10.30pm Sun.*

The Three Horseshoes Hotel

Sheep Street, Rugby CV21 3BX
☎ *(01788) 544585* Christopher Bingham

Greene King IPA, Abbot Ale and Morland Ruddles County usually available, plus one or two guest beers, often from Frankton Bagby, Church End or Adnams breweries.

Central, seventeenth-century inn with open fires and beamed restaurant. Food available 12–2pm and 7–10pm daily. Car park. Children welcome. Accommodation.

OPEN *11am–2.30pm and 7–11pm Mon–Sat; 12–2.30pm and 7–10.30pm Sun.*

The Victoria Inn

1 Lower Hillmorton Road, Rugby CV21 3ST
☎ *(01788) 544374* Mrs White

A freehouse with Cottage Champflower among the brews always available plus two guests such as Hartley XB (Robinson's), Greene King IPA, Hook Norton and Shepherd Neame brews.

A locals' pub just outside the town centre. Two bars, original mirrors in both rooms. Disabled access. Food available at lunchtime only. No children.

OPEN *12–3pm and 6–11pm Mon–Thurs; 12–3pm and 5–11pm Fri; all day Sat; 12–3pm and 7–10.30pm Sun.*

The Coach & Horses

16 New Street, Shipston-on-Stour CV36 4EM
☎ *(01608) 661335* Bob Payne

Hook Norton Best always available plus three guests from a long list including Hook Norton Haymaker, Wye Valley Brew 69, Dorothy Goodbody's Summertime Ale, Ash Vine Toxic Waste, Bateman XXXB and XB.

A 250-year-old village pub in the Cotswolds serving bar and restaurant food at lunchtime and evenings. Car park, garden, accommodation. On the A3400 Birmingham to Oxford road, on the Oxford side of town.

OPEN *11am–11pm (10.30pm Sun).*

The Little Lark

108 Alcester Road, Studley B80 7NP
☎ *(01527) 853105* Mark Roskell

Ushers Best Bitter, Founders and a seasonal brew normally available, plus a guest which is frequently Hobsons Best Bitter or Old Henry, Cannon Royall Arrowhead or Fruiterer's Mild.

An interesting selection of printing paraphernalia is a feature in this real ale house. Food available lunchtimes and evenings Mon–Sat and evenings only Sun. No children.

OPEN *12–3pm and 6–11pm Mon–Fri and Sun; 12–11pm Sat.*

WARWICK

Old Fourpenny Shop

27–9 Crompton Street, Warwick CV34 6HJ
☎ *(01926) 491360* John Richard Siddle

Five guest beers usually served from an extensive selection including Timothy Taylor Landlord, RCH Pitchfork, Greene King Abbot and IPA, and beers from Church End, Abbey, Frankton Bagby, Warwickshire, Eccleshall, Litchfield, Burton Bridge, Bateman and many other independent breweries.

Popular real ale house with restaurant. Food served 12–2pm and 7–10pm daily. Car park. Children over 10 years old welcome.

12–2.30pm and 5.30–11pm Mon–Thurs; 12–3pm and 5–11pm Fri; 12–3pm and 6–11pm Sat–Sun.

★ *The Navigation,* Old Warwick Road, Lapworth
★ *Raglan Arms,* 50 Dunchurch Road, Rugby
★ *The Rose & Crown,* Ratley
★ *The White Swan,* 100 High Street, Henley-in-Arden

Places Featured:

Allesley
Amblecote
Barston
Bilston
Birmingham
Bordesley Green
Brierley Hill
Chapelfields
Coventry
Cradley Heath
Dudley
Enville
Halesowen
Highgate
Hockley

Lower Gornal
Oldbury
Pensnett
Sedgley
Shelfield
Shustoke
Smethwick
Solihull
Stourbridge
Tipton
Walsall
West Bromwich
Willenhall
Wollaston
Wolverhampton

THE BREWERIES

BATHAMS LTD

The Delph Brewery, Delph Road, Brierley Hill
DY5 2TN
☎ *(01384) 77229*

MILD ALE 3.5% ABV
BEST BITTER 4.3% ABV
No better brew when on form.

Plus seasonal beers.

THE BEOWULF BREWING CO.

Waterloo Buildings, 14 Waterloo Road, Yardley,
Birmingham B25 8JR
☎ *(0121) 706 4116*

HAMA 3.8% ABV
Golden, with nutty flavour and dry
hoppy bitterness.

NOBLE BITTER 4.0% ABV
Dry, with powerful bitterness.

WIGLAF 4.3% ABV
Golden and malty with strong hoppy flavours.

SWORDSMAN 4.5% ABV
Pale, refreshing and fruity.

HEROES BITTER 4.7% ABV
Golden and hoppy with some sweetness.

MERCIAN SHINE 5.0% ABV
Pale and hoppy with dry finish.

Plus seasonal brews.

ENVILLE ALES

Enville Brewery, Cox Green, Enville, Stourbridge
DY7 5LG
☎ *(01384) 873728*

CHAINMAKER MILD 3.6% ABV
Dark, with some sweetness and smooth
malty finish.

BEST BITTER 3.8% ABV
Bitter, well-balanced with good hoppiness.

SIMPKISS BITTER 3.8% ABV
Gold-coloured, quenching and well-hopped.

NAILMAKER MILD 4.0% ABV
Dark and sweeter with dry finish.

CZECHMATE SAAZ 4.2% ABV
Dry and fruity in the Czechoslovakian style.

WHITE 4.2% ABV
A clear, refreshing wheat beer.

ALE 4.5% ABV
Pale yellow, honeyed sweetness and hoppy
finish.

PORTER 4.5% ABV
Dark, complex roast malt and fruit, and dry
finish.

GINGER BEER 4.6% ABV
Excellent summer brew, delicate ginger flavour.

PHOENIX IPA 4.8% ABV
Superb IPA using new Phoenix hop variety.

GOTHIC ALE 5.2% ABV
Black and rich, with honey flavours.

Plus occasional brews.

HIGHGATE & WALSALL BREWING CO. LTD

Sandymount Road, Walsall WS1 3AP
☎ *(01922) 644453*

DARK MILD 3.4% ABV
GOLDEN ALE 3.7% ABV
Light, delicate hoppiness.
SADDLERS BEST BITTER 4.3% ABV
Balanced and full-flavoured.
BLACK PIG 4.4% ABV
OLD ALE 5.1% ABV
Rich, powerful flavours.
Plus seasonal brews.

HOLDEN'S BREWERY

PO Box 20, George Street, Woodsetton, Dudley DY1 4LN
☎ *(01902) 880051*

STOUT 3.5% ABV
Dark with bitter, malty flavour.
MILD 3.7% ABV
Malty and well-balanced.
BITTER 3.9% ABV
Gold-coloured, quenching session beer.
XB 4.1% ABV
Refreshing and hoppy with some sweetness.
SPECIAL 5.1% ABV
Golden, balanced and far too easy to drink.

THE WOLVERHAMPTON & DUDLEY BREWERIES PLC

PO Box 26, Park Brewery, Bath Road, Wolverhampton WV1 4NY
☎ *(01902) 711811*

HANSON'S MILD 3.3% ABV
Maltiness throughout.
BANKS'S ORIGINAL 3.5% ABV
BANKS'S BITTER 3.8% ABV
Hoppy, with a good combination of flavours.

THE PUBS

ALLESLEY

Rainbow Inn and Brewery

73 Birmingham Road, Allesley Village, Coventry CV5 9GT
☎ *(024) 7640 2888*

Piddlebrook and Firecracker brewed and served on the premises plus one guest beer.

Brewing started in October 1994 providing ale only for the pub and a few beer festivals. Production at the two-barrel plant takes place twice a week. An unpretentious pub in a village location. Grade II listed building dating from around 1650. Bar and restaurant food served at lunchtime and evenings. Parking, garden. Children allowed. Just off the main A45 at Allesley.

PIDDLEBROOK 3.8% ABV
FIRECRACKER 4.8% ABV

OPEN *11am–11pm.*

AMBLECOTE

The Maverick

Brettell Lane, Amblecote, Stourbridge DY8 4BA
☎ *(01384) 824099 Mark Boxley*

A freehouse with Banks's Bitter and Mild always available plus one guest pump perhaps serving Enville Ale or a Kimberley brew.

A town pub with an American Western theme. One bar, beer garden. Bar snacks and burgers available all day. Children allowed.

OPEN *All day, every day (except Wed–Thurs 3–11pm).*

The Swan

10 Brettell Lane, Amblecote, Stourbridge
☎ *(01384) 76932 Mr G Cook*

Two weekly changing guest beers served, often from Eccleshall, Batham, Cains, Smiles, Hook Norton, Young's, Lees, Elgood's, Brakspear, Ruddles, Daleside or Tisbury.

A traditional town pub with comfortable lounge, bar, darts and juke box. Beer garden. No food. No children.

OPEN *12–2.30pm and 7–11pm Mon–Fri; 12–11pm Sat; 12–3pm and 7–10.30pm Sun.*

BARSTON

The Bulls Head

Barston Lane, Barston, Solihull B92 0JV
☎ *(01675) 442830* Mr M Bradley

Fuller's London Pride plus a guest beer regularly available from a large countrywide selection.

Traditional village pub with garden, dating back to the 1490s. No machines or music. Food served 12–2pm and 7–8.30pm Mon–Sat. Car park. Children welcome.

11am–2.30pm and 5.30–11pm Mon–Fri; 11am–11pm Sat; 12–10.30pm Sun.

BILSTON

The Olde White Rose

20 Lichfield Street, Bilston WV14 0AG
☎ *(01902) 498339* John Denston

Twelve real ale pumps serve the crème de la crème from Shepherd Neame, Hop Back and all the other popular independent and micro-breweries; the list is endless!

Situated in the heart of the Black Country, this is a lounge-style pub currently undergoing extension. Food available every day until 9pm. Children allowed, with designated play area inside and out. Plans for a beer garden. Easy accessible on the Snowhill–Wolverhampton Metro (tram) although be careful not to confuse it with The White Rose in the same town.

12–11pm Mon–Sat; 12–4pm and 7–10.30pm Sun.

BIRMINGHAM

The Anchor

308 Bradford Street, Birmingham B5 6ET
☎ *(0121) 622 4516* Gerry Keane

A freehouse with a good selection of real ales. Four or five available during the week and up to eight at weekends. Favourites include RCH Pitchfork, Exmoor Gold and ales from Daleside, Church End and Wye Valley. Three major beer festivals held each year (March, May and October), plus themed weekends, e.g. Burns' Night, St Patrick's Day, Easter Beers.

Situated outside the city centre, a well-preserved three-bar pub in a Grade II listed building. Local CAMRA Pub of the Year 1996 and 1998. Food available at lunchtime and evenings. Children allowed in the beer garden May–October (weather permitting!).

11am–11pm (10.30pm Sun).

Figure of Eight

236–9 Broad Street, Birmingham B1 2HG
☎ *(0121) 633 0917* Tom Taylor

Enville Ale and Wadworth 6X usually available in a range of up to 12 real ales. Others are served on a guest basis, and may include beers from breweries such as Enville, Springhead, Wyre Piddle, Timothy Taylor, Hop Back, Hook Norton, Shepherd Neame and Greene King.

Busy, JD Wetherspoon's freehouse, popular with all ages, serving the largest number of real ales in the area. Food available 10am–10pm Mon–Sat and 12–9.30pm Sun. No children.

10am–11pm Mon–Sat; 12–10.30pm Sun.

The Old Fox

54 Hurst Street, Birmingham B5 4TD
☎ *(0121) 622 5080* Pat Murray

Marston's Pedigree and Morland Old Speckled Hen always available plus two guests, changed twice-weekly, such as Wychwood The Dog's Bollocks, Trash and Tackle or Burton Bridge brews.

An eighteenth-century town freehouse with stained-glass windows, situated in a modern area near the Hippodrome. Food available 12–8pm daily in a separate dining area. Outside seating. No children.

11.30am–11pm (10.30pm Sun).

The Old Joint Stock

Temple Row West, Birmingham B2 5NY
☎ *(0121) 200 1892* Alison Turner

Fuller's London Pride, Chiswick and ESB are permanently available, plus Fuller's seasonal ale and a Beowulf brew which changes every three weeks.

A Fuller's Ale and Pie House. Large pub in traditional style, balcony area, club room and function room for hire. Food served 12–8.30pm Mon–Sat. Patio area. No children.

11am–11pm Mon–Sat; closed Sun.

The Pavilion

229 Alcester Road South, Kings Heath, B14 6DT
☎ *(0121) 441 3286* Peter Galley

Banks's Original and Bitter plus Marston's Pedigree regularly available.

Friendly community local. Food served every lunchtime and evening. Car park. No children.

12–11pm (10.30pm Sun).

BORDESLEY GREEN

The Tipsy Gent

157 Cherrywood Road, Bordesley Green,
Birmingham B9 4XE
☎ *(0121) 772 1858* Paul and Jackie Rackam

A freehouse with Fuller's London Pride among its permanent features, plus one guest, such as Exmoor Gold, changed weekly. Smaller and independent brewers favoured.

A traditional one-bar town pub with stone floors and open fires. Food available Mon–Fri lunchtimes only. Beer garden. No children.

11am–11pm (10.30pm Sun).

BRIERLEY HILL

The Bull & Bladder

10 Delph Road, Brierley Hill DY5 2TN
☎ *(01384) 78293* Mr Wood

Bathams Mild, Best and XXX always available.

Also known as The Vine, this is the brewery tap for Bathams, which is situated behind. A multi-roomed pub with open fires. Bar food available at lunchtime. Car park, garden, children's room.

12–11pm Mon–Sat; 12–4pm and 7–10.30pm Sun.

CHAPELFIELDS

The Nursery Tavern

38–9 Lord Street, Chapelfields, Coventry
CV5 8DA
☎ *(024) 7667 4530* Harry Minton

Four guest ales usually featured from breweries such as Church End, Fat God's, Wolf, RCH and Hampshire.

A small, 150-year-old, village-style pub in a town location. Beams, wooden floors. Bar snacks available Mon–Fri; breakfasts Sat–Sun and Sunday lunches. Children allowed in the back room and garden.

11am–11pm Mon–Sat; 12–10.30pm Sun.

COVENTRY

The Old Windmill

22 Spon Street, Coventry CV1 3BA
☎ *(024) 7625 2183* Lynn Ingram

Marston's Pedigree, Morland Old Speckled Hen and a Banks's ale always available, plus two guests such as Badger Tanglefoot or beers from breweries such as Church End, Orkney, Buchanan and other micros.

A Grade II listed Tudor building situtated in the town centre. The oldest pub in Coventry with beams, stone floor, old range in one bar and inglenook fireplaces. Food available at lunchtime in non-smoking restaurant. Children allowed in the restaurant only.

11am–11pm Mon–Sat; 12–3pm and 7–10.30pm Sun.

CRADLEY HEATH

The Waterfall

132 Waterfall Lane, Cradley Heath B64 6RG
☎ *(0121) 561 3499* Marie Smith

Nine beers always available including brews from Bathams. Also Enville Ale, Holden's Special, Hook Norton Old Hooky and Marston's Pedigree. Plus guests such as Oak Double Dagger, Titanic White Star, RCH Fiery Liz and Gibbs Mew Bishop's Tipple plus something from Burton Bridge and Wood.

A traditional Black Country pub. Bar food available at lunchtime and evenings. Car park, garden with waterfall, children's room. Also function room for party and quiz nights, etc. Up the hill from the old Hill Station.

12–3pm and 5–11pm Mon–Thurs; all day Fri–Sun.

DUDLEY

Little Barrell

68 High Street, Dudley DY1 1PY
☎ *(01384) 235535* Mrs Day

Wadworth 6X always available plus three guests such as Morland Old Speckled Hen, Holden's XB, Shepherd Neame Bishop's Finger, Wychwood Hobgoblin or King & Barnes brews. Seasonal and celebration beers as available.

A small, traditional town pub with wooden floors. One bar, dining area. Food available at lunchtime only. Children allowed if eating.

11am–11pm (10.30pm Sun).

ENVILLE

The Cat Inn
Bridgnorth Road, Enville, Nr Stourbridge DY7 5MA
☎ *(01384) 872209* Mrs Lisa M Johnson

Enville Ale and Everards Beacon regularly served with other Enville beers often available.

A traditional country inn with real fires in winter. Food served 12–2pm and 7–9pm Mon–Fri and 12–2pm Sat. Car park. Children welcome at lunchtime, but no special facilities.

OPEN *12–3pm and 7–11pm (10.30pm Sun).*

HALESOWEN

Edward VII
88 Stourbridge Road, Halesowen B63 3UP
☎ *(0121) 550 4493* Patrick Villa

Banks's Traditional Cask ale permanently available plus one guest changing every three weeks. Beers might include Everards Tiger, Enville White or Marston's Bitter.

B eautiful, well-thought-out, comfortable pub/restaurant with two bars and outside seating. Food served every lunchtime and Tues–Sat evenings. Children allowed. Located on the A458, next to Halesowen Town Football Club.

OPEN *12–3pm and 5–11pm Mon–Thurs; 11am–11pm Fri–Sat; 12–10.30pm Sun.*

The Waggon & Horses
21 Stourbridge Road, Halesowen B63 3TU
☎ *(0121) 602 2082* Peter Rawson

Bathams Bitter, Enville Simpkiss and Ale, and something from Everards always available plus up to ten guests (800 per year) from far and wide.

A West Midlands Victorian boozer. Bar food available at lunchtime. Car parking. Children allowed.

OPEN *12–11pm (10.30pm Sun).*

HIGHGATE

The Lamp Tavern
157 Barford Street, Highgate, Birmingham B5 6AH
☎ *(0121) 622 2599* Eddie Fitzpatrick

A freehouse with Stanway Stanney Bitter, Everards Tiger, Marston's Pedigree and Church End Grave Digger always available, plus one guest pump serving beers such as Shepherd Neame Bishop's Finger or Church End What the Fox's Hat.

A small, friendly village pub situated near the town. Bar snacks available at lunchtime. No children.

OPEN *All day Mon–Sat; 12–3pm and 8–10.30pm Sun.*

HOCKLEY

Black Eagle
16 Factory Road, Hockley, Birmingham B18 5JU
☎ *(0121) 523 4008* Tony Lewis

Marston's Pedigree, Timothy Taylor Landlord and something from Beowulf regularly available plus two guest beers, perhaps from Wye Valley, Church End or Burton Bridge.

P opular award-winning pub with two small front lounges, a large back lounge, snug and restaurant. Original Victorian back bar. Beer garden. Well known locally for good food. Bar meals 12.15–2.30pm and 5.30–9.30pm, restaurant 7–10.30pm. Children welcome to eat.

OPEN *11.30am–2.30pm and 5.30–11pm Mon–Fri; 11.30am–11pm Sat; 12–10.30pm Sun.*

The Church Inn
22 Great Hampton Street, Hockley, Birmingham B18 6AQ
☎ *(0121) 515 1851* Mr Wilkes

Morland Old Speckled Hen and a Bathams ale always available, plus one guest.

A Victorian town pub with one servery and two adjoining rooms. Food available at lunchtime and evenings. Children allowed.

OPEN *11.45am–11pm Mon–Fri; 11.45am–3pm and 6–11pm Sat; closed Sun.*

LOWER GORNAL

The Fountain Inn
8 Temple Street, Lower Gornal
☎ *(01384) 24277* Alan Davis

Enville Ale, Holden's Special, Everards Tiger and Old Original always available, plus five rotating guests. Two real ciders also served.

A comfortable freehouse with a warm and pleasant atmosphere. Bar food served at lunchtime and evenings. Parking, garden and function room. Children allowed.

OPEN *12–3pm and 6–11pm Mon–Fri; 12–11pm Sat; 12–4pm and 7–10.30pm Sun.*

OLDBURY

The Waggon & Horses
Church Street, Oldbury B69 3AD
☎ *(0121) 552 5467* Andrew Gale

Enville Ale, Marston's Pedigree, plus something from Holden's always available. Also a traditional mild. Many guests (200 per year) including Bateman Yellow Belly, Timothy Taylor Landlord, Berrow Topsy Turvy, Red Cross OBJ, Greene King Abbot Ale, Brains Reverend James Original and many more.

A Victorian, Grade II listed building with tiled walls, copper ceiling and original brewery windows. Bar food available at lunchtime and evenings. Car parking. Children allowed when eating. Function room with capacity for 40 people. At the corner of Market Street and Church Street in Oldbury town centre, next to the library.

OPEN *12–3pm and 5–11pm Mon–Thur; 11am–11pm Fri; 11am–3pm and 6–11pm Sat; 12–3pm and 7–10.30pm Sun.*

PENSNETT

The Holy Bush Inn
Bell Street, Pensnett, Brierley Hill DY5 4HJ
☎ *(01384) 78711* Ian Trafford

Batham Mild and Bitter always available.

A small two-bar pub with beer garden. No food. Children allowed.

OPEN *All day, every day.*

SEDGLEY

The Beacon Hotel
129 Bilston Street, Sedgley, Dudley DY3 1JE
☎ *(01902) 883380*

Sarah Hughes Pale Amber, Suprise and Dark Ruby always available, plus Snowflake from Nov to Feb. Various guest beers (150 per year) served on a daily basis.

The Sarah Hughes Brewery, which operates on the premises, reopened in 1987 after a 30-year closure, and now supplies around 500 pubs with guests beers. Visitors welcome for brewery tours, but booking is essential. Children's room, plus beer garden with play area.

PALE AMBER 4.0% ABV
SURPRISE 5.0% ABV
DARK RUBY MILD 6.0% ABV
SNOWFLAKE 8.0% ABV

OPEN *12–2.30pm and 5.30–10.45pm Mon–Thur; 12–2.30pm and 5.30–11pm Fri; 11.30am–3pm and 6–11pm Sat; 12–3pm and 7–10.30pm Sun.*

SHELFIELD

The Four Crosses Inn
1 Green Lane, Shelfield, Walsall WS4 1RN
☎ *(01922) 682518* Mr Holt

A freehouse with Marston's Pedigree and Banks's Bitter and Mild always available, plus two weekly changing guests from smaller and micro-breweries such as Burton Bridge and Ash Vine.

A traditional two-bar pub on the outskirts of town. Games in the bar, beer garden. No food. No children.

OPEN *All day Mon–Sat; 12–3pm and 7–10.30pm Sun.*

SHUSTOKE

The Griffin Inn
Church Road, Shustoke B46 2LP
☎ *(01675) 481567*

At least six Church End brews plus Marston's Pedigree always available. Also 200 guest beers per year.

A large country freehouse with oak beams and open fires set in large grounds. The Church End brewery is next to the pub. Bar food is available at lunchtime (except Sunday). Car park, garden. Children allowed in the conservatory and grounds. Take the B4114 from Coleshill.

GRAVEDIGGERS 3.8% ABV
WHAT THE FOX'S HAT 4.2% ABV
WHEAT A BIX 4.2% ABV
M-REG GTI 4.4% ABV
PEWS PORTER 4.5% ABV
OLD PAL 5.5% ABV

OPEN *12–3pm and 7–11pm Mon–Sat; 12–2.30pm and 7–10.30pm Sun.*

SMETHWICK

The Bear Tavern
500 Bearwood Road, Smethwick B66 4BX
☎ *(0121) 429 1184* Brendan Gilbride

Marston's Pedigree and Morland Old Speckled Hen always available plus five weekly changing guests. Regulars include Hardys and Hansons Kimberley Best and Greene King Abbot.

A locals' pub built after the Second World War, although there has been a pub on the site for 300 years. A mix of the traditional and modern. Four bars, fireplace, beer garden, disabled access. Food available all day. Children allowed.

OPEN *All day, every day.*

SOLIHULL

The Harvester

Tanhouse Farm Road, Solihull B92 9EY
☎ *(0121) 742 0770* Mrs Harwood

A freehouse with Charles Wells Bombardier always available plus two guests such as Morland Old Speckled Hen. Beers served are always between 3.7% and 5% ABV.

A modern community pub with two bars, pool room, dining area in lounge, garden. Food available at lunchtime and evenings. Children allowed.

OPEN 12–2.30pm and 6–11pm Mon–Thurs; 12–3pm and 6–11pm Fri–Sat; 12–3pm and 7–10.30pm Sun.

STOURBRIDGE

Hogshead

21–6 Foster Street, Stourbridge DY8 1EL
☎ *(01384) 371040* David Collins

Fourteen beers including ten guest ales regularly available. Examples include Enville White, Fuller's London Pride, Timothy Taylor Landlord, Marston's Pedigree, Wadworth 6X or something from Black Sheep, Brakspear or many others.

Hogshead original design, town-centre pub with ten beers on long front bar and four gravity-dispensed beers on back bar. Background music during the day, livelier in the evenings. Air-conditioned. Food available all day. Children welcome in designated areas until 8pm. Situated in pedestrian precinct.

OPEN 12–11pm (10.30pm Sun).

The Robin Hood Inn

196 Collis Street, Amblecote, Stourbridge DY8 4EQ
☎ *(01384) 821120*

Bathams Bitter, Enville Ale, Everards Beacon, Tiger and Old Original always available plus three guests (120 per year) such as Timothy Taylor Landlord, Badger Tanglefoot, Shepherd Neame Bishop's Finger, Fuller's ESB, Exmoor Gold and Hook Norton Old Hooky.

A family-run, cosy Black Country freehouse. Good beer garden. Non-smoking dining room. Bar and restaurant food available. Parking. Children allowed in the pub when eating. Accommodation.

OPEN 12–3pm and 6–11pm Mon–Sat; 12–10.30pm Sun.

TIPTON

The Port 'n' Ale

178 Horseley Heath, Great Bridge, Tipton DY4 7DS
☎ *(0121) 557 7249* Kevin Taylor

A freehouse with Greene King Abbot, RCH Pitchfork, Moorhouse's Pendle Witches and Badger Tanglefoot always available, plus two guest pumps regularly serving RCH beers or something like Burton Bridge Summer Ale or Cotleigh Barn Ale. Some 120 different ales were served during the period March to July 1999.

A Victorian pub situated out of town. Bar, lounge and beer garden. Basic food served, including fish and chips and sandwiches. Children allowed in the garden only. Just down the road from Dudley Port railway station.

OPEN 12–3pm and 5–11pm Mon–Fri; 12–11pm Sat; 12–4.30pm and 7–10.30pm Sun.

The Rising Sun

116 Horseley Road, Tipton DY4 7NH
☎ *(0121) 530 9780* Penny McDonald

RCH Pitchfork, Banks's Bitter and Original, plus three regularly changing guest beers usually available, perhaps from Burton Bridge, Church End, Hobsons, Holden's, Beowulf, Ash Vine, Wye Valley, Cottage, Eccleshall or many others.

Friendly, locals' pub with large beer garden. Food served 12–2pm Mon–Sat. No children.

OPEN 12–2.30pm and 5–11pm Mon–Fri; 12–3pm and 5–11pm Sat; 12–3pm and 7–10.30pm Sun.

WEST BROMWICH

The Old Crown

56 Sandwell Road, West Bromwich B70 8TG
☎ *(0121) 525 4600* Mr Patel

A freehouse with three hand pumps serving an ever-changing selection of ales such as Fuller's London Pride, Young's Special, Cottage Somerset or something from Church End, Enville, Burton Bridge, Wye Valley or Hydes' Anvil, to name but a few.

An open-plan town pub. Food available at lunchtime and evenings in a non-smoking area – home-cooked curries, balti and tikka masala are specialities. Children allowed in the non-smoking area only, until 9pm.

OPEN 11am–4pm and 5–11pm Sun–Fri; all day Sat.

The Vine

152 Roebuck Street, West Bromwich B70 6RD
☎ *(0121) 553 2866* Mr Patel

A freehouse with two real ales always available. Breweries featured include Wood, Lichfield and Wye Valley, among others.

A traditional two-bar pub with beams and gardens. Children's play area. Food available at lunchtime and evenings – barbecues and currys are specialities. Children allowed. Situtated out of town.

OPEN *11.30am–2.30pm and 5–11pm Mon–Thurs; all day Fri–Sun.*

The Brewer's Droop

44 Wolverhampton Street, Willenhall WV13 2PS
☎ *(01902) 607827* Ruth Faulkner

A freehouse with Bathams Bitter and Charles Wells Eagle IPA always available, plus a range of guests changing twice-weekly, such as Holden's Special and Badger Tanglefoot.

A traditional town-centre pub decorated with bric-a-brac, particularly relating to motorbikes. Two bars, pool table. Food available at lunchtime and evenings. Children allowed until 9pm.

OPEN *12–3.30pm and 6–11pm Mon–Thurs; all day Fri–Sat; 12–4pm and 7–10.30pm Sun.*

The Falcon Inn

Gomer Street West, Willenhall WV13 2NR
☎ *(01902) 633378* Mick Taylor

A freehouse with Hyde's Bitter and Mild, Banks's Mild, Greene King Abbot and Timothy Taylor Landlord, plus a Porter or a Stout always available. Also a wide range of guests, for example, Red Cross OBJ, Freeminer Celestial Steam Gale, Bunces Danish Dynamite, RCH Pitchfork, Fuller's ESB, Archers Golden, Ringwood 4X, Freeminer Deep Shaft Stout and Slaughter Porter or beers from Wye Valley, Hop Back or Burton Bridge. Beers changed at least every three days, but the record is 1hr 50mins!

A 1930s back-street boozer with stone floors, beams and vines. Bar and lounge, non-smoking area, beer garden. Children allowed until 8.30pm.

OPEN *12–11pm (10.30pm Sun).*

Tap & Spile

5 John Street, Walsall WS2 8AF
☎ *(01922) 627660* John Davies

Charles Wells Eagle IPA usually available plus seven guest beers which change regularly, totalling around 40 per month. These may include beers from Bateman, Wychwood, Arundel, Hoskins, Fuller's, Harviestoun, Hydes', Hop Back, Highwood, Hook Norton, Orkney or any other independent brewery.

Small, traditional back-street pub with great atmosphere. Friendly staff and chatty customers. Food available 12–2pm Mon, 12–2pm and 6.30–9pm Tues–Sat. Children welcome.

OPEN *12–3pm and 5.30–11pm Mon–Thurs; 12–11pm Fri–Sat; 12–3pm and 7–10.30pm Sun.*

The Princess

115 Bridgnorth Road, Wollaston, Stourbridge DY8 3NX
☎ *(01384) 443687* Ralph and Kay Vines

Wadworth 6X, Charles Wells Bombardier, Greene King Abbot Ale and Banks's Original are permanent fixtures, plus a monthly changing guest beer.

Single bar with wooden floor, quarry tiles and an interesting selection of mirrors and artefacts. Food served lunchtimes only. Car park. Children welcome, but no special facilities.

OPEN *11am–11pm Mon–Sat; 12–10.30pm Sun.*

Chindit

113 Merridale Road, Wolverhampton
☎ *(01902) 425582* John Ralph Smith

Four guest beers available, changing twice weekly, and totalling around 350 different beers each year. Favourite breweries include Hop Back, Harviestoun, Daleside and Wychwood. The Chindit held its first beer festival in 1999 with 30 different beers available and it is planned to be an annual event.

Cosy, two-room pub named after a Second World War regiment – the only pub in the world so named. Live music on Friday evenings and barbecues in summer, weather permitting. Children welcome until 7.30pm. Play area. Located one mile from town centre, on the west side of Wolverhampton.

OPEN *12–11pm (10.30pm Sun).*

The Exchange Vaults

Cheapside, Wolverhampton WV1 1TS
☎ *(01902) 714219* Steven Durling

Up to five real ales available. Marston's Pedigree, one other Marston's ale and a Banks's ale are on permanently plus guests from Marston's, Banks's or Hardys and Hansons.

The old Corn Exchange, this is the only pub in the Civic Centre area. One bar, outside seating, food available every day from 11am–5pm. Children allowed if eating. Situated between St Peter's Church and the Civic Centre.

OPEN *11am–11.30pm (10.30pm Sun).*

Great Western

Sun Street, Wolverhampton
☎ *(01902) 351090* Kevin Michael Gould

Batham Bitter, Holden's Mild, Black Country Bitter and Special Bitter regularly available.

Friendly pub with non-smoking dining room. Food served 11.45am–2.15pm Mon–Sat. Car park. Situated two minutes' walk from railway station. Children welcome in conservatory if dining.

OPEN *11am–11pm Mon–Sat; 12–3pm and 7–10.30pm Sun.*

Newhampton

Riches Street, Wolverhampton WV6 0DW
☎ *(01902) 745773* Betty Carnegie

Marston's Pedigree, Charles Wells Bombardier and a daily changing guest beer regularly available, such as Timothy Taylor Landlord or something from Enville.

Traditional community pub, an 'oasis' with with bowling green, garden and children's play area. Home-made food served 12–2pm Mon–Sun. Children very welcome.

OPEN *11–11pm Mon–Sat; 12–10.30pm Sun.*

Tap & Spile

35 Princess Street, Wolverhampton WV1 1HD
☎ *(01902) 713319* Jason Caskerino (Manager)

Mansfield Highgate Dark Mild and Tap & Spile Premium always available, plus up to six guest ales of which Charles Wells Bombardier, Wychwood Hobgoblin, Badger Tanglefoot and Fuller's London Pride are regular features.

A locals' town pub with wooden floors, open fire, one main bar and snug rooms. Food available 12–4pm. Beer garden. Children allowed until 7pm.

OPEN *All day Mon–Sat; 12–3pm and 7–10.30pm Sun.*

Places Featured:

THE BREWERIES

ARCHERS ALES LTD

Penzance Drive, Swindon SN5 7JL
☎ *(01793) 879929*

 VILLAGE BITTER 3.5% ABV
Malty, with hop and fruit notes.
BEST BITTER 4.0% ABV
Bitter with some sweetness.
BLACK JACK PORTER 4.6% ABV
Dark, roasted malt, winter brew.
GOLDEN BITTER 4.7% ABV
Superb balance, a classic beer.
Plus seasonal brews.

ARKELLS BREWERY LTD

Kingsdown Brewery, Swindon SN2 6RU
☎ *(01793) 823026*

 2B 3.2% ABV
Light and quenching with good bitter
hoppiness.
3B 4.0% ABV
Amber, balanced and hoppy.
KINGSDOWN ALE 5.0% ABV
Smooth, rounded and flavour-packed.
Plus seasonal brews.

THE HOP BACK BREWERY PLC

*Unit 22–4, Batten Road, Downton Business
Centre, Downton, Salisbury SP5 3HU*
☎ *(01725) 510986*

 GFB 3.5% ABV
Smooth and full-flavoured for gravity.
BEST BITTER 4.0% ABV
Well-balanced, easy-drinking.
ENTIRE STOUT 4.5% ABV
Powerful roast malt flavour.
SUMMER LIGHTNING 5.0% ABV
Superb, pale and quenching with good hoppiness.
THUNDERSTORM 5.0% ABV
Mellow wheat beer.
Plus seasonal and occasional brews.

MOLE'S BREWERY

5 Merlin Way, Bowerhill, Melksham SN12 6TJ
☎ *(01225) 708842*

 TAP 3.5% ABV
Malty with clean, balancing bitterness.
BEST BITTER 4.0% ABV
Golden with quenching, hoppy finish.
BARLEYMOLE 4.2% ABV
Pale, hoppy brew with malty finish. Occasional.
MOLEGRIP 4.3% ABV
Rounded, balanced Autumn ale.
LANDLORD'S CHOICE 4.5% ABV
Darker, with hops, fruit and malty finish.
HOLY MOLEY 4.7% ABV
Good malt flavour with hop balance. Occasional.
BREW 97 5.0% ABV
Malty with fruity sweetness and good hoppiness.
MOEL MOEL 6.0% ABV
Winter warmer.

STONEHENGE ALES (BUNCES BREWERY)

The Old Mill, Mill Road, Netheravon, Salisbury SP4 9QB
☎ *(01980) 670631*

 BENCHMARK 3.5% ABV
Malt flavours with good balancing hoppy bitterness.

PIGSWILL 4.0% ABV
Mellow and hoppy.

BEST BITTER 4.1% ABV
Refreshing malt and fruitiness with bitter finish.

HEEL STONE 4.3% ABV
Quenching fruity flavour.

GREAT DANE 4.6% ABV
Real lager.

DANISH DYNAMITE 5.0% ABV
Golden and far too easy to drink!

OLD SMOKEY 5.0% ABV
Rich and smoky.

Plus seasonal brews.

TISBURY BREWERY 2000

Oakley Business Park, Dinton, Salisbury SP3 5EU
☎ *(01722) 716622*

 STONEHENGE BITTER 3.8% ABV
Full-flavoured session bitter.

ARCHIBALD BECKETT 4.3% ABV
Superb balance

NADDERJACK 4.3% ABV
Gold-coloured, with bittersweet flavour.

EL FRESCO 4.5% ABV
Summer brew.

FANFARE 4.5% ABV
Spring brew.

OLD MULLED ALE 4.5% ABV
Winter brew.

RED NUT ALE 4.5% ABV
Autumn brew.

OLD WARDOUR 4.8% ABV
Dark with rich roast malt and fruit flavour. Sept–Mar.

Plus seasonal brews.

WADWORTH & CO. LTD

Northgate Brewery, Devizes SN10 1JW
☎ *(01380) 723361*

 HENRY'S ORIGINAL IPA 3.6% ABV
Well-balanced and smooth, with malt throughout.

SUMMERSAULT 4.0% ABV
Quenching, lager-style beer.

6X 4.3% ABV
Rich, with malt flavours.

FARMERS GLORY 4.5% ABV
Deep-coloured and smooth.

THE PUBS

BERWICK ST JOHN

The Talbot Inn
The Cross, Berwick St John, Nr Shaftsbury SP7 0HA
☎ *(01747) 828222* Wendy and Roy Rigby

Adnams Broadside and Best plus Wadworth 6X regularly available.

Typical country inn in Chalke Valley below Cranbourne Chase. Food served lunchtimes and evenings Tues–Sat. Car park. Children welcome at lunchtime.

12–2.30pm and 6.30–11pm Mon–Sat; 12–2.30pm and 7–10.30pm Sun.

BOX HILL

The Quarrymans Arms
Box Hill, Corsham SN13 8HN
☎ *(01225) 743569* John Arundel

Wadworth 6X, Mole's Best Bitter and Butcombe Bitter regularly available. Two or three guest beers are also served, often from Bath Ales, Abbey Ales or Cottage.

A 300-year-old miners pub, tucked away in the Wiltshire countryside, high above the Colerne Valley. Popular with pot-holers, cavers, walkers and cyclists. Food served 12–3pm and 7–10pm daily. Car park. Children welcome. Very difficult to find, so ring for directions.

11am–3pm and 6–11pm Mon–Thurs; 11am–11pm Fri–Sat; 12–10.30pm Sun.

BRADFORD-ON-AVON

The Beehive
Trowbridge Road, Bradford-on-Avon BA15 1UA
☎ *(01225) 863620* Mrs C Crocker

A freehouse with Butcombe ales always available plus five guests such as Fuller's London Pride, Burton Bridge Draught Excluder, Dobbins' Drop, Blackpool Bitter and Stairway to Heaven (aka Celestial Gateway).

A pub situated next to the home of Sir John Betjeman, on the side of the canal. One bar, no music, open fires. Beer garden features a boules pitch and an antique pump dating from 1880. Also open for coffee. Food available every lunchtime and Mon–Sat evening. Children allowed.

12–2.30pm and 7–11pm (10.30pm Sun).

CHARLTON

The Horse & Groom
The Street, Charlton, Malmesbury SN16 9DL
☎ *(01666) 823904* Nicola King

Archers Village and Wadworth 6X always available, plus three guests such as Uley Old Spot, Smiles Best, Abbey Bell Ringer or Ridleys Spectacular.

A traditional country village pub with beams, fires and wooden floors. Two bars, beer garden, accommodation. Food served at lunchtime and evenings in a separate dining area. Well-behaved children allowed.

12–3pm and 7–11pm Mon–Fri; all day Sat–Sun.

CHIPPENHAM

The Peterborough Arms
Dauntsey Lock, Chippenham SN15 4HD
☎ *(01249) 890409* Nicky Brown

Wadworth 6X and Archers Best always available plus weekly rotating guests. Favourites include Weltons Predator, RCH Pitchfork and Tripple FFF Afterglow.

A two-bar, family-run, traditional country freehouse with oak beams, fires and non-smoking dining area. Large beer garden with trampoline and other play equipment. Extensive menu of home-made food changes weekly and includes vegetarian options plus traditional Sunday roasts. Large function room available for parties, wedding receptions, etc. Children and dogs welcome. Ample parking. Visit our website at: www.peterborougharms.co.uk

12–2.30pm and 6–11pm Mon–Fri; all day Sat–Sun and spring/autumn bank holidays.

CORSHAM

The Two Pigs
38 Pickwick, Corsham SN13 0HY
☎ *(01249) 712515* Dickie and Ann Doyle

Stonehenge Pigswill always available plus three guests (200 per year) including Church End brews, Hop Back Summer Lightning, Greene King Abbot and Wood Shropshire Lad. Guest ales rotating constantly, two in ABV range 4.1–4.6% and one at 5%+ ABV.

A traditional wood-panelled pub with stone floors. No food. Parking nearby. Covered courtyard, No children. Live blues music on Monday. On the A4 between Chippenham and Bath.

7–11pm Mon–Sat; 12–2.30pm and 7–10.30pm Sun.

CORSLEY

The White Hart

Lane End, Corsley, Nr Warminster BA12 7PH
☎ *(01373) 832805* Mr S and Mrs E Middleton

Oakhill Best Bitter, Mendip Gold, Yeoman and 2K regularly available.

Welcoming, traditional pub with good mix of clientele and comprehensive menu. Food served lunchtimes and evenings. Car park. Children's room, menu and high chairs.

OPEN *11.30am–depends on custom; 6–11pm Mon–Sat; 12–3pm and 7–10.30pm Sun.*

CORTON

The Dove Inn

Corton, Nr Warminster BA12 0SZ
☎ *(01985) 850109* W Harrison-Allan

Oakhill Best Bitter, Brakspear Bitter and Fuller's London Pride usually available, plus two to four guest beers from a varied selection.

Tastefully refurbished, traditional pub tucked away in a beautiful and tranquil village close to the River Wylye. Restaurant and garden. Food served 12–2.30pm and 7–9.30pm every day. Car park. Children welcome. Newly developed en-suite accommodation. For further information, visit the web site at www.thedove.co.uk

OPEN *12–3pm and 6–11pm Mon–Sat; 12–11pm Sat; 12–10.30pm Sun.*

DEVIZES

The British Lion

9 Estcourt Street, Devizes SN10 1LQ
☎ *(01380) 720665* Michael Dearing

A rotating session bitter always available at £1.40 a pint, such as Wychwood Shires, Tisbury Best Bitter, Ash Vine Bitter, Oakhill Bitter plus two guests (about 100 a year) from Ash Vine, Abbey Ales, Bath Ales, Butts, Cottage, Goff's, Hop Back, Mole's, Moor, Oakhill, RCH, Stonehenge (Bunces), Wychwood, Wye Valley, York. Also winter specials and two real ciders.

A straightforward locals' community pub for all ages. Car park and garden. On the main Swindon (A361) road, opposite The Green.

OPEN *11am–11pm Mon–Sat; all day Sun.*

EAST KNOYLE

The Fox & Hounds

The Green, East Knoyle, Salisbury SP3 6BN
☎ *(01747) 830573* Andrew Knight

A freehouse with Smiles Golden Brew, Ringwood Fortyniner and Wadworth 6X always available, plus a minimum of three guests from breweries such as Church End or Hampshire. Ales from smaller breweries stocked whenever possible.

A country village pub with beams, slate floors, conservatory and garden. Food available at lunchtime and evenings. Children allowed in the conservatory and garden.

OPEN *11am–2.30pm and 6–11pm (10.30pm Sun).*

EASTON ROYAL

Bruce Arms

Easton Royal, Nr Pewsey SN9 5LR
☎ *(01672) 810216* WJ and JA Butler

Wadworth 6X and a Butts brew usually available. Other guests such as Ringwood Best Bitter may also be served.

Popular, traditional pub with many original features, situated on the B3087. Only cheese and onion rolls/sandwiches served lunchtimes and evenings. Car park. Children welcome in lounge, skittle alley or pool room. Website: www.brucearms.co.uk

OPEN *11am–2.30pm and 6–11pm Mon–Sat; 12–2.30pm and 7–10.30pm Sun.*

EBBESBOURN WAKE

The Horseshoe Inn

Ebbesbourne Wake SP5 5JF
☎ *(01722) 780474*

Wadworth 6X, Ringwood Best and Adnams Broadside always available straight from the barrel, plus a guest (12 per year) perhaps from Bateman, Poole, Felinfoel, Fuller's, Tisbury or Hop Back breweries.

A remote, old-fashioned unspoilt pub hung with old tools of a bygone age. Bar and restaurant food available lunchtime and evenings (except Monday). Car park, garden, accommodation. Children are allowed if eating. From Salisbury (A354), turn right to Bishopston, Broadchalke then on to Ebbesbourne Wake.

OPEN *11.30am–3pm and 6.30–11pm.*

The Swan

Longstreet, Enford, Nr Pewsey SN9 6DD
☎ *(01980) 670338* Bob Bone

A good choice of real ales available, changing regularly but usually including brews from Smiles, Fuller's, Ringwood and Shepherd Neame.

Old thatched and beamed pub with open fires. Bar food available at lunchtime and evenings. Car park, garden, restaurant. Easy to find.

12–3pm and 7–11pm Mon–Sat; 12–4pm and 7–10.30pm Sun.

The Wheatsheaf

High Street, Figheldean, Nr Salisbury SP4 8JJ
☎ *(01980) 670357*

Hop Back brews always available plus a couple of guests (20 per year) including ales from Titanic, Eldridge Pope, Young's, Exmoor, Hook Norton and Wychwood.

A single-bar pub with open fire and alcoves. Family room, garden. Bar food available lunchtime and evening (not Monday). Off the A345, north of Amesbury.

12–3pm and 7–11pm (closed Monday lunchtime).

The White Hart

Ford, Nr Chippenham SN14 8RP
☎ *(01249) 782213* Peter and Kate Miller

Badger Tanglefoot permanently available, plus six guest pumps serving a constantly changing selection. Examples include Shepherd Neame Spitfire, Morland Old Speckled Hen and Black Sheep Bitter. There are usually three beers served straight from the barrel.

Old coaching inn off the A420 on the edge of a river. One main bar, restaurant and buttery. Bar food available at lunchtime. Restaurant open at lunchtime and evenings. Car parks, river terrace, accommodation. Children allowed in the buttery.

11am–3pm and 5–11pm Mon–Sat; usual hours Sun.

The Cuckoo Inn

Hamptworth Road, Hamptworth, Nr Salisbury SP5 2DU
☎ *(01794) 390302* Ray Proudley

Wadworth 6X, Badger Tanglefoot, Cheriton Pots Ale, Hop Back Summer Lightning and GFB always available plus three guest beers from a long list including brews from Bunces, Adnams, Ringwood, Hampshire, Shepherd Neame and Cottage breweries.

A 300-year-old thatched pub in the New Forest. Bar food available at lunchtime and evenings. Car park, garden, play area, petanque area, children's room. Just off the A36 near Hamptworth golf course.

11.30am–2.30pm and 6–11pm Mon–Fri; 11.30am–11pm Sat; 12–3pm and 7–10.30pm Sun.

The Queen's Head

23 The Street, Hullavington, Chippenham SN14 6DP
☎ *(01666) 837221* Yvette Hicks

A freehouse with Archers Village always available, plus guests changing every fortnight. Wadworth 6X and Morland Old Speckled Hen are favourites, as are beers from the Adnams and Berkeley breweries.

An old-style country pub with two open coal fires, beams and pine furniture. New restaurant is scheduled to open late 2000. Bed and breakfast available. Children welcome. Just five minutes from J17 of the M4.

6–11pm Mon; 12–3pm and 5–11pm Tues–Thurs; 12–11pm Fri–Sat; 12–10.30pm Sun.

The Jolly Huntsman

Kington St Michael, Chippenham
☎ *(01249) 750305* MI and CVS Lawrence

Wadworth 6X, Badger Tanglefoot, Wickwar Brand Oak Bitter and Mole's Tap Bitter regularly served, plus a guest beer from a wide selection of independent breweries around the country.

Welcoming village pub with en-suite accommodation. Food served lunchtimes and evenings. Car park. Children welcome.

11.30am–2.30pm and 6.30–11pm Mon–Sat; 12–3pm and 7–10.30pm Sun.

LACOCK

The Bell Inn

Bowden Hill, Lacock, Chippenham SN15 2PJ
☎ *(01249) 730308*
Alan and Heather Shepherd

Wadworth 6X and Smiles Best always available, plus three monthly changing guests from breweries such as Wickwar, Bateman, Adnams and Tisbury.

A traditional rural freehouse built in converted cottages. One bar, dining area, beer garden. Food available lunchtimes and evenings. Children allowed.

OPEN *11.30am–2.30pm and 6–11pm in summer; 11.30am–2.30pm and 7–11pm in winter.*

The Rising Sun

32 Bowden Hill, Lacock, Nr Chippenham SN15 2PP
☎ *(01249) 730363* Howard and Sue Sturdy

Five beers always available including Mole's Tap, Best, Landlord's Choice, Brew 97 and Black Rat. Guests ales also served.

A Cotswold stone pub with flagstone floors and open fires. Bar food available at lunchtime and evenings (not Mon or Sun evenings), roasts served on Sun until 3.30pm. Car park, garden. Live music Wed evenings plus alternate Sun from 3pm. Children and dogs allowed. Turn into village, then go up Bowden Hill.

OPEN *11.30am–3pm Tues–Sat (closed Mon lunchtime); 6–11pm Mon–Sat; 12–10.30pm Sun.*

LITTLE CHEVERELL

The Owl

Low Road, Little Cheverell, Devizes SN10 4JS
☎ *(01380) 812263* Sally Buckle

A freehouse with Wadworth 6X always available plus three constantly changing guests from independent breweries such as Hop Back, Oak Hill, Ash Vine, Ringwood or Uley.

A country pub with beams and a woodburning stove. One bar, separate dining area. Large streamside beer garden. Food available at lunchtime and evenings. Children allowed.

OPEN *12–2.30pm and 7–11pm Tues–Sat; 12–3pm and 7–10.30pm Sun; closed Mon.*

LOWER CHICKSGROVE

The Compasses Inn

Lower Chicksgrove, Tisbury, Salisbury SP3 6NB
☎ *(01722) 714318* Jonathan and Caren Bold

A freehouse with Wadworth 6X always available, plus guests from the Tisbury brewery.

A beamed pub with open fires and wooden floors situated in a country hamlet. Small dining area, beer garden, accommodation. Food available Tues–Sun lunchtime and Tues–Sat evenings. Well-behaved children allowed.

OPEN *11am–3pm and 6–11pm Tues–Sat; 12–3pm and 6–10.30pm Sun; closed Mon except bank holidays, but then closed Tues.*

MALMESBURY

The Smoking Dog

62 High Street, Malmesbury SN16 9AT
☎ *(01666) 825823*
Ricki Mattioli and Vicky Morgan

Wadworth 6X, Brains SA and Reverend James Original, and Archers Best always available, plus at least three guests. These might be Gibbs Mew Bishop's Finger, Fuller's London Pride or a Young's ale, or seasonal and more obscure ales from smaller breweries. A porter is always available in winter.

A traditional small-town pub with log fires, beams and wooden floor. No music or machines. Food available in an à la carte restaurant, plus bar snacks all day. Beer garden. Children allowed.

OPEN *11.30am–11pm Mon–Sat; 12–10.30pm Sun.*

MARSTON MEYSEY

The Old Spotted Cow

Marston Meysey SN6 6LQ
☎ *(01285) 810264* James and Denise Kelso

Fuller's London Pride, Wickwar Brand Oak Bitter and Timothy Taylor Landlord usually available, plus a regularly changing mystery guest beer. Guess what it is and you win four pints!

Friendly, attractive, nineteenth-century country inn with large, yet intimate, open stone bar and two feature fireplaces. Situated on the edge of award-winning village. Food served lunchtimes and evenings Tues–Sat, lunchtimes only Sun, (no food Mon). Separate restaurant. Car park. Large, safe children's play area with activities. Accommodation. Touring caravan parking facilities.

OPEN *11.30am–11pm Mon–Sat; 12–10.30pm Sun.*

MELKSHAM

The Red Lion
1–3 The City, Melksham SN12 8DA
☎ *(01225) 702960* Alexander Cuthbert

A Bath Ales beer and Church End Gravediggers are regularly available, plus guest beers which might be from Wood, Mighty Oak, Wychwood, Exmoor, Brakspear, Fuller's, Smiles, Greene King, Hydes' Anvil, Young's, Bateman, Wickwar or Marston's.

Grade II listed building dating from 1220 and the only real ale pub in town. Food served 12–2pm Mon–Fri. Car park. No children. Located opposite the Avon Rubber Tyre Factory.

11am–2.30pm and 5–11pm Mon–Thurs and Sat; 11am–11pm Fri; 12–3pm and 7–10.30pm Sun.

NORTH WROUGHTON

The Check Inn
Woodland View, North Wroughton, Nr Swindon SN4 9AA
☎ *(01793) 845584* Doug Watkins

Six hand pumps, soon to be eight, serve a constantly changing range of beers from around the UK and Eire.

Single bar pub with separate lounge (eating) area and plans for extension. Family- and dog-friendly. Traditional pub games and barbecue. Food served lunchtimes and evenings Mon–Fri and all day at weekends. Car park. Children welcome. Directions: from the A361 Swindon–Devizes, take immediate first right after the dual carriageway over the M4.

11.30am–3.30pm and 6.30–11pm Mon–Thurs; 11.30am–11pm Fri–Sat; 12–10.30pm Sun.

PEWSEY

The Cooper's Arms
37–9 Ball Road, Pewsey SN9 5BL
☎ *(01672) 562495* Mr Dainton

A freehouse with Wadworth 6X and Oakhill Mendip Gold always available, plus four guests from local breweries such as Hop Back, Tisbury, Stonehenge, Ringwood, Cottage or Butts whenever possible.

A thatched country pub in a picturesque area. No food. Beer garden. Function room. Live music. Children allowed.

6–11pm Mon–Fri (closed lunchtimes); 12–3pm and 6–11pm Sat; 12–3pm and 6–10.30pm Sun.

QUEMERFORD

The Talbot Inn
Quemerford, Calne SN11 0AR
☎ *(01249) 812198* Paul Picken

Wadworth 6X always available plus up to four guests such as Morland Old Speckled Hen, Shepherd Neame Spitfire, Fuller's London Pride, Elgood's Greyhound or Exmoor Hart.

A village pub with a reputation for good food and real ales. One bar, wooden floors, beams, children's play area, large beer garden and car park. Conservatory doubles as dining area. Food available at lunchtime and evenings. Children allowed in the conservatory and garden only.

11am–11pm Mon–Sat; 12–10.30pm Sun.

ROWDE

The George & Dragon
High Street, Rowde, Devizes SN10 2PN
☎ *(01380) 723053* Tim Withers

A freehouse with three hand pumps serving a selection of real ales from local West Country breweries whenever possible, or other smaller and micro-breweries. Breweries regularly featured include Abbey Ales, Tisbury, Ash Vine and Hop Back.

A seventeenth-century village pub with beams, wooden floor and open fires. One bar, dining area and beer garden. Food available Tues–Sat lunchtime and evenings. Children allowed.

12–3pm and 7–11pm (10.30pm Sun).

SALISBURY

The Blackbird Inn
30 Churchfields Road, Salisbury SP2 7NW
☎ *(01722) 802828* Mr Leonard

Up to four real ales available. Breweries regularly featured include Hop Back, Stonehenge, Tisbury, Ringwood, Hampshire, Cottage and Isle of Skye. An annual beer festival is held on the last three days of August, with a selection of 12 real ales.

A one-bar pub situated at the back of the railway station. No music or machines. Light snacks available at lunchtime, rolls only in the evenings. Children allowed in the back yard only.

12–3pm and 5–11pm Mon–Thurs; all day Fri–Sat; 12–6pm Sun (closed Sun pm).

The Deacon Arms

118 Fisherton Street, Salisbury SP2 7QT
☎ *(01722) 504723* Frank Keay

A freehouse with Hop Back GFB always available plus two guests including, perhaps, Cheriton Best, RCH Pitchfork or Hop Back Summer Lightning.

A community pub with two bars, wooden floors, open fires in winter and air conditioning in summer. Accomodation. No food. Children allowed.

OPEN 5–11pm Mon–Fri; 12–11pm Sat; 12–10.30pm Sun.

Devizes Inn

53 Devizes Road, Salisbury SP2 7LQ
☎ *(017220) 327842* B P O'Malley

Hop Back GFB and Summer Lightning usually available.

Locals' town pub near the railway station. En-suite accommodation with discount if you mention *The Real Ale Pub Guide*. No food. Car park. Children welcome.

OPEN 4.30–11pm Mon–Thurs; 2–11pm Fri; 12–11pm Sat; 12–10.30pm Sun.

The Star Inn

69 Brown Street, Salisbury SP1 2AS
☎ *(01722) 327137* Mrs Bugler

A freehouse with Wadworth 6X, Fuller's London Pride and Oakhill Triple Crown always available, plus two guests such as Hop Back GFB or Bunces Sign of Spring.

A traditional one-bar town pub on the ring road. Rolls available. Children allowed.

OPEN 11am–11pm (10.30pm Sun).

Tom Brown's

225 Wilton Road, Salisbury SP2 7JY
☎ *(01722) 335918*

A Goldfinch Brewery tied house with a range of Goldfinch beers rotated on three pumps and always available: Tom Brown's Best, Flashman's Clout, Midnight Blinder and Midnight Sun.

A basic one-bar town pub for real ale drinkers. No food. No children.

OPEN 6–11pm Mon–Fri; 12–3pm and 6–11pm Sat; 12–3pm and 6–10.30pm Sun.

The Village Freehouse

33 Wilton Road, Salisbury SP2 7EF
☎ *(01722) 329707*

Oakhill Mendip Gold plus Abbey Somerset and Bellringer always available. Also three guests, constantly changing.

A small street-corner pub with a friendly atmosphere. Bar snacks available at lunchtime and evenings. Children allowed. Two minutes from Salisbury railway station.

OPEN 4–11pm Mon; 12–11pm Tues–Sat; 12–5pm and 7–10.30pm Sun.

The Wig & Quill

1 New Street, Salisbury SP1 2PH
☎ *(01722) 335665* Ken Stanforth

A Wadworth managed house with 6X and IPA from the wood, and a seasonal ale plus Hophouse Varietals all year round. Other guest ales from The Red Shoot brewery, Mayhem brewery and others.

A city-centre pub with an atmosphere that resembles a village local. A mix of the traditional and modern with one bar and three adjoining areas, open fires and beer garden. Food served at lunchtime 12–2.30pm. Children welcome.

OPEN 11am–11pm Mon–Sat; 12–3pm and 7–10.30pm Sun.

The George Inn

London Road, Shrewton, Salisbury SP3 4DH
☎ *(01980) 620341* Tony Clift

A freehouse with Ushers Best and Wadworth 6X always available plus a choice of two guests.

A remote country pub with traditional beams, open fires, one main bar, large covered patio area, skittle alley and a 26-seater restuarant. Food available at lunchtime and evenings. Children allowed. Beer festival held every August Bank Holiday.

OPEN 11.30am–3pm and 6–11pm Mon–Fri; all day Sat–Sun in summer, regular hours in winter.

The Carriers Arms

Highworth Road, South Marston, Nr Swindon
☎ *(01793) 822051* Val and Dave Fletcher

Ushers Best and seasonal brews usually available. A larger selection of beers may be available soon.

Traditional, village-centre, two-bar pub with separate dining area and patio. Car park. Children welcome when eating, but no special facilities.

OPEN 12–2.30pm and 6.30–11pm Mon–Sat; 12–3pm and 7–10.30pm Sun.

STAPLEFORD

The Pelican Inn

Warminster Road, Stapleford, Salisbury SP3 4LT
☎ *(01722) 790241* Mr Pitcher

Ringwood Best, Otter Ale and Greene King Abbot always available, plus one guest. Perhaps Fuller's London Pride or something from a small local or other independent brewer.

A country freehouse with inglenooks, open fireplaces, two linked bars, one large and one small, dining area and beer garden. Food available at lunchtime and evenings. Children allowed in the dining area only.

OPEN *11am–2.30pm and 6–11pm (10.30pm Sun).*

SWINDON

The Famous Ale House

146 Redclife Street, Swindon SN2 2BY
☎ *(01793) 522503* Mr Omara

Archers Village and Golden always available plus a choice of two guest ales such as Morland Old Speckled Hen or Caledonian Golden Promise. New beers on once a week.

An olde-worlde locals' community pub. One bar, restaurant and garden. Food served 12–2.30pm and 6.30–9pm daily. Children allowed in the garden only.

OPEN *11am–11pm (10.30pm Sun).*

The Glue Pot Inn

5 Emlyn Square, Swindon SN1 5BP
☎ *(01793) 523935* Mr Reid

Archers Village, Golden and Best always available, plus one guest such as Fuller's ESB or London Pride, or ales from local or Scottish breweries.

A town pub in the centre of Swindon, located by the railway museum. One small bar, patio. Bar snacks available at lunchtime only. No children.

OPEN *All day, every day.*

The Savoy

38 Regent Street, Swindon SN1 1JL
☎ *(01793) 533970* Val Docherty

A Wetherspoon's pub. Archers Golden, Best and Village always available plus three guest ales. Previous favourites have included Ringwood Old Thumper and Hop Back Summer Lightning but the aim is not to repeat the beers if possible. Beer festivals held every March and October, with 50 real ales at each.

A one-bar town-centre pub. No music or games. Food available all day in non-smoking dining area. Children allowed.

OPEN *10.30am–11pm Mon–Sat; 12–10.30pm Sun.*

The Wheatsheaf

32 Newport Street, Old Town, Swindon SN1 3DP
Sue and Terry Fellows

A Wadworth house with IPA, 6X, Farmers Glory and seasonal brews served. Adnams Southwold and Badger Tanglefoot often available as guest beers.

Traditional town pub with wooden floors and outside seating. Back bar very popular with students. Food available 12–2pm and 5.30–7pm. Children welcome. Accommodation.

OPEN *11am–2.30pm and 5.30–11pm (10.30pm Sun).*

UPTON LOVELL

Prince Leopold

Upton Lovell, Nr Warminster BA12 0JP
☎ *(01985) 850460*
Graham and Pamela Waldron-Bradley

Ringwood Best Bitter and a twice-monthly changing guest beer usually available.

Single-bar freehouse, with garden, pleasantly situated by the River Wylye. En-suite accommodation. Food served 12–3pm and 7–9.30pm daily, with a good reputation locally. Car park. Children welcome.

OPEN *12–3pm and 7–11pm (10.30pm Sun).*

WARMINSTER

The George Inn

Longbridge Deverill, Warminster BA12 7DG
☎ *(01985) 840396* Nicola Broady

Wadworth 6X permanently available plus two guests changed monthly. Ruddles County, Charles Wells Bombardier, Morland Old Speckled Hen and brews from breweries such as Brakspear or Butcombe are featured, plus customer recommendations.

A prettily situated pub with the River Wylie running through the large beer garden. Two bars, terrace, function room and accommodation. Children's play area. Bar food and an à la carte menu available every lunchtime and evening. Children allowed. Located on the main A350.

OPEN *11am–11pm (10.30pm Sun).*

WINTERBOURNE MONKTON

The New Inn

Winterbourne Monkton, Swindon SN4 9NW
☎ *(01672) 539240 Doreen Murrin*

Archers Village and Wadworth 6X permanently on offer, plus one regularly changing guest beer, such as Church End Vicar's Ruin, West Berkshire Dr Hexter's Healer or something from Eccleshall Brewery.

A small country pub overlooking Marlborough Downs and close to Avebury stone circle. Charming restaurant, en-suite accommodation. Food served 12–2.30pm and 6.30–9.30pm daily. Car park. Children's play equipment in garden.

OPEN *11am–3pm and 6–11pm Mon–Fri; 11am–4pm and 6–11pm Sat; 12–5pm and 7–10.30pm Sun.*

WOOTTON BASSETT

Old Nick

61 Station Road, Wootton Bassett, Swindon
☎ *(01793) 848102 Daniel Barclay*

Fuller's London Pride and Archers Best Bitter available, plus a guest beer such as Archers Golden, Shepherd Neame Spitfire or Hook Norton Old Hooky.

A community-based local situated in the old village police station. Specialists in food and real ale with bar menu available every lunchtime and evening. Big screen TV. Outside seating. Children allowed. Small car park. Function room in converted old courthouse.

OPEN *11am–11pm Mon–Sat; 12–11pm Sun.*

WROUGHTON

The Carter's Rest

High Street, Wroughton SN4 9JU
☎ *(01793) 812288 Mrs Woods*

Archers Village, Best and Golden always available, plus four guests changing weekly from breweries such as Tom Hoskins, Smiles and Ash Vine.

A country village pub with two bars and a patio area. Food available at lunchtime only. Children allowed.

OPEN *11.30am–2.30pm and 5–11pm Mon–Thurs; 11am–3pm and 5–11pm Fri; all day Sat–Sun.*

YOU TELL US

- ★ *Angel*, 3 Church Street, Westbury
- ★ *Black Horse*, Wroughton
- ★ *Cross Keys*, 65 Bradenstoke, Bradenstoke
- ★ *Cross Keys*, Lyes Green, Corsley, Warminster
- ★ *Dumb Post*, Dumb Post Hill, Bremhill, Calne
- ★ *George's Railway*, 5 Union Road, Chippenham
- ★ *Goddard Arms*, Wood Street, Clyffe Pypard
- ★ *Golden Fleece*, Folly Lane, Shaw, Melksham
- ★ *Kicking Donkey*, Brokerswood
- ★ *Prince of Wales*, 94 High Street, Dilton Marsh, Westbury
- ★ *Wheatsheaf*, Ermin Street, Swindon
- ★ *Wyndham Arms*, 27 Estcourt Road, Salisbury

Places Featured:

Allerton Bywater
Barnsley
Batley
Beck Hole
Bradford
Brearton
Bridlington
Brompton
Burley
Cawood
Catcliffe
Chapel Haddlesey
Cropton
Denby Dale
Dewsbury
Doncaster
Driffield
Elslack
Flaxton
Guisborough
Gunnerside
Halifax
Harrogate
Haworth
Hebden Bridge
Helperby
Holmfirth
Horbury
Huddersfield
Hull
Ingleton
Keighley
Kirkbymoorside
Knaresborough
Knottingley
Langdale End
Leeds

Linthwaite
Liversedge
Lund
Malton
Mexborough
Middlesbrough
North Duffield
North Howden
Northallerton
Old Mixenden
Ossett
Pontefract
Pool-in-Wharfedale
Pudsey
Ripon
Ripponden
Rotherham
Scarborough
Selby
Sheffield
Shipley
Sowerby Bridge
Staveley
Stokesley
Sutton upon Derwent
Thorne
Thornton-in-Lonsdale
Threshfield
Tockwith
Wakefield
Walsden
Weaverthorpe
Wentworth
Whitby
Wombwell
Wortley
York

THE BREWERIES

ABBEYDALE BREWERY

Unit 8, Aizlewood Road, Sheffield, South Yorkshire S8 0XX
☎ *(0114) 281 2712*

MATINS 3.6% ABV
Pale and flavoursome for gravity.
BEST BITTER 4.0% ABV
Smooth and malty with good hoppiness.
BLACK BISHOP 4.2% ABV
MOONSHINE 4.3% ABV
Fruity easy quaffer.
TURNING POINT 4.5% ABV

WHITE KNIGHT 4.5% ABV
ARCHANGEL 4.7% ABV
Pale and quenching.
DARK ANGEL 4.7% ABV
Dark and rounded.
FIRE ANGEL 4.7% ABV
STORMBRINGER 4.7% ABV
ABSOLUTION 5.3% ABV
Golden, smooth and refreshing.
BLACK MASS 6.6% ABV
Stout, with good hoppiness.
WHITE CHRISTMAS 5.0% ABV
LAST RITES 11% ABV
Smooth toffee sweetness.
Plus The Beer Works range of occasional brews.

BARGE & BARREL BREWING CO.
Park Road, Elland, West Yorkshire HX5 9HP
☎ *(01422) 373623*

 BARGEE 3.8% ABV
Award-winning session beer
BEST BITTER 4.0% ABV
Straw-coloured single malt brew.
NETTLETHRASHER 4.4% ABV
Smooth and rounded flavours.
BLACK STUMP 5.0% ABV
Porter.
LEVELLER 5.7% ABV
Powerful malt and hop flavour.

BARNSLEY BREWERY CO. LTD
Wath Road, Elsecar, Barnsley, South Yorkshire S74 8HJ
☎ *(01226) 741010*

 BITTER 3.8% ABV
Brewed to the original Barnsley Bitter recipe.
OAKWELL 4.0% ABV
Golden, hoppy and smooth.
IPA 4.2% ABV
Malty, pale and full-bodied.
MAYFLOWER 4.5% ABV
Golden and hoppy. Brewed with American hops.
BLACK HEART 4.6% ABV
Stout.
GLORY 4.8% ABV
Ruby-coloured, with rich, smooth flavour.
Plus seasonal and occasional brews.

BLACK DOG BREWERY
St Hilda's Business Centre, The Ropery, Whitby, North Yorkshire YO22 4EU
☎ *(01947) 821467*

 SCALLYWAG 3.6% ABV
Light, hoppy and refreshing summer ale.
WHITBY ABBEY ALE 3.8% ABV
Light and hoppy.
FIRST OUT 4.0% ABV
Hoppy and bitter.
SCHOONER 4.2% ABV
Rounded autumn ale
SYNOD 4.2% ABV
Spring ale.
RHATAS/BLACK DOG SPECIAL 4.6% ABV
Dark, rich and smooth.
WHITBY JET 5.0% ABV
Dark, rich, flavoursome porter. Winter brew.

THE BLACK SHEEP BREWERY
Wellgarth, Masham, Ripon, North Yorkshire HG4 4EN
☎ *(01765) 689227*

 BEST BITTER 3.8% ABV
Golden, well-hopped and refreshing.
SPECIAL 4.4% ABV
Good body, hoppy and bitter.
RIGGWELTER 5.9% ABV
Mouthfilling flavours.

BRISCOE'S BREWERY
16 Ash Grove, Otley, West Yorkshire LS21 3EL
☎ *(01943) 466515*

 ROMBALD'S REVIVER 3.8% ABV
PUDDLED AND BARMY ALE 5.8% ABV

BROWN COW BREWERY
Brown Cow Road, Barlow, Selby, North Yorkshire YO8 8EH
☎ *(01757) 618974*

BITTER 3.8% ABV
Good hoppiness.
JUST 4U 3.9% ABV
Brewed for the Jug Inn, Chapel Haddlesey.
MAIDEN'S CENTURY 4.0% ABV
Light-coloured and quenching.
WOLFHOUND 4.3% ABV
SIMPSON'S NO. 4 4.4% ABV
Roast barley flavour, balancing hop and sweetness.
HOW NOW? 4.5% ABV
Plus occasional brews.

CAPTAIN COOK BREWERY LTD
White Swan, Stokesley, North Yorkshire TS9 5BL
☎ *(01642) 710263*

SUNSET 4.0% ABV
BLACK PORTER 4.2% ABV
SLIPWAY 4.2% ABV
RED GOLD 4.4% ABV

DALESIDE BREWERY
Camwal Road, Starbeck, Harrogate, North Yorkshire HG1 4PT
☎ *(01423) 880022*

NIGHT JAR 3.7% ABV
OLD LUBRICATION 4.1% ABV
OLD LEGOVER 4.1% ABV
SHRIMPER'S ALE 4.1% ABV
CRACKSHOT 4.5% ABV
GREEN GRASS OLD ROGUE ALE 4.5% ABV
MONKEY WRENCH 5.3% ABV
MOROCCO ALE 5.5% ABV

DRUMMONDS BREWERY
443 London Road, Sheffield, South Yorkshire S2 4HJ
☎ *(0114) 255 4024*

BULLDOG 4.0% ABV
DREGS 4.6% ABV

FERNANDES BREWERY
Kirkgate, Wakefield, West Yorkshire
☎ *(01924) 291709*

FRANKLIN'S BREWERY

Bilton Lane, Bilton, Harrogate, North Yorkshire HG1 4DH
☎ *(01423) 322345*

 FRANKLIN'S BITTER 3.8% ABV
FRANKLIN'S BLOTTO 4.7% ABV
FRANKLIN'S DT'S 4.7% ABV
MY BETTER HALF 4.8% ABV

GLENTWORTH BREWERY

Glentworth House, Crossfield Lane, Skellow, Doncaster, South Yorkshire DN6 8PL
☎ *(01302) 725555*

 LIGHTYEAR 3.9% ABV
DONNY ROVER 4.1% ABV
AMBLER GAMBLER 4.3% ABV
LIGHTMAKER 4.5% ABV
WHISPERS 4.5% ABV
FULL MONTY 5.0% ABV
Plus seasonal brews.

GOOSE EYE BREWERY

Ingrow Bridge, South Street, Keighley, West Yorkshire BD21 5AX
☎ *(01535) 605807*

 BARMPOT 3.8% ABV
BITTER 3.8% ABV
Golden and malty with some fruitiness.
BRONTE BITTER 4.0% ABV
Malty and well-balanced.
NO IDEA 4.0% ABV
SUMMER JACKS 4.2% ABV
WHARFEDALE BITTER 4.5% ABV
GOLDEN GOOSE 4.5% ABV
POMMIE'S REVENGE 5.2% ABV
Straw-coloured, soft and smooth.
Plus occasional brews.

H B CLARK & CO. (SUCCESSORS) LTD

Westgate Brewery, Wakefield, West Yorkshire WF2 9SW
☎ *(01924) 372306*

TRADITIONAL BITTER 3.8% ABV
Amber-coloured, with some fruitiness.
CITY GENT 4.2% ABV
Pale golden, fruity and quenching.
FESTIVAL ALE 4.2% ABV
Pale with refreshing fruit flavours.
BLACK CAP BITTER 4.4% ABV
Powerful maltiness with hoppy aroma.
BURGLAR BILL 4.4% ABV
Full-bodied and well-hopped throughout.
OLDEN HORNET 5.0% ABV
Golden and hoppy.
Plus seasonal brews.

HAMBLETON ALES

The Brewery, Holme on Swale, Thirsk, North Yorkshire YO7 4JE
☎ *(01845) 567460*

 BITTER 3.6% ABV
WHITE BOAR 3.7% ABV
For Village Brewer.
BULL 4.0% ABV
For Village Brewer.
STALLION 4.2% ABV
GOLDFIELD 4.2% ABV
STUD 4.3% ABV
OLD RABY 4.8% ABV
For Village Brewer.
NIGHTMARE 5.0% ABV
Plus 4% monthly/seasonal brews.

HUDDERSFIELD BREWERY

Ivy Street East, Huddersfield, West Yorkshire
☎ *(01484) 300028*

TOWN BITTER 3.8% ABV
SILVER STREET BEST 3.9% ABV
HUDDERSFIELD PRIDE 4.4% ABV
WILSONS WOBBLE MAKER 5.0% ABV
All Huddersfield beers are brewed on an occasional basis.

THE HULL BREWERY

144–8 English Street, Hull, East Yorkshire HU3 2BT
☎ *(01482) 586364*

 MILD 3.6% ABV
BITTER 3.8% ABV
ELWOODS BEST BITTER 3.8% ABV
AMBER ALE 4.0% ABV
NORTHERN PRIDE 4.2% ABV
GOVERNOR 4.3% ABV
MICKEY FINN 5.0% ABV
Plus seasonal and occasional brews.

KELHAM ISLAND BREWERY

23 Alma Street, Sheffield, South Yorkshire S3 8SA
☎ *(0114) 249 4804*

 BITTER 3.8% ABV
SHEFFIELDS BEST 4.0% ABV
EASY RIDER 4.3% ABV
PRINCE OF SHEFFIELD 4.5% ABV
CATHEDRAL ALE 5.0% ABV
Dark brew, in support of the Cathedral Millennium fund.
WHEAT BIER 5.0% ABV
Annual brew.
PALE RIDER 5.2% ABV
BETE NOIRE 5.5% ABV
January.
GRANDE PALE 6.6% ABV
August.
Plus two changing monthly brews.

THE KITCHEN BREWERY LTD

Unit J, Shaw Park, Silver Street, Aspley,
Huddersfield, West Yorkshire HD5 9AF
☎ *(01484) 300028*

 DISH WATER 3.8% ABV
TUBBY TANGERINE 4.0% ABV
Blonde colour and refreshing with a hint of
tangerine.
GOBLIN WAITRESS 4.3% ABV
TORMENTED TURNIP 4.5% ABV
Pale and hoppy with some fruity sweetness.
RAISIN STOUT 4.8% ABV
Plus more than 70 seasonal and occasional brews.

MARSTON MOOR BREWERY

Crown House, Kirk Hammerton, York, North
Yorkshire YO26 8DD
☎ *(01423) 330341*

CROMWELL BITTER 3.6% ABV
Light and refreshing with distinctive hop
flavour.
HOLLYDAZE 4.0% ABV
December brew.
PILSENER 4.0% ABV
Refreshing, brewed with Czechoslovakian hops.
PRINCE RUPERT MILD 4.0% ABV
Delicate yet flavoursome light mild.
ROMANCER 4.0% ABV
February special brew.
SUMMER DAZE 4.0% ABV
August brew.
BREWERS PRIDE 4.2% ABV
Smooth, balanced hop flavour.
GEM(INI) 4.5% ABV
June special brew.
HARVEST MOON 4.5% ABV
September brew.
MAD HATTER 4.5% ABV
April special brew.
MERRIE MAKER 4.5% ABV
Award-winning, Yorkshire-style brew.
SCORPIO 4.5% ABV
November brew.
BREWER'S DROOP 5.0% ABV
Easy-drinking, sweeter brew.
TROOPER 5.0% ABV
Dry-hopped version of Brewer's Droop.

NORTH YORKSHIRE BREWING CO.

Pinchinthorpe Hall, Pinchinthorpe, Guisborough
TS14 8HG
☎ *(01287) 630200*

BEST BITTER 3.6% ABV
Pale, refreshing and hoppy.
GOLDEN GINSENG 3.6% ABV
Gold-coloured and hoppy.
MILLENNIUM MILD 3.6% ABV
Dark, with caramel hints and hoppy aftertaste.
PRIOR'S ALE 3.6% ABV
Quenching and very hoppy.
ARCHBISHOP LEE'S RUBY ALE 4.0% ABV
Rounded, Northern ale.
BORO BEST 4.0% ABV
Northern, full-bodied style.
CRYSTAL TIPS 4.0% ABV
Rounded, malty September special.
LOVE MUSCLE 4.0% ABV
February, golden special brew.
HONEY BUNNY 4.2% ABV
Mar–Apr brew.
XMAS HERBERT 4.4% ABV
A festive version of Flying Herbert.
CEREAL KILLER 4.5% ABV
June–July wheat beer.
FOOL'S GOLD 4.6% ABV
Pale and hoppy.
GOLDEN ALE 4.6% ABV
Powerful hoppiness.
FLYING HERBERT 4.7% ABV
Smooth and well-balanced.
LORD LEE 4.7% ABV
Smooth, full-flavoured malt.
WHITE LADY 4.7% ABV
Pale, hoppy October brew.
DIZZY DICK 4.8% ABV
Dark and smooth August brew.
NORTHERN STAR 4.8% ABV
Golden and well-balanced.
ROCKET FUEL 5.0% ABV
Golden brew for November.

ROOSTER'S BREWERY

Unit 20, Claro Court Business Centre, Claro
Road, Harrogate, North Yorkshire HG1 4BA
☎ *(01423) 561861*

SPECIAL 3.9% ABV
Pale, with citrus-fruit freshness.
HOOLIGAN 4.3% ABV
Pale, with some hoppy bitterness.
SCORCHER 4.3% ABV
Pale, with citrus flavours and good hoppiness.
YANKEE 4.3% ABV
Pale, soft and fruity.
CREAM 4.7% ABV
Smooth and soft, with fruit flavours.
ROOSTER'S 4.7% ABV
Golden brown, sweet and fruity.
Plus occasional and seasonal brews. Additional
brews produced under the Outlaw Brewing Co. label.

RUDGATE BREWERY

2 Centre Park, Marston Business Park, Rudgate, Tockwith, York, North Yorkshire YO26 8QF
☎ *(01423) 358382*

 VIKING 3.8% ABV
BATTLEAXE 4.2% ABV
MILD 4.4% ABV
Plus monthly brews.

SAMUEL SMITH OLD BREWERY

High Street, Tadcaster, North Yorkshire LS24 9SB
☎ *(01937) 832225*

 OLD BREWERY BITTER 4.0% ABV
Rounded and flavoursome.

TIMOTHY TAYLOR & CO. LTD

Knowle Spring Brewery, Keighley, West Yorkshire BD21 1AW
☎ *(01535) 603139*

 DARK MILD 3.5% ABV
Mellow and malty with balancing hoppiness.
GOLDEN BEST 3.5% ABV
Balanced, crisp and hoppy.
PORTER 3.8% ABV
Sweeter winter brew.
BEST BITTER 4.0% ABV
Refreshing, hoppy and bitter.
LANDLORD 4.3% ABV
Distinctive combination of malt, hops and fruit.
RAM TAM 4.3% ABV
Landlord with added caramel.

TIGERTOPS BREWERY

Oakes Street, Wakefield, West Yorkshire
☎ *(01229) 716238*
Constantly changing beer range.

WAWNE BREWERY

14 Greens Lane, Wawne, East Yorkshire HU7 5XT
☎ *(01482) 835400*

Brewery may move shortly.

 MONKS MILD 3.2% ABV
ST. PETER'S BITTER 3.8% ABV
WAGHEN BITTER 4.1% ABV
Plus occasional brews.

WEST YORKSHIRE BREWERY

Victoria Buildings, Burnley Road, Luddendenfoot, Halifax, West Yorkshire HX2 6AA
☎ *(01422) 885930*

 BAHT'AT 3.8% ABV
YORKSHIREMAN 4.1% ABV
Pale and malty with dry hoppy finish.
SEARNOWT 4.5% ABV
Plus monthly brews.

YORK BREWERY

Toft Green, Micklegate, York YO1 1JT
☎ *(01904) 621162*

MILDLY MAD 3.3% ABV
Dark, with smooth chocolate maltiness.
STONEWALL 3.7% ABV
Malty with hoppy finish.
BRIDESHEAD 4.0% ABV
Well-balanced with some fruitiness.
REFEREE'S REVENGE 4.0% ABV
Balanced and quenching.
SHEILA'S GOLD 4.1% ABV
Hoppy, easy quaffer.
YORKSHIRE TERRIER 4.2% ABV
Gold-coloured with good hoppy bitterness.
SUMMER BREEZE 4.5% ABV
Fruit, hop and malt flavours with some sweetness.
WET 'N WILD 4.5% ABV
Mellow and well-balanced.
EARTH MOVER 4.6% ABV
Dark, with hoppy malt bitterness.
STOCKING FILLER 4.8% ABV
Robust and rich with distinctive flavour.
CREAM OF THE CROP 5.0% ABV
Refreshing, citrus fruit flavour.
OLD LAG 5.0% ABV
Real Lager
CENTURION'S GHOST ALE 5.0% ABV
Millennium brew.

THE PUBS

ALLERTON BYWATER

The Boat Inn & Boat Brewery

Boat Lane, Allerton Bywater, Castleford,
West Yorkshire WF10 2BX
☎ *(01977) 552216* Kieron Lockwood

All Boat Brewery ales are brewed on the premises and permanently available. One other monthly special guest.

A small pub with moorings directly outside. Food available every day in a large restaurant with non-smoking areas. Children allowed. For further information, visit the web site at www.boatpub.co.uk

 MAN IN THE BOAT MILD 3.5% ABV
AIRTONIC 3.6% ABV
Session bitter.
RATTLER 4.3 % ABV
Light beer.

OPEN *12–3pm and 6–11pm Mon–Fri; all day Sat–Sun.*

BARNSLEY

Miller's Inn

Dearne Hall Road, Barnsley, South Yorkshire
S75 1LX
☎ *(01226) 382888* Mr and Mrs Alan Dyson

A freehouse with Timothy Taylor Landlord and Barnsley Oakwell always available, plus one guest from breweries such as Kitchen, Shepherd Neame or Fuller's.

A riverside two-bar village pub with separate dining area and garden. Food available Wed–Sun lunchtime and Sun–Mon, Wed–Thurs evenings. Children allowed.

OPEN *11.30am–2.30pm and 5.15–11pm Sun–Thurs (closed Tues lunchtime); all day Fri–Sat.*

The Orchard Brewery Bar

15 Market Hill, Barnsley, South Yorkshire S72 PX
☎ *(01226) 288906* Gabriel Savage

The full range of home brews are always available.

A Yorkshire brewpub, with separate fish restaurant upstairs. Food available all day Mon–Sat. Children allowed.

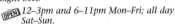 **ORCHARD BEST BITTER 3.9% ABV**
MORETONS 3.9% ABV
TYKE 4.6% ABV

OPEN *11am–11pm (10.30pm Sun).*

BATLEY

The Oaklands

Bradford Road, Batley, West Yorkshire
WF17 5PS
☎ *(01924) 444181*

Up to six beers available. Always something from local breweries plus at least three guests from Wild's, Timothy Taylor or Tomlinson's.

A busy circuit pub. Bar food available at lunchtime and evenings. Car park, garden. Children allowed up to 7pm.

OPEN *12–3pm and 5–11pm; all day Fri–Sat.*

BECK HOLE

Birch Hall Inn

Beck Hole, Goathland, North Yorkshire
YO22 5LE
☎ *(01947) 896245*

A wide choice of beers always available, including Black Sheep Bitter and local brews from Cropton, Black Dog and Daleside Brewery. Many more guests through the year from further afield.

Tiny, traditional unspoilt pub with two bars dating from 1600s. CAMRA pub of the year. No juke box or games machines. Bar food available at lunchtime and evenings. Garden. Children allowed. Between Pickering and Whitby.

OPEN *11am–11pm in summer; usual hours in winter.*

BRADFORD

The Beehive Inn

583 Halifax Road, Bradford, West Yorkshire
BD6 2DU
☎ *(01274) 678550* Kevin Guster

Two guest ales always available, regulars include Yorkshire ales like Timothy Taylor Landlord and Black Sheep Bitter, but also beers from any brewery in the country. Seasonal ales for Christmas and Bonfire Night when possible.

A one-bar locals' pub on the outskirts of Bradford. Bar snacks available all day. Children allowed.

OPEN *11am–11pm (10.30pm Sun).*

The Castle Hotel

*20 Grattan Road, Bradford, West Yorkshire
BD1 2LU*
☎ *(01274) 393166* James Duncan

Mansfield Riding and Riding Mild always available plus seven guest beers (200 per year) from brewers such as Goose Eye, Ridleys, Brains, Moorhouse's, Marston's, Eldridge Pope, Jennings, Wadworth, Shepherd Neame and many more.

A pub built like a castle in 1898. Bar food is served at lunchtime from Monday to Thursday and until 7.30pm on Friday and Saturday. Parking at weekends and evenings. Children not allowed. Located in the city centre.

11.30am–11pm Mon–Sat; closed Sun.

The Corn Dolly

*110 Bolton Road, Bradford, West Yorkshire
BD1 4DE*
☎ *(01274) 720219* Mr Duncan

Up to 12 beers available. Moorhouse's Bitter, Black Sheep and Black Bull always available, plus four guests (500 per year) from brewers including Fuller's, Charles Wells, Wadworth and Goose Eye.

CAMRA Bradford Pub of the Year 1993 and 1994. Bar food is available at lunchtime. Car park and garden. Situated off Forster Square.

11.30am–11pm.

The Fighting Cock

*21–3 Preston Street, Bradford, West Yorkshire
BD7 1JE*
☎ *(01274) 726907* Kevin Quill

At least ten beers on sale. Brews from Timothy Taylor and Black Sheep always available plus many guests (200 per year) from Greene King, Fuller's, Archers, Jennings and Ringwood etc.

A friendly back-to-basics original ale house. Bar food available at lunchtime. Go left on Thornton Road from the cinema in the city centre, then left again at the lights.

11am–11pm Mon–Sat; 11am–3pm and 7–10.30pm Sun.

Haigy's Bar

*31 Lumb Lane, Bradford, West Yorkshire
BD8 7QU*
☎ *(01274) 731644* Mrs Haig

A freehouse serving Greene King Abbot, Timothy Taylor Landlord and a Black Sheep ale plus two weekly changing guests from breweries such as Fuller's.

An edge-of-town pub with traditional decor, painted in Bradford City colours, but with a modern feel. Games, pool, disco at weekends. Disabled access, beer garden. Food available at lunchtime and evenings. Children allowed in the afternoons only.

5pm–1am Mon–Thurs; 12pm–1am Fri–Sat; closed Sun except Festival for Yorkshire Day.

The Idle Cock

Bolton Road, Bradford, West Yorkshire BD2 4HT
☎ *(01274) 639491* Jim Wright

Samuel Smith OBB, Black Sheep Special and Timothy Taylor Landlord always available plus several guests (130 per year) including Tomintoul Stag, Hop Back Summer Lightning, Fuller's London Pride, Daleside Old Legover, Joseph Holts etc.

A York stone pub with two separate bars, part wood, part flagstone floors, wooden bench seating. A proper no-frills alehouse. Bar food is available. Parking and garden. Follow the 'Idle' signs along Bolton Road for approximately two miles from the city centre.

11.30am–11pm Mon–Sat; 12–3pm and 7–10.30pm Sun.

The Shearbridge

*111 Great Horton Road, Bradford,
West Yorkshire BD7 1PS*
☎ *(01274) 732136* Rob Heir

Marston's Pedigree among the beers always available plus up to four guests, such as Harviestoun Schiehallion or a Black Sheep ale.

A students' pub with beams, wooden floors and beer garden. Food available at lunchtime and evenings. No children.

12–11pm (10.30pm Sun).

BREARTON

The Malt Shovel

Brearton, Nr Knaresborough, North Yorkshire HG3 3BX
☎ *(01423) 862929* Mr Mitchell

Five beers always available – up to 100 guests per year. Favourites include Daleside Nightjar, Durham Magus, Rudgate Ruby Mild, Black Sheep Bitter and Daleside brews.

A sixteenth-century beamed village inn, with open fires in winter. Bar food available at lunchtime and evenings. Car park, garden. Children allowed. Off the B6165.

OPEN *12–2.30pm and 6.45–11pm Tues–Sat; 12–2.30pm and 7–10.30pm Sun.*

BRIDLINGTON

The Old Ship Inn

90 St John's Street, Bridlington, East Yorkshire YO16 7JS
☎ *(01262) 670466*

Up to seven beers always available.

A two-bar country pub with dining area and beer garden. Food available. Children allowed.

OPEN *11am–11pm (10.30pm Sun).*

BROMPTON

The Crown Inn

Station Road, Brompton, Northallerton, North Yorkshire DL6 2RE
☎ *(0160) 977 2547* Mrs Addington

Two guest ales such as Marston's Pedigree in addition to the two regular brews.

A traditional country inn with one bar, coal fires and a small garden. There are plans to serve food in the near future. Children allowed.

OPEN *12–3pm and 7–11pm Mon–Thurs; all day Fri–Sun.*

BURLEY

The Fox & Newt

9 Burley Street, Burley, Leeds, West Yorkshire LS3 1LD
☎ *(01132) 432612* Roy Cadman

A wide range of guest ales always available. Regulars include Young's Special, Greene King Abbot, Timothy Taylor Landlord, Wadworth 6X, Marston's Pedigree, Fuller's London Pride and Caledonian 80/-. The beers are changed weekly.

An old-style pub with a wooden floor. Food available at lunchtime only in a separate dining area. Children allowed for lunches only.

OPEN *All day, every day.*

CAWOOD

The Ferry Inn

2 King Street, Cawood, Selby, North Yorkshire YO8 3TL
☎ *(01757) 268515*
Lynn Moore, Phillip Daggitt and Dee Ellershaw

A freehouse serving Mansfield Bitter, Black Sheep Special and Timothy Taylor Landlord plus one constantly changing guest ale.

A sixteenth-century village inn with stone floor, beams, log fires and beer garden. Bar food available at lunchtime and evenings. Separate dining area planned. Children allowed. Near the river.

OPEN *5–11pm Mon–Tues; 12–3pm and 5–11pm Wed–Thurs; 12–11pm Fri–Sun.*

CATCLIFFE

The Waverley

Nursery Bungalow, Brinsworth Road, Catcliffe, Rotherham, South Yorkshire S60 5RW
☎ *(01709) 360906* Ron Woodthorpe

A freehouse with four hand pumps serving a range of guest brews. Regular breweries supported include Glentworth, Slaters (Eccleshall), Drummonds, Banks's and Timothy Taylor.

A large suburban pub with separate lounge and children's room, garden and play area. Disabled access and toilets. Food available at lunchtime and evenings. Children allowed in children's room only.

OPEN *12–4pm and 6–11.30pm Mon–Fri; all day Sat; 12–4pm and 7–10.30pm Sun.*

CHAPEL HADDLESEY

The Jug Inn

Chapel Haddlesey, Selby, North Yorkshire
☎ *(01757) 270307* Sydney Bolton

A Brown Cow brew is usually available, plus three guest beers, often from Glentworth, Rudgate, Barnsley, Cropton, Ash Vine, Eccleshall, Goose Eye, Kelham Island or Tiger Tops.

Welcoming village pub with beamed ceilings and open coal fires. Food served 12–2.30pm and 6–9.30pm daily in small dining room. Beer garden. Car park. Children's play area in beer garden.

OPEN *12–2.30pm and 6–11pm Mon–Fri; 12–11pm Sat; 12–10.30pm Sun.*

CROPTON

The New Inn

Cropton, Nr Pickering, North Yorkshire
YO18 8HH
☎ *(01751) 417310* Sandra Lee

Home of the Cropton Brewery, so a selection of Cropton beers always available.

Cropton Brewery was established in 1984 in the basement of the New Inn in this tiny moorland village. It owes its existence to the deep-seated local fear that, one day, the harsh moors winter weather would prevent the beer waggon from getting through. The brewery's reputation has since spread and, as demand exceeded capacity, a new purpose-built brewery was constructed in an adjacent quarry. Bar and restaurant food is served at lunchtime and evenings. Car park, garden, children's room, accommodation.

KING BILLY BITTER 3.6% ABV
TWO PINTS BEST BITTER 4.0% ABV
HONEY GOLD 4.2% ABV
SCORESBY STOUT 4.2% ABV
UNCLE SAM'S BITTER 4.4% ABV
BACKWARDS BITTER 4.7% ABV
MONKMAN'S SLAUGHTER BITTER 6.0% ABV

11am–3pm and 6.30–11pm; all day Sat.

DENBY DALE

The White Hart

380 Wakefield Road, Denby Dale, Huddersfield,
West Yorkshire HD8 8RT
☎ *(01484) 863572* Mrs Donna M Brayshaw

Between two and four guest beers usually available, often from the Barge & Barrell Brewery.

Friendly, village-centre pub with an open fire in winter. Beer garden and Tuesday night quiz with free buffet. Food served 12–2.30pm daily. Car park. Children welcome when eating.

12–3.30pm and 6–11pm Mon–Thurs;
12–11pm Fri–Sat; 12–3.30pm and
7–10.30pm Sun.

DEWSBURY

West Riding Licensed Refreshment Rooms

Dewsbury Railway Station, Wellington Road,
Dewsbury, West Yorkshire WF13 1HF
☎ *(01924) 459193* Paul Kloss and Mike Field

A freehouse with Black Sheep Bitter and Timothy Taylor Landlord always available, plus up to five guests from breweries such as Ossett, Durham, Abbeydale and Kelham Island. Close links with local breweries.

Situated in the railway station and doubling as a waiting room, this is a real ale pub with one central bar, wooden floors and beer garden. Live music on Thursdays. Music festival venue. Food available every lunchtime, plus Tuesday nights (Pie Nights) and Wednesday nights (Curry Nights). Children allowed in designated areas. On Trans-Pennine route – four trains an hour in each direction.

11am–11pm (10.30pm Sun).

DONCASTER

The Hallcross

33–4 Hallgate, Doncaster, South Yorkshire
DN1 3NL
☎ *(01302) 328213*

Home of the Stocks Brewery, so Stocks brews produced and served on the premises.

The brewery was established in 1981 behind the pub. It is owned and run by Cooplands, a Doncaster bakers, on the site of the first shop, which was opened in 1931 to sell home-made sweets. The pub is of traditional Victorian style with a beer garden. Bar food is served at lunchtime and evenings. Parking, children allowed.

BEST BITTER 3.9% ABV
Light hoppy ale brewed for the northern taste.

SELECT 4.7% ABV
Premium ale of smooth and slightly malty character.

ST LEDGER PORTER 5.1% ABV
Award-winning, almost black, full-flavoured ale with deep fruit and roast malt flavours. A hoppy finish.

GOLDEN WHEAT 4.7% ABV

OLD HORIZONTAL 5.4% ABV
Strong ale with a distinctive nutty flavour, good body and excellent head retention, flavoured with a delicate blend of Fuggles and Goldings hops.

11am–11pm.

The Salutation

*14 South Parade, Doncaster, South Yorkshire
DN1 2DR*
☎ *(01302) 368464* Lisa Potts

Marston's Pedigree is always available at this renowned real ale pub, plus five guests (500 per year), which are changed regularly.

A 300-year-old pub with one bar and a haunted cellar. Food available every day. Function room, beer garden. Just outside the town centre. Families welcome.

All day, every day.

Bell In Driffield

*46 Market Place, Driffield, East Yorkshire
YO25 6AN*
☎ *(01377) 256661* Mr GAF Riggs

Two beers available weekdays and three or four at weekends from a range of around thirty locals beers, often including something from York, Hambleton or Highwood.

Characterful, eighteenth-century inn retaining many original features. Food served 12–1.30pm and 7–9.30pm daily. Car park. No children under 12.

*11am–2.30pm and 6–11pm Mon–Sat;
12–3pm and 7–10.30pm Sun.*

The Tempest Arms

Elslack, Nr Skipton, North Yorkshire
☎ *(01282) 842450* Garry Kirkpatrick

Jennings Bitter, Cumberland, Cockerhoop and Sneck Lifter regularly available plus a guest beer, perhaps Adnams Broadside or a Jennings seasonal brew.

A hotel situated in its own grounds in a rural setting with bar, restaurant and function room. Food available lunchtimes and evenings Mon–Fri and all day at weekends. Car park. Children's play area.

11am–11pm Mon–Sat; 12–10.30pm Sun.

The Blacksmiths Arms

Flaxton, York, North Yorkshire YO60 7RJ
☎ *(01904) 468210* Mrs Alison Jordan

Black Sheep Bitter and Timothy Taylor Landlord regularly available.

A 250-year-old country freehouse with separate non-smoking dining area serving home-cooked food Mon–Sat evening, lunchtime and evening Sun. Car park. Children welcome.

*7–11pm Mon–Sat; 12–3pm and
7–10.30pm Sun.*

The Tap & Spile

*11 Westgate, Guisborough, North Yorkshire
TS14 6BG*
☎ *(01287) 632983* Angela Booth

Tap & Spile Premium (brewed by Mansfield), always available plus six guests (200 per year) which may include Hambleton ales and those from Hull Brewery, Cotleigh, Big Lamp and Durham.

Plenty of olde-worlde charm, a beamed ceiling, non-smoking room, snug and beer garden. Bar food available at lunchtime. Parking. Children allowed. Situated on the main street in Guisborough.

*11.30am–11pm Mon–Sat; 12–3pm and
7–10.30pm Sun.*

The Kings Head

Gunnerside, North Yorkshire
☎ *(01748) 886261* R Hooton

A Black Sheep beer, Swaled Ale Old Gang Bitter and Kings Brew usually available.

Traditional Dales walkers' pub. Food served 11am–9pm daily. Children welcome.

11am–11pm (10.30pm Sun).

Tap & Spile

1 Clare Road, Halifax, West Yorkshire HX1 2HX
☎ *(01422) 353661* Chris Dalton

Black Sheep Bitter, Big Lamp Bitter, Fuller's London Pride always available, plus up to four guests, not repeated if possible, from breweries such as Broughton Ales, Fuller's, Hop Back and Hambleton.

A traditional town pub in a listed building, with one bar and a dining area. Plans for a beer garden. Food available at lunchtime only. No children.

All day, every day.

The Three Pigeons Ale House

*1 Sunfold, South Parade, Halifax, West Yorkshire
HX1 2LX*
☎ *(01422) 347001* Jeff Amos

A freehouse with Timothy Taylor Landlord and Best and Black Sheep Bitter and Special always on offer, plus three guests such as Timothy Taylor Golden Best, Church End Gravedigger and Shepherd Neame Dark Mild.

A unique, unspoilt 1930s Art Deco pub just outside the city centre. Real fires, one bar and three parlour rooms. Patio at front. Food available at lunchtime and evenings. Children allowed in designated area.

12–11pm (10.30pm Sun).

The Alderman Fortune

51 Parliament Street, Harrogate, North Yorkshire HG1 2RE
☎ *(01423) 502759* Elaine Airey

A good selection of up to seven guest ales, regularly featuring Timothy Taylor Landlord, Daleside Greengrass or other Daleside ale, and Black Sheep Best and Special, but also many other seasonal and celebration ales. Beers from the local Daleside brewery stocked whenever possible.

A traditional one-bar town pub (formerly The Pump Rooms) with wooden floors, low ceilings and poetry on the walls. Food available every lunchtime. No children.

OPEN *12–11pm daily.*

The Tap & Spile

Tower Street, Harrogate, North Yorkshire HG1 1HS
☎ *(01423) 526785* Roger Palmer

No permanent beers, but a constantly changing range of guest ales. Rooster's and Daleside are regular breweries featured, but two new beers are served every week.

A two-bar pub situated just off the town centre. Stone walls, half-carpet in public bar and lounge, one non-smoking, fireplace. Patio at front. Food available at lunchtime only. Children allowed in non-smoking room only.

OPEN *All day, every day.*

The Fleece

Main Street, Haworth, Nr Keighley, West Yorkshire BD22 8DA
☎ *(01535) 642172* Mr and Mrs Fletcher

The complete range of Timothy Taylor beers (six in all) are always on offer. A Taylor's tied house, but special in that they always stock the complete range and most pubs only stock one or two.

Traditional old coaching inn with three small rooms downstairs and a meeting room upstairs. Pool room, outside seating. No food. Well-behaved children allowed.

OPEN *12–11pm (10.30pm Sun).*

The Fox & Goose

9 Heptonstall Road, Hebden Bridge, West Yorkshire HX7 6AZ
☎ *(01422) 842649* Robin Starbuck

Goose Eye Bitter always available plus three guest beers (400 per year) including Exmoor Gold, Old Mill Bitter, Fuller's London Pride and Orkney Dark Island.

A small, friendly three-roomed pub with a wide variety of customers. Foreign bottled beers also stocked. Bar food is available at lunchtime and evenings. Garden. Children allowed. Off the A646.

OPEN *11.30am–3pm and 7–11pm.*

The Golden Lion Inn

Main Street, Helperby, York, North Yorkshire YO61 2NT
☎ *(01423) 360870*
Pippa and Richard Heather

A freehouse with four guest beers always available, including premium and strong beers for adventurous drinkers!

A traditional village country inn with stone floor and two log fires. Bar food always available. Home-cooked meals and 'nibbles' menu available weekends and weekday evenings (except Mon–Tues). A warm welcome for all, including families.

OPEN *12–11pm (10.30pm Sun).*

The Farmer's Arms

2–4 Liphill Bank Road, Holmfirth, West Yorkshire HD7 1LG
☎ *(01484) 683713* Mr Drummond

Six beers always available including Black Sheep Bitter. Guests might include Black Sheep Special and Eastwood's Best Bitter.

An eighteenth-century pub. Bar food available. Parking nearby. Garden and function room. Small parties catered for. Accommodation. Children allowed. Off the A635.

OPEN *6–11pm Mon–Fri; 12–11pm Sat; 12–10.30pm Sun.*

HORBURY

Boon's

6 Queen Street, Horbury, Wakefield,
West Yorkshire WF4 6LP
☎ *(01924) 280442* John Bladen

Timothy Taylor Landlord and Clark's Bitter regularly available, with up to four guest beers often from Adnams, Orkney, Shepherd Neame, Wychwood, Elgood's, Everards, Weltons, Ushers, Thwaites, Rebellion, Nethergate, Jennings, Hoskins, Greene King, Fuller's, Daleside, Bateman or Burton Bridge.

Traditional, single-bar olde-worlde pub with patio and beer garden. Established as a pub c.1710, it retains an open fire, beams and flagged floor. Walls hung with sporting pictures. Food served 12–2pm Mon–Tues and Thurs–Sat. Children welcome in beer garden and patio only.

11am–3pm and 5–11pm Mon–Thur; 11am–11pm Fri–Sat; 12–10.30pm Sun.

The King's Arms

27 New Street, Horbury, Wakefield,
West Yorkshire WF4 6NB
☎ *(01924) 264329* Mike Davidson

A Marston's house with Pedigree, Bitter and others available, plus one guest pump regularly featuring a Banks's ale.

A one-bar village pub with wooden floors in bar area. Pool and games area. Conservatory, dining area, garden. Food currently available 5–7 pm. Children allowed.

3–11pm Mon–Thurs; 12–11pm Fri–Sat; 12–4pm and 7–10.30pm Sun.

HUDDERSFIELD

The Old Court Brewhouse

Queen Street, Huddersfield, West Yorkshire
HD1 2SL
☎ *(01484) 454035*

Four Old Court Brewery beers produced and served on the premises.

A brewpub with the brewery part raised up from the lower floor and visible from the public bar. This listed building was formerly the county court. Bar and restaurant food available at lunchtime and evenings (Mon–Sat). Metered parking, garden.

COPPERS 3.4% ABV
M'LUD 3.5% ABV
1825 4.5% ABV
MAXIMUM SENTENCE 5.5% ABV
Ring for details.

Rat & Ratchet

40 Chapel Hill, Huddersfield, West Yorkshire
HD1 3EB
☎ *(01484) 516734*

Fourteen ales at all times. Three home brews plus Adnams Best, Bateman Mild, Mansfield Old Baily, Marston's Pedigree, Timothy Taylor Landlord and several more.

The brewery opened at the Rat and Ratchet in December 1994. A popular pub with beer festivals and special events held regularly.

THE GREAT GNAWTHERN 4.0% ABV
THE GREAT ESCAPE 4.2% ABV
CRATCHET'S CHRISTMAS CRACKER 4.3% ABV
12–11pm.

HULL

The Duke of Wellington

104 Peel Street, Spring Bank, Hull, East Yorkshire
HU3 1QR
☎ *(01482) 329603* Shaun Miller

Timothy Taylor Landlord and Greene King Abbot Ale, plus between three and six guest beers, such as Jennings Cockerhoop, Morland Old Speckled Hen, Adnams Broadside, Bateman XB, Brains SA or something from Black Sheep or Robinson's.

Converted eighteenth-century cottages in traditional pub style, with bar, pool room and beer garden. Big screen TV with free bar snacks for football matches. Car park. Children welcome.

5–11.30pm Mon–Thurs; 12–11.30pm Fri–Sat; 12–10.30pm Sun.

Minerva Hotel

Nelson Street, Hull, East Yorkshire HU1 1XE
☎ *(01482) 326909* Eamon (Scotty) Scott

Timothy Taylor Landlord and one or two guest beers regularly available, often from Orkney, Aviemore, Tomintoul, Harviestoun, Broughton, Rooster's, Young's, Abbeydale, Concertina, Woodforde's or Oakham.

Traditional, nineteenth-century pub built on the banks of the River Humber and packed with maritime memorabilia. Three main bars, plus nooks and possibly the smallest snug in Britain which seats three. Large portions of home-cooked food served lunchtimes and evenings Mon–Thurs, lunchtimes only Fri–Sun. Children welcome if taking a meal. Situated at the top of Queens Street.

11am–11pm Mon–Sat; 12–10.30pm Sun.

Springbank Tavern

29 Spring Bank, Hull, East Yorkshire HU3 1AS
☎ *(01482) 581879* Mr and Mrs JF Egan

Mansfield Bitter, Riding Bitter and Riding Mild always available plus up to three guests per week including Black Dog Mild and Timothy Taylor Landlord, with the emphasis on small breweries.

A one-room alehouse with traditional games (darts and dominoes). Students and locals provide mixed clientele. Background music, but no juke box. Bar food available 12–2pm daily. Street parking, disabled facilities. Children allowed in the bar for meals. Just off the city centre.

11am–11pm Mon–Sat; 12–3pm and 7–10.30pm Sun.

Ye Olde Black Boy

150 High Street, Hull, East Yorkshire HU1 1PS
☎ *(01482) 326516* Barry Fenn

Nine guest beers served (300 per year), from Hambleton, Rooster's, Cropton, North Yorkshire and Bateman breweries.

The first Tap & Spile charter house. The original building dates back to 1331. Traditional wood-panelled walls and floors. Upstairs bar open for food at lunchtimes and on Friday and Saturday evenings. Bar food available at lunchtime and evenings. Parking. Children allowed in the upstairs bar when having food. Situated on the Old High Street, next to the River Hull.

12–3pm and 7–11pm Mon–Thurs; all day Fri–Sun.

The Wheatsheaf Inn

22 High Street, Ingleton, North Yorkshire LA6 3AD
☎ *(01524) 241275* Mr Thompson

A freehouse with Black Sheep Bitter and Special, Riggwelter and Moorhouse's Pendle Witches Brew among the beers always available.

An olde-worlde one-bar country pub with dining area and beer garden. Disabled access. Accommodation. Food available at lunchtime and evenings. Children allowed.

12–11pm (10.30pm Sun).

The Old White Bear

6 Keighley Road, Crosshills, Keighley, West Yorkshire BD20 7RN
☎ *(01535) 632115*

Two brews produced and served on the premises plus guests beers.

The owner ran the Goose Eye Brewery from 1978 to 1991 but wanted to produce a fuller beer using natural water and ingredients, so he started production in the old stables here in 1993. The pub was built in 1735 and retains its original beams. Bar and restaurant food available at lunchtime and evenings. Car park, small garden. Children allowed if kept under control.

BITTER 3.9% ABV
BARNSLEY BITTER 3.9% ABV

11.30am–3pm and 5–11pm Mon–Thurs (not Mon lunch); 11.30am–11pm Fri–Sat; 12–4pm and 7–10.30pm Sun.

The Worth Valley Inn

1 Wesley Place, Halifax Road, Keighley BD21 5BB
☎ *(01535) 603539* Kevin Sutcliffe

Castle Eden ale permanently available, plus a range of changing guest real ales.

Situated very near to the Keighley and Worth Valley railway, this is a small local with passing trade from the railway. Plans for refurbishment. Food available lunchtimes and evenings. Children allowed.

11am–11pm Mon–Sat; 12–10.30pm Sun.

The George & Dragon Hotel

17 Market Place, Kirkbymoorside, North Yorkshire YO62 6AA
☎ *(01751) 433334* Mrs E Walker

Timothy Taylor Landlord and a Black Sheep beer usually available.

Cosy, beamed bar with blazing log fire in winter, plus a collection of cricket, rugby and golf memorabilia for the sports enthusiast. Food served 12–2.15pm and 6.30–9.15pm Mon–Sat and 7–9.15pm Sun. Car park. Children welcome – there is an enclosed garden, but no other special facilities.

10am–11pm Mon–Sat; 12–10.30pm Sun.

Blind Jacks

19 Market Place, Knaresborough, North Yorkshire HG5 8AL
☎ *(01423) 869148* David Llewellyn

A traditional alehouse with five beers always available including Timothy Taylor Landlord, Village Brewer's White Boar and Bull Premium, Black Sheep Bitter and Daleside Green Grass, plus three rotating guest beers from independent breweries including Hambleton Bitter, Daleside Legover, Crompton Two Pints and Goose Eye ales.

A seventeenth-century listed building, beamed with wooden floors and lots of mirrors. Children and dogs allowed in. Parking nearby.

OPEN *5.30–11pm Mon; 4–11pm Tue–Thur; 12–11pm Fri–Sat; 12–10.30pm Sun.*

The Steam Packet Inn

Racca Green, Knottingley, West Yorkshire WF11 8AT
☎ *(01977) 677266*
Helen Mellor and Mark Spriggs

A freehouse with Kent Garden Brewery ales, plus two guests, changing every weekend, from Beartown and Wye Valley, among others.

A small-town pub with lounge bar, public bar, function room and beer garden. Currently under refurbishment. No food. Children allowed but not at the bar.

OPEN *All day, every day.*

Moorcock Inn

Langdale End, Scarborough, North Yorkshire.
☎ *(01723) 882268* Susan Mathewson

A Daleside beer and Malton Golden Chance are regularly available, plus a guest beer.

Unspoilt, two-bar country pub with hatch servery. No music or machines. Food served every lunchtime and evening during the summer; Thur–Sun evenings and Sat–Sun lunch in the winter. Well-behaved children welcome until 9pm. Situated at the Scarborough end of Forrest Drive.

OPEN *Summer: 11.30am–2.30pm and 6.30–11pm Mon–Sat; 12–3pm and 7–10.30pm; Winter: 6.30–11pm Wed–Sat; 7–10.30pm Sun (ring first to be sure).*

The City of Mabgate

45 Mabgate, Leeds, West Yorkshire LS9 7DR
☎ *(01132) 457789* Mr K Broughton

Black Sheep Bitter and Timothy Taylor Landlord among the brews always available plus up to four guests such as Fuller's London Pride or other beers from smaller breweries such as Rooster's and Durham. Beers change frequently, usually every day, the record is Eldridge Pope Royal Oak, which changed after two hours!

A town-centre pub, winner of CAMRA's Pub of the Year 1998. Two bars, non-smoking area and garden. Food available 12–2pm Mon–Fri. Children allowed until 7pm.

OPEN *12–11pm Mon–Sat; 12–4pm and 7.30–10.30pm Sun.*

The Duck & Drake

43 Kirkgate, Leeds, West Yorkshire LS2 7DR
☎ *(0113) 246 5806* Mr and Mrs Morley

Timothy Taylor Landlord always available plus six guests (300 per year) from breweries including Jennings, Clark's, Exmoor, Rooster's and Pioneer. Also real cider.

A traditional alehouse with wooden floors, coal fires, bare boards and live bands. Bar food served at lunchtime. Get to Leeds market and ask for directions.

OPEN *All day, every day.*

The Eagle Tavern

North Street, Sheepscar, Leeds, West Yorkshire LS2 1AF
☎ *(0113) 245 7146* Mr Vaughan

A Samuel Smith tied house. Old Brewery Bitter always available, plus other seasonal ales. CAMRA Yorkshire Pub of the Year 1995.

An 1826 Georgian building close to the city centre. Bar food available at lunchtime and evenings. Occasional live music. Parking. Ten minutes walk out of the city centre. B&B accommodation.

OPEN *11.30am–2.30pm and 5.30–11pm Mon–Fri; 11.30am–2.30pm and 6–11pm Sat; 12–3pm and 7–10.30pm Sun.*

The Old Vic

17 Whitecote Hill, Leeds, West Yorkshire
LS13 3LB
☎ *(0113) 256 1207 Craig Seddon*

A freehouse with Timothy Taylor Landlord and Black Sheep Bitter among the brews always available, plus four guests from breweries such as Coach House and Hambleton.

Three rooms plus a function room decorated with old Bramley photographs. Patio. Disabled access and toilets. Situated on the outskirts of town. No food. Well-behaved children allowed.

OPEN *4–11pm Mon–Thurs; 2–11pm Fri; 11am–11pm Sat; 12–3pm and 7–10.30pm Sun.*

LINTHWAITE

Sair Inn

Lane Top, Linthwaite, Huddersfield,
West Yorkshire HD7 5SG
☎ *(01484) 842370*

A dozen Linfit beers are brewed and served on the premises.

Home of the award-winning Linfit Brewery, which began production in 1982 for the Sair Inn and free trade, and increased its capacity in 1994. The pub is a traditional nineteenth-century inn with four rooms, stone floors and open fires. Parking in road, children's room.

DARK MILD 3.0% ABV
BITTER 3.7% ABV
CASCADE 4.2% ABV
GOLD MEDAL 4.2% ABV
SPECIAL 4.3% ABV
AUTUMN GOLD 4.7% ABV
ENGLISH GUINEAS STOUT 5.3% ABV
OLD ELI 5.3% ABV
LEADBOILER 6.6% ABV
ENOCH'S HAMMER 8.6% ABV

OPEN *7.30–11pm Mon–Fri; 12–11pm Sat–Sun and public holidays.*

LIVERSEDGE

The Black Bull

37 Halifax Road, Liversedge, West Yorkshire
WF15 6JR
☎ *(01924) 403779 Mr Toulson*

A freehouse with Timothy Taylor Landlord and Black Sheep Special always available, plus four guests such as Samuel Smith Old Brewery Bitter, Glentworth Light Year or a Clark's brew. Also seasonals, specials and celebration ales as available.

Two bars, beamed ceilings. Disabled access at rear. No food. Children allowed in the afternoons only. Situated out of town.

OPEN *12–4pm and 7–11pm Mon–Thurs; all day Fri; 11am–4pm and 7–11pm Sat; 12–4pm and 7–10.30pm Sun.*

The Cross Keys

283 Halifax Road, Liversedge, West Yorkshire
WF15 6NE
☎ *(01274) 873294 Paul George Stephenson*

Marston's Bitter and Pedigree regularly available.

Open-plan, community-style pub, with Sky TV and regular quiz nights. Food served Sat lunchtimes and Wed–Sat evenings. Car park.

OPEN *5–11pm Mon–Fri; 11am–11pm Sat; 12–10.30pm Sun.*

LUND

The Wellington Inn

19 The Gren, Lund, Driffield, East Yorkshire
YO25 9TE
☎ *(01377) 217294 Russell Jeffrey*

A freehouse with Timothy Taylor Landlord and Dark Mild and Black Sheep Best always available, plus one other constantly changing guest ale, usually from local Yorkshire micro-breweries.

A two-bar country village pub with three log fires, flag floors and patio. Bar food available at lunchtime and a separate restaurant is open in the evenings. Children allowed

OPEN *7–11pm only Mon; 12–3pm and 7–11pm Tues–Sat (10.30pm Sun).*

MALTON

The Kings Head

5 Market Place, Malton, North Yorkshire
YO17 7LP
☎ *(01653) 692289 Caroline Norris*

Four guest beers regularly available, which may include Ruddles County, Marston's Pedigree or Morland Old Speckled Hen.

Traditional-style pub with lounge bar and tap room. A la carte menu and sandwiches available 12–2.30pm and 7–9pm Tues–Sat, and 12–2.30pm Sun. Car park opposite pub. No children.

OPEN *11am–3pm and 7–11pm Mon–Sat; 12–3pm and 7–10.30pm Sun.*

Suddaby's Crown Hotel

Wheelgate, Malton, North Yorkshire YO17 7HP
☎ *(01653) 697580* RN Suddaby

Malton Pale Ale, Double Chance, Pickwick's Porter, Crown Bitter, Dogbreath and Owd Bob available plus guests.

The Malton Brewery Company was formed in 1984 in the converted stables behind Suddaby's Crown Hotel. The first pint was pulled in February 1985. The pub is a traditional inn, full of character and located in the town centre. It is popular with locals and visitors alike. No background music or juke box, but pub games and TV showing the latest starting prices for the day's horse racing meetings. Bar food served lunchtimes Fri–Sat. Sandwiches available Mon–Thurs lunchtimes. Parking, children's room. Accommodation.

PALE ALE 3.3% ABV
Hoppy and refreshing.
DOUBLE CHANCE BITTER 3.8% ABV
Fruity with good hoppy bitterness.
PICKWICK'S PORTER 4.2% ABV
Dark, smooth and malty.
CROWN BITTER 4.5% ABV
Smooth, with balanced flavours.
DOGBREATH 4.9% ABV
Mid-brown balanced beer with a hoppy, bitter finish.
OWD BOB 6.0% ABV
A winter special.

11am–11pm Mon–Sat; 12–4pm and 7–10.30pm Sun.

MEXBOROUGH

The Falcon

12 Main Street, Mexborough, South Yorkshire S64 9DW
☎ *(01709) 513084* Mr Seedring

Old Mill Bitter always available plus several seasonal, celebration or guest ales.

A traditional brewery tap room situated out of the town centre. No food. No children.

All day Mon–Sat; 12–3pm and 7–10.30pm Sun.

MIDDLESBROUGH

Doctor Browns

135 Corporation Road, Middlesbrough, North Yorkshire TS1 2RR
☎ *(01642) 213213* Tony Linklater

Black Sheep Best Bitter and Special Strong Bitter always available plus many guest beers. Everards Tiger and Bateman XXXB are regular features, as are a range of seasonal ales.

Live music at weekends and a quiz every Monday night. Food available 12–2pm and summer evenings 5–8pm. Disabled facilities.

12–11pm (10.30pm Sun).

The Isaac Wilson

61 Wilson Street, Middlesbrough, North Yorkshire TS1 1SB
☎ *(01642) 247708* Norma Hardisty

Up to six guests, with Timothy Taylor Landlord a regular feature.

A town pub with food available 11am–10pm daily. No music or TV. Non-smoking area, disabled access. No children.

All day, every day.

NORTH DUFFIELD

The King's Arms

Main Street, North Duffield, Selby, North Yorkshire YO8 5RG
☎ *(01757) 288492* Martin Lamb

A freehouse with Black Sheep Bitter always available plus up to three guests such as Timothy Taylor Landlord or ales from Greene King, Adnams or local independent brewers.

A village pub with one bar, beamed ceilings and inglenook fireplace. Bar food available, plus restaurant menu in non-smoking restaurant during evenings only. Children allowed. Beer garden.

4–11pm Mon–Fri; all day Sat–Sun.

NORTH HOWDEN

Barnes Wallis Inn
Station Road, North Howden, Nr Goole,
East Yorkshire DN14 7LF
☎ *(01430) 430639* Philip Teare

Hambleton Best Bitter and Black Sheep Best Bitter regularly served, with a constantly changing range of three guest beers which are rarely repeated unless requested. Previous beers have been from Black Dog, Whitby, Kitchen, York, Brown Cow, Selby, Malton, Cropton, Marston Moor, Eccleshall, Rooster's and many more.

Traditional, small, real ale house with a permanent exhibition of Barnes Wallis (and other) prints. Large main garden and small sheltered one. Barbecue. Food available 12–2pm Tues–Sun and 7–9pm Fri–Sat. Large car park. Children welcome, but no special facilities. Situated adjacent to railway station.

7–11pm Mon; 12–2pm and 5–11pm Tues–Fri; 12–11pm Sat; 12–10.30pm Sun.

NORTHALLERTON

The Tanner Hop
2 Friarage Street, Northallerton, North Yorkshire DL6 1DP
☎ *(0160) 977 8482* Brian Simpson

Four guest ales always available. Two beer festivals held each year, each offering 12 different brews.

A very busy, lively town freehouse built in a converted furniture warehouse. All wooden floors, old wooden chairs and empty beer barrels. Jenga games available. Live music. Bar snacks available. Function room with catering for parties. Children allowed.

7–11pm Mon–Wed; 7–12pm Thurs; 7pm–1am Fri; 2pm–1am Sat; 12–10.30pm Sun.

OLD MIXENDEN

The Hebble Brook
2 Mill Lane, Old Mixenden, Halifax,
West Yorkshire HX2 8UH
☎ *(01422) 242059* Teresa Ratcliffe

Black Sheep Special always available plus Old Mill Nellie Dean most of the time. Also up to five guests such as Thwaites Bloomin' Ale and Daniels Hammer or Banbury Old Vic.

A country community pub with lounge and games room. Stone floors in the games room, open fires, wooden ceilings in lounge, garden. Food currently available at lunchtime. No children.

12–3pm and 5.30–11pm Mon–Thurs; all day Fri–Sun.

OSSETT

The Brewer's Pride
Low Mill Road, Healey Road, Ossett,
West Yorkshire WF5 8ND
☎ *(01924) 273865* Sally Walker

A brewpub, home of the Ossett Brewing Company. Excelsior and Special Bitter always available as well as Timothy Taylor Landlord. Also up to four guests from breweries such as Durham, Morland, Coach House and Cottage.

A traditional real ale house in an old stone building in the old Healy Mills area. No music, etc. Open fires, beer garden. The Ossett Brewing Co. is on site with brewery tours available. Food available 12–2pm Mon–Sat; and Wednesday evenings. Children allowed up to 8pm.

12–3pm and 5.30–11pm Mon–Thurs; all day Fri–Sun and bank holidays

PONTEFRACT

The Counting House
Swales Yard, Pontefract, West Yorkshire WF8 1DG
☎ *(01977) 600388* Louise Horner

No permanent beers, just a changing range of up to eight ales from breweries such as Black Sheep, Jennings, Old Mill and Four Rivers.

A town pub on two levels in a medieval building. Food available at lunchtime only. Children allowed.

11am–3pm and 7–11pm (10.30pm Sun).

The Tap & Spile
28 Horsefair, Pontefract, West Yorkshire WF8 1NX
☎ *(01977) 793468* Marcus Bonam

Jennings Cumberland Ale always available, plus a changing range of up to nine guests.

Two beer festivals per year, usually in May and November. Situated opposite Pontefract bus station.

12–11pm Mon–Sat; 12–3pm and 7–10.30pm Sun.

POOL-IN-WHARFEDALE

The Hunter's Inn

Harrogate Road, Pool-in-Wharfedale, Nr Otley,
North Yorkshire LS21 2PS
☎ *(0113) 284 1090* Geoff Nunn

Seven guest beers always available (300+ per year), including brews from Abbeydale, Black Sheep, Cropton, Daleside, Durham, Enville, Everards, Fuller's, Goose Eye, Hook Norton, Sarah Hughes, Jennings, Kelham Island, Moorhouse's, Oakham, Greene King, Rooster's, Outlaw, Ossett, Rudgate, Slaters (Eccleshall), Hambleton, Black Dog, Marston Moor and many others from all over the country.

Pub with real ale, real fire and real characters, from bikers to business people. Warm, friendly welcome. Bar food available 12–2.30pm every day except Tuesdays. Car park, garden patio with tables and chairs, pool table, juke box, stone fireplace. Children are allowed but not encouraged too much (no play area). One mile from Pool-in-Wharfedale, on the Harrogate road. Seven miles from Harrogate.

OPEN *All day, every day.*

PUDSEY

The Commercial Hotel

48 Chapetown, Pudsey, West Yorkshire LS28 8BS
☎ *(0113) 2577153* Michelle Farr

A freehouse serving a range of real ales.

A lively town pub with Friday evening disco, Saturday evening '60s and '70s music and live entertainment once a month. Free dripping and black pudding on the bar on Sundays. Patio. No children.

OPEN *All day, every day.*

RIPON

One Eyed Rat

51 Allhallowgate, Ripon, North Yorkshire
HG4 1LQ
☎ *(01765) 607704*

Timothy Taylor Landlord and Black Sheep Bitter always available, plus four guests, constantly changing, which may be from Rooster's, Durham, Hambledon, Fuller's or any other independent brewery. No beers from national breweries served. A real freehouse.

Unspoilt, terraced pub, very popular. Superb beer garden. No food, no music, no TV, but fine ales and good conversation. Children allowed in beer garden only.

OPEN *6–11pm Mon–Wed; 12–2pm and 6–11pm Thur–Fri; 12–3pm and 6–11pm Sat; 12–3pm Sun.*

RIPPONDEN

The Old Bridge Inn

Priest Lane, Ripponden, Sowerby Bridge,
West Yorkshire HX6 4DF
☎ *(01422) 822595*
Ian Beaumont and Timothy Walker

Moorhouse's Premier, Black Sheep Best Bitter, Timothy Taylor Golden Best, Best Bitter and Landlord regularly available, plus a guest beer which might be from Kitchen, Old Mill, Burton Bridge, Joseph Holt, Fuller's, St Austell or Gale's.

Historic pub in lovely riverside setting which has been in the same ownership since 1963. Open fires in winter and flowers in summer. Award-winning window boxes and hanging baskets all year round. Full bar menu available every lunchtime and snacks weekday evenings but no food Sat–Sun evenings. Car park. Children welcome until 8.30pm.

OPEN *12–3pm and 5.30–11pm Mon–Fri; 12–11pm Sat; 12–10.30pm Sun.*

ROTHERHAM

Limes

38 Broom Lane, Rotherham, South Yorkshire
☎ *(01709) 363431* E.Daykin

Camerons Strongarm, plus Banks's Bitter and Original regularly available.

This is a popular hotel situated on the outskirts of the town centre with a small hotel atmosphere. Food served all day, every day. Car park. Children welcome, but no special facilities.

OPEN *11am–11pm Mon–Sat; 12–10.30pm Sun.*

SCARBOROUGH

The Highlander

15–16 The Esplanade, Scarborough,
North Yorkshire YO11 2AF
☎ *(01723) 373426* Mrs Dawson

Young's IPA among the brews always available, plus up to five guests such as Barnsley Bitter, Black Dog Whitby Abbey Ale, Wyre Piddle Piddle in the Wind, Wychwood Dog's Bollocks and Fisherman's Whopper. Also a good selection of whiskies.

On the South Cliff Esplanade, a traditional pub with real fires. Food available at lunchtime only in a separate dining area. Children allowed until 6pm. Patio. Accommodation.

OPEN *11am–11pm (10.30pm Sun).*

The Hole in the Wall

26 Vernon Road, Scarborough, North Yorkshire YO11 2NH
☎ *(01723) 373746* Ann Pearson

A freehouse with Shepherd Neame Master Brew, Fuller's ESB and one Durham brewery beer always available, plus a constantly changing range of guests such as Timothy Taylor Landlord and ales from across the country – Orkneys to Cornwall – served as available. Some 2500 beers served over 18 years.

A traditional wooden-floored real ale pub in a town location. No music, no games. Food available at lunchtime only. No children. Dogs welcome.

OPEN *11.30am–2.30pm and 7–11pm Mon–Fri; 11.30am–3pm and 7–11pm Sat; 12–3pm and 7–10.30pm Sun.*

Indigo Alley

4 North Marine Road, Scarborough, North Yorkshire YO12 7PD
☎ *(01723) 381900* Graham Forrest

Six regularly changing guest beers perhaps from Rooster's, Timothy Taylor, Kelham Island, Swale, Hambleton and many more. Over 300 different ones in nine months.

Basic, town-centre pub specialising in ever-changing guest beers and live music on Tues, Wed, Thurs and Sun evenings. No food. No children.

OPEN *12–11pm (10.30pm Sun). Extra hours Fri–Sun Jun–Aug.*

The Scalby Mills Hotel

Scalby Mills Road, Scarborough, North Yorkshire YO12 6RP
☎ *(01723) 500449* Julia Bennett

Daleside Monkey Wrench and Old Lubrication always available, plus a selection of guests including, perhaps, Daleside Nightjar, Barnsley Bitter, Fools Gold or Crackshot.

A seaside freehouse built in an old mill with the Cleveland Way behind it. Two bars, original stonework and beams. Outside seating. Food available at lunchtime only. Children allowed until 6pm. Dogs allowed in the smaller of the two bars. Situated near the Sealife Centre.

OPEN *All day, every day.*

The Tap & Spile

94 Falsgrave Road, Scarborough, North Yorkshire YO12 5AZ
☎ *(01723) 363837*
IM Kilpatrick and V Office

Big Lamp Bitter always available plus guest ales including Bateman, Jennings and Old Mill brews and Tap & Spile Premium. Also two guest ciders.

A lovely old coaching inn with low beams, old Yorkshire stone floor and non-smoking room. Bar food available 11.30am–3pm Mon–Fri, 11.30am–4.30pm Sat, 12.30–3pm Sun. Car park, garden, children's room. Turn left out of the railway station, going towards the roundabout.

OPEN *11am–11pm.*

SELBY

The Albion Vaults

1 The Crescent, New Street, Selby, North Yorkshire YO8 4PT
☎ *(01757) 213817* Patrick Mellors

An Old Mill Brewery tied house serving only Old Mill ales. Old Traditional and Bullion always available, plus either Old Curiosity, Spring Eternal or Nellie Dean.

An old dark-wood pub with brick fireplaces, taproom and lounge. Beer garden, disabled access. Food available at lunchtime and evenings. Organises brewery tours of The Old Mill Brewery, which is four miles away, during October–April. Children allowed up to 7pm.

OPEN *12–11pm (10.30pm Sun).*

The Royal Oak

70 Ousegate, Selby, North Yorkshire YO8 4NJ
☎ *(01757) 291163* Simon Compton

Three guest pumps with ales such as Timothy Taylor Landlord, Eccleshall Top Totty or Swale Indian Summer Pale Ale.

A real ale pub comprising a balance of the traditional and the modern: live music in a Grade II listed building with wooden floors and original beams. Beer garden. No food. Children allowed on Sunday afternoons only.

OPEN *12pm–close.*

SHEFFIELD

The Broadfield

*Abbeydale Road, Sheffield, South Yorkshire
S7 1FR*
☎ (0114) 255 0200
Hannah Creasy and Martin Bedford

Guests such as Morland Old Speckled Hen, Wadworth 6X and brews from Kelham Island and Black Sheep are served. Only popular beers, such as Kelham Island Pale Rider, are repeated, and requests are encouraged!

A two-bar pub with snooker and pool room and beer garden. Just out of the town centre. Food available 12–7pm daily, plus Sunday breakfast at 11am. Children allowed if eating.

11am–11pm Mon–Sat; 11am (for breakfast)–10.30pm Sun.

Cask & Cutler

*1 Henry Street, Infirmary Road, Sheffield,
South Yorkshire S3 7EQ*
☎ (0114) 249 2295 Neil Clarke

Seven regularly changing guest beers (3000 beers served to date), including a pale, hoppy bitter, a mild and a stout or porter. Main breweries used are Durham, Glentworth, Ossett, Tigertops, Townes and Oldershaw. No nationals. Also serve Weston's Old Rosie cider. There are plans to open a micro-brewery at the rear of the pub.

A largely unspoilt, two-roomed street-corner local. On-street parking. Real fire in cold weather. Situated 100 yards from Shalesmoor supertram stop. Adjacent to the junction of the A61 and B6079, one mile north of the city centre.

5.30–11pm Mon; 12–2pm and 5.30–11pm Tues–Thur; 12–11pm Fri–Sat; 12–3pm and 7–10.30pm Sun.

The Fat Cat

*23 Alma Street, Sheffield, South Yorkshire
S3 8SA*
☎ (0114) 249 4801

Kelham Island brews plus six guest beers, constantly alternating. In total, the pub has now served more than 3,100 guest ales.

This olde-worlde pub is a Kelham Island Brewery tap, with no music, no machines, real fires and ten real ales. It is situated in a back street near the city centre. Food served at lunchtime. Parking, garden, children's room.

12–3pm and 5.30–11pm Mon–Sat; 12–3pm and 7–10.30pm Sun.

The Frog & Parrot

Division Street, Sheffield, South Yorkshire S1 4GF
☎ (0114) 272 1280 Mr Perkins

A brewpub with a selection of own brews always available. Guests served between June and September, one at a time, such as Marston's Pedigree or a Castle Eden ale.

A one-bar town pub, a young person's venue, particularly at weekends. Bar food available at lunchtime from 12–2pm and 12" pizzas served in the evenings until 11pm. No children.

MR DOO'S 3.4% ABV
RECKLESS 4.6% ABV
ARMAGEDDON 6.2% ABV
CONQUEROR 6.9% ABV
ROGER AND OUT 12.6% ABV
Served in third-of-a-pint measures.

11am–11pm (10.30pm Sun).

Morrissey's East House

19 Spital Hill, Sheffield, South Yorkshire S4 7LG
☎ (0114) 272 6916 Rita Fielding

A freehouse with Timothy Taylor Landlord and Abbeydale Moonshine among the beers always available, plus one guest such as Morland Old Speckled Hen or Timothy Taylor Dark Mild or Golden Best.

A student pub, situated conveniently close to the local curry houses! No food. Children allowed until 8pm.

Closed during day; 6–11pm Mon–Sat; 7–10.30pm Sun.

The New Barrack Tavern

*601 Penistone Road, Sheffield, South Yorkshire
S6 2GA*
☎ (0114) 234 9148 James Birkett

Abbeydale Moonshine, Wentworth WPA, Barnsley Bitter and five guest beers usually available. Breweries featured include Abbeydale, Wentworth, Rooster's, Wye Valley, Kitchen, Kelham Island, Concertina, Swale, Osset, Rudgate, Okells, Timothy Taylor, Brakspear, Holt, Hydes' Anvil, Woodforde's, Beartown, Cains, Oakham, Skinner's, Hop Back, Daleside and many others.

Large, award-winning pub offering a wide selection of draught and bottled beers and excellent food. Regular live music. Non-smoking room and attractive beer garden. Food served 12–2.30pm and 6–8pm Mon–Fri, 12–2.30pm Sat–Sun. Children welcome in the back room and beer garden only.

12–11pm (10.30pm Sun).

The Old Grindstone
3 Crookes, Sheffield, South Yorkshire S10 1UA
☎ *(0114) 266 0322* Margaret Shaw

Up to six guest ales such as Glentworth Full Monty and Little Gem. The repeating of beers is generally avoided.

A one-bar local community pub. Food available at lunchtime and evenings. No children.

All day, every day.

SHIPLEY

Fanny's Ale & Cider House
63 Saltaire Road, Shipley, Nr Bradford, West Yorkshire
☎ *(01274) 591419* S Marcus Lund

Old Mill Bitter and Timothy Taylor Landlord regularly available, plus four guest beers such as Fuller's London Pride, Timothy Taylor Ram Tam, Black Sheep Bitter, Glentworth Whispers, Daleside Monkey Wrench, Rooster's Yankee or Cream and many others.

Olde-worlde alehouse with wooden floorboards and open fire, full of brewery memorabilia. Gas lighting still used in the lounge bar. Food served 11.30am–2pm Mon–Sat. Free car park nearby. Children welcome at lunch times only.

11am–11pm Mon–Sat; 12–10.30pm Sun.

SOWERBY BRIDGE

The Moorcock Inn
Norland, Sowerby Bridge, West Yorkshire HX6 3RP
☎ *(01422) 832103* Mr Kitson

A freehouse with Samuel Smith Old Brewery Bitter always available plus two guest ales including, perhaps, Coach House Innkeeper's Special Reserve or Phoenix Old Oak Bitter.

A one-bar country pub with wooden beams, restaurant and outside area. Food available at lunchtime and evenings. Children allowed. Disabled access.

12–3pm and 5.30–11pm (10.30pm Sun).

The Moorings
Canal Basin, Sowerby Bridge, West Yorkshire HX6 2AG
☎ *(01422) 833940* Tony Mulgraw

Black Sheep Special among the brews always available plus three guests, often from Ossett (such as Silver King, Silver Link, Quick Silver or Silver Fox) but also from Moorhouse's and Kitchen.

A small family-run pub with good quality beers, food and service. Beams, stone walls, wooden floors. Seating on canal side. Food available at lunchtime and evenings. Children allowed.

12–11pm (10.30pm Sun).

The Navigation Inn
47 Holmes Road, Sowerby Bridge, West Yorkshire HX6 3LF
☎ *(01422) 831636* Andy Dawson

Two Tom Eastwood beers always available plus one guest such as Moorhouse's Navigation (a house brew produced especially for The Navigation Inn).

An old country village pub near a boatyard. Two bars, two gardens. Holiday cottage next door available for rent. Food available Wed–Sun lunchtime and evenings. Children allowed.

12–3pm and 4.30–11pm Mon–Thurs; all day Fri–Sun.

STAVELEY

The Royal Oak
Main Street, Staveley, Nr Knaresborough, North Yorkshire HG5 9LD
☎ *(01423) 340267*

Four beers always available plus two guests (25 per year) from small independent breweries.

A typical country pub, cosy, friendly, with open fires and two bars. Bar and restaurant food available at lunchtime and evenings (not Sunday and Monday evenings). Car park, garden, children's play area.

12–3pm and 6–11pm Mon–Sat; 12–5pm and 7–10.30pm Sun.

STOKESLEY

The White Swan
1 West End, Stokesley, Middlesbrough, North Yorkshire TS9 5BL
☎ *(01642) 710263*
June Harrison and Brian Skipp

A brewpub with the full range of Captain Cook Brewery beers brewed on site and always available in the pub. Also occasional guests such as Castle Eden Ale.

A market town pub with one bar, open fire, background music and traditional pub games. Brewery on premises, tours available. Winner of the National Ploughman's Award 1997. Ploughman's (selection of 20 cheeses), pâtés and cold pies only. No children.

11.30am–3pm and 5.30–11pm Mon–Thurs; all day Fri–Sun.

SUTTON UPON DERWENT

St Vincent Arms

Main Street, Sutton upon Derwent, East Yorkshire
☎ *(01904) 608349* Philip Hopwood

Fuller's Chiswick, London Pride and ESB and Timothy Taylor Landlord always available plus guests including Adnams Extra, Old Mill Bitter, Charles Wells Bombardier, Mansfield Old Baily and seasonal and special ales.

About 200 years old, with white-washed walls. Two bars, four rooms, open fires. Bar and restaurant food available at lunchtime and evenings. Car park, beer garden, non-smoking room. Children allowed. On main road through village.

OPEN *11.30am–3pm and 6–11pm Mon–Sat; 12–3pm and 7–10.30pm Sun.*

THORNE

Canal Tavern

South Parade, Thorne, Doncaster, South Yorkshire DN8 5DZ
☎ *(01405) 813688* Mr Murrigton

A freehouse with one guest ale changing weekly and not repeated if at all possible. Examples have included Thwaites Bloomin' Ale, Greene King Triumph and Marston's Pedigree.

A two-bar canalside country pub with dining area. Coal fires in winter, waterside beer garden. Food available at lunchtime and evenings. Children allowed, if eating.

OPEN *11am–3pm and 5.30–11pm Mon–Fri; all day Sat–Sun.*

THORNTON-IN-LONSDALE

The Marton Arms

Thornton-in-Lonsdale, Near Ingleton, North Yorkshire LA6 3PB
☎ *(01524) 241281* Colin Elsdon

Fifteen real ales always on offer with Black Sheep Bitter, Black Sheep Special, Dent Bitter, Dent T'Owd Tup, Timothy Taylor Golden Best, Oakhill Best Bitter and Oakhill Mendip Gold as permanent fixtures plus guests from breweries such as Bateman, Hart, Jennings, Robinson's, Arundel, Hampshire, Ash Vine and Shepherd Neame to name but a few. Over the last ten years in excess of 1000 beers from over 250 different breweries have been sold.

Dating from the twelfth century, this old coaching inn is steeped in history. Cask Marque approved. Food available all opening hours. Well-behaved children allowed. Over 200 malt whiskies. En-suite accommodation. Situated one mile north of Ingleton off A65, close to junction of A786/A65. See our website at www.martonarms.co.uk

OPEN *Lunchtimes June–Sept only; otherwise 6–11pm Mon–Fri; all day Sat–Sun.*

THRESHFIELD

Old Hall Inn

Threshfield, Grassington, Skipton, North Yorkshire
☎ *(01756) 752441* Ronald C Matthews

Timothy Taylor Best Bitter and Landlord regularly available.

Traditional country pub with dining room, patio and beer garden. Food served 12–2pm and 6–9.30pm daily. Car park. Children welcome.

OPEN *12–3pm and 6–11.30pm Mon–Sat; 12–3pm and 7–10.30pm Sun.*

TOCKWITH

The Spotted Ox

Westfield Road, Tockwith, York, North Yorkshire YO26 7PY
☎ *(01423) 358387* James Ray

A freehouse with a selection of three cask ales always available, constantly changing.

A country pub with three bars decorated with the pump clips of past beers sold. Food available at lunchtime and evenings. Beer garden. Children allowed.

OPEN *All day in summer; in winter 11am–3pm and 5.30–11pm Mon–Thurs; all day Fri–Sun.*

WAKEFIELD

The Talbot & Falcon

58 Northgate, Wakefield, West Yorkshire WF1 3AP
☎ *(01924) 201693* Glen Plunkett

Marston's Pedigree and Timothy Taylor Landlord always available plus a range of guest ales such as Hop Back Summer Lightning, Badger Tanglefoot and something form Broughton and Tomintoul. Also specials from breweries such as Leatherbritches and Malcolm's of Grimsby when available. Beer Festivals held four to six times a year.

A traditional town-centre pub under refurbishment. Plans for dining area. Disabled access. Food available 12–7pm. Children allowed. Located by the bus station.

OPEN *11am–11pm (10.30pm Sun).*

The White Hart

*77 Westgate End, Wakefield, West Yorkshire
WF2 9RL*
☎ *(01924) 375887*
Debbie Chetwood and David Hobson

Six real ales always available from a wide range of independent breweries. Beers changed weekly.

A traditional alehouse with flagstone floors and real log fires in winter. All-year-round beer garden, which is covered and heated in winter. Free supper served on Tuesdays, Wednesdays and Sundays. Well-behaved children allowed.

OPEN *12–11pm (10.30pm Sun).*

The Cross Keys Inn

*649 Rochdale Road, Walsden, Todmorden,
West Yorkshire*
☎ *(01706) 815185* Ken Muir

Timothy Taylor Landlord, Black Sheep Bitter, Charles Wells Bombardier and three weekly changing guest beers usually available.

L ively pub, set on the side of the Rochdale Canal. Food served 12–2pm and 5–8pm Mon–Sat, 12–8pm Sun. Children welcome.

OPEN *12–11pm (10.30pm Sun).*

Star Country Inn

*Weaverthorpe, Malton, North Yorkshire
YO17 8EY*
☎ *(01944) 738273*
Susan and David Richardson

Camerons Bitter permanently available, plus two guest beers often from Hambleton, Durham, Eccleshall, Rooster's or Ash Vine.

T raditional country inn, well-known locally for good food. Food served 7–9pm Wed–Mon and 12–2pm Sat–Sun. Car park. Children welcome, but no special facilities. Accommodation. For further information, visit the web site at www.thestarinn.net

OPEN *7–11pm Mon–Fri; 12–4pm and 7–11pm Sat; 12–4pm and 7–10.30pm Sun.*

The George & Dragon

*85 Main Street, Wentworth, Rotherham,
South Yorkshire S62 7TN*
☎ *(01226) 742440* Gary and John Sweeting

A freehouse always serving Timothy Taylor Landlord, plus a good selection of guests, not repeated if possible, from breweries such as Ossett, Glentworth and Oakham.

A country village pub with two bars, two real fires and stone floors. Breakfast served 10am–12pm; lunch served 12–2.30pm and evening meals served 5.30–9pm in a separate dining area. Large beer garden with children's playground. Children allowed if eating.

OPEN *10am–11pm (10.30pm Sun).*

The Duke of York

*Church Street, Whitby, North Yorkshire
YO22 4DE*
☎ *(01947) 600324* Laurie Bradley

Whitby's Black Dog Special often available plus two guests such as Timothy Taylor Landlord and Adnams Regatta.

A seafaring pub, a mix of the traditional and the modern, with oak beams and modern decor. Food available 12–9pm. Children allowed.

OPEN *All day, every day.*

Tap & Spile

*New Quay Road, Whitby, North Yorkshire
YO21 1DH*
☎ *(01947) 603937* Mr Fleming

Mansfield Tap & Spile always available, plus four guests such as Daleside Country Style and Four Rivers Moondance. Around 450 beers served in the past five years. Celebration and seasonal ales where possible.

A three-roomed town pub with two bars, wooden floors and beams and one non-smoking room. Food available every day from 12pm. Children allowed in designated area. Entertainment most nights (generally Folk music and Irish bands, Blues on Wednesday). Located by the railway station.

OPEN *All day, every day.*

WOMBWELL

Royal Oak Hotel

13 Burch Street, Wombwell, South Yorkshire
☎ *(01254) 883541* Helen Jones

Five real ales available from a long list including Brewery on Sea Spinnaker Bitter and Bateman brews.

A 1920s-style town-centre pub. Bar food available at lunchtime and evenings. Car park, accommodation. Children allowed at restricted times.

OPEN *11am–11pm Mon–Sat; 12–10.30pm Sun.*

WORTLEY

Wortley Arms Hotel

Halifax Road, Wortley, South Yorkshire S35 7DB
☎ *(0114) 288 2245* Brian Morrisey

Timothy Taylor Landlord and Dark Mild, Wortley Bitter and Oakwell Barnsley Bitter always available, plus a range of guests.

A classic sixteenth-century coaching inn with inglenook fireplace. No background music, no gaming machines. Food served lunchtimes and evenings and all day Fri–Sun. Soup and a roll, plus tea and coffee, available all day, every day. Car park, children's room, non-smoking room. En-suite accommodation. Popular with walkers and cyclists on Trans-Pennine and Timberland trails.

OPEN *11am–11pm (10.30pm Sun).*

YORK

The Blue Bell

53 Fossgate, York, North Yorkshire YO1 9TF
☎ *(0190) 465 4904* Mr T Worrall

Marston's Pedigree always available, plus up to five constantly changing guest ales.

The smallest pub in York with the oldest pub interior in York (last decorated in 1903). Two small rooms with bar in between and drinking corridor. Lookalike real fires! Sandwiches available until 4pm Mon–Sat. No children.

OPEN *12–11pm (10.30pm Sun).*

The Maltings

Tanners Moat, York, North Yorkshire YO1 16HU
☎ *(01904) 655387* Maxine Collinge

Black Sheep Bitter always available plus six guests changing daily (700 per year). Too many to mention but with an emphasis on small, independent brewers. Beer festivals twice a year. Also Belgian bottled and draught beers, fruit wines and four traditional ciders.

S mall city-centre freehouse. CAMRA Yorkshire Pub of the Year 1994–95 and Cask Ale Pub of Great Britain 1998. Pub grub served at lunchtime. Situated on Lendal Bridge. Further information available on website www.maltings.co.uk

OPEN *11am–11pm Mon–Sat; 12–10.30pm Sun.*

Spread Eagle

98 Walmgate, York, North Yorkshire
☎ *(01904) 635868* Michael Dandy

Seven or eight beers always available. Guests including Mansfield Riding Bitter and Old Baily and Timothy Taylor Landlord.

P opular Victorian-style freehouse. Bar and restaurant food available at lunchtime and evenings. Garden. Children allowed.

OPEN *11am–11pm Mon–Sat; 12–10.30pm Sun.*

The Tap & Spile

29 Monkgate, York, North Yorkshire
☎ *(01904) 656158* Andy Mackay

Eight cask ales always available, usually including a beer from Black Sheep, Big Lamp or Rooster's. Traditional ciders and a range of fruit wines also served.

A traditional alehouse, with bar food and full menu available at lunchtimes only, plus traditional roasts on Sundays. Car park, beer garden. Evening Press Pub of the Year 1999 and local CAMRA Pub of the Season, Spring 2000.

OPEN *11.30am–11.30pm Mon–Sat; 12–10.30pm Sun.*

YOU TELL US

★ *Beer Street*, Nowell's Yard, Dewsbury
★ *The Black Horse Inn*, The Green, Altwick
★ *The Brewer's Arms*, 10 Pontefract Road, Snaith
★ *The Concertina Band Club*, 9a Dolcliffe Road, Mexborough
★ *The Crown*, Main Street, Dishforth
★ *The Elm Tree*, 5 Elm Tree Square, Embsay
★ *The Fleece*, Ripponden Bank, Barkisland, Ripponden
★ *George & the Dragon*, Main Street, Melmerby
★ *Hill Inn*, Chapel-le-Dale
★ *The Keighley & Worth Railway Buffet Car*, The Station, Keighley
★ *Keystones*, 4 Monkgate, York
★ *The Kirklands Hotel*, 605 Leeds Road, Outwood

★ *The Lord Rosebery*, 85–7 Westborough, Scarborough
★ *The Lundhill Tavern*, Beechhouse Road, Hemingfield
★ *The Midhopestones Arms*, Mortimer Road, Midhopestones
★ *Milestone*, 12 Peaks Mount, Waterthorpe, Sheffield
★ *The Mission*, Posterngate, Hull
★ *The Packhorse Hotel*, Carr Lane, Laithwaite
★ *The Queen's Head*, Wednesday Market, Beverley
★ *The Station Hotel*, Knott Lane, Easingwold
★ *The Tap & Spile*, Flemingate, Beverley
★ *The Tap & Spile*, 26 Sackville Street, Bradford
★ *The Tap & Spile*, Spring Bank, Hull
★ *The Tap & Spile*, High Street, Northallerton
★ *The Waggon & Horses*, 48 Gillygate, York
★ *The Zetland Hotel*, 9 High Street, Marske

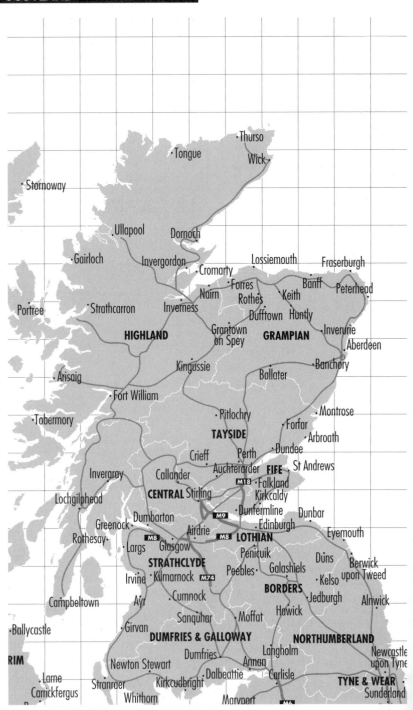

ARRAN BREWERY
Cladach, Brodick, Isle of Arran
☎ *(01770) 302353*

 ALE 3.8% ABV
DARK 4.3% ABV
BLONDE 5.0% ABV

AVIEMORE BREWERY CO. LTD
Unit 12, Dalfaber Industrial Estate, Aviemore PH22 1PY
☎ *(01479) 812060 (Brewery tours)*

 HIGHLAND IPA 3.6% ABV
Refreshing and hoppy.
RUTHVEN BREW 3.8% ABV
Copper-coloured and malty with delicate bitterness.
STRATHSPEY 4.2% ABV
Dark, hoppy and complex.
WOLFE'S BREW 4.6% ABV
Dark and well-balanced.
WEE MURDOCH 4.8% ABV
Powerful malt flavour with some hoppiness.
CAIRNGORM 5.0% ABV
Golden, refreshing and far too easy to drink.

BELHAVEN BREWERY CO.
Spott Road, Dunbar EH42 1RS
☎ *(01368) 862734*

 60/- 2.9% ABV
Roast character with smooth malty palate.
70/- 3.5% ABV
Nutty with a light sweet finish.
SANDY HUNTER'S TRADITONAL ALE 3.6% ABV
Malty and nutty palate with hoppy nose and flavour.
IPA 4.0% ABV
80/- 4.2% ABV
Malty and nutty.
ST ANDREW'S ALE 4.9% ABV
Well-balanced and distinctive with dry after-palate.
90/- 8.0% ABV
Smooth and rounded.
Plus seasonal brews.

BLACK ISLE BREWERY
Taeblair, Munlochy IV8 8NZ
☎ *(01463) 811871*

 GOLDEN EAGLE 3.6% ABV
Seasonal brew.
RED KITE 4.2% ABV
YELLOW HAMMER 4.3% ABV
Seasonal brew.
WAGTAIL 4.5% ABV
Seasonal porter.

BRIDGE OF ALLAN BREWERY
Queen's Lane, Bridge of Allan, Stirling SK9 4HD
☎ *(01786) 834555*

 STIRLING DARK MILD 3.2% ABV
STIRLING BITTER 3.7% ABV
STIRLING BRIG 4.1% ABV
BANNOCKBURN 4.2% ABV
STIRLING IPA 4.2% ABV
Plus seasonal ales.

BROUGHTON ALES LTD
Broughton ML12 6HQ
☎ *(01899) 830345 (Brewery tours)*

 GREENMANTLE ALE 3.9% ABV
Maltiness, with bittersweet flavour, and hoppy finish.
SPECIAL BITTER 3.9% ABV
As above, but dry-hopped.
CLIPPER IPA 4.2% ABV
DISCOVERY ALE 4.2% ABV
MERLIN'S ALE 4.2% ABV
Gold-coloured, with dry hop flavour combined with malt.
SCOTTISH OATMEAL STOUT 4.2% ABV
Powerful, malty flavour and hoppy bitterness.
80/- 4.2% ABV
THE GHILLIE 4.5% ABV
Hoppy fruit flavours throughout.
BLACK DOUGLAS 5.2% ABV
Dark and malty.
OLD JOCK 6.7% ABV
Dark copper-coloured, with fruit and roast flavours.

BURNTISLAND BREWING CO.
Burntisland Brewery, High Street, Burntisland KY3 9AA
☎ *(01592) 873333*

 BLESSING OF BURNTISLAND 3.8% ABV
ALEXANDER'S DOWNFALL 4.3% ABV
DOCKYARD RIVETS 5.1% ABV
Excellent, lager style.

CALEDONIAN BREWING CO.
42 Slateford Road, Edinburgh EH11 1PH
☎ *(0131) 3371286 (Brewery tours)*

DEUCHARS IPA 3.8% ABV
Pale, well-hopped and refreshing. Ever-popular.
80/- 4.1% ABV
Golden, full-flavoured award winner.
GOLDEN PROMISE 5.0% ABV
Light-coloured, hoppy organic beer.
Plus monthly special brews.

FISHERROW BREWERY

Unit 12, Duddingston Yards, Duddingston Park
South, Edinburgh EH15 3NX
☎ *(0131) 621 5501*

 INDIA PALE ALE 3.8% ABV
Golden, refreshing and full-bodied for
gravity.

GOLDEN HEAVY 4.0% ABV
Pale and malty with delicate hoppy aftertaste.

BURGH BITTER 4.2% ABV
Golden and refreshing with some sweetness.

NUT BROWN ALE 4.8% ABV
Full-flavoured, traditional brown ale.

EXPORT PALE ALE 5.2% ABV
Pale, refreshing easy-quaffer.
Plus monthly brews.

HARVIESTOUN BREWERY LTD

Devon Road, Dollar FK14 7LX
☎ *(01259) 742141*

 WEE STOATER 3.6% ABV
BROOKER'S BITTER & TWISTED 3.8% ABV
Blond with refreshing citrus fruit
flavours.

TURNPIKE 4.1% ABV

PTARMIGAN 4.5% ABV
Pale, with Bavarian hops.

SCHIEHALLION 4.8% ABV
Superb, real cask lager.
Plus seasonal and occasional brews.

HEATHER ALE CRAIGMILL BREWERY

Craigmill, Strathaven ML10 6PB
☎ *(01357) 529529*

 PALEY ALEY 3.9% ABV
FRAOCH 4.1% ABV
Heather ale – available all year.

KELPIE 4.4% ABV
Brewed with seaweed.

GROZET 5.0% ABV
Gooseberry wheat beer – available Aug–Nov.

PICTISH 5.3% ABV
Heather ale – available Dec–Mar.

EBULUM 6.5% ABV
Elderberry black – available Oct–Jan

THE INVERALMOND BREWERY

Inveralmond Way, Inveralmond, Perth PH1 3UQ
☎ *(01738) 449448*

 INDEPENDENCE 3.8% ABV
Well-balanced malt and hops with some
spiciness.

OSSIAN'S ALE 4.1% ABV
Golden and hoppy.

THRAPPLEDOUSER 4.3% ABV
Amber, quenching with good hoppiness.

LIA FAIL 4.7% ABV
Smooth, dark and full-flavoured.

THE ISLE OF SKYE BREWING CO. (LEANN AN EILEIN) LTD

Uig IV51 9XY
☎ *(01470) 542477 (Brewery tours)*

 YOUNG PRETENDER 4.0% ABV
Gold-coloured and lightly hopped with
dry finish.

RED CUILLIN 4.2% ABV
Slightly malty, with some fruit and hoppy finish.

HEBRIDEAN GOLD 4.3% ABV
Smooth with good hoppy bitterness.

BLACK CUILLIN 4.5% ABV
Stout-like, with hints of chocolate and honey.

BLAVEN 5.0% ABV
Golden, fruity and well-balanced.

MOULIN BREWERY

11–13 Kirkmichael Road, Moulin, Nr Pitlochry,
Perthshire PH16 5EW
☎ *(01796) 472196*

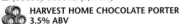 **MOULIN LIGHT ALE 3.7% ABV**
BRAVEHEART 4.0% ABV
ALE OF ATHOL 4.5% ABV
OLD REMEDIAL 5.2% ABV

THE ORKNEY BREWERY

Quoyloo, Sandwick KW16 3LT
☎ *(01856) 841802 (B/tours)*

 HARVEST HOME CHOCOLATE PORTER
3.5% ABV

NORTHERN LIGHT 3.8% ABV
Golden, refreshing and mellow.

RAVEN ALE 3.8% ABV
Superb malt, hop, citrus fruit flavours and
nuttiness.

DRAGONHEAD STOUT 4.0% ABV
Black, powerful roast maltiness, with nutty
flavours.

THE RED MACGREGOR 4.0% ABV
Mellow and malty with nut and hoppy finish.

DARK ISLAND 4.6% ABV
Smooth, flavour-packed and easy to drink.

SKULLSPLITTER 8.5% ABV
Beautifully smooth and hoppy with dry finish.

SULWATH BREWERS LTD

The Brewery, King Street, Castle Douglas
DG7 1DT
☎ *(01556) 504525*

CUIL HILL 3.6% ABV
Pale amber, and bursting with fresh malt
and hops.

HAWKHILL BEST 3.8% ABV
Traditional-style, occasional brew.

JOHN PAUL JONES 4.0% ABV
Malty occasional brew.

CRIFFEL 4.6% ABV
Rounded malt and hop flavours with delicate
bitterness.

KNOCKENDOCH 5.0% ABV
Deep roast malt flavour and hoppy aftertaste.
Plus occasional brews.

TOMINTOUL BREWERY
Mill of Auchriachan, Tomintoul, Ballindalloch AB37 9EQ
☎ *(01807) 580333*

STAG 4.1% ABV
Hoppy with balancing, soft maltiness.
NESSIE'S MONSTER MASH 4.4% ABV
Rounded, with malt flavours.
WILD CAT 5.1% ABV
Complex malt and fruit, with powerful hoppiness.

TRAQUAIR HOUSE BREWERY
Traquair Estate, Innerleithen EH44 6PW
☎ *(01896) 831370 (B/tours)*

STUART 4.5% ABV
Summer brew.
BEAR ALE 5.0% ABV
Full-bodied and fruity with good dryness in the hoppy finish.

VALHALLA BREWERY
New House, Baltasound, Unst ZE2 9DX
☎ *(01957) 711348*

SUMMER DIM 4.0% ABV
AULD ROCK 4.5% ABV
Smooth, malty and full-bodied robust hoppiness.
WHITE WIFE 4.8% ABV

Places Featured:

Allanton
Auchencrow
Bonchester Bridge
Denholm
Eyemouth
Galashiels

Greenlaw
Innerleithen
Newcastleton
Peebles
St Mary's Loch

THE PUBS

ALLANTON

The Allanton Inn
Allanton, Duns, Berwickshire TD11 3JZ
☎ *(01890) 818260* John Ward

A freehouse with four pumps offering a range that changes weekly. Ales from Northumberland, Border and Belhaven breweries are all popular.

A country inn with pool, darts and a juke box. Restaurant, en suite bed and breakfast. Food at lunchtime and evenings. Children allowed. Signposted.

OPEN *12–2.30pm Mon–Fri; 6–11pm Mon–Wed; 6pm–12am Thurs; 6pm–1am Fri, all day Sat–Sun.*

AUCHENCROW

The Craw Inn
Auchencrow, Berwickshire
☎ *(018907) 61253* Trevor Wilson

Caledonian Deuchars IPA plus a regularly changing guest, perhaps from Orkney, Caledonian or other Scottish and small English regional breweries.

Family-run, eighteenth-century, listed country inn in small, attractive Borders village. Bar and restaurant food served 12.30–2.30pm and 7–9.30pm daily. Car park. Children welcome. En-suite accommodation.

OPEN *12–2.30pm and 6–11pm Mon–Thurs; 12–12 Fri–Sat; 12.30–11pm Sun.*

BONCHESTER BRIDGE

Horse & Hound Hotel

Bonchester Bridge, Hawick TD9 8JN
☎ *(01450) 860645* Mr and Mrs Hope

Maclay, Charles Wells and Border brews always available plus a guest beer (20 per year) perhaps from Longstone, Bateman, Jennings, Caledonian, Belhaven or Holt breweries.

A former coaching inn dating from 1704 with comfortable accommodation and non-smoking areas. Bar and restaurant food is available at lunchtime and evenings. Car park. Children's certificate. Hawick is seven miles from Carter Bar on the England–Scotland border.

OPEN *11.30am–3pm and 6–11pm.*

DENHOLM

Auld Cross Keys Inn

Main Street, Denholm, Roxburghshire TD9 8NU
☎ *(01450) 870305* Peter Ferguson

A freehouse with eight pumps offering real ales supplied through the Broughton brewery, rotated and constantly changing.

Public bar, lounge bar, function room. Food lunchtimes and evenings, plus Sunday carvery. Children allowed.

OPEN *5–11pm Mon; 11am–2.30pm and 5–11pm Tues–Wed; 11am–2.30pm and 5pm–12am Thurs; 11am–2pm and 5pm–1am Fri; all day Sat and Sun.*

EYEMOUTH

The Ship Hotel

Harbour Road, Eyemouth, Berwickshire TD14 5HT
☎ *(01890) 750224* Mr RD Anderson

Leased from Carlsberg Tetley, this pub has Caledonian 80/- and Border Farne Island Pale Ale always available. A guest, changed frequently in summer, is also offered. Caledonian Deuchars IPA is a popular choice.

A local fishermen's pub and family-run hotel near the harbour with lounge bar and separate dining area. Food at lunchtime and evenings. Children allowed.

OPEN *All day, every day.*

GALASHIELS

Ladhope Inn

33 High Buckholmside, Galashiels, Borders TD1 2HR
☎ *(01896) 752446* Mrs Johnston

A freehouse with a varied range of constantly changing ales.

On the main road; first pub on the A7. Toasted sandwiches only. Children allowed.

OPEN *All day, every day.*

GREENLAW

Cross Keys Inn

3 The Square, Greenlaw, Duns TD10 6UD
☎ *(01361) 10247* Mary O'Brian

Two real ales always available, regulars including Timothy Taylor Landlord and Caledonian Deuchars IPA.

A very old-fashioned freehouse with one bar and a restaurant area. Food at lunchtime and evenings. Children allowed.

OPEN *Closed daily between 2.30 and 5pm.*

INNERLEITHEN

Traquair Arms Hotel

Traquair Road, Innerleithen, Borders EH44 6PD
☎ *(01896) 830229* Mr Anderson

A freehouse with real ales on three pumps offering the local Traquair House Bear Ale on draught. Broughton Greenmantle Ale and Black Douglas also often available plus occasional others.

A country-style pub with one bar and separate dining area. Food served all day. Children allowed.

OPEN *All day, every day.*

NEWCASTLETON

The Grapes Hotel

16 Douglas Square, Newcastleton, Roxburghshire TD9 0QD
☎ *(01387) 375245* Jim McDonald

Up to eight pumps operating, with Caledonian Deuchars IPA among the beers always available. Guests are changed monthly.

A small hotel with restaurant. Food at lunchtimes and evenings. Children allowed until 8.30pm (residents later).

OPEN *All day, every day.*

PEEBLES

Green Tree Hotel
41 Eastgate, Peebles EH45 8AD
☎ *(01721) 720582* Mervyn Edge

Caledonian 80/- is permanently available, plus one or two guest beers such as Timothy Taylor Landlord or something from Broughton Ales.

Lively, traditional hotel bar. Food served 12–2.30pm and 5–8.30pm. Car park. Children welcome.

OPEN *11am–midnight daily.*

ST MARY'S LOCH

Tibbie Shiels Inn
St Mary's Loch, Selkirk, Borders TD7 5LH
☎ *(01750) 42231* Mrs Brown

A freehouse offering Broughton Greenmantle Ale and Belhaven 80/-.

A remote coaching inn with a non-smoking dining area. Food at lunchtime and evenings. Children allowed.

OPEN *All day, every day (closed Mon–Wed from November–Easter.*

Places Featured:
Alva
Bridge of Allan
Dollar
Dunblane
Falkirk

Pool of Muckhart
Sauchie
Stirling
Tillicoultry

THE PUBS

ALVA

Cross Keys Inn
120 Stirling Street, Alva, Clackmannanshire FK12 5EH
☎ *(01259) 760409* Mrs Michie

Tied to Maclay with three of the brewery's ales always available. Up to three guests, changed weekly, may include Brains Buckley's Best or Maclay 80/- and Wallace IPA.

An old-fashioned pub with two bars. Food at lunchtime and evenings. Children allowed.

OPEN *All day, every day.*

BRIDGE OF ALLAN

The Queen's Hotel
24 Henderson Street, Bridge of Allan, Stirling, Stirlingshire FK9 4HD
☎ *(01786) 833268* Mr Ross

A freehouse with beers Stirling Brig, Bitter, IPA and Dark Mild from the local Bridge of Allan Brewery permanently available, plus seasonal specials. Also Burton brews.

A two-bar pub with restaurant and occasional live entertainment. Food at lunchtime and evenings. Children allowed.

OPEN *All day, every day.*

DOLLAR

Castle Campbell Hotel
11 Bridge Street, Dollar, Clackmannanshire FK14 7DE
☎ *(01259) 742519* Tara Watters

A freehouse with real ale on two pumps. Usually Fuller's London Pride and one of the local Harviestoun ales.

A traditional, very busy pub with a separate dining area and lounge bar. Food at lunchtime and evenings. Children allowed.

OPEN *All day, every day.*

The King's Seat Inn
19 Bridge Street, Dollar, Clackmannanshire FK14 7DE
☎ *(01259) 742515* Mr and Mrs McGuee

Seven beers always available from a constantly changing range (300 per year) including Fuller's London Pride, Timothy Taylor Landlord, Orkney Dark Island, Eldridge Pope Thomas Hardy and others from Adnams, Caledonian, Jennings, Harviestoun, Burton Bridge and Greene King breweries.

A village inn serving families (with a children's certificate). Bar and restaurant food available at lunchtime and evenings. Parking. Accommodation. Dollar is on the main A91 road between Stirling and St Andrews.

OPEN *11am–2.30pm and 5pm–12am Mon–Sat; 12.30–2.30pm and 6.30–11pm Sun.*

The Lorne Tavern

17 Argyll Street, Dollar, Clackmannanshire
FK14 7AR
☎ *(01259) 743423* Jim Nelson

A freehouse with Harviestoun and Abbeydale brews always available. Two pumps, changed every four days, offer guests which include regulars from Backdykes and Inveralmond breweries. Others featured include the Maclay range.

A traditional local with separate restaurant. Children allowed in the dining room.

OPEN All day, every day.

The Tappit Hen

Kirk Street, Dunblane, Perthshire FK15 0AL
☎ *(01786) 825226* Eric Billett

Up to four real ales changed weekly including something from Belhaven.

A one-bar community pub. No food. No children. Opposite the cathedral.

OPEN All day, every day.

Eglesbrech Brewing Company

Upstairs At Behind The Wall, 14 Melville Street, Falkirk FK1 1HZ
☎ *(01324) 633338* C Morris

The Eglesbrech range of beers is normally available, plus a Caledonian brew and a range of guest beers often from Harviestoun, Caledonian, Broughton, Maclay, Belhaven and Orkney.

Recently extended town-centre complex with restaurant, café bar and conservatory. Food served all day. Car park opposite. Children welcome.

OPEN 11am–midnight Sun–Thurs; 11am–1am Fri–Sat.

The Muckhart Inn

Pool of Muckhart, Muckhart, Clackmannanshire
FK14 7JN
☎ *(01259) 781324* Derek Graham

A freehouse and micro-brewery serving Devon Original, Pride and Thick Black plus others.

A one-bar pub with beamed ceilings and log fires. Food at lunchtime and evenings. Children allowed.

OPEN All day, every day.

Mansfield Arms

7 Main Street, Sauchie, Nr Alloa,
Clackmannanshire FK10 3JR
☎ *(01259) 722020* John Gibson

Three beers brewed and served on the premises.

CAMRA Scottish Pub of the Year in 1993, started brewing in May 1994. The four-barrel brewhouse was built from spare parts and discarded equipment and now produces cask ales in the English tradition. Food is available in the bar until 9pm. Car park, garden. Children allowed. Just north of Alloa.

DEVON ORIGINAL 3.8% ABV
DEVON THICK BLACK 4.1% ABV
DEVON PRIDE 4.6% ABV

OPEN 11am–midnight.

The Birds & Bees

Easter Cornton Road, Causewayhead, Stirling
FK9 5PB
☎ *(01786) 463384*
Lesley Anderson and Raymond Stevenson

A freehouse with three real ales on the menu. Caledonian 80/- and Deuchars IPA always available, plus one guest a week.

A traditional farmhouse-style pub with log fires, beer garden and French boules. Voted one of the best places to eat in local Tourism Awards 1999 – food available lunchtimes and evenings. Children welcome.

OPEN 11am–3pm and 5pm–midnight Mon–Thurs; all day Fri–Sun.

The Woolpack

1 Glassford Square, Tillicoultry,
Clackmannanshire FK13 6AH
☎ *(01259) 750332* Mr D McGhee

A freehouse with Harviestoun Ptarmigan 85/- and Orkney Dark Island always available. A guest beer, changed every two days, is also offered.

Built around 1700, a one-bar pub with restaurant and children's room. Food served all day. No children in the bar. Off the beaten track, no signposts. Head towards the Glen.

OPEN All day, every day.

Places Featured:

Bladnoch
Canonbie
Castle Douglas
Dalbeattie
Dumfries
Gatehouse of Fleet
Glenluce

Haugh of Urr
Kirkcudbright
Langholm
Lockerbie
Newton Stewart
Portpatrick
Thornhill

THE PUBS

BLADNOCH

The Bladnoch Inn

Bladnoch, Wigtown, Nr Newton Stewart,
Wigtownshire DG8 9AB
☎ *(01988 402200)* Peter McLaughlin

Freehouse with up to nine beers available including Sulwath Criffel and Morland Old Speckled Hen. Others from breweries such as Belhaven are rotated twice-weekly.

A country inn and restaurant overlooking the river next to the old distillery. Food at lunchtime and evenings. Children allowed.

All day, every day.

CANONBIE

The Riverside

Canonbie DG14 0UX
☎ *(013873) 71295/71512* Mr and Mrs Phillips

Caledonian IPA and an organic lager always available plus occasional, alternating guest beers.

A civilised English-style country inn on the River Esk. Bar and restaurant food available at lunchtime and evenings. Car park and garden. Accommodation. Children allowed. Situated 14 miles north from the M6 junction 44.

11am–2.30pm and 6.30–11pm.

CASTLE DOUGLAS

The Royal Hotel

17 King Street, Castle Douglas,
Kirkcudbrightshire DG7 1AA
☎ *(01556) 502040* Mrs Bennett

A freehouse with Orkney Dark Island and Caledonian Deuchars IPA always available.

A small, family-run hotel with two bars and a separate restaurant. Children allowed.

All day, every day.

DALBEATTIE

The Pheasant Hotel

1 Maxwell Street, Dalbeattie DG5 4AH
☎ *(01556) 610345* Bill Windsor

A freehouse with either Caledonian Deuchars IPA or Harviestoun Bitter and Twisted always available.

A high-street community pub, with TV and folk club. Second-floor dining area. Food at lunchtime and evenings. Children allowed.

All day, every day.

DUMFRIES

Douglas Arms

Friars Vennel, Dumfries DG1 2RQ
☎ *(01387) 256002* Mrs A Whitefield

Broughton Greenmantle Ale, Merlin's Ale, The Ghillie, Black Douglas and Old Jock always available plus one guest beer (150 per year) to include Whim Magic Mushroom Mild and Hartington Bitter.

An old-style pub with a real coal fire. No food available. Situated in the town centre.

11am–11pm Sun–Thurs; 11am–midnight Fri–Sat.

The New Bazaar

38 Whitesands, Dumfries DG1 2RS
☎ *(01387) 268776* Ian McConnell

A freehouse with Belhaven St Andrews and Sulwath Knockendoch always available plus two guest beers daily (over 300 a year) from a list of breweries including Bateman, Adnams, Ash Vine, Titanic, Moorhouse's, Tomintoul and Greene King, as well as many new brews.

A traditional Victorian public house consisting of public bar, lounge and games room. The public bar has an old-fashioned gantry stocked with more than 200 malt and other whiskies. Lounge has real coal fire. No food available. Car park. The pub overlooks the River Nith.

All day, every day.

The Ship Inn
St Michael Street, Dumfries DG1 2P7
☎ *(01387) 255189 Mr T Dudgeon*

Timothy Taylor Landlord, Morland Old Speckled Hen, Charles Wells Bombardier, Marston's Pedigree and two regularly changing guest beers usually available, perhaps from Orkney, Everards, Brakspear, Harviestoun, Broughton, Fuller's, Badger, Greene King, Holt, Hook Norton, Hop Back, Jennings or Adnams.

Seven ales on handpump and four directly from the barrel in this friendly alehouse. No TV or music, just good conversation. No food. No children.

OPEN *11am–2.30pm and 5–11pm Mon–Sat; 12.30–2.30pm and 6.30–11pm Sun.*

Tam O'Shanter
117 Queensberry Street, Dumfries DG1 1BH
☎ *(01387) 254055 Doreen Johnston*

Caledonian Deuchars IPA always available plus four guests, changed frequently, from a broad selection.

A traditional pub with upstairs restaurant. Food all day. Children allowed.

OPEN *All day, every day.*

Masonic Arms
Ann Street, Gatehouse of Fleet, Nr Castle Douglas Kirkcudbrightshire DG7 2HU
☎ *(01557) 814335 Paul Irvin*

A freehouse with up to seven ales available.

A traditional, English-style country inn with one bar, restaurant and conservatory. Food at lunchtime and evenings. Children allowed.

OPEN *Lunchtimes, and evenings from 5pm.*

Kelvin House Hotel
53 Main Street, Glenluce, Newton Stewart, Wigtownshire DG8 0PP
☎ *(01581) 300303 Christine Holmes*

A freehouse offering three real ales, one changed once or twice a week. Orkney Red MacGregor and Burtonwood Top Hat always on the menu, with one guest from a good selection that may include Timothy Taylor Landlord and Orkney Dark Island.

An hotel off the A75, with residents' lounge, dining lounge, public bar and restaurant. Food at lunchtime and evenings, all day at weekends. Children allowed.

OPEN *11am–3pm and 5–11.30pm Mon–Fri; all day Sat–Sun.*

Laurie Arms Hotel
Haugh of Urr, Castle Douglas, Kirkcudbrightshire DG7 3YA
☎ *(01556) 660246 William Rundle*

A freehouse offering four real ales including Timothy Taylor Landlord and Orkney Red MacGregor, with guests from many different breweries changed weekly.

An old country pub with log fires and separate dining area. CAMRA Pub of the Year for Scotland 1999. Food at lunchtime and evenings. Children allowed.

OPEN *11.45am–2.30pm and 5.30pm–midnight.*

Selkirk Arms Hotel
High Street, Kirkcudbright, Kirkcudbrightshire DG6 4JG
☎ *(01557) 330209 Mr and Mrs J Morris*

A freehouse with Sulwath Criffel always available. A guest, changed weekly, might be Fuller's London Pride or other independent ale.

A Georgian hotel with public and lounge bars and a bistro. Food at lunchtime and evenings. Children allowed.

OPEN *All day, every day.*

The Crown Hotel
High Street, Langholm DG13 0GH
☎ *(01387) 380247*
Mr A Barrie and Miss D Bailey

Orkney brews always available in this freehouse plus a guest beer changed weekly.

An eighteenth-century coaching house with five bars and a dining area. Food served. Children allowed.

OPEN *All day, every day.*

Somerton House Hotel
35 Carlisle Road, Lockerbie DG11 2DR
☎ *(01576) 202583 Alex Arthur*

A freehouse always offering Caledonian Duchars IPA and Broughton Greenmantle. A guest is changed each week. Favourites include beers from Fuller's, Jennings and Caledonian breweries.

An hotel built in the 1880s with a separate dining area. Food served at lunchtime and evenings. Children allowed.

OPEN *All day, every day.*

NEWTON STEWART

The Creebridge House Hotel

Newton Stewart, Wigtownshire DG8 6NP
☎ *(01671) 402121* Mr Chris Walker

A freehouse with Sulwath Criffel and Cuil Hill ales always available. Two guests served each week, with favourites such as Bridge of Allan Sheriff Muir and Timothy Taylor Landlord.

A country-style pub built in 1760, with one large bar, brasserie and restaurant. Award-winning food available for lunch and dinner. Children's certificate. Real ale weekends held in March and November.

12–2.30pm Mon–Sun; 6–11pm Mon–Thurs; 6pm–midnight Fri–Sat; 6.30–11pm Sun.

PORTPATRICK

Harbour House Hotel

53 Main Street, Portpatrick, Stranraer, Wigtownshire DG9 8JW
☎ *(01776) 810456* Ian Cerexhe

A freehouse with two real ale pumps. Black Sheep Best Bitter always available plus a guest beer during the summer.

Central hotel on the seafront with lounge bar overlooking the harbour. Outside seating and music most weekends. Separate dining area. Food at lunchtime and evenings. Children allowed.

All day, every day.

THORNHILL

Buccleuch & Queensberry Hotel

112 Drumlanrig Street, Thornhill, Dumfriesshire DG3 5LU
☎ *(01848) 330215* David A Spencer

Two regularly changing guest beers available, perhaps from Belhaven, Fraoch, Isle of Skye, Orkney, Bateman, Harviestoun, Caledonian or Cains.

A family-run hotel built in 1851 as a coaching inn, situated in the centre of a conservation village. Traditional lounge bar with open fire and friendly staff. A haven for fishermen, walkers and golfers. Food served 12–2.30pm and 5.30–9.30pm daily. Car park. Children welcome.

11am–midnight Mon–Wed; 11am–1am Thurs–Sat; 12.30pm–midnight Sun.

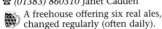

Places Featured:

Aberdour   Kettlebridge
Anstruther   Kirkcaldy
Ceres   Leslie
Earlsferry   Leven

THE PUBS

ABERDOUR

Cedar Inn

20 Shore Road, Aberdour KY3 0TR
☎ *(01383) 860310* Janet Cadden

A freehouse offering six real ales, changed regularly (often daily).

A friendly locals pub with two bars and lounges. Food at lunchtime and evenings. Children allowed.

OPEN *All day, every day.*

ANSTRUTHER

Dreel Tavern

16 High Street, Anstruther KY10 3DL
☎ *(01333) 310727* Mr Scarsbrook

A freehouse with Orkney Dark Island a permanent fixture. Three guest beers, changed weekly, are also offered and these may include Timothy Taylor Landlord, Morland Old Speckled Hen and Caledonian 80/-, or any of the full range of Harviestoun brews.

A sixteenth-century coaching inn with an extensive non-smoking dining area. Food at lunchtime and evenings. Children allowed.

OPEN *All day, every day.*

CERES

Ceres Inn

The Cross, Ceres, Cupar KY15 5NE
☎ *(01334) 828305* Ms LA and Miss JAL Rout

Two guest beers regularly available, perhaps Harviestoun Bitter and Twisted, Caledonian Deuchars IPA, Belhaven IPA or 80/- or something from Houston Brewery.

Traditional olde-worlde bar with good atmosphere, situated in the centre of Ceres. Bar food served 12–2pm Wed–Mon, high teas 4.30–7pm Sat–Sun. Car park. Children's menu.

OPEN *11.30am–3pm and 5–late daily.*

EARLSFERRY

Golf Tavern (19th Hole)

Links Road, Earlsferry KY9 1AW
☎ *(01333) 330 610* Douglas Duncanson

Caledonian Deuchars IPA, Broughton Greenmantle and an occasional guest beer served.

Small village pub with wood panelling and gas lamps in the bar. Homemade soup and snacks available. Children welcome in the lounge bar until 8pm.

OPEN *11am–1am daily in season; 11am–2.30pm and 5pm–1am daily out of season.*

KETTLEBRIDGE

Kettlebridge Inn

9 Cupar Road, Kettlebridge
☎ *(01337) 830232* James Alkman

Five beers always available from a list that runs into hundreds.

A traditional village coaching inn in Fife golfing country on the A914 road to St Andrews. Open fires, lounge bar and restaurant. Local CAMRA Pub of the Year 1994 and 1999. Bar and restaurant food available at lunchtime and evenings. Street parking, garden. Children allowed in restaurant only.

OPEN *12–2.30pm Mon–Sat; 5–7pm Mon; 5–11pm Tues–Thurs; 5–midnight Fri–Sat; 12.30–2.30pm and 5–11pm Sun.*

KIRKCALDY

Betty Nicol's

297 High Street, Kirkcaldy KY1 1JL
☎ *(01592) 642083* Mrs Nicol

A freehouse with Orkney Dark Island, Caledonian Deuchars IPA and Backdykes Malcolm range always available, plus a guest. Morland Old Speckled Hen, Timothy Taylor Landlord and Fuller's London Pride are regularly featured but many others also stocked as available.

Olde-worlde pub with separate room for children. Snacks and toasties only.

OPEN *All day, every day.*

Harbour Bar

469 High Street, Kirkcaldy KY1 2SN
☎ *(01592) 264270*

Home of the Fyfe Brewing Company offering the full range of Fyfe beers. Also guests from Belhaven Brewery and elsewhere.

The brewery is located in an old sailworks behind and above the pub. Auld Alliance, the first brew, was launched in May 1995 and there are now four more beers available, with further plans for expansion. The plant size is for two and a half barrels, with a ten-barrel per week restriction. The Harbour Bar is a traditional ale house. Snacks are available at lunchtime and evenings. Parking. Children not allowed.

ROPE OF SAND 3.7% ABV
Golden IPA-style brew.
AULD ALLIANCE 4.0% ABV
Ruby-coloured and heavily hopped.
LION SLAYER 4.2% ABV
Golden bitter.
FYFE FYRE 4.8% ABV
Straw-coloured and fruity.
CAULD TURKEY 6.0% ABV
Dark and dangerous.

11am–2.30pm and 5–midnight Mon–Thurs; 11am–midnight Fri–Sat; 12.30pm–midnight Sun.

Burns Tavern

187 High Street, Leslie, Glenrothes KY6 3DB
☎ *(01592) 741345* Margaret Wilkie

A freehouse, but with an agreement with Carlsberg-Tetley for a limited period, offering four real ales. Caledonian Duchars IPA and 80/- always available. One guest beer chosen each month by the customers is also always on offer.

An old Scottish pub with well-equipped en-suite rooms. Only snacks available, with plans to expand the menu soon. Children allowed.

All day, every day.

Hawkshill Hotel

Hawkslaw Street, Leven KY8 4LS
☎ *(01333) 427033* Mrs Rossiter

A freehouse with Timothy Taylor Landlord always available, plus a guest beer changed weekly. Favourites include Orkney Dark Island, Exmoor Gold and Kelham Island Pale Rider.

A family inn with function room, separate dining area and beer garden. Food available lunchtimes and evenings. Children allowed.

11am–2.30pm and 6–12am Mon–Thurs; 11am–midnight Fri–Sat; 12pm–12am Sun.

Places Featured:

Aberdeen	Portsoy
Elgin	Ruthven
Findhorn	Stonehaven
Methlick	Tomintoul

THE PUBS

ABERDEEN

Archibald Simpson

5 Castle Street, Aberdeen AB9 8AX
☎ *(01224) 621365 Angus W Gould*

 Caledonian 80/- and Deuchars IPA regularly served plus one or two guest beers. Tomintoul Wild Cat often available.

It's not difficult to imagine this Grade I listed building as it used to be: a Clydesdale Bank. Now a JD Wetherspoon freehouse situated on the corner of Union and King Streets. Food served all day, every day. Children welcome until 6pm if eating a meal.

11am–midnight Mon–Sat.

The Blue Lamp

121–3 Gallowgate, Aberdeen AB25 1BU
☎ *(01224) 647472 Mr Brown*

A freehouse with Caledonian 80/- and Duchars IPA always available. plus up to five guest beers. Regulars include Isle of Skye Young Pretender and many others from small Scottish breweries.

A pub combining the traditional and the contemporary, with live entertainment at weekends. Two bars, one with an early 1960s feel, the other spacious. Small function room available to hire. Sandwiches only. No children.

All day Mon–Sat; 12.30–3.30pm and 6.30–11pm Sun.

Carriages Bar & Restaurant

101 Crown Street, Aberdeen AB11 6HH
☎ *(01224) 595440/571593 Jim Byers*

Caledonian Deuchars IPA and a Castle Eden brew regularly available, plus five regularly changing beers such as Marston's Pedigree, Wadworth 6X, Fuller's London Pride, Shepherd Neame Spitfire, Greene King Abbot Ale, Orkney Dark Island or something from Aviemore, Isle of Skye, Tomintoul, Houston or any other independent brewery.

Carriages is a freehouse and part of the Brentwood Hotel. Personally run by the director/licensee, who is a fount of local knowledge, it has a relaxed, informal atmosphere. A hot buffet lunch is served 12–2pm Mon–Fri; dinner in the restaurant 6–9.45pm Mon–Sun. Car park. Children welcome in lounge area and restaurant, when eating. Special children's menu available.

12–2.30pm and 5pm–midnight Mon–Sat; 6–11pm Sun.

The Prince of Wales

7 St Nicholas Lane, Aberdeen AB10 1HF
☎ *(01224) 640597 Steven Christie*

A freehouse with Inveralmond Prince of Wales and Caledonian 80/- always on the menu. Four guest beers, changed weekly, may include Isle of Skye Red Cuillin and Young Pretender, Timothy Taylor Landlord or Orkney Dark Island, but ales from other independents also available as and when.

A classic city-centre Victorian bar. No music. Food available at lunchtime. Children allowed.

All day, every day.

Tap & Spile

Aberdeen Airport, Dyce, Aberdeen
☎ *(01224) 722331 D Regan*

Two guest beers regularly served, such as Caledonian IPA, 80/- or Marston's Pedigree.

Airport bar. Food served 8am–5pm. Children welcome.

8am–9.45pm daily.

ELGIN

Sunninghill Hotel

Hay Street, Elgin, Morayshire IV30 1NH
☎ *(01343) 547799* Winnie Rose

A freehouse offering five real ales. Guests changed weekly, from Scottish breweries such as Isle of Skye, Orkney and Tomintoul.

A hotel lounge bar. Food at lunchtime and evenings. Children allowed.

11am–2.30pm and 5–11pm Mon–Fri; 11am–11pm Sat; 12.30–11pm Sun.

FINDHORN

Crown & Anchor Inn

Findhorn, Nr Forres, Morayshire IV36 3YF
☎ *(01309) 690243* Mrs Heather Burrell

A freehouse serving at least four real ales and up to seven in summer. Regulars include Timothy Taylor Landlord, Fuller's ESB and Bateman brews.

Built in 1739, a pub offering bed and breakfast accommodation, live entertainment and a lounge area. Food at lunchtime and evenings. Children allowed.

All day, every day.

Kimberley Inn

Findhorn, Nr Forres, Morayshire IV36 0YG
☎ *(01309) 690492* Mrs Hessel

A freehouse with real ale on two pumps in the winter and up to four in summer. Timothy Taylor Landlord and Orkney The Red MacGregor among those always on the menu. Guests may include Black Sheep Best Bitter or other ales from the Orkney brewery.

A one-bar village pub with non-smoking area and views across the bay. Food at lunchtime and evenings. Children allowed.

All day, every day.

METHLICK

The Gight House Hotel

Sunnybrae, Methlick, Ellon, Aberdeenshire AB41 7BP
☎ *(01651) 806389* Les Ross

Three real ale pumps serve a regularly changing range of beers, with Timothy Taylor Landlord, Black Sheep Bitter and Marston's Pedigree featured often, plus Scottish brews such as Isle of Skye Red Cuillin.

A freehouse with lounge, restaurant, two conservatories, children's play area and large garden with putting green. Food served at lunchtime and evenings Mon–Sat and all day Sun. Situated about 20 miles from Aberdeen. Find Methlick and you will not be far away!

12–2.30pm and 5pm–midnight Mon–Fri; all day Sat–Sun.

PORTSOY

The Shore Inn

The Old Barbour, Church Street, Portsoy, Banffshire AB45 2QR
☎ *(01261) 842831* Mr Hill

A freehouse with Isle of Skye Red Cuillin among the brews always available. A guest, changed weekly, is also offered.

A traditional, 300-year-old pub, overlooking a seventeenth-century harbour. Separate restaurant. Food all day. Children allowed.

All day, every day.

RUTHVEN

Borve Brew House

Ruthven, Huntly, Aberdeenshire AB54 4SR
☎ *(01466) 760343*

The full range of Borve Brews are produced and available on the premises.

The Borve Brew House is a former school house converted into a small brewery. It relocated to Ruthven, a hamlet in the foothills of the Grampian mountains, in 1988, having originated at Borve, on the Isle of Lewis, in 1983. The beer is available bottled or on draught. No food. Car park. Children not allowed.

BORVE ALE 4.0% ABV
A session ale.

TALL SHIPS IPA 5.0% ABV

BORVE EXTRA STRONG 10% ABV
A connoisseur's beer.

Also various seasonal specials.

11am–11pm Mon–Sat; 11am–2.30pm and 6.30–11pm Sun.

STONEHAVEN

The Marine Hotel
9–10 Shorehead, Stonehaven AB3 2JY
☎ *(01569) 762155* Mr and Mrs Duncan

Timothy Taylor ales always available plus four guests (200 per year) perhaps from Orkney, Harviestoun and Tomintoul breweries, plus a wide range of English ales.

The pub overlooks the harbour and has a large bar with a juke box and pool table. Bar and restaurant food served at lunchtime and evenings. Local seafood. Parking. Follow the signs to the harbour.

OPEN *11am–midnight.*

TOMINTOUL

The Glen Avon Hotel
1 The Square, Tomintoul, Ballindalloch, Banffshire AB37 9ET
☎ *(01807) 580218* Robert Claase

A freehouse always offering Tomintoul Wild Cat, Stag and Nessie's Monster Mash. Guest beers changed weekly on two pumps in summer.

A country pub with log fires and separate dining area. Food at lunchtime and evenings. Children allowed.

OPEN *All day, every day.*

HIGHLANDS & ISLANDS

Places Featured:

Aviemore	Lochranza
Avoch	Melvich
Carrbridge	Nairn
Dingwall	Sligachan
Inverness	Stromness
Kingussie	Ullapool

THE PUBS

AVIEMORE

Old Bridge Inn
Dalfaber Road, Aviemore, Inverness-shire PH22 1PX
☎ *(01479) 811137* Mr Reid

Aviemore Ruthven Brew and a house bitter always available in this freehouse, plus a varied selection of guests.

Set in a rural location next to the River Spey. Separate dining area. Food at lunchtime and evenings. Children allowed.

OPEN *All day, every day.*

AVOCH

The Station Hotel
Bridge Street, Avoch, Moray, Ross-shire IV9 8GG
☎ *(01381) 620246* David Graham

A freehouse with two guests, changed twice-weekly, which may include regulars such as Mansfield Old Baily or other occasional features.

A country village pub with two bars and a conservatory. Food at lunchtime and evenings. Children allowed.

OPEN *All day, every day.*

CARRBRIDGE

Cairn Hotel

Carrbridge, Inverness-shire PH23 3AS
☎ *(01479) 841212* A E Kirk

Black Isle Red Kite, Caledonian 80/- and Deuchars IPA, Isle of Skye Red Cuillin, Aviemore Ruthen and Cairngorm regularly available, plus something perhaps from Houston or Tomintoul.

Family-owned, traditional freehouse in ideal touring area. Situated in the centre of the village, well visited by locals and tourists alike. Food served 12–2.15pm and 6–8.30pm. Car park. Children's certificate. En-suite accommodation.

OPEN 11am–midnight Mon–Fri; 11am–1am Sat; 11am–11pm Sun.

DINGWALL

The National Hotel

High Street, Dingwall, Ross-shire IV15 9HA
☎ *(01349) 862166*

Roseburn Bitter, Gynack Glory and Black Five (all from Iris Rose brewery) served, plus a couple of guests such as Black Sheep Best Bitter.

An elegant Georgian hotel with two bars and dining area, owned by the man behind the Irisrose Hotel Group. Food lunchtimes and evenings. Children allowed.

OPEN All day, every day.

INVERNESS

Blackfriars

93–5 Academy Street, Inverness
☎ *(01463) 233881* Alexander MacDiarmid

Three or four guest beers regularly available, often from Morland and Black Isle.

Old Scottish alehouse, situated close to Inverness bus and railway stations. Food available. Children's certificate.

OPEN 11am–midnight Mon–Wed; 11am–1am Thur–Fri; 11am–11.45pm Sat; 12.30–11pm Sun.

Clachnaharry Inn

17–19 High Street, Clachnaharry Road, Inverness PH38 4NG
☎ *(01463) 239806* David Irwin

A freehouse offering four real ales, three from the cask. Regular favourites include Tomintoul Wild Cat and Nessie's Monster Mash, Adnams Broadside and Morland Old Speckled Hen.

A traditional old coaching inn next to the railway and canal. Lounge and public bar. The beer garden used to be a train platform. Food served all day. Children allowed in lounge only.

OPEN All day, every day.

The Heathmount Hotel

Kingsmills Road, Inverness IV2 3JU
☎ *(01463) 235877* Angus Murray

A freehouse with Maclay 80/- and Isle of Skye Red Cuillin always on offer. Plus a couple of guests that might include Shepherd Neame Spitfire.

Newly renovated pub, modern with an old touch. Smoking and non-smoking areas in the restaurant. Food at lunchtime and evenings. Children allowed. One minute from the town centre.

OPEN All day, every day.

KINGUSSIE

The Royal Hotel

High Street, Kingussie, Inverness-shire PH21 1HX
☎ *(01540) 661898* Carl Justice

The pub forms part of the Iris Rose micro-brewery, producing 12 of its own ales. Up to nine beers available, including home brews and several guests.

A 52-bedroom hotel with a brewer's bar seating about 200 people and offering live entertainment. The restaurant serves food all day. Children allowed.

SUMMER ALE 3.5% ABV
CARL'S BEST BITTER 3.7% ABV
ROSEBURN BITTER 3.8% ABV
GYNACK GLORY 4.4% ABV
CRAIG BHEAG LAGER 4.4% ABV
STRATHSPEY HEAVY 4.6% ABV
BLACK 5 5.0% ABV
IPA 5.1% ABV
ZOE'S OLD GRUMPY 7.2% ABV

OPEN All day, every day.

LOCHRANZA

Catacol Bay Hotel

Catacol, Lochranza, Brodick, Isle of Arran KA27 8HN
☎ *(01770) 830231* Dave Ashcroft

A freehouse with Caledonian Deuchars IPA and Arran Brewery ales always available plus up to three guest beers.

Easy-going, family-orientated pub, with lounge bar, dining room and pool room. Food all day till 10pm. Children allowed. Website: www.catacol.co.uk

OPEN All day, every day.

MELVICH

Melvich Hotel & Far North Brewery

Melvich, Thurso, Caithness & Sutherland KW14 7YJ
☎ *(01641) 531 206* Peter Martin

Real Mackay 1042 brewed on the premises and usually available, plus a guest beer often from Aviemore or Orkney breweries.

A country hotel with two bars and a restaurant, overlooking the Pentland Firth to Orkney. Food served 6–8.15pm daily. Car park. Children welcome.

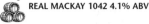 **REAL MACKAY 1042 4.1% ABV**

OPEN *11am–11pm Mon–Thurs; 11am–12.45am Fri; 11am–11.45pm Sat; 12.30–11pm Sun.*

NAIRN

The Invernairne Hotel

Thurlow Road, Nairn, Moray IV12 4EZ
☎ *(01667) 452039* Mrs Wilkie

Isle of Skye Red Cuillin always available plus one or two guests, changed fortnightly, which may include Belhaven brews or Fuller's London Pride.

A freehouse with a lounge bar and dining area. Regular live music. Food served evenings only. Children allowed.

OPEN *5pm–12.30am all week.*

SLIGACHAN

The Sligachan Hotel

Sligachan, Isle of Skye IV47 8SW
☎ *(01478) 650204* Iain Campbell

A freehouse with eight real ale pumps in the public bar and one in the lounge bar. Beers from the Isle of Skye Brewery always available, plus frequently changing guest ales such as Caledonian 80/- and Deuchars IPA.

A 100-year-old building with a main public bar, lounge bar, pool tables. Live music. The only pub on the island that is licensed to open at 11am on Sundays! Food at lunchtime and evenings. Children allowed until 8pm – the pub has the largest outdoor play area on the island.

OPEN *All day, every day.*

STROMNESS

The Stromness Hotel

Victoria Street, Stromness, Isle of Orkney KW16 3AA
☎ *(01856) 850298* Leona Macleod

A freehouse with Orkney The Red MacGregor and Dark Island always available.

The largest hotel in Orkney, with 42 bedrooms. A separate restaurant serves food at lunchtime and evenings. Children allowed.

OPEN *All day, every day.*

ULLAPOOL

The Ferryboat Inn

Shore Street, Ullapool, Ross-shire IV26 2UJ
☎ *(01854) 612366* Richard Smith

A freehouse offering six real ales. Regulars come from the Orkney brewery, others from further afield such as Wadworth 6X.

An old-fashioned one-bar pub with coal fire and separate restaurant area. Food served at lunchtime and evenings. Children allowed.

OPEN *All day, every day.*

Places Featured:

Belhaven
East Linton
Edinburgh
Haddington

Linlithgow
Mid-Calder
North Berwick
South Queensferry

THE PUBS

BELHAVEN

The Mason's Arms

8 High Street, Belhaven, Dunbar, East Lothian EH42 1NP
☎ *(01368) 863700* Brian Porteous

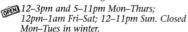 Belhaven 80/- or St Andrew's Ale usually available, or occasionally Sandy Hunter's Traditional Ale.

Traditional country inn, situated between West Barns and Dunbar. Bar, separate lounge and restaurant. Food served in summer only, 12–2.30pm and 6–9pm daily. Children welcome until 9pm, with grass play area set within the beer garden.

12–3pm and 5–11pm Mon–Thurs; 12pm–1am Fri–Sat; 12–11pm Sun. Closed Mon–Tues in winter.

EAST LINTON

The Drover's Inn

5 Bridge Street, East Linton, East Lothian EH40 3AG
☎ *(01620) 860298* Michelle Findlay

A freehouse with Adnams Broadside and Caledonian 80/- always on the menu. Two guests, changed most days, include regular choices such as Inveralmond Lia Fail or Hardy Country Bitter.

An old-fashioned pub-restaurant with one bar. Smoking and non-smoking dining areas and bistro. Live entertainment and folk bands on Wednesdays. Food at lunchtime and evenings. Children allowed.

11am–2.30pm and 5pm–midnight Mon–Sat; all day Sun.

EDINBURGH

The Bow Bar

80 West Bow, Edinburgh EH1 2HH
☎ *(0131) 226 7667* Chris Smalley

Caledonian 80/- and Deuchars IPA, and Timothy Taylor Landlord always available, plus five constantly changing guests, including a couple from Scotland and the rest from other independent breweries – from Orkney to Cornwall. A good range of cask ales.

Take a step back in time to a genuine freehouse offering an unparalleled selection of real ales and malt whiskies. Bar food at lunchtime. Children not allowed.

11am–11.15pm.

Cambridge Bar

20 Young Street, Edinburgh EH2 4JB
☎ *(0131) 225 4266* Mr Newman

Caledonian 80/- and Deuchars IPA always on offer plus five guest pumps serving a weird and wonderful variety of cask ales.

Edinburgh's original cask ale house. Full menu available lunchtimes, plus snacks in the evenings. Children allowed.

All day Mon–Sat; closed Sun.

Carter's Bar

185 Morrison Street, Edinburgh EH3 8DZ
☎ *(0131) 623 7023* Richard Treadgold

Owned by the Belhaven brewery, so Belhaven 70/-, St Andrew's Ale and Caledonian 80/- always available. Two guest beers change weekly; Marston's Pedigree and Caledonian Deuchars IPA are often featured.

Traditional wooden interior with feature gallery view into the bar. Rolls only. Children under 14 not allowed.

All day, every day.

The Cask & Barrel

115 Broughton Street, Edinburgh EH1 3RZ
☎ *(0131) 556 3132* Patrick Mitchell

Caledonian 80/- and Deuchars IPA are among the brews permanently available plus five guest beers from breweries such as Hop Back, Harviestoun, Mauldons, Hambleton, Cotleigh, Coach House, Shepherd Neame and Larkins.

A large horseshoe bar with a wide range of customers. Food available at lunchtime. From the east end of Queen Street, turn left off York Place.

OPEN *11am–midnight.*

Cloisters Bar

26 Brougham Street, Edinburgh EH3 9JH
☎ *(0131) 221 9997* Benjamin Budge

A freehouse with Caledonian Deuchars IPA and Village White Boar always available. Guests changed once or twice a week. Dent Aviator, Timothy Taylor Landlord and Caledonian 80/- are regularly featured. Others include B&T, Smiles Golden Brew, Spinnaker Buzz and Ringwood Fortyniner.

A central, old-fashioned, church-like pub, with one bar. No TV or music. Food lunchtimes only. Children allowed.

OPEN *All day, every day.*

The Cumberland Bar

1–3 Cumberland Street, Edinburgh EH3 6RT
☎ *(0131) 558 3134* Miss S Young

Caledonian Deuchars IPA and 80/- always on the menu. Guests, changed twice a week, may include Timothy Taylor Landlord, Kelham Island Pale Rider, Fuller's ESB or Greene King Abbot Ale.

A traditional one-bar alehouse. Food at lunchtime only. No children.

OPEN *All day, every day.*

The Guildford Arms

1 West Register Street, Edinburgh EH2 2AA
☎ *(0131) 556 4312* Paul Cronin

Caledonian 80/-, Deuchars IPA, Orkney Dark Island, Harviestoun Waverley 70/- and Schiehallion permanently available plus seven guest beers (260+ per year) including Traquair Bear Ale and Festival Ale, plus a massive selection from all over England.

A beautiful Jacobean pub. Restaurant food available at lunchtime. At the east end of Princes Street, behind Burger King.

OPEN *11am–11pm Mon–Wed; 11am–midnight Thurs–Sat; 12.30–11pm Sun.*

Halfway House

24 Fleshmarket Close, High Street, Edinburgh EH1 1BX
☎ *(0131) 225 7101* John Ward

A freehouse offering five real ales. Regulars include Caledonian, York and Backdykes brews.

Small city-centre pub serving an age group predominantly 25 to 50. Rolls only. No children. Close to Waverley Central train station.

OPEN *All day, every day.*

Homes Bar

102 Constitution Street, Leith, Edinburgh EH6 6AW
☎ *(0131) 553 7710* Patrick Fitzgerald

A freehouse with five real ales served on custom-made hand pumps. Guest beers a speciality.

A traditional one-room friendly bar, with interesting decor featuring antiques. All-day breakfasts and snacks served 12–3pm daily.

OPEN *All day, every day.*

Leslie's Bar

45 Ratcliffe Terrace, Edinburgh EH9 1SU
☎ *(0131) 667 5957* Gavin Blake

A freehouse with real ale on six pumps. Bass, Belhaven 80/-, Caledonian 80/- and Deuchars IPA, plus Timothy Taylor Landlord always available. One guest beer also offered, which is often a Maclay brew.

Unchanged in 100 years, with an old-fashioned gantry and open fire. One bar. Pies only. No children.

OPEN *All day, every day.*

Old Chain Pier

32 Trinity Crescent, Edinburgh EH5 3ED
☎ *(0131) 552 1233* Mr Nicol

Caledonian Deuchars IPA, Black Sheep Best Bitter and Timothy Taylor Landlord are more or less permanent fixtures here, plus one guest, changed every two days. Regulars include brews from Harviestoun and Moorhouse's.

A local with very mixed clientele, young and old. Non-smoking area. Food from 12–9.30pm. Children allowed.

OPEN *All day, every day.*

Royal Ettrick Hotel

13 Ettrick Road, Edinburgh EH10 5BJ
☎ *(0131) 228 6413* Mrs EM Stuart

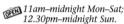 Caledonian 80/- and Maclay Kanes Amber Ale always available, plus four guest beers from a large range that may include Timothy Taylor Landlord, Castle Eden Conciliation Ale, Titanic Best, Hook Norton Old Hooky, or Broughton, Greene King and Adnams ales.

Part of a mansion and conservatory built in 1875 in the leafy suburbs. Bar and restaurant food available at lunchtime and evenings. Morning and afternoon teas also served. Car park, garden, banqueting and conference facilities. Weddings catered for. Children allowed. Accommodation.

11am–midnight Mon–Sat; 12.30pm–midnight Sun.

Southsider

3–5 West Richmond Street, Edinburgh EH8 9EF
☎ *(0131) 667 2003* Colin Mallon

Two Maclay brews always available plus two guests. The emphasis is on smaller breweries, and a large selection of lager-style beers is also served.

A lounge and public bar, popular with locals and students. Extensive menu available 10am–7pm daily. Fully refurbished. No children. Car park in the city centre.

11.30am–midnight.

The Starbank Inn

64 Laverock Road, Edinburgh EH5 3BZ
☎ *(0131) 552 4141* Scott Brown

A freehouse with Belhaven 80/-, IPA, St Andrew's Ale, Sandy Hunter's Traditional Ale and Timothy Taylor Landlord always available. Five guests, changed weekly, may include Tomintoul brews or those from Aviemore and other small and micro-brewers.

Traditional, old-fashioned pub with one bar, overlooking the River Forth. Separate non-smoking dining area. Food at lunchtime and evenings. Children allowed.

All day, every day.

The Steading

118–20 Biggar Road, Edinburgh EH10 7DU
☎ *(0131) 445 1128* Ray Simpson

A freehouse with Caledonian Duchars IPA, Timothy Taylor Landlord and Orkney and Belhaven brews always available. Plus a guest, changed weekly. Brains Reverend James Original Ale is a favourite.

A country inn with two bars, one smoking, one non-smoking, plus a separate dining area. Food served all day. Children allowed.

All day, every day.

HADDINGTON

Waterside Bistro and Restaurant

1–5 Waterside, Nungate, Haddington, East Lothian EH41 4BE
☎ *(01620) 825674* James Findlay

Regular guests in this freehouse include Belhaven brews, Caledonian Deuchars IPA, Marston's Pedigree and Timothy Taylor Landlord.

An old, restored cottage overlooking the River Tyne and the abbey. Separate dining area. Food at lunchtime and evenings. Children allowed.

11am–2.30pm and 5–11pm.

LINLITHGOW

The Four Marys

65 High Street, Linlithgow EH49 7ED
☎ *(01506) 842171* Eve and Ian Forrest

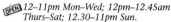 Belhaven 80/- and St Andrew's, Caledonian Deuchars and an Orkney ale always available plus nine guest beers (400 per year) that may include something from Harviestoun.

A traditional pub with antique furniture and stone walls. The bar has masses of mementoes of Mary Queen of Scots, who was born at Linlithgow Palace. Food available lunchtimes and evenings Mon–Sat and all day Sun. Parking. Children allowed. Two real ale festivals held every year, with 20 real ales at each. Opposite the entrance to Linlithgow Palace.

12–11pm Mon–Wed; 12pm–12.45am Thurs–Sat; 12.30–11pm Sun.

MID-CALDER

Torpichen Arms

36 Bank Street, Mid-Calder, Livingston, West Lothian EH53 0AR
☎ *(01506) 880020* Helen Hill

Caledonian 80/- and Deuchars IPA always available, plus guests, changed weekly. Harviestoun, Nethergate, Robinson's, Tomintoul and Cains breweries are regularly featured.

Old village pub with weekend entertainment. Bed and breakfast. Lunches only. Children allowed until 8.30pm.

All day, every day.

NORTH BERWICK

Nether Abbey Hotel

*20 Dirleton Avenue, North Berwick, East Lothian
EH39 4BQ*
☎ *(01620) 892802* Stirling Stewart

A freehouse with Belhaven beers always on the menu. Guests may include Caledonian Deuchars IPA, Marston's Pedigree, Orkney Dark Island, Kelham Island Pale Rider and Timothy Taylor Landlord.

A hotel with a warm, friendly atmosphere, situated in a leafy Victorian avenue, and run by the Stewart family for the past 40 years. One main bar, brasserie and beer garden, plus first-class accommodation. Lunches, suppers, bar snacks and children's menu always available. Annual beer festival every February features over 50 ales, plus live music and all-day food. Free parking. Families welcome – the hotel has a children's outdoor play area. For more details visit our website at: www.netherabbey.co.uk

OPEN All day, every day.

SOUTH QUEENSFERRY

The Ferry Tap

*36 High Street, South Queensferry, Nr Edinburgh
EH30 9HN*
☎ *(0131) 331 2000* Brian Inglis

A freehouse always offering Caledonian 80/- and Deuchars IPA plus Orkney Dark Island. Guests are changed weekly, one in winter, two in summer.

Old-fashioned real ale house with one bar and lounge. Food served at lunchtimes; snacks only in evenings. No children.

OPEN All day, every day.

Places Featured:

Arrochar	Hamilton
Ayr	Houston
Biggar	Inverary
Castlecary	Inverkip
Cove	Johnstone
Darvel	Kilmarnock
Dumbarton	Largs
Dundonald	Lochwinnoch
Furnace	Lugton
Glasgow	Paisley
Gourock	Troon

THE PUBS

ARROCHAR

The Village Inn

*Arrochar, Lochlong, Argyll and Bute
G83 7AX*
☎ *(01301) 702279* Josie Andrade

A pub managed by Maclay Brewery, with Maclay Wallace IPA always on the menu. Two guests are changed weekly and may include Orkney Dark Island.

Olde-worlde village pub with two bars and separate dining area. Food served all day. Children allowed.

OPEN All day, every day.

AYR

Burrowfields Café Bar

13 Beresford Terrace, Ayr KA7 2EU
☎ *(01292) 269152* Daniel Kelly

Real ale on three pumps in this freehouse. Regular guests, changed weekly, include brews from Caledonian, St Giles in the Wood, Greene King and Cains.

Live music once a week, TV and lounge bar. Food at lunchtime and evenings. Children allowed at lunchtime.

OPEN All day, every day.

Geordie's Byre

103 Main Street, Ayr KA8 88U
☎ *(01292) 264325*

Caledonian 80/- and Deuchars IPA always available plus three guest beers (450 per year) from Orkney (Skullsplitter) to Cornwall and Devon (Summerskill Whistle Belly Vengeance).

A friendly freehouse managed by the owners. Decorated with memorabilia and Victoriana. No food. Children not allowed. Located 50 yards from the police headquarters on King Street.

OPEN *11am–11pm (midnight Thurs–Sat); 12.30–11pm Sun.*

The Crown Inn

109–11 High Street, Biggar, Lanarkshire ML12 6DL
☎ *(01899) 220116* Mr and Mrs A Barrie

A freehouse offering real ale on four pumps, two in each bar. Regular guests include Adnams Broadside, Morland Old Speckled Hen, Shepherd Neame Spitfire and Wadworth 6X.

A seventeenth-century pub with two bars, recently refurbished. Beer served all day. Beer garden. Children allowed.

OPEN *All day, every day in summer; lunchtimes and evenings in winter.*

Castlecary House Hotel

Main Street, Castlecary, Cumbernauld, Lanarkshire G68 0HB
☎ *(01324) 840233* Mr McMillan

Freehouse with Caledonian Deuchars IPA among the brews always available. Two guests, changed fortnightly, might include brews from Harviestoun, Belhaven and Caledonian.

Traditional pub. Food at lunchtimes and evenings. Children allowed.

OPEN *All day, every day.*

Knockderry Hotel

204 Shore Road, Cove, Nr Helensburgh, Argyll G84 0NX
☎ *(01436) 842283* Ian Johnston

A freehouse with real ale on three pumps. Regular guests, changed weekly, include brews from Orkney, Maclay Wallace IPA and Broadsword, Isle of Skye Red Cuillin and Black Cuillin.

A 12-bedroom, family-run hotel on the shores of Loch Long, built in 1851. Food served in separate restaurant. Children allowed.

OPEN *All day, every day.*

Loudounhill Inn

Darvel, Ayrshire KA17 0LY
☎ *(01560) 320275* Graham Wellby

Tied to the Belhaven Brewery. One guest, changed weekly, may be Orkney The Red MacGregor.

An old, one-bar coaching inn, with restaurant area. Lounge also used as a function room. Food at lunchtime and evenings. Children allowed. On the main A71, one mile east of Darvel.

OPEN *All day, every day (closed Tues night and Wed lunch).*

Cutty Sark

105 High Street, Dumbarton G82 1LF
☎ *(01389) 762509* Mr Fennell

Tied to Punch Taverns, with Belhaven St Andrew's Ale always available. A weekly guest beer might well be Orkney Dark Island.

A town-centre pub with lounge bar and a mixed clientele. Food at lunchtime only. Children allowed.

OPEN *All day, every day.*

Castle View

29 Main Street, Dundonald, Kilmarnock, Ayrshire KA2 9HH
☎ *(01563) 851112* Iain Fisher

Part of the Wilson Boyle development. Caledonian 80/- or Deuchars IPA are regularly featured. Alternatives from Orkney and Harviestoun.

Restaurant-dominated, with two bars. Food at lunchtime and evenings. Children allowed. Just off the B739.

OPEN *All day, every day.*

Furnace Inn

Furnace, Inverary, Argyll PA32 8XN
☎ *(01499) 500200* Gordon Pirie

A freehouse with four or five beers always available. Guests, changed weekly, often include brews from Orkney, St Giles in the Wood.

A country-style pub, with one bar, oak beams and fires. Food served all day. Children allowed.

OPEN *All day, every day.*

GLASGOW

Athena Greek Taverna

780 Pollokshaws Road, Strathbungo, Glasgow,
Lanarkshire G42 2AE
☎ *(0141) 424 0858* Nicholas Geordiades

Six beers always available from a list of 200 guests that may include Otter Bright and beers from Rooster's, Yates, Belhaven, Caledonian and Shardlow breweries.

A café-style bar and adjacent Greek Cypriot restaurant serving Greek and European food. Children allowed. Situated beside Queen's Park railway station, not far from Shawlands Cross.

OPEN *11am–2.30pm and 5–11pm Mon–Sat; closed Sun.*

The Counting House

2 St Vincent Place, Glasgow, Lanarkshire
G1 2DH
☎ *(0141) 248 9568* Phil Annet

This freehouse hosts a real ale festival in the spring, when there may be 50 brews on sale. The rest of the time, Tomintoul Wild Cat and Caledonian Deuchars IPA are among the beers always available. Guests change weekly, and Shepherd Neame Spitfire is a regular.

A converted Bank of Scotland building with original fixtures and fittings, including the safe. Ninety tables. Food available all day. No children.

OPEN *All day, every day.*

Maclachlan's Bar

57 West Regent Street, Glasgow G2AE
☎ *(0141) 332 0595*

A range of own brews and Heather Ale always available plus two guests, usually from Scottish breweries.

A very Scottish bar with slate floor and stone bar. Around 100 malt whiskies also available. Food (specialising in venison, pheasant and salmon) available every day. No children.

MACLACHLAN'S IPA 3.8% ABV
KOLSH 4.1% ABV
Lager-style beer.
STRAWBERRY BLONDE 4.1% ABV
Fruit beer.
KIRKCULLEN 6.5% ABV
Winter ale. Porridge beer made with porridge oats.

OPEN *11am–11.45pm Mon–Sat; 12.30–11.45pm Sun.*

Station Bar

55 Port Dundas Road, Glasgow, Lanarkshire
☎ *(0141) 332 3117* Michael McHugh

A freehouse with Caledonian Deuchars IPA always available plus a guest, which might be Caledonian Edinburgh Strong Ale or Fuller's ESB.

A traditional city-centre local with one bar. Snacks and rolls available. Children usually allowed until about 6pm.

OPEN *All day, every day.*

Tap

1055 Sauchiehall Street, Glasgow G3 7UD
☎ *(0141) 339 0643* Gary Hamilton

Caledonian Deuchars IPA and 80/- usually served, with guest beers such as Heather Ale Fraoch and Marston's Pedigree.

Traditional bar in a residential area catering mainly for student clientele. Specialising in jazz, with live music at weekends. A light-hearted and welcoming pub favoured by musicians and arty types. Food served 12–9pm. No children. Situated directly opposite Kelvingrove Art Gallery in West End.

OPEN *12–11pm Sun–Thurs; 12 noon–midnight Fri–Sat.*

Tennents Bar

191 Byres Road, Hillhead, Glasgow G12
☎ *(0141) 341 1024* Alison O'Conner

Up to 12 beers available from a guest list (100 per year) that may include Fuller's London Pride, Morland Old Speckled Hen and Marston's Pedigree.

A large public bar with a friendly atmosphere and no music. Bar and restaurant food is available at lunchtime and evenings. A refurbishment has recently taken place. Adjacent to Glasgow University and Hillhead subway.

OPEN *11am–11pm Mon–Thurs; 11am–midnight Fri–Sat; 12.30–11.30pm Sun.*

The Three Judges

141 Dumbarton Road, Partick Cross, Glasgow
G11 6PR
☎ *(0141) 337 3055* Helen McCarroll

Maclay 80/-, Broadsword and Wallace IPA always available plus five guest beers (250 per year) from independent and micro-breweries, old and new.

A lively West End pub. Bar food is served at lunchtime and evenings. Parking available. Near Kelvin Hall underground.

OPEN *11am–11pm Sun–Thurs; 11am–midnight Fri–Sat.*

GOUROCK

Spinnaker Hotel

121 Albert Road, Gourock, Renfrewshire
☎ *(01475) 633107* Stewart McCartney

Belhaven 80/- regularly available, plus three guest beers often from Caledonian, Orkney, Houston or Castle Eden.

Small hotel, situated a quarter of a mile west of the town centre, with panoramic views over the River Clyde and Cowal Peninsula. Food available all day every day. Children welcome.

11am–12am Mon–Thurs; 11am–1am Fri–Sat; 12.30pm–12am Sun.

HAMILTON

The George Bar

18 Campbell Street, Hamilton, Lanarkshire ML3 6AS
☎ *(01698) 424225* Lynn Adams

A pub tied to Maclay, with three rotating guest beers always available. Regulars include Maclay 70/- and Heather Fraoch Ale.

A traditional-style, town-centre pub with small back room. Food at lunchtime. Children allowed. Can be tricky to find because of the one-way system!

All day, every day.

HOUSTON

The Fox & Hounds

South Street, Houston, Johnstone, Renfrewshire PA6 7EN
☎ *(01505) 612991* Jonathan Wengel

A freehouse and brewpub. Home of the Houston Brewing Company, so home brews are always on the menu, plus guests, changed weekly, such as Isle of Skye Red Cuillin or Coniston Bluebird.

A traditional coaching inn with three bars and a separate restaurant area. Food at lunchtime and evenings. Children allowed.

KILLELLAN 3.7% ABV
Golden, mellow ale.
BAROCHAN 4.0% ABV
Ruby-coloured and smooth.
ST PETER'S WELL 4.2% ABV
Fruity wheat beer made with continental hops.
FORMAKIN 4.3% ABV
Clean, tawny-coloured and nutty.

All day, every day.

INVERARY

The George Hotel

Main Street East, Inverary, Argyll PA32 8TT
☎ *(01499) 302111* Donald Clark

Real ale on up to three pumps in this freehouse. Guests are changed weekly, regulars include Broughton Greenmantle Ale and Belhaven St Andrew's Ale. Others might well come from the Houston Brewing Company.

An old-fashioned country house with two bars and a function room. Beer garden. Food served all day. Children allowed.

All day, every day.

INVERKIP

Inverkip Hotel

Main Street, Inverkip, Greenock, Renfrewshire PA16 0AS
☎ *(01475) 521478* Mr Hardy and Mr Cushley

A freehouse with real ale on three pumps. Belhaven and Caledonian Breweries tend to supply much of the range.

A family-run pub with dining area and separate restaurant. TV in the public bar. Food at lunchtime and evenings. Children allowed.

All day, every day.

JOHNSTONE

Coanes

26 High Street, Johnstone, Renfrewshire PA5 8AH
☎ *(01505) 322925* Michael Coane

A freehouse always offering Caledonian 80/- and Deuchars IPA and Orkney Dark Island. Guests, changed weekly, may include favourites such as Orkney The Red MacGregor, Greene King Abbot Ale, Adnams Broadside or Marston's Pedigree or other occasional features.

An olde-worlde pub with a bar and lounge. Food available at lunchtime and evenings from Wed to Sat. Children allowed up to 8pm if eating.

All day, every day.

KILMARNOCK

The Hunting Lodge

14–16 Glencairn Square, Kilmarnock, Ayrshire KA1 4AH
☎ *(01563) 322920* Mr Little

A freehouse with real ale on up to seven pumps. Caledonian Deuchars IPA and Shepherd Neame Spitfire always available. Guests, changed weekly might include Timothy Taylor Landlord, Morland Old Speckled Hen, Greene King Abbot Ale and Fuller's London Pride.

Olde-worlde Georgian pub with three bars and a separate eating area. Food at lunchtime and evenings. Children allowed.

11am–3pm and 5pm–midnight Mon–Wed; all day Thurs–Sun.

LARGS

The Clachan Bar

14 Bath Street, Largs, Ayrshire KA30 8BL
☎ *(01475) 672224*

Tied to the Belhaven brewery, but with a wide selection of ales available, including Belhaven IPA and guest beers.

A traditional pub with pool room. Meals and bar snacks served 11am–6pm daily, with toasties occasionally available later! Children welcome if eating.

All day, every day.

LOCHWINNOCH

The Brown Bull

33 Main Street, Lochwinnoch, Renfrewshire PA12 4AH
☎ *(01505) 843250*

A freehouse with Orkney Dark Island always on offer plus three guest pumps with ales changing weekly.

Olde-worlde one-bar pub and restaurant. Coal fire in winter. Restaurant open Thurs–Sun evenings (booking advised). Children allowed until 8pm.

All day, every day.

LUGTON

Lugton Inn

1 Lochlibo Road, Lugton, Ayrshire KA3 4DZ
☎ *(01505) 850267* Christopher Lynas

Home of the Lugton Brewery, so the full range of Lugton brews permanently available.

An old coaching inn in a village near Glasgow with open fires and copper wedge wire floor. Bar and restaurant food served at lunchtime and evenings. Car park, garden, children's room, accommodation. Children allowed.

LUGTON GOLD 5.0% ABV
A lager brewed in the traditional German fashion.

JOHN BARLEYCORN 5.0% ABV
Originally brewed for Burns's birthday using four types of barley, one hop and honey.

BLACK HEART 5.0% ABV
A traditional porter.

All day, every day.

PAISLEY

Gabriels

33 Gauze Street, Paisley, Renfrewshire PA1 1EX
☎ *(0141) 887 8204* Michael O'Hare

A freehouse with Caledonian Deuchars IPA and ales from the Houston Brewing Company always available. Guests change weekly and may include Fuller's London Pride, Cotleigh and Harviestoun ales.

An oval bar with traditional decor on the walls. Separate dining area and restaurant. Food all day. Children allowed.

All day, every day.

TROON

Dan McKay's Bar

69 Portland Street, Troon KA10 6QU
☎ *(01292) 311079* Dan McKay

A freehouse with Belhaven 80/-, Caledonian 80/- and Deuchars IPA always on offer. Plus a guest beer, changed once or twice a week, which might be Timothy Taylor Landlord, Wadworth 6X, Young's Special or Fuller's London Pride.

Traditional establishment, leaning towards a café bar, with TV, live music and jazz. Food at lunchtime and evenings. Children allowed during the day.

All day, every day.

Places Featured:

Abernethy	Dundee
Blairgowrie	Inverkeilor
Broughty Ferry	Kinross
Carnoustie	Moulin
Clova	Perth
Comrie	Strathtummel

THE PUBS

ABERNETHY

Cree's Inn
Main Street, Abernethy, Perthshire PH2 9LA
☎ *(01738) 850714* Brian Johnston

A freehouse offering beers on four pumps. The range changes every week, but favourites include Belhaven 80/-, Marston's Pedigree, Greene King Abbot Ale and Caledonian Deuchars IPA and 80/-.

A one-bar country pub with separate restaurant attached, open all day. Children allowed. Accommodation.

OPEN *11am–2.30pm and 5–11pm Mon–Fri; all day Sat–Sun.*

BLAIRGOWRIE

Rosemount Golf Hotel
Golf Course Road, Blairgowrie, Perthshire PH10 6LJ
☎ *(01250) 872604* Mr E Walker

A freehouse with beers from Inveralmond Brewery always available, plus a guest, changed more frequently in summer. Caledonian Deuchars IPA is one favourite.

A family-run hotel, with one bar and a dining area with overspill for non-smokers. Food at lunchtime and evenings. Children allowed.

OPEN *All day, every day.*

The Stormont Arms
101 Perth Street, Blairgowrie, GH10 6DT
☎ *(01250) 87312* Lewis Forbes Paterson

Three beers usually available often from Caledonian, Inveralmond, Houston, Belhaven, Tomintoul or Orkney.

Traditional pub with lots of mirrors, favoured by sporting types. No food. Car park. No facilities for children.

OPEN *11am–2.30pm and 5–11pm Mon–Thurs; 11am–11pm Fri–Sun.*

BROUGHTY FERRY

Fisherman's Tavern
12 Fore Street, Broughty Ferry, Dundee DD5 2AD
☎ *(01382) 775941* Mrs M Buntin

Belhaven 60/-, 80/- and St Andrew's Ale plus Maclay 80/- always available. Also three guest beers (600 per year) which include Traquair Bear Ale, Harviestoun Schiehallion, Buchan Gold, Belhaven Festival Gold and Sandy Hunter's, Maclay Wallace IPA, plus beers from every corner of England and Wales. Also Belgian and German bottled beers.

A 300-year-old listed building, formerly a fisherman's cottage. Bar and restaurant food available at lunchtime and evenings. Parking, secluded walled garden. Children welcome. Accommodation. Situated by the lifeboat station at Broughty Ferry.

OPEN *11am–midnight Mon–Sat; 12.30pm–midnight Sun.*

CARNOUSTIE

The Stag's Head Inn
61 Dundee Street, Carnoustie, Angus DD7 7PN
☎ *(01241) 852265* Mr Duffy

A freehouse with real ale on four pumps. Guest ales, which change constantly, may include Timothy Taylor Landlord, Caledonian 80/- or Orkney Dark Island.

A locals' pub with two bars. Food served at lunchtime and evenings in the summertime. Children only allowed in the pool table area.

OPEN *All day, every day.*

CLOVA

Clova Hotel

Glen Clova, Nr Kirriemuir, Angus DD8 4QS
☎ *(01575) 550222* Graham Davie

A freehouse with Broughton Greenmantle Ale among the brews always available. Guests, changed weekly, might include Caledonian Deuchars IPA.

A two-bar country hotel, with separate dining area. Food at lunchtime and evenings. Children allowed.

OPEN *All day, every day.*

COMRIE

Royal Hotel

Melville Square, Comrie, Perthshire
☎ *(01764) 679200* Edward Gibbons

Caledonian 80/-, Deuchars IPA and guest beer such as Caledonian Golden Promise, Timothy Taylor Landlord or something from Aviemore, Harviestoun or Inveralmond may be available.

Large open fireplace, church pews and stone walls with ornate, hardwood gantry and bar counter. Pool table and Sky TV. Food served lunchtimes and evenings Mon–Fri, and all day Sat–Sun and bank holidays. Car park. Children welcome in the lounge bar or in large walled beer garden.

OPEN *11am–11pm Mon–Thurs; 11am–midnight Fri–Sat; 12–11pm Sun.*

DUNDEE

Drouthy Neebors

142 Perth Road, Dundee, Angus DD1 4JW
☎ *(01382) 202187* Kirstin Wilson

A pub tied to the Belhaven Brewery, so their range is generally served, but Caledonian 80/- and others may be available as well.

Old, traditional Scottish pub. Food served at lunchtime and evenings. Children allowed from 12–3pm.

OPEN *All day, every day.*

Mickey Coyle's

21–3 Old Hawkhill, Dundee
☎ *(01382) 225871* Ann Taylor

Broughton Greenmantle usually available, plus two changing guest beers perhaps from Caledonian, Timothy Taylor, Inveralmond, Orkney, Maclay or Houston.

Traditional, family-run pub. Food available lunchtimes and evenings Mon–Sat. Car park. Well-behaved children welcome.

OPEN *11am–3pm and 5–11.30pm Mon–Thurs; 11am–11.30pm Fri–Sat; 7–11pm Sun.*

The Phoenix Bar

103 Nethergate, Dundee, Angus DD1 4DH
☎ *(01382) 200014* Alan Bannerman

A freehouse always offering Orkney Dark Island, Caledonian Deuchars IPA and Timothy Taylor Landlord.

A traditional, one-bar pub with TV and music. Food served lunchtimes and evenings. No children.

OPEN *All day, every day.*

Speedwell Bar

165–7 Perth Road, Dundee, Tayside DD2 1AS
☎ *(01382) 667783* Jonathan Stewart

A freehouse with real ale on three pumps. Regulars include Timothy Taylor Landlord, Fuller's London Pride, Belhaven brews and Caledonian Deuchars IPA.

An Edwardian pub, unchanged since 1902. One bar, two rooms (one non-smoking). Bar snacks only. Children allowed until 6pm.

OPEN *All day, every day.*

INVERKEILOR

The Chance Inn

Main Street, Inverkeilor, Arbroath, Angus DD11 5RN
☎ *(01241) 830308* Mrs Lee

A freehouse offering three real ales, changed weekly.

Two bars, two recommended restaurants plus accommodation. Food served lunchtimes and evenings. Children allowed. Scottish Tourist Board 3 Star rated.

OPEN *12–3pm and 5–12pm Mon–Fri; all day Sat–Sun.*

KINROSS

The Muirs Inn

49 Muirs, Kinross
☎ *(01577) 862270* Paul Chinnock

Orkney Dark Island and Belhaven 80/- always available plus up to six guest beers (100 per year) perhaps from the Harviestoun or Border breweries. Also Scottish wines and whiskies.

A traditional Scottish country inn. Bar and restaurant food available at lunchtime and evenings. Car park and courtyard. Children allowed. Accommodation. M90 junction 6, then follow signs for the A922. At the T-junction, the inn is diagonally opposite to the right.

OPEN *All day, every day.*

MOULIN

Original Moulin Inn

Moulin Hotel, 11–3 Kirkmichael Road, Moulin,
By Pitlochry, Perthshire
☎ *(01796) 472196* Heather Reeves

Home of the Moulin Brewery with the full range of own ales normally available.

Seventeenth-century coaching inn situated in the village square, with open fires, beams and stone walls. Originally, it was the traditional meeting house for the Parish. Extended in 1880 and again in 1970. Food served all day, every day. Car park. Children welcome away from the bar area.

MOULIN LIGHT ALE 3.7% ABV
BRAVEHEART 4.0% ABV
ALE OF ATHOLL 4.5% ABV
OLD REMEDIAL 5.2% ABV

12–11pm Sun–Thurs; 12–11.45pm Fri–Sat.

PERTH

Greyfriars

15 South Street, Perth, Perthshire PH2 8PG
☎ *(01738) 633036* Jeanette Nicholson

A freehouse with Friar's Tipple, the exclusive house ale brewed locally by Inveralmond Brewery, always available. Guests include regular favourites Caledonian Deuchars IPA, Timothy Taylor Landlord and Morland Old Speckled Hen.

An old-fashioned pub with stone walls and non-smoking dining room upstairs. The clientele tends to be 25 and upwards. Home-made food at lunchtime only. Accompanied children welcome at lunchtimes.

All day, every day.

Lovat Hotel

90–2 Glasgow Road, Perth, Tayside PH2 0LT
☎ *(01738) 636555* Mr Andrew Seal

A freehouse with real ale on four pumps, one rotated each week. The nearby Inveralmond brewery suppplies Lia Fail, Ossian and others.

Two bars, accommodation, food at lunchtime and evenings. Children allowed. On the outskirts of Perth, a mile from Broxton roundabout.

11am–2.30pm and 5pm–midnight.

STRATHTUMMEL

Loch Tummel Inn

Strathtummel, Nr Pitlochry, Perthshire
PH16 5RP
☎ *(01882) 634272* Michael Marsden

A freehouse with Moulin Braveheart always available.

A coach house on the road to the Isles, built by the Duke of Argyll. Food at lunchtime and evenings. Children allowed.

All day, every day.

YOU TELL US

★ *Allan Ramsay Hotel*, Main Street, Carlops
★ *The Cross Keys Inn*, The Green, Ancrum
★ *The Cellar Bar*, 79 Stirling Street, Airdrie
★ *The Crow's Nest*, Tomintoul
★ *Goblin'ha Hotel*, Main Street, Gifford
★ *Hoolit's Nest*, Paxton
★ *Weston Tavern*, 27 Main Street, Kilmaurs
★ *Wynd Tower*, 57–63 High Street, Fraserburgh

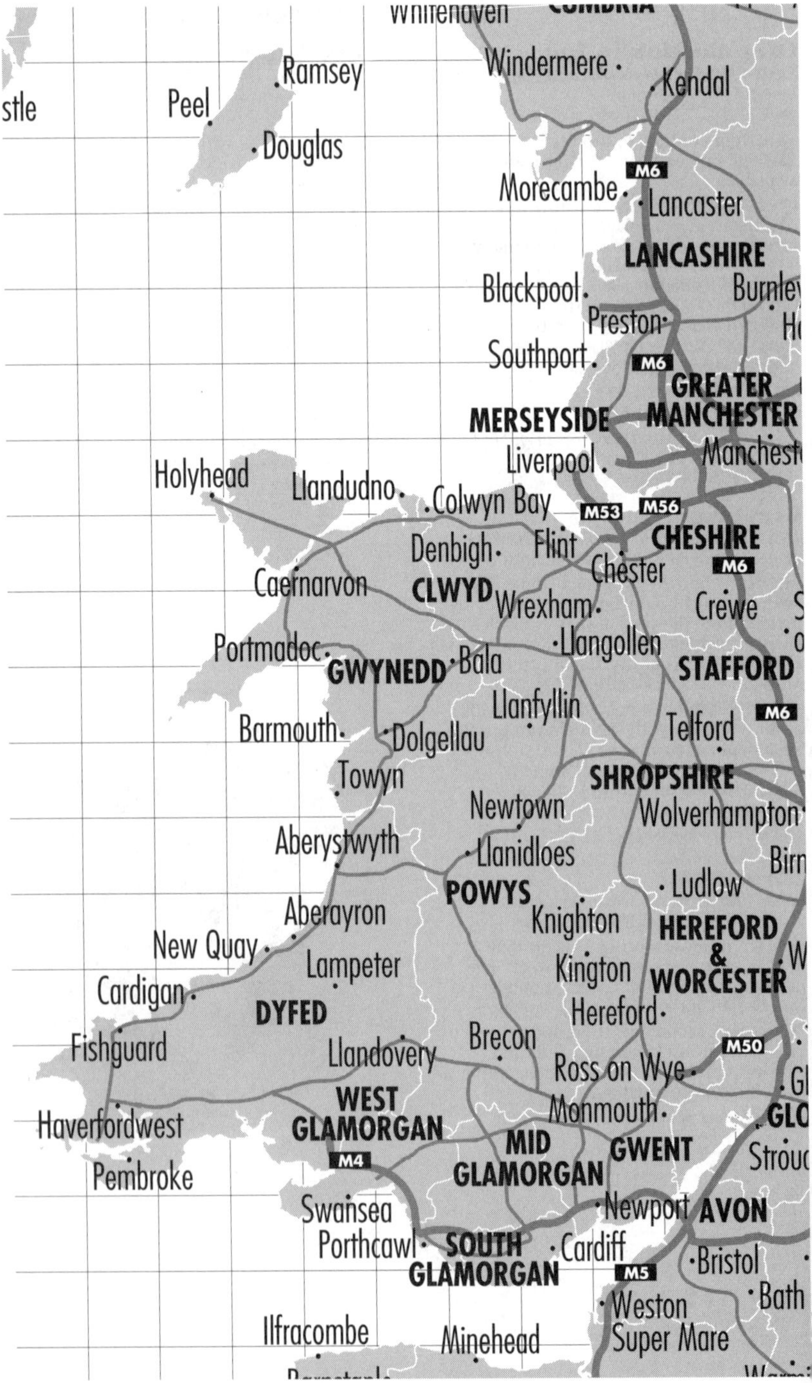

Whitehaven

CUMBRIA

Windermere ·

· Kendal

Ramsey ·

Peel ·

stle

· Douglas

Morecambe ·

M6

· Lancaster

LANCASHIRE

Blackpool ·

Burnley

Preston ·

H

Southport ·

M6

GREATER
MANCHESTER

MERSEYSIDE

Manchest

Holyhead

Liverpool ·

Llandudno ·

· Colwyn Bay

M53

M56

CHESHIRE

Denbigh ·

· Flint

· Chester

M6

Caernarvon

CLWYD

Wrexham ·

Crewe

S

Portmadoc ·

· Llangollen

o

GWYNEDD

· Bala

STAFFORD

Llanfyllin

Barmouth ·

· Dolgellau

Telford

M6

· Towyn

SHROPSHIRE

Newtown

Wolverhampton ·

Aberystwyth

· Llanidloes

Birn

POWYS

· Ludlow

Aberayron

Knighton

HEREFORD
&
WORCESTER

New Quay ·

Lampeter

Kington

Cardigan ·

Hereford ·

W

DYFED

Fishguard

Llandovery

Brecon

Ross on Wye ·

M50

Gl

Haverfordwest

Monmouth ·

GLO

WEST
GLAMORGAN

MID
GLAMORGAN

GWENT

Stroud

Pembroke

M4

Newport

AVON

Swansea

Porthcawl ·

SOUTH
GLAMORGAN

· Cardiff

· Bristol

· Bath

M5

· Weston
Super Mare

Ilfracombe

Minehead

BRAGDY CEREDIGION BREWERY

2 Brynderwen, Llangrannog SA44 6AD
☎ *(012239) 654099*

 GWRACH DU (BLACK WITCH) 4.0% ABV
Porter.

BARCUD COCH (RED KITE) 4.3% ABV
Red in colour, with fruit flavours.

CWRW 2000 (ALE 2000) 5.0% ABV
Red, with fruit and chocolate flavours.

CWRW GWYL (FESTIVAL ALE) 5.0% ABV
Gold-coloured and smooth.

Y DDRAIG AUR (THE GOLD DRAGON) 5.0% ABV
Gold in colour and full-flavoured.

YR HEN DARW DU (THE OLD BLACK BULL) 6.2% ABV
Powerful stout.

BULLMASTIFF BREWERY

14 Bessemer Close, Leckwith, Cardiff CF1 8DL
☎ *(01222) 665292*

GOLD BREW 3.8% ABV
BEST BITTER 4.0% ABV

CARDIFF DARK 4.2% ABV

JACK THE NIPPER 4.3% ABV

SPRING ALE 4.5% ABV
Seasonal.

SUMMER MOULT 4.5% ABV
Seasonal.

THOROUGHBRED 4.5% ABV

SOUTHPAW 4.7% ABV
Seasonal.

BRINDLE 5.0% ABV

SON OF A BITCH 6.0% ABV

MAD DOG 8.2% ABV
Christmas brew.

MOGADOG 10.0% ABV

COTTAGE SPRING BREWERY

Gorse Cottage, Graig Road, Upper Cwmbran, Gwent NP44 5AS
☎ *(01633) 482543*

DRAYMAN'S BITTER 3.5% ABV
DRAYMAN'S GOLD 3.8% ABV

CROW VALLEY BITTER 4.2% ABV

FULL MALTY 5.2% ABV
Malty cross between a bitter and mild.

FELINFOEL BREWERY CO. LTD

Farmers Row, Felinfoel, Llanelli SA14 8LB
☎ *(01554) 773357*

DRAGON BITTER 3.4% ABV
Light, refreshing and hoppy.

CAMBRIAN BEST 3.8% ABV
Easy-drinking, hoppy brew.

DOUBLE DRAGON 4.2% ABV
Rich, malty and smooth with balancing hoppiness.

PEMBROKE BREWERY CO.

Eaton House, 108 Main Street, Pembroke SA71 4HN
☎ *(01646) 682517 (Brewery tours)*

DARKLIN MILD 3.5% ABV
TWO CANNONS EXTRA 3.6% ABV

SAND WHISTLE 3.8% ABV
Summer ale.

DIAMOND LAGER 4.1% ABV

GOLDEN HILL ALE 4.5% ABV

OLD NOBBY STOUT 4.5% ABV

OFF THE RAILS 5.1% ABV

SIGNAL FAILURE 6.0% ABV
Winter ale.
Plus occasional brews.

PLASSEY BREWERY

The Plassey, Eyton, Wrexham LL13 0SP
☎ *(01978) 780922 (Brewery tours)*

PLASSEY BITTER 4.0% ABV
BLACK DRAGON STOUT 4.5% ABV

FUSILIER 4.5% ABV

CWRW TUDNO 5.0% ABV

DRAGON'S BREATH 6.0% ABV

SA BRAIN AND CO. LTD

The Old Brewery, St Mary Street, Cardiff CF1 1SP
☎ *(01222) 399022 (Brewery tours)*

BUCKLEY'S IPA 3.4% ABV
BRAINS DARK 3.5% ABV
Chocolate and nut flavours, with a dry finish.

BRAINS BITTER 3.7% ABV
Refreshing. Well-balanced with some sweetness.

BUCKLEY'S BEST BITTER 3.7% ABV
Smooth and nutty with balancing hoppiness.

BRAINS SA 4.2% ABV
Powerful malt flavour with bittersweet finish.

BUCKLEY'S REVEREND JAMES 4.5% ABV
Full-flavoured and complex.

TOMOS WATKIN AND SONS LTD
The Castle Brewery, 113 Rhosmaen Street,
Llandeilo SA19 6EN
☎ *(01558) 824140 (Brewery tours)*

WATKINS' WHOOSH 3.7% ABV
Dark amber beer with light bitterness.
WATKINS BB 4.0% ABV
Malty, with moderate bitter flavour and floral hoppiness.
MERLIN'S STOUT 4.2% ABV
Dark, with powerful liquorice flavour.
WATKINS OSB 4.5% ABV
Award-winning, malty with delicate hoppiness.
Plus seasonal ales.

WARCOP COUNTRY ALES
Unit 3 Century Park, Valley Way, Swansea
Enterprise Park SA6 8RP
☎ *(01792) 775333*

PIT SHAFT 3.4% ABV
Dark mild.
ARC 3.5% ABV
Light, hoppy session beer.
PITSIDE 3.7% ABV
Delicate and malty.
PIT PROP 3.8% ABV
Dark mild.
BLACK AND AMBER 4.0% ABV
Dark, full-flavoured with balancing hoppiness.
CASNEWYDD 4.0% ABV
Light, quaffer.
HILSTON PREMIER 4.0% ABV
Dry and refreshing.
STEELER'S 4.2% ABV
Red and malty.
FURNACE 4.5% ABV
Ruby, malty beer with dry finish.
RIGGERS 4.5% ABV
Golden version of Furnace.
DOCKER'S 5.0% ABV
Golden, fruity and full-bodied.

MID-WALES

Places Featured:

Aberedw	Llanwrtyd Wells
Aberystwyth	Machynlleth
Cwmann	Montgomery
Goginan	Pengenffordd
Howey	Pisgah
Llanbadarn Fynydd	Rhayader
Llangynwyd	Rhydowen
Llanidloes	Tregaron

THE PUBS

ABEREDW

The Seven Stars Inn
Aberedw, Builth Wells, Powys LD2 3UW
☎ *(01982) 560494 Deena Jones*

A freehouse with three pumps and two guests from a range that has included Shepherd Neame Early Bird, Everards Tiger, Wood Shropshire Lad, Wye Valley brews and many others from micro- and small breweries.

A traditional, two-bar olde-worlde pub with log fires, darts and quoits, no fruit machines or juke box. Food available at lunchtime and evenings in the restaurant. Children allowed.

12–3pm and 7.30–11pm (10.30pm Sun).

ABERYSTWYTH

The Coopers Arms
Northgate Street, Aberystwyth, Ceredigion
SY23 2JT
☎ *(01970) 624050 Mrs Somers*

A Felinfoel Brewery tied house with two pumps serving Felinfoel ales and occasional guests.

Live music, no juke box or fruit machines. Well-mixed clientele of locals and students. No food. Children allowed.

11am–11pm Mon–Sat; 12–10.30pm Sun.

Flannery's Brewery Tap
High Street, Aberystwyth, Dyfed SY23 1JG
☎ *(01970) 612334* Miss Flannery

A freehouse and micro-brewery serving own beers plus two guests such as Fuller's London Pride. The guests change monthly.

An old one-bar pub with food available at lunchtime and evenings. Children allowed.

OPEN *11am–11pm Mon–Sat; 12–10.30pm Sun.*

CWMANN

The Ram Inn
Cwmann, Lampeter, Carmarthenshire SA48 8ES
☎ *(01570) 422556* Wynne and Mary Davies

A freehouse offering Archers Golden Bitter plus one or two guest beers changed frequently, from national and smaller breweries.

An old drover's pub one mile outside Lampeter on the Llandovery Road, dating from around 1560, with a dining room, bar and garden. CAMRA Best Pub in Wales 1997 and 4th Best Pub in Britain 1997. Food available at lunchtime and evenings. Children allowed.

OPEN *All day, every day.*

GOGINAN

The Druid Inn
Goginan, Aberystwyth, Ceredigion SY23 3NT
☎ *01970 880650* William John Howell

A freehouse with three real ales always available. Banks's Bitter and Brains brews are regulars, while other gusests changed monthly might include Cottage Champflower Ale.

The building dates back to 1730, when it was used by the local mining community. Bar, pool room, function room. A beer garden under construction. No juke box or games machines. Food available all day in a separate dining room. Children allowed. On the A44 heading into Aberystwyth.

OPEN *11am–11pm Mon–Sat; 12–10.30pm Sun.*

HOWEY

The Drovers Arms
Howey, Llandrindod Wells, Powys LD1 5PT
☎ *(01597) 822508* Mr Day

A freehouse serving its own Drovers Ale, plus guests, usually Welsh.

A stylish Victorian red-brick inn. Back bar for drinking has real fire, no juke box, no fruit machines and no pool table. Non-smoking dining room serves fresh, traditional, award-winning food lunchtimes and evenings. British Cheese Board Award and Heart Beat Wales Award. No children under 14 please. Accommodation available. Website: www.drovers-arms.co.uk

OPEN *12–2.30pm and 7–11pm (10.30pm Sun); closed Tues lunchtime.*

LLANBADARN FYNYDD

The New Inn
Llanbadarn Fynydd, Llandrindod Wells, Powys LD1 6YA
☎ *(01597) 840378* Robert Barton

A freehouse with two real ale pumps changed at least monthly. Wood Shropshire Lad and brews from Eccleshall (Slaters) and Wye Valley are among those usually stocked.

A traditional ale and food house with log fires. Food available lunchtimes and evenings in a separate restaurant. Children allowed. Located on main A483 between Newton and Llandrindod Wells.

OPEN *10.30am–3pm and 5.30–11pm in summer; 12–2.30pm and 7–11pm in winter.*

LLANIDLOES

The Coach & Horses Inn
12–13 Smithfield Street, Llanidloes, Powys SY18 6EJ
☎ *(01686) 412266* Tony Cox

A freehouse servings Brains brews plus two guests changed weekly. These might include Robinson's Best, Everards Tiger, Shepherd Neame Early Bird and Spitfire, Ash Vine Bitter or Tomintoul Grand Slam.

An edge-of-town, family-orientated pub with children's room, patio and aviary. Live entertainment every second Saturday. Food available all day, every day except Tuesday.

OPEN *5–11pm Mon–Thurs; 12–11pm Fri–Sat; 12–10.30pm Sun.*

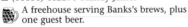

The Red Lion

8 Longbridge Street, Llanidloes, Powys SY18 6EE
☎ *(01686) 412270* Mandy James

A freehouse serving Banks's brews, plus one guest beer.

A modernised, ten-bedroom hotel with a friendly atmosphere. Open fires, patio garden. Restaurant food and bar meals available lunchtimes and evenings. Children allowed in the restaurant only.

OPEN *11.30am–3pm and 7–11pm (10.30pm Sun).*

LLANWRTYD WELLS

Stonecroft Inn

Dolecoed Road, Llanwrtyd Wells, Powys LD5 4RA
☎ *(01591) 610332/610327*

Four regularly changing beers, perhaps from Brains, Dunn Plowman, Wye Valley or Flannerys.

W elcoming country pub situated in the smallest town in Britain and popular with cyclists and visitors. Large riverside beer garden. Bar food served Fri–Sun lunchtime and every evening. Hot basket snacks available at other times. Car park. Children welcome. For further information, visit the web site at www.stonecroft.co.uk

OPEN *5–11pm Mon–Thurs; 12–11pm Fri–Sat; 12–10.30pm Sun.*

MACHYNLLETH

The Wynnstay Hotel

Maengwyn Street, Machynlleth, Powys SY20 8AE
☎ *(01654) 702941* Nigel Edwards

A freehouse with Greene King IPA usually available, plus two regularly changing guests such as Wadworth 6X, Morland Old Speckled Hen, Timothy Taylor Landlord and Greene King Abbot Ale.

A comfortable bar in an old coaching inn with open fire. Large bar at the rear with beer garden. Restaurant (evenings) and quality bar meals (lunchtimes and evenings). Children welcome. Accommodation, parking.

OPEN *All day, every day.*

MONTGOMERY

The Dragon Hotel

1 Market Square, Montgomery, Powys SY15 6PA
☎ *(01686) 668359* Mrs Michaels

A freehouse serving guest beers on one pump. Brains brews and Fuller's London Pride are regular favourites.

A hotel bar with food available at lunchtime and evenings. Children allowed.

OPEN *11am–11pm Mon–Sat; 12–10.30pm Sun.*

PENGENFFORDD

The Castle Inn

Pengenffordd, Talgarth, Powys LD3 0EP
☎ *(01874) 711353* Paul Mountjoy

A freehouse with three pumps serving alternating guest ales. Brains Rev James Original, Shepherd Neame Spitfire and Bateman XXXB are often, plus others from breweries such as SP Sporting Ales, Cottage and others.

A rural country inn with separate dining area. B&B, plus barn-style dormitory accommodation in the middle of the hills: a good walking area at 1,000 feet. Food available at lunchtimes and evenings. Children allowed.

OPEN *11am–3pm and 7–11pm (10.30pm Sun).*

PISGAH

The Halfway Inn

Devil's Bridge Road, Pisgah, Aberystwyth, Dyfed SY23 4NE
☎ *(01970) 880631*

Three beers always available (30 per year) including Felinfoel brews plus Wadworth 6X, Bateman XXX, Hook Norton Old Hooky, Shepherd Neame Spitfire, Fuller's London Pride and Ringwood Old Thumper.

A traditional olde-worlde hostelry 700 feet up with magnificent views of the Cambrian mountains. Bar and restaurant food available at lunchtime and evenings. Car park and garden. Children allowed. Accommodation. Halfway along the A4120 Aberystwyth to Devil's Bridge road. Note, this is not the Pisgah near Cardigan.

OPEN *11.30am–2.30pm and 6.30pm–11pm Mon–Sat; 12–3pm and 7–10.30pm Sun.*

RHAYADER

The Cornhill Inn

West Street, Rhayader, Powys LD6 5AB
☎ *(01597) 810869* P Vaughan

Morland Old Speckled Hen and Brains Reverend James Original regularly available, plus frequently changing guest beers.

A seventeenth-century freehouse with olde-worlde charm. Low beams and open fires. Bar food available at lunchtimes and evenings. Parking. Children allowed. Accommodation. On the road to Elan Valley.

OPEN *11am–3pm and 7–11pm (10.30pm Sun).*

RHYDOWEN

The Alltyrodyn Arms
Rhydowen, Llandysul, Ceredigion SA44 4QB
☎ *(01545) 590319* Derrick and Jean Deakin

A freehouse serving three or four real ales. Archers Golden and Everards Tiger are regularly available plus hundreds of others constantly changing.

A sixteenth-century pub with a restaurant serving food all day, a pool room, beer garden with fish pond and waterfall. B&B and self-catering accommodation available. Children allowed in the bar until 9pm.

11am–11pm Mon–Sat; 12–4pm Sun.

TREGARON

The Talbot Hotel
Main Square, Tregaron, Ceredigion SY25 6JL
☎ *(01974) 298208* Graham Williams

A freehouse with three handpumps serving a wide range of real ales.

An old, traditional pub offering a friendly welcome. Beer garden. Open fires, separate restaurant, accommodation, beer garden. Restaurant and bar food available at lunchtime and evenings. Ample parking. Children allowed.

11am–11pm Mon–Sat; 12–10.30pm Sun.

Places Featured:

Abergele
Bangor
Betws-y-Coed
Betws-yn-Rhos
Bodedern
Brynford
Caernarfon
Caerwys
Cilcain
Colwyn Bay
Cymau
Denbigh
Dulas
Gorsedd

Llandudno
Llangollen
Lloc
Mochdre
Mold
Morfa Nefyn
Northop
Old Colwyn
Penysarn
Rhewl
Rhyd Ddu
Ruthin
St Asaph
Waunfawr

THE PUBS

ABERGELE

The Bull Hotel

Chapel Street, Abergele, Conwy LL22 7AW
☎ *(01745) 832115* Alan Yates

Lees GB Mild and JW Bitter regularly available.

Family-run pub situated just outside Conwy town on the Llanwrst road. Restaurant and music-free main bar. Food served Wed–Mon 11am–2pm and 6.30–8.30pm. Car park. Children welcome. Accommodation.

OPEN *11am–3pm and 6–11pm Wed–Mon; 11am–3pm and 7–11pm Tues.*

BANGOR

The Castle (Hogshead)

Glanrafon, off High Street, Bangor, Gwynedd LL57 1LH
☎ *(01248) 355866* Mark Fisher

A Whitbread tied house with up to ten hand pumps plus four beers served straight from the barrel. Regular guests include Timothy Taylor Landlord, Fuller's London Pride, Caledonian 80/- and Marston's Pedigree. Has served more than 500 beers in the past three years.

A roomy pub with a large open single floor, dark wood floors, background music. Non-smoking area, wheelchair access. Food available 12–7pm. Children allowed. Opposite the Cathedral, close to the railway station.

OPEN *11am–11pm Mon–Sat; 12–10.30pm Sun.*

The Tap & Spile

Garth Road, Bangor, Gwynedd LL57 2SW
☎ *(01248) 370835* Dean Ibbitson

Greene King Triumph, Otter Ale and a Tap & Spile own brew usually available on eight guest pumps. No permanent beers. Beers changed daily.

A suburban pub with B&B. Food lunchtimes and evenings. No children. Located by the pier.

OPEN *All day, every day.*

BETWS-Y-COED

Pont-Y-Pair Hotel

Holy Head Road, Betws-y-Coed LL24 0BN
☎ *(01690) 710407* E Adam and Ann Watkins

Marston's Pedigree and Green King Abbot Ale usually available.

Small hotel situated in the heart of Snowdonia with lots of rural pursuits close by. Home-cooked food available 11am–2pm and 6–9pm daily. Children welcome.

OPEN *11am–11pm Mon–Sat; 12–10.30pm Sun.*

BETWS-YN-RHOS

The Wheatsheaf

Betws-yn-Rhos, Abergele, Conwy LL22 8AW
☎ *(01492) 680218* Raymond Perry

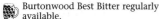 Morrells Varsity, Marston's Best and Pedigree regularly available.

Inn with olde-worlde atmosphere and lots of brass, first licensed in 1640. Food every lunchtime and evening. Car park. Beer garden with Wendy house and high chairs available.

OPEN *12–3pm and 6–11pm Mon–Fri; 12–11pm Sat; 12–10.30pm Sun.*

BODEDERN

The Crown Hotel

Church Street, Bodedern, Nr Holyhead, Anglesey
☎ *(01407) 740 734* Robert Aled Michael

Burtonwood Best Bitter regularly available.

Traditional two-bar pub with pool room. Real fires in winter. Food served 12–2pm and 6–8pm daily. Car park. Children welcome, but no special facilities.

OPEN *12–2pm and 5–11pm Mon–Sat; 12–10.30pm Sun.*

BRYNFORD

The Llyn y Mawn Inn

Brynford Hill, Brynford, Holywell, Flintshire CH8 8AD
☎ *(01352) 714367* Martin Jackson

A freehouse serving up to six brews every week. Welsh ales are favoured, plus others from small breweries.

CAMRA Welsh Pub of the Year 1995 and 1997. Typical Welsh long house with restaurant and gardens. Real fires, background music. Food available Tues–Sun evenings plus Sat–Sun lunchtimes. Well-behaved children allowed. Adjacent to the A55 expressway, and can be seen from there.

OPEN *5.30–11pm Mon–Fri (not lunchtime); 12–3pm and 6–11pm Sat; 12–3pm and 7–10.30pm Sun.*

CAERNARFON

The Alexandra Hotel

North Road, Caernarfon, Gwynedd LL55 1BA
☎ *(01286) 672871* Ken Moulton

A Whitbread tied house serving a range of guests. Regulars include Wadworth 6X, Morland Old Speckled Hen and Marston's Pedigree. The guest list changes fortnightly.

A local pub with B&B accommodation. Tables outside. No food. Children allowed in the afternoons only.

OPEN *11am–11pm Mon–Sat; 12–10.30pm Sun.*

Y Goron Fach

Hole in the Wall Street, Caernarfon, Gwynedd LL55 1RF
☎ *(01286) 673338* Mr Williams

A freehouse permanently serving Flannery's Celtic Ale, plus Fuller's London Pride, Brains St David's Ale and Adnams bitters as regular guests on two pumps.

A town pub with two bars and a garden. Food served at lunchtimes and evenings in the summer, lunchtime only in winter. Children allowed.

OPEN *All day, every day.*

CAERWYS

The Travellers' Inn

Pen y Cefn, Caerwys, Mold, Clwyd CH7 5BL
☎ *(01352) 720251* Kevin Jones

A freehouse and brewpub with Marston's Pedigree regularly available plus various other guests rotated on the two remaining pumps.

A family pub and restaurant with food available all day. Children allowed. Located on the A55

🛢 **ROY MORGAN'S ORIGINAL 3.8–3.9% ABV**
🛢 **OLD ELIAS 5.2% ABV**

OPEN *11am–11pm Mon–Sat; 12–10.30pm Sun.*

CILCAIN

The White Horse

The Square, Cilcain, Mold, Flintshire CH7 5NN
☎ *(01352) 740142* Mr Jeory

A freehouse with two hand pumps serving a wide range of beers on rotation. Exmoor Gold, Greene King Abbot, Marston's Pedigree and Fuller's London Pride are regularly featured. Others might include beers from Wood or Cottage breweries. The range changes every other day.

A small, cosy village pub, unspoilt for 150 years, spread over four rooms with real fires and beams. No juke box or pool table. Food available at lunchtime and evenings. No children.

OPEN *12–3pm and 6.30–11pm Mon–Fri; 11am–11pm Sat; 12–10.30pm Sun.*

COLWYN BAY

The White Lion Inn

Llanelian-yn-Rhos, Colwyn Bay, Conwy
LL29 8YA
☎ *(01492) 515807* Jack Cole

A freehouse with three real ales usually available from a wide range that changes fortnightly.

A traditional stone-built Welsh country inn with slate floor, log fires and beams. B&B accommodation and non-smoking dining area. Food available at lunchtime and evenings. Children allowed.

OPEN *11am–3pm and 6–11pm Mon–Sat; 12–3pm and 7–10.30pm Sun.*

CYMAU

Ye Olde Talbot Inn

Cymau Lane, Cymau, Nr Wrexham, Clwyd
☎ *(01978) 761410* L J Mee

Hydes' Anvil Bitter permanently available, plus a changing seasonal beer every two months.

A traditional drinkers' pub. No food. Car park. Children welcome.

OPEN *7–11pm Mon–Thurs; 12–4pm and 7–11pm Fri–Sun.*

DENBIGH

The Eagle Inn

Back Row, Denbigh, Denbighshire LL16 3TE
☎ *(01745) 813203* Mr Evans

A freehouse serving up to eight real ales. Morland Old Speckled Hen is popular but all real ales are considered.

A large pub with a snooker room, pool, darts etc. The pub runs quiz nights and a cricket team. Food currently available at lunchtime only although expansion is planned. Children allowed if eating.

OPEN *11am–11pm Mon–Sat; 12–10.30pm Sun.*

DULAS

Pilot Boat Inn

Dulas, Amlwch, Anglesey
☎ *(01248) 410205 Mark Williams*

A Robinson's tied house serving Best Bitter.

Traditional country pub in an area of outstanding natural beauty. Popular with locals and tourists alike. Food served 12–9.30pm daily. Car park. Children's menu and play area. Situated on the A5025.

OPEN *11.30am–11pm Mon–Sat; 12–10.30pm Sun.*

GORSEDD

The Druid Inn

Gorsedd, Holywell, Flintshire CH8 8QZ
☎ *(01352) 710944* Ken Doherty

A freehouse usually serving Marston's Pedigree plus four or five others from an extensive range that favours the smaller and micro-breweries rather than nationals.

A listed twelfth-century long house, with oak beams and log fires. The separate restaurant serves food every evening and Sunday lunchtime. Children allowed. Located off the A5026, two miles west of Holywell.

OPEN *7–11pm Mon–Sat (closed lunchtimes except Sun); 12–3pm and 7–10.30 Sun.*

LLANDUDNO

The Queen Victoria

Church Walks, Llandudno, Conwy LL30 2HL
☎ *(01492) 860949* Mr J Vaughan-Williams

A freehouse serving Banks's brews and up to five others.

A Victorian pub, comfortable, family-orientated. Food is a speciality, served in a separate restaurant and available at lunchtime and evenings. Children allowed. Situated near the pier.

OPEN *11am–11pm Mon–Sat; 12–10.30pm Sun.*

LLANGOLLEN

The Sun Inn

49 Regent Street, Llangollen, Denbighshire
LL20 8HN
☎ *(01978) 860233*
Alan Adams and Paul Lamb

A freehouse offering six real ales that could well include Weetwood Old Dog and Wye Valley brews. Four Belgian beers and two real ciders also available.

A friendly, old, beer-drinker's pub with a good atmosphere. Food available at lunchtime and early evening. Take the A5 towards Llangollen.

OPEN *11am–11pm Mon–Sat; 12–10.30pm Sun.*

LLOC

Roak Inn

Lloc, Nr Holywell, Flintshire CH8 8RD
☎ *(01352) 710049* T Swift

Burtonwood Bitter and Top Hat usually available.

Small, friendly, family-run two-bar pub with dining room. Large car park with picnic benches. Food available lunchtimes and evenings Mon–Sat. Children welcome.

OPEN *12–11pm (10.30pm Sun).*

MOCHDRE

The Mountain View

7 Old Conwy Road, Mochdre, Colwyn Bay, Conwy LL28 5AT
☎ *(01492) 544724* Malcolm Gray

A Burtonwood Brewery tied house serving Burton Best and Top Hat permanently plus regular rotating guests including, perhaps, Everards Tiger, Bateman XXX, Gales HSB and Caledonian brews. Also a 'Brewery Choice' of a seasonal brew like Black Parrot.

A village pub with restaurant and large garden. Food available at lunchtimes and evenings. Children allowed.

OPEN *All day, every day.*

MOLD

Y Pentan

New Street, Mold, Flintshire CH7 1NY
☎ *(01352) 758884* Tim Hughes

A tied pub serving beers from the Marston's and Banks's breweries plus a regularly changing guest from the Banks's range of cask ales (including seasonal brews).

A pub in the town centre, with public bar and L-shaped lounge. Food available Mon–Sat lunchtime (not Sun).

OPEN *11am–3pm and 6.30–11pm Mon, Tues, Thurs; 11am–11pm Wed, Fri, Sat; 12–10.30pm Sun.*

MORFA NEFYN

Cliffs Inn

Beach Road, Morfa Nefyn, Gwynedd LL53 6BY
☎ *(01758) 720356* Glynne Roberts

A freehouse with two pumps usually serving one English and one Welsh ale, the Welsh brew usually from Brains.

A food-orientated pub with good beer. Outside patio. Food available at lunchtime and evenings in a separate dining area. Children allowed.

OPEN *12–3pm and 6–11pm (10.30pm Sun).*

NORTHOP

Stables Bar at Soughton Hall

Soughton Hall Country House Hotel and Restaurant, Northop, Flintshire CH7 6AB
☎ *(01352) 840577* Mr Rodenhurst (owner); Alexander John (bar manager)

A freehouse serving real ales from Flannery's and Hanby Breweries. There are three dedicated Flannery pumps and three others serving brews rotated weekly. Small and micro-breweries preferred.

An unusual location, set in the old stable block of the hotel complex. The hayloft has been converted into a restaurant. Beer garden and wine shop. Food available at lunchtime and evenings. Children allowed. Located off the A55 Flint/Northop junction

OPEN *11am–11pm Mon–Sat; 12–10.30pm Sun.*

OLD COLWYN

The Red Lion

385 Abergele Road, Old Colwyn, Colwyn Bay, Conwy LL29 9PL
☎ *(01492) 515042* Wayne Hankie

A freehouse serving seven cask ales, four of which are constantly rotated. Brains SA, Charles Wells Bombardier, Greene King Abbot Ale and Morland Old Speckled Hen usually available plus many, many more. Some 400 brews have been served over the past two years.

A village pub on the main road with a double lounge bar, open fires and no music in lounge. The public bar has a pool table, TV and juke box. No food. Children not allowed. A regional pub of the year.

OPEN *5–11pm Mon–Fri; 11am–11pm Sat; 12–10.30pm Sun.*

PENYSARN

Y Bedol

Penysarn, Anglesey, Gwynedd LL69 9YR
☎ *(01407) 832590* Steven and Sheila Hughes

A selection of three Robinson's ales always available.

Warm, friendly pub with beer garden, pool room, karaoke and quiz nights and occasional local Welsh entertainment. Bar food available evenings. Children allowed.

OPEN *11am–11pm Mon–Sat; 12–10.30pm Sun.*

RHEWL

The Drovers Arms
Rhewl, Ruthin, Denbighshire LL15 2UD
☎ *(01824) 703163* Charles Gale-Hasleham

A freehouse serving three real ales. Tries to specialise in Welsh beers from small and micro-breweries. Coach House Honeypot and brews from Vale and Flannery's Breweries are often featured.

A 300-year-old pub and an old meeting place for drovers. An English Civil War skirmish took place on the bridge outside the pub. Large garden with tables, barbecues in nice weather. Food available at lunchtime and evenings. Well-behaved children allowed. The landlord used to own the Vale and Clwyd (now Flannery's) Breweries.

OPEN 12–3pm (not Mon) and 7–11pm; 12–10.30pm Sun.

RHYD DDU

The Cwellyn Arms
Rhyd Ddu, Gwynedd LL54 6TL
☎ *(01766) 890321* Graham Bamber

A freehouse serving nine real ales, perhaps Dorothy Goodbody's Warming Wintertime Ale (Wye Valley), Cottage Great Western Ale, Young's Special, Fuller's London Pride, Thwaites Bitter, Wadworth 6X and Old Timer, Gales HSB, Charles Wells Bombardier, Adnams Broadside, Coach House Gunpowder Strong Mild or McGuinness Feather Plucker Mild.

A country inn with B&B accommodation and cottages to let. Restaurant, beer garden, children's adventure playground. Bunkhouses and camping on nearby 25-acre area leading to Cwellyn Lake. Food available all day every day. At the foot of Mount Snowdon, on the Caernarfon/ Beddgelert road.

OPEN 11am–11pm Mon–Sat; 12–10.30pm Sun.

RUTHIN

Red Lion
Cyffylliog, Ruthin, Denbighshire LL15 2DN
☎ *(01824) 710664* Mrs CF Kimberley Jones

JW Lees Bitter regularly available and also seasonal beers from the same brewery.

Friendly, family-run country pub with lots of character. Caters for everyone, including family meals and bed and breakfast. Food served 7–10pm Mon–Fri and 12–10pm Sat and Sun. Car park. Children welcome.

OPEN 7–11pm Mon–Fri, 12–11pm Sat–Sun.

ST ASAPH

The Kentigern Arms
High Street, St Asaph, Clwyd LL17 0RG
☎ *(01745) 584157* Mrs Redgrave

A freehouse offering up to seven real ales. Popular brews come from Marston's, Cottage and other smaller breweries. The varied and unusual range changes every two weeks.

A seventeenth-century coaching inn with beams and open fires. A separate small room can be used for children or as a dining room. Four bedrooms available. Food available at lunchtimes only. Children allowed.

OPEN 12–3pm and 7–11pm (10.30pm Sun).

WAUNFAWR

The Snowdonia Parc Hotel
Beddgelert Road, Waunfawr, Gwynedd LL55 4AQ
☎ *(01286) 650409* Karen Humphreys

A brewpub in which the landlady's son Gareth provides the beer, usually up to around 5% ABV. Marston's Bitter and Pedigree are among a range of real ales always available, plus occasional local beers. Up to four beers in total in summer.

A village pub in beautiful surroundings. Campsite, family room. Food available at lunchtime and evenings. Play area with play equipment and safety surface. On the A4085 Roman road from Caernarfon to Beddgelert. From July 2000 the pub will be a terminus for the reinstated Welsh Highland Railway from Caernarfon.

OPEN 11am–11pm Mon–Sat and 12–10.30pm Sun in summer; 12–2pm and 6–11pm in winter.

Places Featured:

Abercrave	Llanvihangel Crucorney
Bassaleg	Machen
Bettws Newydd	Mumbles
Bishopston	Newport
Blackmill	Pant
Blaenavon	Penallt
Bridgend	Pontardawe
Chepstow	Raglan
Clytha	Rassau
Gilwern	Sebastopol
Glan-y-Llyn	Shirenewton
Heol y Plas	Swansea
Kenfig	Talybont-on-Usk
Llanbedr	Tondu
Llandogo	Tredunnock
Llandovery	Trellech
Llangorse	Upper Llanover
Llangynwyd	Usk
Llanrhidian Gower	Ystalyfera
Llantilio Crossenny	

THE PUBS

ABERCRAVE

The Copper Beech Inn
133 Heol Tawe, Abercrave, Swansea,
West Glamorgan SA9 1XS
☎ *(01639) 730269* Philip and Paul Colman

A family-run freehouse. Young's Special and Brains brews usually available, plus guests served on one pump (changed weekly) from breweries such as Wye Valley and Cottage.

A local's pub, with function room and beer garden. Families welcome. Food available at lunchtimes and evenings.

11am–11pm Mon–Sat; 12–10.30pm Sun.

BASSALEG

The Tredegar Arms
4 Caerphilly Road, Bassaleg, Newport, Gwent
NP1 9LE
☎ *(01633) 893247* David Hennah

A Whitbread tied house with up to nine hand pumps and six beers from the barrel. Up to 13 brews available, changing weekly. Regulars include Shepherd Neame Spitfire, Timothy Taylor Landlord and beers from Wychwood and Caledonian. Two beer festivals are held each year, in May and August.

A busy wayside inn; near junction 28 of the M4. Large beer garden, ample car parking. Food available lunchtime and evenings. Children allowed.

11am–11pm Mon–Sat; 12–10.30pm Sun.

BETTWS NEWYDD

The Black Bear

Bettws Newydd, Usk, Monmouthshire NP15 1JN
☎ *(01873) 880701*
Gillian and Stephen Molyneux

A freehouse with four real ales available at any one time, all straight from the barrel. The range changes every couple of weeks.

An old one-bar country pub with fine restaurant and beer garden. Families welcome. Food available at lunchtime and evenings except Sunday evening. Accommodation. Children allowed. Three miles outside of Usk

12–2pm and 6–11pm Mon–Sat (closed Mon lunch); 12–10.30pm Sun; all day on bank holidays.

BISHOPSTON

The Joiners' Arms

50 Bishopston Road, Bishopston, Swansea, West Glamorgan SA3 3EJ
☎ *(01792) 232658* Genevieve Davies

Home of the Swansea Brewing Company. Up to eight pumps serve the full range of brews.

A traditional village pub with mixed clientele, no juke box. Local and regional CAMRA award winner for 1999. Food available at lunchtime and in the evenings. Children allowed.

11.30am–11pm Mon–Sat; 12–10.30pm Sun.

BLACKMILL

The Ogmore Junction Hotel

Blackmill, Mid Glamorgan CF35 6DR
☎ *(01656) 840371* John Nicholas

Up to six pumps serving a range of beers that changes regularly.

A country pub with beams and log fires, beer garden and car park. Backs on to the River Ogmore. Food is available in the separate restaurant at lunchtime and evenings. Children allowed in a designated area. Situated not far from the M4 on the main road to the Rhondda Valley. A fortnightly sheep sale is held behind the pub from the end of July to the end of December.

11am–11pm Mon–Sat; 12–10.30pm Sun.

BLAENAVON

Cambrian Inn

Llanover Road, Blaenavon, Gwent NP4 9HR
☎ *(01495) 790327* J and P Morgans

Blaenavon Pride and Glory and Brains brews always available, plus a guest (50 per year) such as Morland Old Speckled Hen.

A typical Welsh mining village pub. Darts, pool, cards, etc. No food. Street parking opposite the pub. Children not allowed.

6–11pm Mon–Thurs; 12–11pm Sat; 12–3pm and 7–10.30pm Sun.

BRIDGEND

The Famous Pen y Bont Inn

Derwen Road, Bridgend, Mid Glamorgan CF31 1LH
☎ *(01656) 652266* Ruth and Jim Simpson

A Scottish and Newcastle pub, with Wadworth 6X and Marston's Pedigree always available, and plans to introduce guest beers in the future.

A small, friendly, comfortable pub. Food is available at lunchtime and evenings. No children. Located near the railway station – formerly the Railway Hotel.

11am–11pm Mon–Sat; 12–10.30pm Sun.

CHEPSTOW

The Coach & Horses

Welsh Street, Chepstow, Monmouthshire NP6 5LN
☎ *(01291) 622626* Ralph Thomas

A Brains tied pub, with the brewery's ales on three pumps and three guests. Regular visitors include Morland Old Speckled Hen.

A family pub with B&B accommodation and food available at lunchtime and evenings in a separate dining area. A beer festival is held every July to coincide with the Chepstow Carnival, when up to 20 different beers are available.

11am–11pm Mon–Sat; 12–10.30pm Sun.

CLYTHA

Clytha Arms
Clytha, Gwent NP7 9BW
☎ *(01873) 840206* Mr and Mrs Canning

Hook Norton Best is among those beers permanently available, plus three guests (360 per year) from breweries such as Freeminer, Felinfoel, RCH, Wye Valley, Jennings, Fuller's, Harviestoun, Exmoor and Adnams. A mild is always available.

A large old dower house with restaurant and traditional bar. Bar and restaurant food available at lunchtime and evenings. Car park, garden, accommodation. Children allowed. Located on the old Abergavenny to Raglan road.

OPEN *6–11pm Mon; 11.30am–3pm and 6–11pm Tues–Fri and Sun; 11am–11pm Sat.*

GILWERN

Bridgend Inn
Main Road, Gilwern, Gwent
☎ *(01873) 830939* Mrs P D James

Up to four real ales always available including Felinfoel brews. Guests include Fuller's London Pride and ESB, also Wadworth 6X and IPA.

Canalside, olde-worlde pub. Bar and restaurant food available at lunchtime and evenings. Car park, patio and garden. Children allowed for meals.

OPEN *12–2pm and 7–11pm Mon–Thurs; 12–11pm Fri–Sat; 12–10.30pm Sun.*

GLAN-Y-LLYN

Fagin's Ale & Chop House
Cardiff Road, Glan-y-Llyn, Mid Glamorgan
☎ *(029) 2081 1800* Jeff Butler

Five beers always available from a range that may include Shepherd Neame Bishop's Finger, Greene King Abbot, Morland Old Speckled Hen and many more.

A converted terraced house. Former CAMRA Pub of the Year. Bar and restaurant food available at lunchtime and evenings. Function room. Children allowed.

OPEN *12–11pm (10.30pm Sun).*

HEOL Y PLAS

Ye Olde Red Lion
Heol y Plas, Llannon, Carmarthenshire SA14 6AA
☎ *(01269) 841276* Steven Ireland

A Felinfoel Brewery tied house with two pumps serving Felinfoel ales.

A rural sixteenth-century pub with oak beams and log fires. Non-smoking and smoking dining areas. Food available every evening plus Saturday and Sunday lunchtimes. Children welcome.

OPEN *5–11pm Mon–Fri; 11am–11pm Sat; 12–10.30pm Sun.*

KENFIG

The Prince of Wales Inn
Kenfig, Mid Glamorgan CF33 4PR
☎ *(01656) 740356* Richard Ellis

A freehouse serving up to four real ales at any one time. Tomas Watkin OSB and Fuller's London Pride are regularly available, plus a range of others, changing constantly, from a huge list that might include St Austell Tinners Ale or Morland Old Speckled Hen.

An olde-worlde pub with three open fires, a lounge and a function room (which houses the Sunday School). Food is available at lunchtime and evenings. Children allowed in the separate dining area.

OPEN *11am–4.30pm and 6–11pm Mon–Thurs; 11am–11pm Fri–Sun (10.30pm Sun).*

LLANBEDR

The Red Lion Inn
Llanbedr, Crickhowell, Powys NP8 1SR
☎ *(01873) 810754* Mr Sloan

A freehouse serving two real ales from breweries such as Wye Valley or Bateman.

A quiet 300-year-old pub with beams and real fires. Non-smoking room and garden. Nearby campsite situated in a very beautiful spot in the Black Mountains. Food available lunchtimes and evenings. Children allowed.

OPEN *7–11pm Mon–Fri; 12–2.30pm Wed–Fri; 11am–11pm Sat; 12–4pm and 7–10.30pm Sun.*

LLANDOGO

The Sloop Inn

Llandogo, Monmouthshire NP5 4TW
☎ *(01594) 530291* Eddie Grace

A freehouse with two real ales always on at any one time and more in summer. One session and one stronger ale always available.

Recently redecorated. Describes itself as more of an inn than a pub, family-orientated with accommodation and garden. Set in a beautiful village location in the Wye Valley. Food available every lunchtime and evening. On the A466.

OPEN *12–2.30pm and 5.30–11pm Mon–Fri, 11am–11pm Sat–Sun (10.30pm Sun); all day, every day in summer.*

LLANDOVERY

The White Swan

47 High Street, Llandovery, Carmarthenshire SA20 0DE
☎ *(01550) 720816* Ray Miller

A freehouse specialising in beers up to 4.2% ABV. Two always available, changed every two weeks.

A town pub offering darts, pool and a mixed local clientele. No juke box or fruit machines. No food. Children and dogs are welcome. The last pub on the way out of Llandovery, near the supermarket.

OPEN *12–3pm and 7–11pm (10.30pm Sun).*

LLANGORSE

The Castle Inn

Llangorse, Brecon, Powys LD3 7UB
☎ *(01874) 658225* Mr Williams

A freehouse with two pumps serving ales from a range including Bateman XB, Morland Old Speckled Hen and many more.

An olde-worlde village inn with a 27-seater restaurant. Food available at lunchtime and evenings. Children allowed under supervision.

OPEN *12–3pm and 6–11pm Mon–Fri; 11am–11pm Sat; 12–10.30pm Sun.*

LLANGYNWYD

The Old House

Llangynwyd, Maesteg, Mid Glamorgan CF34 9SB
☎ *(01656) 733310* Richard David

A freehouse with Brains SA permanently available plus guests from Marillwyd.

An old, traditional pub with three bars and a garden. Food available at lunchtimes and evenings. Children allowed.

OPEN *All day, every day.*

LLANRHIDIAN GOWER

The Greyhound Inn

Old Walls, Llanrhidian Gower, Swansea, West Glamorgan SA3 1HA
☎ *(01792) 391027* Peter and Sally Green

A freehouse with six real ales available. Bullmastiff, Marston's, Morland and Wadworth brews are regular examples plus brews from the nearby Swansea Brewing Company.

An old, comfortable, family- and food-orientated pub, in the middle of nowhere, with coal fires. The beer garden has play equipment. Separate restaurant specialises in fish, fresh oysters, Indian and vegetarian food. Located in a ramblers walking area.

OPEN *11am–11pm Mon–Sat; 12–10.30pm Sun.*

LLANTILIO CROSSENNY

The Hostry Inn

Llantilio Crossenny, Abergavenny, Gwent NP7 8SU
☎ *(01600) 780278* Pauline and Michael Parker

A freehouse offering up to three real ales. Bullmastiff and Cardiff brews regularly available plus one from Wye Valley or elsewhere.

A small, welcoming, country pub on Offa's Dyke ramblers path. Skittle alley, function room, non-smoking restaurant and non-smoking area in the bar. Food available lunchtime and evenings. Well-behaved children allowed. Located on the B4233, halfway between Monmouth and Abergavenny.

OPEN *11am–11pm Mon, Tues, Fri, Sat, Sun (10.30pm); closed lunchtime Oct–Mar.*

LLANVIHANGEL CRUCORNEY

Skirrid Mountain Inn

Llanvihangel Crucorney, Abergavenny, Monmouthshire NP7 8DH
☎ *(01873) 890258* Heather Grant

Ushers Best, Founders and seasonal beers, usually available.

Historic, twelfth-century country inn of unique character, believed to be the oldest pub in Wales and situated in the beautiful Black Mountains. Well-known locally for good food and a friendly welcome. Food served all day, every day, except Sunday and Monday evenings. Car park. Well-behaved children welcome, but no special facilities.

OPEN *11am–3pm and 6–11pm Mon–Fri; 11am–11pm Sat; 12–10.30pm Sun.*

The White Hart Inn

Nant y Ceisiad, Machen, Newport, Gwent
NP1 8QQ
☎ *(01633) 441005* Alan Carter

A freehouse which, over the last four years, reckons to have served 1,700 different beers on five handpumps. Small and micro-breweries from all over the British Isles have featured.

A very olde-worlde pub, designed as the interior of ship (the captain's cabin came from the Empress of France). Food available at lunchtime and evenings in a separate dining area which seats 100 people. Play area and beer garden. Children allowed. Located just off the main road (A448).

11am–11pm Mon–Sat; 12–10.30pm Sun; closed 3.30–6pm in winter.

The Park Inn

23 Park Street, Mumbles, Swansea,
West Glamorgan SA3 4DA
☎ *(01792) 366738* Mr Francis

A freehouse with two guest pumps which change too frequently to list. Timothy Taylor Landlord and brews from Cottage are just two examples. Over 200 beers served over the past two years.

A small, traditional, one-bar local. No food. No children.

12–3.30pm and 5.30–11pm Mon–Fri; 11am–11pm Sat; 12–10.30pm Sun.

St Julian's Inn

Caerleon Road, Newport, Gwent NP6 1QA
☎ *(01633) 258663* Mr S J Williams

A Unique Brewing Company pub serving four beers with two guests changed twice-weekly. Wadworth 6X and Everards Tiger are regulars. Other brewers supported include Wye Valley, Cottage and B&T.

A pretty, family pub in a scenic location with balcony overlooking the River Usk. Food available Mon–Sat lunchtime and evenings. Children allowed.

11am–11pm Mon–Sat; 12–10.30pm Sun.

Wetherspoons

Cambrian Retail Centre, Cambrian Road,
Newport, Gwent NP9 4AD
☎ *(01633) 251752* Paul McDonnell

Five handpumps serving a wide range of real ales that change on a weekly basis.

A busy pub with a wide-ranging clientele, old and young. Particularly lively in the evenings. Food available at lunchtime and evenings. No children. Next to the railway station.

11am–11pm Mon–Sat; 12–10.30pm Sun.

Pant Cad Ifor Inn

Pant, Merthyr Tydfil, Mid Glamorgan
CF48 2DD
☎ *(01685) 7723688* Phillip Williams

Up to six real ales available, with regulars including Everards Tiger, Shepherd Neame Bishop's Finger and Young's brews.

A small country pub on the outskirts of town with a separate dining area. There is a steam railway 100 yards up the road. Coach parties are catered for. Food is available at lunchtime only. Children allowed.

11am–11pm Mon–Sat; 12–10.30pm Sun.

The Boat Inn

Lone Lane, Penallt, Monmouth, Gwent MP5 4AJ
☎ *(01600) 712615* Don and Pat Ellis

Wadworth 6X and Greene King IPA are always available straight from the barrel, plus approximately six others, some from a rolling rota of about ten regulars, including Oakhill Bitter, and other occasionals.

A small riverside inn on the England–Wales border built into the hillside, with stone floors and simple decor. Live music on Tuesday and Thursday evenings. Very cosy with no juke box or games machines. Bar food available at lunchtimes and evenings. Car park on the side of the river, terrace gardens with ponds, streams and waterfalls. Children allowed. The car park is in Redbrook (Gloucestershire) on the A466, next to a football field. Follow the footpath over an old railway bridge across the Wye.

11am–11pm Mon–Sat; 12–10.30pm Sun.

PONTARDAWE

The Pontardawe Inn
Herbert Street, Pontardawe, Swansea,
West Glamorgan SA8 4ED
☎ *(01792) 830791* Mr P Clayton

A freehouse serving 170 guest beers per year. Shepherd Neame Early Bird and Everards Tiger are often available, plus a constantly changing range on seven pumps plus one straight from the barrel.

An olde-worlde pub with no juke box and no pool table. Festival-orientated with music from all around the world. Four beer festivals and one music festival held every year. Food served at lunchtime and in the evenings in a separate 28-seater restaurant. Children allowed until 9pm.

OPEN *11am–11pm Mon–Sat; 12–10.30pm Sun.*

RAGLAN

The Ship Inn
High Street, Raglan, Monmouthshire NP15 2DY
☎ *(01291) 690635* Jane Tucker

A freehouse serving up to two guest beers at any one time, changed weekly.

A sixteenth-century olde-worlde coaching inn with beams and log fires. There is a well in the cobblestoned forecourt. Food available at lunchtime and evenings. Children allowed. Located just off the High Street, opposite the supermarket.

OPEN *11am–11pm Mon–Sat; 12–10.30pm Sun.*

RASSAU

Rhyd u Blew
Rassau Road, Rassau, Ebbw Vale, Gwent
NP23 5PW
☎ *(01495) 308935* Lyn Collins

Up to four real ales available, changing all the time.

Out-of-town, open-plan, community pub with a beer garden. Food available Mon–Fri lunchtimes. No children. Located off the A465.

OPEN *12–3pm and 6.30–11pm Mon–Fri; 11.30am–3pm and 6–11pm Sat; 12–3pm and 7–10.30pm Sun.*

SEBASTOPOL

The Open Hearth
Wern Road, Sebastopol, Pontypool, Torfaen
NP4 5DR
☎ *(01495) 763752* Gwyn Philips

A freehouse with seven real ales always available. Regular favourites include Greene King Abbot Ale and Archers Golden Bitter.

A busy pub on the canal side, with excellent food and beer reputation. Winner of three regional CAMRA awards. Food available in a separate non-smoking restaurant. No juke box or pool table. Mixed clientele of all ages. Children welcome, with children's room provided.

OPEN *11.30am–4.30pm and 6–11pm Mon–Fri; 11am–11pm Sat; 12–4pm and 7–10.30pm Sun.*

SHIRENEWTON

The Carpenters Arms
Shirenewton, Nr Chepstow, Monmouth
☎ *(01291) 64121* James Bennet

Fuller's London Pride, Wadworth 6X and Marston's Pedigree usually available with one or two guest beers, such as Timothy Taylor Landlord, Greene King Abbot Ale, Gale's HSB, Fuller's ESB, Ringwood Old Thumper or Young's Special.

Atmospheric, traditional country inn crammed with antiques and memorabilia. Profusion of colour from the hanging baskets in summer months. Food served 12–2pm and 7–9.30pm Mon–Sat (until 10pm Fri–Sat). Car park. Family room. Located on the B4235 Chepstow/Usk road, just outside the village.

OPEN *11am–2.30pm and 6–11pm (10.30pm Sun).*

SWANSEA

The Glamorgan Hotel
88 Argyle Street, Swansea, West Glamorgan
SA1 3TA
☎ *(01792) 455120* Vince Carr

Two real ales on the guest pumps including Camerons Strongarm, Marston's Bitter and Banks's Bitter.

A broad-based local, no juke box. Food available lunchtime and evenings. Children allowed in the afternoons only.

OPEN *11am–11pm Mon–Sat; 12–10.30pm Sun.*

The New Inn

The Lone, Swansea, West Glamorgan SA6 5SU
☎ *(01792) 842839* Glynn Hopkin

A Whitbread-owned pub with up to seven real ales. Brains Dark, Morland Old Speckled Hen, Fuggles Imperial IPA and Fuller's London Pride are regularly available plus Greene King Abbot and others from time to time.

A village inn with a restaurant and function room. Food available at lunchtime and evenings. Children allowed.

OPEN *11am–3pm and 6–11pm Mon–Thurs; 11am–11pm Fri–Sat; 12–4pm and 7–10.30pm Sun.*

The Potters Wheel

85–6 The Kingsway, Swansea, West Glamorgan SA1 5JE
☎ *(01792) 465113* Nerys Jones

A JD Wetherspoon's pub with up to 16 real ales available.

A town-centre pub on the high street. No music, games or pool, non-smoking area. Food available all day. No children.

OPEN *11am–11pm Mon–Sat; 12–10.30pm Sun.*

TALYBONT-ON-USK

The Star Inn

Talybont-on-Usk, Brecon, Powys LD3 7YX
☎ *(01874) 676635* Mrs Coakham

A constantly changing range of 12 beers, including brews from Felinfoel, Freeminers, Bullmastiff, Wadworth and Crown Buckley.

A riverside and canalside site, with lovely garden. Bar and restaurant food is available at lunchtime and evenings. Parking, garden, live music on Wednesdays. Children allowed. Accommodation. Less than a mile off the A40 between Brecon and Abergavenny (Brecon six miles, Abergavenny 14 miles).

OPEN *11am–11pm (10.30pm Sun) in summer; otherwise closed 3–6pm.*

TONDU

Llynfi Arms

Maesteg Road, Tondu, Bridgend CF32 9DP
☎ *(01656) 720010* Pearl Fowler

One guest beer always available and changing every two weeks, from smaller independents such as Cottage, Ash Vine, Fisherrow or Tomos Watkins.

The pub is close to Tondu railway station, and has two model trains running around the ceiling of the lounge bar. Food served 12–2pm and 7–9.30pm Wed–Sat and 12–2pm Sun. Booking advised Fri–Sun. Children welcome in the lounge bar at lunchtime.

OPEN *1–4pm and 7–11pm Mon–Tues; 12–4pm and 7–11pm Wed–Sat; 12–3pm and 7–10.30pm Sun.*

TREDUNNOCK

The Newbridge Inn

Tredunnock, Usk, Monmouthshire NP5 1LY
☎ *(01633) 450227* Robert Noone

A freehouse with four pumps and serving two guests from smaller breweries such as Wye Valley.

A recently totally refurbished pub on the banks of the River Usk. A traditional country pub atmosphere. Food available at lunchtime and evenings. Children allowed. Village signposted off the Caerlon–Usk road.

OPEN *11am–11pm Mon–Sat; 12–10.30pm Sun.*

TRELLECH

The Lion Inn

Trellech, Nr Monmouth, Monmouthshire NP25 4PA
☎ *(01600) 860322* Tom and Debbie Zsigo

A freehouse with three guest pumps, changed weekly. Fuller's London Pride and Wadworth 6X are usually available plus another from a smaller brewery, such as Bath, Wychwood or Lees.

A stone-fronted, sixteenth-century typical country pub with open fire, no fruit machines or juke box. Favours traditional pub games such as bar billiards and bar skittles plus many social evenings. Prize-winning food available every lunchtime and all evenings except Sunday. Well-behaved children and dogs allowed, but no dogs in the lounge.

OPEN *12–3pm and 7–11pm Mon; 12–3pm and 6–11pm Tues–Fri; 6.30–11pm Sat; closed Sunday evenings.*

The Trekkers

The Narth, Nr Trellech, Monmouthshire
NP5 4QG
☎ *(01600) 860367* Mr and Mrs Flower

 A freehouse with two guest ales changed fortnightly. Greene King Abbot, Shepherd Neame Spitfire and Smiles Golden regularly available.

A local country pub, in the style of a log cabin, family-orientated with beer garden, swings and skittle alley. Traditional, home-made, British-bought food available in separate dining area lunchtimes and evenings. It is advisable to book for Sunday lunch.

11am–2.30pm and 6–11pm Mon–Sat; 12–3pm and 7–10.30pm Sun.

UPPER LLANOVER

The Goose & Cuckoo Inn

Upper Llanover, Abergavenny, Monmouthshire
NP7 9ER
☎ *(01873) 880277*
Ann and John McDonald Cullen

 A freehouse with three pumps, usually serving either a Brains ale or Wadworth 6X.

A small, isolated, picturesque country pub with a real fire. No juke box or games machines, traditional card games. Beer garden. Food available every lunchtime and all evenings except Thursday. Well-behaved children allowed.

11.30–3pm and 7–11pm Tues–Sat; 12–3pm and 7–10.30pm Sun; closed Monday unless bank holiday.

USK

The Greyhound Inn

1 Chepstow Road, Usk, Monmouthshire
NP5 1BL
☎ *(01291) 672074* Bob and Annette Burton

A freehouse serving four beers including those from RCH, Brakspear, Greene King, Wye Valley, Shepherd Neame and Freeminer. The beers change fortnightly.

An early sixteenth-century pub on the edge of town. Bar, no juke box. Food available lunchtime and evenings. Children allowed.

12–3pm and 6.30–11pm Mon–Sat; 12–3pm and 7–10.30pm Sun.

The Kings Head Hotel

18 Old Market Street, Usk, Monmouthshire
NP5 1AL
☎ *(01291) 672963* S Musto

A freehouse with four pumps serving a wide range of guests.

A fifteenth-century pub with accommodation. Open fireplace, function room and restaurant serving food at lunchtime and evenings. Children allowed.

All day, every day.

YSTALYFERA

Wern Fawr Inn

47 Wern Road, Ystalyfera, Swansea SA9 2LX
☎ *(01639) 843625* Mr Will Hopton

The home of the Bryncelyn Brewery with the full range of own brews permanently available. All the home ales are named on a Buddy Holly theme. Also one guest, often from Wye Valley.

A village pub dating back to the 1850s. Background music is 1960s and 70s. No food. Beer garden. Children allowed.

BUDDY MARVELLOUS 4.0% ABV
Dark ruby mild beer.
OH BOY 4.5% ABV
A light-coloured ale with good aroma and taste.
CHH BITTER 4.5% ABV
A rich red-brown bitter with a good malt and hop balance.

7–11pm only Mon–Sat; 12–3pm and 7–10.30pm Sun.

Places Featured:

Felinfoel	Llansaint
Haverfordwest	Mynydd y Garreg
Horeb	Narbeth
Llanddarog	Pembroke
Llandeilo	Upper Cwmtwrch

THE PUBS

FELINFOEL

The Royal Oak
*Felinfoel Road, Felinfoel, Carmarthenshire
SA14 8LA*
☎ *(01554) 751140* Mrs M Cleland

Tied to the nearby Felinfoel Brewery, with two handpumps serving the Felinfoel ales.

An old-fashioned local opposite the brewery, with food available at lunchtime and evenings. Children allowed.

All day, every day.

HAVERFORDWEST

King's Arms Hotel
23 Dew Street, Haverfordwest, Dyfed
☎ *(01437) 763726* Chris Hudd

Six beers always available from a list of approximately 150 brews per year.

An old, beamed and flagstoned pub in the town, just past the library. Street parking, function room. No children.

*11am–3pm and 6–11pm Mon–Sat;
12–3pm and 7–10.30pm Sun.*

HOREB

The Waunwyllt Inn
*Horeb Road, Five Roads, Horeb, Llanelli,
Carmarthenshire SA15 5AQ*
☎ *(01269) 860209* Shaun Pawson

A freehouse with four pumps serving a constantly changing selection of real ales. Popular recent brews include Shepherd Neame Bishop's Finger, Everards Tiger and others from Cottage, Brecknock and Tomos Watkin.

A popular country inn in a quiet hamlet outside Llanelli. Close to the Celtic Trail cycle route. Large beer garden, non-smoking dining area, five en suite bedrooms. Food available at lunchtime and evenings. Children allowed. From Llanelli, take the B4309 towards Carmarthen.

*11am–11pm Mon–Sat and 12–10.30pm
Sun in summer; 12–3pm and 6.30–11pm
in winter.*

LLANDDAROG

The White Hart Inn
Llanddarog, Carmarthenshire SA32 8NT
☎ *(01267) 275395* PA Coles

Cwrw Du and Cwrw Blasus regularly available from the on-site brewery.

A 600-year-old pub in a beautiful village with open log fire, oak beams, antiques and ancient carved furniture. Beer garden. Food available 11.30am–3pm and 6.30–10pm daily. Car park. Children welcome. Situated just off the A48 on the B4310.

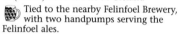 **CWRW DU 4.0% ABV**
CWRW BLASUS 4.5% ABV

11.30am–3pm and 6.30–11pm.

LLANDEILO

The Castle Hotel
*113 Rhosmaen Street, Llandeilo, Dyfed
SA19 6EN*
☎ *(01558) 823446* Simon Williams

A Tomas Watkins tied house with award-winning ales such as Whoosh, Best, Old Style Bitter and Merlin's Stout permanently available. Other seasonal guests rotated on one hand pump.

A town-centre pub with two bars serving five adjoining rooms, 65-seater restaurant, beer garden. Bar and restaurant food served lunchtimes and evenings. Children allowed. Easy, free parking. Local CAMRA Pub of the Year 1999.

All day, every day.

LLANSAINT

The King's Arms
*13 Maes yr Eglwys, Llansaint, Nr Kidwelly,
Carmarthenshire SA17 5JE*
☎ *(01267) 267487* John and Debbie Morris

A freehouse serving three regularly changing beers.

Separate smoking and non-smoking dining areas – bar and restaurant food served lunchtimes and evenings. Log fire in season, beer garden, car park. Children allowed. Follow signs for Llansaint from Kidwelly – the pub nestles under the church tower.

*12–3pm and 6–11pm (10.30pm Sun);
closed Tues lunchtimes.*

MYNYDD Y GARREG

The Prince of Wales

Heol Meinciau, Mynydd y Garreg, Kidwelly,
Carmarthenshire SA17 4RP
☎ *(01554) 890522* Gail and Richard Pickett

Six beers always available from a list that includes brews from Wye Valley, Bullmastiff, Black Sheep, Cottage and various Welsh micro-breweries. Please phone ahead for details of beers currently on tap.

A 200-year-old cottage pub with a collection of cinema memorabilia and bric-à-brac. Bar and restaurant food available at lunchtime and evenings. Car park and garden. No children. Take the Mynydd y Garreg turn from the Cydweli bypass, then just over a mile on the right.

OPEN *5–11pm (10.30pm Sun).*

NARBETH

The Kirkland Arms

East Gate, St James Street, Narbeth, Dyfed
SA67 7DB
☎ *(01834) 860423* Mr Edger

A Felinfoel Brewery tied pub with guest beers rotated on one pump. These might include York Yorkshire Terrier, Swansea Bishopswood Bitter, Wadworth 6X and many others changed on a weekly basis.

An old, traditional pub with pool table, games machines and beer garden. Fresh rolls and sandwiches served every day. Children allowed.

OPEN *11am–11pm Mon–Sat; 12–10.30pm Sun.*

PEMBROKE

The Castle Inn

17 Main Street, Pembroke, Pembrokeshire
SA71 4JS
☎ *(01646) 682883* Nigel Temple

A freehouse usually serving Charles Wells Bombardier and Wadworth 6X plus up to two guests.

A very old pub with long and narrow stone walls and beams. No food. Children allowed.

OPEN *11am–11pm Mon–Sat; 12–10.30pm Sun.*

The First & Last

London Road, Pembroke Dock, Pembrokeshire
SA72 6TX
☎ *(01646) 682687* Richard Maynard

A freehouse with Charles Wells Bombardier or Brains SA usually available plus one other.

A local community pub with beer garden. Light lunches only served. Children allowed at lunchtime only.

OPEN *11am–11pm Mon–Sat; 12–10.30pm Sun.*

UPPER CWMTWRCH

The George IV Inn

Upper Cwmtwrch, Swansea Valley,
Carmarthenshire
☎ *(01639) 830441* PA Coles

Cwrw Blasus regularly available, brewed at the Coles family brewery, the White Hart Inn, Llanddarog.

Rural, olde-worlde, riverside pub with large beer garden. Open-plan kitchen serving food during opening hours. Car park. Children's play equipment in the garden.

OPEN *11.30am–3pm and 6.30–11pm.*

YOU TELL US

★ *The Brittannia Inn*, Pentre Road, Halkyn, Holywell, Flintshire
★ *The Castle Hotel*, 113 Rhosmaen Street, Llandeilo, Dyfed
★ *Garrd Fon*, Beach Road, Felinheli, Gwynedd
★ *Gawain and the Green Knight*, Golftyn Lane, Connah's Quay, Deeside, Clwyd
★ *The Nag's Head*, Abercych, Pembrokeshire
★ *The New Inn*, Bedwellty, Blackwood, Gwent
★ *Wynnstay Arms Hotel*, Maengwyn Street, Macgynlleth, Powys

Places Featured:

Bangor
Belfast

Hillsborough
Saintfield

THE BREWERIES

HILDEN BREWERY
Hilden House, Grand Street, Hilden, Lisburn
BT27 4TY
☎ *(01846) 663863*

GREAT NORTHERN PORTER 4.0% ABV
HILDEN ALE 4.0% ABV
MOLLY MALONE 4.6% ABV
SPECIAL RESERVE 4.6% ABV
Plus occasional brews.

THE PUBS

BANGOR

The Esplanade Bars
12 Ballyhome Esplanade, Bangor, Co Down
BT20 5LZ
☎ *(02891) 270954* Maeve Gillespie

A freehouse with Whitewater Glen Ale always available plus two guests such as Whitewater Cascade or one of the Highwood Tom Wood brews.

A public bar with TV and juke box, dining area and restaurant. Food available at lunchtime and evenings. Children allowed.

All day, every day.

BELFAST

Beaten Docket
48 Great Victoria Street, Belfast, Co Antrim
BT2 7BB
☎ *(028) 9024 2986* Joseph McLarnon

Beers from Whitewater, Cains and Tom Wood breweries plus guests such as Wadworth Old Timer.

A designer-style pub with lots of mahogany and brass. Food served daily 10am–7pm. Children allowed. Opposite the railway station.

All day, every day.

HILLSBOROUGH

Hillside Restaurant & Bar
21 Main Street, Hillsborough, Co Down
BT26 6AE
☎ *(01846) 382765* Ian Carmichael

Whitewater Solstice Pale Ale and Belfast Special always available, plus two guests guests such as Hop Back GFB.

A pub with bistro and à la carte restaurant serving food at lunchtime and evenings. Children allowed.

All day, every day.

SAINTFIELD

The White Horse
Main Street, Saintfield, Co. Down
☎ *(028) 9751 0417/1143* Craig W Spratt

Five beers usually available, which may include Whitewater Belfast Special and Glen Ale plus three different guest ales each week.

Fine, long, four-storey building situated in the middle of a quaint, old, market town and conservation area. Good food and friendly, intimate atmosphere. Food served all day, every day. Free parking nearby. Children's menu, high chairs and family room provided.

11.30am–11.30pm Mon–Sat.

YOU TELL US

★ *The Anchor Bar*, 9 Bryansford Road, Newcastle
★ *The Botanic Inn*, 23–7 Malone Road, Belfast
★ *The Burrendale Hotel*, Castlewellan Road, Newcastle
★ *The Dirty Duck*, 2 Kennegar Road, Holywood
★ *The Kitchen Bar*, 16 Victoria Square, Belfast
★ *Lavery's Gin Palace*, 12–16 Bradbury Place, Belfast
★ *Monico Bars*, 17 Lombard Street, Belfast
★ *Portside Inn*, 1 Dargan Road, Belfast
★ *Woody's Cellars*, 607 Shore Road, Newtownabbey, Co Antrim

Places Featured:

JERSEY
Grouville
St Brelade
St Helier
St Laurence
St Ouen
St Peter's Village

GUERNSEY
Castel
Forest
St Peter Port

THE GUERNSEY BREWERY CO. LTD

South Esplanade, St Peter Port, Guernsey GY1 1BJ
☎ *(01481) 720143*

BRAYE MILD 3.7% ABV
Malty, toffee flavour. Balancing hops.
SUNBEAM BITTER 4.2% ABV
Smooth, well-balanced. Dry bitter finish.
Plus seasonal brews.

RW RANDALL LTD

PO Box 154, Vauxlaurens Brewery, St Julian's Avenue, St Peter Port, Guernsey GY1 3JG
☎ *(01481) 720134*

MILD 3.4% ABV
PATOIS ALE 5.0% ABV
Plus occasional brews.

Seymour Inn

La Rocque, Grouville, Jersey JE3 9BU
☎ *(01534) 854558* Gary Boner

Guernsey Sunbeam and Tipsy Toad Jimmy's usually available. The Tipsy Toad special brews are also served.

Traditional country pub with two lounges, bar and beer garden. Food served 12–2pm and 6–8pm Mon–Sat. Car park. Children welcome.

OPEN 10am–11pm Mon–Sat; 11am–11pm Sun.

The Old Smugglers Inn

Ouaisne Bay, St Brelade, Jersey JE3 8AW
☎ *(01534) 41510* Nigel Godfrey

A freehouse usually serving ales from the Ringwood Brewery and occasional others from Brains, Randalls and elsewhere.

A very olde-worlde traditional country pub with no music or machines. Two bar areas and restaurant. Food served at lunchtime and evenings. Children allowed.

OPEN All day, every day.

Lamplighter

Mulcaster Street, St Helier, Jersey JE2 3NJ
☎ *(01534) 723119* Dave Ellis

Marston's Pedigree usually available, plus a guest beer which might be Wadworth 6X.

Gas-lit pub with old wooden beams, rafters and soft, pewter bar top. No music or video games. Food served 12–2pm daily. Children welcome but no special facilities. Situated close to St Helier bus station.

OPEN 9.30am–11pm.

The Prince of Wales Tavern

8 Hilgrove Street, St Helier, Jersey JE2 4SL
☎ *(01534) 737378* Graeme Channing

Marston's Pedigree and Wadworth 6X usually available.

Small, original old tavern with lovely beer garden at the rear. Food served 11am–2.30pm Mon–Fri. No children.

OPEN 10am–11pm Mon–Sat; 11am–2pm Sun.

The Tipsy Toad Townhouse
57–9 New Street, St Helier, Jersey
☎ *(01534) 615000 Sheila Gallagher*

 Mostly serves a selection of keg ales from The Jersey Brewery, but still worth a visit as Tipsy Toad Brewery's Jimmy's Bitter and Mmad are also permanently available.

A pub in a converted warehouse with three function rooms for live music etc. Winner of CAMRA's Pub of the Year award. Bar and restaurant food available at lunchtime and evenings. Parking nearby. Children allowed.

(OPEN) *11am–11pm.*

The British Union
Main Road, St Lawrence, Jersey JE3 1NL
☎ *(01534) 861070 Alan Cheshire*

 Guernsey Bitter and other Guernsey brews always available.

An open-plan pub with two bars and games room. Small beer garden. Food available at lunchtime and evenings. Children allowed. Opposite St Lawrence Church

(OPEN) *All day, every day.*

Le Moulin de Lecq
Greve de Lecq, St Ouen, Jersey JE3 2DT
☎ *(01534) 482818 Shaun Lynch*

Guernsey Sunbeam and Tipsy Toad Jimmy's Bitter available plus occasional others from Tipsy Toad and Guernsey Breweries.

Built around a twelfth-century flour mill with working parts inside and outside the bar. One bar and small upstairs lounge, large outside seating area and adventure playground. Summer barbecues. Food served every lunchtime and Mon–Sat evenings. Children welcome. In the north-west of the island.

(OPEN) *All day, every day.*

The Star
La Grande Route de St Pierre, St Peter's Village, Jersey JE3 7AA
☎ *(01534) 485556*

 Home of The Tipsy Toad Brewery. One cask ale is permanently brewed on the premises, plus seasonal specials.

Jersey's first brewpub is situated in renovated and restored Victorian premises. The result is a cosy pub with a family atmosphere. The brewing process can be observed through a wall of windows. Bar food is available at lunchtime and evenings. Family room and conservatory, outdoor children's play area. Baby-changing facilities and disabled toilets.

JIMMY'S BITTER 4.2% ABV
DIXIES WHEAT BEER 4.1% ABV
Summer.
NAOMH PADRAIG'S PORTER 4.4% ABV
Autumn.
FESTIVE TOAD 8.0% ABV
Christmas.

(OPEN) *10am–11.30pm.*

Hotel Fleur du Jardin
Kings Mills, Castel, Guernsey GY5 7JT
☎ *(01481) 257996 Keith Read*

Guernsey Brewery Sunbeam plus one other local beer regularly served.

Fifteenth-century country inn with olde-worlde atmosphere, serving bar and restaurant meals at lunchtimes and evenings. Lovely beer garden. Car park. Children welcome.

(OPEN) *11am–11.45pm Mon–Sat; 12–3pm Sun (Sun evenings by prior arrangement, if eating).*

Venture Inn
New Road, (Rue de la Villiaze), Forest, Guernsey GY8 0HG
☎ *(01481) 263211 Tony and Kay Mollet*

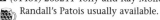 Randall's Patois usually available.

Country pub in the heart of the farming community. Log fire in the lounge during winter months. SIS Tele Betting, big screen TV, pool and darts in locals' bar. Food served May–Sept 12–2pm and 6–9pm Mon–Sat; Oct–Apr, 12–2pm Mon–Thurs, 12–2pm and 6–9pm Mon–Sat. Car park. Children's menu.

(OPEN) *10.30am–11.45pm Mon–Sat.*

Cock & Bull

2 Lower Hauteville, St Peter Port, Guernsey
☎ *(01481) 722660* Stephen Taylor

Ringwood Best Bitter, Fortyniner, Old Thumper and a guest beer available which may include something from Stonehenge, Shepherd Neame, Hop Back, Palmers, Rebellion, Skinner's, Greene King or Crouch Vale.

Pub on three levels with some wooden flooring and wide mix of clientele, including university students. Acoustic music and Irish music on Thursdays. Light snacks served 12–2pm Mon–Fri. Children welcome at lunchtimes. Situated at the top of Cornet Street, on the way to Victor Hugo's house.

11.30am–2.30pm and 4–11.45pm Mon–Thurs; 11.30am–11.45pm Fri–Sat; closed Sun.

The Drunken Duck

The Charroterie, St Peter Port, Guernsey GY1 1EL
☎ (01481) 725045 Marita Priaulx

One of two freehouses bringing guest beers into Guernsey. A Ringwood brew is always available plus two guest beers (80 per year) which might include Hop Back Summer Lightning and Wheat Beer, Morland Old Speckled Hen, Hadrian Centurian and Shepherd Neame Spitfire.

A small, friendly pub for young and old. Live music each week. Food available all day from 12pm. Parking from 5pm. Bar billiards.

11am–11.45pm Mon–Sat; 12–3.30pm Sun.

Prince of Wales Bars

Manor Place, St Peter Port, Guernsey GY1 2JN
☎ *(01481) 720166* Mrs Julie Lane

Wadworth 6X regularly available, plus a guest beer perhaps Morland Old Speckled Hen, Badger Tanglefoot or something from Tipsy Toad or Guernsey Brewery.

Town-centre freehouse, a rarity in Guernsey, with two bars known as The Coal Hole and The Prince Bar. Known locally for well-kept real ales. Food served at lunchtime only. Children welcome, but no special facilities. Situated opposite the Court House.

10am–11.45pm.

The Ship & Crown

Pier Steps, The Esplanade, St Peter Port, Guernsey
☎ *(01482) 721368* Mark Pontin

Various Guernsey Brewery beers regularly available plus additional Tipsy Toad brews.

Large, lively, single-bar town pub with excellent views over the harbour. Walls covered in pictures of local shipwrecks and local history, including the German occupation during the Second World War. Food served 11am–3pm Mon–Sat, plus 12–3pm and 6–10pm Sun. Car park. Children welcome until 3pm.

11am–11.45pm Mon–Sat; 12–3pm and 6–10pm Sun.

YOU TELL US

★ *The Coronation Inn*, 36 High Street, St Anne, Alderney
★ *Le Friquet Hotel*, Castel, Guernsey
★ *The Royal Hotel*, Le Grande Route de Faldouet, St Martin, Jersey

Places Featured:

Ballaugh	Laxey
Castletown	Peel
Douglas	Ramsey

THE BREWERIES

BUSHY'S BREWERY

Mount Murray, Bradden
☎ *(01624) 661244*

CASTLETOWN BITTER 3.5% ABV
RUBY 1874 MILD 3.5% ABV
BUSHY'S EXPORT BITTER 3.8% ABV
MANANNAN'S CLOAK 3.8% ABV
SUMMER ALE 3.8% ABV
Seasonal.
CELTIBRATION 4.0% ABV
Occasional.
OYSTER STOUT 4.2% ABV
Very occasional.
OLD BUSHY TAIL 4.5% ABV
OLD SEA DOG 4.5% ABV
OLD SHUNTER 4.5% ABV
Occasional.
PISTON BREW 4.5% ABV
Brewed for the TT races.
LOVELY JUBBELY 5.2% ABV
Winter brew.

THE PUBS

BALLAUGH

The Raven Inn

Main Road, Ballaugh
☎ *(01624) 897272* Steven Barrett

Okells Mild and Bitter regularly served.

Small, friendly country pub next to
Ballaugh Bridge. Good selection of home-
cooked food served every lunchtime and
Fri–Sat evenings. Traditional pub games and
TV. Children welcome at lunchtime only and
in the separate bistro during opening hours.

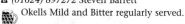 *12–11pm Mon–Thurs; 12pm–midnight
Fri–Sat; 12–11pm Sun. Times may vary
during winter months.*

CASTLETOWN

The Sidings

Station Road, Castletown
☎ *(01624) 823282* Norman Turner

Marston's Pedigree, Bushy's Castletown
Bitter, Mild, Manannan's Cloak and
seasonal brew usually available, plus two
guest beers which might be from Bushy's,
Everards, Greene King, Timothy Taylor, Wye
Valley, Morland or Charles Wells.

Welcoming, traditional, beer-orientated
pub which was once the railway station
and is now situated alongside it. Chip-fat-free
atmosphere! Bar snacks served 12–2.30pm.
Car park. Beer garden. Children welcome at
lunchtime only.

*11.30am–11pm Mon–Thurs;
11.30am–midnight Fri–Sat; 12–10.30pm
Sun.*

DOUGLAS

Albert Hotel

3 Chapel Row, Douglas IM1 2BJ
☎ *(01624) 673632* Geoff Joughin

Okells Mild, Bitter and Jough Manx Ale
(house bitter) usually served. Occasional
brews from Okells may also be available.

Town-centre, working man's local
adjacent to the bus terminal. No food. No
children.

*10am–11pm Mon–Thurs; 10am–midnight
Fri–Sat; 12–11pm Sun.*

Old Market Inn

Chapel Row, Douglas IM1 2BJ
☎ *(01624) 675202* Irene Large

Okells Bitter and Bushy's Bitter regularly
served.

A friendly atmosphere is to be found in this
small, seventeenth-century tavern,
popular with all ages. No food. No children.

*11am–11pm Mon–Wed; 10am–midnight
Thurs–Fri; 12–3pm and 7–11pm Sun.*

Saddle Inn

Queen Street, Douglas
☎ *(01624) 673161* William Beattie

 Cains Bitter and Okells Bitter and Mild regularly available, plus guest beers often from Cains, Coach House or Okells.

Friendly quayside pub, popular with locals, visitors and motorcyclists throughout the year. Various memorabilia on display. No food.

⟨OPEN⟩ *11.30am–11pm Mon–Thurs; 11.30am–midnight Fri–Sat; 12–3.30pm and 7–11pm Sun.*

LAXEY

Queens Hotel

New Road, Laxey
☎ *(01624) 861195* James Robert Hamer

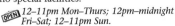 Old Laxey Bosun Bitter, Bushy's Ruby Mild and Export regularly available, plus a guest beer which might, perhaps, be something from Cains Brewery.

Friendly village pub with single, open-plan bar and pool area. Large beer garden and adjacent to the electric railway. The Laxey wheel is near by. Toasted sandwiches available. Car park. Children welcome, but no special facilities.

⟨OPEN⟩ *12–11pm Mon–Thurs; 12pm–midnight Fri–Sat; 12–11pm Sun.*

PEEL

The White House

2 Tynwald Road, Peel IM5 1LA
☎ *(01624) 842252* Jamie Keig

A freehouse serving Okells Mild and Bitter, Bushy's Bitter and Timothy Taylor Landlord plus regular guests.

A traditional pub with one main bar and four small adjoining rooms. Live local music every Saturday. TV. Light bar snacks served in the bar area. Children allowed until 9pm.

⟨OPEN⟩ *11am-11pm Mon-Thurs;11am–midnight Fri–Sat; 12–3pm and 7–10.30pm Sun.*

RAMSEY

The Stanley Hotel

West Quay, Ramsey
☎ *(01624) 812258* Colin Clarke

Okells Mild and Bitter are permanent features, plus a guest beer from Coach House is also often available.

A small pub near the harbour. Food served 12–3pm daily. Children welcome at lunchtime only.

⟨OPEN⟩ *11.30am–11pm (10.30pm Sun).*

The Trafalgar Hotel

West Quay, Ramsey
☎ *(01624) 814601* James Kneen

Okells Bitter, Cains Mild and Bitter usually available, plus a regularly changing guest beer which is often from Bushy's or Old Laxey.

Small, friendly and very traditional quayside pub, known for well-kept ales. Traditional, home-cooked food served at lunchtimes. Children welcome at lunchtime only.

⟨OPEN⟩ *11am–11pm Mon–Thurs; 11am–midnight Fri–Sat; 12–3pm and 7–10.30pm Sun.*

YOU TELL US

★ *Samuel Webb,* Marina Road, Douglas
★ *The Shore Hotel,* Shore Road, Laxey (brewpub)
★ *The Tramshunters Arms,* Sefton Hotel, Harris Promenade, Douglas

READER RECOMMENDATIONS

Research for the next edition of the guide is already underway and, to ensure that it will be as comprehensive and up-to-date as possible, we should be grateful for your help.

We hope that you will agree that every pub included this year is in the book on merit, but ownership and operation can change both for better and for worse. Equally, there are bound to be hidden gems that have so far escaped our attention and that really ought to be included next time around.

So, if what you discover does not live up to expectations, or if you know of another pub that we cannot afford to be without, please let us know. Either fill in the forms below or send your views on a separate piece of paper to:

The Editor, The Real Ale Pub Guide
Foulsham, Bennetts Close, Slough, Berkshire, SL1 5AP.

Alternatively, you can leave your comments on our web site at www.foulsham.com

Please let us know if you would like additional forms. Every reply will be entered into a draw for one of five free copies of next year's guide. Thank you very much for your help.

Pub name: _____

Address: _____

Already in the guide? Yes ☐ No ☐

Comments: _____

_____

_____

Your name: _____

Your address: _____

_____

Tel: _____

Pub name: _____

Address: _____

Already in the guide? Yes ☐ No ☐

Comments: _____

_____

_____

Your name: _____

Your address: _____

_____

Tel: _____